VISUAL QUICKSTART GUIDE

MICROSOFT OFFICE 2008

FOR MACINTOSH

Steve Schwartz

Peachpit Press

Visual QuickStart Guide

Microsoft Office 2008 for Macintosh

Steve Schwartz

Peachpit Press
1249 Eighth Street
Berkeley, CA 94710
(510) 524-2178
(510) 524-2221 (fax)

Find us on the Web at: www.peachpit.com
To report errors, please send a note to errata@peachpit.com
Peachpit Press is a division of Pearson Education

Editors: Nancy Peterson and Cliff Colby
Production Coordinator: Lisa Brazieal
Compositor: Steve Schwartz
Indexer: FireCrystal Communications
Cover Design: Peachpit Press

ISBN 13: 978-0-321-53400-2

ISBN 10: 0-321-53400-X

9 8 7 6 5 4 3 2 1

Printed and bound in the United States of America

Dedication:

In memory of my dear friend, Marjorie.

Special Thanks to:

- Nancy Peterson, Lisa Brazieal, and Cliff Colby (Peachpit Press)
- Emily Glossbrenner (FireCrystal Communications)
- Paul Robichaux
- Aimee Martin, Rosalie Duryee, and Tara Mulchy (Edelman)
- Bill Gladstone and Ming Russell (Waterside Productions)
- Pat McMillan, Andy Ruff, and the other members of the MacBU

TABLE OF CONTENTS

Part IV: Microsoft PowerPoint 279

PART V: MICROSOFT ENTOURAGE 339

Introduction

Welcome to *Microsoft Office 2008 for Macintosh: Visual QuickStart Guide*. In the pages that follow, you'll find all the information and instructions you need to quickly become productive with Office 2008.

Like other titles in the *Visual QuickStart* series, this book was written primarily as a reference. Unlike a book on a single program, however, this one covers *four* major applications. Rather than discuss every command and procedure in excruciating detail (as you'd expect in a one-program book), the focus of this book is on commands and procedures you're most likely to actually *use*.

The Office 2008 Editions and This Book

Like previous versions of Office, there are multiple editions of Office 2008. Each of the three editions includes the core Office applications: Word, Excel, PowerPoint, and Entourage (with My Day). Each edition in the list below contains all features of the lesser editions. Following are the differences between the three editions:

- **Office 2008 for Mac: Home & Student Edition.** This is the base edition. It includes full versions of the four core applications, but Entourage provides no Exchange Server support. (In general, only corporate and institutional users have Exchange accounts.)
- **Office 2008 for Mac.** This edition adds Exchange Server support in Entourage and includes Automator workflows for automating Office tasks.
- **Office 2008 for Mac: Special Edition.** In addition to the programs in the other editions, this edition includes Microsoft Expression Media to help organize and manage the digital media on your Mac.

This Visual QuickStart guide is appropriate for all three editions of Office 2008 for Mac. It covers the four core Office applications and Entourage's Exchange Server support (Chapter 28). However, it does *not* discuss Microsoft Expression Media.

How to Use This Book

This is a book for beginning to intermediate users of Microsoft Office for Mac. If you're using Office for the first time, switching from a Windows version to the Macintosh version, or already know the basics but want to get more out of your investment in Office, this book is for you. If you learn better from step-by-step instructions and lots of graphic examples than from reference manuals that just describe what the menu commands do, this book is also for you. Most of all, if you know what you want to do and want to get started in the shortest possible time, this book is *definitely* for you.

I've worked hard to create a book that will let you turn to the directions for any procedure, learn what it does, and do it yourself. A screen shot illustrates every significant step. The goal is to give you all the information you need and none that you don't, making you productive as quickly as possible. Along the way, you'll find tips that offer helpful information about many of the procedures.

To make it easy for you to find the information you need at any given moment, the book is divided into major sections called *parts*.

- Part I provides an introduction to essential Office procedures.
- Parts II through V are devoted to the four core Office applications: Word, Excel, PowerPoint, and Entourage (with My Day).
- Part VI explains how to use the Office applications together. You'll also learn about Office's many Internet-related features.

About Word

Word 2008, the word-processing component of Microsoft Office, is used to create letters, memos, invoices, proposals, reports, forms, brochures, catalogs, labels, envelopes, and just about any other type of printed or electronically distributed document that you can imagine.

You can type text into Word and insert almost any kind of graphic, formatting the text and graphics into sophisticated documents with cover pages, tables of contents, running headers and footers, tables, footnotes, cross-references, page numbers, and indexes. If your needs aren't that expansive, you can also create simple letters and memos with Word's easy-to-use features.

Word's approach, like that of the other applications in Office, is visual. As you work in a document, you see all the text, graphics, and formatting exactly as it will appear when you print.

Word works in concert with the other Office applications. It can display numbers and charts from Excel worksheets, as well as slides from PowerPoint. And you can flag Word documents for follow-up in your Entourage to-do list.

About Excel

Excel 2008, the Office spreadsheet application, is used to track, calculate, and analyze data. If you want to view numeric information graphically, you can use Excel to create professional charts in dozens of formats.

After typing numbers into a row-and-column cell grid in an Excel worksheet, you can enter formulas into adjacent cells that total, subtract, multiply, or divide the numbers. You can also enter *functions,* special Excel formulas that perform complex calculations—from sums and averages to sophisticated financial computations, such as net present value. Excel can even calculate statistics.

You can also use Excel to create, maintain, and import lists and databases. You can accumulate text and numeric records, as well as sort, search, filter, and extract data from a database. Excel works especially well with FileMaker Pro databases.

About PowerPoint

PowerPoint 2008 is the presentation component of Office. You use it to create slides, handouts, and other materials you might use during a stand-up dog-and-pony show. You can even use PowerPoint to present *slide shows*—electronic presentations that you run on your computer screen or on a projection device in front of an audience.

PowerPoint comes with dozens of professionally designed templates that take care of the presentation's look, allowing you to focus on its message. It also includes sample presentation outlines to help you get a start on the content.

PowerPoint's powerful arsenal includes bulleted and numbered text slides, graphs, tables, organization charts, clip art, animations and movies, and drawing tools.

If you need to convey your PowerPoint presentation to an even wider audience, you can convert it to a QuickTime movie, a Web-based slide show that can be viewed with any Web browser, or a set of pictures that can be viewed on a video iPod.

About Entourage

Entourage 2008 helps you manage your life and your communications. Use it to send and receive email, read and post to newsgroups, and maintain your calendar, address book, to-do list, and notes.

You can flag Office documents for follow-up in your to-do list, remind yourself of appointments and events, and link related Entourage items, such as messages, contact records, and appointments.

The Project Center helps you organize and view Office materials related to a particular project. Although all projects are created in Entourage, they can be accessed from any Office application.

My Day is a widget-style application that shows your upcoming events and to-do items. Although My Day draws its data from Entourage, it runs separately from it. Now you can view your calendar and to-do list regardless of whether Entourage is currently running.

What's New in Office 2008?

Office 2008 for Mac has many new features. Here are some of the most significant ones. (Changes listed below apply primarily to Word, Excel, and PowerPoint.)

What's new in all Office programs?

- Office is now optimized for both PowerPC and Intel Macs.
- For compatibility with Office 2007 (Windows), Office 2008 documents use a new file format that's based on XML (Extensible Markup Language). However, you can still save in earlier formats to enable owners of those Office versions to read your documents.
- You can click icons in the Elements Gallery (found beneath each application's toolbars) to quickly add common and complex items to Office documents, such as SmartArt, WordArt, tables, and charts.
- Several new tabs have been added to the Office Toolbox: the Object Palette (all applications), Formula Builder (Excel), and Custom Animation (PowerPoint). The Toolbox is also available in Entourage, but includes only the Scrapbook, Object Palette, and Reference Tools tabs.
- Attractive, customizable graphic elements called SmartArt can be added to any Office document. You can use them to create bullet points or illustrate relationships, for example.
- Office charts for Word and PowerPoint are now created by entering and editing data in Excel.
- In addition to creating PDF (Portable Document Format) files in the Print dialog box, PDF is now a file format option in Save/Save As dialog boxes.

What's new in Word 2008?

- A publishing layout view has been added, enabling you to create more complex and special-purpose documents, such as flyers, newsletters, brochures, catalogs, posters, and CD labels. A variety of desktop publishing templates are provided.
- Document elements can be selected from the Elements Gallery to add a stylish cover page or insert a table of contents into the current document. Creating headers, footers, and bibliography entries are also simplified.
- Fonts can now include *ligatures* (characters that combine two or more separate characters for improved appearance or readability).

What's new in PowerPoint 2008?

- To give your slides a consistent look, you can choose from approximately 50 themes that specify the layout, fonts, and colors used.
- Slideshows can be sent to iPhoto to be turned into pictures that you can display on a video iPod.
- You can use an Apple Remote to control slideshows.
- When moving an object, dynamic guides simplify the process of aligning objects to one another or centering them on the slide.

What's new in Excel 2008?

- If you need help creating worksheets, Excel includes over two dozen templates called ledger sheets. Use them to record your stock portfolio data, create a budget, manage a business or personal checkbook, or generate invoices, for example.
- Rather than constantly consulting Help, you can use the Formula Builder tab of the Office Toolbox to help you create formulas. Formula Builder provides a description of each Excel function and prompts for the necessary arguments.
- As you type, Formula AutoComplete displays drop-down lists of function names and defined names from which you can choose. Typing =S, for example, displays a list of all functions and defined names that begin with S.

What's new in Entourage 2008?

- You no longer need to launch Entourage just to check your schedule. A new application called My Day shows upcoming events and tasks. You can also use it to quickly create new tasks and mark existing ones as having been completed.
- Spotlight searches can locate text in messages or attachments. You can also use Spotlight to search for Entourage contact records.
- Entourage 2008 includes improved junk email filtering. Warnings regarding possible phishing attempts are also provided.
- Messages and contacts marked as To Do are added to a special To Do List that also includes your created tasks. (The normal Tasks list does not include to-do items.)
- Entourage toolbars can be customized by adding, removing, or rearranging icons.
- If you have an Exchange Server account, you can create an Out of Office message that will automatically be sent in response to incoming messages while you're away.

Part I: Introduction

1 Essential Office Techniques

Many basic operations in Office 2008, such as starting a new document, opening an existing document, saving your work, using common interface elements, working with various types of content, and getting help, apply to all or most Office applications. Rather than repeat this information throughout the book, we'll cover it here.

Launching Office Applications

You can launch Office applications in the same manner as other OS X applications—plus some Office-specific ways.

To launch an Office application:

- *Do one of the following:*
  - ▲ Click the application icon in the Dock (**Figure 1.1**).
  - ▲ Open the Microsoft Office 2008 folder (**Figure 1.2**) and double-click the application icon.
  - ▲ Double-click an alias for the Office application. (To create an alias for a program or document, select its file icon and choose File > Make Alias. Then move the alias to a convenient location, such as the Desktop.)
  - ▲ From the New tab of the Project Gallery in any open Office application, create a new document in another Office application.

The application launches. Depending on your Preferences settings, the Project Gallery appears (see the next section) or a new, blank document appears.

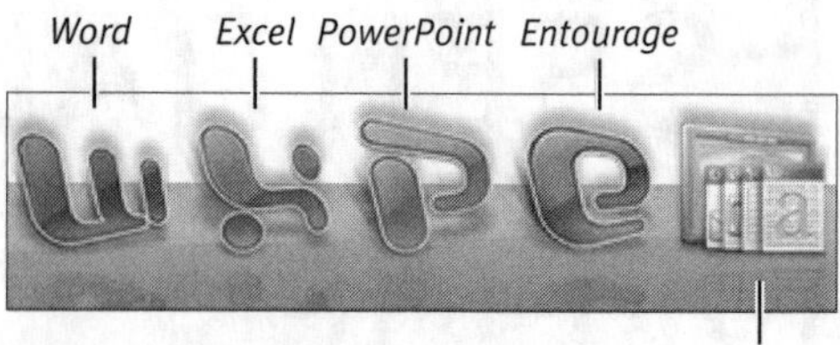

Figure 1.1 If the Office applications are in the Dock, click an icon to launch the application.

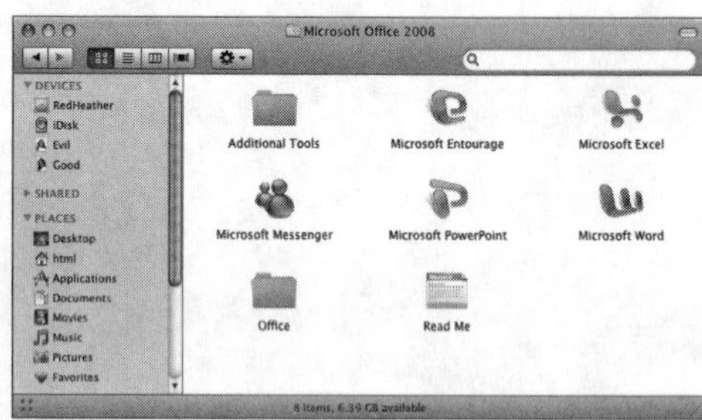

Figure 1.2 You can also launch an Office application by double-clicking its icon.

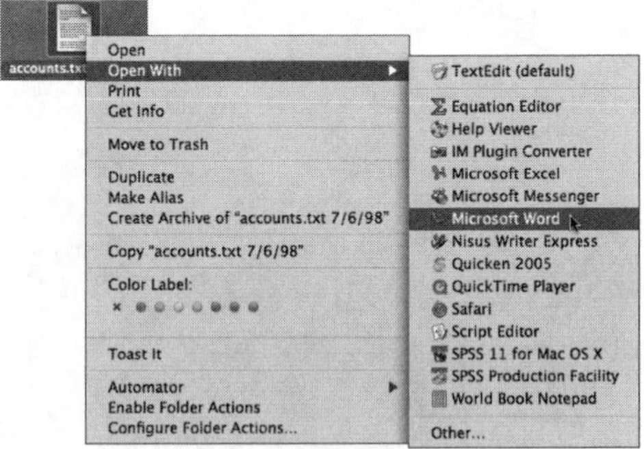

Figure 1.3 To open a compatible document (such as this text file) in a specific Office application, choose the program from the pop-up menu.

To launch an Office application while opening one or more documents:

- *Do one of the following:*
  - Double-click an Office document icon or document alias. (For example, double-clicking a Word document will launch Word—if it isn't already running—and open the document.)
  - Drag the icon of a compatible document onto an Office application icon. (For example, you can drag a compatible worksheet onto the Excel icon.)
  - Select one or more document icons of the same type, Control-click one of them, and choose the appropriate Office application from the Open With submenu (**Figure 1.3**).
  - Within Entourage or another mail application, double-click or open an Office document that's attached to an email message.

  The application launches and the selected document or documents open.

✔ Tips

- There is no right or preferred way to launch an Office application or open its documents. Use any method that's convenient at the moment. (Of course, the more methods you learn, the more likely you'll always find one that's convenient.)
- Where you store your Office documents is up to you. Many users store them in folders within the Documents folder, for example. You may want to keep a few frequently used documents on the Desktop. *Where* the documents are stored isn't important. That you know where they're stored is *extremely* important. When saving an Office document, be sure to pay attention to its location on disk.

Launching Entourage from My Day or Office Reminders

If you double-click a scheduled event, to do item, or task in My Day, Entourage will launch and open the item. Similarly, you can launch Entourage and open a selected event or task by:

- Double-clicking the reminder in Office Reminders
- Selecting the reminder in Office Reminders and choosing File > Open Item (⌘O)

Using the Project Gallery

A feature introduced in Office 2001 called the *Project Gallery* gives you access to standard blank documents, templates and wizards (which provide substantial amounts of document formatting and content), and recently opened documents.

To use the Project Gallery:

1. *Do one of the following:*
   - ▲ Launch an Office application. (If the Project Gallery hasn't been disabled, it will open on program launch.)
   - ▲ Choose File > Project Gallery (or press Shift⌘P).
   - ▲ Click the Microsoft Project Gallery icon in the Dock (see Figure 1.1).

   The Project Gallery appears.
2. *Do one of the following:*
   - ▲ *To create a new document* for this or another Office application (regardless of whether it is currently running), click the New tab (**Figure 1.4**). Select Blank Documents from the Category list, select a document type from the thumbnails, and click Open.
   - ▲ *To create a document from a template or wizard,* click the New tab (Figure 1.4), and select My Templates or another category that contains templates, such as Labels or Stationery. Select a template or wizard thumbnail, and click Open.
   - ▲ *To open a document on which you recently worked,* click the Recent tab (**Figure 1.5**). Select a time period from the Date pane, select a document from the ones listed, and click Open.

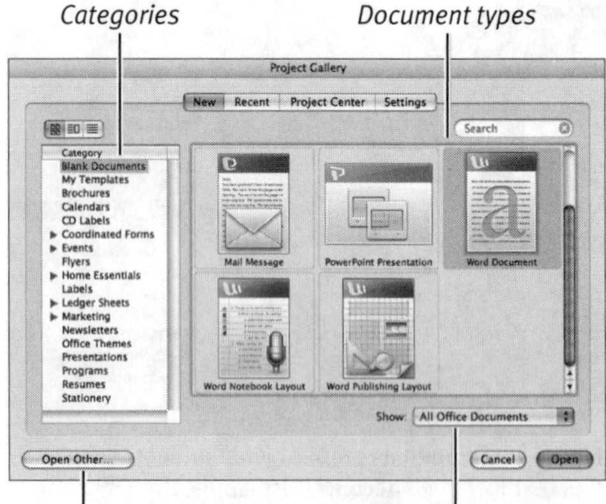

Figure 1.4 To create a new document, select Blank Documents, select the thumbnail of the type of document you want to create, and click Open.

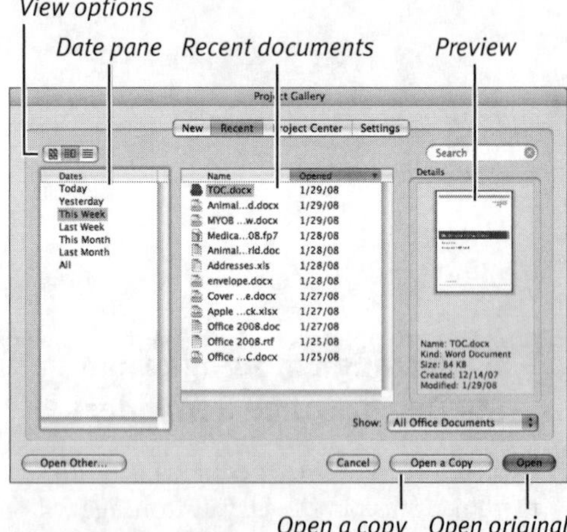

Figure 1.5 You can open a document on which you've worked by selecting it from the list on the Recent tab.

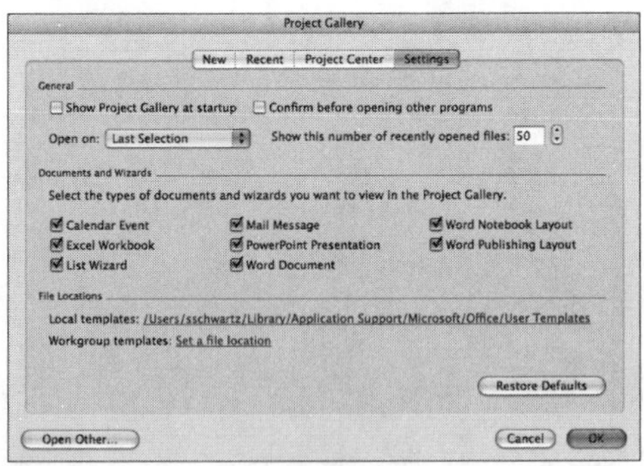

Figure 1.6 Set Project Gallery preferences on the Settings tab of the Project Gallery window.

- ▲ *To open a file associated with a Project Center project,* click the Project Center tab, select a document, and click Open.
- ▲ *To open an existing document* (other than the ones displayed), click the Open Other button, select a document from the Open dialog box that appears, and click Open.

  When the Project Gallery is opened from within an Office application, the Open Other button is available on all tabs. However, when the Project Gallery is launched from the Dock, the Open Other button is *not* displayed.
- ▲ *To set Project Gallery preferences,* click the Settings tab (**Figure 1.6**). If you'd rather not see the Project Gallery each time you launch an Office application, for instance, remove the check mark from Show Project Gallery at startup.

✔ Tips

- You can view documents as a gallery (thumbnails) or a text list by clicking the appropriate view icon at the top of the Project Gallery (see Figure 1.5).
- You can limit the kinds of documents shown in the Project Gallery by picking a file type from the Show drop-down menu (see Figure 1.4). For example, you can elect to list only Excel documents.
- On the Recent tab, you can optionally open a *copy* of a recent document rather than the original—effectively treating the file as a template or stationery document. Select a file and click the Open a Copy button (see Figure 1.5).

Creating a New Document

Unless you work exclusively with documents created by others, you'll also want to create new documents of your own. You can create a new blank document in these ways:

- **Word.** Choose File > New Blank Document (**Figure 1.7**).
- **PowerPoint.** Choose File > New Presentation.
- **Excel.** Choose File > New Workbook.
- **All.** Press ⌘N or click the New icon on the Standard toolbar. (In Word, clicking the New icon displays a drop-down menu.)

✔ Tips

- If you don't make a choice in the Project Gallery window and click Cancel to dismiss it, a new blank document is automatically created for you.
- If the option to Show Project Gallery at startup isn't checked on the Project Gallery's Settings tab (see Figure 1.6) or in the Office applications' Preferences, launching Word, PowerPoint, or Excel causes a new document to automatically be created.
- As explained in the previous section, you can also create a new document in the Project Gallery window. Click the New tab, select Blank Documents from the Category list, select the type of Office document you want to create, and click Open (see Figure 1.4).
- If you decide that a new document isn't needed, click the document's red close button. If you've typed anything into the document, don't save it when you're prompted.

Figure 1.7 Create a new document, such as this one in Word, when you want to start from scratch.

Figure 1.8 Select a category in the left pane to view available templates and wizards. To restrict the list to application-specific templates and wizards, choose the application from the Show drop-down menu.

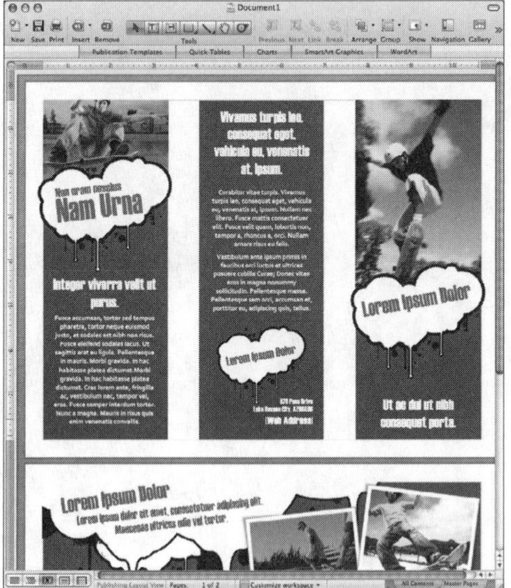

Figure 1.9 Word includes desktop publishing templates that open in the new Publishing Layout View.

Templates and Wizards

Office 2008 includes a diverse collection of templates and wizards that you can use to create impressive documents without having to become a design professional.

Templates are formatted documents to which you add your own content. *Wizards* are short multiple-step or tabbed procedures that ask you questions about the document you want to produce and then create the document based on your answers. If you like, you can edit the resulting document when the wizard is finished.

Creating a document from a template

A *template* is a partially formed document that contains text, styles, and formatting. You can start a document with a template, and then modify the content and formatting.

To create a document from a template:

1. If the Project Gallery isn't open, choose File > Project Gallery (Shift⌘P) or click the Project Gallery icon in the Dock.

   The Project Gallery opens.

2. Click the New tab (**Figure 1.8**). In the Category list, select the type of document you want to create. (To expand a category, click the triangle beside it.)

   Document thumbnails appear in the main pane.

3. *Optional:* Choose the specific Office program from the Show drop-down menu.

4. Select a template thumbnail and click Open.

   A copy of the template opens (**Figure 1.9**).

5. Fill in the content, edit and format the document, and then save the document.

✔ Tips

- When creating a new document from a template, you're working with a *copy*—not the original template. To remind you, Word names the copy *Document* rather than using the template name. As long as you save the copy with a new name or in a different location, changes you make to the copy won't affect the template.
- You can also base a new document on any recently used Office document—treating your own documents as templates. In the Project Gallery, click the Recent tab, select a document, and click Open a Copy.

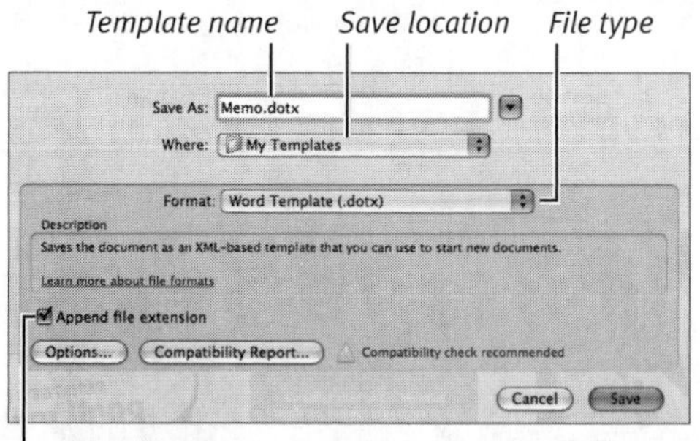

Figure 1.10 Select *application* Template as the format when saving a file as a template.

Saving a document as a template

You don't have to rely exclusively on the provided Office templates. You may find it useful to save your *own* documents as templates, allowing you to reuse them with minor changes whenever you like.

To save a document as a template:

1. Create an Office document with the desired formatting. Delete text and other material that you don't want saved as part of the template, while retaining any text you'll want to use in new documents.

   In a Word fax-form template, for example, you might leave your contact information intact and add a placeholder (such as "Message text here") for the message text.
2. Choose File > Save As.
3. In the dialog box that appears, choose *application* Template from the Format drop-down menu (**Figure 1.10**).
4. Enter a name for the template in the Save As text box.
5. From the Where drop-down list, choose a location in which to save the template.

   Normally, you should accept the default folder (My Templates) for personal templates, but you're free to save them to other locations.
6. Click the Save button.

   The document is saved as a template.

✔ Tip

- For compatibility with Office 2007 for Windows, Mac template files use these file extensions: Word (.dotx), Excel (.xltx), and PowerPoint design (.potx). When saving any Office template or document, the appropriate file extension is added automatically (unless you remove the check mark from Append file extension).

Modifying an existing template

You can modify the templates provided with Office, as well as any files of your own that you've saved as templates. In this way, you can create templates that better serve your needs.

To modify a template:

1. In the Office application in which the template was created, choose File > Open (⌘O).
   The Open dialog box appears.
2. Choose *application name* Templates from the Enable drop-down menu.
3. Navigate to the `Microsoft Office 2008:Office:Media:Templates` folder. Open additional folders as necessary until you find the template that you want to change (**Figure 1.11**).
4. Select the template and click Open.
5. Make the necessary edits and formatting changes to the template.
6. *Do one of the following:*
   - ▲ To save the modified template without overwriting the original, choose File > Save As, edit the template name (if desired), and save it in the My Templates folder or another folder of your choosing (**Figure 1.12**).
   - ▲ To replace the original template with the modified one, choose File > Save (⌘S).

✔ Tip

- Unless you're certain you'll never need the original template again, it's more prudent to modify a *copy* of the template, saving it with a new filename. To open a copy of a template for modification, choose Copy from the Open drop-down menu in the Open dialog box (Figure 1.11).

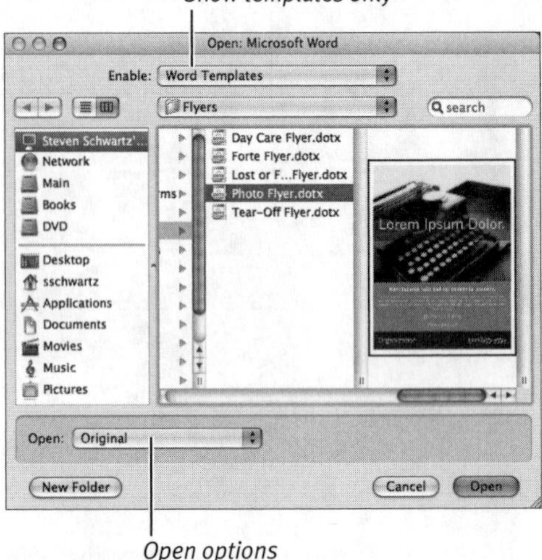

Figure 1.11 Select the template that you want to modify (OS X 10.4.11/Tiger shown).

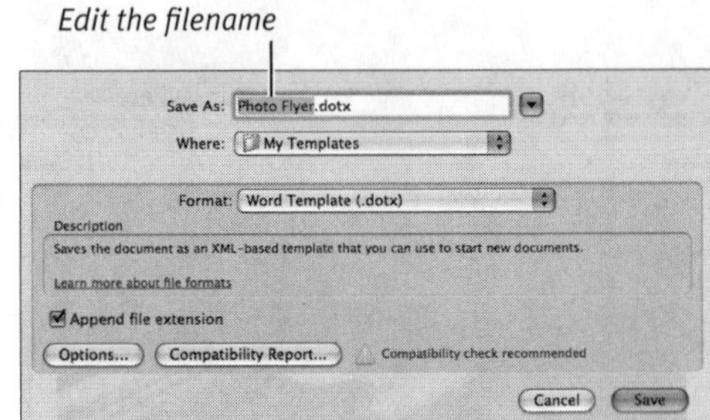

Figure 1.12 To avoid overwriting the original template, save the edited version with a different filename or in a different folder. (To make it easily accessible for use in Office, save it in My Templates.)

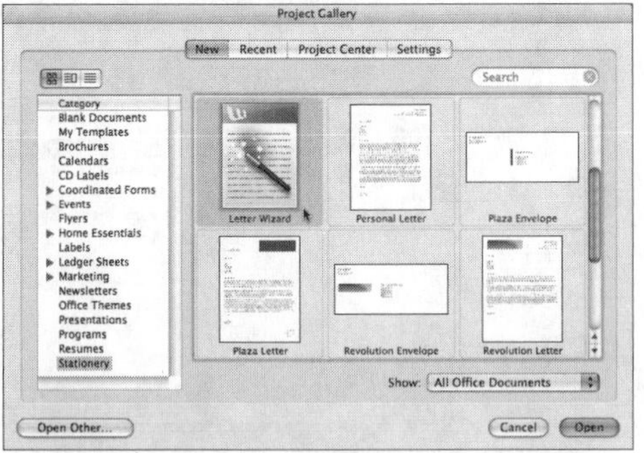

Figure 1.13 The Letter Wizard thumbnail is selected in the Project Gallery.

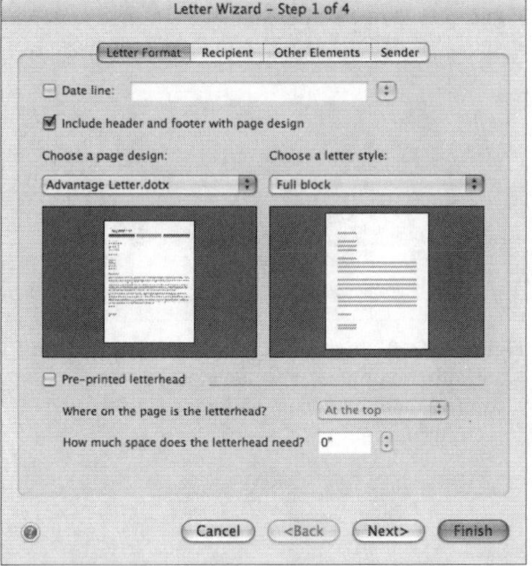

Figure 1.14 Enter the information requested by the wizard and set options as you like.

Working with wizards

Wizards step you through the process of creating a specific type of document. They generally provide sample text that you can use, too. In Word, for example, you can use wizards to create letters, brochures, menus, catalogs, and labels.

To use a wizard:

1. If the Project Gallery isn't open, choose File > Project Gallery (Shift⌘P) or click the Project Gallery icon in the Dock.
2. On the New tab, select a category from the Category list.
3. In the main pane, select the wizard for the type of document you want to create (**Figure 1.13**) and click Open. (Wizard thumbnails have a magician's wand.)

   The wizard appears (**Figure 1.14**).
4. Follow the steps presented by the wizard. Each step prompts you for more detail to help generate a customized document.
5. To complete the wizard, click Finish, Save & Exit, or OK. (Button labels vary.)

   The resulting document includes the information you entered and the options selected.
6. Make any necessary changes to the document and save the file.

✔ Tips

- Not every wizard has the word *Wizard* in its filename.
- You can move from one section of a multi-page wizard to another by clicking Next, Back, or a specific tab.

Opening Existing Documents

Unless you use every document you create only once (a *very* unlikely occurrence), you'll need to open documents you've previously saved on disk.

To reopen a saved file:

1. Choose File > Open, click the Open icon on the Standard toolbar, or press ⌘O.
2. In the Open dialog box (**Figure 1.15**), navigate to the location on disk where the file is stored.
3. From the Open drop-down menu (**Figure 1.16**), *choose one of the following:*
   - ▲ **Original.** Open the original for editing.
   - ▲ **Copy.** Open a copy for editing, protecting the original from changes.
   - ▲ **Read-Only.** Open the document for viewing. If you edit the document, you can save the changes only if you use a different filename and/or location.
4. To open the document, double-click the document's filename or select the filename and click Open.

✔ Tips

- If the file you want to open is one you've recently used, it may appear in the File > Open Recent list (**Figure 1.17**). If so, you can open it by choosing its name.
- You can also open documents by choosing them from the Recent tab of the Project Gallery.
- Another way to open a document is to double-click its icon on the Desktop or in the folder in which the file is stored. See "Launching Office Applications," earlier in this chapter.

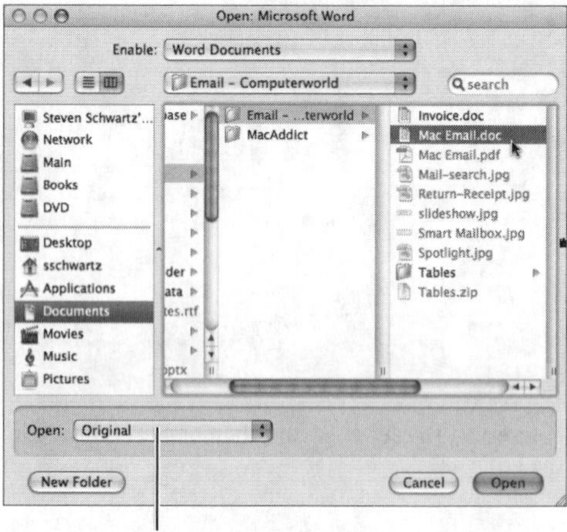

Figure 1.15 To open an existing document, choose it in the Open dialog box (OS X 10.4.11/Tiger shown).

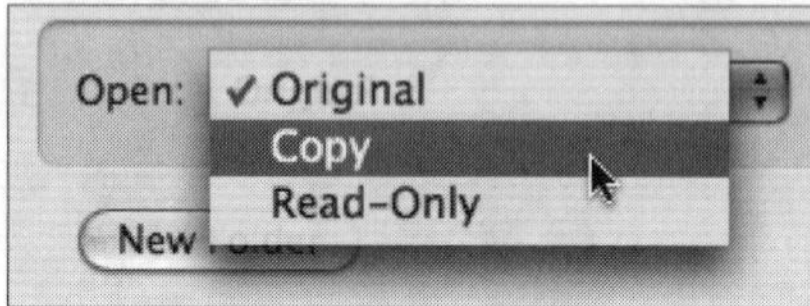

Figure 1.16 Although you'll usually want to work with the original, you can elect to open a copy or open the document for viewing only (read-only mode).

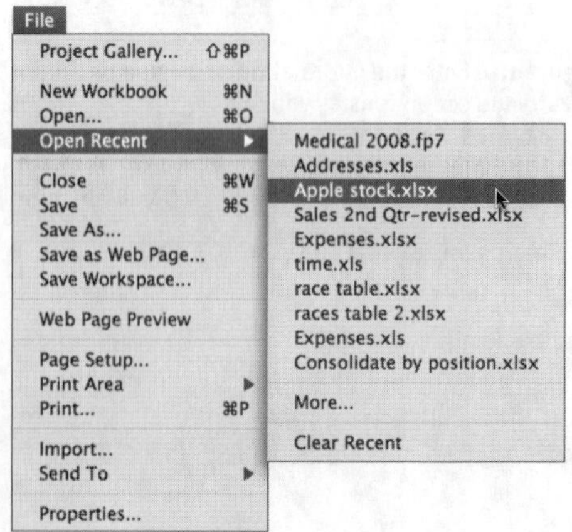

Figure 1.17 You can also open a file by choosing its name from the File > Open Recent submenu.

Figure 1.18 To save the current document, click the Save icon on the Standard toolbar.

Expand or collapse the Where area

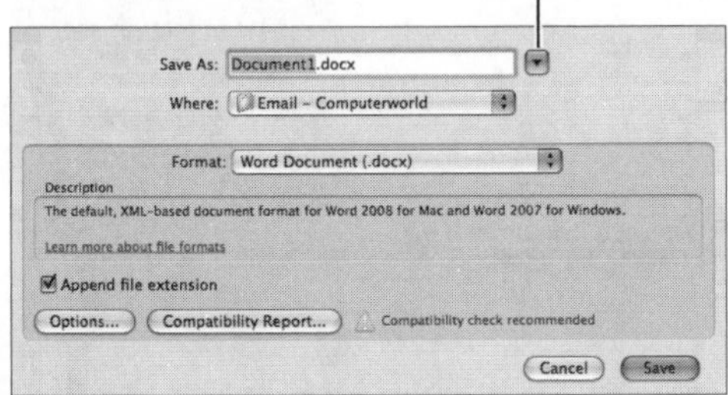

Figure 1.19 To save a new document or to save an old one using a new name or location, enter the necessary information in the Save As dialog box.

Enable AutoRecover

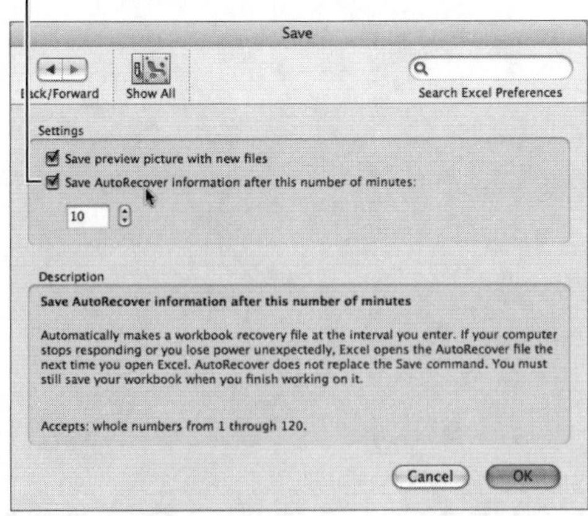

Figure 1.20 By enabling AutoRecover, you can ensure that you never lose more than a few minutes' work.

Saving Your Work

It's a good idea to save your work frequently to guard against data loss.

To save your work:

1. Choose File > Save, press ⌘S, or click the Save icon on the Standard toolbar (**Figure 1.18**).

   If the document was previously saved, the new version of the file automatically overwrites the old one.

2. If this is the first time you've saved the document (or if you've chosen File > Save As), a Save As dialog box appears (**Figure 1.19**).

3. Enter a filename in the Save As text box.

4. Choose a file format from the Format drop-down menu.

5. Click the Where drop-down menu to select a location in which to store the document.

   If you need to navigate to a drive or folder that isn't listed, click the triangle icon to expand the Where area.

6. Click Save or press Return.

✔ Tips

- To save a previously saved document to a new location or using a new name (preventing the original copy from being overwritten), choose File > Save As rather than File > Save.

- Word, Excel, and PowerPoint can be instructed to automatically save documents at user-defined intervals. This is known as *AutoRecover*. To enable Auto-Recover and specify a time interval, choose *program name* > Preferences and open the Save category (**Figure 1.20**).

Working with Text

Text is an important part of most Office documents. Whenever an application is ready for you to type, a blinking insertion mark appears in the document. Whatever you type appears at the text insertion mark.

Setting the text insertion mark

To revise or add to existing text, you must move the insertion mark to the spot where you want to make the change.

To set the insertion mark:

- *Do one of the following:*
  - ▲ Move the I-beam cursor to the spot where you want to position the insertion mark. Click to set the insertion mark (**Figure 1.21**).
  - ▲ If the text insertion mark is currently set in a normal Word document, an Excel cell, or a PowerPoint text block, you can move the insertion mark by pressing the arrow keys, Pg Up, Pg Dn, or any of the other keyboard shortcuts listed in **Table 1.1**.

✓ Tip

- In Excel, the insertion mark can be in the data entry box on the formula bar or in the cell (**Figure 1.22**), depending on where you're performing the editing or data entry.

Office lets you easily share information between its applications. The three main methods are to copy, embed, or link information from one application to another.

Text insertion mark I-beam cursor

Figure 1.21 Whatever you type will appear at the text insertion mark.

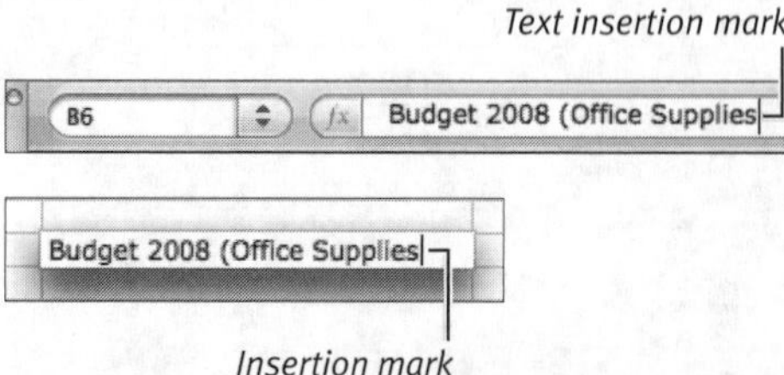

Figure 1.22 In Excel, the insertion mark can be in the formula bar (top) or in the cell you're editing (bottom).

Table 1.1

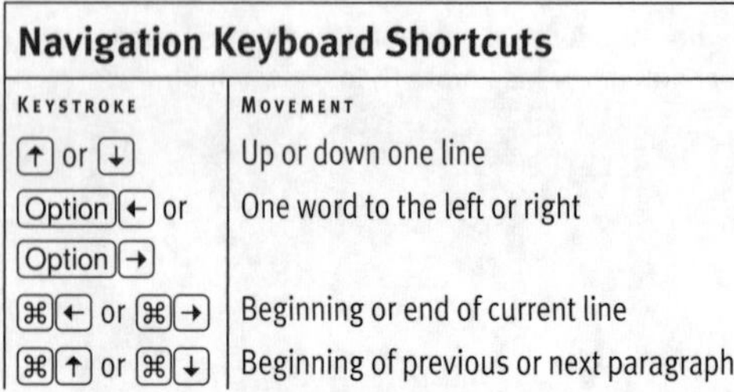

Navigation Keyboard Shortcuts

Keystroke	Movement
↑ or ↓	Up or down one line
Option ← or Option →	One word to the left or right
⌘ ← or ⌘ →	Beginning or end of current line
⌘ ↑ or ⌘ ↓	Beginning of previous or next paragraph

Selected text

When you link rather than embed an object, the object remains in the original application's document. A *copy* of the object—linked to the original—is displayed in the second application.

Figure 1.23 Click and drag to create a text selection. The selected text is highlighted.

Selecting text

Before you can edit, replace, delete, or format text, you must first *select* it. Any operation you then perform will affect the selected text.

To select text using the mouse:

- *Do any of the following:*
  - Click at one end of a section of text to set the text insertion mark and drag to the other end to select the text (**Figure 1.23**). A selection can be as little as one character or can contain many consecutive paragraphs.
  - To select text on consecutive lines, click to set the insertion mark at the beginning of the selection and either drag through the lines you want to select or Shift-click at the end of the selection.
  - You can make multiple, noncontiguous text selections. You might, for example, want to select several headings to simultaneously apply the same formatting to them. Hold down ⌘ to make multiple selections.
  - Double-click anywhere within a word to select it. Triple-click anywhere within a paragraph to select it.

✔ Tips

- A Preferences setting ensures that the entire first and last word of a selection are highlighted. If you want to be able to select *parts* of words, choose *application name* > Preferences, select the Edit heading, and remove the check mark from When selecting, automatically select entire word.
- To select an entire line of text in a Word document, click in the left margin of the line. To select multiple lines, click in the margin to the left of a line and then drag down through the lines.

To select text using the keyboard:

1. Use the arrow keys or mouse to set the insertion point at one end of the text that you want to select.
2. Hold down Shift and press arrow keys (or the keys shown in Table 1.1) to extend the selection.

✔ Tips

- Use Shift Option ← or Shift Option → to select a word at a time.
- Use Shift ↓ or Shift ↑ to select multiple lines of text.
- To select from the insertion mark to the beginning or end of the current line, press Shift ⌘ ← or Shift ⌘ →, respectively.

Moving text

To move text in a document, you can either use Edit > Cut (⌘X) and Edit > Paste (⌘V) or drag and drop. *Drag and drop* is a simplified cut and paste, accomplished by selecting text and then dragging it to a new location in the document. You can even drag text from one document to another or from one application window to another.

To drag and drop text:

1. Select the text to be moved.
2. Place the cursor over the selected text.

   The cursor changes to an arrow pointer (**Figure 1.24**).
3. Press and hold the mouse button, and drag the pointer to the destination.

   A text insertion mark shows the spot where the dragged text will reappear (**Figure 1.25**).
4. Release the mouse button to drop the text at the new location (**Figure 1.26**).

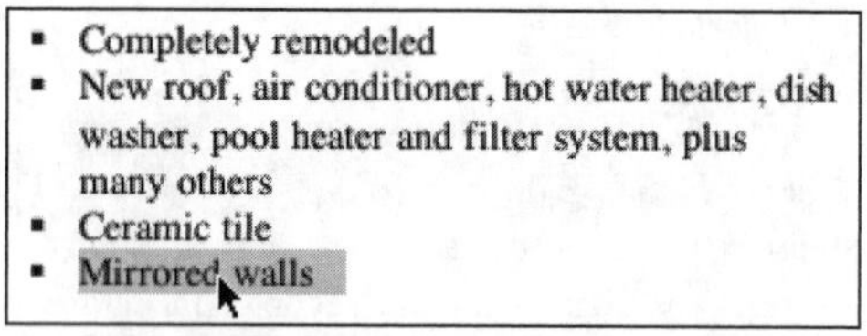

- Completely remodeled
- New roof, air conditioner, hot water heater, dish washer, pool heater and filter system, plus many others
- Ceramic tile
- Mirrored walls

Figure 1.24 When the cursor is moved over a text selection, it becomes an arrow pointer.

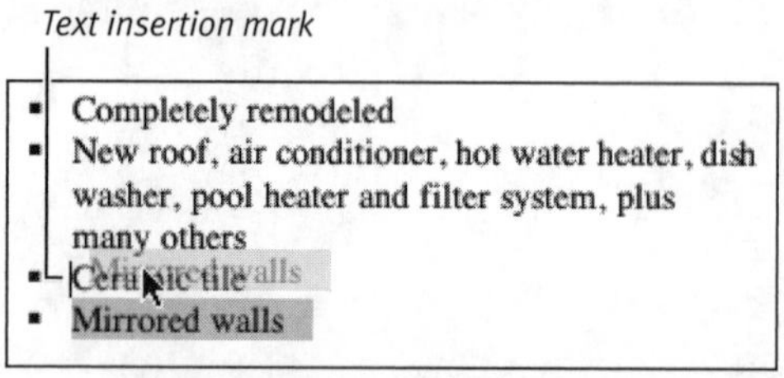

Text insertion mark

- Completely remodeled
- New roof, air conditioner, hot water heater, dish washer, pool heater and filter system, plus many others
- Ceramic tile
- Mirrored walls

Figure 1.25 Drag the arrow pointer to the destination. A text insertion mark shows where the dragged text will appear.

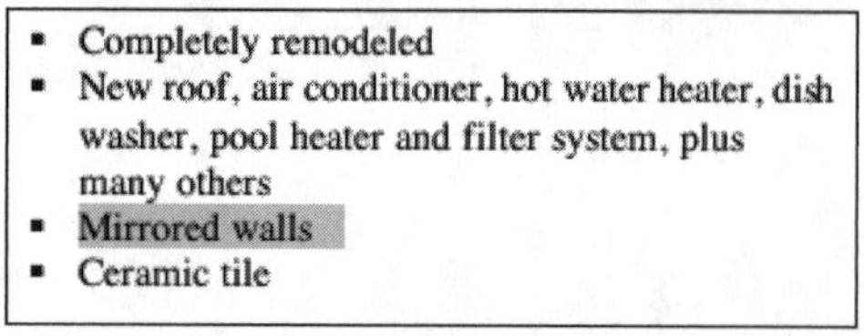

- Completely remodeled
- New roof, air conditioner, hot water heater, dish washer, pool heater and filter system, plus many others
- Mirrored walls
- Ceramic tile

Figure 1.26 Release the mouse button to drop the text. In this example, the "Mirrored walls" bullet has been moved up one paragraph.

Rachel Johnson

Figure 1.27 To replace this selected last name with another, there's no need to press Delete. Just type the new last name.

✔ Tips

- To *copy* text rather than move it (leaving the original text intact), press Option as you drag.
- A drag and drop between documents is treated as a copy rather than a cut. That is, following the operation, the original material remains in the source document.
- You can also use drag and drop to copy or move other kinds of objects, such as graphics and charts.
- You can use drag and drop to drag a text selection from Office 2008 onto the Desktop, creating a *picture clipping*.

Replacing text

To replace text in a document or dialog box, select the text and type over it (**Figure 1.27**). Doing so simultaneously deletes the text and replaces it with the new text. (It isn't necessary to first delete the old text.)

Working with Pictures and Other Objects

Drawings, charts, WordArt, clip art, scanned images, and other items you can select in an Office document are *objects*. After selecting an object (by clicking or dragging through it), you can reposition it on the page by dragging. You can also drag objects into other documents—including documents in other applications. To copy rather than move an object, hold down Option as you drag.

To format an object, you must select it and then choose a formatting command, as described in the following steps.

To format an object:

1. Select the object that you want to format.
2. *Do one of the following:*
   - ▲ Choose a command or click an icon on the Formatting Palette (**Figure 1.28**) or the Drawing toolbar (**Figure 1.29**).
   - ▲ Double-click the object to open a relevant formatting dialog box.
   - ▲ From the Format menu, choose an appropriate command (such as Picture or WordArt).

✔ Tips

- If the Formatting Palette isn't visible, you can display it by choosing View > Formatting Palette or by clicking the Toolbox icon on the Standard toolbar.
- In Office 2004, object-specific toolbars appeared automatically. In Office 2008, many of them appear as sections in the Formatting Palette.
- For more information about using the Formatting Palette, see the next section.
- For assistance with text formatting, see Chapter 4.

Figure 1.28 When you select an object (such as this WordArt), the Formatting Palette displays commands that are relevant to formatting the object.

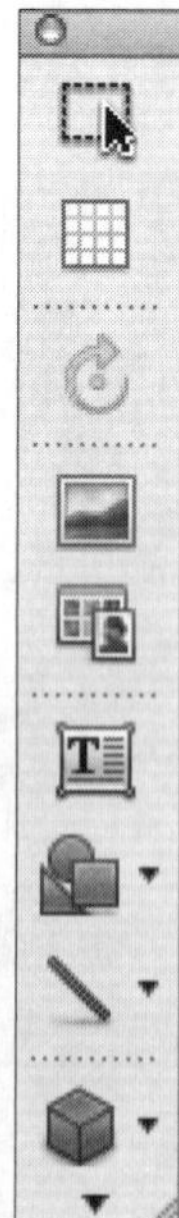

Figure 1.29 You can modify many objects by choosing commands and options from the Drawing toolbar.

Figure 1.30 Click the Format Painter icon on the Standard toolbar.

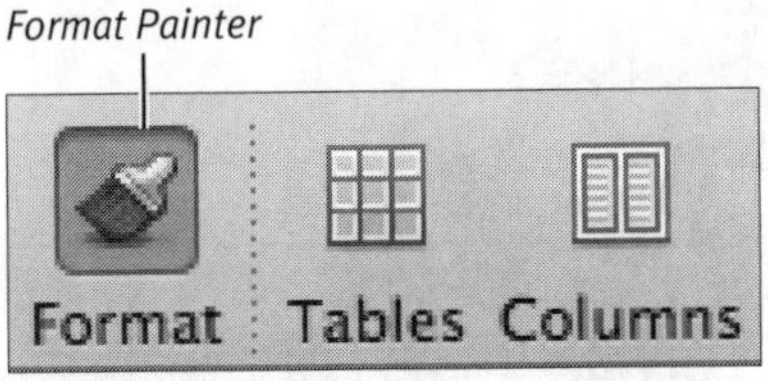

Format Painter

Format Tables Columns

Figure 1.31 Double-click the Format Painter icon to lock it.

Using the Format Painter

Rather than laboriously recreate complex formatting, you can use the Format Painter (**Figure 1.30**) to copy the formatting of selected text and objects and apply it to other text and objects.

To use the Format Painter:

- *Do any of the following:*
  - To copy character formatting from one text string to another, select the source string, click the Format Painter toolbar icon, and then drag-select the target text string. When you release the mouse button, the formatting is applied to the target text.
  - To copy a paragraph format, select the entire source paragraph (including the paragraph mark at its end), click the Format Painter toolbar icon, and then click anywhere in the target paragraph (or drag through multiple paragraphs).
  - To copy object formatting, select the source object, click the Format Painter toolbar icon, and then click the target object.

✔ Tips

- To copy formatting to *multiple* objects, text strings, or paragraphs, select the source text or object and double-click the Format Painter toolbar icon (**Figure 1.31**). One by one, apply the formatting to as many target objects, text strings, or paragraphs as you wish. When you're done, click the Format Painter icon again.
- In Excel, you can use the Format Painter to quickly duplicate cell formatting. Examples of copied formatting include number formats (such as Currency with two decimal places), cell shading, and borders.

Undoing and Redoing Actions

If you make a mistake, you can often correct it by *undoing* the action. You can choose Edit > Undo *action* or click the Undo icon on the Standard toolbar.

Office 2008 programs allow unlimited Undos. If you find that you made a mistake several actions ago, you can step back from the most recent action to the one you need to fix, reversing (undoing) each one. And if, after undoing an action, you change your mind, you can *redo* what you've undone.

To undo one or more actions:

1. To undo your most recent action, *do any of the following:*
   - Choose Edit > Undo *action* (⌘Z).
   - Click the Undo icon on the Standard toolbar (**Figure 1.32**).
2. To undo *multiple* recent actions, *do any of the following:*
   - Repeatedly choose Edit > Undo *action,* press ⌘Z, or click the Undo icon.
   - Click the down arrow beside the Undo toolbar icon and select the actions that you want to correct (**Figure 1.33**).

   In order from most to least recent, each action is undone.
3. To reverse (redo) the effect of one or more Undo commands, *do any of the following:*
   - Choose Edit > Redo *action* (⌘Y).
   - Click the Redo toolbar icon (Figure 1.32).
   - Click the down arrow beside the Redo toolbar icon, and choose the number of actions that you want to redo (Figure 1.33).

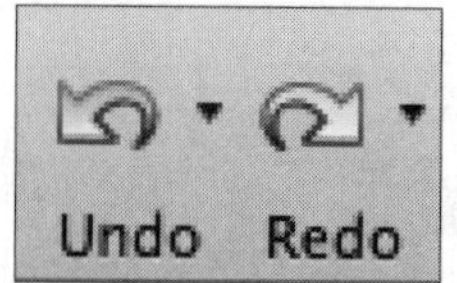

Figure 1.32 Undo and Redo icons can be found on the Standard toolbar.

Figure 1.33 Open the Undo menu and choose the actions to undo.

Repeating an Action

You'll occasionally find yourself repeating an action over and over. For example, if you decide to change the font, color, or style of a particular heading level in a Word document, there's no need to laboriously choose the same formatting command for each heading. Instead, after you select a heading, apply the Repeat command.

Redo and Repeat share the same keyboard shortcut. To apply your most recent action or command to a new selection, choose Edit > Repeat (⌘Y).

The Elements Gallery

Visually, the most obvious difference between Office 2008 and 2004 is the addition of the Elements Gallery (**Figure 1.34**, page bottom) to Word, Excel, and PowerPoint. Its purpose is to simplify the process of inserting various material into Office documents. The tabs of the Elements Gallery can be found immediately above the document area.

To insert an Elements Gallery item:

1. Depending on the item you're inserting, *you may need to do one of the following:*
   - ▲ Set the text insertion mark to indicate where the item, such as a Word table, will be placed.
   - ▲ Select data (from which to create a chart in Excel, for example).
   - ▲ Select the object with which the item will interact, such as a PowerPoint slide or an object on a slide.
2. Click an Elements Gallery tab.

   The Elements Gallery opens and displays a set of thumbnails.
3. Some items are organized into groups, such as the Document Elements in Word (Figure 1.34). If so, click the button of the group you want to view.
4. If there are more thumbnails than can be shown, click the scroll arrows to view the others.
5. Click a thumbnail to insert or apply that item.

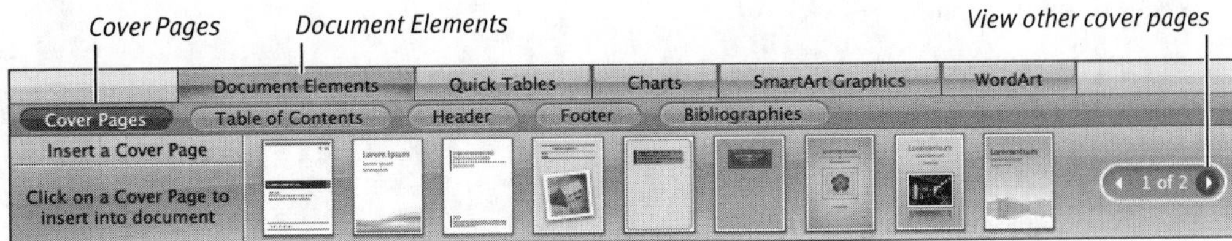

Figure 1.34 To add a cover page to the current Word document, click a thumbnail in the Elements Gallery.

The Toolbox

Many useful utilities can be found on the tabs of the floating Toolbox. Although the Toolbox is available in all four Office applications, some tabs are application-specific, such as Formula Builder (Excel) and Citations (Word).

To introduce you to the Toolbox, this section covers the Scrapbook and Compatibility Report tabs. Other tabs are discussed throughout the book, such as Reference Tools (dictionary, encyclopedia, thesaurus) in Chapter 2, Object Palette in Chapter 5, and Project Palette in Chapter 30.

To open or close the Toolbox:

1. To open the Toolbox, click the Toolbox icon on the Standard toolbar (**Figure 1.35**) or choose View, followed by the name of a Toolbox tab.

   The Toolbox opens (**Figure 1.36**) to the tab you last used or the tab you specifically chose. To switch to another tool, click its tab at the top of the window.

2. To close the Toolbox, click the Toolbox icon again, click the window's red close button, or choose the name of the current (checked) tab from the View menu.

✔ Tips

- To move the Toolbox, drag its title bar.
- To collapse or expand the Toolbox, click its green zoom button.
- To collapse or expand sections of any Toolbox tab, click the triangle that precedes the section name.
- There's no Toolbox icon in Entourage nor is there a Toolbox command in the View menu. To open the Toolbox in Entourage, choose a specific tab from the Tools > Toolbox submenu.

Figure 1.35 Click the Toolbox icon on the Standard toolbar. When the Toolbox is open (as it is here), its icon is dark.

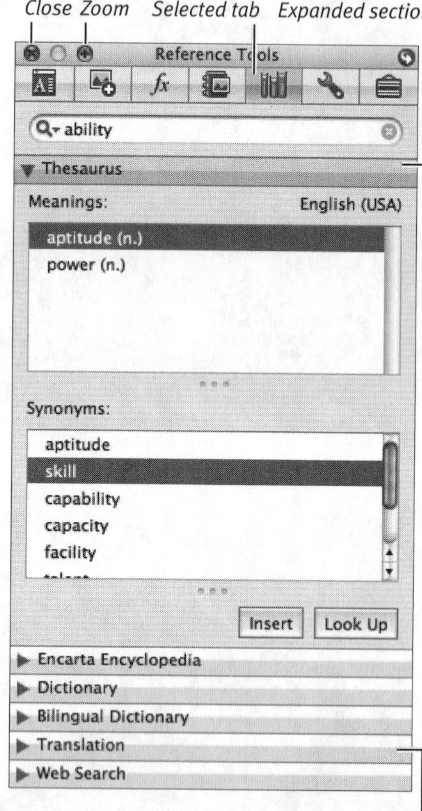

Figure 1.36 The Toolbox.

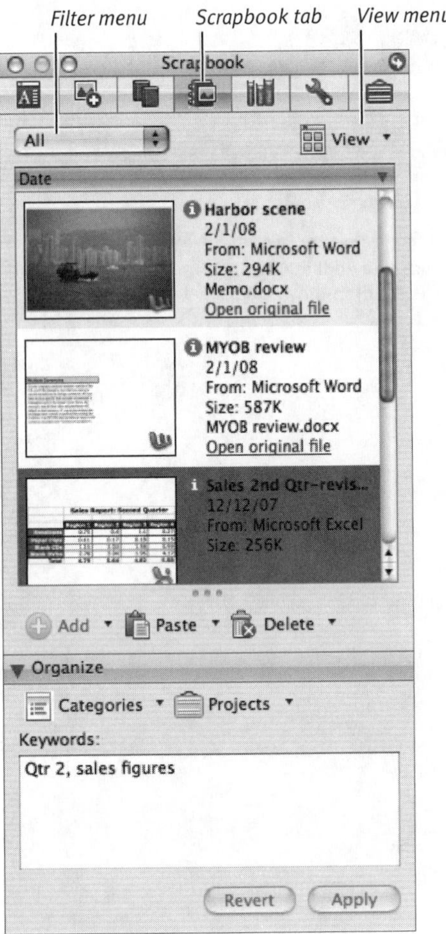

Figure 1.37 Use the Scrapbook to store text and graphic clips.

Figure 1.38 Click the Add drop-down menu to store information from the current selection, Clipboard, or a file.

The Scrapbook

In Mac OS X, the *Clipboard* is a temporary repository for copied (⌘C) or cut (⌘X) material. The material can then be pasted (⌘V) into the same document, a different document, or even a document of another application. For instance, you can copy an image in Photoshop and paste it into a Word document.

Unlike the Clipboard, material stored in the Scrapbook isn't temporary. It remains there until you delete it, and it can be pasted into any Office document. You can store material that is selected within an Office document, copied or cut material from the Clipboard, or complete files.

To add an item to the Scrapbook:

1. Open the Toolbox and click the Scrapbook tab (**Figure 1.37**).
2. *Do one of the following:*
   - ▲ Select an item in an open Office document, such as text, a graphic image or another object, or a cell range. Drag the item into the Scrapbook or click the Scrapbook's Add button.
   - ▲ To add the contents of the Clipboard as a Scrapbook item, click the down arrow beside the Add button and choose Add from Clipboard (**Figure 1.38**).
   - ▲ To add a file as a Scrapbook item, click the down arrow beside the Add button and choose Add File (see Figure 1.36). In the Choose a File dialog box that appears, select the file that you want to add and click Choose.

The material is added as a new Scrapbook item (called a *clip*).

To insert a clip into a document:

1. *Optional:* Click in an active document to place the insertion mark where you want to paste the Scrapbook clip.
2. In the Scrapbook, select a clip to be pasted. The selected item is shaded in blue.
3. *Do one of the following:*
   - ▲ Drag the clip to the desired location in the document and release the mouse button.
   - ▲ Click the Paste button at the bottom of the Scrapbook window. The clip is added to the document at the current insertion mark.
   - ▲ Click the down arrow beside the Paste button (**Figure 1.39**) and choose Paste as Plain Text. The selected text clip is pasted, but its formatting is ignored.
   - ▲ Click the down arrow beside the Paste button (Figure 1.39) and choose Paste as Picture. The clip is pasted into the document as a graphic object.

✔ Tip

- ■ To simultaneously paste multiple Scrapbook items into a document, ⌘-click to select each item and then click Paste. You can also use this technique to delete multiple items.

Figure 1.39 Additional options are available in the Paste drop-down menu.

Setting Toolbox Preferences

To view or set preferences for the Toolbox or one of its palettes, click the Toolbox Settings icon on the right side of the title bar. Set display options for the Toolbox in the top half of the window. To change the preferences for a particular palette, choose its name from the drop-down Palette menu.

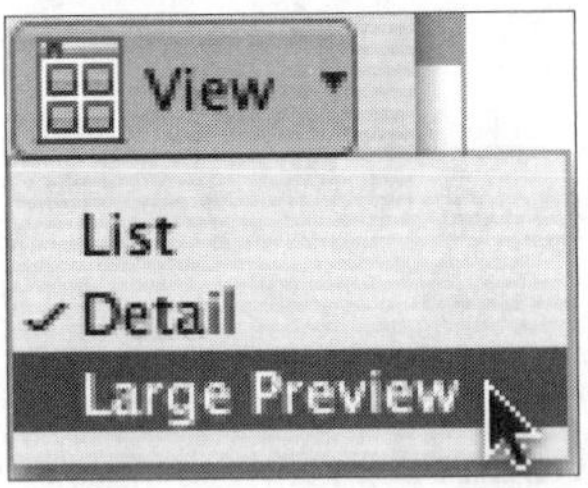

Figure 1.40 To change the manner in which clips are displayed, open the View drop-down menu.

To organize your Scrapbook clips:

◆ *Do any of the following:*

▲ To change the clip display mode, choose an option from the View drop-down menu (**Figure 1.40**).

▲ To add a descriptive name to a clip, double-click the clip. Replace the selected clip name with one of your choosing.

▲ To associate a selected clip with a category, project, or keywords, expand the Organize section of the Scrapbook. Choose categories and projects from the drop-down lists. To add keywords, type them in the Keywords box, separated by commas.

▲ To delete one or more selected clips, click the Delete button at the bottom of the window.

▲ To delete all or just the visible clips from the Scrapbook, click the down arrow beside the Delete button, choose the appropriate command, and confirm the deletion in the dialog box that appears.

Filtering the Clip List

If your Scrapbook contains a lot of clips, you can filter it to show only those that match a criterion. Choose a command from the drop-down menu at the top of the window (**Figure 1.41**). To restore the complete list, choose All.

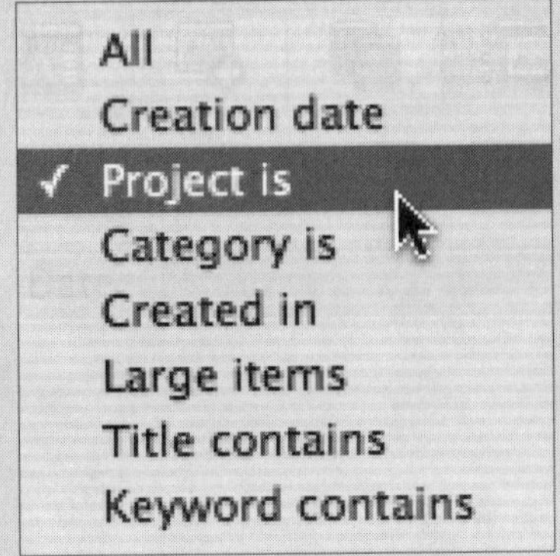

Figure 1.41 Choose a filter option from the drop-down menu. Then enter any other requested information.

Compatibility Report

Many users are concerned about the cross-platform compatibility of their documents, as well as whether users of older versions of Office will be able to open documents created in the newest version. In Office 2008, this should be less of a concern because you can check any document for potential compatibility issues and optionally correct them.

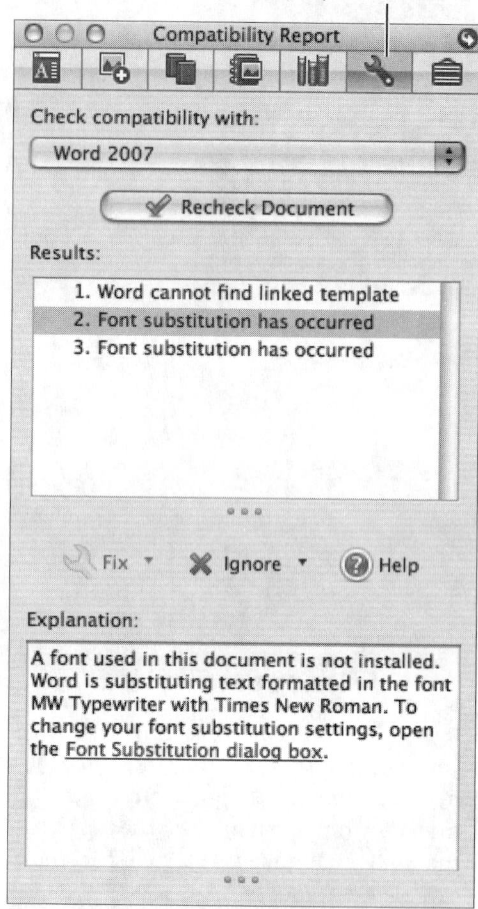

Figure 1.42 Use the Compatibility Report palette to determine if the current document has potential compatibility problems.

To create a compatibility report:

1. In Office 2008, open the document you want to check.
2. Open the Toolbox. Click the Compatibility Report tab.
3. If you know the version of Office that the document's intended recipient uses, select it from the drop-down list.
4. Click the Check Document button.

   Compatibility issues, if any, appear in the Results box (**Figure 1.42**). The button label changes to "Recheck Document."
5. One by one, select each numbered item that appears in the Results box.

   An explanation of the compatibility issue appears in the Explanation box.
6. For each compatibility issue, you can click Fix or Ignore.

   However, as shown in Figure 1.42, not all issues can be corrected in this manner. Some must be fixed manually by following the Explanation text.

✔ Tip

- Each application's Preferences has a Compatibility section where you can specify how compatibility issues will be handled.

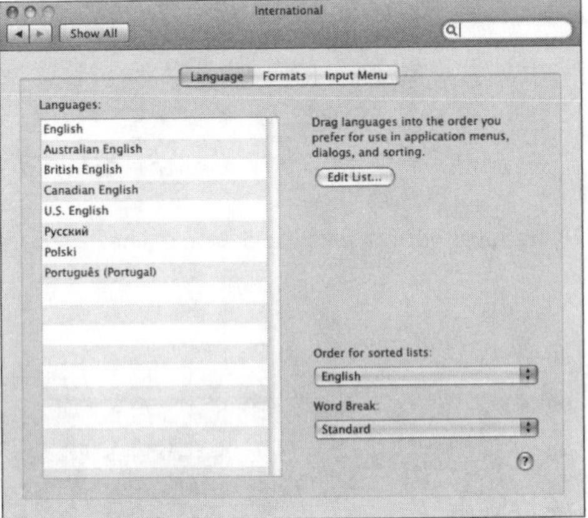

Figure 1.43 Use the International System Preferences to instruct OS X to support languages other than English on your computer.

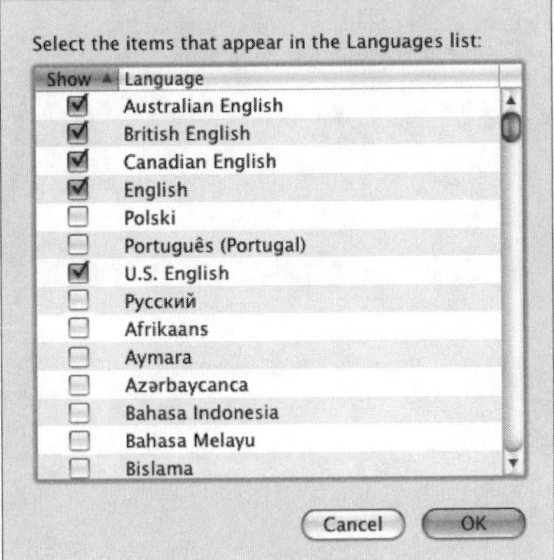

Figure 1.44 Check the languages that you want OS X to support.

Working in Other Languages

Via its Unicode language support, Office 2008 can display a variety of foreign (non-Roman) characters. You can view and edit documents in many languages, mix languages in a document, and set preferences to match the conventions and requirements of particular languages. You can also use foreign characters in filenames.

To set OS X's foreign language support:

1. Open System Preferences and click the International icon.
2. Select the Language tab of the International dialog box (**Figure 1.43**).
3. If the language you want to use isn't in the Languages list box, click the Edit List button to add languages (**Figure 1.44**).

   After adding a language, you can change the list's order by dragging items up or down in the Languages list.
4. Click the other tabs to set your preferred date, time, and number styles, as well as the keyboard layout. Close the dialog box.

To mark text as a different language:

1. Select the text. Choose Tools > Language. The Language dialog box appears.
2. Select the text's language from the list, and then click OK.

   During spelling checks, the appropriate foreign language dictionary will be used to check the selected text.

✔ Tip

- To specify a new language for the spelling checker to use, select the language in the Language dialog box and click Default. Confirm the change by clicking Yes.

Flagging Files for Followup

You can flag any Office document for followup at a later time. For instance, if you want to be reminded to review a budget worksheet two hours before the scheduled meeting, you can flag it for followup. At the appointed date and time, a reminder will pop onscreen. The Office Reminders program (see Chapter 23) is responsible for displaying all Office-related reminders.

To flag a document for followup:

1. Make the document active in the Office program in which it was created.
2. Choose Tools > Flag for Follow Up.
   The Flag for Follow Up dialog box appears (**Figure 1.45**).
3. Specify the date and time at which you want to be reminded, and then click OK.
   The flagged document is recorded as a new Entourage task.
4. At the designated time, a reminder dialog box will appear (**Figure 1.46**). Double-click the document's item to launch the appropriate Office application and open the document.

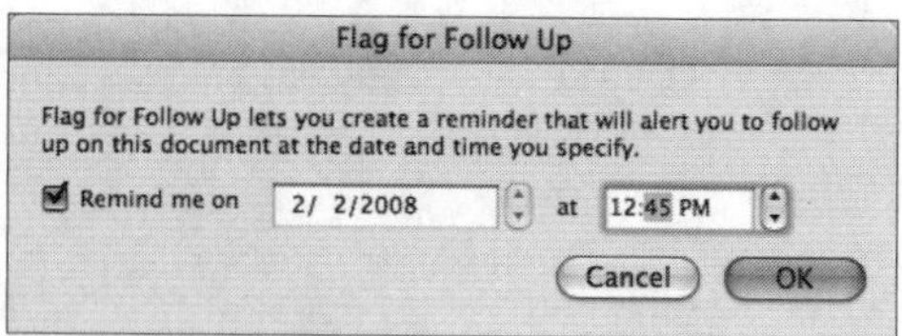

Figure 1.45 Specify a followup date and time.

Figure 1.46 To open the document, double-click its task in the Office Reminders dialog box.

✔ Tips

- Like other tasks, you can also use the Office Reminders window to mark the document followup as complete (by clicking its check box), request that you be reminded again later (by clicking the Snooze button), or dismiss the reminder but leave the item as incomplete in the Tasks list (by clicking Dismiss).
- For more information about using the Office Reminders window and working with tasks, see Chapters 23 and 24.

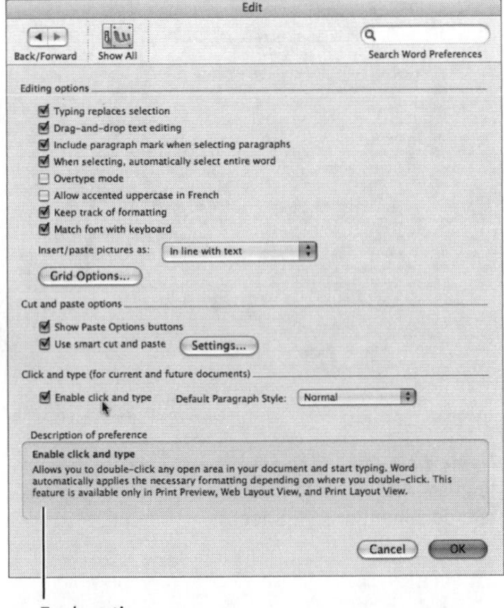

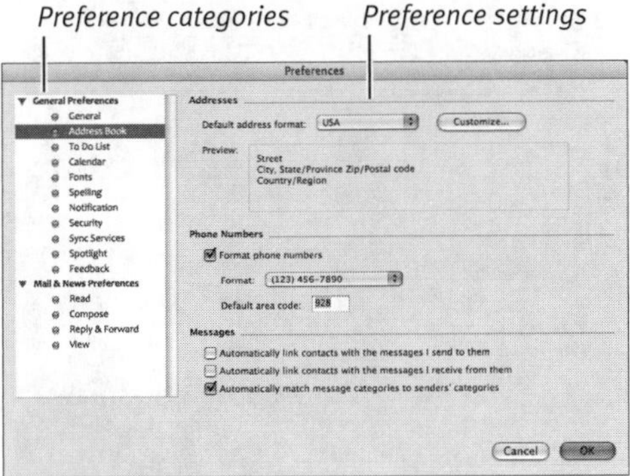

Figure 1.47 Edit preferences (Word, top) and Address Book preferences (Entourage, bottom).

Customizing and Setting Preferences

Although the Office applications are preconfigured in a way that will suit the average user's needs, you're free to customize them, if you wish. There are two ways to do this:

- Modify settings in the application's Preferences dialog boxes.
- Customize toolbars, menus, and keyboard shortcuts.

To change Preferences for a program:

1. With the program running, choose *program name* > Preferences (for example, Word > Preferences) or press ⌘,.

   The Preferences dialog box appears (**Figure 1.47**).

2. There are three styles of Preferences dialog boxes:

   - Entourage uses the Office 2004 style in which categories are listed on the left.
   - Word and Excel preferences are presented in the style of OS X System Preferences. Click an icon to view that preference category.
   - In PowerPoint, preference icons are strung across the top of the dialog box. As in Word and Excel, you click an icon to view that preference category.

   Click an icon (Word, Excel, or PowerPoint) or select a category (Entourage).

   The selected preferences appear. When the cursor is rested over a preference item (Word and Excel Preferences only), an explanation appears in the bottom pane.

3. Set preferences as you wish.
4. Repeat Steps 2 and 3 for other preference categories, if desired.
5. Click OK to save the new settings.

To customize Word, Excel, or PowerPoint toolbars or menus:

1. With the application running, choose View > Customize Toolbars and Menus.

   The Customize Toolbars and Menus dialog box appears.

2. **Default toolbars.** Click the Toolbars and Menus tab of the dialog box (**Figure 1.48**). Click check boxes of the toolbars that should automatically be displayed whenever you run the application.

   Word only: From the Save in drop-down menu, choose the current document (to associate the selected toolbars with only that document) or a style sheet name, such as Normal.dotm (to associate the toolbars with all Word documents based on that style sheet).

3. **Customized toolbars and menus.** You can customize toolbars and menus by adding icons, controls, and commands. (To modify a toolbar, the toolbar must be onscreen. You can display it by clicking its check box on the Toolbars and Menus tab of the dialog box. To create a toolbar from scratch, click the New button.)

   Click the Commands tab of the dialog box. *Do any of the following:*

   ▲ To add an icon to a toolbar, select it in the Commands pane and drag it into position on the toolbar.

   ▲ To add a command to a menu, drag the command from the Commands pane onto the menu title in the mini-menu bar (**Figure 1.49**). The menu will drop down. Drag the command to its destination position within the menu and release the mouse button.

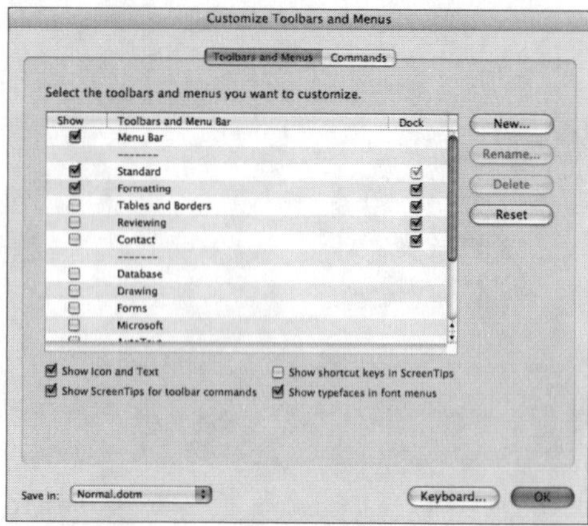

Figure 1.48 Add and remove check marks to specify toolbars that will automatically appear with the current document or style sheet.

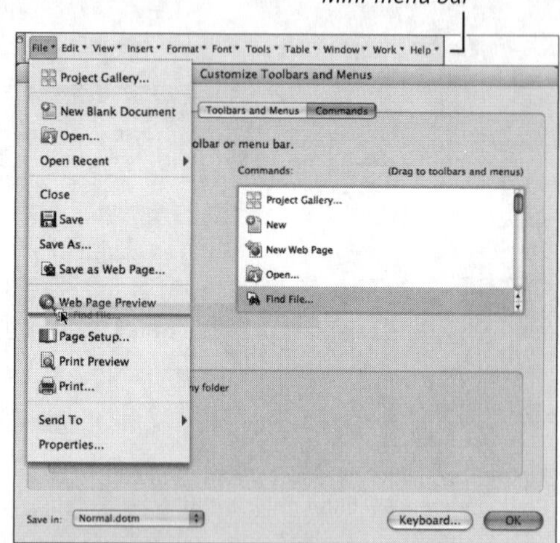

Figure 1.49 To add a command to a menu, drag it from the Commands section of the dialog box into the destination mini-menu.

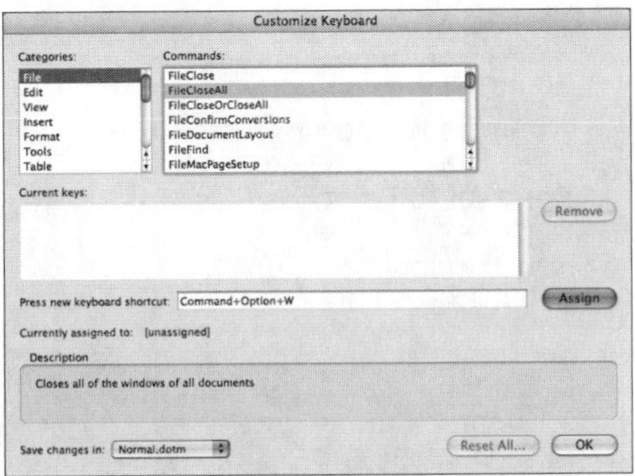

Figure 1.50 Use the Customize Keyboard dialog box to create new keyboard shortcuts for Word or Excel.

- If you later decide to remove an added command or toolbar icon, select the Commands tab of the Customize Toolbars and Menus dialog box. Drag the command out of the mini-menu or drag the icon off the toolbar.

4. **Customized Keyboard (Word and Excel only).** In the Customize Toolbars and Menus dialog box, click the Keyboard button (see Figure 1.48). The Customize Keyboard dialog box (**Figure 1.50**) is used to add or change keyboard shortcuts.

   Word only: From the Save changes in drop-down menu, choose the current document (to associate the new shortcuts with only that document) or a style sheet name, such as Normal.dotm (to associate the shortcuts with all Word documents based on that style sheet).

   In the Categories list, select a menu category. In the Commands list, select the command whose shortcuts you want to change. The current shortcuts assigned to that command (if any) are displayed.

   Do any of the following:

   - To add a new shortcut, click in the Press new keyboard shortcut box, press the key combination, and then click Assign or Add. (Be sure that no other command is already associated with the key combination before you click Add or Assign!)
   - To remove a keyboard shortcut, select it in the Current keys list and click Remove.
   - To restore the default keyboard shortcuts, select the style sheet or document name from the Save changes in drop-down menu and click Reset All.

✔ Tip

- For Entourage customization instructions, see Chapter 20.

Automator Workflows

If you have any version of Office 2008 other than the Home and Student edition, Office includes Automator actions sets. By employing and combining actions, you can create Automator workflows that automate complex or repetitive Office activities.

To view the Office 2008 actions, launch Automator by double-clicking its icon in the Applications folder. Then select an Office application from the Library list.

For information about using Automator to create workflows, switch to the Finder, choose Help > Mac Help, and search for `automator`. In Automator, choose Help > Automator Help.

Managing Windows

Regardless of the Office application you're using, you will occasionally work on multiple documents. You can use the Window menu (**Figure 1.51**) or click buttons to arrange, switch among, and manage the windows.

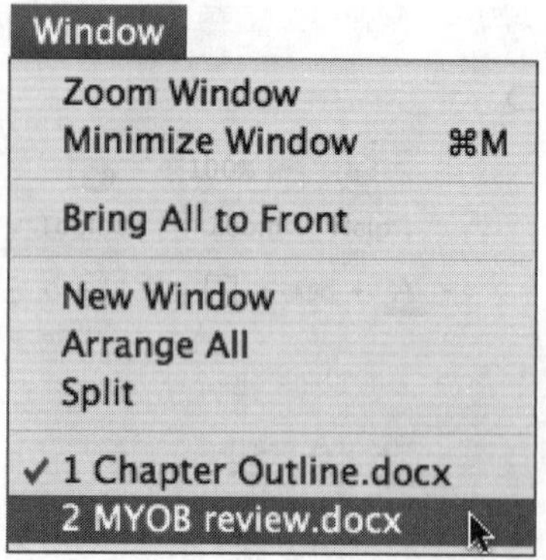

Figure 1.51 Window menu (Word).

To manage document windows:

- *Do any of the following:*
  - **Make a document active.** To make a different document active, click anywhere in its window or choose its name from the bottom of the Window menu.
  - **Minimize a document.** To minimize the active document, click the yellow button in the window's upper-left corner (**Figure 1.52**), double-click the window's title bar, choose Window > Minimize Window, or press ⌘M.

    To restore a minimized document, click its Dock icon or choose its name from the Window menu.
  - **Hide toolbars.** To hide or reveal the toolbars above the document area, click the button in the upper-right corner of the document window.
  - **Arrange All.** Choose this command to display all open documents at the same time. Windows are reduced as necessary to fit them onscreen.

    To work with one of the documents at its full size and position, choose Window > Zoom Window or click the zoom button (Figure 1.52). Repeat this procedure to restore the window to its Arrange All position.
  - **Close a document.** Click the close button (Figure 1.52), choose File > Close, or press ⌘W.

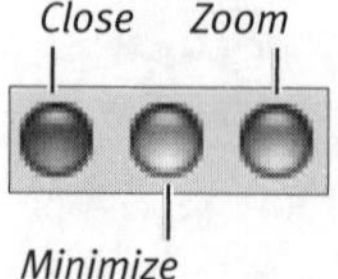

Figure 1.52 By clicking buttons at the top of any document, you can close, minimize, or zoom its window.

✔ Tip

- The Zoom button and the Zoom Window command toggle a window between its *current* location and size and its *last* location and size.

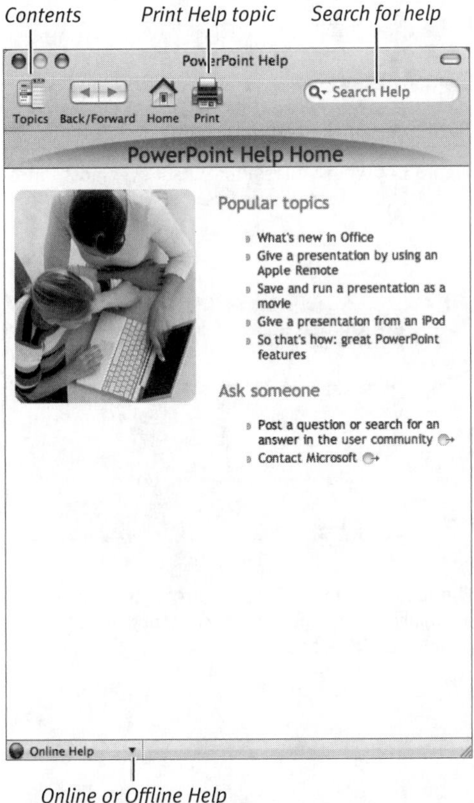

Figure 1.53 Your primary source of help (other than this book) is the application's Help window.

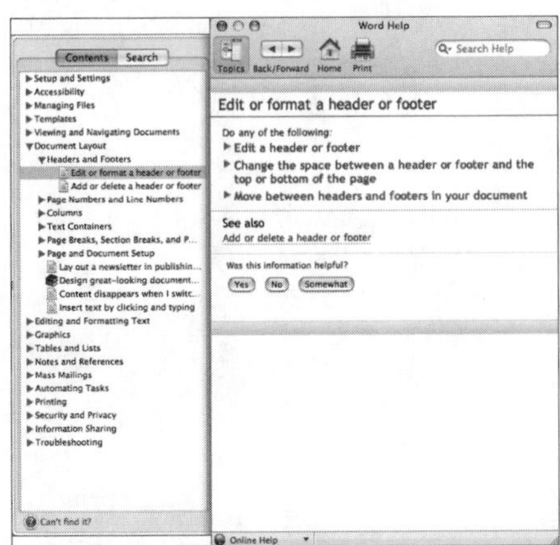

Figure 1.54 Help topics and search results appear in the drawer on the left.

Getting Help

Office 2008 provides several sources of help:

- You can use the detailed Help system provided with each Office application.
- You can get pop-up ScreenTips (also called ToolTips) for toolbar icons, controls, and other interface elements.
- You can visit Microsoft's Web site for tips and other information.

To use application Help:

1. Choose Help > *application* Help (⌘?).
   The Help system opens (**Figure 1.53**).
2. *Do one of the following:*
   - In the toolbar at the top of the Help window, click Topics to display a list of major topics. The list is presented in a drawer that pops out of the left side of the window.
   - Enter a keyword or phrase in the Search box and press Return to search for related Help text. Potential topic matches appear in the drawer.
3. Click an item in the drawer on the left (**Figure 1.54**) to display a Help topic or to expand a topic to display a list of subtopics, any of which you can click to view the associated Help text.
4. To navigate backward and forward through multiple help screens, click the arrow icons in the toolbar. In the body of the window, blue underlined text is a clickable link to another Help section.

To display a ScreenTip or ToolTip:

- Move the pointer over any icon, button, or other Office element, and then wait a second or two.

  A yellow ScreenTip appears (**Figure 1.55**).

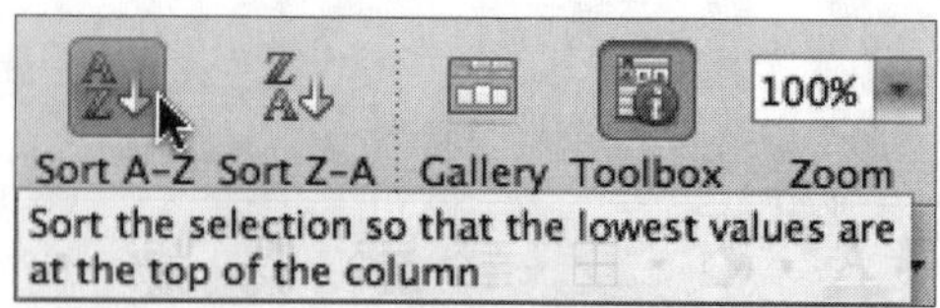

Figure 1.55 When you rest the cursor over most Office elements, a ScreenTip appears.

✔ Tips

- The Help system can draw its information from material stored on your hard disk during the installation (Offline Help) or from Microsoft's site (Online Help). To choose a Help source, click the down arrow in the bottom-left corner of the Help window (see Figure 1.53).
- To visit an Office application's Web site in your default browser, choose Help > Visit the Product Web Site.
- To manually check for available updates to the current Office application, choose Help > Check for Updates. The Microsoft AutoUpdate dialog box appears (**Figure 1.56**). Click the Check for Updates button.
- Microsoft AutoUpdate can be configured to automatically check for updates on a repeating schedule. Click the Automatically radio button and choose a schedule from the drop-down menu.
- To see a list of all installed updates (as well as the Office programs you've registered), click View Installed Updates.

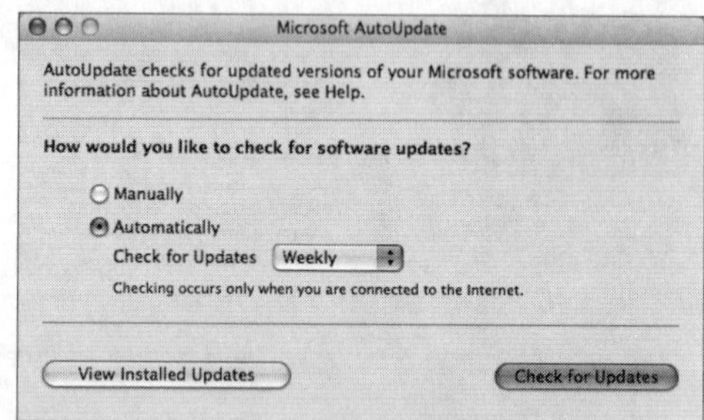

Figure 1.56 Microsoft AutoUpdate can be used to manually or automatically check for and install updates to Office 2008.

Part II: Microsoft Word

2

Introducing Word 2008

Expanding on the material in Chapter 1, this chapter covers additional elementary features that are specific to Word. While you can get along fine without mastering the material in this chapter, a familiarity with it will make your Word experience more productive.

Other chapters in Part II explain document and text formatting; adding images to Word documents; designing tables; working in other views to create outlines, notebooks, and publications; and employing more advanced features to create documents for school and business.

The Word Interface

If this is the first time you've used Word, you should begin by familiarizing yourself with the Word window and its components (**Figure 2.1**). They'll be referred to throughout the chapters in Part II of this book.

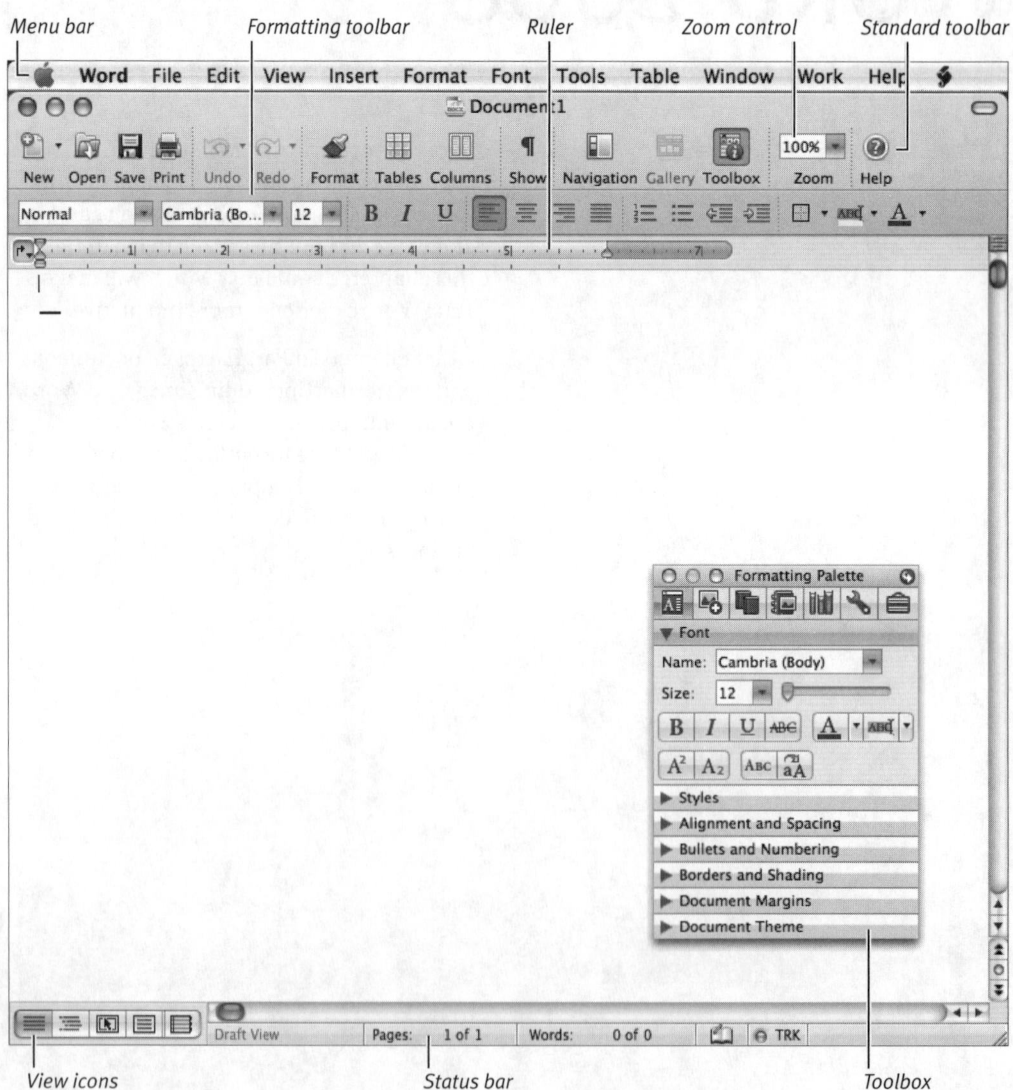

Figure 2.1 The Word window.

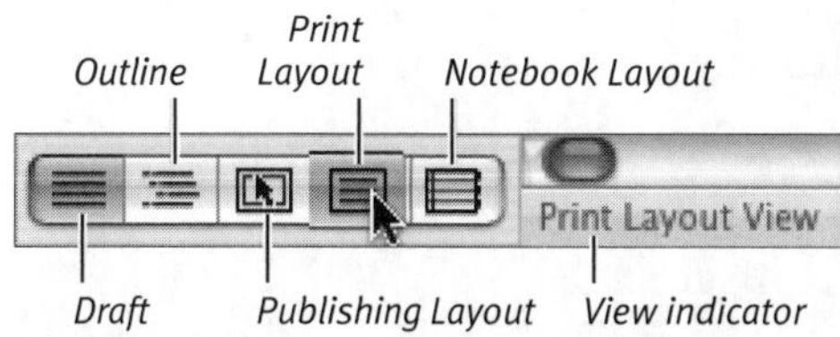

Figure 2.2 You can switch to most views by clicking an icon at the bottom of the document window.

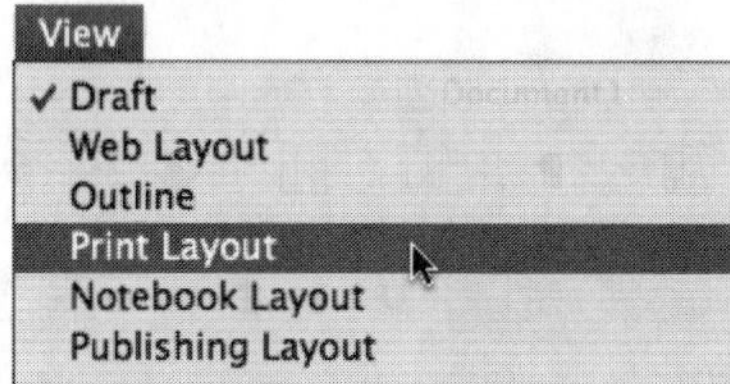

Figure 2.3 You can also change views by choosing a command from the top section of the View menu.

Changing views

Different *views* enable you to work with or view a document in different ways. You can pick from Draft, Web Layout, Outline, Print Layout, Notebook Layout, and Publishing Layout views (see **Table 2.1**).

To change views:

- *Do one of the following:*
  - Click the Draft, Outline, Publishing Layout, Print Layout, or Notebook Layout icon in the bottom-left corner of the document window (**Figure 2.2**).
  - Choose a view from the View menu (**Figure 2.3**).

✔ Tips

- Many of the views have been renamed in Office 2008. The only *new* view, however, is Publishing Layout view.
- Web Layout view is only accessible from the View menu.
- Although Print Layout view constantly displays useful layout information (such as margins, page breaks, and so on), writing in Word is usually fastest when done in Draft view.
- To use "click and type" (discussed later in this chapter), you must be in Print Layout, Web Layout, or Notebook Layout view.

Table 2.1

Word Document Views

View	Purpose
Draft	Shows text formatting in a simplified page layout that lends itself well to most standard writing tasks.
Outline	Shows the document's structure and allows you to rearrange text by dragging headings.
Print Layout	Shows the document as it will look when printed, including the page borders, margins, headers and footers, columns, and frames that contain images.
Web Layout	Shows the document as it would appear in a Web browser.
Notebook Layout	Used to quickly record notes and ideas (both in text and audio form).
Publishing Layout	Using layout tools, you can create complex documents, such as newsletters, brochures, and flyers.

Changing the magnification

Depending on the resolution setting in the Displays System Preferences, what you're working on, and your eyesight, you may want to increase or decrease the magnification for the current document. Select a new setting from the Zoom control's drop-down list on the Standard toolbar (see Figure 2.1) or choose View > Zoom (**Figure 2.4**).

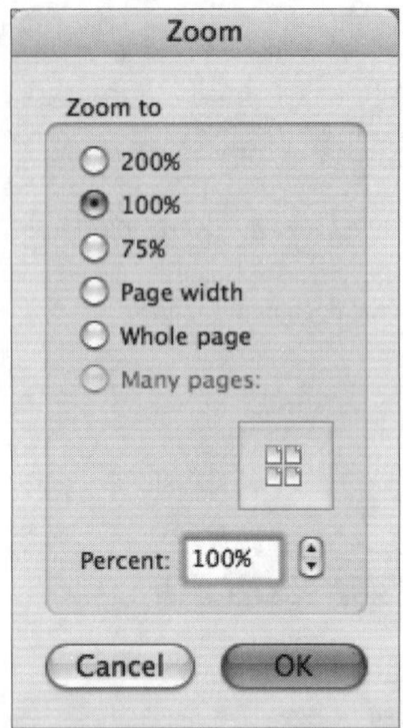

Figure 2.4 In addition to selecting the most common magnifications, you can set a specific magnification level in the Zoom dialog box.

Showing/hiding toolbars

As is the case in all Office 2008 applications, you can show or hide individual toolbars whenever you like. Some toolbars, such as the Outlining toolbar, are context-sensitive and appear automatically based on what you're doing. To display or remove a toolbar, choose its name from the View > Toolbars submenu. Checked toolbars are displayed; unchecked ones are hidden.

✔ Tips

- Some toolbars, such as the Standard and Formatting toolbars, appear at the top of the document window. Others, such as the Drawing toolbar, float and can be resized or moved around the screen (**Figure 2.5**).
- A floating toolbar can be removed by clicking its close button.
- Many toolbar functions are also available on the tabs of the Toolbox. For instance, you can select text-formatting options from the Formatting toolbar or the Formatting Palette.

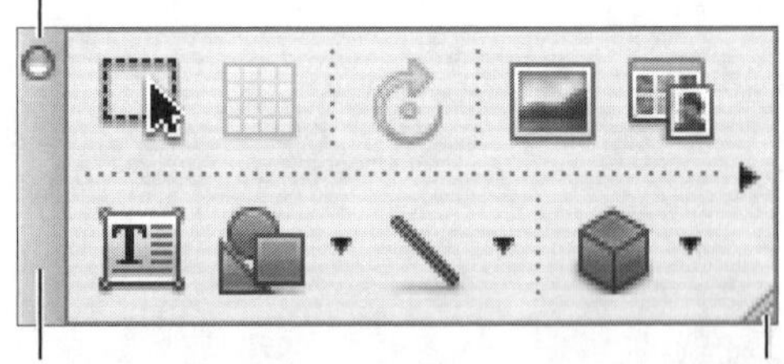

Figure 2.5 Floating toolbars can be moved, resized, or reshaped.

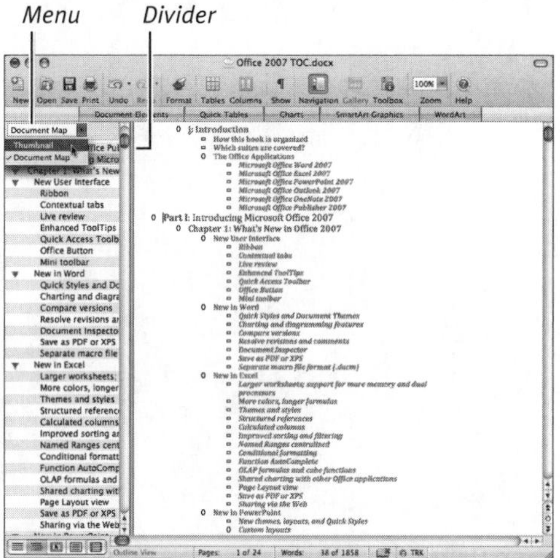

Figure 2.6 Use the navigation pane to navigate large documents.

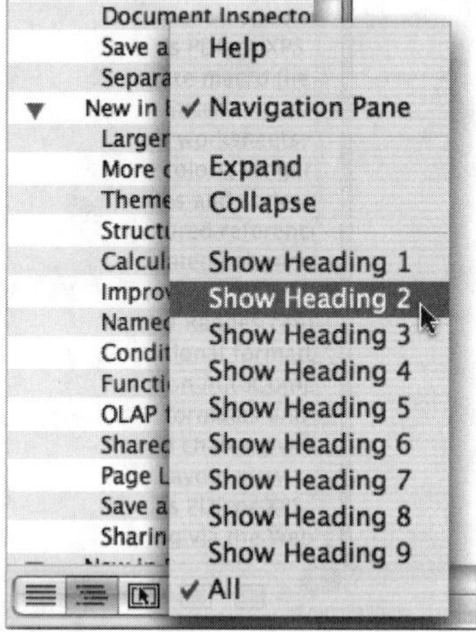

Figure 2.7 Choose a Show Heading command to specify the heading levels to be shown.

Using the navigation pane

You can use the navigation pane to immediately jump to any page or heading in the current document. As such, it's especially useful in long documents, such as manuals and reports.

To use the navigation pane:

1. To show or hide the navigation pane (on the left side of the document window), choose View > Navigation Pane or click the Navigation Pane icon on the Standard toolbar.
2. The navigation pane (**Figure 2.6**) has two display modes, determined by your choice from the drop-down menu above the pane:
   - ▲ **Thumbnail.** Displays miniature representations of document pages.
   - ▲ **Document Map.** Displays headings in the current document.

   You can switch display modes by choosing the other command.
3. To move to a new location in the current document, *do one of the following:*
   - ▲ When Thumbnail is chosen, click a page thumbnail.
   - ▲ When Document Map is chosen, click a heading.

✔ Tips

- You can change the width of the navigation pane by dragging the divider to the left or right.
- In Document Map view, you can control the specific heading levels displayed by Control-clicking in the navigation pane (**Figure 2.7**). Choose a Show Heading command to display all headings that are that level or higher. You can also expand and collapse heading levels as needed.

Entering Text

If you're new to computing, you'll find that entering text in a word-processing document is only a little different than using a typewriter—different but *much* simpler.

As in most computer programs, the blinking vertical line (called the *text insertion mark*) indicates where the next character you type will appear. Type as you would with a typewriter. The main differences include the following:

- You press Return only to begin a new paragraph—*not* to begin a new line in the same paragraph.
- You'll note that the lines of a paragraph are automatically adjusted to include as many words as possible. This occurs via a feature called *word wrap*. If you add or delete text in a paragraph, the entire paragraph rewraps to accommodate the changes.
- Typing a word-processing document doesn't have to be a linear process—as it must with a typewriter. For example, although you *can* backspace over errors (by pressing Delete), you can also just select incorrect text and type over it. (The first character you type automatically deletes the selected text.)
- You can click anywhere within existing text to change the text insertion mark. Then you can insert more text at that spot, correct an error, or perform edits.

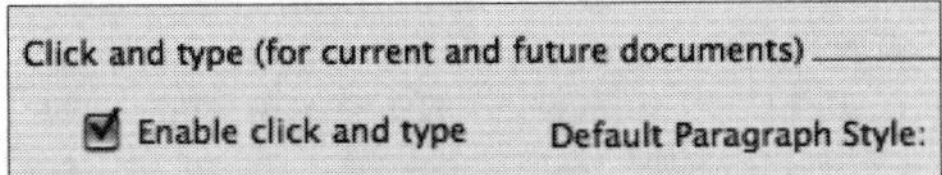

Figure 2.8 Enable click and type in the Edit dialog box.

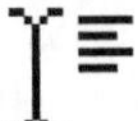

Figure 2.9 The click and type cursor changes to show the paragraph formatting that will be applied.

Click and type

Click and type is a Word feature that you can think of as a form of automatic paragraph formatting. You can click in any blank area of your document to enter text at that spot. In a new document, for example, you could click near the right margin or halfway down the page. Click and type is available in Print Layout, Web Layout, and Notebook Layout views, but not in Draft or Outline view.

To enable and use click and type:

1. Choose Word > Preferences (⌘,).
   The Word Preferences dialog box appears.
2. In the Authoring and Proofing Tools section, click the Edit icon to display the Edit preferences.
3. Near the bottom of the dialog box, ensure that Enable click and type is checked (**Figure 2.8**). Click OK.
4. Switch to a view in which click and type is supported: Print Layout, Web Layout, or Notebook Layout.
5. Move the cursor to a blank spot on the page where you'd like to type.
   As you move, the cursor changes shape to reflect the type of paragraph formatting that will be applied to the text (**Figure 2.9**). The shapes include align left, align right, center, left indent, left text wrap, and right text wrap.
6. Double-click to set the new text insertion mark and begin typing.
   Word inserts the necessary blank paragraphs and tabs to fill the document to the beginning of the new text.

Showing/hiding nonprinting characters

Whether you're entering, editing, or proofing text, it can be helpful to see the normally invisible, nonprinting characters: spaces, tabs, returns, and line breaks (**Figure 2.10**). Displaying nonprinting characters is very useful when you're looking for multiple tab characters where only one should be or when you're trying to eliminate incorrect punctuation, such as blank paragraphs or extra spaces between words or sentences.

You can show or hide these characters as you work on any Word document. See **Table 2.2** for a list of nonprinting characters.

To show/hide nonprinting characters:

◆ Click the Show all nonprinting characters icon on the Standard toolbar (**Figure 2.11**).

✔ Tips

■ The Show all nonprinting characters (¶) icon works as a toggle. Click it once to show nonprinting characters and a second time to hide them.

■ Showing nonprinting characters is particularly useful in the proofing/editing stage—after you've finished the writing. (Having nonprinting characters visible while *creating* a document, on the other hand, can be distracting.)

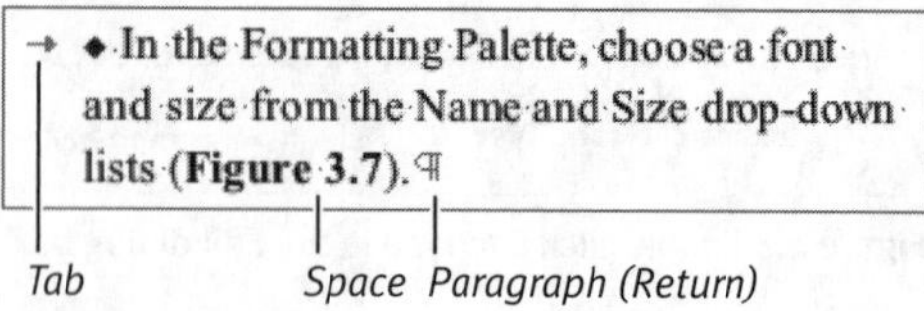

Figure 2.10 When displayed, non-printing characters are a faint gray.

Figure 2.11 The Show all nonprinting characters icon is the paragraph symbol (¶).

Table 2.2

Non-printing Characters	
SYMBOL	CHARACTER
· (dot)	Space
→	Tab
↵	Line break (new line, same paragraph)
¶	End of paragraph

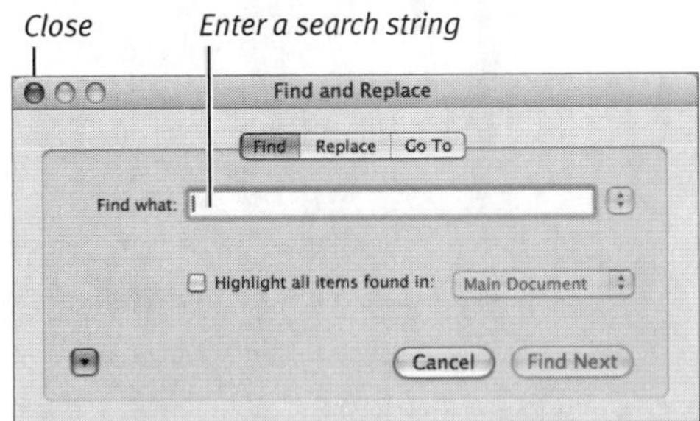

Figure 2.12 Enter the text you want to find in the Find what box.

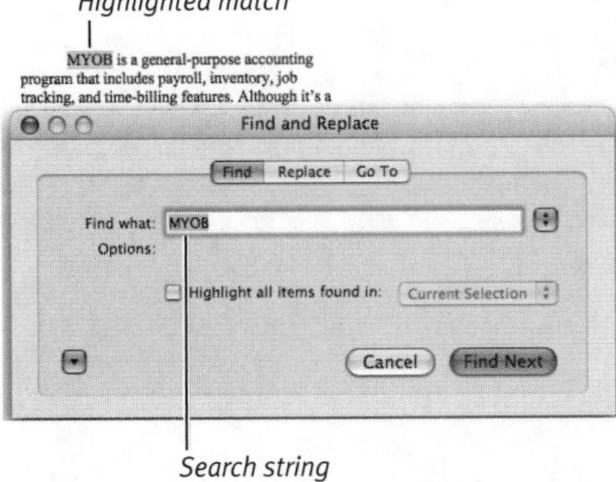

Figure 2.13 When a Find or Find and Replace search locates a match, Word scrolls as necessary to highlight the found text.

Editing: Beyond the Basics

Basic editing techniques were discussed in Chapter 1. In this section, you'll learn to search for and replace text, use Office's AutoText feature to automatically enter text for you, and use smart buttons to speed common editing and formatting tasks.

Finding and replacing text

You can instruct Word to search for and optionally replace words or phrases. For example, if you can't remember the page on which you referred to Apple's annual report, you could perform a Find on the phrase `annual report`. Or suppose your company recently changed its name from Johnson Plumbing Supplies to Widgets Inc. Using the Replace command, you can replace every instance of the old name with the new one. On the next page, see **Table 2.3** for a list of special Find/Replace options.

To find text:

1. Choose Edit > Find (⌘F).

   The Find and Replace dialog box appears (**Figure 2.12**). The Find tab is selected.

2. Type a search string in the Find what box.

3. *Do either of the following:*

   ▲ To find the next instance of the search string, click Find Next.

   Word searches for the string, starting from the current text insertion mark. If the string is found, it's highlighted (**Figure 2.13**).

   ▲ To find and highlight *all* instances of the search string, click the Highlight all items found in check box, choose an option from the drop-down menu (such as Main Document or Current Selection), and click Find All.

continues on next page

4. *Do either of the following:*
   - ▲ To search for the next occurrence of the text (when searching for individual instances), click Find Next. Repeat as necessary to find other matches.
   - ▲ If you're done searching, click the Cancel or Close button.

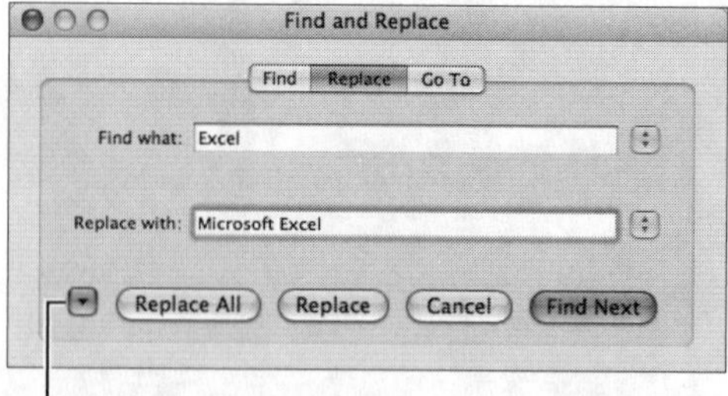

Figure 2.14 Type the search text in the Find what box and the replacement text in the Replace with box.

To replace text:

1. *Do one of the following:*
   - ▲ Choose Edit > Replace (Shift⌘H). The Find and Replace dialog box appears. The Replace tab is selected (**Figure 2.14**).
   - ▲ Choose Edit > Find (⌘F). The Find and Replace dialog box appears. Click the Replace tab.
2. Type a search string in the Find what box.
3. In the Replace with box, type the replacement string. Click Find Next.

   Word searches for the text. If an instance is found, it's highlighted in the document.
4. *Do one of the following:*
   - ▲ Click Replace to replace the text and search for the next instance, if any.
   - ▲ Click Find Next to ignore this instance and search for the next occurrence.

   Repeat this step until you're done or until Word has finished searching.
5. Click Cancel or Close to dismiss the dialog box.

Table 2.3

Special Find/Replace Options

Option	Description
Match case	Finds words that contain the same combination of upper- and lowercase characters
Find whole words only	Finds only complete words (for example, "art" finds only "art," not "artist")
Use wildcards	Allows you to enter a code to specify a special character combination to find (for example, "?" will match any single character)
Sounds like	Finds text that sounds like the search string
Find all word forms	Finds all variations of the chosen word (for example, "apple" and "apples")

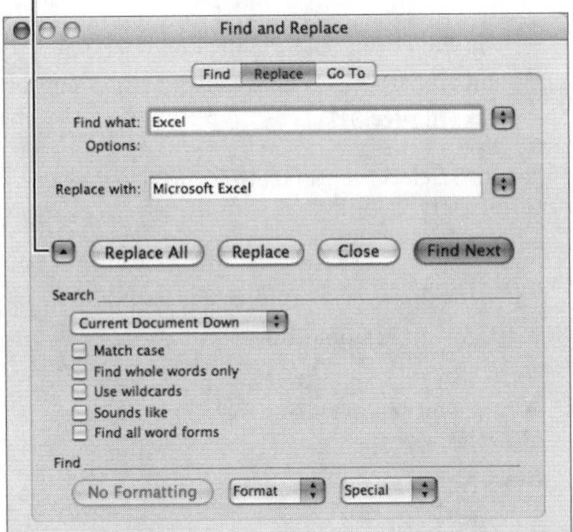

Figure 2.15 Click the triangle to expand the Find and Replace dialog box to show advanced search options (see Table 2.3 on the previous page).

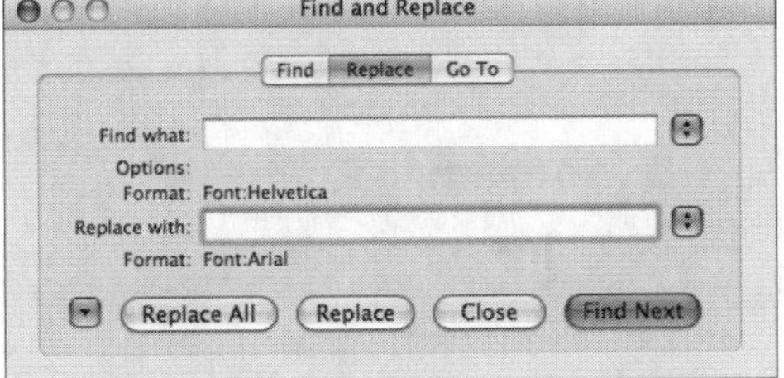

Figure 2.16 By including only format options in the Find what and Replace with boxes, you can replace one font with another throughout a document.

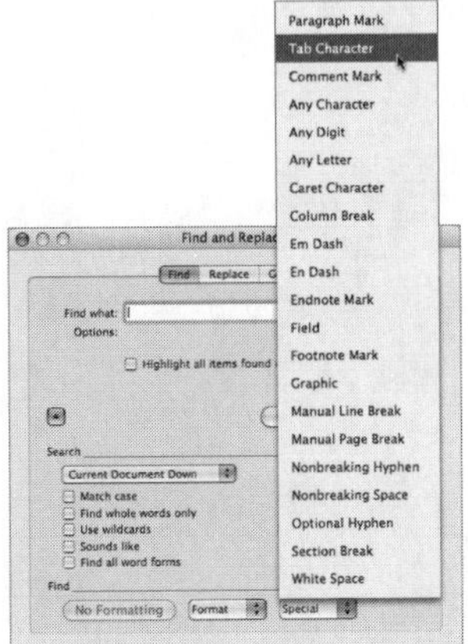

Figure 2.17 To include a special character in a Find or Replace string, choose it from this menu.

✔ Tips

- When performing a new Find or a Find/Replace, you can repeat a search by clicking the arrow to the right of the Find what text box. Search terms you've previously used appear in a drop-down list. The arrow to the right of Replace with provides a list of the recently used replacement text strings.
- When performing a Replace, you can click Replace All to simultaneously replace all occurrences of the search string.
- Click the triangle in the bottom-left corner of the dialog box to display additional search options (**Figure 2.15**). For instance, Finds are normally case insensitive. If you want to find terms that match a specific capitalization, click the Match case check box. To hide the additional search options, click the triangle again.
- You can also base a search on a font, effect, or style by choosing options from the Format drop-down menu (Figure 2.15). For example, you could replace all instances of Helvetica text with Arial (**Figure 2.16**).
- To clear formatting from the find and replace strings, click No Formatting.
- To specify a search direction (down, up, or all) or to search all open documents rather than just the active one, choose an option from the drop-down menu at the top of the expanded search options.
- To include a special character such as a tab or paragraph mark in a search, open the Special menu and choose a character (**Figure 2.17**). The symbol for the chosen character is automatically added to the search string. (In the example shown in Figure 2.17, `^t` is inserted to represent a tab character.)

Automatically entering text

The AutoText feature is designed to help you avoid repetitively typing text. AutoText allows you to quickly insert any amount of frequently used text into a document—from one word to multiple paragraphs.

2. → Do one of the following: ¶

→ ◆ In the Formatting Palette, choose a font and size from the Name and Size drop-down lists (Figure 3.7). ¶

Figure 2.18 Select the text that will become the new AutoText entry.

To create an AutoText entry:

1. In the active document, select the text from which you want to create an AutoText entry (**Figure 2.18**).

   The selected text must consist of at least five characters.

2. Choose Insert > AutoText > New.

   The Create AutoText dialog box appears and suggests a name.

3. *Optional:* Replace the suggested name with one of your own (**Figure 2.19**).

   If you want to be able to insert the entry using AutoComplete, make sure that the name contains at least four characters.

4. Click OK to add the text to the list of available AutoText entries.

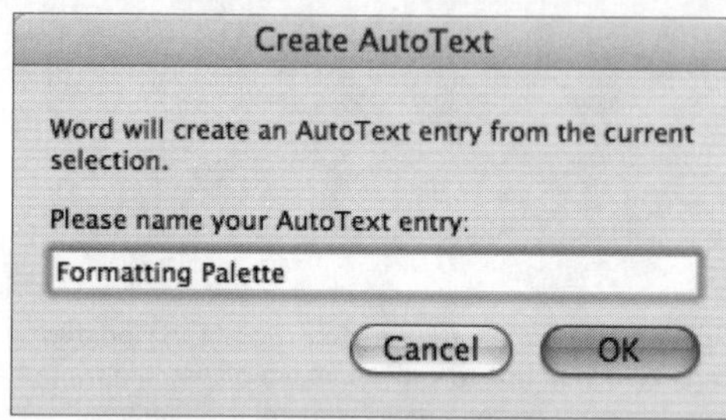

Figure 2.19 The Create AutoText dialog appears and suggests a name for the new entry. Edit it as desired.

To insert an AutoText entry:

1. As you type, Word watches for the name of an AutoText entry. When it detects one, a yellow box containing the AutoText entry's name appears (**Figure 2.20**).

2. *Do one of the following:*

   ▲ To accept the AutoText replacement, press Enter or Return.

   ▲ To ignore the proposed AutoText replacement, continue typing.

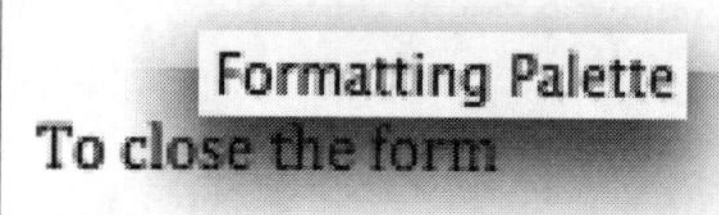

Figure 2.20 Whenever you type four characters that are a possible AutoText entry, you are offered the opportunity to insert it.

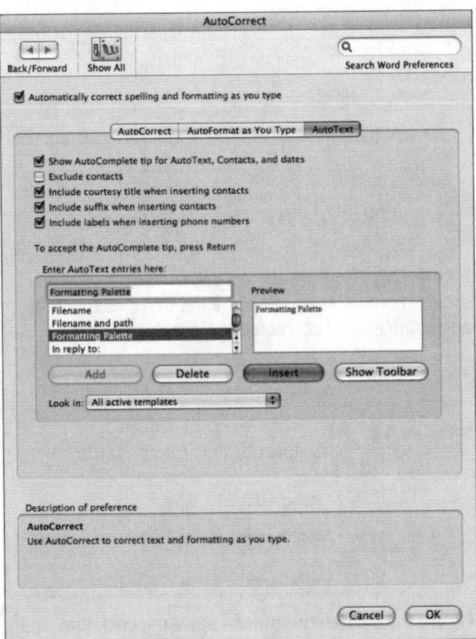

Figure 2.21 You can delete AutoText entries, as well as specify the classes of entries to use, in the AutoCorrect dialog box.

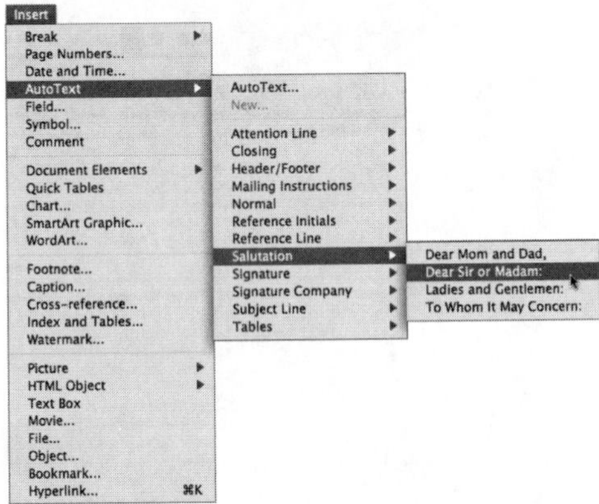

Figure 2.22 You can also insert an AutoText entry by choosing it from an Insert > AutoText submenu or from the floating AutoText toolbar (View > Toolbars > AutoText).

✔ Tips

- You can use AutoText to enter lengthy medical, legal, or technical terms. AutoText is also great when writing letters that use standard opening and closing lines.
- To delete an AutoText entry, choose Insert > AutoText > AutoText. On the AutoText tab of the AutoCorrect dialog box (**Figure 2.21**), select the entry in the list box and click the Delete button.
- You can also insert AutoText by choosing Insert > AutoText > AutoText, selecting the entry from the list in the AutoCorrect dialog box (Figure 2.21), and clicking Insert.
- Another way to make an AutoText entry is to choose it from one of the Insert > AutoText submenus (**Figure 2.22**). Word provides dozens of common AutoText entries to get you started. You'll find your personal entries in the document template in which they were stored; typically, this is the Normal template.
- By default, the names of your Entourage contacts are also available as AutoText entries. To exclude them, check the Exclude contacts check box in the AutoCorrect dialog box (Figure 2.21).

Working with smart buttons

To make certain edits more flexible, Word, Excel, and PowerPoint provide smart buttons. A *smart button* is a pop-up icon that displays a menu of options when clicked. There are two types of smart buttons: AutoCorrect Options and Paste Options.

The Replace list of words, phrases, and symbols in the AutoCorrect dialog box (**Figure 2.23**) determines which text will automatically be substituted for other text as you type. For instance, if you type (c), a copyright symbol (©) is substituted. Common typos, such as ones caused by transposing letters, are also corrected. After an autocorrection occurs, you can click the AutoCorrect Options button to modify the correction.

Paste Option buttons are immediately available after pasting or using drag and drop. You can specify that the pasted or dropped text keep its original formatting or that it adopt the formatting of surrounding text.

To use an AutoCorrect Options button:

1. After an autocorrection, move the cursor over the corrected text.

   A blue underline appears under the text.

2. Move the cursor over the blue underline to reveal the AutoCorrect Options button. Click the button to open the menu (**Figure 2.24**).

3. *Do one of the following:*
   - ▲ Choose Undo or Change back to restore the original, uncorrected text.
   - ▲ Choose Stop Automatically Correcting *condition* to prevent future instances from being corrected and to delete the item from the Replace list.
   - ▲ Choose Control AutoFormat Options to change your AutoCorrect settings.

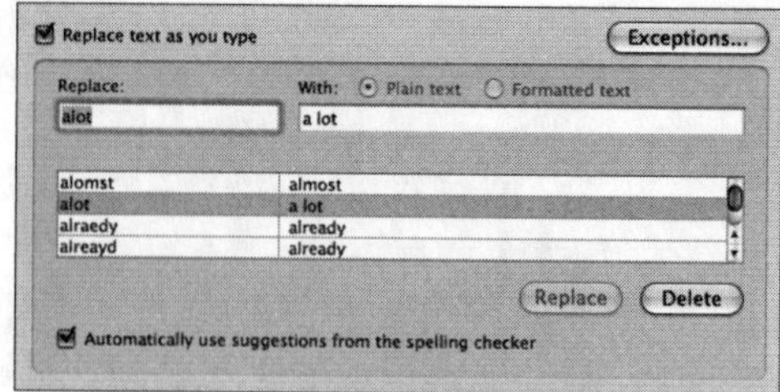

Figure 2.23 The AutoCorrect tab of the AutoCorrect dialog box contains a Replace list of items that will automatically be corrected in your documents.

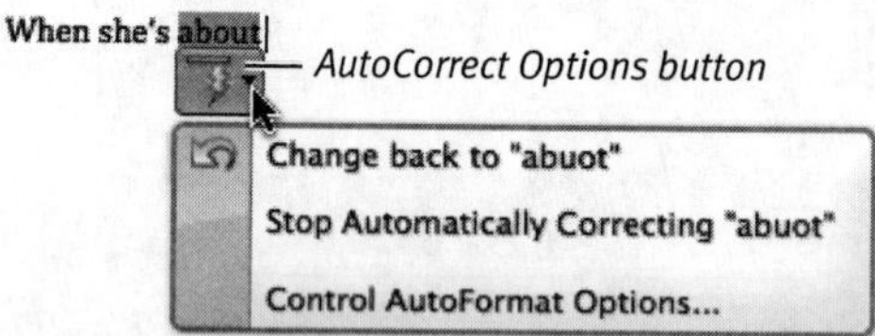

Figure 2.24 When the button appears, click it to open the drop-down menu.

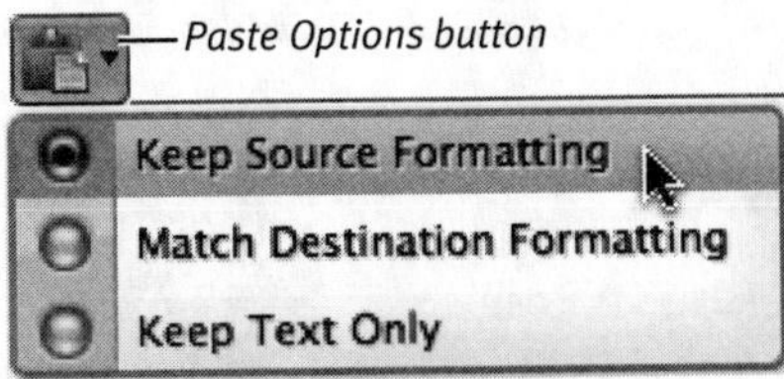

Figure 2.25 Use the Paste Options button to control the formatting of pasted text.

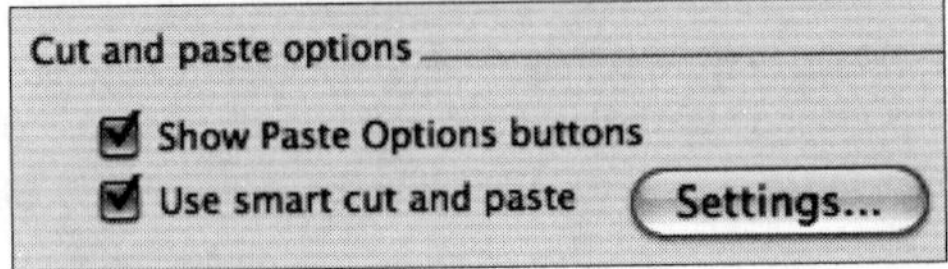

Figure 2.26 You can enable or disable Paste Options buttons in the Cut and paste options section of the Edit dialog box.

To use a Paste Options button:

1. Immediately after most paste or drag-and-drop operations, a Paste Options button appears (**Figure 2.25**).
2. Click the button to reveal its menu, and *do one of the following:*
   - ▲ Choose Keep Source Formatting to keep the original formatting for the pasted or dropped text.
   - ▲ Choose Match Destination Formatting to make the pasted text match the formatting of surrounding text.
   - ▲ Choose Keep Text Only to strip the formatting from the pasted or dropped text. (For instance, red italicized text would be reduced to plain black text.)

✔ Tips

- There is no time limit for clicking an AutoCorrect Options button. As long as you haven't closed and reopened the document, a button will be available for each autocorrection made in the session.
- On the other hand, a Paste Options button must be used immediately.
- After undoing an AutoCorrect, you can later "redo" the correction by clicking the button and choosing Redo AutoCorrect.
- Paste Options buttons can be a nuisance. To prevent them from appearing, choose Word > Preferences, and click the Edit icon. In the Edit dialog box, uncheck Show Paste Options buttons (**Figure 2.26**) and click OK.
- Other ways to open the AutoCorrect dialog box include the following:
  - ▲ Choose Word > Preferences and then click the AutoCorrect icon.
  - ▲ Choose Tools > AutoCorrect.
  - ▲ Choose Insert > AutoText > AutoText.

Proofing Your Work

It's a good idea to check your work before letting anyone else see it. Word 2008 provides tools you can use to check your spelling and grammar, find synonyms when you're stuck for a word, and look up definitions.

Improving your writing

You can avoid common errors and typos by performing a spelling and grammar check on each document. Use the Thesaurus and Dictionary tools to enliven your writing and ensure that you're using words correctly.

To check spelling and grammar:

1. Choose Tools > Spelling and Grammar or press Option⌘L.

   The Spelling and Grammar dialog box appears (**Figure 2.27**). The spelling checker flags possible misspellings and the grammar checker identifies questionable grammar.

2. As it examines the document, Word stops at each questionable word or phrase. For each instance, *do one of the following:*
   - ▲ To accept one of the entries in the Suggestions list, highlight the suggestion and click Change.
   - ▲ To leave the word or phrase as is and continue the spelling check, click Ignore. To ignore all instances of the word or phrase in the current document, click Ignore All.
   - ▲ To add the current spelling of a flagged word to your user dictionary and also accept the spelling as correct, click Add. (Adding a word to the user dictionary prevents Word from flagging it as a misspelling in other documents.)
   - ▲ Manually edit the text in the upper box. Click Change to accept your edits or Undo Edit to restore the original text.

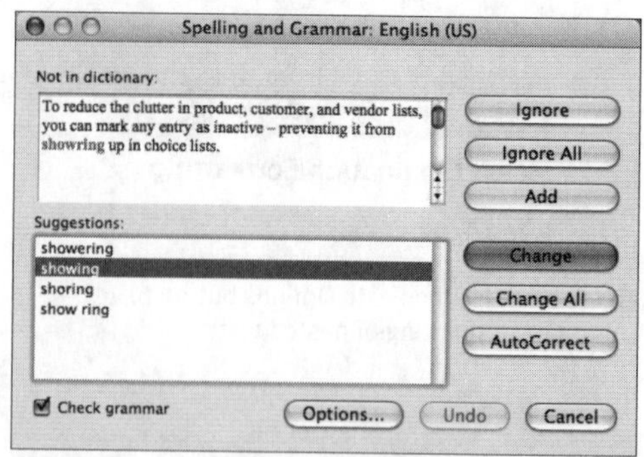

Figure 2.27 Word suggests corrections for most spelling and grammatical issues that it finds.

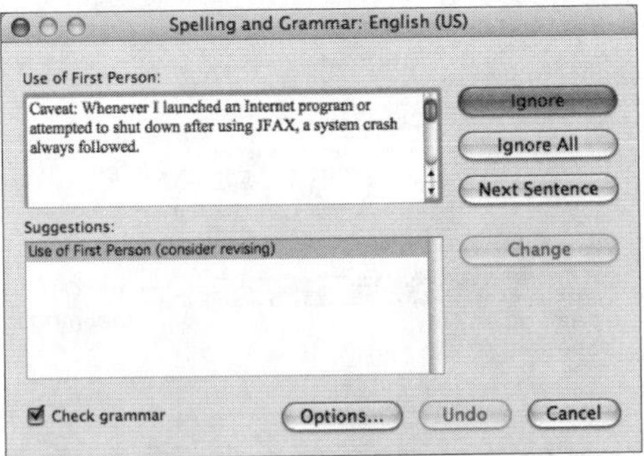

Figure 2.28 When questionable grammar is found, you can accept a suggestion, ignore this instance or all instances, or skip this error and jump to the next.

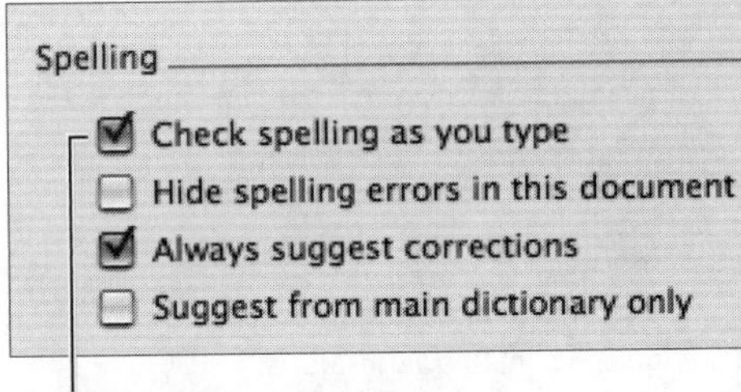

Figure 2.29 To instruct Word to automatically mark misspelled words as you type, this Spelling preferences item must be checked.

3. When a possible grammatical error is identified, the dialog box and its options change (**Figure 2.28**). For each flagged error, *do one of the following:*
   - ▲ To ignore the error for this or all instances in the document, click Ignore or Ignore All, respectively.
   - ▲ To accept a selected correction in the Suggestions box, click Change.
   - ▲ To examine the next identified error (without making a judgment on the current problem), click Next Sentence.
   - ▲ Manually edit the text. Click Change to accept the edits or Undo Edit to restore the original text.
4. An alert box appears when the spelling and grammar checks are complete. Click OK to dismiss it.

✔ Tips

- To immediately end a spelling/grammar check, click the Cancel button.
- To restrict a check to only part of a document, select the text prior to issuing the Spelling and Grammar command.
- Unless you've changed the Spelling and Grammar preferences (**Figure 2.29**), Word automatically checks your spelling as you type. Suspect words are marked with a squiggly red underline.
- As you type, Word automatically corrects common misspellings. To add your own words to the AutoCorrect list, choose Tools > AutoCorrect. Enter the misspelling in the Replace box and the correctly spelled word in the With box.
- To disable grammar checking, remove the check mark from Check grammar in the Spelling and Grammar dialog box (Figure 2.28). Or in Spelling and Grammar preferences, remove the check mark from Check grammar with spelling.

To replace a word with a synonym:

◆ *Do one of the following:*

▲ Select the word or phrase you want to replace. Choose Tools > Thesaurus. The Reference Tools tab of the Toolbox appears, showing information for the selected word or phrase (**Figure 2.30**). Select the closest meaning from the Meanings list, select a synonym from the Synonyms list, and click Insert.

▲ Display the Reference Tools tab of the Toolbox. (If the Toolbox isn't open, click the Toolbox icon on the Standard toolbar or choose View > Reference Tools.) In the Thesaurus section, type or paste a word or phrase into the search box, and then press Return. Select a meaning, select a synonym, and click Insert.

✔ Tip

■ To view the definition for the selected synonym, click Look Up. To view the definition for the original term or phrase, expand the Dictionary section.

To look up a word's definition:

◆ *Do one of the following:*

▲ Select the word in your document and choose Tools > Dictionary.

▲ Control-click the word and choose Look Up > Definition from the pop-up menu that appears.

The Reference Tools tab of the Toolbox is selected. The Dictionary section displays the definition (**Figure 2.31**).

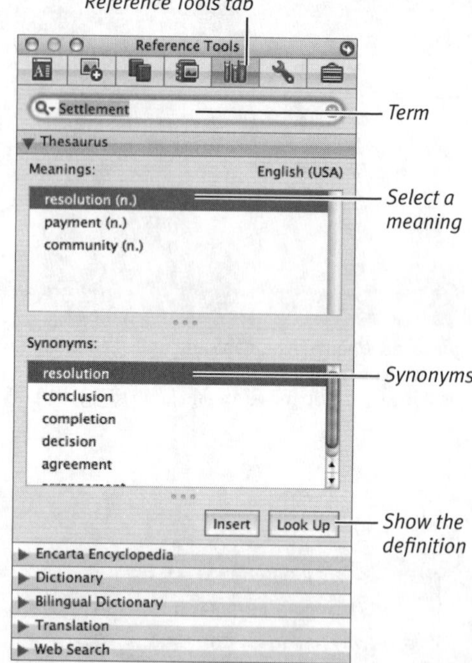

Figure 2.30 The Reference Tools tab of the Toolbox contains a thesaurus, dictionary, and encyclopedia.

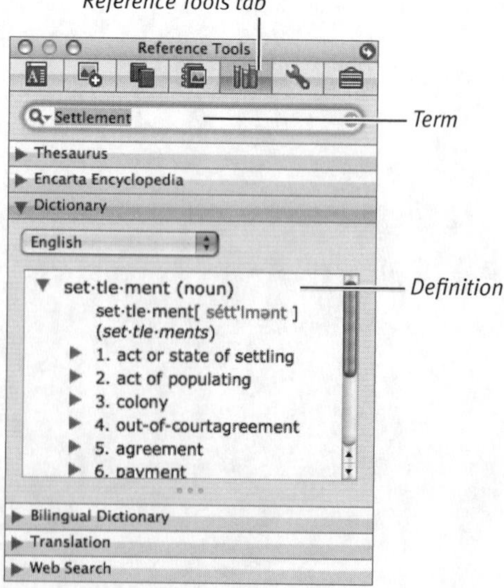

Figure 2.31 You can look up a word's definition in the Dictionary.

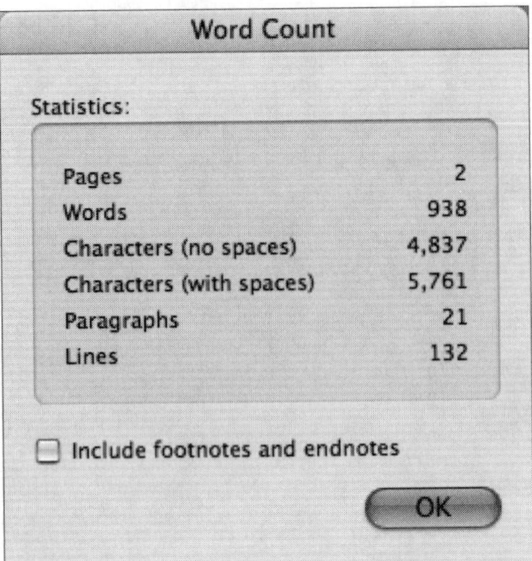

Figure 2.32 To view a word count and other useful document statistics, choose Tools > Word Count.

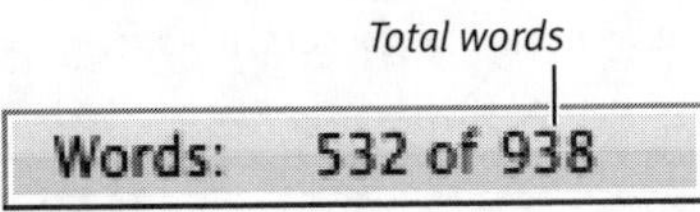

Figure 2.33 You can also view the word count in the status bar.

✔ Tips

- At the bottom of every Word window are two numbers (**Figure 2.33**). The first is the word in which the text insertion mark is located, counting from the beginning of the document. The second is the number of words in the document.
- If text is selected, the first number at the bottom of the page is the word count for the selected words.

✔ Tips

- You can also type or paste words into the search box to view a definition.
- You can use the Web to expand the information available to you concerning the text in the search box by doing the following:
  - ▲ Open the Encarta Encyclopedia section to read related encyclopedia articles.
  - ▲ Open the Web Search section to perform a Web search for the term. Click links to view them in your browser.

Calculating a word count

Sometimes you may need to know a document's exact word count or similar statistics. Word count is important when you're writing to a particular length, as may be the case with magazine articles or homework assignments.

To calculate the word count:

1. *Do one of the following:*
   - ▲ To calculate statistics for a portion of the document, begin by selecting that part of the document.
   - ▲ To calculate statistics for an entire document, ensure that nothing is selected.
2. Choose Tools > Word Count.

   The Word Count dialog box appears (**Figure 2.32**). It contains information about your document, including the page count and the number of words, lines, and paragraphs in your document
3. Click OK to dismiss the dialog box.

Tracking Changes

You may collaborate with others on certain Word documents. For instance, you might be creating a group report for school, working on a departmental budget with members of your staff, or writing a magazine or journal article that needs to incorporate an editor's comments. As the author, you can review the comments and changes of others, as well as accept or reject each one.

To track changes to a document:

1. Choose View > Toolbars > Reviewing. The Reviewing toolbar appears.
2. Click the Track Changes icon on the toolbar (**Figure 2.34**, page bottom). When Track Changes is enabled, the icon is darkened and changes you make are recorded. The TRK indicator at the bottom of the document window turns blue.
3. Choose a display option from the Display for Review drop-down menu:
   - ▲ **Original.** Display the original, unedited document (as it would look if all changes were rejected).
   - ▲ **Original Showing Markup.** Display insertions and formatting changes in balloons. Deleted text is struck through.
   - ▲ **Final.** Display the document as if all changes have been accepted.
   - ▲ **Final Showing Markup.** Display deletions in balloons. Insertions and formatting changes remain visible in the document text (**Figure 2.35**).

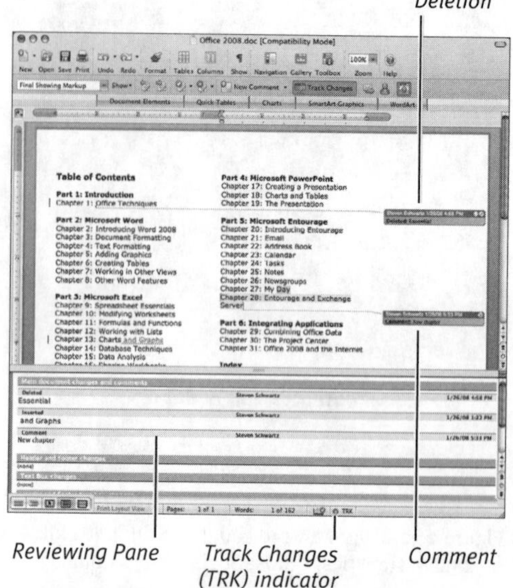

Figure 2.35 You'll do most of your work with Final Showing Markup chosen. You can accept or reject changes, as well as make other necessary edits.

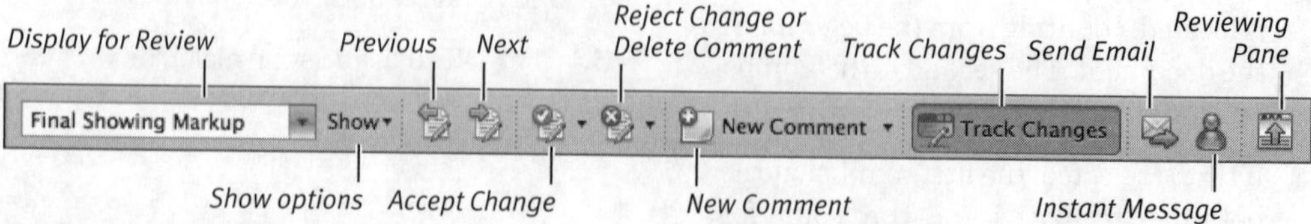

Figure 2.34 When track changes is enabled (the darkened icon), the Reviewing toolbar is extremely useful.

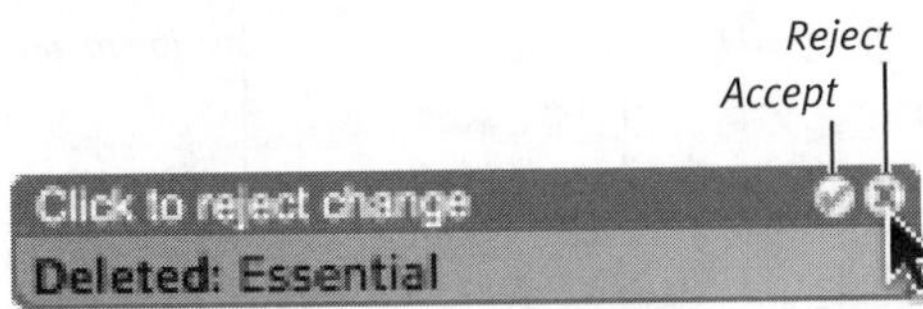

Figure 2.36 You can reject or accept an edit (or delete a comment) by clicking an icon in the related balloon.

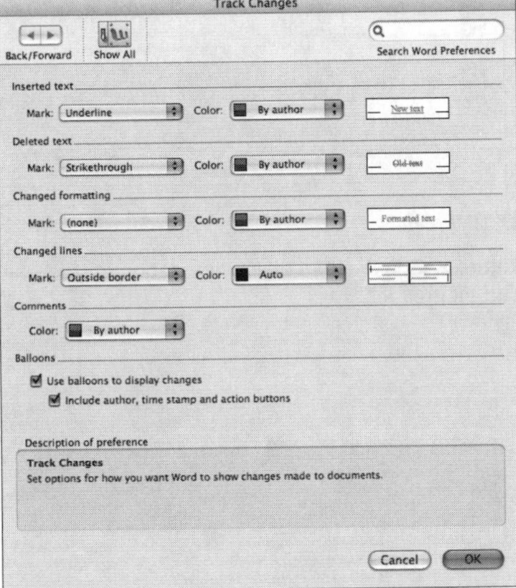

Figure 2.37 Although the default settings will usually suffice, you can alter the Track Changes preferences.

Comparing Document Versions

You can also compare different versions of a document. Open the current version of the document, and choose Tools > Track Changes > Compare Documents. In the Choose a File dialog box, select a document to compare with the open document. Word generates and displays a comparison document that shows all differences between the two files.

4. To insert a comment, select the text on which you want to comment (or position the text insertion mark within it). Choose Insert > Comment or click the New Comment icon on the Reviewing toolbar.

   A new comment line is added to the Reviewing Pane at the bottom of the document window. Enter your comment.

5. To delete a comment or reject an edit, *do one of the following:*
   - Click the Reject button in the associated balloon (**Figure 2.36**).
   - In the Reviewing Pane, select the top line of the edit or comment. Click the Reject Change/Delete Comment icon on the Reviewing toolbar.
   - Control-click the comment or edit in the body of the document. Choose Reject Change or Delete Comment from the pop-up menu that appears.

6. To accept an edit, *do one of the following:*
   - Click the Accept button in the balloon.
   - In the Reviewing Pane, select the top line of the edit. Click the Accept Change icon on the Reviewing toolbar.
   - Control-click the edit in the body of the document. Choose Accept Change from the pop-up menu that appears.

✔ Tips

- You can jump directly from one edit or comment to another by clicking the Next and Previous toolbar icons.
- To show or hide the Reviewing Pane, click the Reviewing Pane toolbar icon.
- You can send email or an instant message to the author of a selected comment or edit by clicking a toolbar icon.
- To alter the Track Changes preferences (**Figure 2.37**), click the Show toolbar icon (see Figure 2.34) and choose Preferences.

Printing Word Documents

Like other applications in Office 2008, Word provides an assortment of print options. The step list below discusses those options that you are most likely to use.

To print a Word document:

1. Open the Word document that you want to print.
2. *Optional:* To print only part of the current document, select that text.
3. Choose File > Print (⌘P).
   The Print dialog box appears (**Figure 2.38**), open to the Copies & Pages section.
4. Select a connected printer from the Printer drop-down list.
5. Specify the number of copies and range of pages to print.
   The Selection option for Pages is only available if you preselected part of the document in Step 2.
6. *Optional:* To change Page Setup options (paper size, orientation, and paper feed method), click the Page Setup button.
7. *Optional:* To set Word-specific options, choose Microsoft Word from the drop-down section menu. Choose an option from the Print What drop-down menu (**Figure 2.39**). If you're doing two-sided printing, you can also elect to print just the odd or even pages.
   Choose Copies & Pages from the drop-down menu to return to the main Print dialog box screen.
8. Turn on the printer and click Print.
   The print job is sent to the selected printer.

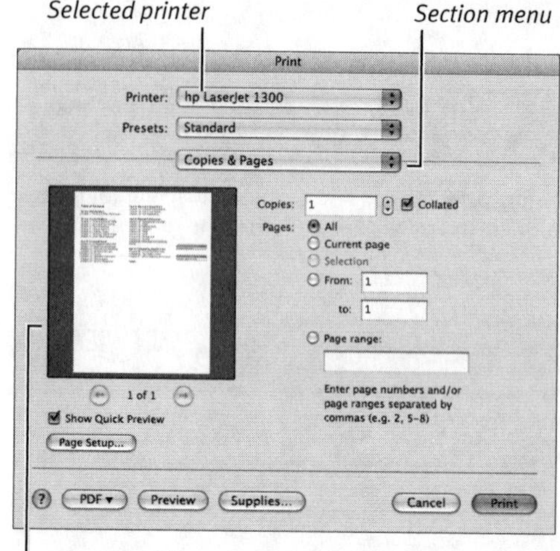

Figure 2.38 In the Print dialog box, set options for the current print job.

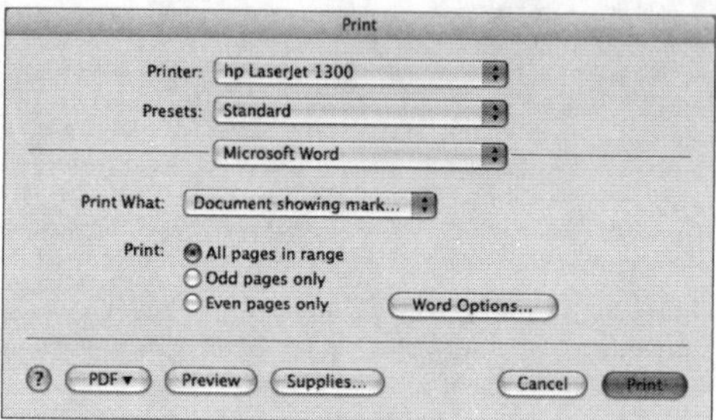

Figure 2.39 Set Word-specific options, such as printing a document showing changes, in the Microsoft Word section of the Print dialog box.

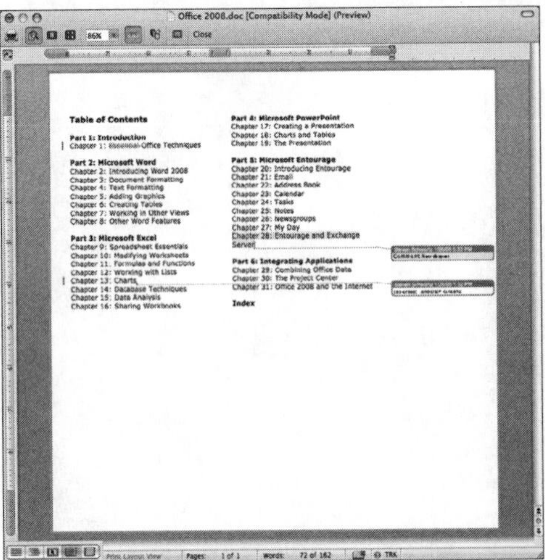

Figure 2.40 You can determine what the printout will look like using the current print settings by choosing File > Print Preview.

OS X 10.4.11/Tiger

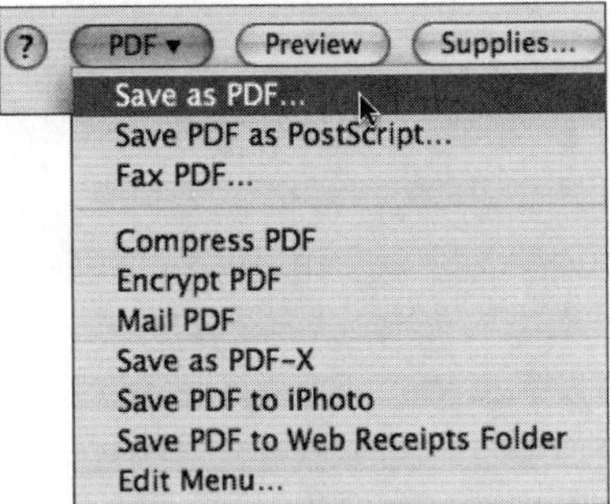

OS X 10.5/Leopard

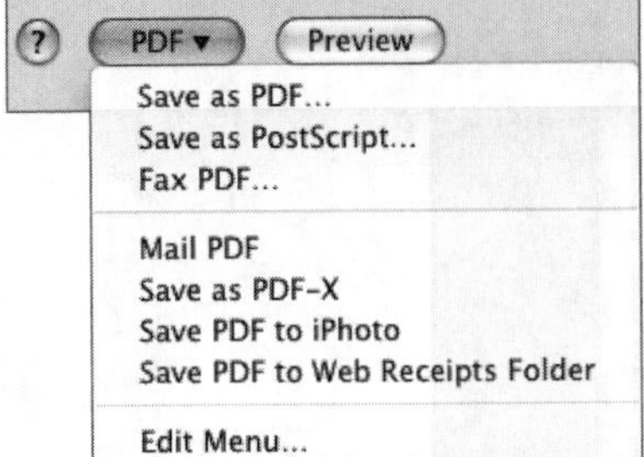

Figure 2.41 You can create a variety of PDFs from any Mac document. Options depend on the version of OS X you're running.

✔ Tips

- You can preview a printout onscreen by choosing File > Print Preview (**Figure 2.40**). It's often a good idea to request a print preview prior to printing. You can use it to ensure that page breaks, margins, and the like will be as you expect.

  Click icons above the window to interact with the print preview:

  - To change the magnification, select the Magnifier and click. Or you can choose a magnification setting from the zoom drop-down menu.
  - Click the Print One Copy icon to print from Print Preview mode.
  - Click the Close icon to return to the normal document window.

- To print the complete document using the current print settings, click the Print icon on the Standard toolbar. Printing commences immediately—without displaying the Print dialog box.

- If you save a document after printing it, the print settings are saved, too. This makes it easy to repeat complex print jobs.

- To share a Word document with someone who doesn't have Word, click the PDF button in the Print dialog box and choose Save as PDF (**Figure 2.41**). A cross-platform PDF file will be generated that can be opened in Preview or Adobe Reader. The recipient will be able to read the document onscreen and print it, if desired.

- When change tracking is enabled, you can include the edits and comments in the printout by choosing Final Showing Markup or Original Showing Markup from the Display for Review menu on the Reviewing toolbar (see Figure 2.34).

3

Document Formatting

Unlike character and paragraph formatting (discussed in Chapter 4), *document formatting* applies to an entire document (or, in some cases, only to selected document sections). You can use document formatting commands to alter the page orientation, set margins, or specify a custom paper size on which to print a memo or an envelope, for example.

You can add columns to create a newsletter or magazine layout, divide a document into sections (as you might do for a manual or report), and force pages and columns to break exactly where you want. As you choose new settings, Word automatically adjusts the text to fit the specified orientation, margins, paper size, number of columns, and so on.

Paper Size and Orientation

Word's default printout setting is 8 ½" x 11" *portrait* (vertical orientation). The choices you make for paper size and orientation are applied to the current document only. New documents revert to the default settings.

To change paper size or orientation:

1. Choose File > Page Setup.
   The Page Setup dialog box appears (**Figure 3.1**).
2. Choose Page Attributes from the Settings drop-down menu. Select a destination printer from the Format for list of installed printers.
3. To set the page orientation, click the portrait icon for a standard vertical printout or a landscape icon for a horizontal printout.
4. *Do one of the following:*
   - ▲ Select a standard paper size from the Paper Size drop-down list.
   - ▲ To use a nonstandard paper size, select Manage Custom Sizes from the Paper Size drop-down list. In the Custom Page Sizes dialog box (**Figure 3.2**), select a defined paper size and click OK.

     To define a *new* paper size, click the plus (+) icon, enter the dimensions in the Width and Height text boxes, select a target printer, specify mandatory margins, name the size, and click OK. Select the new size from the Paper Size drop-down list.
5. *Optional:* To proportionately scale the printout to better fit the selected paper size, enter a number in the Scale text box.
6. Click OK to close the dialog box.
   The document is modified to match the new Page Setup settings.

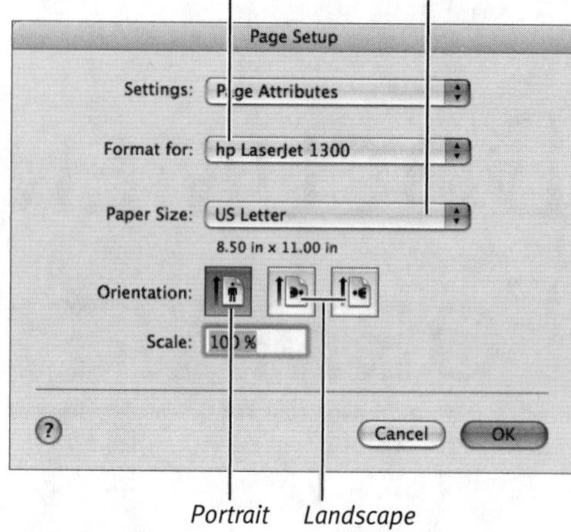

Figure 3.1 Specify a paper size and orientation in the Page Setup dialog box.

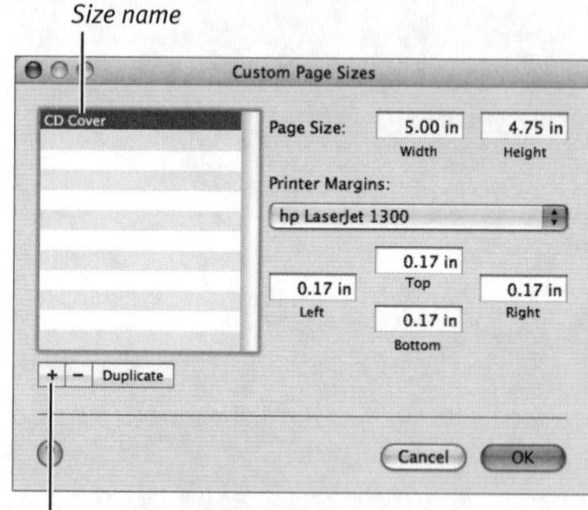

Figure 3.2 You can define a custom paper size if you need to print on nonstandard paper.

✔ Tips

- To see how the new settings will affect the printed version of the document, switch to Print Layout view (View > Print Layout) or choose File > Print Preview.
- When you define a custom paper size, it will be available in every program installed on your Mac.

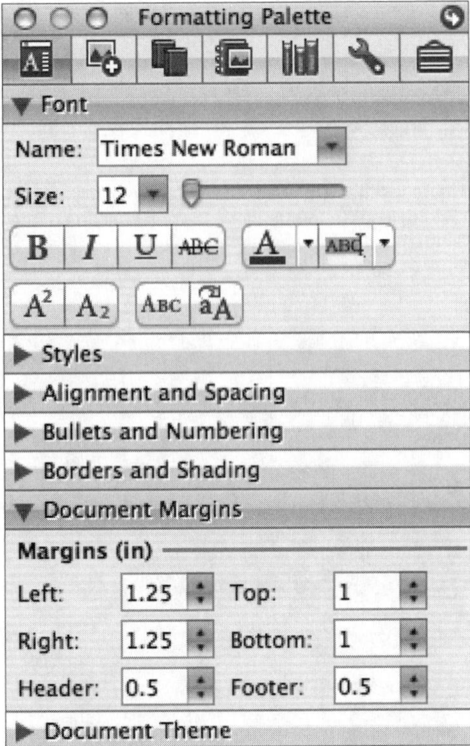

Figure 3.3 You can set basic margins in the Document Margins section of the Formatting Palette.

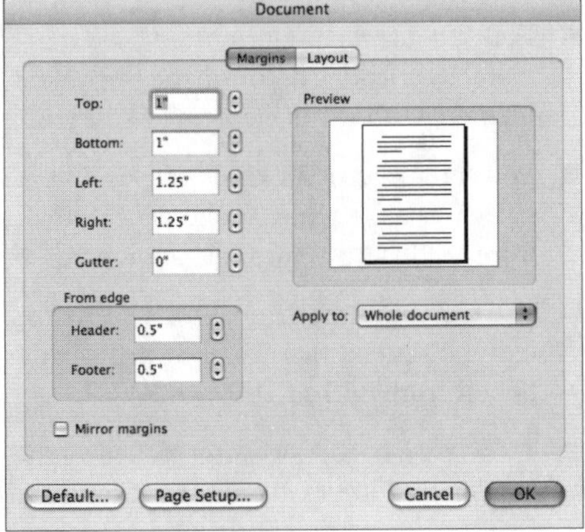

Figure 3.4 The Document dialog box offers more extensive margin options.

Margins

Margins are the blank borders around each document page. Although Word has default margin settings, you can vary the margins to fit the dictates of the current document—to print on odd-sized paper or to squeeze a few extra lines of text onto each page, for example.

To change the margins:

- *Do one of the following:*
  - Expand the Document Margins section of the Formatting Palette (**Figure 3.3**). Enter new Left, Right, Top, and/or Bottom margins.
  - Choose Format > Document. On the Margins tab of the Document dialog box (**Figure 3.4**), enter margin settings and click OK.

  The new margin settings are applied to the document.

✔ Tips

- The Document dialog box (Figure 3.4) has other margin options that you may find useful:
  - Specify a gutter margin if you're preparing the document for binding. (The *gutter* is extra space added to the edge of pages that will be bound. This prevents the binding from obscuring the printing.)
  - Click the Mirror margins check box when creating a book, magazine, or another two-sided publication. This makes the outer margin on left pages match those of right pages, while also creating matching inner margins.
- Margin settings are applied to an entire document or section. However, you can set different *indents* for selected paragraphs in the Paragraph dialog box.

Headers and Footers

Headers and footers display the same reference information at the top or bottom of every document page. You can include any information you want, such as your name, document title, current date, or page numbers, for example.

To insert headers and footers:

1. Choose View > Header and Footer.

   Word switches to Print Layout view (**Figure 3.5**), and the Header and Footer section of the Formatting Palette is expanded (**Figure 3.6**).

   If the Formatting Palette isn't visible, choose View > Toolbox > Formatting Palette or click the Toolbox icon on the Standard toolbar.
2. You can edit the header or the footer. To switch between them, click the Switch Between Header and Footer icon (Figure 3.6) or click in the element you wish to edit (that is, the header or the footer).
3. A header or footer can contain any combination of text, graphics, and special items, such as page numbers or today's date. Type the desired text. Insert special items by clicking icons or choosing commands from the Insert menu.
4. Use tabs to separate and position header and footer elements.
5. When you're done editing, click the Close button (Figure 3.5) beneath or above the header or footer area.

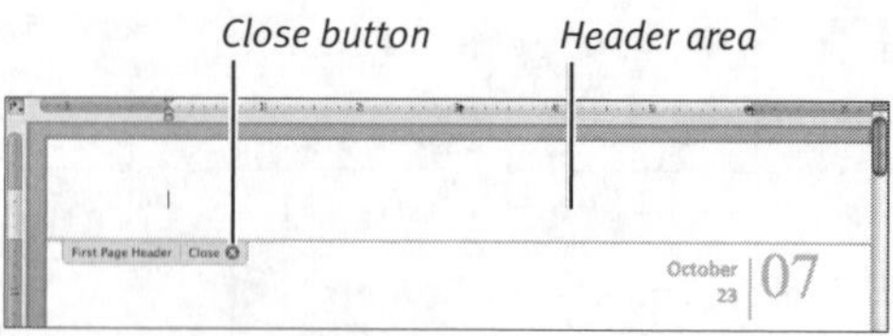

Figure 3.5 Create a header or footer by typing and by clicking icons in the Header and Footer section of the Formatting Palette (see Figure 3.6).

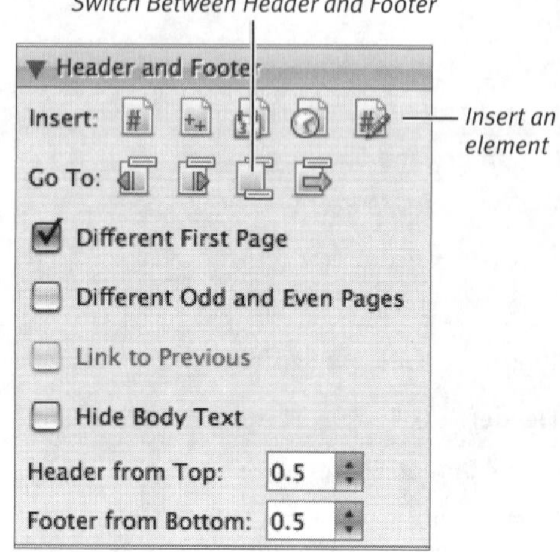

Figure 3.6 The Header and Footer section of the Formatting Palette.

✔ Tips

- In Print Layout view (View > Print Layout), you can create or edit a header or footer by double-clicking in the appropriate area of the page. Click the Close button (Figure 3.5) when you're done.
- You can insert a preformatted header or footer by selecting one from the Document Elements tab of the Elements Gallery.
- You can insert other kinds of special text, such as the filename, by choosing items from the Insert > AutoText submenu.
- You can make more room for a header or footer by adjusting Header from Top and Footer from Bottom (Figure 3.6).
- To delete a header or footer, delete all the header or footer text and other elements.
- To specify a different (or no) header or footer on page 1, click the Different First Page check box (Figure 3.6).

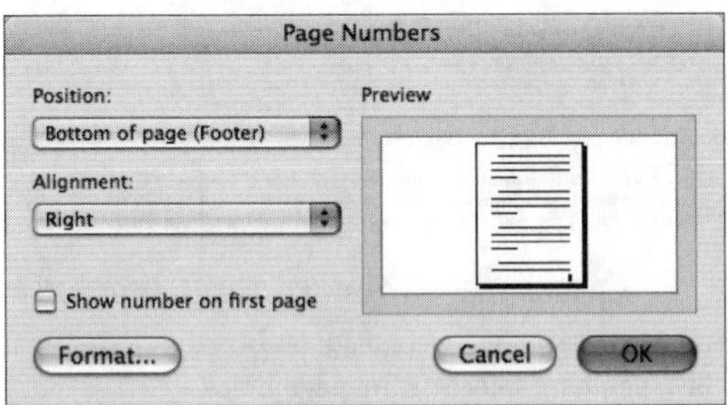

Figure 3.7 Indicate where you want the page numbers to appear, their alignment, and whether the first page will be numbered.

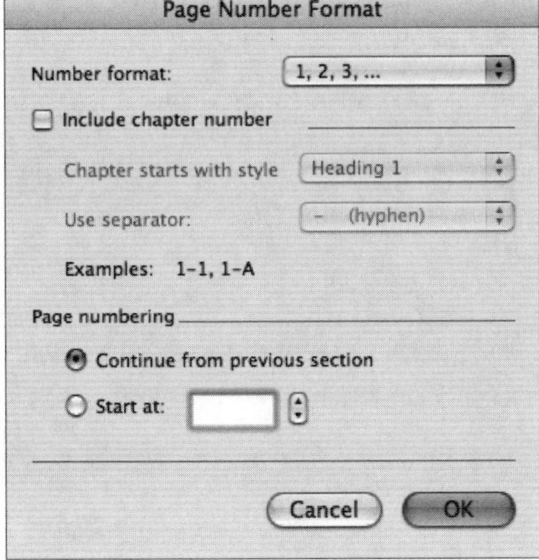

Figure 3.8 The Page Number Format dialog box provides additional options, such as whether to use chapter-relative page numbering.

✔ Tips

- You can precede each page number with the word Page. Be sure to separate the Page text and page number placeholder with a space.
- You can also insert a page number placeholder when editing the header or footer. Click the Insert Page Number icon in the Header and Footer section of the Formatting Palette.

Page Numbers

Page numbers in a header or footer improve a document's organization and make it easy for readers to keep their place.

To number a document's pages:

1. Choose Insert > Page Numbers.

   The Page Numbers dialog box appears (**Figure 3.7**).

2. Specify the page number's position and alignment:
   - ▲ You can place numbers in the header or footer (Position) and align them to the right, left, or center (Alignment).
   - ▲ The Inside and Outside alignment choices apply if you have mirrored pages, as when creating a book.

3. If you want the first page's number to be displayed, click the Show number on first page check box. Otherwise, the first visible number will be on the second page.

4. To set or change the page number format, click the Format button. The Page Number Format dialog box appears (**Figure 3.8**). *Do any of the following:*
   - ▲ Choose a numbering style from the Number format drop-down menu.
   - ▲ To use chapter-relative numbering (as in 13-1, 13-2, and so on), click the Include chapter number check box, and then choose a style and separator from the two drop-down menus.
   - ▲ You can also elect to continue page numbering from a previous section (as in a book, for instance) or designate a starting page number.

   Click OK to close the Page Number Format dialog box.

5. Click OK to close the Page Numbers dialog box.

Inserting Page Breaks

Word inserts an *automatic page break* whenever text fills a page. In Draft view, an automatic page break is shown as a blue line. If you want a page to break *before* you've filled the page (to avoid splitting a table across two pages, for example), you can insert a *manual page break*.

To insert a page break:

1. Position the insertion mark at the beginning of the line where you want the new page to start.
2. Choose Insert > Break > Page Break.

✔ Tips

- To delete a manual page break in Draft view, select the break (**Figure 3.9**) and press Delete. To delete a manual page break in Print Layout view, position the insertion mark just before the first character of the new page and press Delete.
- You cannot delete or move an automatic page break. You can, however, insert a manual page break above it.
- Use Widow/Orphan control to ensure that Word doesn't leave a single line of text at the page top or bottom when it breaks a page. Select the errant paragraph, choose Format > Paragraph, click the Line and Page Breaks tab in the Paragraph dialog box (**Figure 3.10**), check Widow/Orphan control, and click OK. Word will repaginate as necessary to eliminate the widow or orphan text.
- To prevent a heading and the following paragraph from being split across two pages, select the heading, choose Format > Paragraph, click the Lines and Page Breaks tab, and check the option to Keep with next (Figure 3.10).

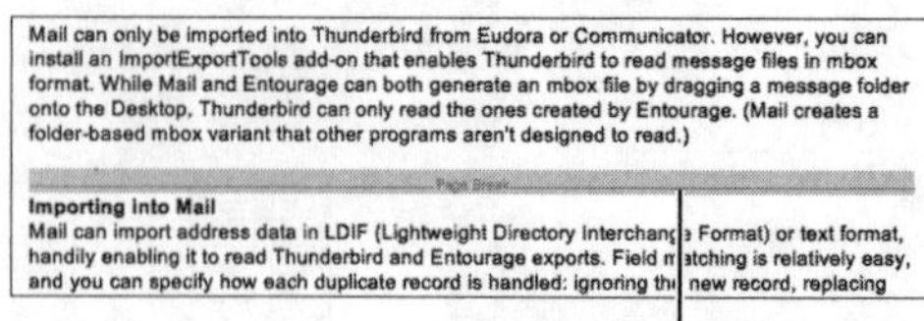

Mail can only be imported into Thunderbird from Eudora or Communicator. However, you can install an ImportExportTools add-on that enables Thunderbird to read message files in mbox format. While Mail and Entourage can both generate an mbox file by dragging a message folder onto the Desktop, Thunderbird can only read the ones created by Entourage. (Mail creates a folder-based mbox variant that other programs aren't designed to read.)

Page Break

Importing into Mail

Mail can import address data in LDIF (Lightweight Directory Interchan[illegible] Format) or text format, handily enabling it to read Thunderbird and Entourage exports. Field m[illegible]tching is relatively easy, and you can specify how each duplicate record is handled: ignoring th[illegible] new record, replacing

Selected manual page break

Figure 3.9 To remove a manual page break in Draft view, begin by selecting the page break.

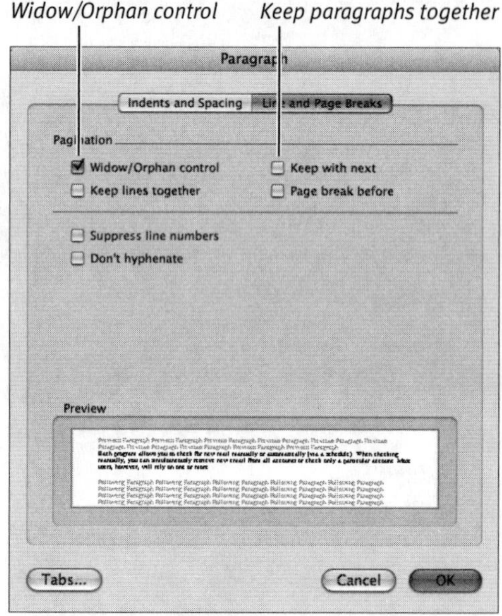

Figure 3.10 In the Paragraph dialog box, you can tell Word to handle widows and orphans and prevent two paragraphs from being split between pages.

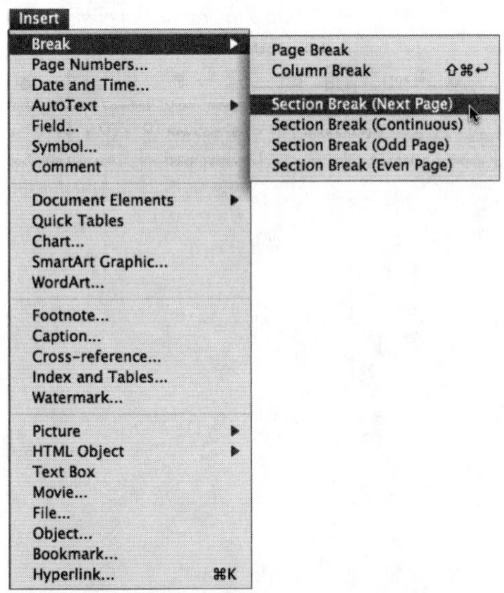

Figure 3.11 Choose the type of section break to insert.

Creating Multiple Sections

A document can contain multiple sections, each with different document formatting attributes, such as different margins, page numbering schemes, and headers and footers. For example, an annual report might contain different sections for the title page, introduction, body, and financial information.

A new document contains only one section until you insert a section break. See **Table 3.1** (page bottom) for section break options.

To create multiple sections:

1. Place the insertion mark where you want the new section to begin.
2. Choose Insert > Break, and choose one of the section break types from the submenu (**Figure 3.11**).

   In Draft view, Word inserts a double line marked with the text "Section Break," followed by the break type (**Figure 3.12**).

Section break indicator

6/10/03	cash	Mohave Community College	$50.00	GED testing fee
8/6/03	cash	Visions	$425.00	Theft of glasses (casualty)

Section Break (Next Page)

The information in this document is confidential and is the property of Steven Schwartz.

Figure 3.12 A new section break appears.

Table 3.1

Section Breaks

Break Type	Description
Next Page	Starts a new section at the top of the next page.
Continuous	Starts a new section without moving the text after the section break to a new page. If the previous section has multiple columns, Word evens out the column bottoms.
Odd Page	If the section break falls on an even page, Word starts the new section on the next page. Otherwise, it leaves the next even page blank and starts the new section on the next odd page.
Even Page	If the section break falls on an odd page, Word starts the new section on the next page. Otherwise, it leaves the next odd page blank and starts the new section on the next even page.

✔ Tips

- Like page breaks, the Section Break indicator text and double lines are normally visible only in Draft and Outline views. However, you can also make them visible in Print Layout view by clicking the ¶ (Show all non-printing characters) icon on the Standard toolbar.
- To remove a section break, switch to Draft or Outline view, highlight the Section Break indicator, and press Delete.
- To apply document formatting options to a section, select some text in the section and choose Format > Document. The Document dialog box appears. Click the appropriate tab (**Figure 3.13**), alter the layout and margin settings, choose This section from the Apply to drop-down menu, and click OK.
- To apply document formatting to *multiple* sections, select some text from the sections and choose Format > Document. Specify settings in the Document dialog box, choose Selected sections from the Apply to drop-down menu, and click OK.

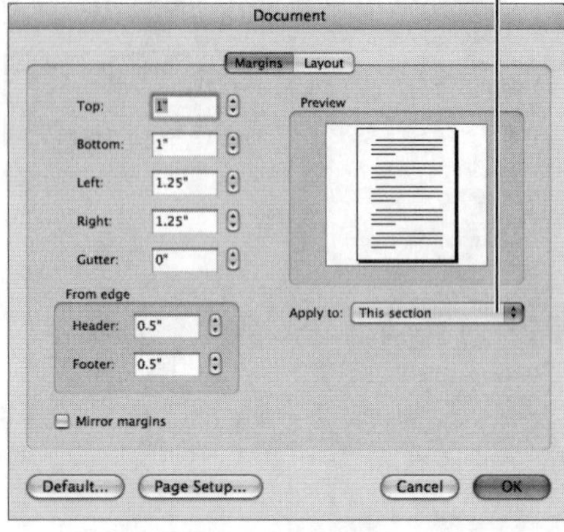

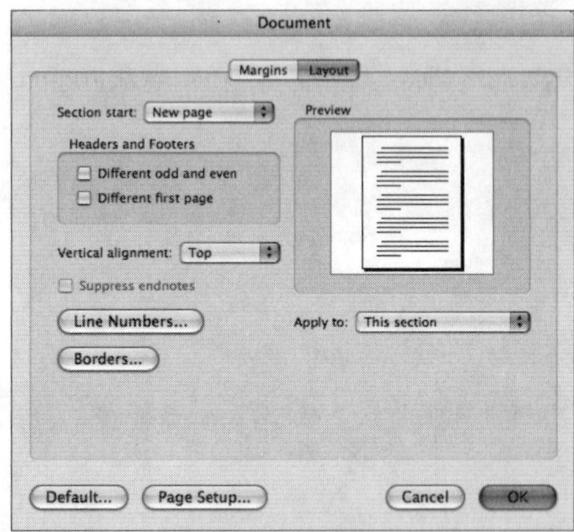

Figure 3.13 To set new formatting for one or more selected sections, make the necessary changes on the Margins (top) and Layout (bottom) tabs of the Document dialog box.

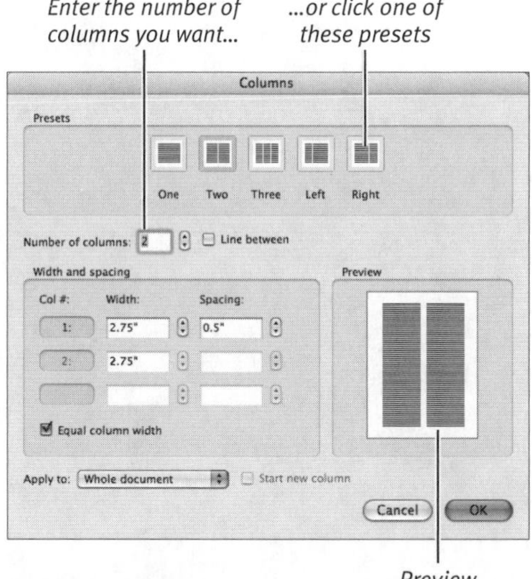

Figure 3.14 In addition to specifying the number of columns, you can set column widths and the space between them in the Columns dialog box.

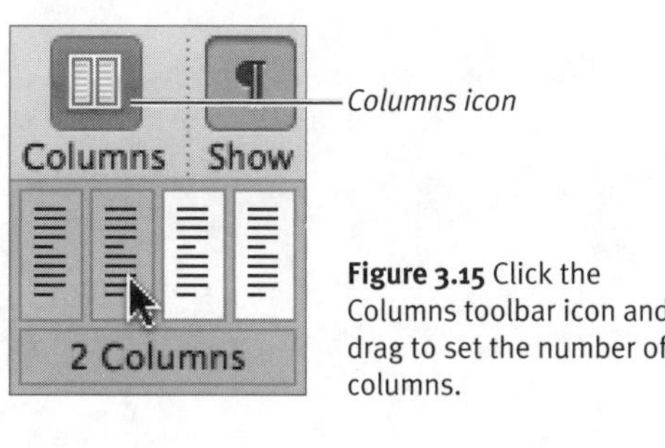

Figure 3.15 Click the Columns toolbar icon and drag to set the number of columns.

Setting a Document Background

Occasionally, you might like to swap the usual white page background for something dressier. To add a background color, pattern, texture, gradient, or picture to the current document, choose View > Toolbars > Background or Format > Background. Select options in the floating Background toolbar that appears.

Multiple Columns

A new Word document normally starts as a single large column. However, if you want to lay out a newsletter or break up your text with pictures, for example, you can create additional columns.

To set up multiple columns:

1. Choose Format > Columns.

   The Columns dialog box appears (**Figure 3.14**).

2. In the Columns dialog box, click one of the Presets or enter a number in the Number of columns text box.
3. *Optional:* To add a vertical line between each pair of columns, click the Line between check box.
4. In the Width and spacing section of the dialog box, specify the width and space between for each column. (To make all columns the same width, click the Equal column width check box.)
5. Choose an option from the Apply to drop-down menu.
6. Click OK.
7. Switch to Print Layout view (View > Print Layout) to see the effect of the column settings.

✔ Tips

- You can quickly set the number of columns by clicking the Columns icon on the Standard toolbar and then dragging until you reach the requisite number of columns (**Figure 3.15**).
- After creating multiple columns, you can change the number of columns or other column-related settings by returning to the Columns dialog box.

Text Formatting

In Chapter 3, you learned to apply document-level formatting, such as setting the page size, orientation, and margins. In this chapter, you'll discover the many ways you can format the text in your documents. There are two types of formatting that can be applied to selected text: character and paragraph.

- *Character formatting* refers to the font, size, styles, and color applied to—and that only affects—selected text within a paragraph.
- *Paragraph formatting* concerns itself with formatting that affects entire paragraphs. In addition to setting a default font for the paragraph, formatting can include line spacing, space before and after the paragraph, alignment, and so on.

To make it simpler to consistently format a document's text, you can define and apply character and paragraph styles, as explained at the end of this chapter.

Character Formatting

You can change the look of selected text by applying different font, size, style, and color formatting. You can format text in several ways, as described below. Use any method that's convenient for you.

To apply character formatting:

1. Select the text you want to format.

   Using normal selection techniques, you can select individual characters, words, paragraphs, or the entire document.

2. *Do any of the following:*
   - ▲ Click the Formatting Palette tab in the Toolbox. In the Font section (**Figure 4.1**), select any combination of font, size, color, highlighting, and style effects.
   - ▲ Choose Format > Font or press ⌘D. On the Font tab of the Font dialog box (**Figure 4.2**), select font, size, color, and effects, and then click OK.
   - ▲ Select font, size, color, highlighting, and style options from the icons and drop-down menus on the Formatting toolbar (**Figure 4.3**).

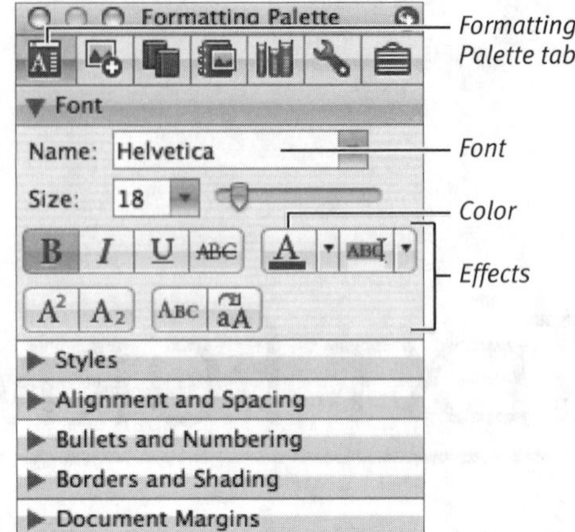

Figure 4.1 You can apply most types of character formatting by selecting options from the Formatting Palette.

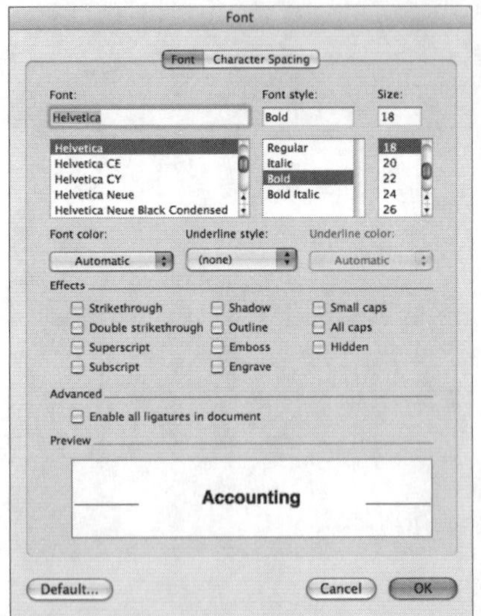

Figure 4.2 For more complex formatting needs, you can select options from the Font dialog box.

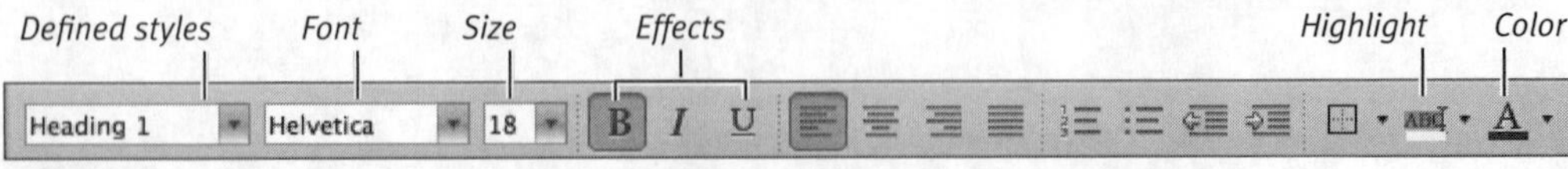

Figure 4.3 Basic character formatting options can be selected from the Formatting toolbar.

Figure 4.4 Show or hide the Toolbox by clicking this icon on the Standard toolbar.

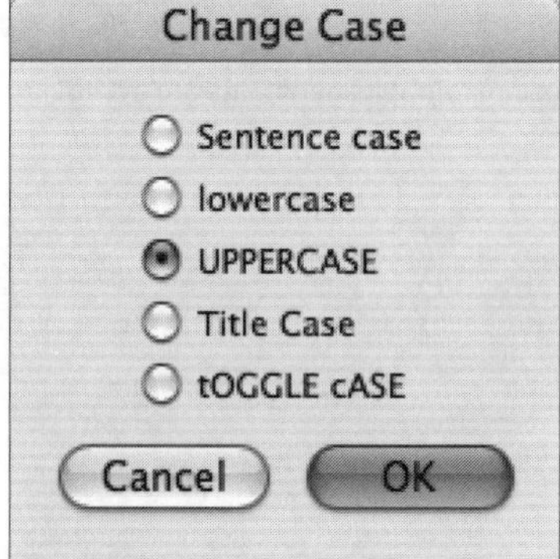

Figure 4.5 You can change the case of selected text by selecting an option in this dialog box.

Table 4.1

Font Effect Keyboard Shortcuts	
SHORTCUT	DESCRIPTION
⌘B	Boldface
⌘I	Italic
⌘U	Underline
⌘Shift K	Small caps
⌘Shift A	All capital letters
Shift F3	Cycle through case selections

✔ Tips

- To show or hide the Formatting Palette, you must open or close the Toolbox. Choose View > Formatting Palette or click the Toolbox icon on the Standard toolbar (**Figure 4.4**). To show or hide the Formatting toolbar, choose View > Toolbars > Formatting.
- To restore selected text to the standard font and size for the paragraph, select the text and choose Clear Formatting from the Styles section of the Formatting Palette (see Figure 4.1) or from the Style drop-down list on the Formatting toolbar (see Figure 4.3).
- To increase the size of selected text by one point, press ⌘Shift>. To decrease the size by one point, press ⌘Shift<.
- You can use keyboard shortcuts (**Table 4.1**) to apply the most common font effects to selected text.
- The font effect icons (such as Bold), as well as their keyboard shortcuts, work as toggles. Issue them once to apply the formatting; issue them again to remove the formatting.
- You can change the letter case of selected text by choosing Format > Change Case. Select an option from the Change Case dialog box (**Figure 4.5**) and click OK.
- Applying a bold or italic effect to selected text is *not* the same as using the actual bold or italic version of a font, if one is available. By choosing the bold version of a font (Arial Bold or Baskerville Italic, for example), you will normally get more aesthetically pleasing and typographically correct text than you will by applying the bold or italic effect.

Paragraph Formatting

Some formatting is paragraph-specific. That is, rather than affecting individual words or sentences, it affects the entire paragraph. Common paragraph formatting that you can apply includes alignment, indents, tab stops, and line spacing. You can also create bulleted or numbered lists, and add borders or shading.

Setting paragraph alignment

Each paragraph in a document can be aligned left, center, right, or justified (**Figure 4.6**), as explained below:

- *Left* is the most common alignment setting and is the default. Text in a left-aligned paragraph is flush with the left margin and ragged on the right margin.
- *Center-aligned* paragraphs are horizontally centered between the left and right margins and are ragged on both sides. Center alignment is sometimes used for titles and section heads.
- *Right-aligned* paragraphs are flush with the right margin and ragged on the left.
- *Justified* paragraphs are aligned flush with both the left and right margins. You'll often see this in newspapers and magazines. The spacing between words is automatically adjusted as needed to maintain the flush margins.

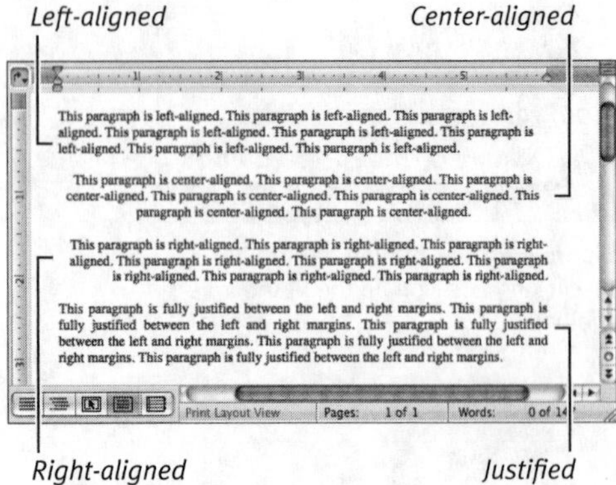

Figure 4.6 These paragraph alignments are available in Word.

New vs. Existing Text

You can apply formats to text and paragraphs before or after you've typed them:

- When you apply a character or paragraph format to existing text, only that text is affected.
- When you apply a character format before you type, all text that follows will have the same format until you choose another character format.
- When you apply a paragraph format before you type, its format dictates the format of following paragraphs.

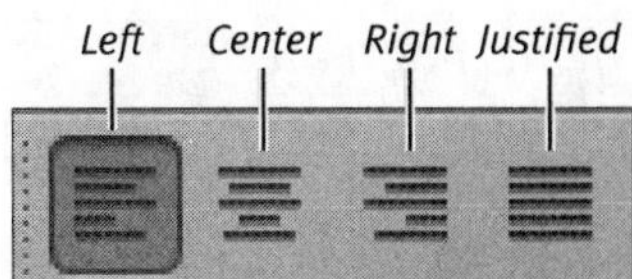

Figure 4.7 One of the quickest ways to set alignment is to click an icon on the Formatting toolbar.

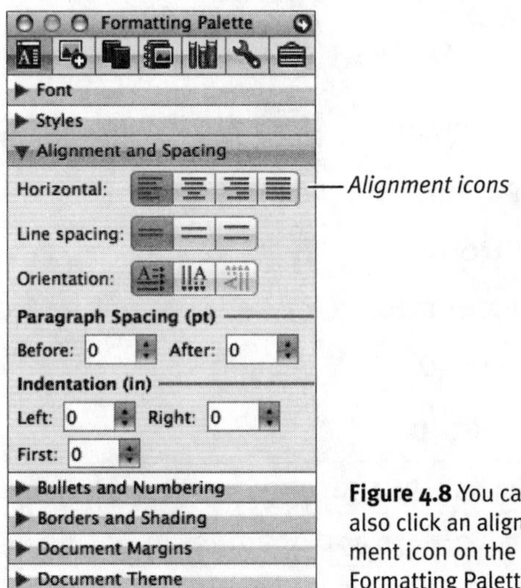

Figure 4.8 You can also click an alignment icon on the Formatting Palette.

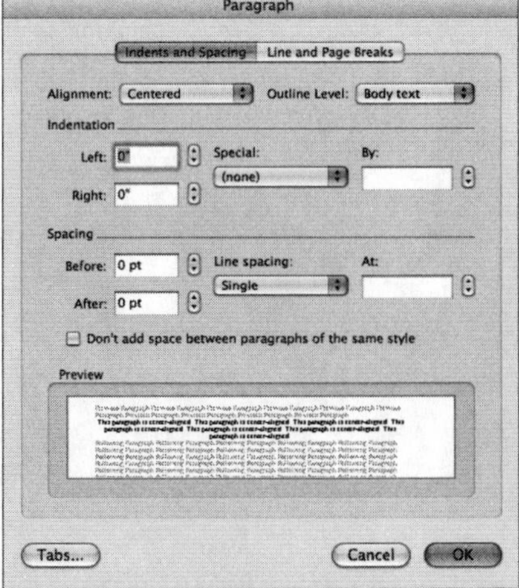

Figure 4.9 Although it's more convenient when you have multiple options to set, you can also set alignment in the Paragraph dialog box.

To set alignment for a paragraph:

1. Select one or more paragraphs whose alignment you want to change.
2. *Do one of the following:*
   - ▲ Click an alignment icon on the Formatting toolbar (**Figure 4.7**).
   - ▲ Expand the Alignment and Spacing section of the Formatting Palette, and click an alignment icon (**Figure 4.8**).
   - ▲ Choose Format > Paragraph. The Paragraph dialog box appears. On the Indents and Spacing tab, choose an alignment from the Alignment drop-down menu (**Figure 4.9**) and click OK.

   The selected paragraph(s) are aligned as directed.

✔ Tip

- When you're typing and press Return to end a paragraph, the next paragraph automatically takes on the alignment of the paragraph you just completed.

Indenting paragraphs

An *indent* is space between a paragraph and the left or right margin. Indents can be used to set off quotations from surrounding text (left and right indents), format body paragraphs in a business letter or school report (first line indents), and create bulleted or numbered lists (hanging indents).

Before setting an indent, you must first select the paragraph(s). Selecting a paragraph for formatting is different from selecting a word. You don't have to select the *entire* paragraph; it's sufficient to just click somewhere within it. To select multiple contiguous paragraphs, drag through them. To select multiple non-contiguous paragraphs, you can ⌘-double click a word in each one.

You can set paragraph indents using the Formatting Palette, the Paragraph dialog box, or the ruler. You can create the following types of indents in Word:

- **Left.** Indents the paragraph from the left margin.
- **Right.** Indents the paragraph from the right margin.
- **First.** Indents only the first line of the paragraph.
- **Hanging.** Indents the entire paragraph except for the first line.

To indent paragraphs using the Formatting Palette:

1. Select the paragraph(s).
2. Expand the Alignment and Spacing section of the Formatting Palette.
3. In the Indentation area, set the Left, Right, and/or First indent (**Figure 4.10**).

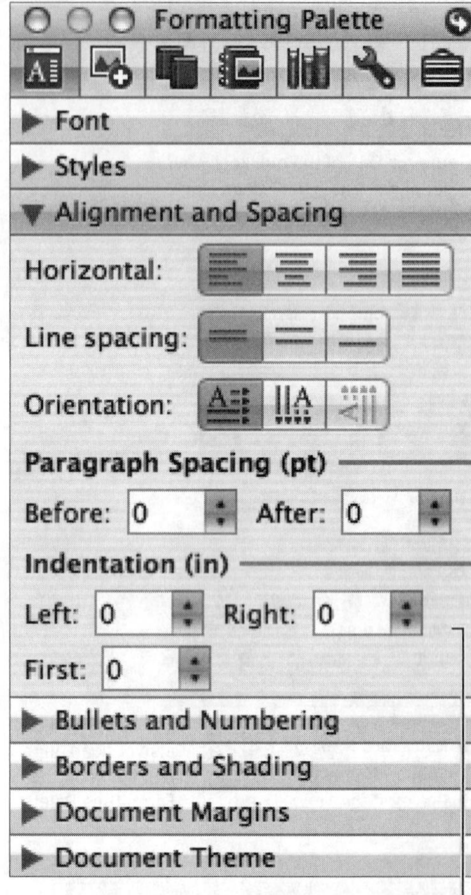

Figure 4.10 You can specify a left, right, or first line indent in the in the Alignment and Spacing section of the Formatting Palette.

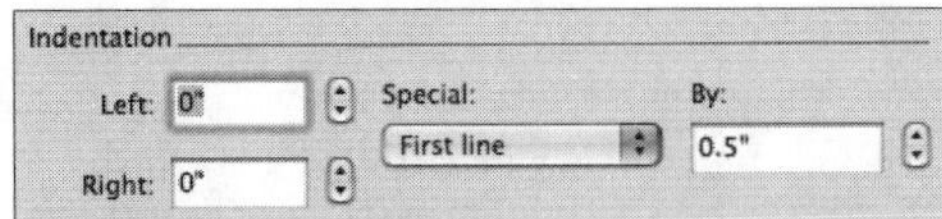

Figure 4.11 For greater precision in setting indents, use these options on the Indents and Spacing tab of the Paragraph dialog box.

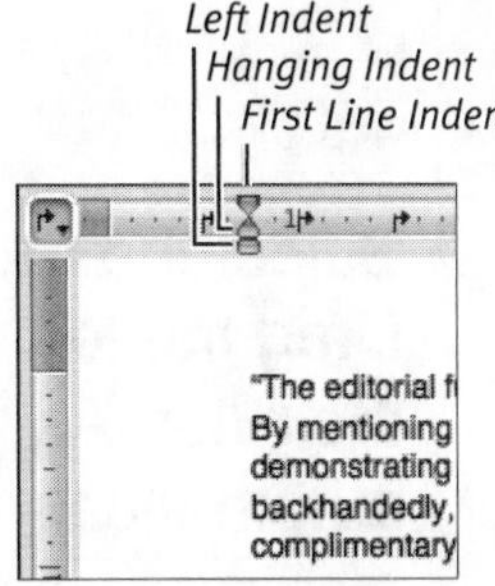

Figure 4.12 Align these three indent markers to create a block (to format a quotation, for example).

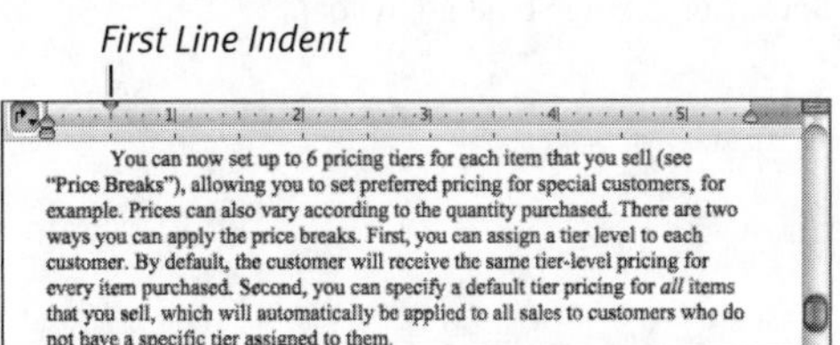

Figure 4.13 Move the First Line Indent marker slightly to the right to create a paragraph style that is commonly used in business and education documents.

To indent paragraphs using the Paragraph dialog box:

1. Select the paragraph(s).
2. Choose Format > Paragraph or press Option ⌘ M.
   The Paragraph dialog box appears.
3. Switch to the Indents and Spacing tab.
4. *Do any of the following:*
   - ▲ In the Indentation section of the tab (**Figure 4.11**), change the values for Left and/or Right. The numbers correspond to the ruler that appears above the document text.
   - ▲ To set a first line or hanging indent, choose First line or Hanging from the Special drop-down menu and then enter a value in the By text box.
5. Click OK to apply the new settings to the selected paragraph(s).

To indent paragraphs using the ruler:

- ◆ To create a uniform or flush indent, move the First Line Indent marker so it is directly above the Hanging and Left Indent markers (**Figure 4.12**). Then click and drag the square base of the Left Indent marker. The three markers will move together.
- ◆ To set a first line indent, move the First Line Indent marker (**Figure 4.13**). Note that it moves independently of the other indent markers.
- ◆ To create a hanging indent, move the First Line Indent marker to the left of the Left Indent marker and move the Hanging Indent marker to the position where the indent will begin.
- ◆ To set the indent for the right side of a paragraph, move the Right Indent marker.

✔ Tips

- Click the Decrease Indent or Increase Indent icons on the Formatting toolbar (**Figure 4.14**) or the same icons in the Bullets and Numbering section of the Formatting Palette to decrease or increase the left indent.
- When entering text for the first line of a paragraph that's formatted with a hanging indent, enter the bullet character or number, press [Tab], and then type the paragraph text (**Figure 4.15**). If the paragraph has multiple lines, all lines after the first will automatically align to the Hanging Indent marker.
- Word also has options for *directly* creating numbered and bulleted lists, as explained later in this chapter.

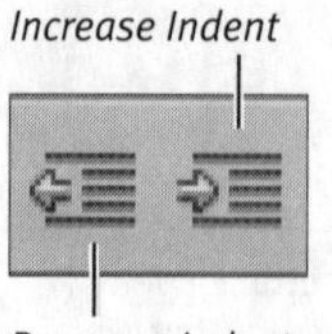

Figure 4.14 Click these toolbar icons to decrease or increase a paragraph's left indent by 0.5".

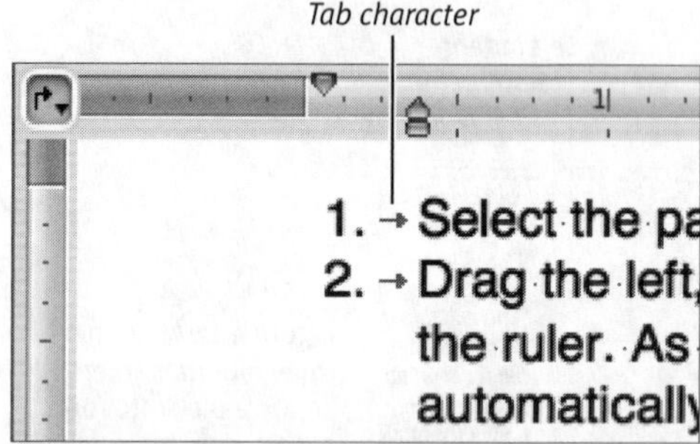

Figure 4.15 A tab separates each bullet character or number from the text. (To show/hide tabs, click the Show icon on the Standard toolbar.)

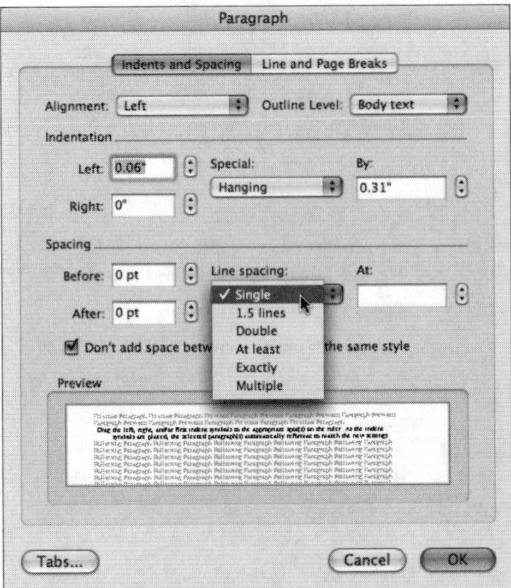

Figure 4.16 For precise line spacing needs, you can choose a setting from the Line spacing drop-down menu in the Paragraph dialog box.

Setting line spacing

Being able to modify line spacing is especially useful if you're creating a document that has space restrictions or when it must follow line-spacing requirements set by an editor or teacher. The most common line spacings are single, 1.5, and double. You can also specify an exact value.

To set line spacing for a paragraph:

1. Select the paragraph or paragraphs for which you want to set line spacing.
2. *Do either of the following:*
   - ▲ In the Formatting Palette, expand the Alignment and Spacing section, and then click one of the Line spacing icons (see Figure 4.10).
   - ▲ Choose Format > Paragraph or press Option⌘M. The Paragraph dialog box appears. On the Indents and Spacing tab, choose a line spacing option from the Line spacing drop-down menu (**Figure 4.16**) and click OK.

✔ Tips

- Line spacing is a paragraph—not a document—formatting option. When you set line spacing, it is applied only to the currently selected paragraphs. To apply the same line spacing to an entire document, choose Edit > Select All (or press ⌘A) prior to setting the line spacing.
- The Paragraph dialog box has additional line spacing options. *At least* is designed to accommodate graphics and large font sizes. It sets line spacing to the minimum amount necessary to prevent clipping the tops of text. *Exactly* generates a fixed line spacing of a set amount. *Multiple* enables you to increase or decrease line spacing by a percentage. A setting of `1.2` would increase line spacing by 20 percent, for example.
- You can also specify the amount of blank space above and beneath each paragraph. In the Alignment and Spacing section of the Formatting Palette (see Figure 4.10) or on the Indents and Spacing tab of the Paragraph dialog box (Figure 4.16), set an amount for Before and/or After (in points).

Setting tab stops

Tab stops are often used to align text and numbers in neat columns. For example, you can use tabs to create tables in which the entries are aligned on their left edges, right edges, or decimal points (**Figure 4.17**).

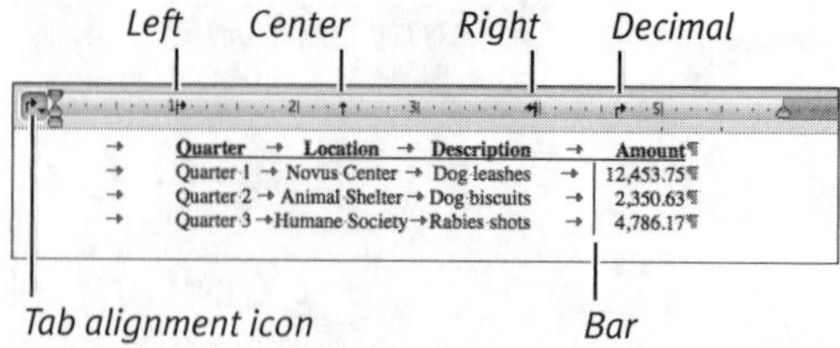

Figure 4.17 By judiciously choosing and setting tab stops, you can create perfectly aligned tables.

To set tabs:

1. Select the paragraph(s) for which you want to set tab stops.
2. Click the tab alignment icon to the left of the ruler, and choose the type of tab you want to set (**Figure 4.18**).
3. Click the ruler at the location where you want to place the tab stop.
   If the placement is off, you can drag the marker to another spot on the ruler.
4. To add more tab stops for the selected paragraph(s), repeat Steps 2 and 3.
5. If the selected paragraphs don't already contain tabs, insert them as necessary by pressing Tab. Affected text will conform to the new tab stops.

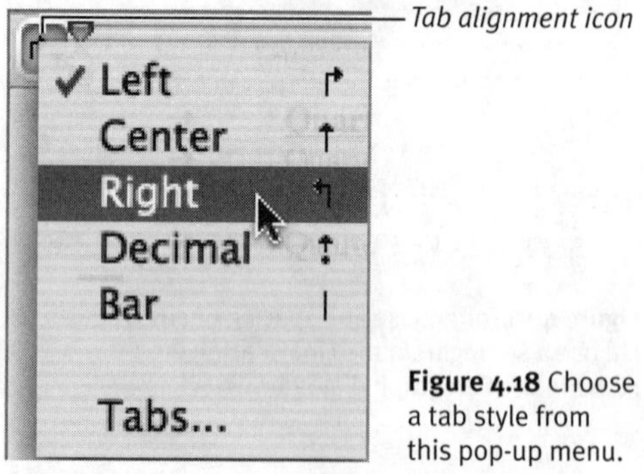

Figure 4.18 Choose a tab style from this pop-up menu.

✓ Tips

- If you need more precise tab settings, choose Format > Tabs and set tabs in the Tabs dialog box (**Figure 4.19**). You can also select a *leader character* (such as a string of periods) that will separate the two text strings. Leaders are sometimes used to separate menu items from prices, for example.
- You can remove a tab stop by dragging it up or down off the ruler. To remove all manually placed tab stops for selected paragraphs, click Clear All in the Tabs dialog box (Figure 4.19).
- The Bar option shown in Figures 4.17–4.19 isn't for aligning text. It inserts a vertical bar at the chosen ruler location.

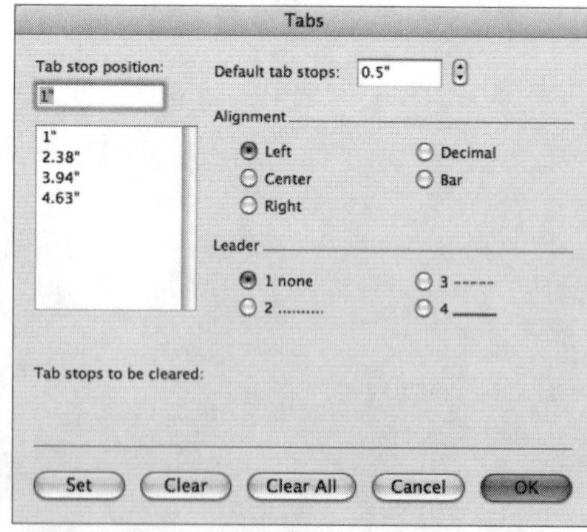

Figure 4.19 To set tab stops precisely or to specify a leader character, use the Tabs dialog box.

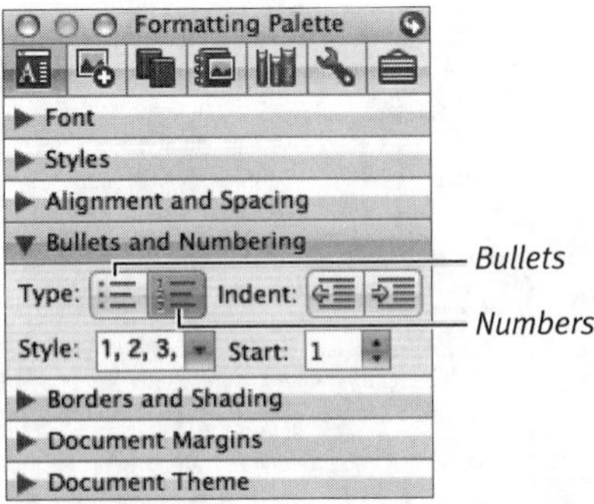

Figure 4.20 Click an icon to enable/disable bullets or numbers for selected paragraph(s).

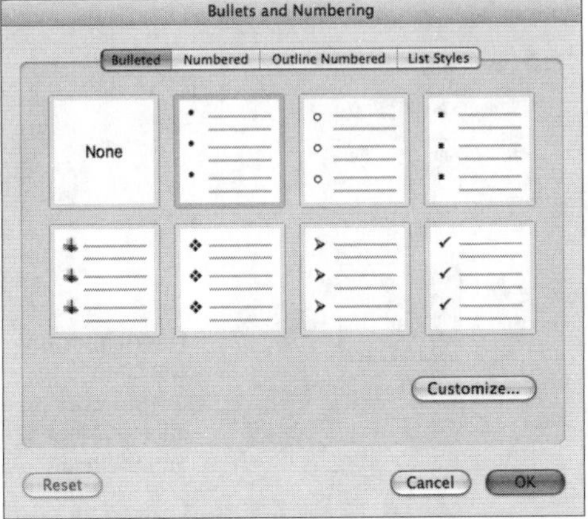

Figure 4.21 Select one of these bullet styles. To use a different character or otherwise alter the bullet settings, click the Customize button.

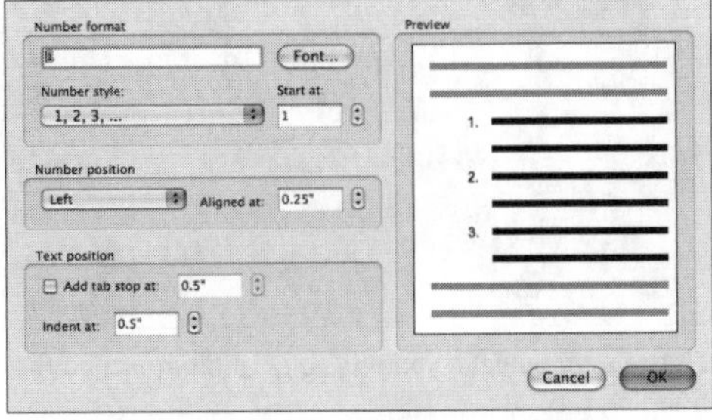

Figure 4.22 In this dialog box, you can change the font, style, alignment, and spacing of numbered lists.

Bulleted and numbered lists

Bullets help break text into readable chunks, making it simpler for a reader to find and digest important points. Word also lets you generate numbered lists, such as points in a contract. The procedures for adding bullets and numbers are very similar. You can apply bullets and numbering to paragraphs before or after you've typed the text.

To create bulleted or numbered lists:

◆ *Do either of the following:*

- ▲ To use the default bullet or numbering style for selected paragraphs, click an icon in the Bullets and Numbering section of the Formatting Palette (**Figure 4.20**) or the same icon on the Formatting toolbar.
- ▲ Choose Format > Bullets and Numbering. On the Bulleted (**Figure 4.21**) or Numbered tab of the Bullets and Numbering dialog box, select a bullet or numbering style and click OK.

The paragraph series becomes a bulleted or numbered list.

✔ Tips

- You can remove bullets or numbers by selecting the paragraphs and clicking the Bullets or Numbering icon again.
- To choose a special bullet character (such as a picture from your hard disk), set the bullet's distance from the text, or specify a new font and format for numbers, click the Customize button in the Bullets and Numbering dialog box. Set options in the dialog box that appears (**Figure 4.22**), and then click OK.
- To quickly change the bullets or numbers in a list, double-click any bullet character or number in your text. The Bullets and Numbering dialog box will open.

Applying borders and shading

Borders and shading can add style to a document or serve to highlight an important paragraph. You can set a border around selected pages, paragraphs, or text. You can do the same with shading.

To apply a border or shading:

1. Select the text to which you'd like to add a border or shading.
2. Choose Format > Borders and Shading. The Borders and Shading dialog box appears (**Figure 4.23**).
3. *Do either of the following:*
   - ▲ To add a border around selected text or selected paragraphs, click the Borders tab.
   - ▲ To add a border around one or more pages, click the Page Border tab.
4. Select a border type: None, Box, Shadow, 3-D, or Custom.
5. *Optional:* If you don't like the default settings, you can specify a different line style, color, and/or width for the border.
6. *Optional:* To adjust the offset that separates the border from the text on each side, click the Options button (**Figure 4.24**).
7. On the Shading tab (**Figure 4.25**), select a shading color in the Fill section and a shading pattern in the Patterns section.
8. From the Apply to drop-down menu, choose the part of the document to which you want to apply the border and/or shading. Click OK.

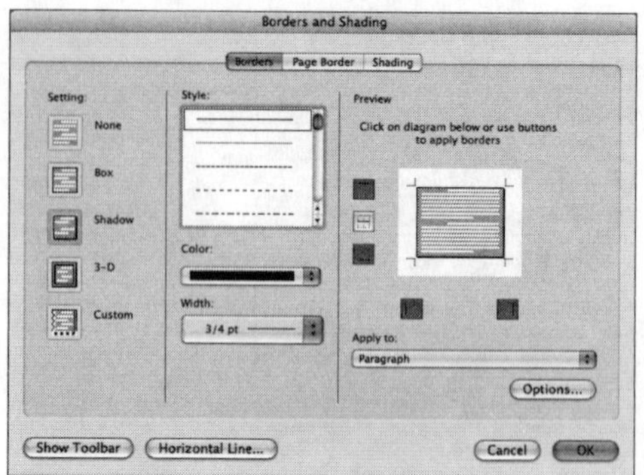

Figure 4.23 Add a border or shading to selected text in the Borders and Shading dialog box.

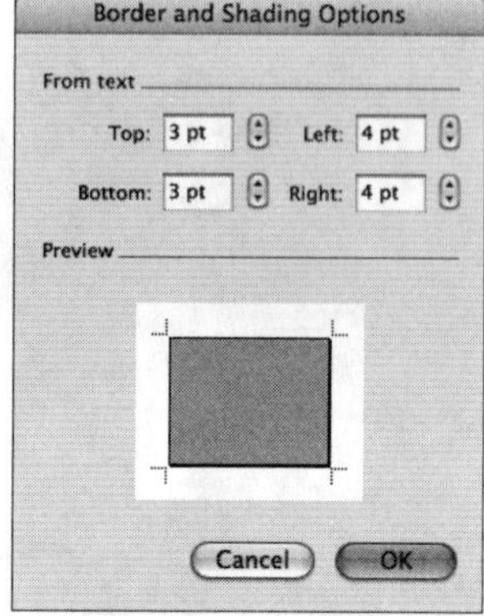

Figure 4.24 You can change the offset between each border edge and the text.

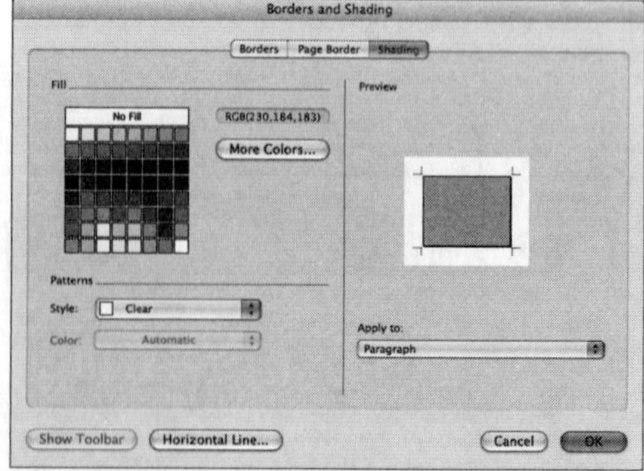

Figure 4.25 Select a shading color and pattern on the Shading tab.

Paragraph Formatting

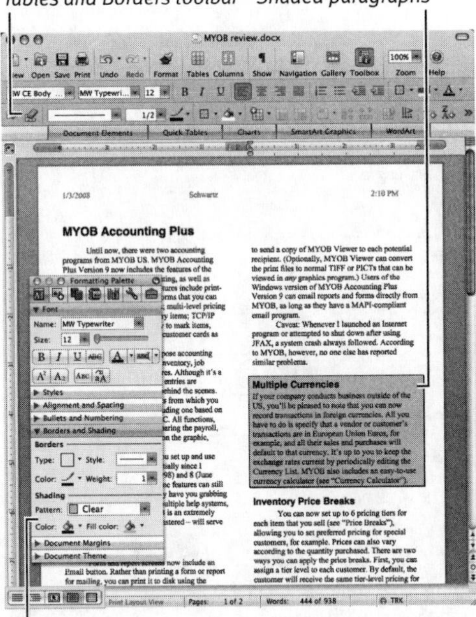

Figure 4.26 You can also select border and shading options from the Formatting Palette.

✔ Tips

- You can also apply borders and shading by choosing options from the Formatting Palette (**Figure 4.26**) or the Tables and Borders toolbar (**Figure 4.27**).
- To add borders only to specific sides, switch to the Borders or Page Border tab of the Borders and Shading dialog box, and then click those sides in the Preview area. You can make each side a different line style, color, and width.

  You can also select individual border lines from the Border Type drop-down palette on the Tables and Borders toolbar (Figure 4.27) or on the Formatting Palette.
- You can remove any line by clicking it in the Preview area of the Borders tab. To remove *all* borders, set Setting to None. You can also clear all borders by setting Type to No Border. (Click the Type icon in the Formatting Palette or the Borders icon on the Tables and Borders toolbar to see this choice.)

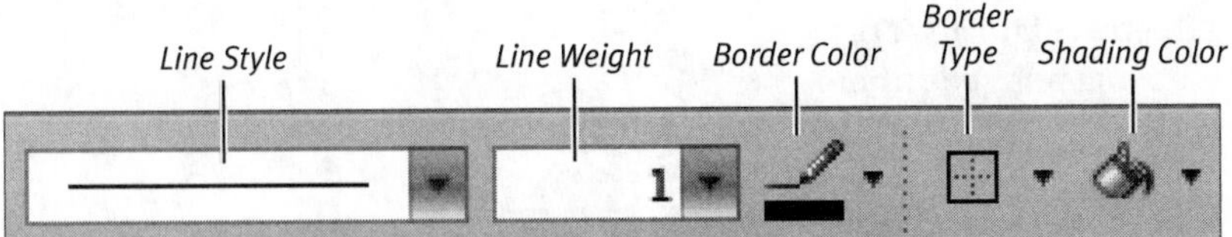

Figure 4.27 Basic border and shading options can be chosen from the Tables and Borders toolbar. (Choose View > Toolbars > Tables and Borders.)

Using Word Styles

A *style* contains text-formatting settings. Using styles, you can quickly apply a specific combination of formatting to characters or paragraphs. A paragraph style named Head A, for example, might contain the formatting for a type of heading, such as its font, space after, and alignment. To format selected text as that type of heading, you'd choose the Head A style from the Style list.

Character styles contain font formatting and are applied to selected characters. *Paragraph styles* are applied to entire paragraphs and contain both font and paragraph formatting. When no specific style is applied, paragraphs use the Normal style and text is formatted with the Default Paragraph Font style.

To apply a style:

1. Display the Formatting toolbar (View > Toolbars > Formatting) or the Formatting Palette (View > Formatting Palette).
2. Select the characters or paragraphs to format.
3. On the Formatting toolbar (**Figure 4.28**) or the Formatting Palette (**Figure 4.29**), select a character or paragraph style from the Style drop-down list.

✔ Tips

- One important reason for using styles is that doing so ensures consistency in the way a document is formatted.
- To quickly remove paragraph or character formatting from selected text, select the Clear Formatting style.
- You can make noncontiguous text selections by ⌘-clicking.

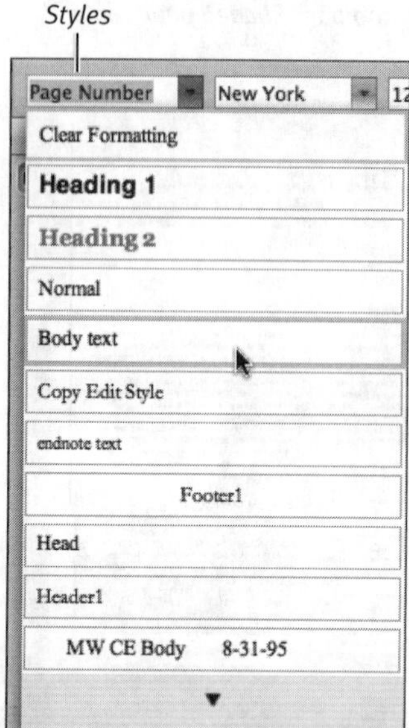

Figure 4.28 You can select a style from the Formatting toolbar...

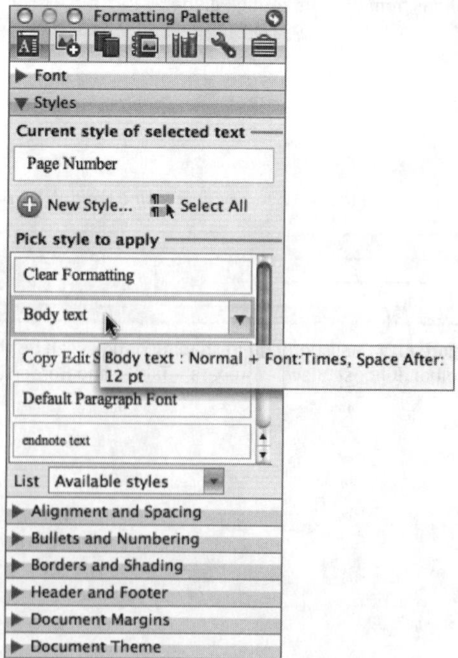

Figure 4.29 ...or from the Styles section of the Formatting Palette.

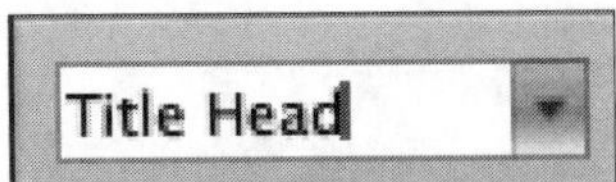

Figure 4.30 To create a new style based on the selected paragraph, type a new name in the Style box.

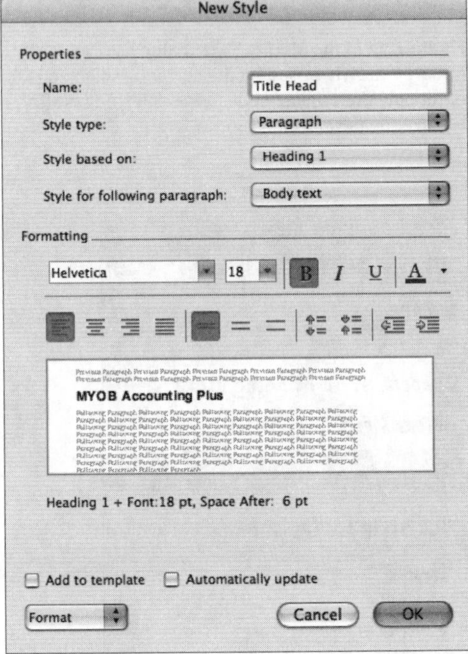

Figure 4.31 You can name and create new styles in the New Style dialog box.

Creating a paragraph style

Generally, you should create paragraph styles when you know you'll need to use the same types of paragraphs throughout a document, such as a custom hanging indent. As explained in the steps that follow, styles are easiest to create "by example."

To create a paragraph style by example using the Formatting toolbar:

1. Apply font and paragraph formatting to a paragraph, and then select the paragraph.
2. Select the current style name in the Style list on the Formatting toolbar.
3. Type the new style name in place of the old one (**Figure 4.30**) and press Return.
   This sets the selected text to the newly named style and adds the new style to the Style list for the current document.

To create a paragraph style by example using the Style dialog box:

1. Apply font and paragraph formatting to a paragraph, and then select or position the text insertion mark within the paragraph.
2. *Do either of the following:*
   - Choose Format > Style. In the Style dialog box, click the New button.
   - In the Styles section of the Formatting Palette, click the New Style button (see Figure 4.29).

   The New Style dialog box appears (**Figure 4.31**).
3. Enter a name for the style in the Name box.
4. Ensure that Paragraph is the Style type and that the *original* style for the selected paragraph is shown as the Style based on.

continues on next page

5. Select a Style for following paragraph from the drop-down list. This is the style Word will automatically apply whenever you use the new style and then press Return to create a new paragraph.
6. *Optional:* If there is additional character or paragraph formatting that you want to include as part of the style definition, specify it in the Formatting section of the dialog box.
7. Click OK to complete the style definition.

   The new style is added to the Style drop-down lists. When you save the document, the style is saved as part of the document.

✔ Tip

- When you create a style in the New Style dialog box, it is *not* automatically applied to the original paragraph. Apply the style after you exit from the dialog box.

To modify a paragraph style by example:

1. Select the paragraph. Apply any desired font and/or paragraph formatting changes.
2. Select the previously applied style from the Style list on the Formatting toolbar.

   The Modify Style dialog box appears (**Figure 4.32**).
3. Select Update the style to reflect recent changes? and then click OK.

   Every paragraph that is currently formatted with this style will be reformatted to match the revised style definition. Other styles based on the modified style will also change as appropriate.

✔ Tip

- You can also modify a style by clicking its drop-down menu in the Formatting Palette and choosing Modify Style (**Figure 4.33**).

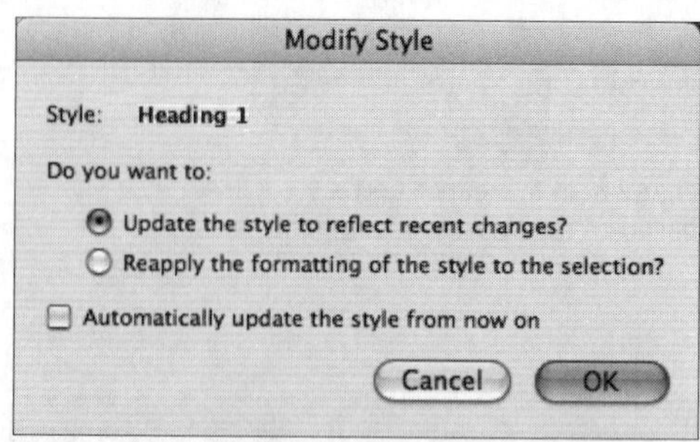

Figure 4.32 In the Modify Style dialog box, you can update the style based on the currently selected text or reapply the original style to the selected text (to remove the new formatting).

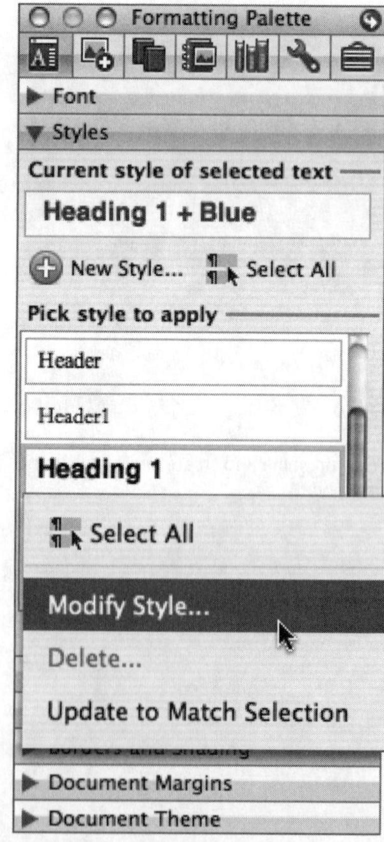

Figure 4.33 To modify a style by changing settings in a dialog box, choose Modify Style from the style's drop-down menu.

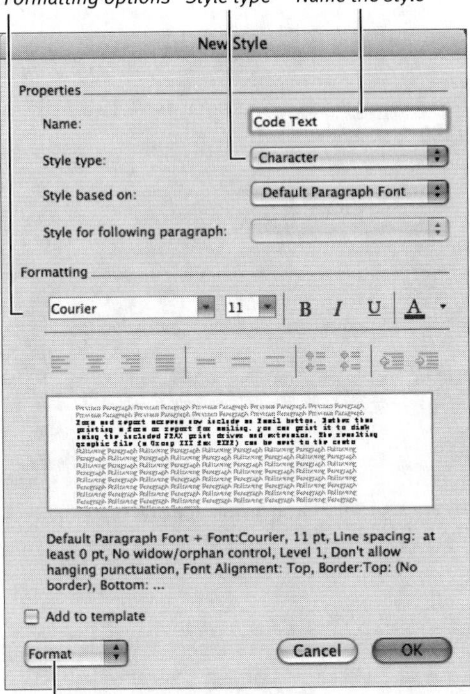

Figure 4.34 Name the new character style and make any desired changes to the formatting.

✔ Tips

- You aren't required to specify *all* formatting options for a character style. For example, if you only select blue as the color while leaving the font information blank, the applied style will simply color selected text without changing the font.
- You can make more extensive formatting changes by choosing options from the Format drop-down menu. For instance, by choosing Font, you can add small caps, strikethrough, or superscript to the style definition.

Creating a character style

Use character styles to apply consistent formatting to selected text. You can apply character styles within a paragraph that already has a paragraph style. The style will only affect the selected word(s) and will only add formatting, such as font, size, or color.

To create a character style by example:

1. Select the formatted text from which you want to create a new character style.
2. *Do either of the following:*
   - ▲ Choose Format > Style. In the Style dialog box, click the New button.
   - ▲ In the Styles section of the Formatting Palette, click the New Style button. Or click the down arrow at the right side the Current style of selected text box and choose New Style.

   The New Style dialog box appears (**Figure 4.34**).
3. In the Name text box, enter a name for the new style or accept the proposed name.
4. Choose Character from the Style type drop-down menu.
5. As necessary, select additional character-formatting options from the Formatting section.
6. Click OK to dismiss the New Style dialog box.

   The new character style is added to the Style lists.

Deleting styles

Although there's little harm in retaining styles that aren't being used in the current document, you're free to delete any style that you've defined. Deleting unnecessary styles can help minimize the clutter in a lengthy Style list. (Note, however, that the default Word styles *cannot* be deleted.)

To delete a style:

1. *Do either of the following:*
   - ▲ Choose Format > Style. Select the style name in the Style dialog box (**Figure 4.35**) and click Delete.
   - ▲ In the Pick style to apply section of the Formatting Palette, click the down arrow beside the style you want to delete. Choose Delete from the menu that appears (see Figure 4.33).

   A confirmation dialog box appears (**Figure 4.36**).
2. Click Yes to delete the style.
3. If the deletion was initiated in the Style dialog box (Step 1), click Close to dismiss the dialog box.

Defined styles for the document

Delete the style

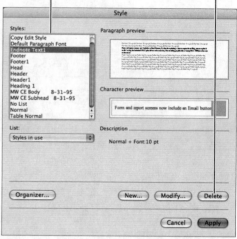

Figure 4.35 Select a style from the Styles list and click the Delete button.

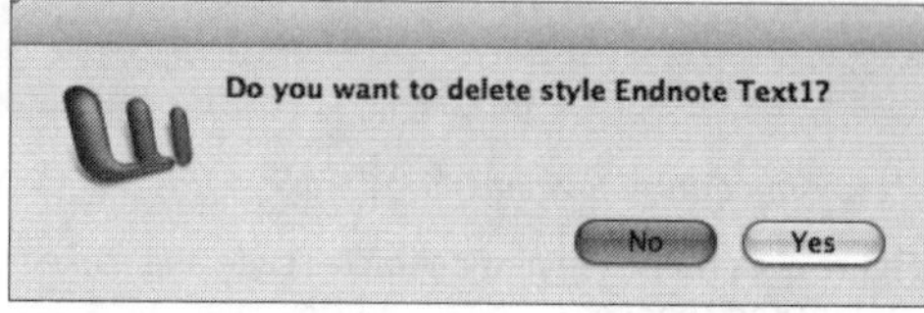

Figure 4.36 Click Yes to confirm the style deletion.

Styles in current document

Figure 4.37 Use the Organizer dialog box to copy styles from one document or template into another.

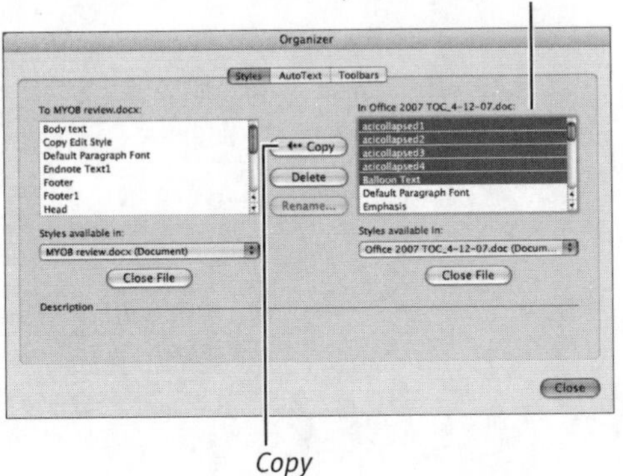

Figure 4.38 From the list on the right, select styles to be copied into the original document.

✔ Tip

- If you select one or more styles that—deliberately or inadvertently—duplicate styles in the current document, a dialog box giving you the opportunity to overwrite duplicates, skip duplicates, or cancel the copy procedure will appear.

Importing styles

Styles that you've defined are only available in the document(s) in which they've been saved. If you'd like to reuse some of these styles, you can import them into other documents.

To import styles:

1. Open the document or template into which you want to import styles.
2. Choose Format > Style.

   The Style dialog box appears (see Figure 4.35).
3. Click the Organizer button.

   The Organizer dialog box appears (**Figure 4.37**), listing the document's defined styles in the left pane. (Click the Styles tab if it isn't currently selected.)
4. Click the Close File button beneath the right pane.
5. Click the Open File button beneath the right pane.

   The Choose a File dialog box appears.
6. Navigate to the folder that contains the file from which you want to import styles, select the file, and click Open. The styles from this document appear in the right pane of the Organizer dialog box.

   By default, the Enable list is set to show Word Templates. If importing from a standard Word file rather than a template, choose Word Documents from the Enable drop-down menu.
7. In the right pane, select the styles you want to import and click the Copy button (**Figure 4.38**).

   You can ⌘-click to select multiple styles.
8. Click Close to dismiss the dialog box.

   The imported styles are now a part of and available for use in the document.

5

Adding Graphics

In this chapter, you'll learn about the many ways you can add and edit graphics in your Word documents:

- You can choose an image from the included clip art collection.
- You can insert images from your hard disk, such as scans, digital photos, or pictures you've downloaded or received in email.
- You can insert pictures from iPhoto.
- You can add predefined shapes called *AutoShapes*.
- You can add artistic text called *WordArt* to your documents.
- You can insert formatted, artistic bullet points and relationship illustrations called *SmartArt* layouts (see Chapter 17).
- You can add Excel charts and graphs to your reports (see Chapters 13, 18, and 29).

✔ Tip

- When scanning images to include in your documents, be aware that most published graphics are copyrighted and cannot be legally used without the permission of the copyright holder. Exceptions are books of royalty-free clip art, as well as royalty-free clip art and photographs that are distributed on disc or electronically.

Inserting Clip Art and Other Images

Clip art, photos, and scans can add color and visual interest to a document. Clip art is great if you're creating a brochure, advertising an event, or hosting a party. And, of course, nothing beats the realism of including your own photographs from iPhoto or elsewhere on your hard disk.

To insert clip art into a document:

1. Choose Insert > Picture > Clip Art or, if the Drawing toolbar is visible, click its Insert Clip Art icon.

   Microsoft Clip Gallery launches, and the Clip Gallery window appears (**Figure 5.1**).
2. Select a clip art category from the list on the left, and then select a picture from the ones shown.
3. *Optional:* To preview the selected image at full size in a separate window, click the Preview check box.
4. Click Insert to insert the picture into your document.

   The picture appears in the document at the text insertion mark.
5. *Optional:* To change the picture's size or formatting, select the picture. Ensure that the Toolbox is open and the Formatting Palette (**Figure 5.2**) is selected.

   To open the Toolbox, click the Toolbox icon on the Standard toolbar or choose View > Formatting Palette.
6. *Optional:* Make any necessary edits, as explained in "Image Editing," later in this chapter.

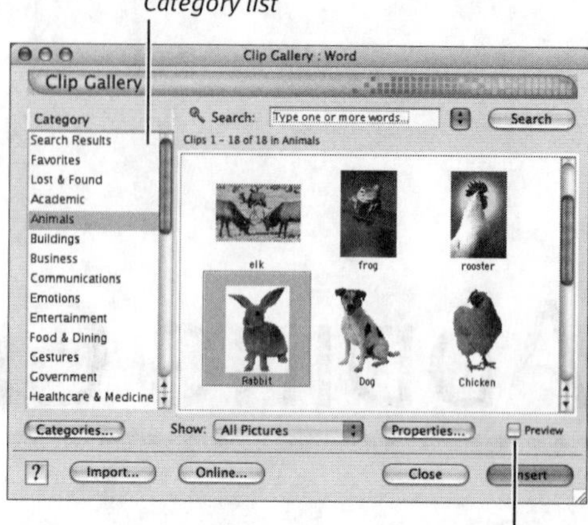

Figure 5.1 Pick from the many high-quality images in the Clip Gallery window.

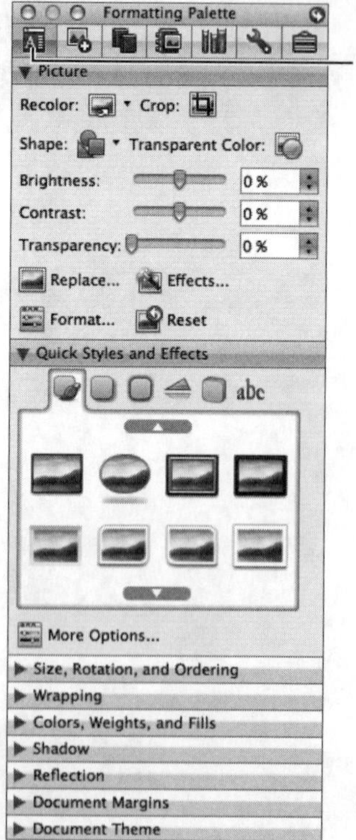

Figure 5.2 You can edit, format, apply special effects, or set text wrap for the image.

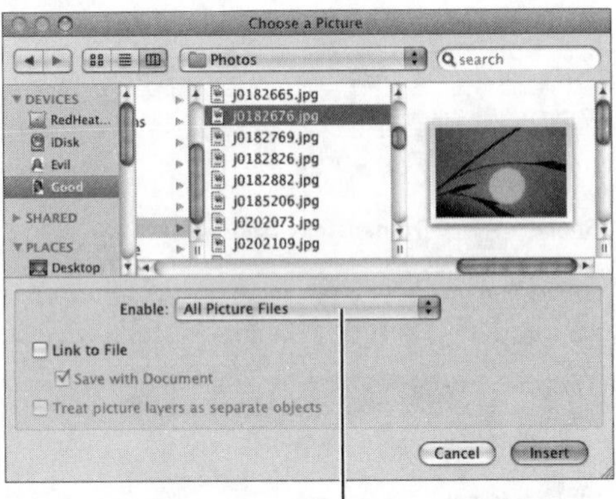

Figure 5.3 Select a picture from your hard disk (OS X 10.5/Leopard shown). Many pictures display a preview when selected.

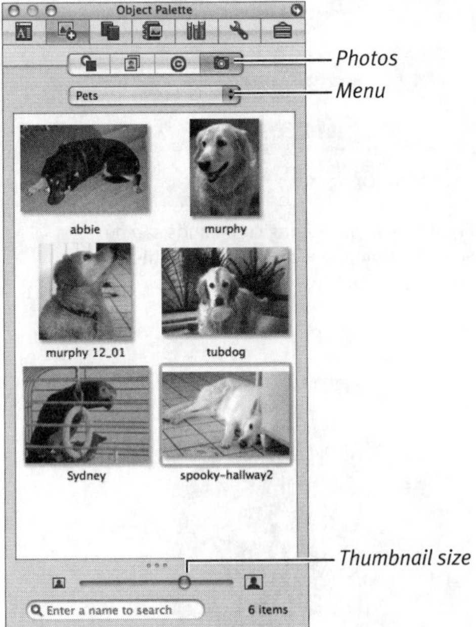

Figure 5.4 You can insert pictures that are stored in iPhoto. Drag the slider to change thumbnail size.

To insert a picture from disk:

1. Choose Insert > Picture > From File or, if the Drawing toolbar is visible, click its Insert Picture icon.

   The Choose a Picture dialog box appears.

2. Navigate to the drive and folder that contains the picture, select it (**Figure 5.3**), and click Insert.

   The image is added to the document.

To insert a picture from iPhoto:

1. Open the Object Palette.

   If the Toolbox is open, select the Object Palette. Otherwise, choose View > Object Palette.

2. Select the Photos tab (**Figure 5.4**).
3. Select a roll, album, or Library from the drop-down menu.
4. Select a photo and drag it onto the document page.

✔ Tip

- Unlike in Office 2004, you can no longer scan or import photos directly into Word. Use Image Capture (in the Applications folder) to transfer scans and digital photos to your hard disk, and then use the procedures in this section to insert them into your Word documents.

Image Editing

Word has a variety of image-editing tools that you can use to correct and edit digital photos, scans, and other *bit-mapped* (dot-based) pictures. Depending on your needs, you may find that a more advanced image-editing application is unnecessary.

To edit a picture:

1. In the Word document, select the picture you want to edit.
2. Editing commands are chosen from the Formatting Palette in the Toolbox. If the Toolbox isn't open, *do one of the following:*
   - ▲ Click the Toolbox icon on the Standard toolbar, and then click the Formatting Palette tab.
   - ▲ Choose View > Formatting Palette.

   The Formatting Palette is displayed (**Figure 5.5**).
3. You can set these options in the Picture section of the Formatting Palette:
   - ▲ **Recolor.** Select an option from this drop-down menu to colorize the picture (changing it to a sepia tone, for example).
   - ▲ **Crop.** To crop a picture (removing unnecessary material from around the subject, for example), click the Crop icon. Then click a handle and drag.
   - ▲ **Shape.** To crop the picture to match a shape (**Figure 5.6**), select an AutoShape from the drop-down submenus.
   - ▲ **Transparent Color.** You can set as transparent all areas in the image that contain a specific color, allowing material in the page's background or lower layers to shine through. Use the special cursor to click the color within the image that will be transparent.

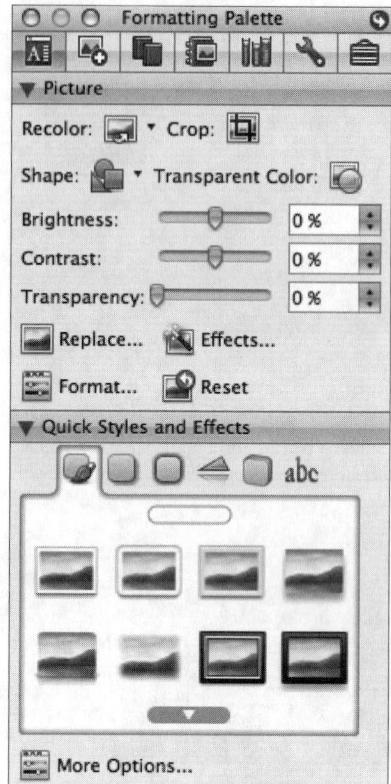

Figure 5.5 Many editing commands can be selected from the Picture section of the Formatting Palette.

Figure 5.6 The image is cropped to match the chosen AutoShape.

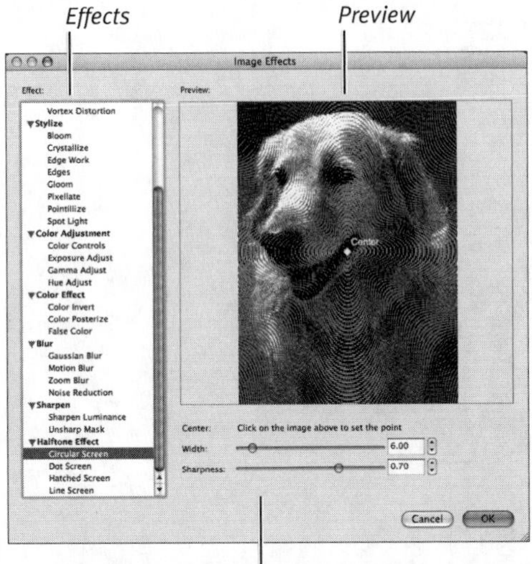

Figure 5.7 In the Image Effects dialog box, select an effect to apply and adjust the sliders. Some effects can be altered by moving the yellow diamond(s) in the Preview area.

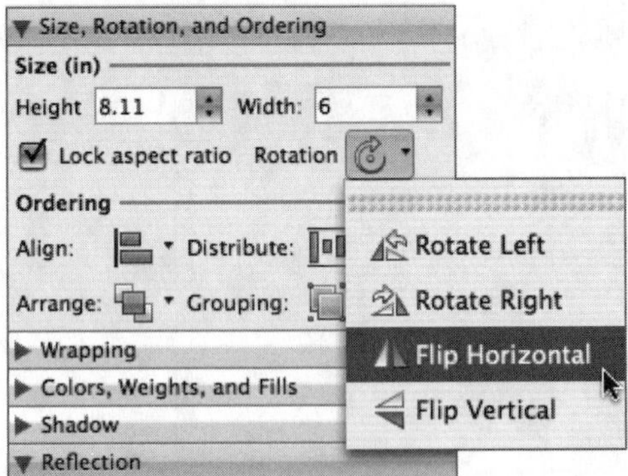

Figure 5.8 Choose a Rotation command (in the Size, Rotation, and Ordering section of the Formatting Palette) to rotate or flip the selected picture.

- **Brightness and Contrast.** Drag a slider or enter a percentage to increase or reduce these properties.
- **Transparency.** Drag the slider or enter a percentage to make the image transparent (allowing text and other materials to show through).
- **Replace.** Click this icon to replace the current image with another one from your hard disk.
- **Effects.** Click this icon to apply an effects filter to the image (**Figure 5.7**).
- **Format.** Click this icon to make changes in the Format Picture dialog box, such as specifying a text wrap or precisely adjusting the image size, contrast, or brightness.
- **Reset.** Click this icon to revert to the original picture.

4. To frame the image, select an option from the various tabs in the Quick Styles and Effects section of the Formatting Palette (see Figure 5.5).
5. To rotate or flip the image, choose a command from the Rotation drop-down menu (**Figure 5.8**). To specify a layering order for the object, choose a command from the Arrange drop-down menu.

✔ Tips

- You can remove the effect of any edit by immediately choosing Edit > Undo (⌘Z). And because Word 2008 supports multiple levels of Undo, you can step backwards through your edits by repeatedly issuing the Undo command.
- To manually rotate a selected picture, click and drag the green rotation handle.
- You can add an artistic reflection beneath a photo by clicking the Reflection check box in the Reflection section of the Formatting Palette and setting options.

Drawing Lines and Shapes

Word provides tools for adding lines and shapes to documents. You can use lines to separate text or create figure callouts, for example. And you can add predefined shapes, such as text balloons and flowchart symbols.

You use the Drawing toolbar or the Shapes tab of the Object Palette to add lines or shapes to a document. If the Drawing toolbar isn't visible, choose View > Toolbars > Drawing. To use the Object Palette, click its tab on the Toolbox or choose View > Object Palette.

To draw lines:

1. *Do either of the following:*
   - ▲ Click the Lines icon on the Drawing toolbar (**Figure 5.9**), and select a line type from the pop-out palette.
   - ▲ Choose Lines from the drop-down menu on the Shapes tab of the Object Palette. Select a line type (**Figure 5.10**).
2. Click in your document where you want to start the line, hold down the mouse button, and drag to complete the line.
3. With the line selected, select color, style, and other settings from the Colors, Weights, and Fills section of the Formatting Palette.

✔ Tips

- To change a line's length or direction, select the line, click a handle at either end, and drag. To move a line to a new position, click and drag the line's middle.
- To restrict the line's angle to 15-degree increments, press Option as you drag.
- You can also change a line's formatting in the Format AutoShape dialog box. To open the dialog box, choose Format > AutoShape or double-click the line.

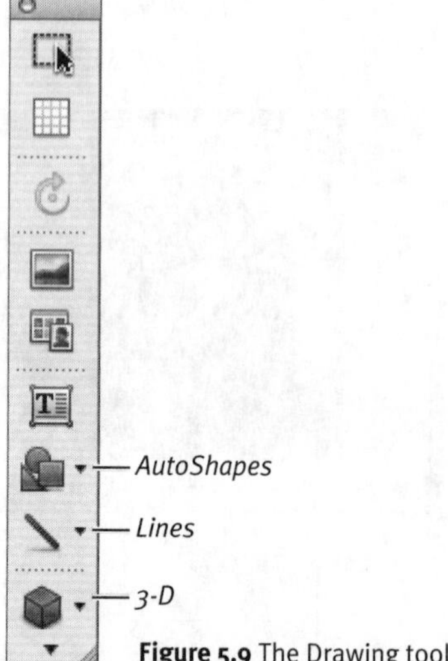

Figure 5.9 The Drawing toolbar.

Figure 5.10 Shapes tab of the Object Palette (showing the Lines group).

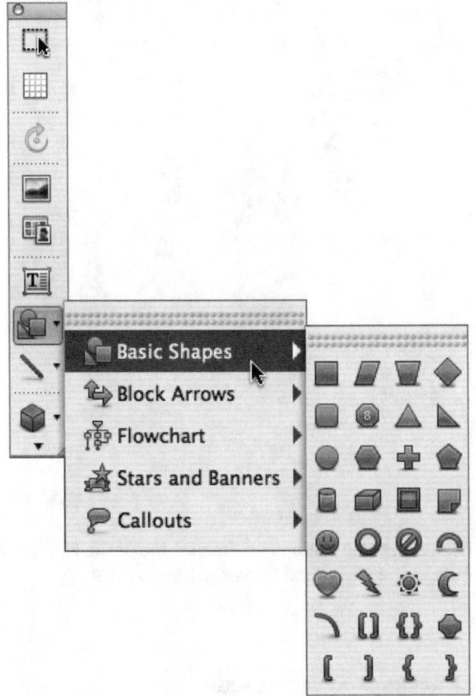

Figure 5.11 Choose a shape from the Auto-Shape submenus.

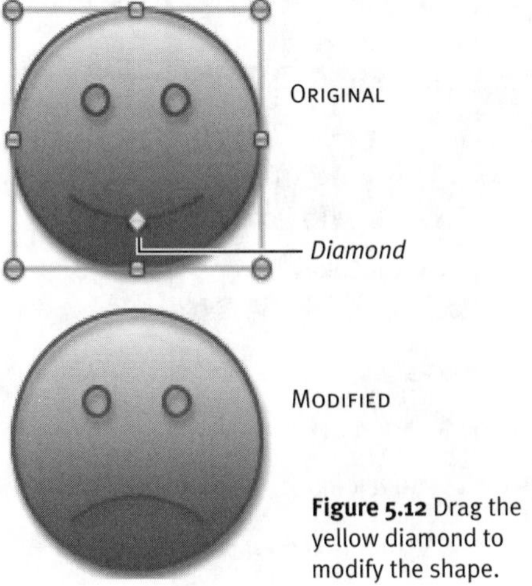

Figure 5.12 Drag the yellow diamond to modify the shape.

To draw a shape:

1. To draw a predefined shape (called an *AutoShape*), click the AutoShapes icon on the Drawing toolbar and choose a shape from one of the submenus (**Figure 5.11**).

   You can also choose an AutoShape from the Shapes tab of the Object Palette.

2. Click and drag to draw the selected shape.

   An AutoShape selected from the Object Palette can be dragged directly onto the page, if you prefer.

✔ Tips

- Another way to create an AutoShape is to choose Insert > Picture > AutoShapes. An AutoShapes toolbar appears from which you can select a shape to draw.
- To draw a proportional AutoShape (creating a square or circle instead of a rectangle or oval, for example), press Shift as you drag.
- To draw an AutoShape or line from its center, press Option as you drag.
- Many AutoShapes contain one or more yellow diamonds that you can drag to change an aspect of the shape (**Figure 5.12**).
- You can make objects three-dimensional by choosing a format from the Drawing toolbar's 3-D palette (see Figure 5.9).
- By picking options from the Formatting Palette, you can change the line style and thickness, color, and rotation angle of a selected shape.
- Certain AutoShapes, such as those in the Callouts submenu, are designed to accept typed or pasted text.
- To delete a line, arrow, or shape, select it and press Delete.

Shape and Line Editing

You can change the size of Auto-Shapes, as well as embellish them with color, shadows, and three-dimensional effects. You can make similar edits on lines.

To resize a line or shape:

1. Select the line or shape.
2. *Do any of the following:*
   - ▲ To non-proportionately resize a shape, click and drag any handle.
   - ▲ If you click and drag a line's handle to resize it, you can also change the angle.
   - ▲ To proportionately resize a shape, press Shift as you drag a corner handle.
   - ▲ Press Shift as you drag a line's handle to ensure that the angle doesn't change as you resize.
   - ▲ To resize a line or shape from its center, press Option as you drag a handle. To proportionately resize from the center, press Shift Option as you drag.
   - ▲ Open the Format AutoShape dialog box. (Double-click the object or choose Format > AutoShape.) Click the Size tab (**Figure 5.13**), and enter a new Height and Width or Scale percentages. To resize proportionately, click the Lock aspect ratio check box.

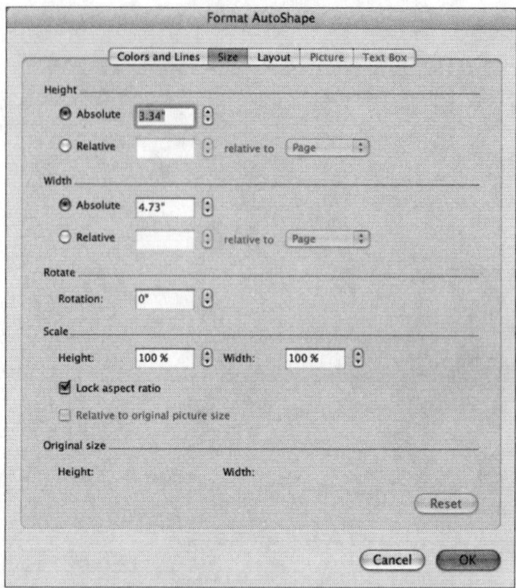

Figure 5.13 Use options on the Size tab of the Format AutoShape dialog box to precisely resize a shape.

To change a line's color:

1. Select the line.
2. In the Colors, Weights, and Fills section of the Formatting Palette, choose a color from the Line Color drop-down menu (**Figure 5.14**).
   The color is applied to the line.

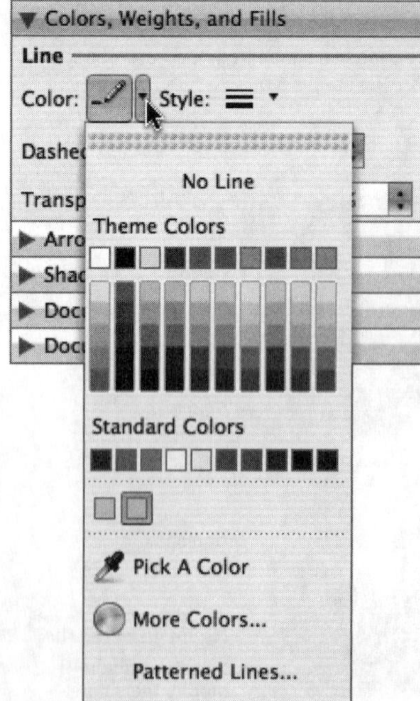

Figure 5.14 Select a new color from the Line Color drop-down menu. To duplicate a color from another object, choose Pick A Color.

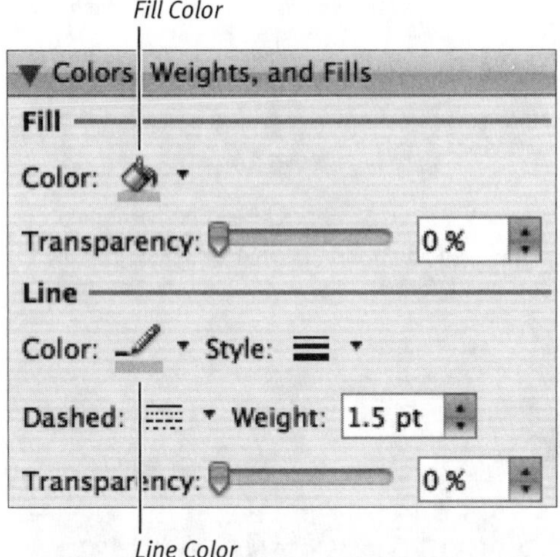

Figure 5.15 To replace a selected shape's fill or outline color, choose new colors from the Fill Color or Line Color drop-down menus.

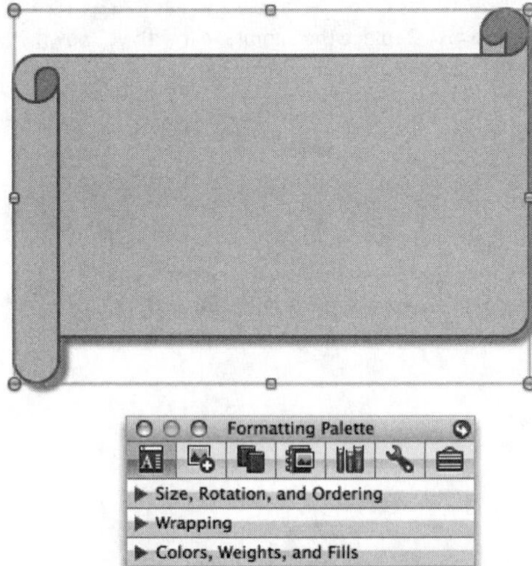

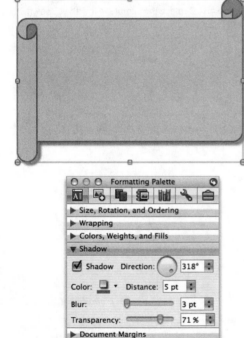

Figure 5.16 Set shadow options for a selected shape in the Shadow section of the Formatting Palette.

To change a shape's color:

1. Select the shape.
2. In the Colors, Weights, and Fills section of the Formatting Palette (**Figure 5.15**), *do either or both of the following:*
   - ▲ To change the shape's main color, choose a color from the Fill Color drop-down menu.
   - ▲ To change a shape's outline color, choose a color from the Line Color drop-down menu.

   The color(s) are applied to the shape.

To apply a shadow or 3-D effect to a shape:

1. Select the shape.
2. *Do one of the following:*
   - ▲ **Shadow.** In the Shadow section of the Formatting Palette (**Figure 5.16**), click the Shadow check box. Change the settings, such as the shadow's size (Distance), as desired.
   - ▲ **3-D effect.** Select an effect from the 3-D pop-out palette on the Drawing toolbar (see Figure 5.9).

✔ Tips

- The Line Color and Fill Color icons each show the most recent color you've applied. To apply that color to another line or shape, simply click the Line Color or Fill Color icon.
- Some shapes can accept both a line and fill color; others can accept only one or the other.
- A shadow can be applied to any type of image (shape, clip art, or photo). A 3-D effect can only be applied to shapes.
- Shadows and 3-D effects are mutually exclusive; you can apply one or the other, but not both.

Creating Artistic Text

WordArt is a graphic text object that Word can display in a number of preset, artistic styles. After creating WordArt, you can modify and fine-tune it using tools in the Formatting Palette.

To insert WordArt:

1. Choose Insert > WordArt or click the WordArt tab in the Elements Gallery.

   The Elements Gallery expands to show the WordArt styles (**Figure 5.17**, page bottom).

2. Select a WordArt category. Scroll through the styles until you see the one you want to use. Click the style's thumbnail.

   A WordArt placeholder appears on the document page (**Figure 5.18**).

3. Double-click the WordArt placeholder. The Edit WordArt Text dialog box appears.

4. Replace the placeholder with your own text. Set the font, size, and style (**Figure 5.19**), and click OK.

   Your WordArt-formatted text appears (**Figure 5.20**).

To modify WordArt:

1. Select the WordArt.

2. *Do any of the following:*

   ▲ To resize WordArt, drag a handle (see Figure 5.18). To move the WordArt, click and drag it to a new location.

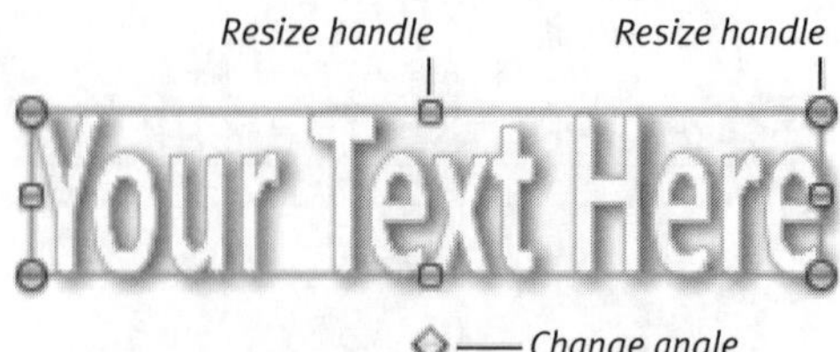

Figure 5.18 A WordArt placeholder appears in the document, formatted to match the selected style.

Figure 5.19 Replace the sample text with your own text. Select a font, size, and style.

Siliconwasteland.com

Figure 5.20 The text is formatted to match the WordArt style and the specified formatting.

Figure 5.17 Select a WordArt style by clicking its icon.

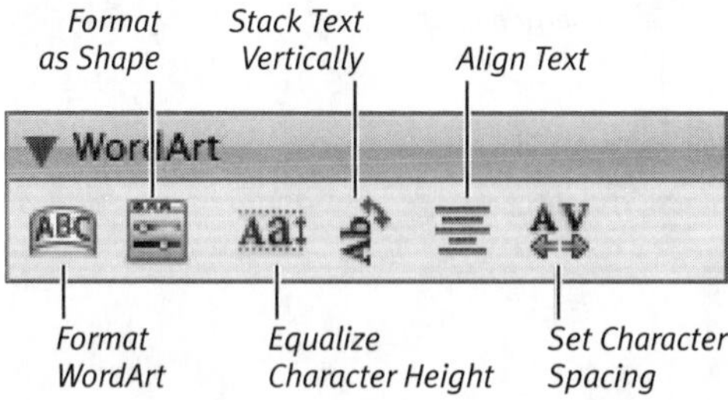

Figure 5.21 WordArt section of the Formatting Palette.

Figure 5.22 You can make the WordArt characters all the same height. Note that punctuation marks (such as the period shown) are also considered characters.

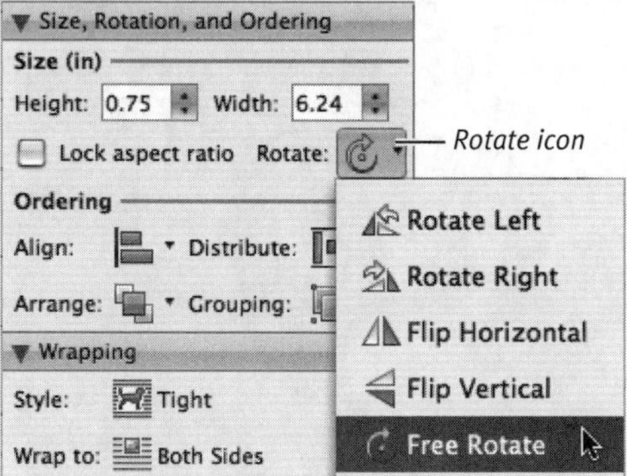

Figure 5.23 You can choose a new rotation angle for the WordArt from the Rotate drop-down menu.

- To edit the text, double-click the WordArt.
- To change the style, select the WordArt and select a replacement style from the Elements Gallery.
- To precisely control the WordArt's appearance, click the Format WordArt icon in the WordArt section of the Formatting Palette (**Figure 5.21**). Make your changes in the Format WordArt dialog box that appears.
- To change the shape of the curve(s) to which the WordArt is bound, click the Format as Shape icon (Figure 5.21) and select a shape from the palette.
- To switch between horizontal and vertical text, click the Stack Text Vertically icon (Figure 5.21).
- To make all characters a uniform height, click the Equalize Character Height icon (Figure 5.21). If you don't like the effect (**Figure 5.22**), click the icon again to reverse it.
- To set a new paragraph alignment or spacing between characters, click the Align Text or Set Character Spacing icon (Figure 5.21).
- To manually change the text angle, click and drag the yellow diamond (see Figure 5.18).
- You can select a new angle from the Rotate icon in the Size, Rotation, and Ordering section of the Formatting Palette (**Figure 5.23**). If you choose Free Rotate, you can drag any corner handle to set the new angle.
- To set the manner in which surrounding text wraps around the WordArt, select options in the Wrapping section of the Formatting Palette or on the Layout tab of the Format WordArt dialog box. (For details, see "Setting Text Wrap," later in this chapter.)

Creating Text Boxes

In Word, you can create text boxes that—unlike normal text—are objects. A *text box* is a rectangular container for text (perfect for emphasizing a quote, for example). You can edit the size, shape, color, and other aspects of a text box, just as you can with a graphic.

To create a text box:

1. Choose Insert > Text Box, or click the Text Box icon on the Drawing toolbar.
2. To draw the box, click and drag from one corner to the opposite corner, and release the mouse button (**Figure 5.24**).
3. Type or paste your text into the box.
4. To set or change the text box's formatting, *do either of the following:*
   - ▲ Choose Format > Text Box, or double-click one of the box's sides. Set options in the Format Text Box dialog box (**Figure 5.25**), and click OK.
   - ▲ Select options from the Text Box and the Colors, Weights, and Fills sections of the Formatting Palette.

✔ Tips

- To create a square text box, press Shift as you draw.
- To change the size or shape of a text box, drag a handle. To resize proportionately, Shift-drag a corner handle.
- To reposition a text box, move the pointer over any of its sides and drag.
- To delete a text box, select it and press Delete.
- You can change the font, size, color, and alignment of text in a text box. Select the text and choose formatting commands from Word's menus, the Formatting toolbar, or the Formatting Palette.

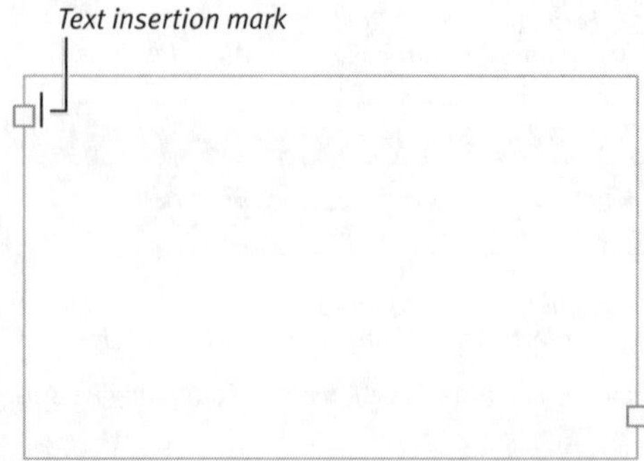

Figure 5.24 The completed text box contains a blinking insertion mark, indicating that it's ready to receive your typed or pasted text.

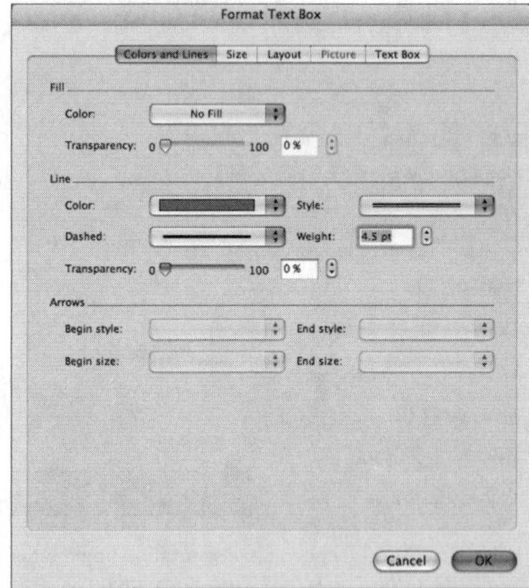

Figure 5.25 On the tabs of the Format Text Box dialog box, you can adjust the text box's size, color, margins, and so on.

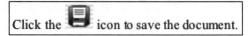

Click the [save icon] icon to save the document.

Figure 5.26 In-line graphics are treated as part of the paragraph in which they're embedded.

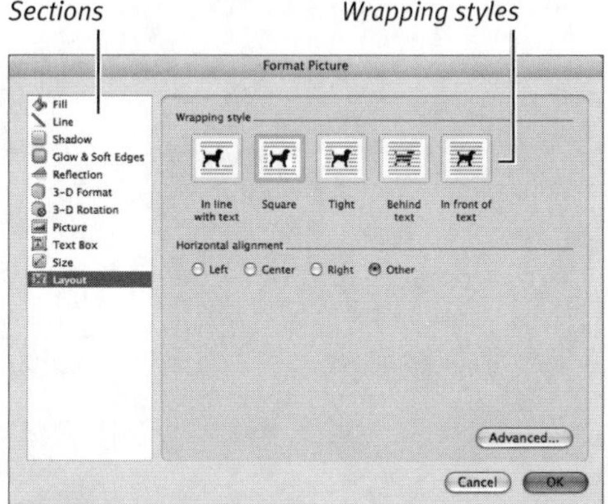

Figure 5.27 Click an icon to specify a wrapping style for the selected object.

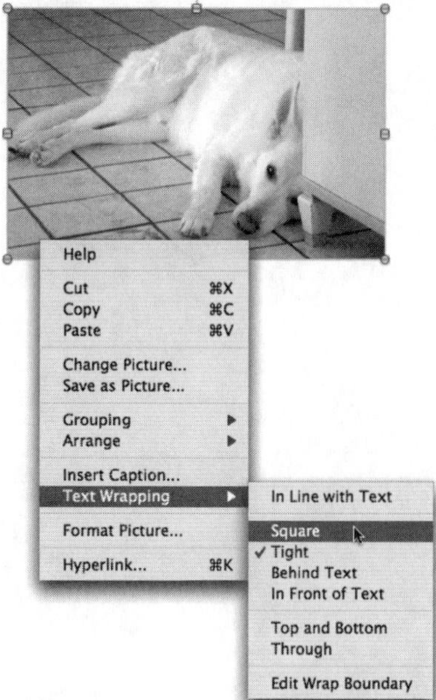

Figure 5.28 You can Control-click photos and clip art to set or change the text wrap.

Setting Text Wrap

Clip art, photos, AutoShapes, and WordArt are all objects. An object's *wrapping style* (also called *text wrap* or *text wrapping*) determines how it interacts with the surrounding text.

Objects can be in-line or floating. An *in-line object* is part of a paragraph and is subject to the paragraph's formatting. As an example, you might include artwork for an icon you want readers to recognize embedded in a sentence (**Figure 5.26**). *Floating objects,* on the other hand, can be freely moved about the page and are not tied to a paragraph.

To set wrapping style for an object:

1. Select the object, and open the Format Picture or Format AutoShape dialog box.

   To do this, double-click the object, click the Format icon in the Picture section of the Formatting Palette, or choose Format > Picture or Format > AutoShape.

2. Select the Layout section (**Figure 5.27**). *Do one of the following:*
   - ▲ To designate the selected object as in-line, click the In line with text icon.
   - ▲ To designate the selected object as floating, click one of the other text wrap icons or click Advanced.

3. Click OK.

   Text wraps around the object as specified.

✔ Tips

- If a newly inserted object is only partially displayed, it has the wrong wrapping style, such as "In line with text."
- You can Control-click a picture or clip art image and choose a command from the Text Wrapping submenu (**Figure 5.28**). You can also set text wrap for a selected object in the Wrapping section of the Formatting Palette.

Creating Tables

It's easy to create tables in Word documents. With the click of a button, you can create and begin entering information into a table. Tables can be included in sales reports, research projects, or data analyses. Or a table can consist of only a list of names and phone numbers. We'll discuss the simplest means of creating tables first, and then move on to building more complex tables.

The procedures in this chapter assume that you're working with an existing Word file. If you don't have a document open, *do one of the following:*

- To add a table to an existing document, choose File > Open, press ⌘O, click the Open toolbar icon, or choose the document from the File > Open Recent submenu.
- To create a table in a new document, choose File > New Blank Document, click the New Blank Document toolbar icon, or press ⌘N.

Inserting a Quick Table

New in Office 2008, Quick Tables are formatted tables that you can insert into documents by merely selecting a table style from the Elements Gallery. Even if you don't see a style that's exactly what you want, you may find it faster to modify a Quick Table than to create a table using the other methods described in this chapter.

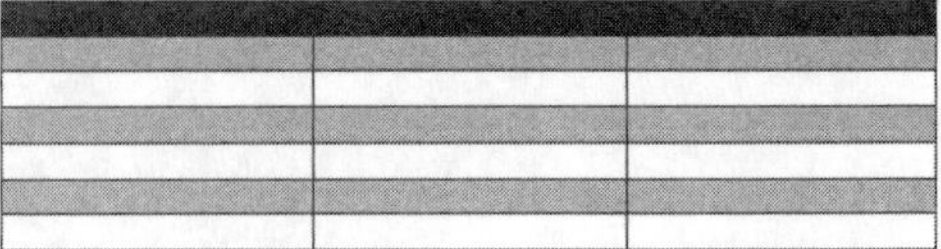

Figure 6.2 A Quick Table style can include cell colors, shading, and fonts.

To add a Quick Table to a document:

1. Position the insertion point in your Word document where you want the table to appear.
2. Click the Quick Tables icon in the Elements Gallery (beneath the toolbars).
   The Quick Tables gallery appears (**Figure 6.1**, page bottom).
3. Select the type of table you want to insert by clicking the Basic or Complex tab.
4. Select a table style by clicking its icon in the Quick Tables gallery. For assistance in selecting a style, *do the following:*
   - ▲ Rest the cursor over any style icon to read a description of the style.
   - ▲ To view additional styles of the current table type, click the arrows on the right side of the gallery.

   A blank table formatted in the selected style appears in your document (**Figure 6.2**). Enter data and change the table formatting as necessary (explained later in this chapter).

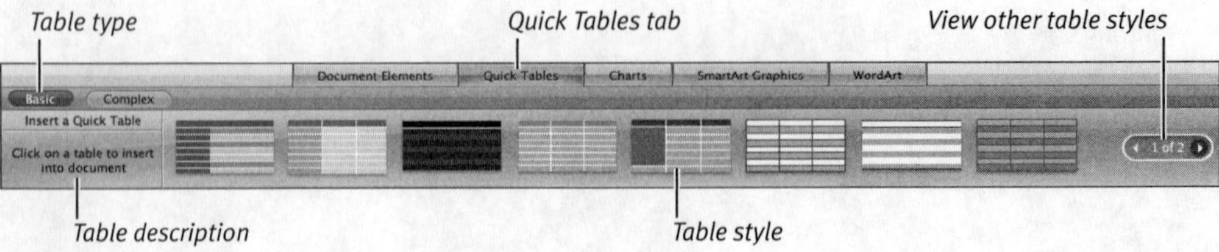

Figure 6.1 Click the Quick Tables tab, and then select a table style.

Figure 6.3 Drag in the Tables palette to specify the desired table size.

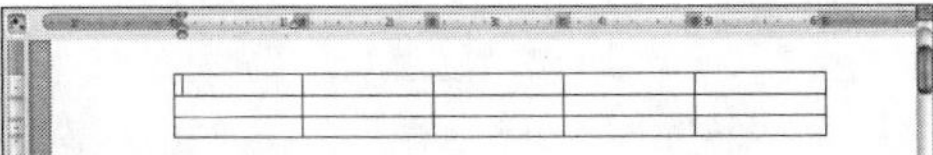

Figure 6.4 An unformatted table appears in the Word document.

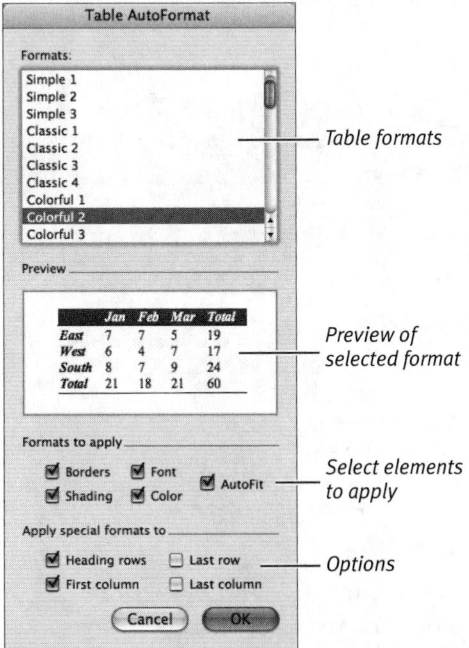

	Jan	Feb	Mar	Total
East	7	7	5	19
West	6	4	7	17
South	8	7	9	24
Total	21	18	21	60

Figure 6.5 Choose Table > Table AutoFormat, and then select a format from the Formats list.

Creating a Simple Table

In addition to selecting Quick Tables, you can create a table by specifying its dimensions and selecting formatting options.

To create a simple table:

1. Click to set the text insertion mark where you want the table to appear.
2. Click the Insert Table icon on the Standard toolbar.
3. In the palette that appears, drag to specify the desired number of columns and rows (**Figure 6.3**).

   An unformatted table appears (**Figure 6.4**). If you don't want to format the table now, you can begin entering text and data. Otherwise, continue with Step 4.
4. To apply a defined format to the table, choose Table > Table AutoFormat.

   The Table AutoFormat dialog box appears (**Figure 6.5**).
5. Select a table style from the Formats list.

   You can choose from variety of formats, such as tables with or without headers, three-dimensional tables, and colored tables. A sample of the selected table format appears in the Preview window.
6. Set formatting options in the bottom section of the dialog box as desired.
7. Click OK.

   The formatting is applied to the table.

✔ Tips

- You can simultaneously insert and format a table by choosing Table > Insert > Table. In the Insert Table dialog box (**Figure 6.6**), specify the numbers of columns and rows, and set the initial column widths. To select a table format, click AutoFormat.
- If the Toolbox is open, you can open the Table AutoFormat dialog box by switching to the Formatting Palette, expanding the Table section, and clicking the Table AutoFormat icon (**Figure 6.7**). The Table section also includes an Insert Table icon, as well as other table-related commands.
- You can apply table formatting at any point—regardless of whether you've begun entering data.
- To show or hide the gridlines in any table, select a cell from the table, and choose Table > Gridlines.

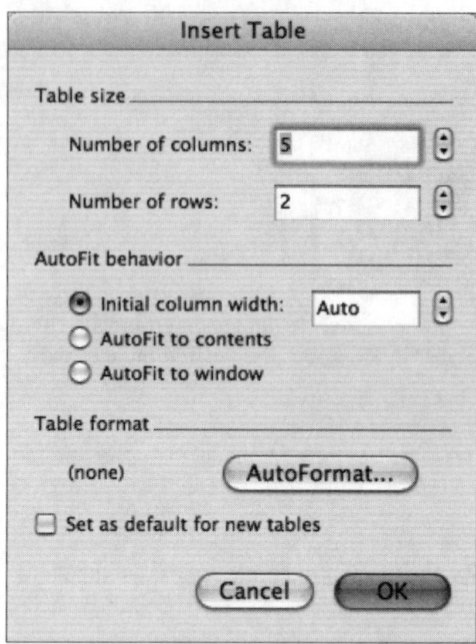

Figure 6.6 In the Insert Table dialog box, set the number of columns and rows for the table.

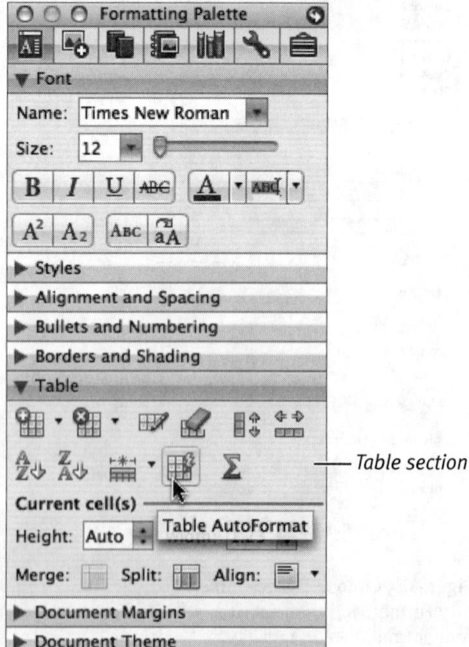

Figure 6.7 Table-related commands can be selected from the Table section of the Formatting Palette.

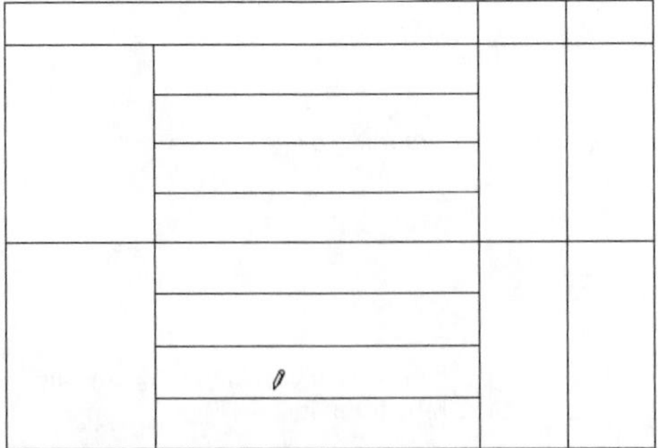

Figure 6.9 Using the Draw Table tool, click and drag to draw the table outline and cell boundaries.

Creating a Table from Scratch

If you have a complex table in mind, you can use Word's table tools to draw it.

To create a table from scratch:

1. Choose Table > Draw Table, or choose View > Toolbars > Tables and Borders.

   The Tables and Borders toolbar appears (**Figure 6.8**, page bottom).

2. Use the Draw Table tool to draw the table outline. (If the tool isn't already selected, click the Draw Table toolbar icon.)

   Click where you want one corner, drag diagonally to the opposite corner, and release the mouse button.

3. Use the Draw Table tool to draw the interior cell boundaries (**Figure 6.9**).

4. When you're done working on the table and ready to begin entering text, click the Draw Table tool icon again.

✔ Tips

- To remove a line, click the Eraser icon on the Tables and Borders toolbar, and then click the line you want to erase. (When drawing with the Draw Table tool, you can temporarily switch to the Eraser tool by pressing Shift.)

- To remove a line you've just drawn, choose Edit > Undo, press ⌘Z, or click the Undo icon on the Standard toolbar.

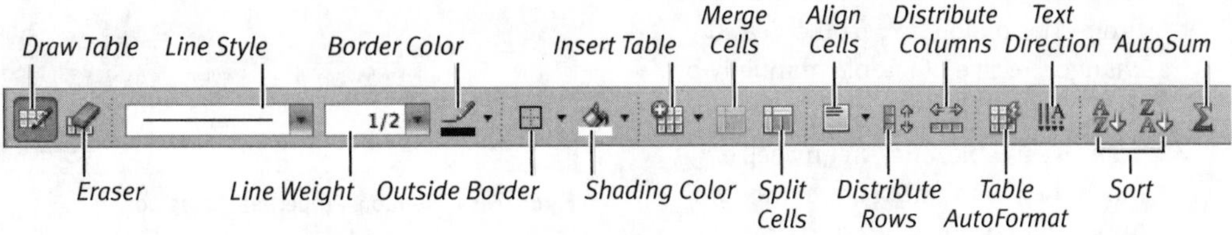

Figure 6.8 Tables and Borders toolbar.

Editing the Table Structure

Once you have created the skeleton of the table, you can fine-tune it using tools in the Tables and Borders toolbar. (Note that you can use these tools to alter *any* Word table.)

To edit the table structure:

- *Do any of the following:*
  - To move a line, click and drag it to a new location (**Figure 6.10**).
  - To change the style, width, or color of a line, choose new options from the Line Style, Line Weight, and Border Color toolbar menus (**Figure 6.11**). Click any line in the table with the drawing tool to apply the new settings to the line. New lines that you draw will also use those settings.
  - To distribute cell heights or widths evenly, click outside the table to clear the tool selection, and then click and drag through the cells you want to adjust. Click the Distribute Rows Evenly or Distribute Columns Evenly icon (**Figure 6.12**) on the Tables and Borders toolbar.
  - To set row heights or column widths precisely, select the cells you want to modify and then choose Table > Table Properties. On the Row or Column tab of the Table Properties dialog box (**Figure 6.13**), enter the new value and click OK.
  - You can change the table width by entering a value in the Preferred width text box on the Table tab of the Table Properties dialog box. You can also change the size of a table manually by dragging its bottom-right corner.
  - To move a table, click in any cell to make the plus symbol appear in its upper-left corner. Click and drag the plus symbol to move the table.

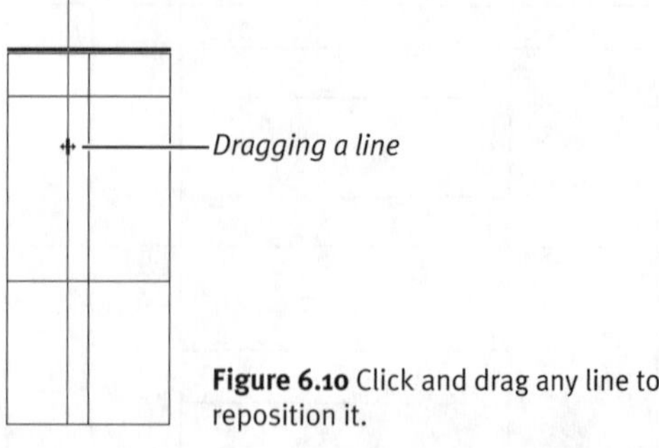

Figure 6.10 Click and drag any line to reposition it.

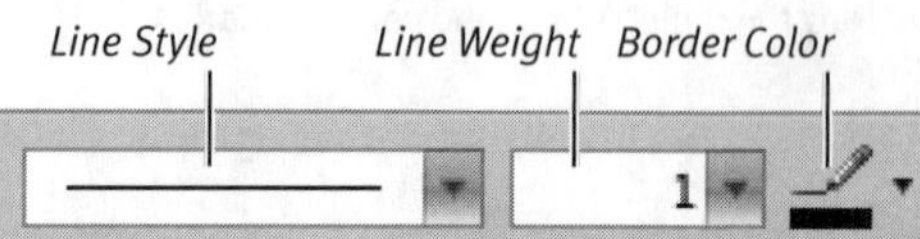

Figure 6.11 To draw or alter the lines in a table, select options from the Tables and Borders toolbar.

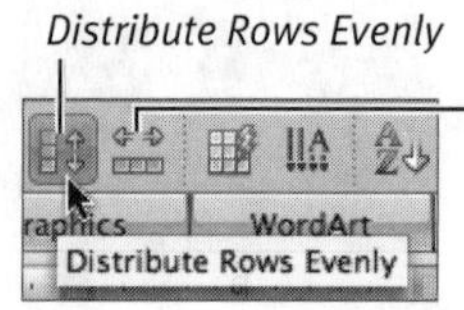

Figure 6.12 You can evenly distribute selected rows or columns.

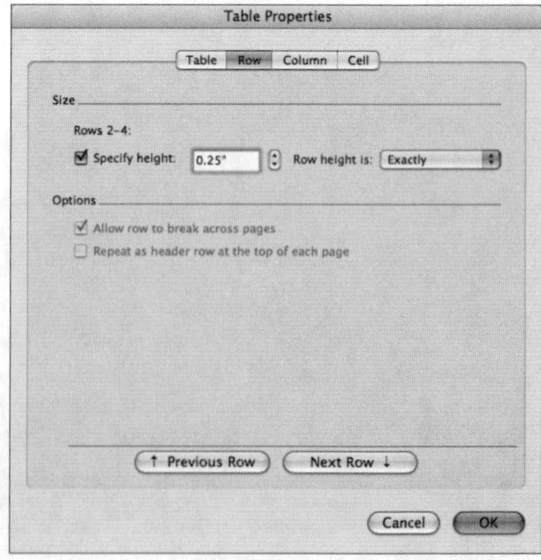

Figure 6.13 The Table Properties dialog box.

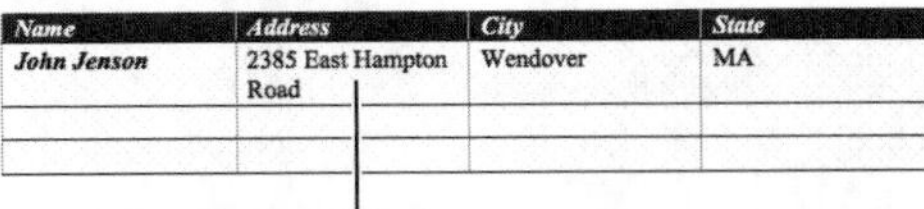

Name	Address	City	State
John Jenson	2385 East Hampton Road	Wendover	MA

Cell with excess text

Figure 6.14 If you enter text that's wider than the cell width, the row height expands as needed to fully display the text.

Sorting a Table

After you've entered a few rows of data, you can sort a table by doing the following:

1. Select or enter any cell in the column on which you want to sort.
2. *Do one of the following:*
   - ▲ To sort alphabetically or from lowest to highest, click the Sort Ascending icon on the Tables and Borders toolbar (see Figure 6.8).
   - ▲ To sort in the reverse order, click the Sort Descending toolbar icon.
   - ▲ To perform a more complex sort, such as sorting on multiple fields or making the sort case sensitive, choose Table > Sort and specify options in the Sort dialog box.

   Note that empty rows, if any, are sorted, too. Header rows, on the other hand, are generally excluded.

Entering Data

After you've placed the table in a document, you can enter your information.

To enter data into a table:

1. Click in the first table cell and then type.

   As you type, the text wraps within the cell as necessary. The entire row will become taller if it needs to accommodate multiple lines of text (**Figure 6.14**).
2. After completing the entry in the first cell, press Tab to move to the cell to its right, and type text in that cell.

   When you reach the rightmost cell of a row, pressing Tab moves the insertion mark to the first cell of the next row.

✔ Tips

- Press Shift Tab to move back one cell.
- If there is already text in a cell when you Tab into it, the text is automatically selected. If you wish, you can delete the entire cell entry by pressing Delete or by typing over it.
- You can move directly to any cell by clicking in it.
- When you finish entering data in the last cell of a table, you can press Tab to create a new row, if you wish.
- Use normal editing procedures to alter and format the information in cells.

Aligning Table Data

Using the Tables and Borders toolbar and the Formatting toolbar, you can change the alignment or orientation of cell data.

To change the alignment or orientation of cell data:

- *Do any of the following:*
  - Select the cells whose alignment you want to change. Click the Cell Alignment icon on the Tables and Borders toolbar and select an alignment from the pop-up palette (**Figure 6.15**).
  - To change the orientation of data within cells, select the cells you want to orient. Click the Change Text Direction icon on the Tables and Borders toolbar (**Figure 6.16**) repeatedly until you get the desired orientation. There are three possible orientations (**Figure 6.17**).

✔ Tips

- You can also set the alignment of selected cells by clicking an alignment icon on the Formatting toolbar. The alignment icons presented (**Figure 6.18**) depend on the text direction in the selected cell(s).
- Another way to change text direction is to select the desired cell(s), and then choose Format > Text Direction. The advantage of this approach is that you can select a *specific* direction in the Text Direction dialog box.
- You can also set text direction or alignment by Control-clicking a selected cell and choosing Text Direction or Cell Alignment from the pop-up menu that appears.
- To specify a table's alignment on the page, select any cell, choose Table > Table Properties, and select Alignment and Text wrapping options on the Table tab.

Figure 6.15 To set alignment for data in selected cells, choose an option from the Cell Alignment palette.

Figure 6.16 To change the orientation of a selected cell's text, click the Change Text Direction icon.

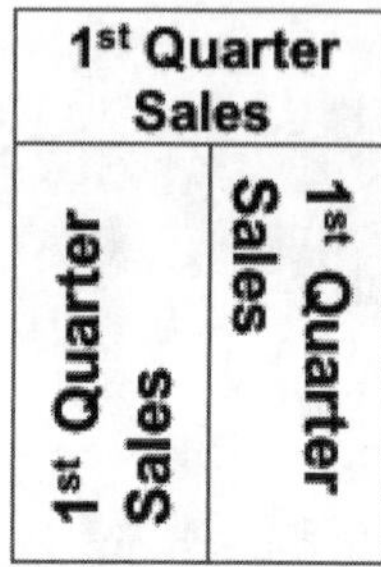

Figure 6.17 You can orient cell text in these directions.

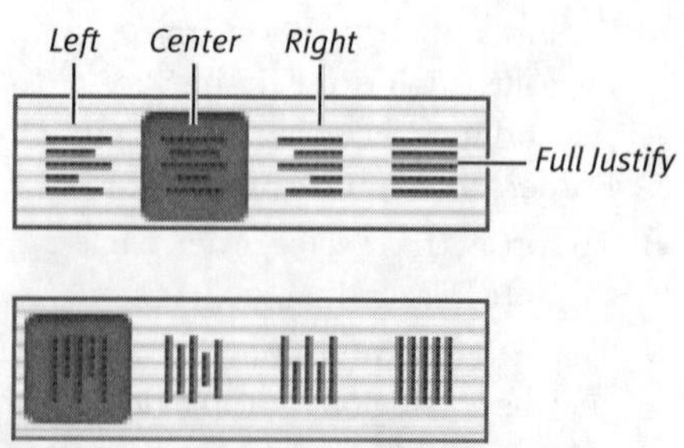

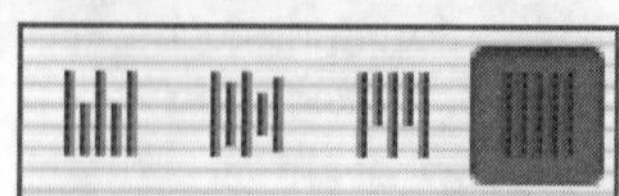

Figure 6.18 To set the alignment of text in selected cells, click these icons on the Formatting toolbar.

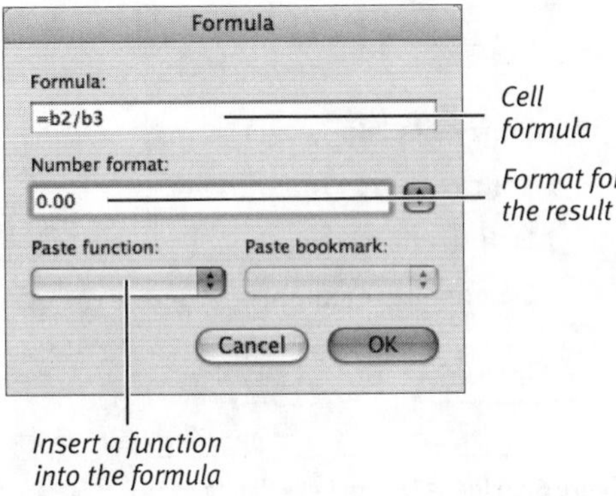

Figure 6.19 Choose Table > Formula and enter a formula in the Formula dialog box.

Working with Numeric Data

Word tables have calculation capabilities that are similar to those of an Excel worksheet. For example, you can use the AutoSum feature to total columns or rows of numeric values. Using the Table > Formula command, you can insert a formula into any cell.

To total a row or column:

- *Do any of the following:*
  - To total values in a column, click in the cell beneath the numbers you're adding, and then click the AutoSum icon on the Tables and Borders toolbar (see Figure 6.8).
  - To total values in a row, click in the cell to the right of the numbers you're adding, and click the AutoSum icon.

✔ Tips

- If you need a blank row for your totals, click in the last row and choose Table > Insert > Rows Below. To add an extra column, click in the rightmost column and choose Table > Insert > Columns to the Right.
- You can perform other calculations with table values. Click in an empty cell where you want to display the result, choose Table > Formula, enter a formula in the Formula dialog box (**Figure 6.19**), and click OK. The calculation result appears in the cell. See Chapter 11 for information about formulas.
- Cells can be referenced as if they were in a worksheet. For example, the top five cells in the first column would be referenced as `A1:A5`.
- You can choose functions from the Paste function drop-down list (Figure 6.19).
- To view the formula in a given cell, select the cell and choose Table > Formula.
- Table formulas do not recalculate automatically. To force a recalculation, reapply the AutoSum or formula to the result cell or Control-click the cell's contents and choose Update Field from the pop-up menu that appears.
- If you need greater calculation capabilities, set up the data and formulas in Excel, copy the cells, and then paste the data into Word as an embedded or linked table. For more information, refer to Chapter 29.

Deleting Cells

You can easily remove cells from a table by deleting the entire table, full rows or columns, or only selected cells.

To delete table cells:

◆ *Do any of the following:*

- ▲ To delete an entire table, click any cell and choose Table > Delete > Table.
- ▲ To delete entire rows or columns, select one or more cells from the row(s) or column(s), and then choose Table > Delete > Rows or Table > Delete > Columns.
- ▲ To delete specific cells in a table, select the cells and choose Table > Delete > Cells. The Delete Cells dialog box appears (**Figure 6.20**). You can delete only the selected cells, moving the rest up or to the left (to close up the deletion), or you can delete entire rows or columns.

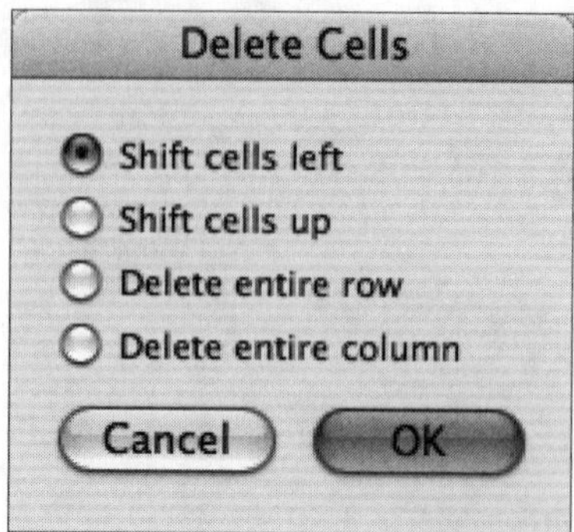

Figure 6.20 In the Delete Cells dialog box, indicate how to adjust the remaining cells after the deletion.

✔ Tips

- You can also make the Delete Cells dialog box appear by selecting the desired cell(s), Control-clicking in the selection, and choosing Delete Cells from the pop-up menu that appears (**Figure 6.21**).
- Deleting a cell, row, or column is not the same as simply clearing the cells' contents. The Delete commands actually *remove* selected cells, rows, or columns from the table. To *clear* one or more cells of the data they contain, select the cells and choose Edit > Clear > Contents.
- If you accidentally delete a table or any part of it, you can restore the deleted portions by immediately choosing the Edit > Undo command, pressing ⌘Z, or clicking the Undo icon on the Standard toolbar.

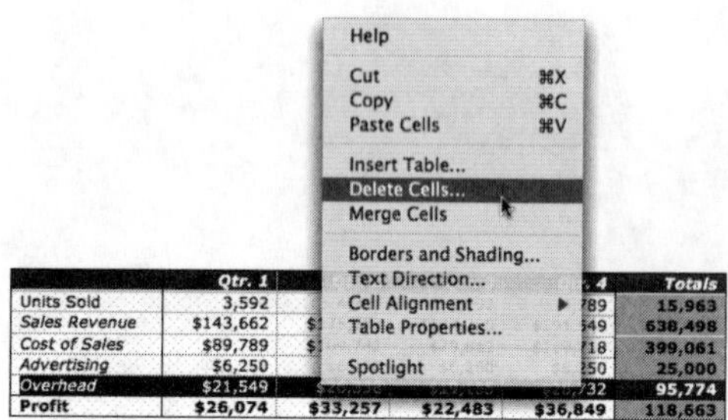

Figure 6.21 You can delete selected cells by Control-clicking them and choosing Delete Cells.

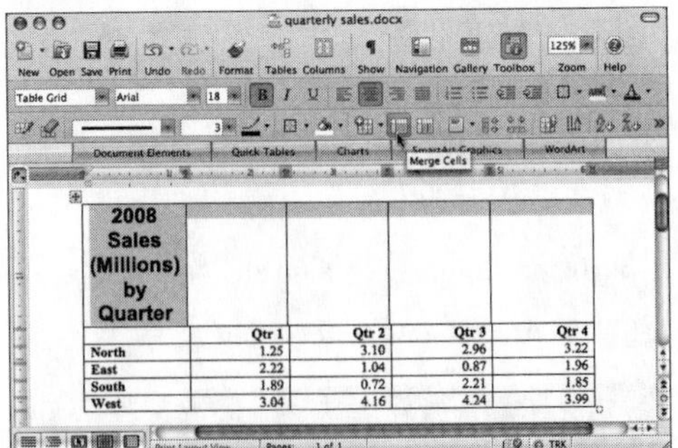

Figure 6.22 Select the cells you want to merge (in this case, the top row) and then click the Merge Cells icon.

Merged cells

2008 Sales (Millions) by Quarter				
	Qtr 1	Qtr 2	Qtr 3	Qtr 4
North	1.25	3.10	2.96	3.22
East	2.22	1.04	0.87	1.96
South	1.89	0.72	2.21	1.85
West	3.04	4.16	4.24	3.99

Figure 6.23 The cells merge, creating a single cell in which to display the table's title.

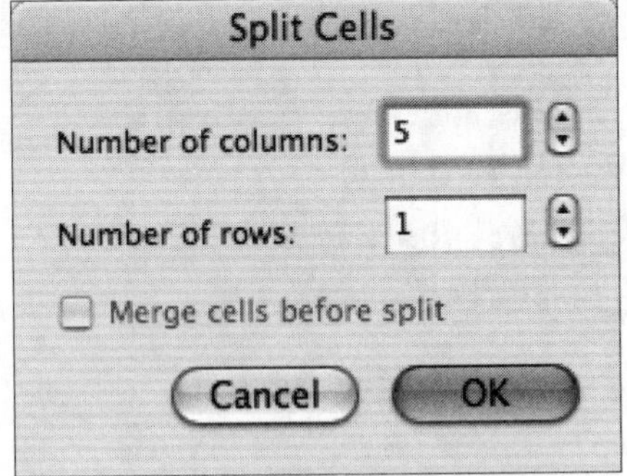

Figure 6.24 When splitting a cell, you specify the number of resulting columns and rows.

Merging and Splitting Cells

Using the Merge Cells command, you can combine two or more adjacent cells into a single cell (to display an extended column or row heading, for example). Similarly, you can use the Split Cells command to split a single cell into multiple cells. Split Cells is also useful for restoring previously merged cells to their original multi-cell structure.

To merge cells:

1. Select two or more adjacent cells to be merged (**Figure 6.22**).
2. Choose Table > Merge Cells or click the Merge Cells icon on the Tables and Borders toolbar (see Figure 6.8).

   The cells merge (**Figure 6.23**).

To split a cell:

1. Select the cell that you want to split into multiple cells.
2. Choose Table > Split Cells or click the Split Cells icon on the Tables and Borders toolbar (see Figure 6.8).

   The Split Cells dialog box appears (**Figure 6.24**).
3. Specify the number of columns and rows into which to split the cell. Click OK.

Adding Rows and Columns

Another way you can change a table layout is by inserting new rows, columns, or cells.

To insert a new row:

1. Click a cell in the row that will serve as the reference for the new row.
2. Choose Table > Insert > Rows Above or Table > Insert > Rows Below, or click the down arrow beside the Insert Table icon on the Tables and Borders toolbar and choose the command (**Figure 6.25**).
   The new row appears.

To insert a new column:

1. Click a cell in the column that will serve as the reference for the new column.
2. Choose Table > Insert > Columns to the Left or Table > Insert > Columns to the Right, or choose the command from the Tables and Borders toolbar (Figure 6.25).
   The new column appears.

To insert new cells:

1. Select the cell or cells that will serve as the reference for the new cell(s).
2. Choose Table > Insert > Cells, or choose the command from the Tables and Borders toolbar (Figure 6.25).
   The Insert Cells dialog box appears (**Figure 6.26**).
3. Select an option and click OK.
   The new cells are inserted into the table, and the surrounding cells are adjusted as necessary.

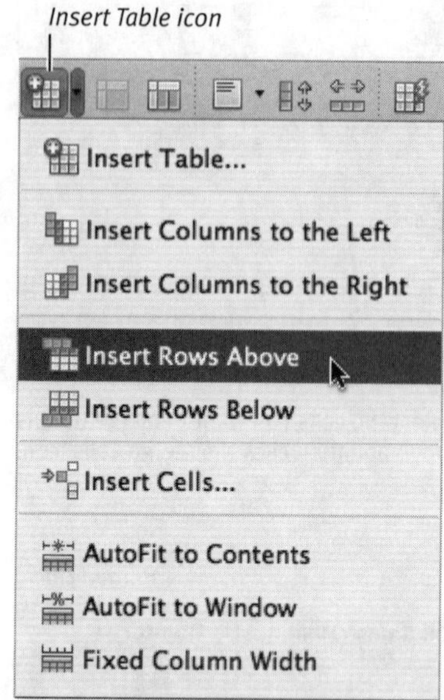

Figure 6.25 Row, column, and cell insertion commands can be chosen from the Insert Table icon's drop-down menu.

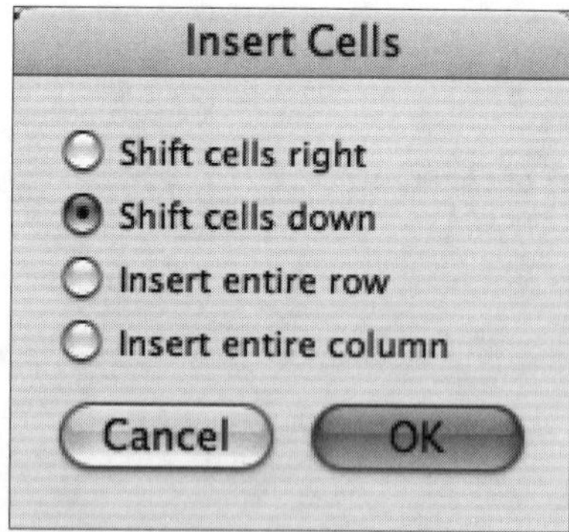

Figure 6.26 When you insert new cells into a table, you must indicate how it will affect the surrounding cells.

✔ Tips

- To insert multiple columns or rows, select the desired number of new columns or rows and then issue the Insert command.
- The Standard toolbar contains an Insert Table/Columns/Cells icon that changes depending on what is currently selected in the table.

Selected cell

	Species	Jan.-June	July-Dec.
Cats	Abyssinian	37	45
	Burmese	12	17
Dogs	Retriever	52	55
	Corgi	23	18
	Total	124	135

Figure 6.27 Select the location where the nested table will be inserted.

Nested table

	Species	Jan.-June	July-Dec.
Cats	Abyssinian	37	45
	Burmese	12	17
Dogs	Retriever Golden | Blonde	52	55
	Corgi	23	18
	Total	124	135

Figure 6.28 The nested table is created within the original table.

Nesting Tables

Nested tables are tables within tables. They can be handy if you have a special subcategory of information that the table needs to reflect. Inserting a nested table is similar to creating a new table.

To insert a nested table:

1. Click in your current table to select a place to insert the nested table (**Figure 6.27**).
2. Click the Insert Table icon on the Standard toolbar (see Figure 6.3) and drag to specify the number of rows and columns for the nested table.

   A nested table appears within your original table (**Figure 6.28**).

✔ Tips

- You can also insert a nested table by choosing the Table > Insert > Table command or by clicking the Insert Table icon on the Tables and Borders toolbar. For instructions on working with the Insert Table dialog box, refer to the first tip following "Creating a Simple Table," earlier in this chapter.
- Like other tables, you can resize a nested table by dragging its lower-right corner.

Borders and Cell Shading

Borders are the lines surrounding cells. *Shading* is a color and pattern fill within cells. The Table > Table AutoFormat command has a collection of templates for borders and shading that you can apply to a table (discussed in "Creating a Simple Table," earlier in this chapter). If you prefer, you can follow the procedure below to set cell borders and shading manually.

To set borders and shading manually:

1. Select the cells whose borders or shading you want to set or change.
2. From the Tables and Borders toolbar, choose a line style, weight, and border color (**Figure 6.29**).
3. Click the Border icon on the Tables and Borders toolbar and select the type of border, such as top, bottom, left, right, or outside, you want to apply to the cells (**Figure 6.30**).
4. To apply shading to the selected cells, click the Shading Color icon on the Tables and Borders toolbar (Figure 6.29). Choose a color from the drop-down palette.

   The completed table can contain any combination of borders and shading (**Figure 6.31**).

✔ Tips

- Word provides another way to draw lines that you may find simpler. From the Tables and Borders toolbar, choose a line style, weight, and border color. Then click the Draw Table icon. Each table line that you click or draw with the pencil cursor will take on the specified settings.
- For more complex border and shading needs, use the Borders and Shading dialog box. Select the cells to format, and then choose Format > Borders and Shading.

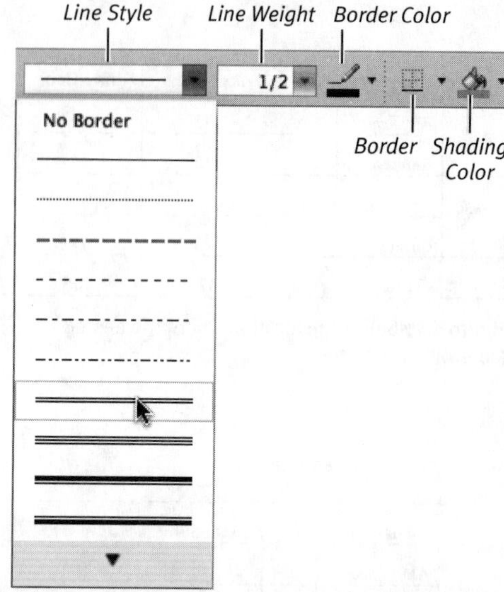

Figure 6.29 Choose a line style, weight, and color from the Tables and Borders toolbar.

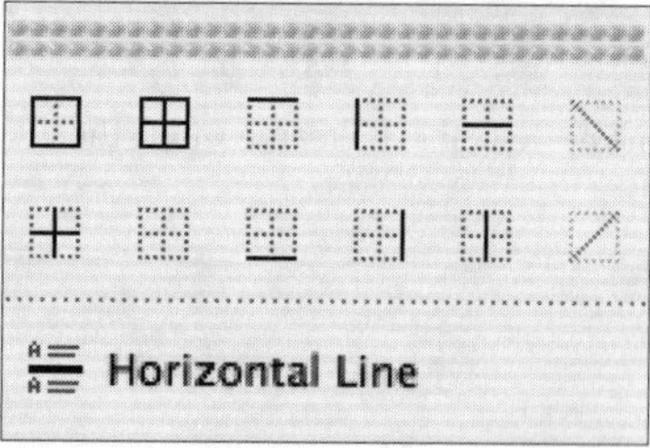

Figure 6.30 From the Borders pop-up palette, choose a border option to apply to the selected cells.

2008 Sales (Millions) by Quarter				
	Qtr 1	Qtr 2	Qtr 3	Qtr 4
North	1.25	3.10	2.96	3.22
East	2.22	1.04	0.87	1.96
South	1.89	0.72	2.21	1.85
West	3.04	4.16	4.24	3.99

Figure 6.31 A table with varied line styles and shade fills often looks more professional.

Converting Text to a Table

You can convert existing text in a Word document into a table.

To convert text to a table:

1. Select the lines of existing text you want to convert into a table (**Figure 6.32**).
2. Choose Table > Convert > Convert Text to Table.

   The Convert Text to Table dialog box appears (**Figure 6.33**).
3. In the Table size section , indicate the number of columns and rows that the table will contain. In the Separate text at section, select the character used to separate data elements.
4. *Optional:* Click AutoFormat to select a format for the table.
5. Click OK to generate the table.

   The selected text is converted into a table (**Figure 6.34**). To adjust the formatting and style, see "Editing the Table Structure" and "Borders and Cell Shading," earlier in this chapter.

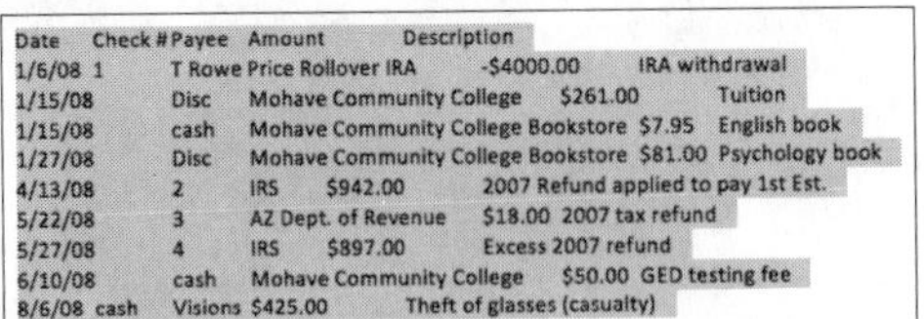

Date Check # Payee Amount Description
1/6/08 1 T Rowe Price Rollover IRA -$4000.00 IRA withdrawal
1/15/08 Disc Mohave Community College $261.00 Tuition
1/15/08 cash Mohave Community College Bookstore $7.95 English book
1/27/08 Disc Mohave Community College Bookstore $81.00 Psychology book
4/13/08 2 IRS $942.00 2007 Refund applied to pay 1st Est.
5/22/08 3 AZ Dept. of Revenue $18.00 2007 tax refund
5/27/08 4 IRS $897.00 Excess 2007 refund
6/10/08 cash Mohave Community College $50.00 GED testing fee
8/6/08 cash Visions $425.00 Theft of glasses (casualty)

Figure 6.32 Select the text you want to convert into a table, and then choose Table > Convert > Convert Text to Table. (In this instance, the text is tab-delimited.)

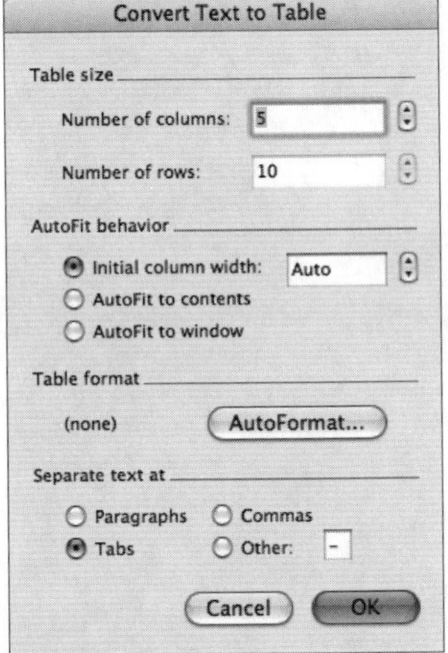

Figure 6.33 If necessary, you can set conversion options in the Convert Text to Table dialog box.

Date	Check #	Payee	Amount	Description
1/6/08	1	T Rowe Price Rollover IRA	-$4000.00	IRA withdrawal
1/15/08	Disc	Mohave Community College	$261.00	Tuition
1/15/08	cash	Mohave Community College Bookstore	$7.95	English book
1/27/08	Disc	Mohave Community College Bookstore	$81.00	Psychology book
4/13/08	2	IRS	$942.00	2007 Refund applied to pay 1st Est.
5/22/08	3	AZ Dept. of Revenue	$18.00	2007 tax refund
5/27/08	4	IRS	$897.00	Excess 2007 refund
6/10/08	cash	Mohave Community College	$50.00	GED testing fee
8/6/08	cash	Visions	$425.00	Theft of glasses (casualty)

Figure 6.34 The selected text is converted into a Word table.

✔ Tips

- To allow Word to convert selected text into an appropriate table *automatically*, click the Insert Table toolbar icon.
- To convert multiple paragraphs into a table, select those paragraphs and choose Table > Convert > Convert Text to Table. Select Paragraphs as the text separator in the Convert Text to Table dialog box.
- If you're converting tab-delimited text into a table, make sure the text doesn't have multiple tab characters between items that should be in adjacent columns—even if removing the extra tabs makes the spacing look wrong.
- You can convert a table back into text by choosing Table > Convert > Convert Table to Text.

7 Outlines, Notebooks, and Publications

Many people—perhaps most—only use Word for traditional word-processing tasks, such as writing letters, memos, and the occasional report. However, Word also has a host of ancillary features and capabilities that you may occasionally find useful. In this chapter, you'll learn to do the following:

- Use Outline View to create outlines
- Use Notebook Layout View to help organize your thoughts
- Design catalogues, menus, newsletters, and other complex publications in the new Publishing Layout View

Outline View

Most of us remember creating outlines in high school or college. Sometimes it was because we were forced to do so as part of an assignment. Other times it was because we found them a useful means of organizing our thoughts for a paper, presentation, or project. If you still find outlines useful or want to explore the ease with which computer-based outlines can be created and organized, you can use Outline View.

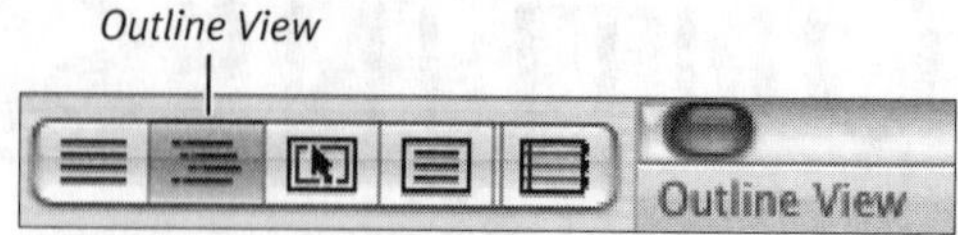

Figure 7.1 You can switch to Outline View by clicking its icon at the bottom of the document window.

Creating an outline

When creating an outline, any document can be switched from Draft or Print Layout View into Outline View. However, it's more common to create a *new* document specifically for this purpose.

To create an outline:

1. In a new document, switch to Outline View by clicking the Outline View icon in the bottom-left corner of the document window (**Figure 7.1**) or by choosing View > Outline.

   The Outlining toolbar (**Figure 7.2**) automatically appears.

2. Type your first item and press Return.

   Word marks it as a Level 1 item, formatted using the Heading 1 style. Each subsequent item (created by pressing Return to generate a new paragraph) will be at the same level as the previous item.

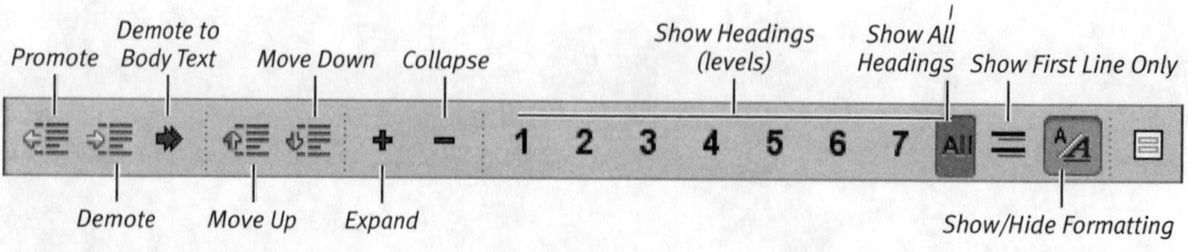

Figure 7.2 The Outlining toolbar.

Chapter 1: Essential Office Techniques
Launching Office Applications
Using the Project Gallery
Creating a New Document

Item to be moved

Figure 7.3 You can promote, demote, or move an item by clicking its outline symbol and then dragging the item to a new position or location.

Other Outliners

While Outline View can certainly serve your basic outlining needs, there are other very capable outliners available for Mac OS X. They have features such as multiple columns (for recording notes, dates, and other items related to each outline point), calculation capabilities, and advanced point-numbering features.

To learn more about two of my favorite Mac OS X outliners, check out:

- *OmniOutliner* (`www.omnigroup.com`)
- *NoteBook* (`www.circusponies.com`)

✔ Tips

- To delete a selected item, press Delete.
- Outline View is designed to make it easy to move material around. You can use it to reorganize normal documents, too.

Working with outlines

In addition to creating new items at the same level as the initial item, you can change an item's level by demoting or promoting it, rearrange and delete items, and change your view of the outline.

To change a selected item's level:

- *Do any of the following:*
  - Click the Promote toolbar icon (see Figure 7.2) or press Control Shift ← to raise an item's level by one.
  - Click the Demote toolbar icon or press Control Shift → to lower an item's level by one.
  - Move the cursor over a point's outline symbol (+ or -). When the cursor becomes a cross (**Figure 7.3**), drag the item to the left or right to promote or demote it to the desired level.
  - Click the Demote to Body Text toolbar icon (see Figure 7.2) to change an item into body text. (This is useful for writing notes and comments related to the item directly above.)

To move an item and its subordinates:

- Select the item and drag it to its new destination within the outline.

To change your view of the outline:

- *Do any of the following:*
  - To show all levels, click the Show All Headings toolbar icon (see Figure 7.2).
  - Click a level number on the toolbar to show only levels that are at that same level or higher.
  - To expand or collapse a selected item by one level, click the Expand or Collapse toolbar item. Each additional click shows or hides one more level.
  - To hide/show an item's subordinate items, double-click its plus (+) symbol.

Notebook Layout View

Introduced in Office 2004, the Notebook Layout View can help organize your thoughts concerning projects, reports, and many other activities. To facilitate note taking, you can insert pictures, freehand drawings, and audio notes. To help arrange your notes, a notebook has section tabs. Each continuously scrolling section can be as long as necessary, encompassing many pages.

To create a new notebook:

◆ *Do one of the following:*

▲ Open the Project Gallery (choose File > Project Gallery, press Shift⌘P, or click the Microsoft Project Gallery icon in the Dock). On the New tab, select the Word Notebook Layout thumbnail in the Blank Documents category, and click Open.

▲ With a new Word document active, click the Notebook Layout View icon at the bottom of the window or choose View > Notebook Layout.

▲ With an existing Word document active, click the Notebook Layout View icon at the bottom of the window or choose View > Notebook Layout. In the dialog box that appears (**Figure 7.4**), click Convert to change the current document into a notebook or click Create New to open a new notebook document.

The Notebook Layout View Standard toolbar appears (**Figure 7.5**, page bottom). Note sections appear in the Formatting Palette (**Figure 7.6**).

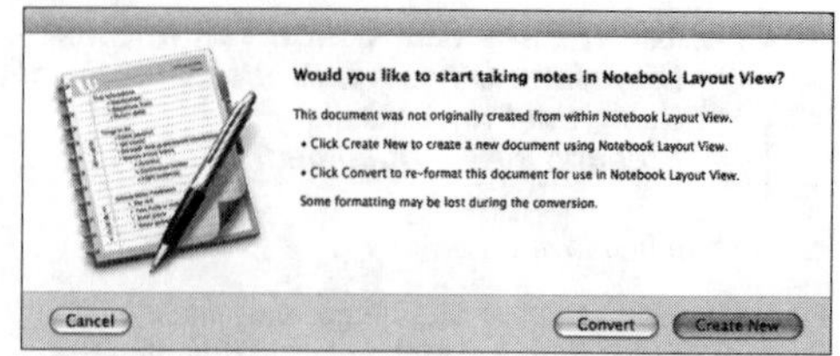

Figure 7.4 You can either convert the current document to a notebook or create a new, blank notebook.

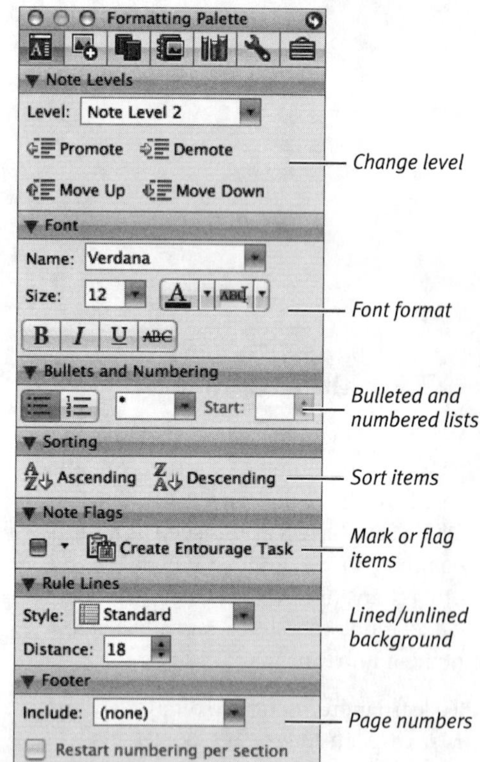

Figure 7.6 Note sections are added to the Formatting Palette.

Figure 7.5 The Standard toolbar is replaced by a toolbar with additional note-related icons and controls.

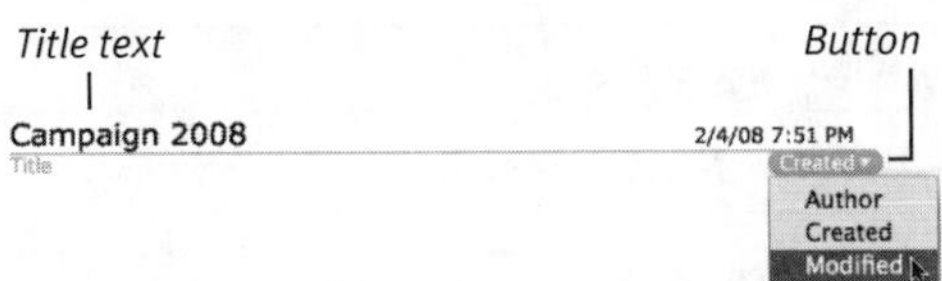

Figure 7.7 Type the notebook's title in the space provided. Choose an additional identifier by clicking the text button on the far right.

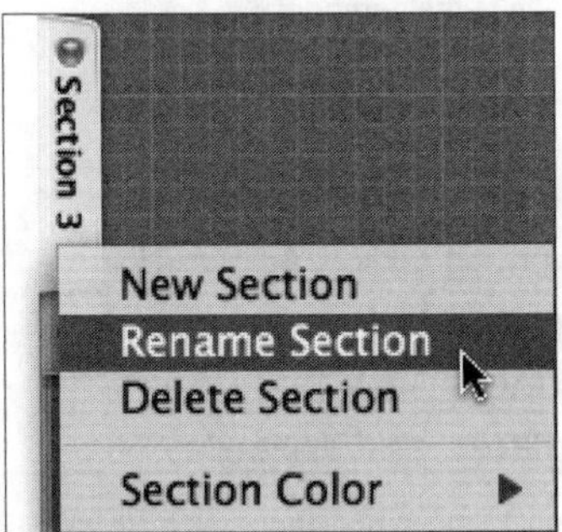

Figure 7.8 You can [Control]-click any section tab and choose commands from this pop-up menu.

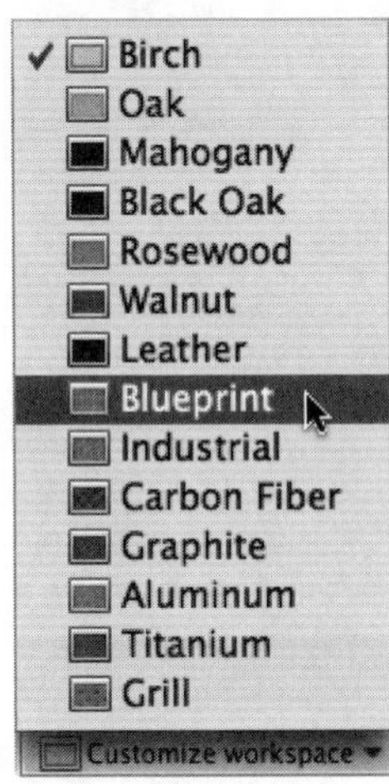

Figure 7.9 You can pick a different background.

Identification and customization

Although you can immediately start entering note text as you would in a Draft/Print Layout View document, you can improve any notebook by adding clear, identifying information and customizing the notebook's "look."

To add a title:

- *Do any of the following:*
  - Type the title on the Title line at the top of the notebook (**Figure 7.7**).
  - You can change the text to the right of the title by clicking the text button (Figure 7.7) and choosing Author, Created, or Modified from the drop-down menu that appears.

To change the section tabs:

- *Do any of the following:*
  - To add a new section to a notebook, click the plus (+) section tab.
  - Rename, delete, or choose a new color for a tab by [Control]-clicking the tab (**Figure 7.8**).
  - Change the order of the section tabs by dragging them up or down.

To change a notebook's appearance:

- *Do any of the following:*
  - On the toolbar, choose a page display option from the Appearance icon's drop-down menu.
  - In the Formatting Palette's Rule Lines section (see Figure 7.6), show/hide the rule lines or change their spacing.
  - Click the Customize Workspace icon (**Figure 7.9**) on the status bar at the bottom of the document window to choose a different background.

Entering notes

Type as you do in a normal document. To start a new note, press Return. Notes can contain multiple lines of text and will automatically wrap as needed.

You can use *click and type* to start a new note anywhere in a section. Just double-click to set the text insertion mark on the line where you want to add the new note.

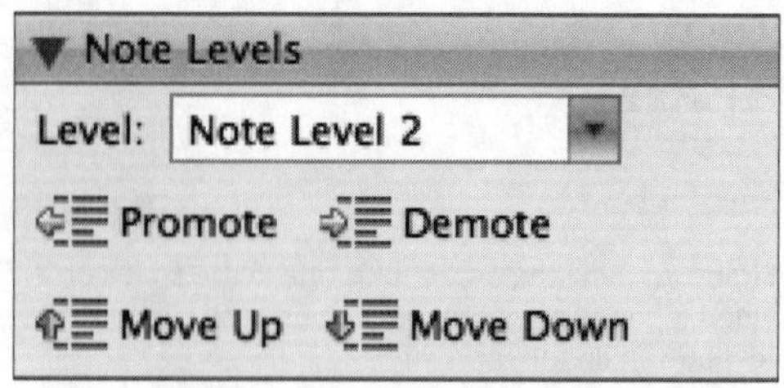

Figure 7.10 In the Note Levels section of the Formatting Palette, you can change the current note's level or move it up or down in the notebook.

Setting levels

Like outline items, notes can be indented to denote subordinate items. To indent (demote) a selected note, press Tab as many times as necessary or click the Demote icon on the Formatting Palette (**Figure 7.10**). To promote a note to a higher level, press Shift Tab or click the Promote icon. You can also demote or promote a selected note by choosing a specific level from the Level drop-down menu.

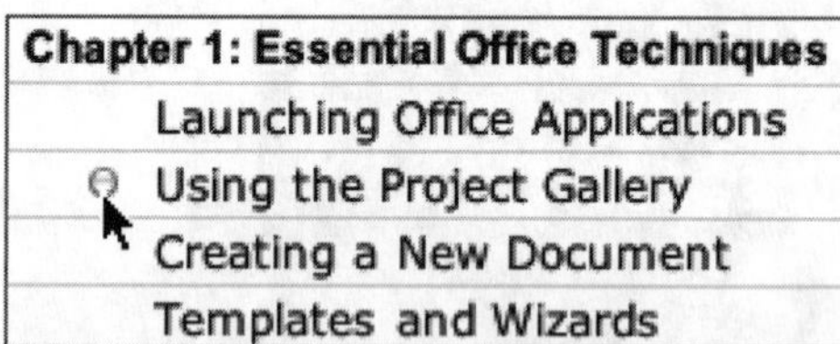

Figure 7.11 When you move the cursor over the left side of a note, a selection symbol appears. You can click the symbol and drag the note to a new location or change its indentation (level).

Reorganizing notes

You can easily rearrange your notes to put them in a new order.

To rearrange notes in a section:

- *Do any of the following:*
  - To move a note and any subordinate notes to a new location, select the note by clicking the symbol to its left. Drag the note(s) to the new position (**Figure 7.11**).
  - Select a note and click the Move Up or Move Down icon on the Formatting Palette (Figure 7.10).

Searching notes for text matches

To find text within a notebook, type a search string in the Quick Search box (see Figure 7.5) and press Return. All matching instances are highlighted. (Matches on other tabs are indicated by highlighted tabs.)

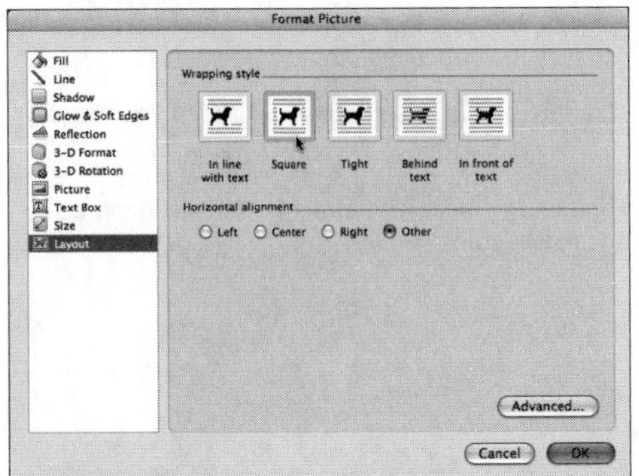

Figure 7.12 To open this dialog box, double-click the image or choose Format > Picture. Select a text wrap style by clicking an icon or the Advanced button.

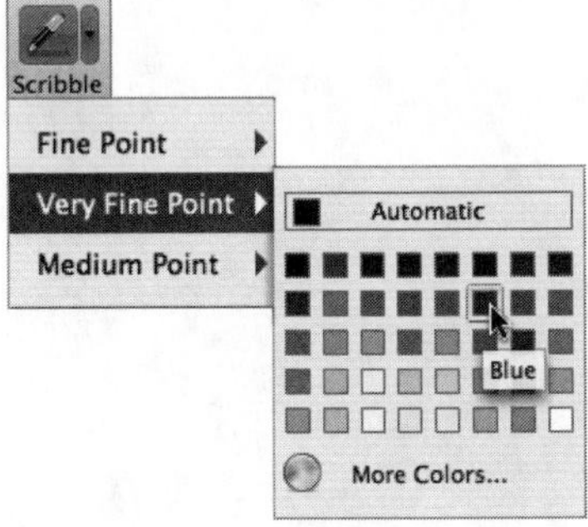

Figure 7.13 You can change the Scribble tool's point size and color.

Adding images, movies, or music

To insert these types of material, choose an item from the Insert > Picture submenu, choose Insert > Movie, or drag a file icon onto the notebook page.

Placed images, movies, and music can be in-line or floating. After selecting the item, you can set a wrapping style on the Layout tab of the Format Picture dialog box (**Figure 7.12**), in the Wrapping section of the Formatting Palette, or by Control-clicking the item.

Making freehand drawings

You can use the Scribble tool to add freehand drawings to a notebook page:

- To draw in the current color and line width, click the Scribble toolbar icon.
- To set a new pen color and/or line width, click the Scribble toolbar icon and choose new settings (**Figure 7.13**).

Recording audio

If you have a microphone, you can record audio notes and add them to the notebook.

To record an audio note:

1. Set the text insertion mark to indicate where you want the recording to appear.
2. Click the Audio toolbar icon. The Audio Notes toolbar appears (**Figure 7.14**).
3. When you're ready, click the Start Recording button and speak into the microphone.

continues on next page

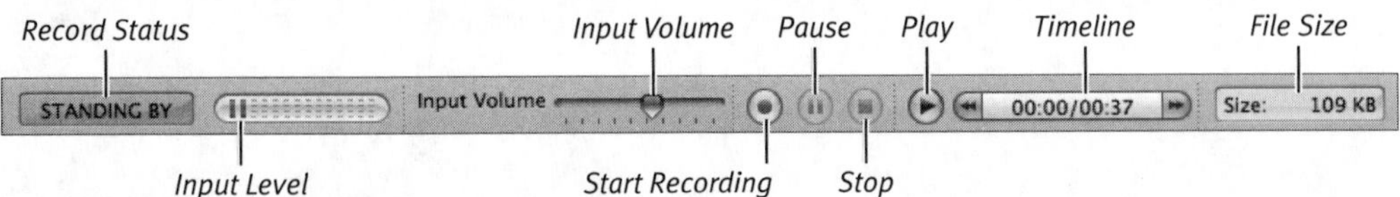

Figure 7.14 Use the Audio Notes toolbar to create and play audio notes.

4. Click Stop to end the recording.

   A speaker icon appears beside the note (**Figure 7.15**).

5. To listen to an audio note, click the speaker icon in the note's margin. Stop or pause playback by clicking a toolbar icon.

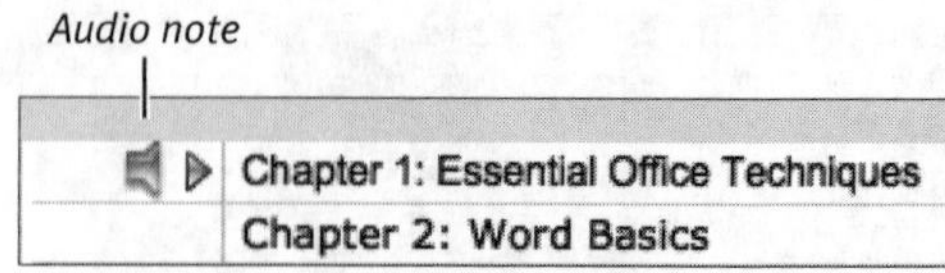

Figure 7.15 A note with attached audio is denoted by a speaker icon.

✔ Tips

- Note text can be formatted by applying fonts, styles, and selective numbering. Select an entire note or specific text and then choose formatting commands from the Format menu, Font menu, or Formatting Palette.
- You can also select a section tab label for editing by double-clicking it.
- To delete an object, click it with the Eraser tool or select it and press Delete.

Publishing Layout View

You can use the new Publishing Layout View for simple desktop publishing tasks, such as creating newsletters, flyers, and brochures. In the past, most people used Print Layout View to create such material. With some effort, it could be accomplished. However, the following Publishing Layout View tools overcome many of the former difficulties of doing layout work in Word:

- **Master pages.** Behind every document page is a master page that can contain static material for the page, such as a corporate logo or page numbers. You can create different masters for odd and even pages, as well as make a separate one that applies only to the first page.
- **Guides.** To make it easier to place text boxes, photos, and other objects, you can add *guides* (lines) to master or content pages. When you print, guides disappear.
- **Text boxes.** Rather than click and type as you do in other Word documents, you decide where you want text to appear on each page by drawing text boxes. You can also create links between text boxes to specify how the text should flow from one text box to the next.

Templates vs. Blank Publications

Although you can start by creating publications from scratch, you'll find it simpler and less confusing to begin by using and experimenting with some of the provided templates. Substitute your own photos or clip art images for the ones in the template, replace the placeholder text with your own copy, and experiment with the layout features, such as adding guides, inserting and removing pages, and creating and linking text boxes.

When you feel you have a handle on the basics, you'll be better prepared to create your own publications from scratch.

Starting a publication

There are a number of ways to start a new publication. Use whichever method is convenient for you.

To create a new blank publication:

- *Do one of the following:*
  - ▲ Open the Project Gallery (choose File > Project Gallery, press Shift⌘P, or click the Microsoft Project Gallery icon in the Dock). On the New tab (**Figure 7.16**), select the Blank Documents category, select the Word Publishing Layout thumbnail, and click Open.
  - ▲ If a publication is currently open or was the most recent document on which you worked, choose File > New Blank Publishing Layout Document (⌘N).
  - ▲ Create a new blank or notebook document. Click the Publishing Layout View icon in the lower-left corner of the document window (**Figure 7.17**) or choose View > Publishing Layout. Click OK in response to the Publishing Layout dialog box.

To create a publication from a template:

- *Do either of the following:*
  - ▲ Open the Project Gallery (see the previous step list). On the New tab, select a template from a publication category, such as Brochures, CD Labels, or Newsletters. Click Open.
  - ▲ Create a blank publication by following the previous step list. Click the Publication Templates tab in the Elements Gallery, click a category button, and click the desired template's thumbnail (**Figure 7.18**).

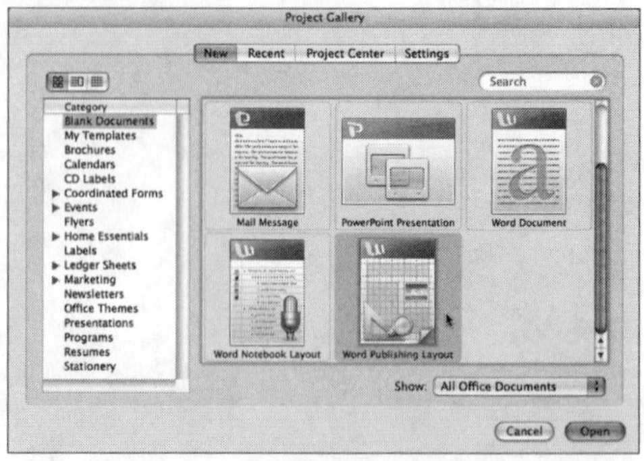

Figure 7.16 The most straightforward way to create a blank publication is to select its thumbnail in the Project Gallery.

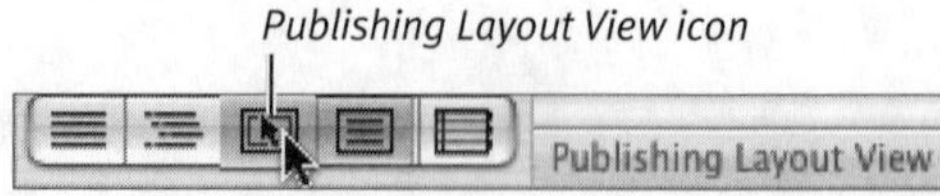

Figure 7.17 If the current document is new, you can change it into a publication by clicking the Publishing Layout View icon at the bottom of the window.

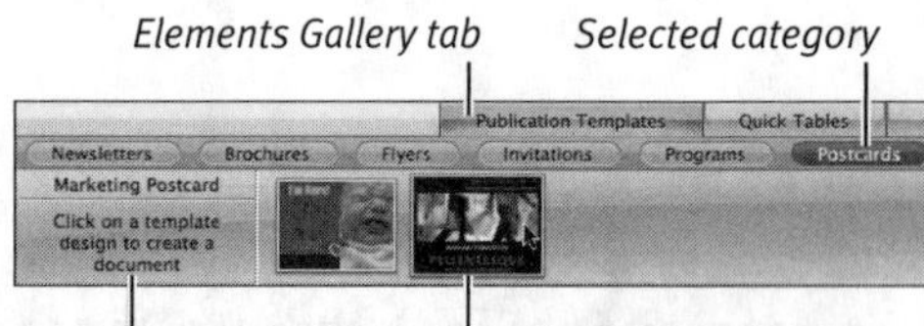

Figure 7.18 You can select a publication template from the Elements Gallery.

✔ Tip

- You can also create a publication from a different type of open Word document. Click the Publishing Layout View icon (Figure 7.17) or choose View > Publishing Layout. In the Publishing Layout dialog box, click Create New to create a blank publication or click Continue to convert the document into a publication.

All Contents Master Pages

Figure 7.19 Click a tab to switch between viewing content and master pages.

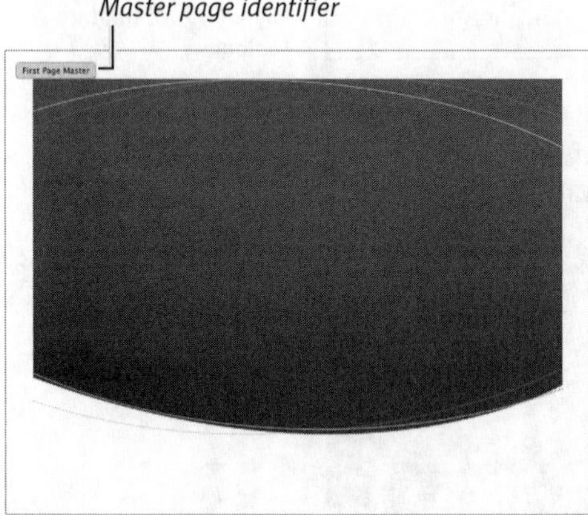

Figure 7.20 This master page for one of the brochure templates contains only this graphic background.

Master and content pages

Every publication page has two layers. In the top layer are the *content pages*. That's where you'll place most of the document's text and photos. Beneath the content layer of every page is a *master page*. Static items, such as running heads, side tabs, page numbers, boilerplate text, and logos, are generally placed on master pages. Unless covered by solid material in the content layer, items on a master page show through.

When you create a blank publication, the initial master page is also blank, allowing you to create it and others from scratch (or ignore them, if they aren't needed). When you select a publication template, on the other hand, master pages already contain material. However, you can replace their contents, change the formatting, or whatever you like.

A publication can have one master page or different masters for even and odd pages (as is the case with many two-sided documents, such as magazines and books). The first page can also have its own master.

To view or edit a master page:

1. *Optional:* To view a particular master page, scroll to its content page.
2. Click the Master Pages tab in the corner of the document window (**Figure 7.19**).

   The master page associated with the current page is displayed (**Figure 7.20**). Each master page is labeled in its upper-left corner. To view other master pages, scroll using the vertical scroll bar.
3. You can add graphics to any master page as you do in other Word documents. To add text, you must create *text boxes* (explained later in this section).
4. When you're done viewing and editing masters, click the All Contents tab.

To insert a new content page:

1. In the All Contents layer, display or select material on the page immediately above where you want the new content page.

   For example, to create a new page 3, display content page 2.

2. Choose Insert > New Page, or click the Insert toolbar icon and choose New Page (**Figure 7.21**).

   The new content page appears.

To insert a new master page:

1. In the All Contents layer, display or select material on the page immediately above where you want a new master page. Note that when inserting a new master page, a new content page is also created.

2. Choose Insert > New Master, or click the Insert toolbar icon and choose New Master (Figure 7.21).

   A new content page is inserted immediately after the current page, along with a new master to be used with this page.

To delete a content page:

1. In the All Contents layer, display or select material on the page you want to delete.

2. Click the Remove toolbar icon (Figure 7.21).

   The page is deleted from the publication.

✔ Tips

- Although you can insert a page in the middle of a publication, it's more common to expand a publication by adding pages to its end.
- If you need to reorganize the pages, choose View > Navigation Pane. Select the thumbnail of the page you want to move and drag it up or down in the page list (**Figure 7.22**).
- When working on master pages, you can specify the types of master pages needed by clicking check boxes in the Formatting Palette (**Figure 7.23**).

Figure 7.21 You can insert or delete pages by clicking icons on the Publishing Layout View Standard toolbar.

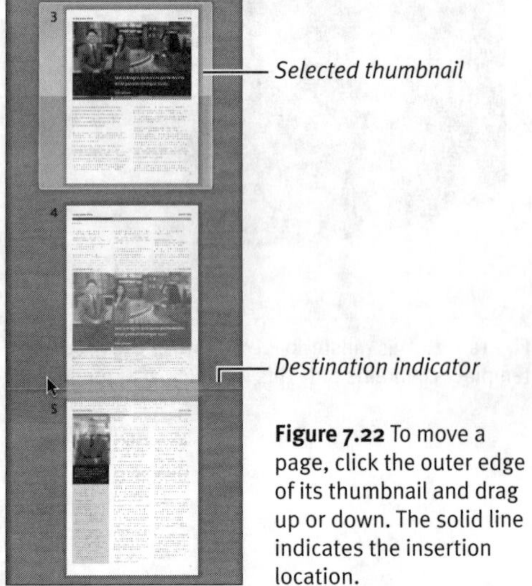

Figure 7.22 To move a page, click the outer edge of its thumbnail and drag up or down. The solid line indicates the insertion location.

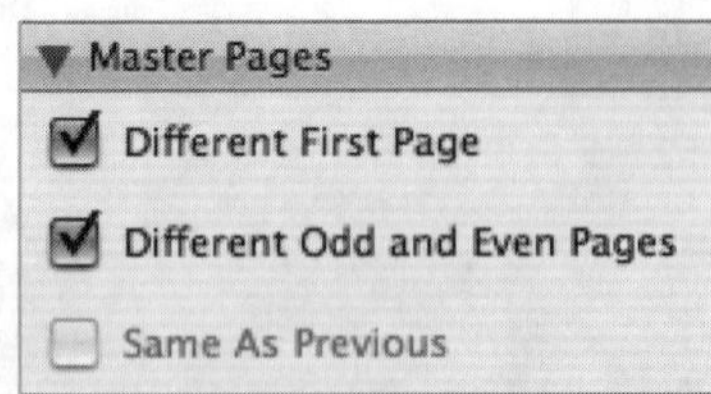

Figure 7.23 Select master page types by clicking their check boxes in the Master Pages section of the Formatting Palette.

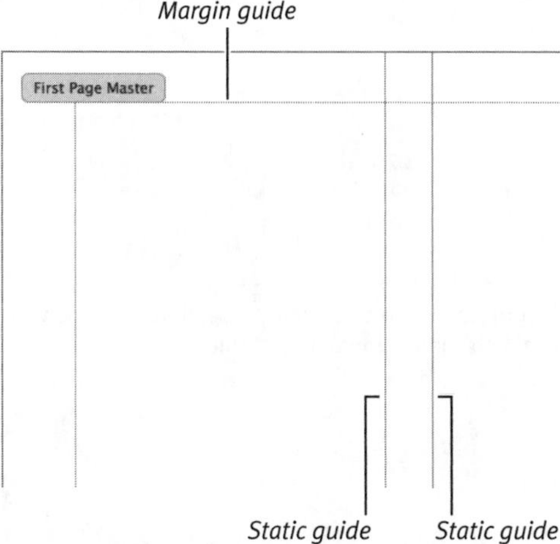

Figure 7.24 The ever-present margin guides show the page margins. Static guides enable you to easily and accurately position objects and text.

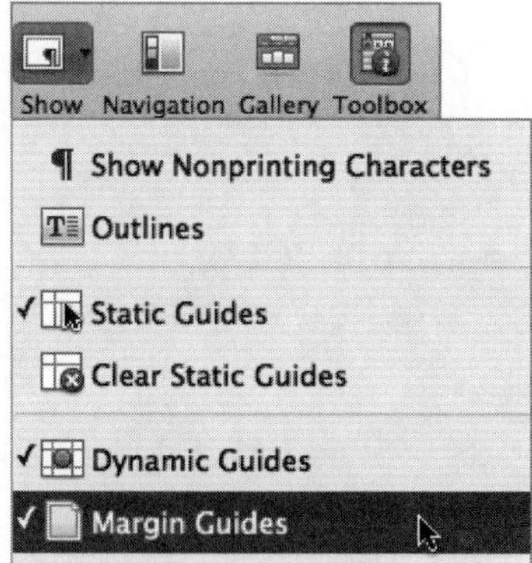

Figure 7.25 Items on the Show drop-down menu work as toggles. Each can be enabled or disabled.

Working with guides

Guides are nonprinting lines that simplify the process of aligning objects and creating precisely sized and placed text boxes in a publication. There are three types of guides: margin, static, and dynamic.

Margin guides show the page margins (top, bottom, left, and right) as a blue bounding rectangle. If you change the margins in the Document Margins section of the Formatting Palette or by choosing Format > Document, the margin guides adjust automatically.

Static guides are manually positioned vertical or horizontal lines that can be added in any quantity to content or master pages (**Figure 7.24**). Their purpose is to help you align placed objects and text boxes. Such items automatically *snap* to the guides. If you place static guides on a master page, they are repeated on all master pages of the same type (for example, Even Page Masters). Static guides placed on a master page are pink; ones placed on a content page are blue.

Dynamic guides appear as you drag an object. They make it easy to precisely place an object by appearing automatically whenever a side or center of the object aligns with something else on the page, such as the page's horizontal or vertical center or the edge or center of another object. Unless you find them intrusive, you should leave dynamic guides enabled.

To enable or disable a guide type:

- Click the Show toolbar icon and choose a guide type from the drop-down menu (**Figure 7.25**).

  Enabled guides are checked; disabled guides are unchecked.

To place static guides:

1. Switch to the layer in which you want to add guides by clicking the All Contents or Master Pages tab (see Figure 7.19).

   Static guides placed in the content layer are specific to the page on which they're placed. Those placed on a master page appear on all master pages of that type, such as Even Master.

2. To add a static guide to the page, move the cursor over the horizontal or vertical ruler. When the cursor changes shape, drag down or across to place the guide.

   As you drag, a ScreenTip shows the guide's position (**Figure 7.26**).

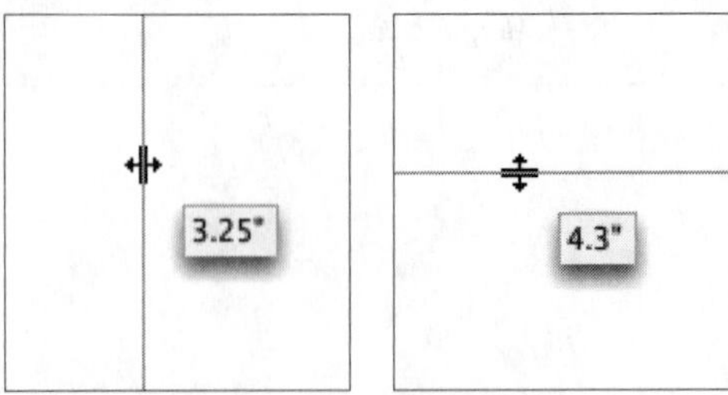

Figure 7.26 To place a static guide, drag from the vertical (left) or horizontal (right) ruler.

✔ Tips

- To reposition a static guide, switch to the layer (content or master) in which the guide exists and move the cursor over the guide. When the cursor changes shape (Figure 7.26), you can drag the guide to a new position on the page.
- To remove a static guide, drag it off the page. Because pages automatically scroll, it's often easier to drag guides off either side of the page than it is to drag them off the top or bottom.
- You can also remove static guides by displaying the appropriate content or master page and then choosing Clear Static Guides from the Show toolbar icon's menu (see Figure 7.25).
- To temporarily hide *all* static guides (regardless of whether they're on a content or master page), choose the Static Guides command from the Show toolbar icon's drop down menu (see Figure 7.25).

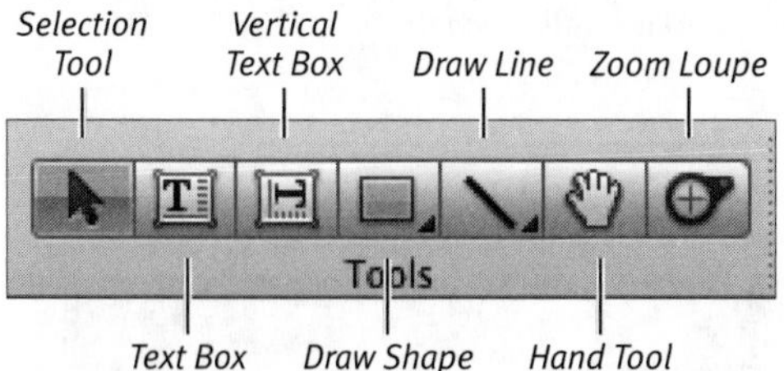

Figure 7.27 To draw a text box, select the Text Box or Vertical Text box tool on the toolbar.

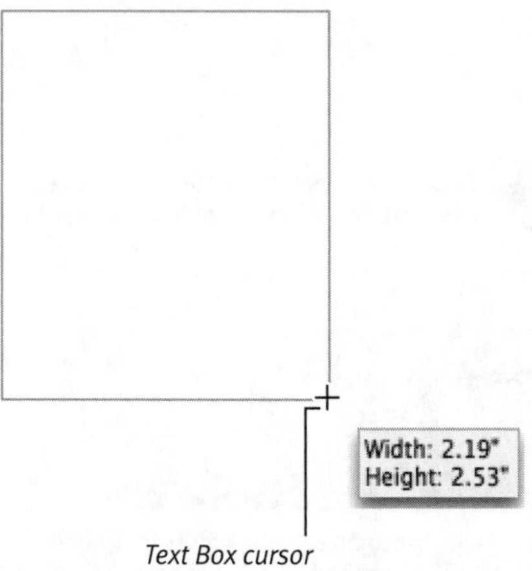

Figure 7.28 As you drag to create the text box, a ScreenTip displays its dimensions.

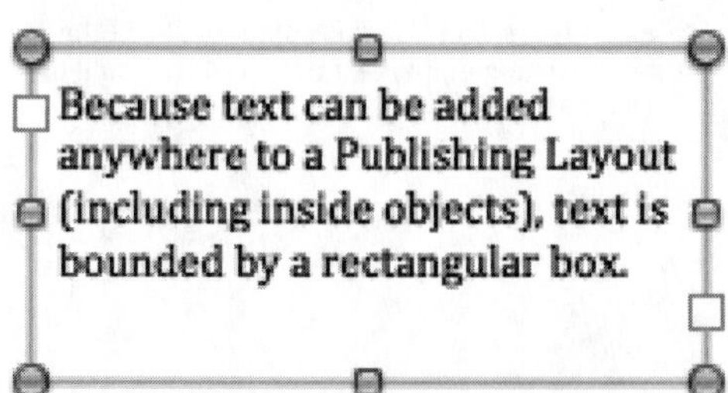

Figure 7.29 A selected text box is surrounded by handles.

Creating text boxes

Because text can be added anywhere to a Publishing Layout (including inside objects), text is bounded by a rectangular box. Either the *text boxes* already exist (templates often include text placeholders) or you can create, size, and position them as required.

To create a text box:

1. *Do one of the following:*
   - ▲ To create a normal text box, select the Text Box tool (⌘2) from the toolbar (**Figure 7.27**).
   - ▲ To draw a box that displays text vertically, select the Vertical Text Box tool (⌘3).
2. Display the content or master page on which you want to create the text box.
3. Click and drag to create the rectangular text box (**Figure 7.28**). Release the mouse button to complete the box.

   The text insertion mark appears in the upper-left corner of the text box.
4. Type or paste your text into the box as you would in a word-processing document.

   Text automatically wraps as needed to fit within the bounds of the box.

✔ Tips

- Like word processing text, you can format selected text within the box by choosing commands from the Format menu, Font menu, or Formatting Palette.
- To apply a single format to *all* text within the box, select the box with the Selection Tool (**Figure 7.29**) and apply formatting.
- To change a box's size, drag any handle. To resize it proportionately, Shift-drag a corner handle. To move a box, select the Selection Tool (Figure 7.27) and drag the box's center.

Linking text boxes

Although you are never required to do so, you can instruct text to *flow* from one box to another. For example, in an article that's spread over a page, across multiple columns, or extending over many pages, you can make the text flow from one box to the next to the next—creating as many *linked text boxes* as you need. If you then edit, delete, or add to the text, the flow is adjusted automatically—just as word wrap occurs automatically in a normal Word document. Linked text boxes constitute a *story*.

At most, a text box can have two links: one forward and one backwards. To this end, every text box has both a forward and a backwards link handle (**Figure 7.30**). The text box from which you are creating the link can be empty or it can contain text. The text box to which you're linking, on the other hand, must be empty.

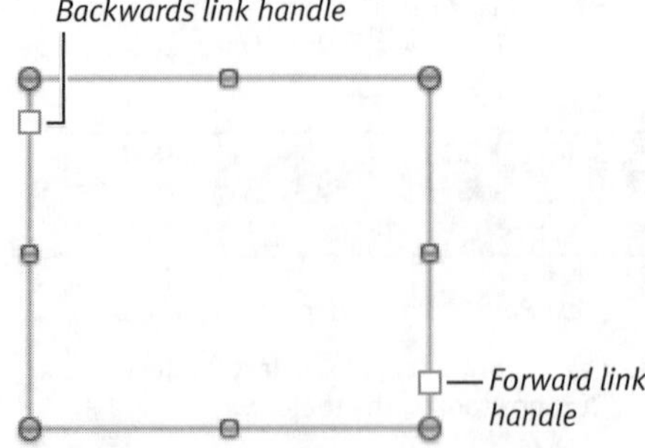

Figure 7.30 To create a link, you can start by clicking a link handle.

Figure 7.31 Use this cursor to draw the new text box to which you'll link.

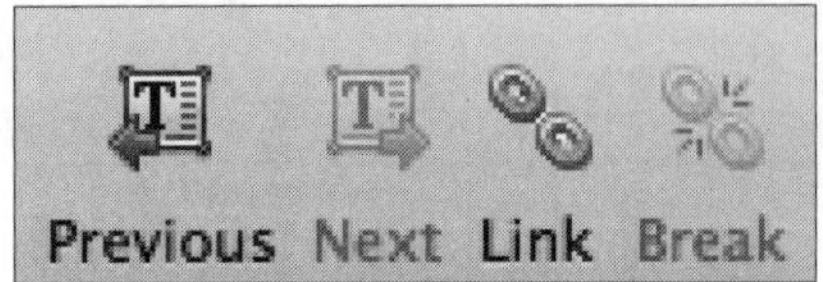

Figure 7.32 To link to an existing empty text box, start by clicking the Link toolbar icon.

Figure 7.33 Use this cursor to select the existing empty text box to which you'll link.

To link text boxes:

1. Click to select the text box from which you want to link (Figure 7.30).
2. *Do one of the following:*
   - **Link to a new text box.** Click the initial box's forward or backwards link handle. Draw the new text box with the special cursor that appears (**Figure 7.31**).
   - **Link to an existing text box.** Click the Link toolbar icon (**Figure 7.32**). Move the special cursor (**Figure 7.33**) over the empty text box to which you want to link and click the box.

   A number appears in the upper-left corner of each linked box to indicate its linking order in the story. Whenever the cursor is passed over a linked text box, the number appears.
3. To create additional links, repeat Step 2.

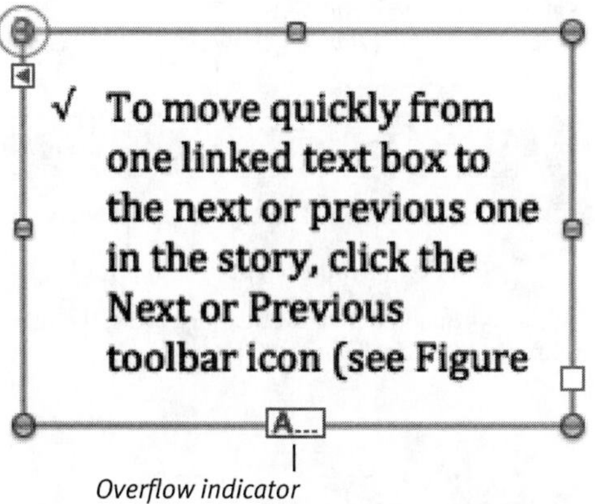

√ To move quickly from one linked text box to the next or previous one in the story, click the Next or Previous toolbar icon (see Figure
A...
Overflow indicator

Figure 7.34 If you see this indicator beneath the final text box in a story, it means there is additional text for you to place.

✔ Tips

- If you change your mind about creating a link, press Esc. If you've just created an unwanted link, choose Edit > Undo Insert Text Box or Edit > Undo Text Box Linking.
- If a story contains more text than can fit in the final text box, a special symbol appears beneath the box (**Figure 7.34**). To view the additional text, increase the size of one or more of the story's text boxes or create additional linked boxes to hold the overflow text.
- The purpose of links is to ensure that text flows between the text boxes. If you discover that text in the initial box breaks badly (ending in the middle of a paragraph or showing only the first line of a paragraph), you can often correct the problem by adjusting the box's height—making it shorter or taller to ensure that the break comes at the desired spot.
- To move quickly from one linked text box in a story to the next or previous one, click the Next or Previous toolbar icon (see Figure 7.32).
- If a story is long, you may prefer to create it in a normal Word document. Then use copy-and-paste or drag and drop to insert it into the Publishing Layout text boxes.
- If it becomes necessary, you can *break* links, creating two sets of links where there is currently one. (Breaking a link is a useful first step when you need to insert a text box in the middle of an existing story.) Select the text box that will be the last link in the story and click the Break icon (see Figure 7.32). All boxes following the selected one will now be empty.
- To remove a linked text box, select it and press Delete. Doing so deletes only the box—*not* the story text the box contains.

Additional Publishing Layout tips

Here are some other Publishing Layout techniques and tips that you may find helpful.

Grouping objects. To prevent two or more objects from moving in relation to one another, you can *group* them to cause Word to treat them as a single object. Select the objects, click the Group toolbar icon, and choose Group from the drop-down menu. Moving one will now cause all to move. If you later need to work individually with the grouped objects, choose Ungroup from the same drop-down menu.

Nudging objects. You can *nudge* a selected text box or object by pressing arrow keys.

Working in layers. If two or more objects overlap, you can specify their layering by selecting an object and choosing a command from the Arrange toolbar icon's menu.

More toolbar tools. The toolbar (**Figure 7.35**) contains other useful tools:

- To switch from another tool, such as the Hand Tool or Zoom Loupe, click the Selection Tool.
- You can create common shapes and line types by choosing items from the Draw Shape or Draw Line drop-down menus and then dragging to draw the shape or line.
- Use the Hand Tool to move around a page by clicking and dragging. It's more precise than using the scroll bars.
- Use the Zoom Loupe to change the magnification. Drag to the right or down to increase the magnification; drag left or up to decrease the magnification.
- You can also set the magnification by choosing an option from the Zoom control (**Figure 7.36**) on the toolbar.

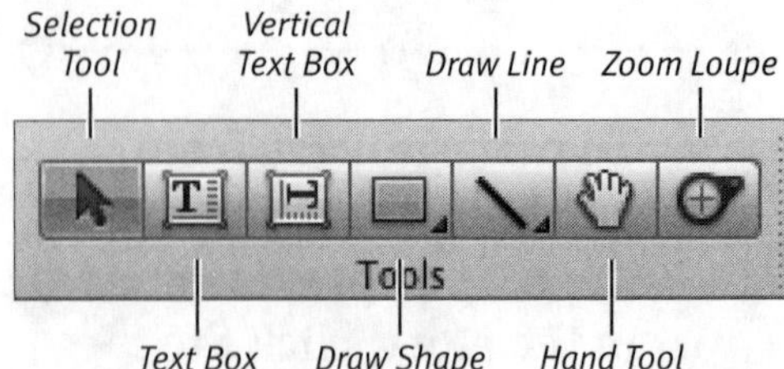

Figure 7.35 In addition to the Text Box tools, the other tools can occasionally be useful.

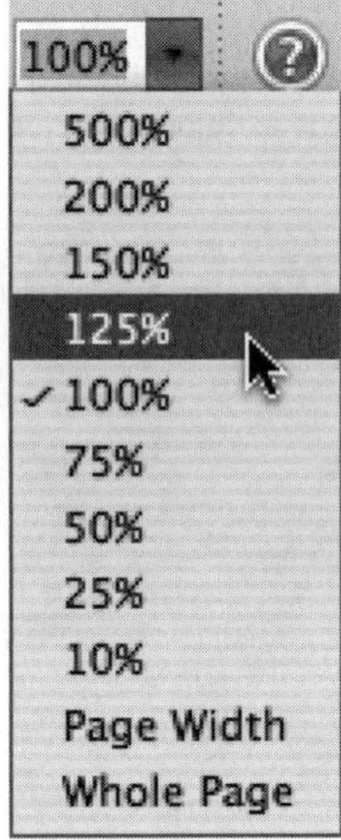

Figure 7.36 You can choose a magnification level from the Zoom control's drop-down menu or type a magnification percentage into its box.

8

OTHER WORD FEATURES

Many people—perhaps most—only use Word for traditional word-processing tasks, such as writing letters, memos, and an occasional report. However, Word also has a host of ancillary features and capabilities that you may occasionally find useful. In this chapter, you'll learn to do the following:

- Use the Contact toolbar to add contact information from your Office Address Book to Word documents
- Select a report cover page from the Elements Gallery
- Create labels and print envelopes
- Use the Mail Merge Manager to create merge documents, such as personalized form letters
- Summarize documents and record important data as document properties

Using the Contact Toolbar

Using the Contact toolbar, you can quickly add name, address, and other contact information from your Office Address Book to letters, labels, and envelopes. (The Office Address Book is normally maintained in Entourage but is also accessible from Word.)

To use the Contact toolbar:

1. Choose View > Toolbars > Contact.

   The Contact toolbar appears above the document window (**Figure 8.1**, page bottom).

2. To insert a contact into your document, position the text insertion mark where you'd like to insert the contact data.

3. Select a contact name from the Contacts drop-down list.

   The contact's name appears in the document at the text insertion mark.

4. If you've recorded a street address, phone number, or email address for the contact, you can also insert that information into the document by clicking the Include Address, Include Phone, or Include E-mail toolbar icon and selecting the data from the drop-down list (**Figure 8.2**).

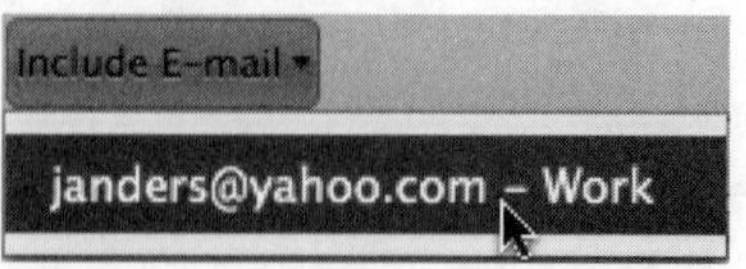

Figure 8.2 You can insert additional information for the currently selected contact.

Figure 8.1 You can use the Contact toolbar to insert contact names and other information from the Office Address Book into your documents.

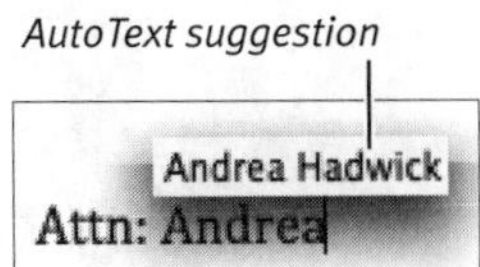

Figure 8.3 If you begin typing the name of a person in your Address Book, Word will offer to insert the name.

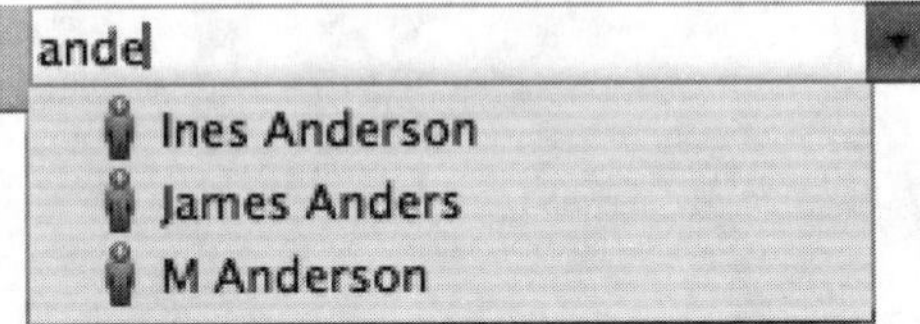

Figure 8.4 To quickly find a contact record, type part of the person's name in the Contacts box.

Figure 8.5 You can create new Address Book records from within Word.

✔ Tips

- You can also enter a contact's name using Word's AutoText feature (see Chapter 2). Start typing the person's name in your document. If the name is in your Address Book, Word will suggest it (**Figure 8.3**). Press Enter or Return to accept the name, or continue typing if it's not the right one.
- If you have many entries in your Address Book, the Contacts drop-down list won't show them all. To see other entries, type part of the person's name in the Contacts box. The contact list will show all possible matches for what you've typed, enabling you to choose the contact (**Figure 8.4**).
- If you scroll the Contacts drop-down list to its end, the last entry reads Open Address Book. Select this entry, select a contact name from the Office Address Book dialog box that appears, and click Insert.
- To create a new contact record, click the Add icon on the Contact toolbar. Enter the information in the dialog box that appears (**Figure 8.5**) and then click Add. For more information on creating Address Book contacts, see Chapter 22.
- To insert a complete address from the Office Address Book at the text insertion mark, choose Tools > Address Book. Select the contact name from the Office Address Book dialog box; choose Default Address, Work Address, or Home Address from the Use drop-down menu; and click Insert.

Adding a Cover Page

To dress up a report or any other important Word document, you can select a cover page from the Elements Gallery. An inserted cover page automatically becomes the document's first page. Each contains placeholders for important text, such as the document title, date, and so on.

To insert a cover page:

1. Switch to Print Layout View. Click the Document Elements tab of the Elements Gallery.
2. If it isn't automatically selected, click the Cover Pages button.

   The first set of thumbnails is displayed (**Figure 8.6**, page bottom).
3. Click the scroll arrows until you see the cover page you want. Click its thumbnail to add the cover page to the document.

   The selected cover page becomes the document's first page.
4. Edit the cover page's text placeholders (**Figure 8.7**).
5. *Optional:* To select a page-numbering format for the document, click the icon at the top of the cover page and choose Format Page Numbers (**Figure 8.8**).

✔ Tip

- To jump to the Cover Pages section, choose Insert > Document Elements > Cover Page.

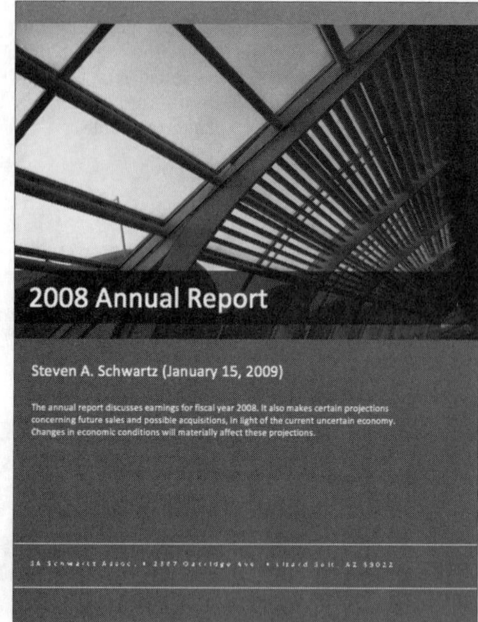

Figure 8.7 A cover page is a useful addition to many reports.

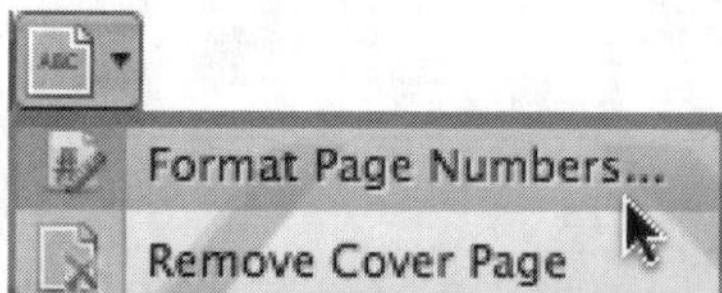

Figure 8.8 By clicking this pop-up icon in the upper-left corner of the cover page, you can select a page-numbering format or remove the cover page.

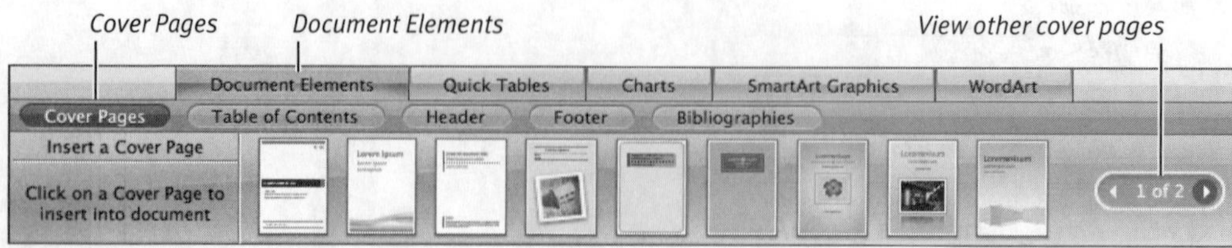

Figure 8.6 To insert a cover page, click its thumbnail.

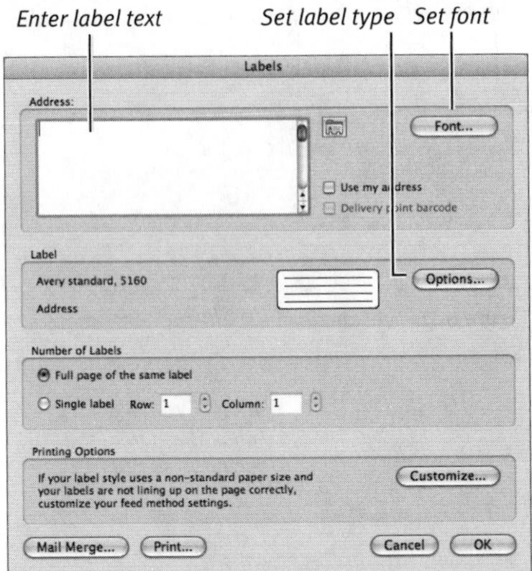

Figure 8.9 Design your label in the Labels wizard.

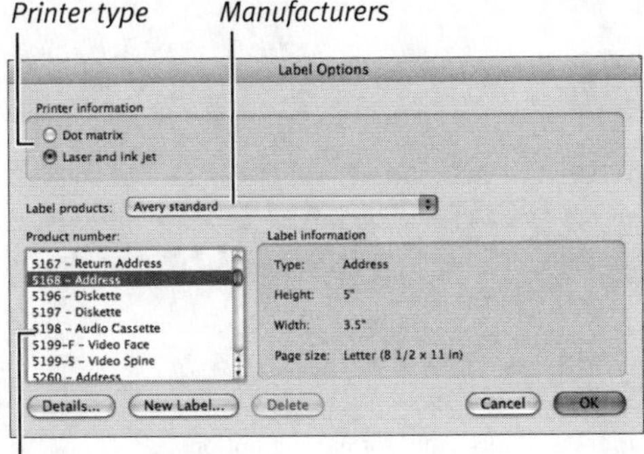

Figure 8.10 Select the label manufacturer, part number, and the type of printer you'll use.

✔ Tips

- This procedure is for printing a *single* label once or many times. For labels with *different* text, such as address labels, see "The Mail Merge Manager" in this chapter.
- If you have 2-up CD or DVD stick-on labels or CD/DVD insert stock, you may be able to use the templates in the CD Labels category of the Project Gallery.

Creating Labels

Word provides templates that you can use to create many kinds of labels, such as mailing labels and name badges. Using the Labels wizard, you can generate a single label or an entire sheet of the same label that will print on popular label manufacturers' stock.

To create labels:

1. *Do either of the following:*
   - ▲ Click the Project Gallery icon in the Dock or choose File > Project Gallery (Shift ⌘ P). On the New tab, select Labels from the Category list, select the Mailing Label Wizard, and click the Open button.
   - ▲ Create a new document by choosing File > New Blank Document (⌘ N), and then choose Tools > Labels.

   The Labels wizard appears (**Figure 8.9**).
2. Click the Options button to open the Label Options window (**Figure 8.10**). Specify the type of printer you'll use, the label manufacturer, and the label's part number. Click OK.
3. Enter the address or other appropriate text in the Address box of the Labels wizard.

   To insert your own address (from your contact record in the Entourage Address Book), click the Use my address check box.
4. Click a radio button to select a printing option: Full page of the same label or Single label. In the latter case, you must also specify the label row and column on which to print.
5. *Optional:* You can alter the font, size, and style of selected text by clicking Font. To set special print options, click Customize.
6. Click OK to create a label document or Print to route the labels to the printer.

Printing Envelopes

Word provides two ways for you to print a business envelope:

- You can use an envelope template. Many of the templates include colorful graphics.
- The Envelope wizard can extract the mailing address from a letter and format it so you can print an envelope. You can also use the Envelope wizard to create and print *any* envelope; it doesn't matter whether the address is extracted from an open document, chosen from the Office Address Book, or entered by hand.

To create an envelope from a template:

1. Open the Project Gallery by clicking its Dock icon or by choosing File > Project Gallery (Shift⌘P).
2. Select the Stationery category from the list on the left side of the dialog box.
3. Select an envelope thumbnail (such as Revolution Envelope) and click Open.

   The envelope template opens in a new document (**Figure 8.11**).
4. Replace the placeholder text with the recipient's name and address. If necessary, you can edit (or enter) the return address.

To create an envelope using the Envelope wizard:

1. *Do one of the following:*
   - Choose Tools > Envelopes.
   - In the Project Gallery, select the Stationery category, select the Envelope Wizard, and click Open.

   The Envelope wizard appears (**Figure 8.12**).

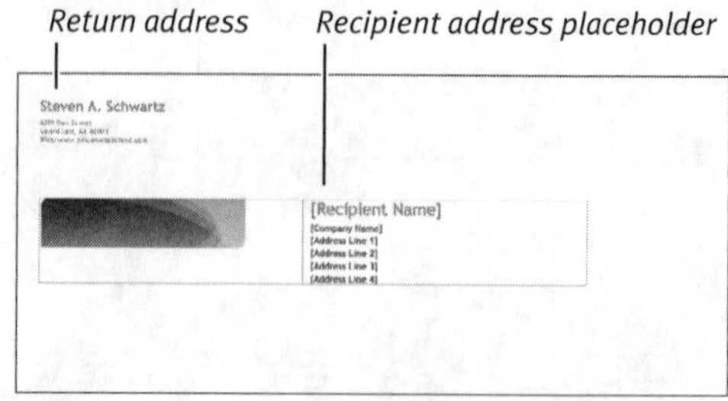

Figure 8.11 An example of a Word envelope template.

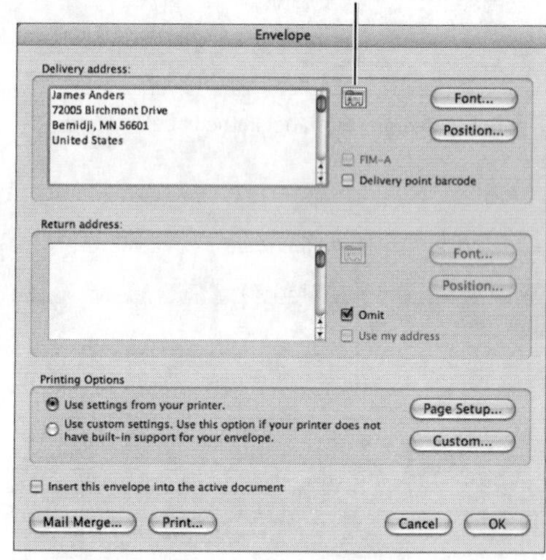

Figure 8.12 Specify the delivery address, the return address (if any), and formatting options.

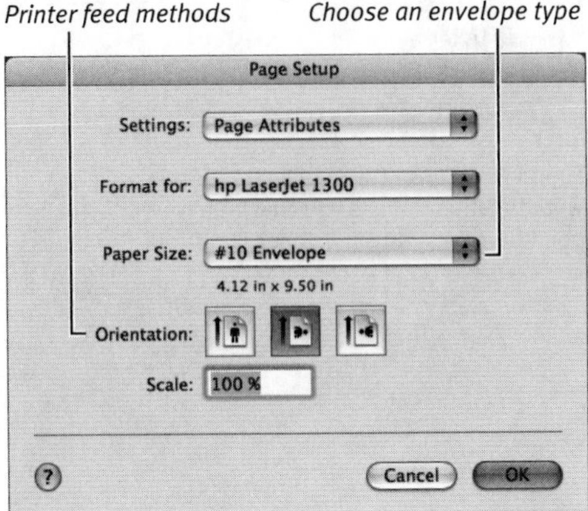

Figure 8.13 Use the Page Setup dialog box to set print options.

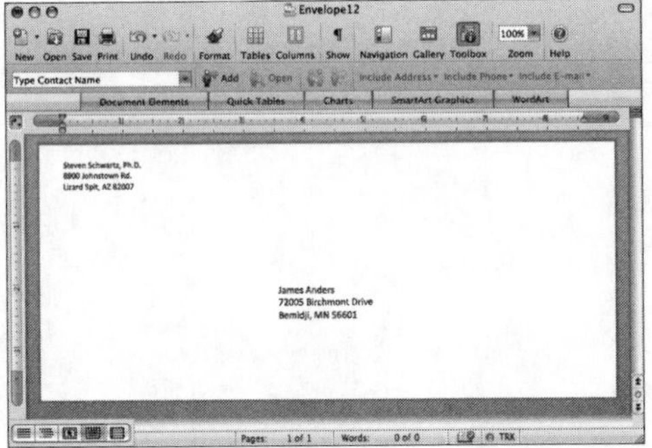

Figure 8.14 Rather than route the envelope directly to your printer, you can generate it as a new Word document.

2. Type or paste the recipient's address in the Delivery address box, or select the address from the Office Address Book by clicking the icon beside the box.
3. To specify a return address in the Return address box, *do one of the following:*
   - ▲ Click the Use my address check box to use your address from the Office Address Book as the return address.
   - ▲ Type or paste a return address into the Return address box.
   - ▲ Click the Address Book icon to select a return address from the Office Address Book.
   - ▲ Click the Omit check box if you're using preprinted envelopes that already contain a return address.
4. *Optional:* Click the Font and Position buttons to make any necessary changes to the format and position of the delivery and return addresses.
5. In the Printing Options section of the wizard, click a radio button to indicate that the envelope will be printed using standard settings for your printer or, in the case of an unsupported envelope size, that custom settings are necessary.
6. Click the Page Setup button to specify the printer to use, envelope size, and feed method (**Figure 8.13**). Click OK.
7. *Do either of the following:*
   - ▲ If you're satisfied with the formatting and are ready to print the envelope, click Print.
   - ▲ If you want to make further changes to the envelope (reducing the line spacing in the addresses or adding a logo, for example), click OK. The envelope is displayed as a new, editable Word document (**Figure 8.14**). Make the desired changes and then print.

✔ Tips

- If the document already contains an obvious address, the Envelope wizard may automatically insert the address into the Delivery address box.
- The Delivery point barcode option in the Envelope wizard (**Figure 8.15**) prints a machine-readable version of the Zip Code on the envelope. This help the USPS process the letter.
- If you're creating reply envelopes, you can print an FIM code by clicking the FIM-A check box in the Envelope wizard. FIMs are necessary *only* for business reply mail. Check with the USPS for more information.
- You can apply fonts selectively. To use a different font or style for just the recipient's name, for example, select the name before clicking the Font button.
- Addresses chosen from the Office Address Book routinely include the country name. For mail within your own country, you'll probably want to delete this line from the return and delivery addresses. Click OK (rather than Print) to create an editable Word document. Make the deletions, and then print the envelope.

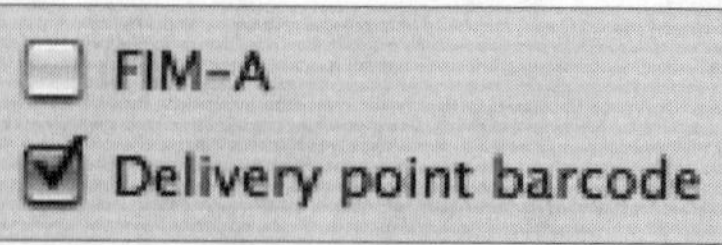

Figure 8.15 These Delivery address options work together. Unless you check Delivery point barcode, you can't check FIM-A.

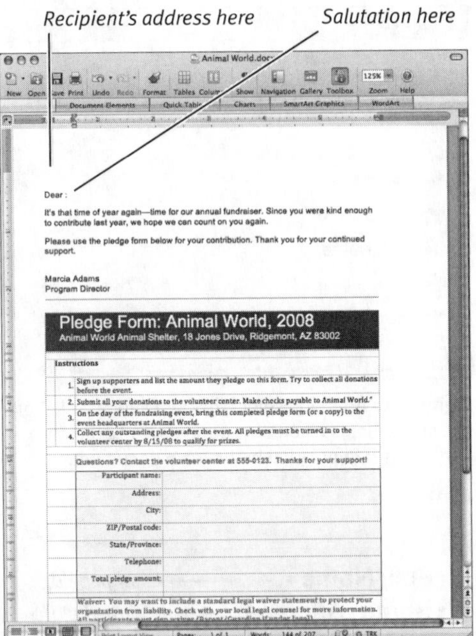

Figure 8.16 This form letter will serve as the main document. Space has been left for the recipient's address and the salutation.

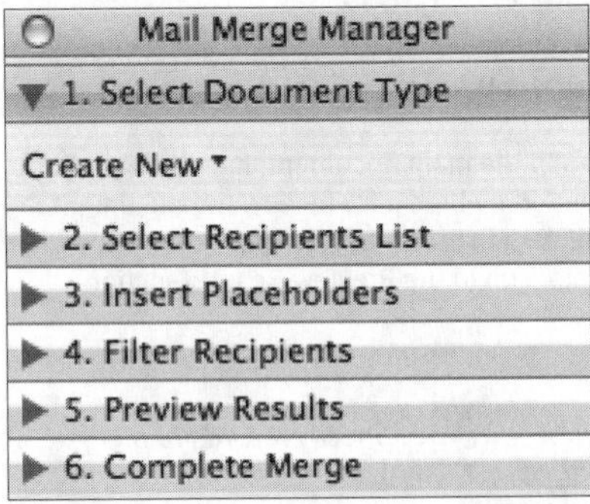

Figure 8.17 Mail Merge Manager palette.

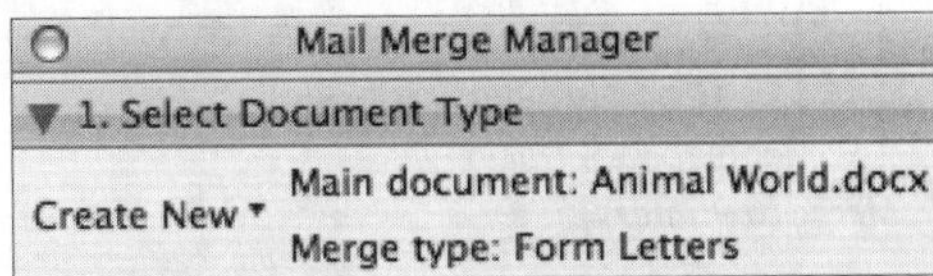

Figure 8.18 This section shows the name of the main document and the type of merge to be performed.

The Mail Merge Manager

Word provides help for creating mail merge letters, labels, and envelopes. It can assist you in creating the *main document* (containing placeholders for the information that changes with each copy), creating or opening the *data source* (for example, a collection of names and addresses), and printing the merged documents. In this example, you'll learn how to create form letters using records in the Office Address Book as the data source.

To generate a merge:

1. Create or open the document you'll use as the main document (**Figure 8.16**).

   You can use a form letter, a label layout, or an envelope layout, for example.

2. Choose Tools > Mail Merge Manager.

   The Mail Merge Manager palette appears (**Figure 8.17**).

3. In the Select Document Type section of the Mail Merge Manager palette, click Create New and choose a merge type (in this case, Form Letters) from the drop-down menu that appears (**Figure 8.18**).

4. Expand the Select Recipients List section, click the Get List icon, and choose one of the following from the drop-down menu:
   - ▲ **New Data Source** steps you through the process of creating a data source from scratch.
   - ▲ **Open Data Source** lets you use data from an existing Word or Excel document.
   - ▲ **Office Address Book** uses contact information from your Address Book.
   - ▲ **FileMaker Pro** lets you import data from selected fields in an existing FileMaker Pro 7.0–9.0 database.

continues on next page

After you've created or opened the data source, the Insert Placeholders section expands to display the fields in the data source—in this example, the Office Address Book (**Figure 8.19**).

5. Drag merge fields from the Insert Placeholders section into position in the main document (**Figure 8.20**).

   The merge fields are placeholders for data from the data source. You can place merge fields on separate lines, together on the same line, or embedded within the text of the main document.

6. If necessary, format the merge fields and add any required spacing or punctuation.

   For example, for the last line of an address, you'd separate City, State, and Zip merge fields with a comma and spaces, like this: `«City», «State» «Zip»`

7. To substitute actual data for the merge fields in the main document, expand the Preview Results section and click the View Merged Data icon. Click the arrow icons to move from one data record to the next, while viewing the results in the main document (Figure 8.20).

8. In the Complete Merge section (**Figure 8.21**), specify the records to merge by choosing an option from the drop-down menu:
   - **All.** Merge all records in the data source.
   - **Current Record.** Merge only the record number selected in the Preview Results section.
   - **Custom.** Specify a range of records (in the From and To boxes) to merge.

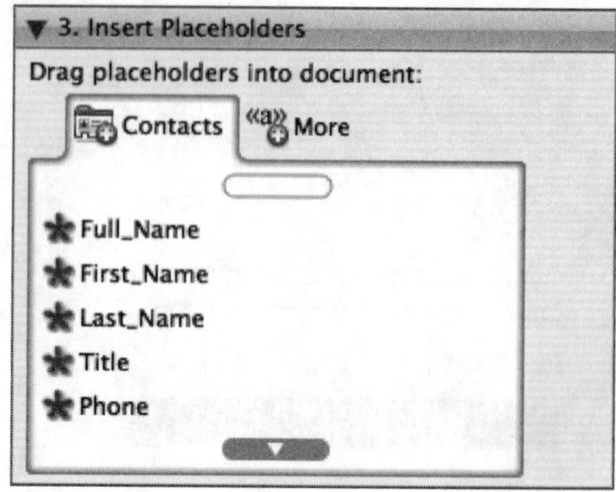

Figure 8.19 After you select the data source, a list of the merge fields it contains appears. Drag the necessary fields into position in the main document.

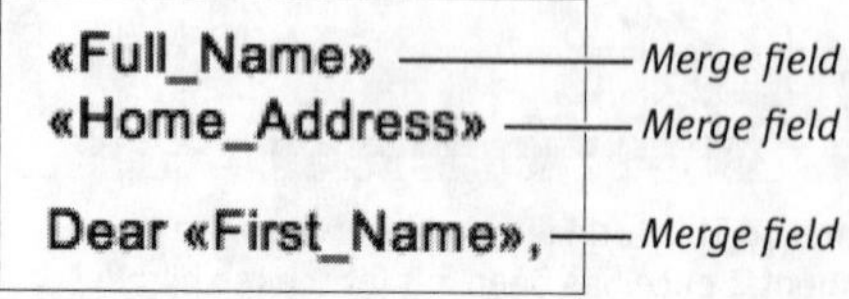

Jonas Griffith
1890 Elmhurst Drive
Littleton, CO 73012

Dear Jonas,

Figure 8.20 In the main document, merge fields (top) are surrounded by brackets. To view the document with merge data in place (bottom), click the View Merged Data icon in the Preview Results section.

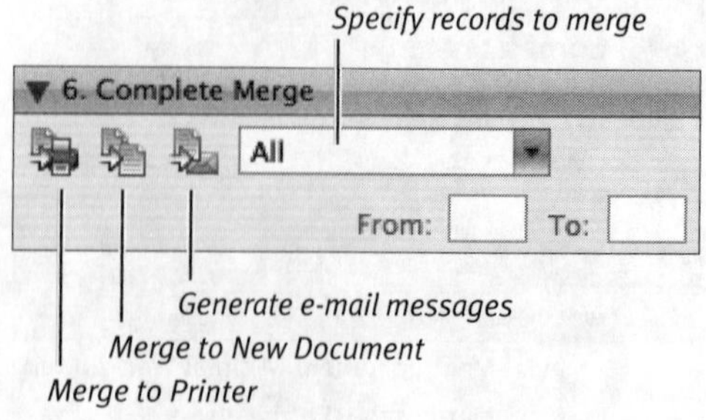

Figure 8.21 In the Complete Merge section, indicate the records that you want to merge.

THE MAIL MERGE MANAGER

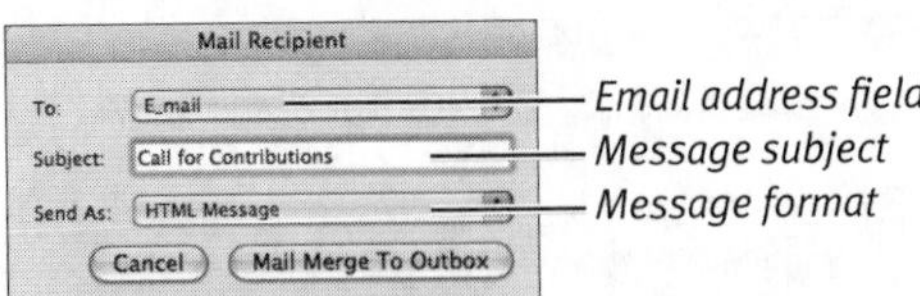

Figure 8.22 Set options in the Mail Recipient dialog box prior to merging to email.

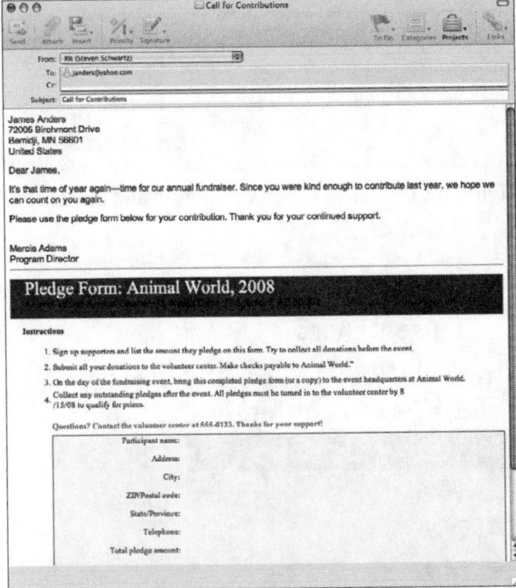

Figure 8.23 When you merge to email, each message generated by the merge is placed in Entourage's Outbox, ready for sending. If necessary, you can edit the messages in Entourage.

9. When the merge document is satisfactory, click one of these buttons in the Complete Merge section (see Figure 8.21):
   - **Merge to Printer.** Routes the merge directly to the printer.
   - **Merge to New Document.** Creates a Word document that you can edit and print later.
   - **Generate e-mail messages.** Sends the merge document(s) to Entourage's Outbox for transmission as email. Enter the requested information in the Mail Recipient dialog box (**Figure 8.22**) and click Mail Merge to Outbox. A separate email message is generated for each recipient (**Figure 8.23**).
10. To dismiss the Mail Merge Manager, click its close button or choose Tools > Mail Merge Manager.

✔ Tips

- At times, you may want to create a merge for just one record. To locate the record, click the Find Record icon in the Select Recipients List section.
- If you aren't certain whether you've chosen the correct records or think that some of them may be incomplete or incorrect, click Merge to New Document. Examine the resulting document, delete unnecessary records, edit any incomplete ones, and *then* print.
- When merging to email, it's a good idea to set Entourage to offline mode prior to generating the merge (choose Entourage > Work Offline). Examine the messages in the Outbox before they're sent and make any necessary edits and deletions. When you're ready to send the messages, choose Entourage > Work Offline again.

Documenting Documents

Depending on the environment in which you work, there are two features you'll either find extraordinarily helpful or marginally useful:

- You can use *AutoSummarize* to condense lengthy material into a few key points.
- If you're in a workgroup or share your documents with others, you can set *document properties* that identify the material and indicate how it's been handled.

To AutoSummarize a document:

1. Open the document you want to summarize and choose Tools > AutoSummarize.

   The AutoSummarize dialog box appears (**Figure 8.24**).
2. *Optional:* Specify the summary length by choosing an option from the Percent of original pop-up menu (**Figure 8.25**).
3. Click a Type of summary icon:
   - ▲ **Highlight key points.** Yellow highlighting is applied to important material. All other document text remains but is formatted light gray.
   - ▲ **Insert an executive summary or abstract at the top of the document.** The summary information is inserted at the beginning of the document.
   - ▲ **Create a new document and put the summary there.** Unlike the other options, this one doesn't change the original document. The summary text is placed in a new, separate document.
   - ▲ **Hide everything but the summary without leaving the original document.** Select this option to view only the summary information or the document with key points highlighted.

   If you want to save the summary information, select the second or third option.

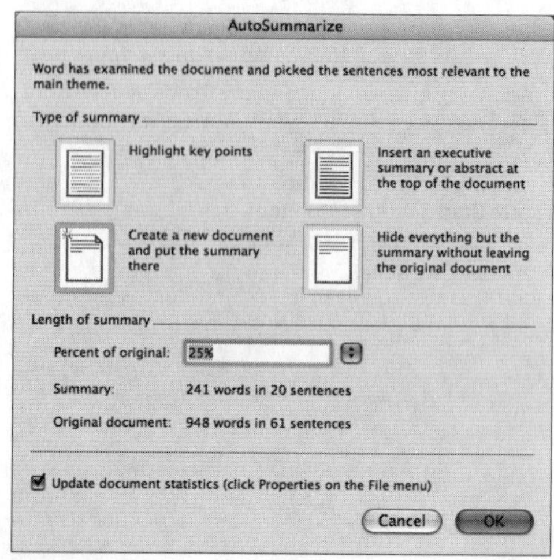

Figure 8.24 Select a summary method and options.

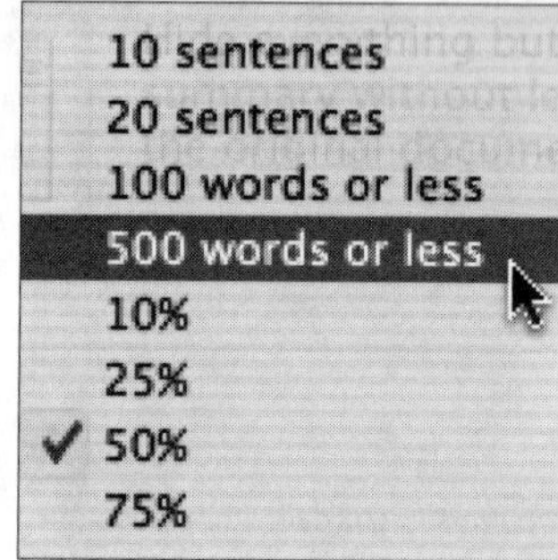

Figure 8.25 Choose the number of sentences, words, or a percentage of the document's length.

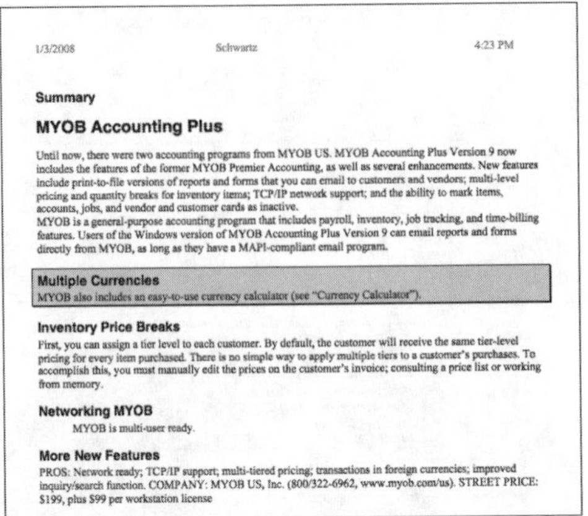

1/3/2008 Schwartz 4:23 PM

Summary

MYOB Accounting Plus

Until now, there were two accounting programs from MYOB US. MYOB Accounting Plus Version 9 now includes the features of the former MYOB Premier Accounting, as well as several enhancements. New features include print-to-file versions of reports and forms that you can email to customers and vendors; multi-level pricing and quantity breaks for inventory items; TCP/IP network support; and the ability to mark items, accounts, jobs, and vendor and customer cards as inactive.
MYOB is a general-purpose accounting program that includes payroll, inventory, job tracking, and time-billing features. Users of the Windows version of MYOB Accounting Plus Version 9 can email reports and forms directly from MYOB, as long as they have a MAPI-compliant email program.

Multiple Currencies
MYOB also includes an easy-to-use currency calculator (see "Currency Calculator").

Inventory Price Breaks

First, you can assign a tier level to each customer. By default, the customer will receive the same tier-level pricing for every item purchased. There is no simple way to apply multiple tiers to a customer's purchases. To accomplish this, you must manually edit the prices on the customer's invoice; consulting a price list or working from memory.

Networking MYOB

MYOB is multi-user ready.

More New Features

PROS: Network ready; TCP/IP support; multi-tiered pricing; transactions in foreign currencies; improved inquiry/search function. COMPANY: MYOB US, Inc. (800/322-6962, www.myob.com/us). STREET PRICE: $199, plus $99 per workstation license

Figure 8.26 Like an abstract for a professional article, the executive summary method places the summary information at the beginning of the document.

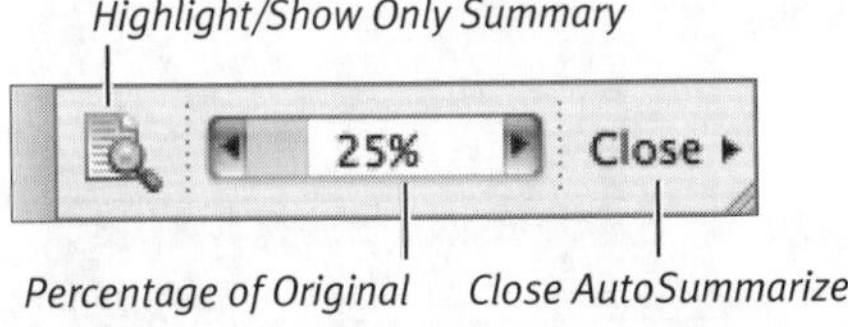

Figure 8.27 The AutoSummarize toolbar.

4. Click OK.

   The document is summarized as specified (**Figure 8.26**).

5. If you selected the first or last summary method in Step 2, an AutoSummarize toolbar appears (**Figure 8.27**). You can use the toolbar to do the following:
   - ▲ Show only the summary or show the full document with highlighting. (This icon works as a toggle.)
   - ▲ Interactively increase or decrease the summary percentage.
   - ▲ Close the toolbar and remove the summary information.

6. *Optional:* If you selected the second or third summary method in Step 2, you can save the summary information.
   - ▲ If you selected Create new document, you can save the summary information by saving the new document. Choose File > Save (⌘S).
   - ▲ If you selected Insert an executive summary, you can save the summary information by saving it as part of the original document (choose File > Save) or as a new document (choose File > Save As and select a new name or location for the file).

✔ Tips

- If you selected the first or last summary method, you can only save the summary information by reissuing the Tools > AutoSummary command and then selecting the second or third method.
- After viewing the summary information, you can prevent the original document from being altered by closing it without saving the changes.

To set or view document properties:

1. With the document open, choose File > Properties.

   The Properties dialog box appears. Only the information on the Summary and Custom tabs can be modified. Information on the other tabs can be viewed, but is set automatically.

2. To alter the information on the Summary tab (**Figure 8.28**), type in the text boxes.

3. To alter the information on the Custom tab (**Figure 8.29**), *do any of the following:*
   - ▲ **Add an item from the Name list.** Select the item from the scrolling list, choose an option from the Type menu, type or select a value in the Value section, and click Add.
   - ▲ **Add an item not in the Name list.** Type the item name in the Name box, choose an option from the Type menu, type or select a value in the Value section, and click Add. (See Figure 8.29 for an example.)
   - ▲ **Delete an item.** Select the item in the Properties list box and click Delete.
   - ▲ **Modify an item.** Select the item in the Properties list box, make the necessary changes to the Type and/or Value, and click Modify.

4. Save the document by choosing File > Save (⌘S).

   Information in the Properties dialog box is automatically saved with the file.

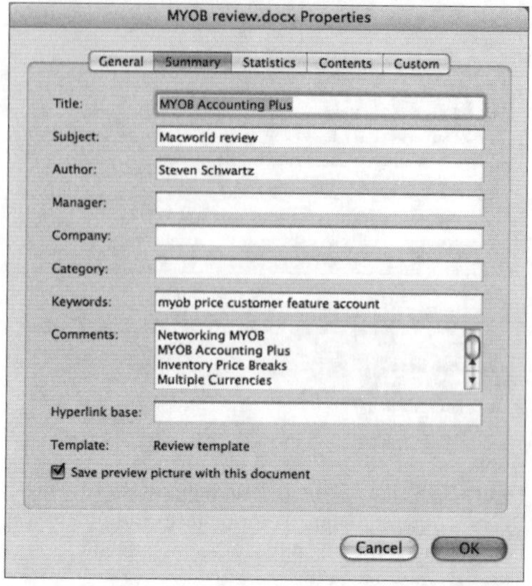

Figure 8.28 On the Summary tab, you can enter basic information, such as the document's title, subject, and author.

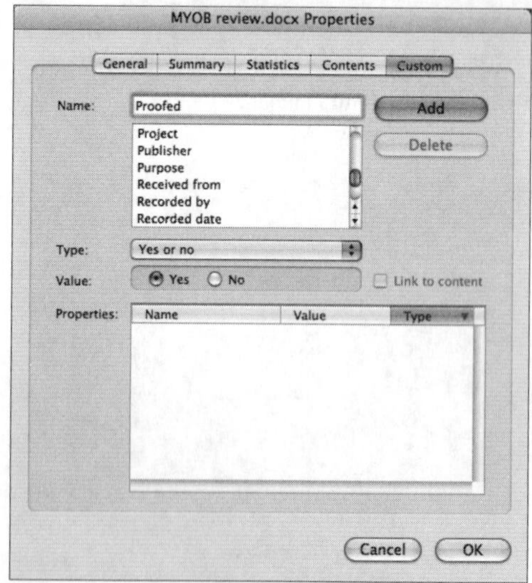

Figure 8.29 On the Custom tab, you can add items to a document's properties, such as its distribution date, recipient names, or the person who approved its distribution.

Part III: Microsoft Excel

Spreadsheet Essentials

As you probably know, Excel is Office 2008's *spreadsheet* application. By working in a grid of columns and rows called a *worksheet*, you can create lists, perform complex calculations, and graph important data.

In this chapter, we'll explore the basic topics you'll need to understand in order to begin using Excel:

- Creating new workbooks
- Understanding the interface and views
- Entering data into cells and navigating a worksheet
- Using AutoFill to intelligently fill ranges
- Editing cell contents and performing Find/Replace procedures
- Documenting cells with comments
- Naming cell ranges
- Importing text files
- Working with workbooks and sheets
- Printing workbooks, worksheets, and selected ranges

This chapter discusses several advanced topics, such as consolidating worksheets. You'll want to refer back to this chapter later.

Creating a New Workbook

A new Excel document is called a *workbook*. Every workbook consists of one or multiple pages known as *sheets* (or *worksheets*). In addition to creating new, blank workbooks, you can base a new workbook on a template by selecting one from the Project Gallery or from the ledger sheets in the Elements Gallery.

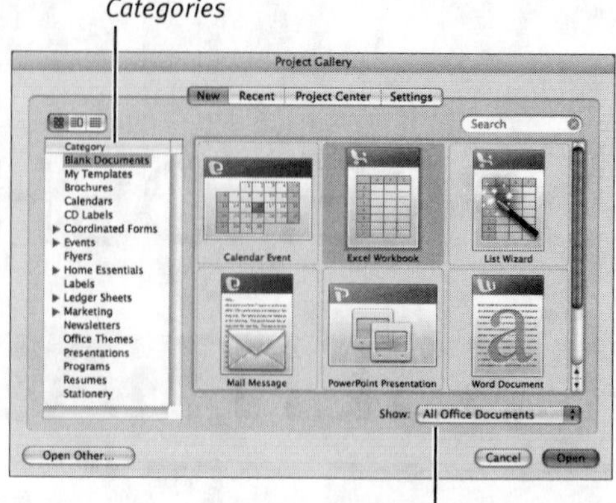

Figure 9.1 On program launch, you can create a new workbook in the Project Gallery by pressing Return.

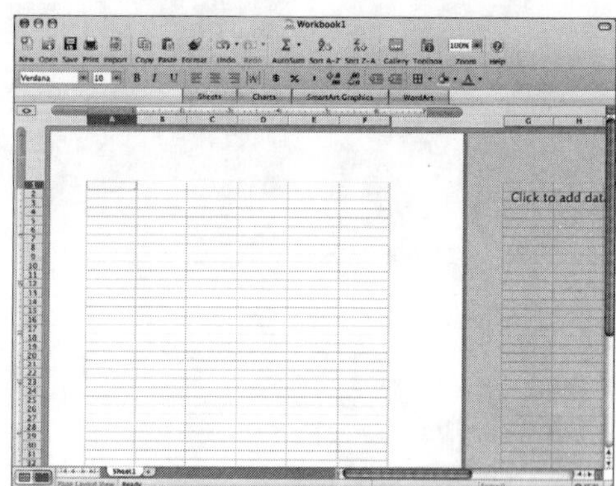

Figure 9.2 A new, blank workbook appears.

To create a new, blank workbook:

- *Do either of the following:*
  - ▲ When you launch Excel, the Project Gallery may appear (**Figure 9.1**). Click the New tab. By default, Blank Documents is selected. Select the Excel Workbook or List Wizard thumbnail, and click Open.
  - ▲ If Excel is already running, choose File > New Workbook, press ⌘N, or click the New icon on the Standard toolbar.

  A new workbook appears (**Figure 9.2**).

To create a workbook from a Project Gallery template:

1. Choose File > Project Gallery (Shift⌘P) or click the Microsoft Project Gallery icon in the Dock.
2. In the Project Gallery window (Figure 9.1), choose Excel Documents from the Show drop-down menu.

   This restricts document and template thumbnails to Excel files.
3. Select a category from the list on the left. These categories contain templates: My Templates, Home Essentials, and Ledger Sheets.
4. Select a template thumbnail in the right side of the window and click Open.

   Excel creates and opens a new workbook based on the selected template.

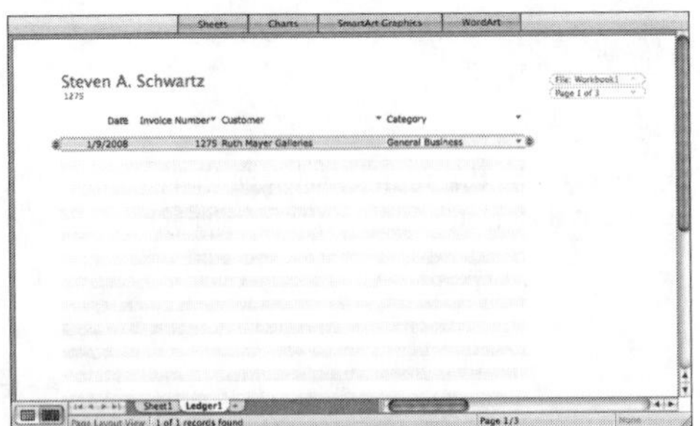

Figure 9.4 Based on the selected template, the new ledger sheet is added to the workbook.

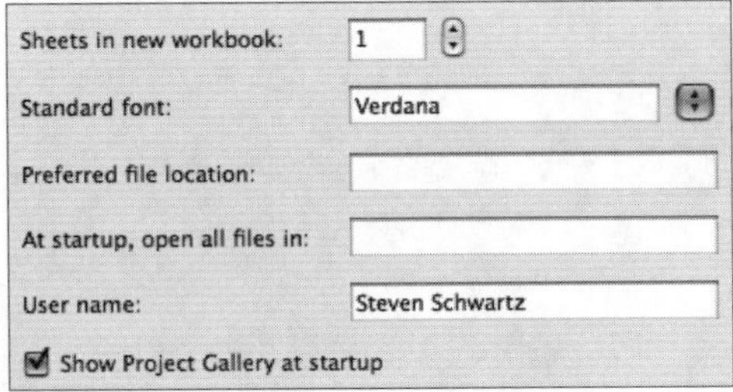

Figure 9.5 In the General section of Preferences, check Show Project Gallery at startup.

To add a ledger sheet to the current workbook:

1. Click the Sheets tab in the Elements Gallery (**Figure 9.3**, page bottom).

   Ledger sheet category buttons appear.

2. Click a category button to view available templates.

   To see a description of a template, rest the cursor on its thumbnail.

3. Select a template to use by clicking its thumbnail.

   A new sheet is added to the current workbook, based on the template (**Figure 9.4**).

✔ Tips

- On Excel's launch, if you close the Project Gallery without opening a new or existing workbook, a new workbook is automatically created.
- Whether the Project Gallery appears at startup is determined by a Preferences setting (**Figure 9.5**). Choose Excel > Preferences, and click the General icon. The number of sheets in a new workbook is also specified in this dialog box.
- You can open the Project Gallery icon in the Dock at any time—even if no Office application is running.
- It isn't necessary to close open workbooks before creating a new one.

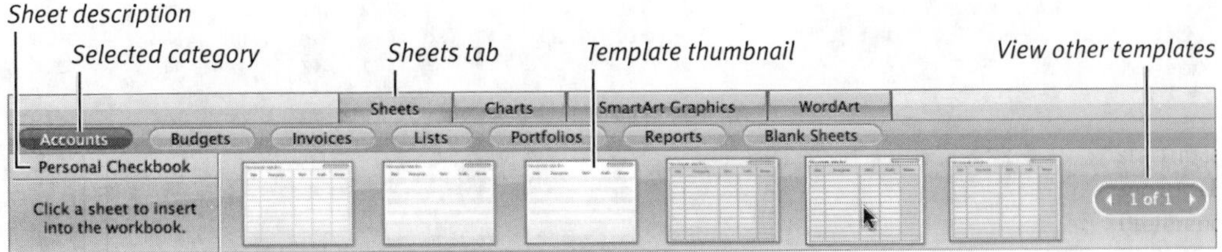

Figure 9.3 Add a ledger sheet to the current workbook by clicking its Elements Gallery thumbnail.

The Excel Interface

The interface components with which you'll need to be familiar are shown in **Figure 9.6**.

Menu bar. Like other Macintosh applications, commands can be chosen by clicking a menu bar heading. For example, to save changes to the current workbook, you click the File menu and choose Save (shown as *File > Save* in this book).

Name box. Part of the formula bar, the Name box (**Figure 9.7**) shows the active cell's address. You can also create English-like names in the Name box that you can use in formulas as shorthand for the cell or range it represents, such as =SUM(Sales) rather than =SUM(A5:A27). Finally, you can enter a cell address or range in the Name box and press Return to immediately go to and select that cell or range in the workbook.

Figure 9.7 Type the address or range that you want to select, and then press Return.

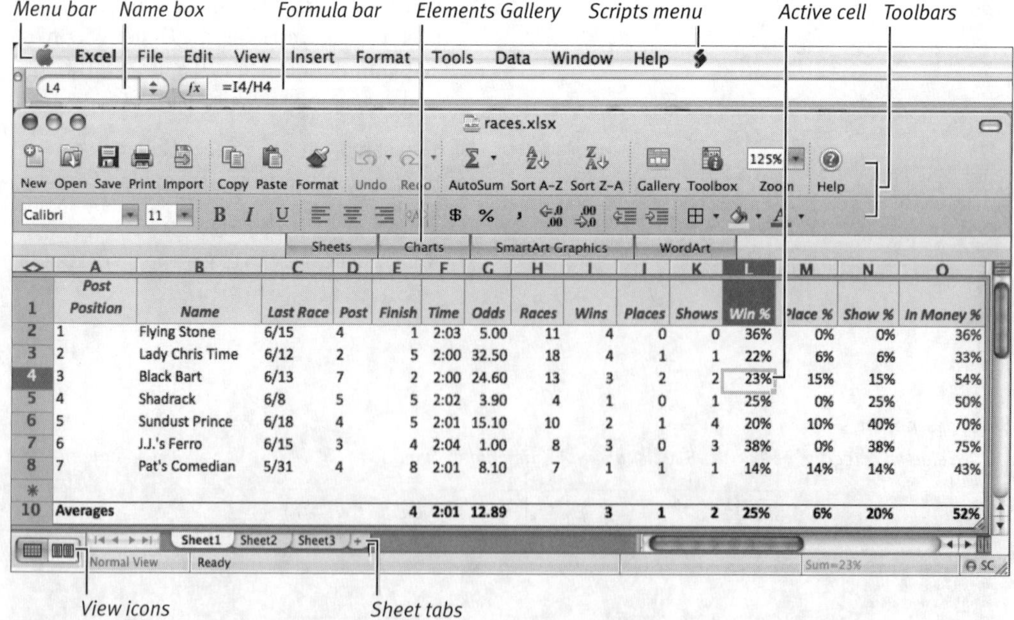

Figure 9.6 The Excel 2008 interface.

Scripts menu

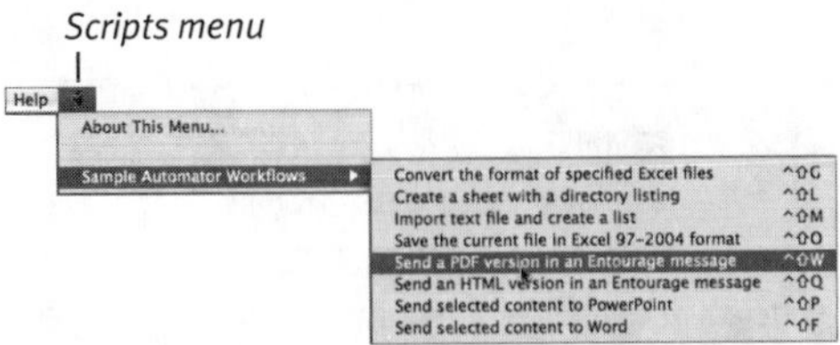

Figure 9.8 You can choose useful special-purpose commands, such as these Sample Automator Workflows, from the Scripts menu.

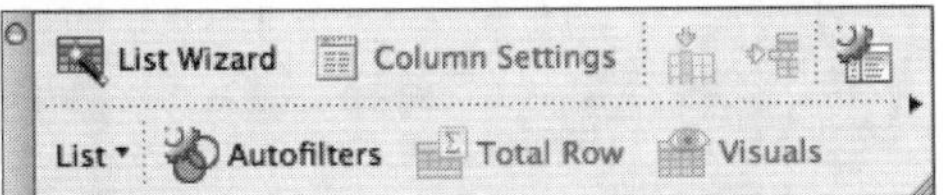

Figure 9.9 Some toolbars are work sensitive and automatically appear when you perform a related function, such as selecting a cell in an Excel list.

Setting Preferences

It's a good idea to review the Excel customization options in Preferences. Because there are so many, the Preferences dialog box was made to look and work like System Preferences. After choosing Excel > Preferences (⌘,), click icons to view different Preference categories. Here are some options you should examine:

- **General.** Sheets in new workbook, default font and size, user name.
- **View.** Settings (show formula bar, preferred view for new sheets), Window options (show page breaks, show formulas, show gridlines).
- **Edit.** Specify the number of decimal places to display.
- **Compatibility.** Default file format.
- **Security.** Passwords, remove personal information from this file on save.

Formula bar. The floating formula bar has two purposes. First, it displays the contents of the active cell. Second, you can use it to enter and edit data and formulas. To show or hide the formula bar, choose View > Formula Bar. (Whether the formula bar automatically appears when you open or create a workbook is determined by an option in View Preferences.)

Elements Gallery. New in Office 2008, each tab presents a different type of Excel material in a scrolling thumbnail list (see Figure 9.3). Click a thumbnail to open the selected item, adding it to the current workbook or sheet. To hide or show the Elements Gallery, choose View > Elements Gallery. After viewing the items for a given tab, such as Charts, click the tab again to close the gallery.

Scripts menu. Click this menu bar menu to run installed AppleScripts and Automator Workflows (**Figure 9.8**).

Active cell. This is another name for the currently selected cell. The cell's address is the intersection of the column and row in which it is located (column L and row 4 in Figure 9.6, for example). Excel automatically highlights the appropriate column and row headings. The cell address is displayed in the name box, and the cell contents (data or a formula) is shown in the formula bar.

Toolbars. A toolbar presents common Excel features grouped by function. Each toolbar appears above the worksheet area or as a floating palette (**Figure 9.9**). You execute toolbar commands by clicking the icons and choosing options from drop-down menus. To show or hide a toolbar, choose View > Toolbars, followed by the toolbar name.

continues on next page

View icons. You can work with the current sheet in either of two views: Normal or Page Layout. In Page Layout View (the default), the sheet is shown as it will print—with margins and page breaks. In Normal View (the preferred setting for entering and editing data), columns and rows are displayed without breaks. Dashed lines show where pages will break when you print.

You can switch views whenever you like by clicking an icon (**Figure 9.10**) or choosing Normal or Page Layout from the View menu. If a workbook has multiple sheets, each one can be set to a different view. You can set the default view (Preferred view for new sheets) in the View section of Preferences.

Sheet tabs. You use the sheet tabs (**Figure 9.11**) to add, delete, name, and switch between worksheets. For information on sheets and sheet tabs, see "Working with Workbooks," later in this chapter.

✔ Tips

- To change the magnification, choose a setting from the Zoom icon on the Standard toolbar. Note that Zoom settings are sheet-specific. Each sheet can have a different magnification, if you like.
- Click the Toolbox icon on the Standard toolbar to show or hide the Toolbox. As you learned in Chapter 1, each Office application makes different tools available on the Toolbox's tabs, such as the Formatting Palette and Formula Builder. You can also open the Toolbox by choosing a specific tab from the View menu.

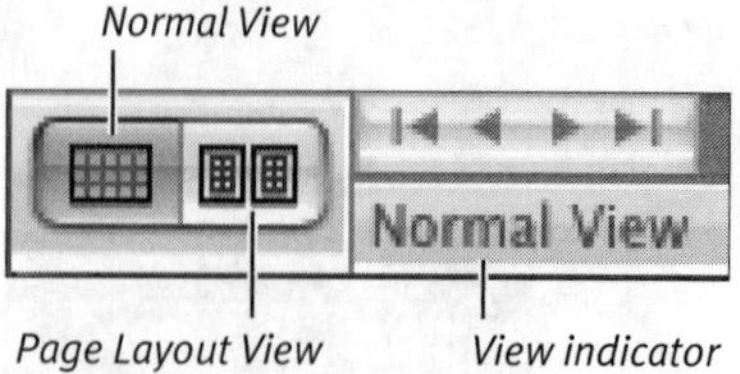

Figure 9.10 The fastest way to change views is to click one of these icons.

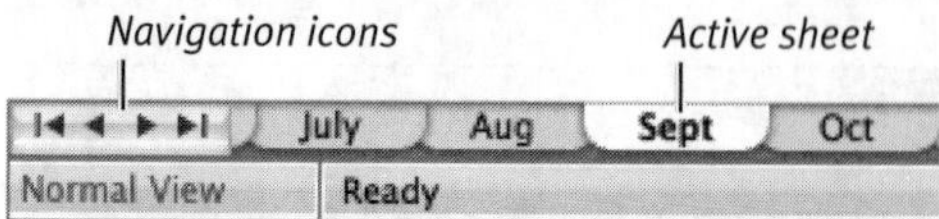

Figure 9.11 A workbook can have many sheets. To make a different sheet active, click its tab. If the sheet name isn't visible, click the navigation icons.

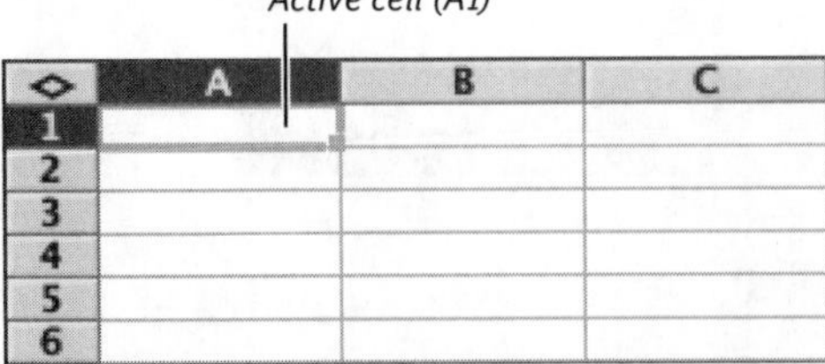

Figure 9.12 In a standard worksheet, each column is named by letter and each row by number. Each cell address, such as A1 or BW723, is the intersection of a particular row and column.

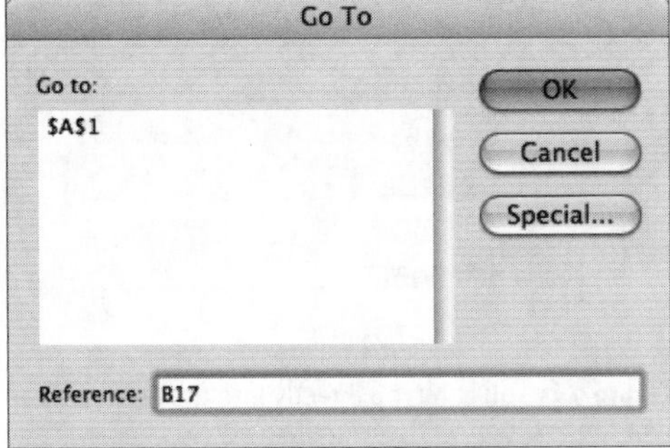

Figure 9.13 Type a cell address and click OK. (If the address was recently used, you can select it from the Go to list.)

Table 9.1

Keyboard Navigation Shortcuts

SHORTCUT	ACTION
↑, ↓, ←, →	Move to the adjacent cell (up, down, left, or right)
Pg Up, Pg Dn	Move up or down one screen
Option Pg Dn, Option Pg Up	Move right or left one screen
Tab, Shift Tab	Move right or left one cell
Enter, Shift Enter	Move down or up one cell
Return, Shift Return	Move down or up one cell
Home	Move to first cell of the row
Control + arrow key	Move to edge of current data
Control Home	Move to cell A1
Control End	Move to last cell in use

Worksheet Navigation

Excel windows work as they do in most other Macintosh applications—with some additional tricks to get you where you want to go.

A sheet is divided into a grid of columns and rows (**Figure 9.12**). The intersection of a column and row is a *cell*. Every column is labeled with a letter (shown in its heading) and every row with a number. The combination of a column letter and row number uniquely identifies each cell, such as G7 or D103. This combination is known as a *cell address*.

To move to a cell:

◆ *Do one of the following:*
  ▲ Scroll as necessary to display the desired cell, and then click the cell.
  ▲ Use the keyboard to navigate to the cell, as explained in **Table 9.1**.
  ▲ Type the cell address in the Name box on the formula bar (see Figure 9.7), and then press Return or Enter.
  ▲ Choose Edit > Go To (Control G). In the Go To dialog box (**Figure 9.13**), enter the address in the Reference box or select it from the Go to list. Click OK.

The cell you click or move to becomes the *active cell*. The address appears in the Name box, and the corresponding column letter and row number are highlighted.

✔ Tips

■ You can use the scroll bars to scroll through a worksheet without changing the active cell.

■ When scrolling, press Control Delete to return immediately to the active cell.

■ If the Name box isn't visible, display the formula bar by choosing View > Formula Bar.

Entering Data into Cells

Data entry is primarily a click-and-type procedure, as explained in the following steps.

To enter data into a cell:

1. Click in a cell to make it the active cell (**Figure 9.14**).
2. In the cell or the formula bar, type the text, number, date, or formula (**Figure 9.15**).

   Formulas must begin with an equal sign (=), as explained in Chapter 11.
3. Complete the entry by pressing a navigation key, such as Return or Enter to move down or Tab to move right.

   Excel evaluates the cell contents and then formats it appropriately.

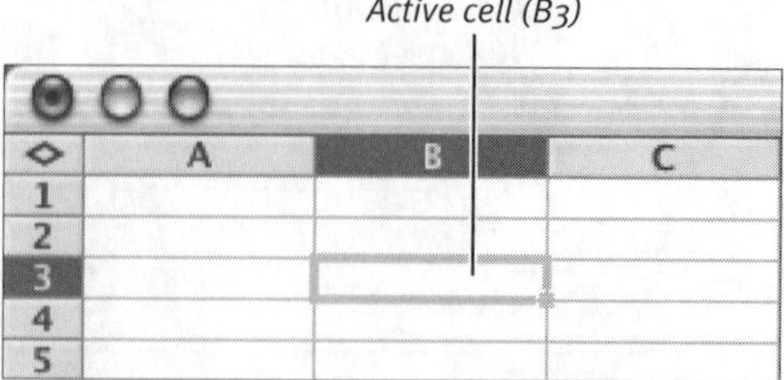

Figure 9.14 The current (or active) cell is surrounded by a thick, gray border. Its column and row heading are highlighted.

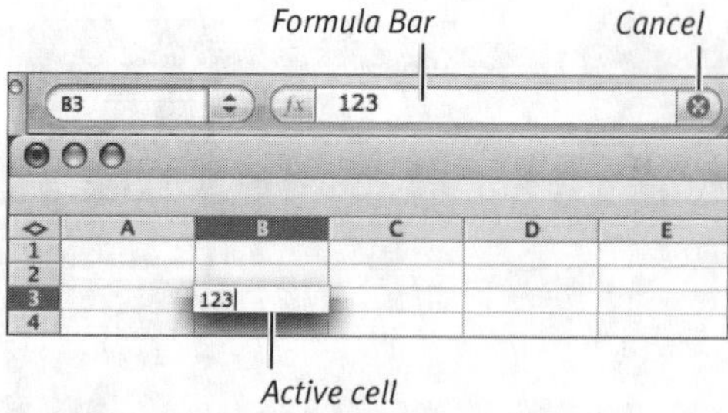

Figure 9.15 You can type directly into the active cell or into the text box on the formula bar.

✔ Tips

- To complete a cell entry, you can also use the keyboard shortcuts shown in Table 9.1.
- If you change your mind about a cell entry, press Esc or click the Cancel icon (X) on the formula bar. If the cell was originally empty, it's cleared; if it contained data or a formula, the data or formula is restored.
- If a text entry you're typing matches one or more others in the same column, Excel provides a drop-down AutoComplete list of all matches (**Figure 9.16**). Click one to accept it, or keep typing to ignore the list. (If you don't find the lists helpful, you can disable AutoComplete in the AutoComplete section of Preferences.)
- Some numbers, such as Zip Codes, are best treated as text rather than numbers. Doing so enables you to preserve any leading zeros, such as `01701`. (If recorded as a number, Excel drops leading zeros.) To prevent this, format the cells as Text prior to entering the data. (See Chapter 10 for formatting instructions.)

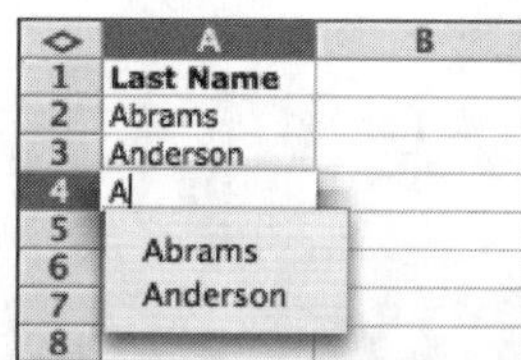

Figure 9.16 An AutoComplete list.

Entering Data into a Range

If you know the cell range into which you'll be entering data, you can speed up the process by first selecting the range.

After you complete the entry for each cell, press Tab to move to the next cell to the right or press Return or Enter to move to the next cell down. When a row or column of the range has been completed, the cursor automatically moves to the beginning of the next row or column.

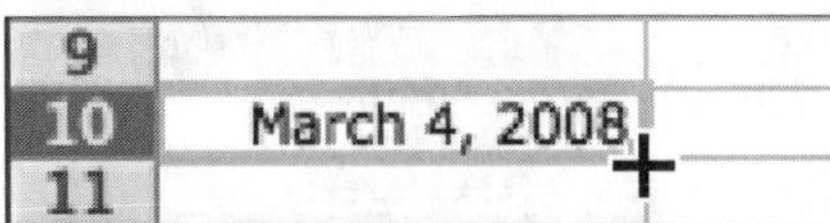

Figure 9.17 Move the cursor over the cell's lower-right corner. It becomes a fill handle.

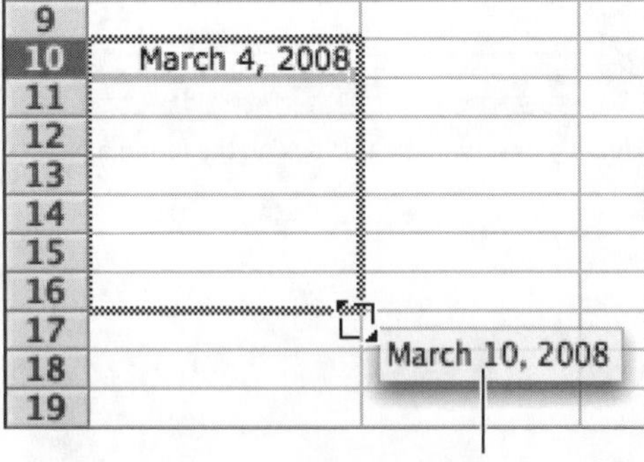

AutoFill ScreenTip

Figure 9.18 Drag to select the range you want to fill.

9	
10	March 4, 2008
11	March 5, 2008
12	March 6, 2008
13	March 7, 2008
14	March 8, 2008
15	March 9, 2008
16	March 10, 2008
17	
18	
19	

AutoFill Options

Figure 9.19 When you release the mouse button, the new data appears.

Filling Cells with a Series

When you need to fill a cell range with consecutive numbers, dates, days of the week, or items that follow a specific pattern (such as every four days), you can use AutoFill to automatically enter the sequence.

To AutoFill a range of cells:

1. In the first cell, type the first number, word, or date of the series.

   Examples include `105`, `Sunday`, `March`, `6/30/04`, `April 1, 2005`, or `Qtr 1`.

2. If the series isn't apparent from the initial cell entry, enter the next item in the series in an adjacent cell (the column to the right or the row below).

3. Select the initial cell or cells. Then move the pointer over the lower-right corner of the lowest or rightmost cell. It becomes a *fill handle* (**Figure 9.17**). Drag to extend the sequence, as desired (**Figure 9.18**).

   As you drag past each cell, the value that will be filled in the current cell is shown in a ScreenTip.

4. Release the mouse button when the destination cells have been selected.

   The sequence appears in the selected cells (**Figure 9.19**).

5. *Optional:* Click the AutoFill Options icon to choose an option, such as Fill Weekdays.

✔ Tips

- If the fill handle doesn't appear, it has probably been disabled in the Edit section of the Preferences dialog box.

- To fill a series of cells with the same text or numeric data, such as `CA` or `0.082`, use a Fill command (such as Edit > Fill > Down) rather than AutoFill. You can also use Fill commands to extend a series of calculated values.

Editing Cell Data

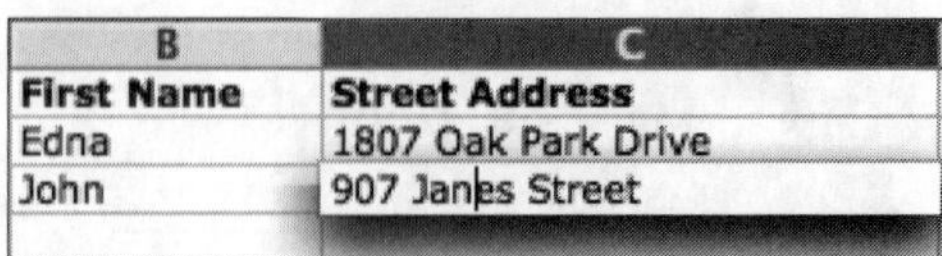

Figure 9.20 You can edit cell data directly in the cell...

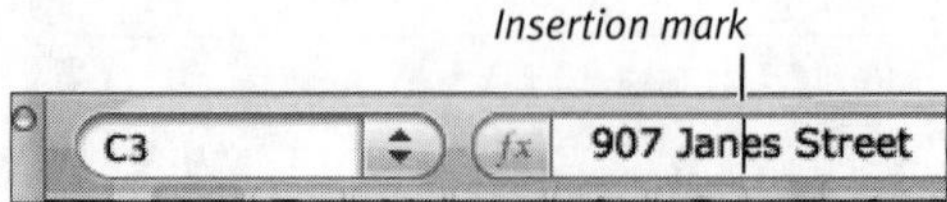

Figure 9.21 ...or in the text box on the formula bar.

The easiest way to change a cell's contents is to select the cell and then type over the current data. But if the cell contains a formula or a lengthy text string, it's often faster to edit the current contents than to retype.

To edit a cell's contents:

1. *Do one of the following:*
   - ▲ Click the cell to select it. (Selecting a cell automatically selects its *entire* contents.) Type to replace/overwrite the contents.
   - ▲ Double-click the cell to set the text insertion mark in the cell's text (**Figure 9.20**).
   - ▲ Click the cell to select it. Set the text insertion mark in the text displayed in the formula bar (**Figure 9.21**).
2. Edit the contents in the cell or in the formula bar using the same techniques as you would if editing text in Word.

   For example, you can delete the previous character or a selection by pressing Delete, insert additional characters, or move left or right within the contents by pressing the left- or right-arrow key.
3. To complete the edit, you can move to another cell; press Return, Enter, Tab; or press any other navigation key.

✓ Tips

- To cancel a revision and leave the original contents of the cell intact, press Esc or click the Cancel icon on the formula bar (see Figure 9.15).
- If you edit a formula or cell data that is referenced by a formula, all affected cells are recalculated when you finish the edit.

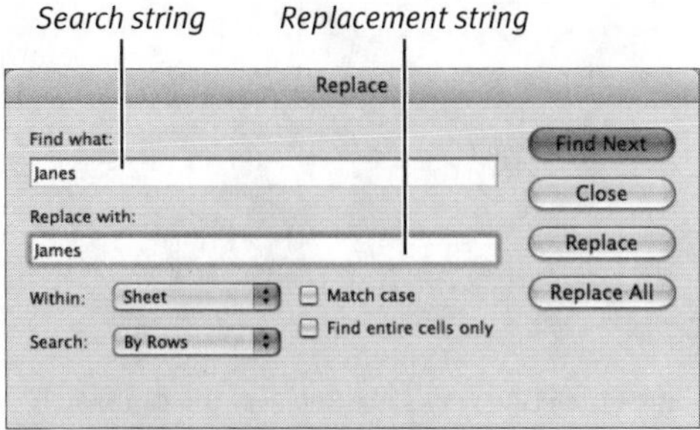

Figure 9.22 Enter Find what and Replace with strings in the text boxes.

B	C
First Name	**Street Address**
Edna	1807 Oak Park Drive
John	907 Janes Street

Selected match

Figure 9.23 When a match is found, Excel scrolls to the cell and selects it.

Finding and Replacing Data

Another way to edit a worksheet is to use the Replace command to search for a string and replace it with another.

To perform a Find/Replace:

1. *Optional:* To restrict your search to a part of the worksheet, select the range.
2. Choose Edit > Replace.
   The Replace dialog box appears.
3. Enter a search string in the Find what text box and a replacement string in the Replace with text box (**Figure 9.22**).
4. From the Within drop-down menu, choose Sheet to search only the active sheet or Workbook to search all sheets.
5. From the Search drop-down menu, choose By Rows or By Columns, depending on how the data is arranged.
   For example, to replace an old company name or address with a new one in a worksheet that restricts those items to one or two columns, a By Columns search is best. If the text could be found in any column, on the other hand, a By Rows search might be better.
6. *Optional:* Click one or both check boxes to restrict matches to those with identical letter case (Match case) or where the Find what string is the *only* data in the found cell (Find entire cells only).
7. To begin the search, click Find Next.
   If Excel finds a match, it highlights it in the worksheet (**Figure 9.23**).

continues on next page

8. For each match, *do one of the following:*
   - ▲ To replace this match with the Replace with string, click Replace.
   - ▲ To skip this match and look for the next one, click Find Next.
   - ▲ To skip this match and end the search immediately, click Close.

   Repeat this step to find any additional matches in the sheet or workbook.

9. If the dialog box doesn't automatically close as the result of an operation (such as a Replace All), click the Close button.

✔ Tips

- To simultaneously search for and replace *all* instances of the match, you can click Replace All at any time. Note, however, that you will not be given an opportunity to view the changes individually, since they are made *en masse.*
- You can undo a Replace All by immediately choosing Edit > Undo Replace (⌘Z).
- The Find what string can also include *wild card characters*, as follows:
  - ▲ **Question mark (?).** A substitute for any single character. For example, `s?ng` would find sang, sing, song, and sung.
  - ▲ **Asterisk (*).** A substitute for any number of characters (including none). `j*n` would find John, Jones, and AJ Loans; that is, any text string that includes a J followed by an N.
- If you want to find certain data but not replace it, choose Edit > Find (⌘F). The Find dialog box (**Figure 9.24**) is similar to the Replace dialog box.
- As a sanity check following a Replace All, you may want to perform a Find, search for the replacement string, and see if the entries look appropriate.

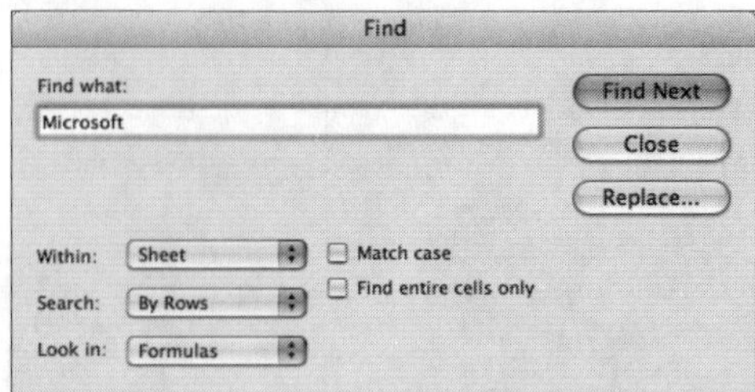

Figure 9.24 Find works like Replace. You can switch from a Find to a Find/Replace by clicking the Replace button.

Sorting Data

Many sheets or certain ranges are organized as rectangular data arrays in which every row is the equivalent of a record and every column is a field. In Excel, such an array can be defined as a list or analyzed using database tools. Whether or not you formally declare an array to be a list, you can periodically sort it by one or multiple fields. For instructions on sorting using the Sort dialog box, refer to "Database Operations" (Chapter 14) and "Sorting a List" (Chapter 12).

You can use the Sort toolbar icons to sort any rectangular data array based on the contents of one of its columns:

1. *Do one of the following:*
   - ▲ To sort the entire array, select any cell within the column on which the sort will be based.
   - ▲ To sort only one column of data while ignoring the surrounding columns, select the columns' cells.
2. Click the Sort A–Z or Sort Z-A icon on the Standard toolbar.

Adding Cell Comments

To document the assumptions underlying a calculation or to explain the meaning of a complex formula, you can attach a *comment* to any cell. Comments are visible only when you want them to be.

To create and manage comments:

1. To attach a comment to a cell, select the cell and choose Insert > Comment.

   A text box appears. If a User Name has been entered in the General section of Preferences (**Figure 9.25**), the name appears in the text box to identify the comment's author. Delete it, if you wish.

2. Enter your comment in the box. When you're finished, click any other cell.

   The comment text box closes and a small triangle appears in the cell's upper-right corner. This is the comment indicator (**Figure 9.26**).

3. To view comments, *do one of the following:*
   - ▲ To view a specific comment, rest the cursor over the cell (**Figure 9.27**).
   - ▲ To view all the comments in a worksheet, choose View > Comments. (To hide the comments, choose View > Comments again.)

✔ Tips

- When you choose View > Comments, the Reviewing toolbar appears (**Figure 9.28**). You can use the toolbar to cycle through the comments, create new comments, delete or edit comments, and so on.
- You can resize a comment box by dragging any of its surrounding handles when creating or editing the comment.
- Since a comment is an object, you can format it (changing its font or color, for example).

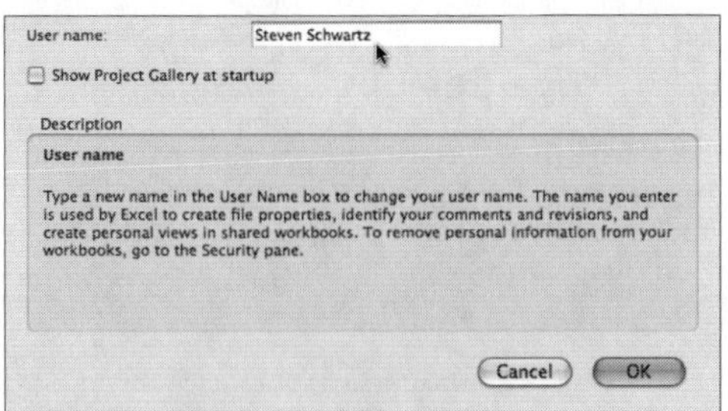

Figure 9.25 If specified in General Preferences, the User name is attached to each comment.

	A	B
1	Last Name	First Name
2	Johnson	Edna
3	Sims	John

Comment indicator

Figure 9.26 The presence of a comment is indicated by a tiny triangle in the cell's upper-right corner.

	A	B	Street
1	Last Name	First Name	Street
2	Johnson	Steven Schwartz:	07
3	Sims	Updated 6/28/08	7 Ja
4			

Figure 9.27 A comment appears when you move the cursor over the cell to which it's attached.

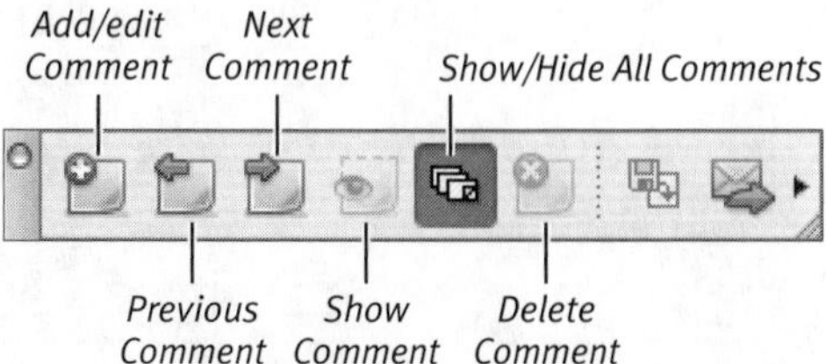

Figure 9.28 The Reviewing toolbar has commands for working with comments.

Naming Cell Ranges

To make it easy to find a particular cell range, create a chart from it, or reference it in a formula, you can assign a name to any cell or range. Such names are called *range names, named ranges*, or *names*.

For example, you could assign the name `April` to a column of April sales figures and refer to it in formulas by name: `=SUM(April)` rather than `=SUM(D3:D14)`. You can assign a name to a single cell, part of a column or row, a group of cells that spans several rows or columns, or a group of nonadjacent cells.

To name a cell range:

1. Select the cells you want to name.
2. In the Name box on the formula bar (**Figure 9.29**), enter the name you want to assign to the selected cells, and press Enter or Return.

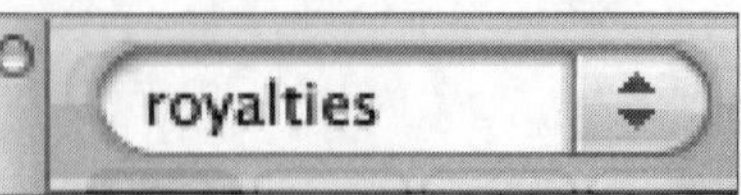

Figure 9.29 In the Name box, enter a name for the selected cell or cell range.

✔ Tips

- The first character of a name must be a letter or an underscore (_). Names may contain multiple words, but they cannot contain spaces. Use an underscore or period instead, such as `Sales.Tax.Pct` or `Sales_Tax_Pct`.
- You can't name a cell while you're changing its contents.
- You can also assign a name to a *constant* (as explained in the following tip), such as defining `SalesTaxPct` as `=0.075`.
- Another way to define names is to choose Insert > Name > Define. In the Define Name dialog box (**Figure 9.30**), enter a name, specify a range or constant in the Refers to box, and click Add. (As shown, all name definitions start with an equal sign.) Click OK when you're done.

NAMING A RANGE

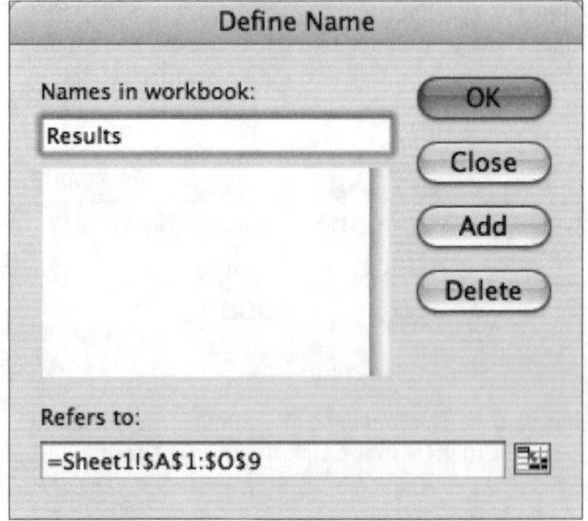

NAMING A CONSTANT

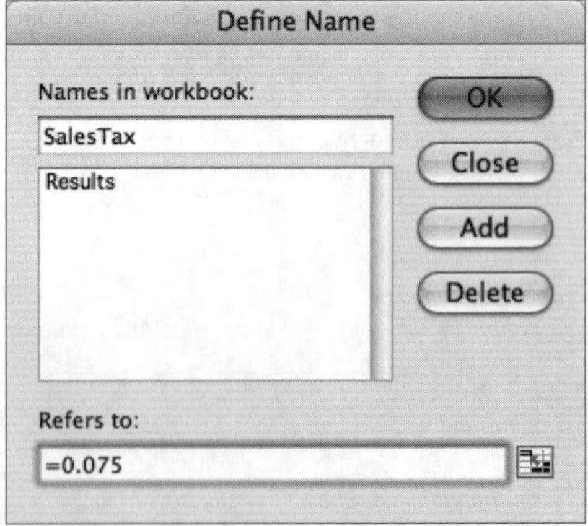

Figure 9.30 You can use the Define name dialog box to create names that refer to a cell or range (top) or a constant (bottom).

Figure 9.31 To go to a named range, you can select it from the Name box's drop-down list.

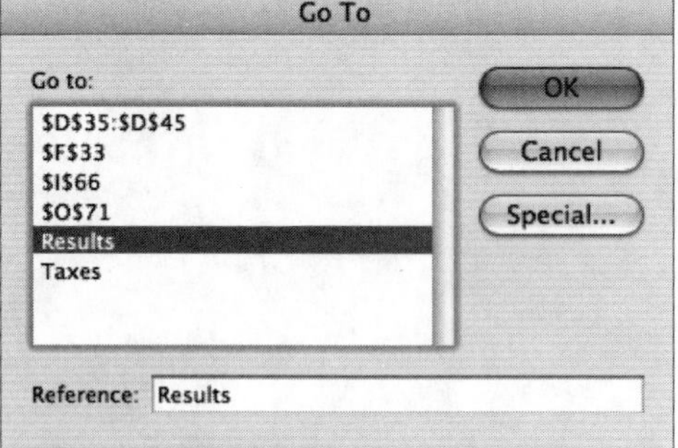

Figure 9.32 You can also go to a named range by selecting its name in the Go To dialog box.

- Another reason to create names is so you can quickly jump to key areas of a sheet. For example, you can name important summary figures, lists, and data areas. To go to and select a named range, *do any of the following:*
  - ▲ Select the name from the Name box's drop-down list (**Figure 9.31**).
  - ▲ Type the name in the Name box.
  - ▲ Choose Edit > Go To (Control G). In the Go To dialog box (**Figure 9.32**), select the name and click OK.
- In a multi-sheet workbook, names can enable you to move directly to areas on *different* sheets. For example, suppose you're tracking sales or expenses by creating a new sheet each month. The totals are likely to be in a different range on each sheet. Assign a name to each month's total range, and then you can jump to any of those ranges—regardless of the sheet that's currently displayed.
- Formulas can reference named ranges on other sheets in the current workbook.

Importing Data from a Text File

Typing data isn't the only way to fill cells. You can import data from a variety of external sources. In Chapter 14, procedures are presented for importing data from FileMaker Pro databases and from Web pages. In this section, you'll learn to import data from text files. Since most major applications can save data or tables as *tab-delimited text files*, it's a very common format for data exchange.

To import data from a text file:

1. In the source program (such as a database, spreadsheet, or word-processing program), export or save the file in a delimited format, such as tab- or comma-delimited.

   In a delimited file, fields are separated from one another by a special character, such as a tab or comma. Each record is a single paragraph, ending with a Return character.

2. Drag the icon of the exported file onto the Excel program icon. (If Excel is in the Dock, you can drag it onto that icon, for example.)

   Excel attempts to open and interpret the file as a new worksheet (**Figure 9.33**).

3. Examine the resulting worksheet. If it's satisfactory, save it as a normal Excel file.

   Choose File > Save As, and change the Format setting to Excel Workbook (.xlsx) or Excel 97-2004 Workbook (.xls).

◇	A	B
1	First Name	Last Name
2	A.	Polland
3	Adam	Engst
4	Adam	Steinberg
5	Aimee	Martin
6	Alex	Blanton
7	Alex	Daniels
8	Alexandra	Krasne
9	Allon	Bendavid

Figure 9.33 Check the new worksheet to see if the data seems to have been reasonably interpreted.

Try It Yourself

To see how importing a text file works, you can create an Excel worksheet from your Entourage Address Book contacts:

1. In Entourage, choose File > Export.

   The Export wizard appears.

2. Select Contacts to a list (tab-delimited text). Click the right arrow icon.

   A Save dialog box appears.

3. Name the export file, select a convenient location for it (such as the Desktop), and click Save.

4. Drag the resulting tab-delimited text file onto the Excel icon (found in the Dock or in the Applications: Microsoft Office 2008 folder).

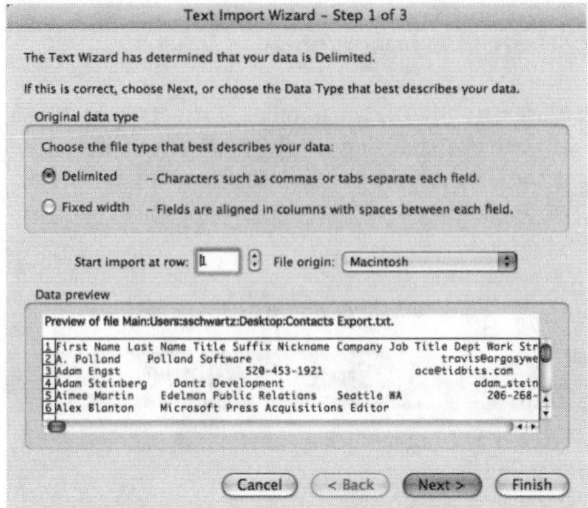

Figure 9.34 The Text Import Wizard presents a series of dialog boxes in which you specify the format of the file being imported.

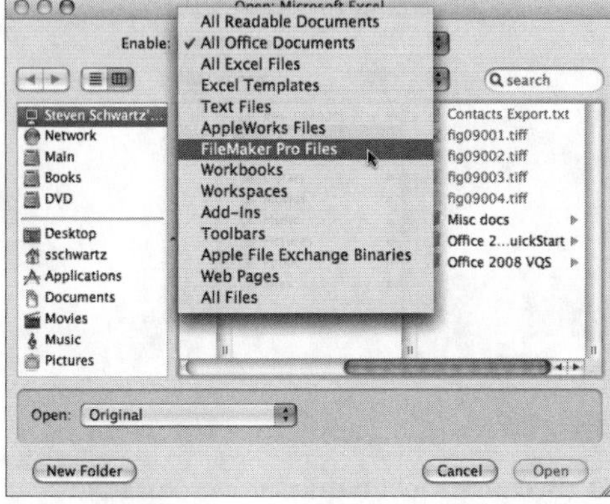

Figure 9.35 In the Open dialog box, open the Enable menu to view a list of Excel-compatible file types.

✔ Tips

- If the result of the drag-and-drop procedure is *not* satisfactory, you can import the data using the Text Import Wizard. Choose Data > Get External Data > Import Text File and follow the Wizard's directions (**Figure 9.34**). The Text Import Wizard can import virtually any consistently delimited file, as well as one in which the data consists of fixed-width fields.
- You can also start the Text Import Wizard by choosing File > Import or by clicking the Import icon on the Standard toolbar. Select Text file in the Import dialog box.
- If you use the File > Open command to open a text file, the Text Import Wizard is automatically invoked.
- When data is exported as text from most applications, any formulas contained in the source data are lost. Instead, the *results* are exported. Thus, following the import into Excel, you may need to reconstruct the formulas in the worksheet.
- Excel can also open some types of files in their native format, such as FileMaker Pro databases and AppleWorks worksheets. When available as an option, this is the preferred method of importing data into Excel.

  For a list of compatible file types, choose File > Open, and then click the Enable pop-up menu in the Open dialog box (**Figure 9.35**).

Working with Workbooks

As mentioned earlier in this chapter, an Excel file is a called a *workbook*. By default, every workbook contains the number of *worksheets* (or *sheets*) specified in the General section of Preferences (**Figure 9.36**). As you'll learn in this section, you can add more sheets to a workbook as needed and delete unnecessary ones, switch from one sheet to another, rename sheets, reference data in any sheet from any other sheet, and consolidate multiple sheets.

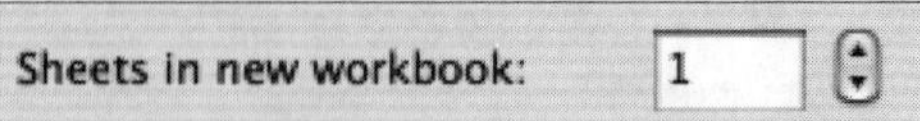

Figure 9.36 Specify the number of sheets in each new workbook by choosing Excel > Preferences and clicking the General icon in the Excel Preferences window.

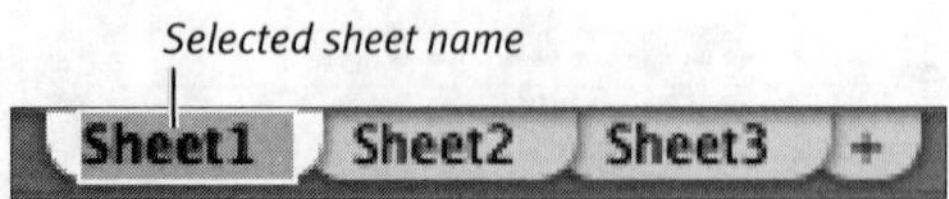

Figure 9.37 Double-click a sheet name to select it for renaming.

Naming sheets

You can replace the default sheet names (Sheet1, Sheet2, and so on) with descriptive names, such as Advertising, July, Personnel, or Budget Summary.

To name or rename a sheet:

1. At the bottom of the workbook window, double-click the tab of the sheet you want to rename.

   The sheet name is selected (**Figure 9.37**).
2. Type a new sheet name or edit the current name.
3. To complete the process, click anywhere else in the sheet or press Return or Enter.

   Sheet names can be a maximum of 31 characters long and may include spaces.

✔ Tips

- To select a sheet's name for editing or renaming, you can also choose Format > Sheet > Rename. Or you can Control-click the tab and choose Rename from the pop-up menu. However, since double-clicking a tab serves the same purpose (selecting the tab name for editing), it's unlikely that you'll ever use these alternate procedures.
- Because sheet names are also used in formulas to indicate where a given cell or range is located, you may want to keep the names relatively short. For instance, `=Income!A17-Expenses!A17` is preferable to `='Income Statement FY 2008'!A17-'Expense Items FY 2008'!A17`.
- If you edit sheet names, the names that appear in any affected formulas are automatically changed to match.
- In a formula, any sheet name that contains a space must be surrounded by single quotes, such as `'Income Statement'`.

Figure 9.39 Click the + icon to add a new sheet to the workbook.

Switching and rearranging sheets

Many of your workbooks will consist of only one sheet (or only one that you're using). But when you're using multiple sheets, it's simple to switch from one to another or to change their order.

To change the active sheet:

- At the bottom of the workbook window (**Figure 9.38**, page bottom), click the tab of the sheet you want to display.
  The selected sheet becomes active.

To rearrange sheets:

- Drag a sheet tab left or right to a new position in the sheet tabs.

✔ Tip

- If the sheet's tab isn't visible, click the arrow icons to scroll through the tabs.

Adding and deleting sheets

There are several ways to add or delete sheets.

To add a sheet:

- *Do one of the following:*
  - Click the Insert Sheet (+) icon to the right of the sheet tabs (**Figure 9.39**).
  - Choose Insert > Sheet > Blank Sheet.
  - Control-click a sheet tab and choose Insert from the pop-up menu. In the Project Gallery window, select the Blank Sheet thumbnail. Click Open.

  A blank sheet is added to the workbook.

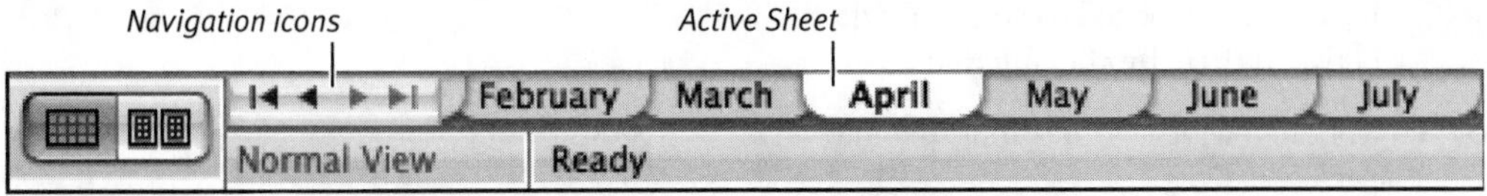

Figure 9.38 To make a different sheet active, click its tab at the bottom of the document window.

To delete a sheet:

- To delete an unwanted sheet, make the sheet active and choose Edit > Delete Sheet. Or [Control]-click the sheet's tab and choose Delete from the pop-up menu.

✔ Tip

- Although you can keep adding sheets to a single workbook, it's more usual to create a new workbook for each new project.

Viewing multiple sheets

Sometimes you may want to view several sheets at the same time. You can accomplish this by opening each sheet in a separate window and then arranging the windows so you can see them all.

To view multiple sheets simultaneously:

1. Choose Window > New Window.

   A copy of the workbook opens in a new window. Repeat for additional copies.

2. In each copy, click the tab of the sheet you want to view.

3. Choose Window > Arrange.

   The Arrange Windows dialog box appears (**Figure 9.40**).

4. Select a window arrangement and click OK.
   - **Tiled.** Arrange windows so that all are visible and as large as possible (**Figure 9.41**).
   - **Horizontal, Vertical.** Arrange windows in horizontal or vertical strips.
   - **Cascade.** Display all windows at full size, cascading downward to the right. Each window overlaps the next, leaving an edge exposed so you can switch between them by clicking that edge.

5. To work in a window, click in it to make it active.

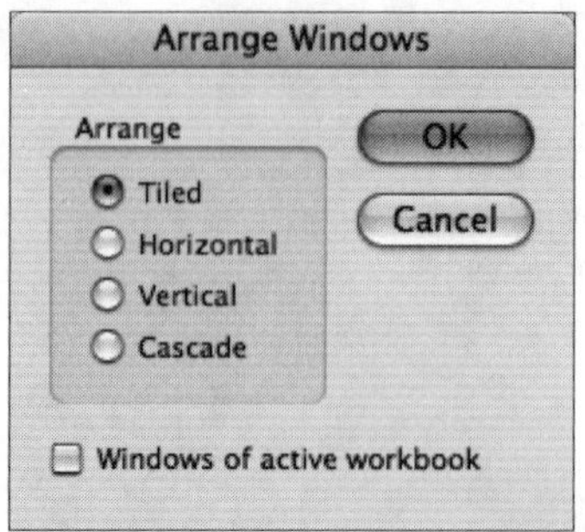

Figure 9.40 Select an arrangement option and click OK.

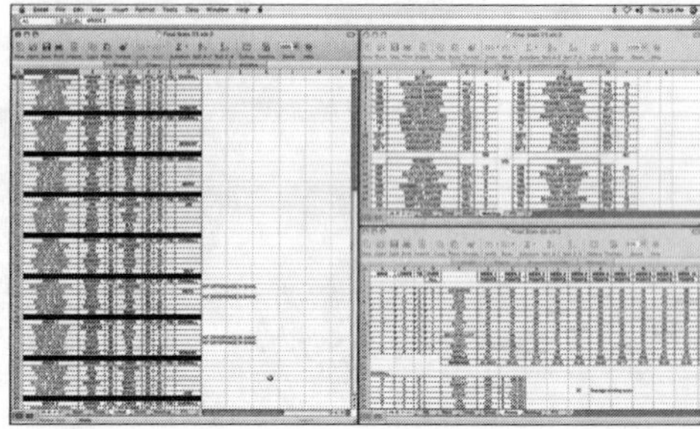

Figure 9.41 This example shows three tiled windows.

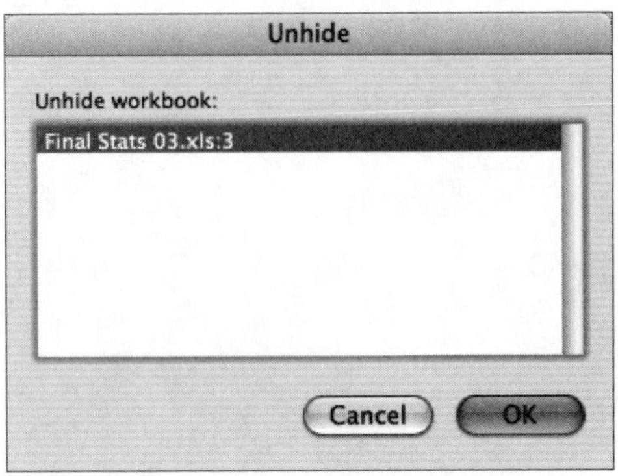

Figure 9.42 Select a window to unhide and click OK.

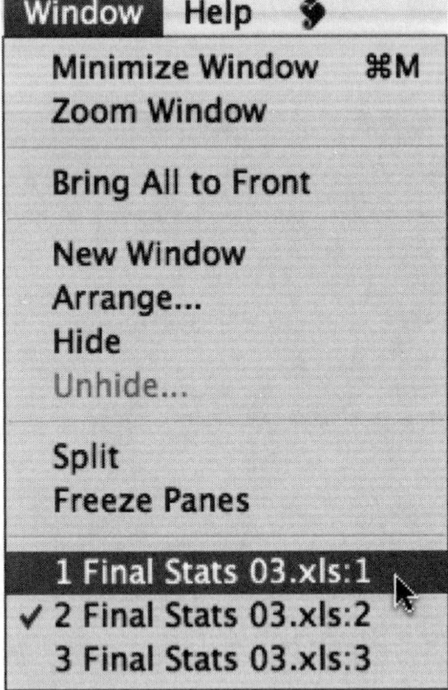

Figure 9.43 Any open workbook or copy can be made active by choosing its name from the Window menu.

✔ Tips

- Each copy name has a number appended to it, such as Sales:1, Sales:2, and Sales:3.
- You can also use the Window arrangement commands to arrange *different* open workbooks—not just multiple copies of a single workbook.
- To make the active workbook fill the screen, click the zoom icon (the green plus) in its title bar. Click the zoom icon again to restore the window to its previous size and screen position.
- To temporarily hide the active window, *do one of the following:*
  - ▲ Click the minimize icon (the yellow minus) in the title bar, double-click the title bar, choose Window > Minimize Window, or press ⌘M. The window moves to the Dock.
  - ▲ Choose Window > Hide.

  To restore a minimized window, click its icon in the Dock. To restore a window that was hidden with the Hide command, choose Window > Unhide. In the Unhide dialog box (**Figure 9.42**), select the window that you want to reveal and click OK.
- If one or more Excel windows are covered by other programs' windows, you can reveal them by choosing Window > Bring All to Front.
- The names of all open workbooks and copies are listed at the bottom of the Window menu (**Figure 9.43**). You can make any open workbook or copy active by choosing its name from this menu.

Referring to data on other sheets

Formulas aren't restricted to cell references to the current worksheet. They can also reference data from other sheets.

To reference another sheet:

1. Click the destination cell for the formula. Type an equal sign (=) to start the formula.
2. As necessary within the formula, you can refer to a cell or range in another sheet by doing either of the following:
   - ▲ Switch to the appropriate sheet, and select the cell or range.
   - ▲ Type the cell reference in the form: *sheet_name!range*
     `August!C17`, for example.
3. If it isn't finished, continue building the formula. To add references to other sheets, repeat Step 2. To complete the formula, press Return or Enter.

   For a complete discussion of formulas, see Chapter 11.

✔ Tips

- If there are named ranges in other sheets, you can enter their names in formulas without worrying about which sheet the data is on. Excel will find the range on any sheet in the current workbook. (See "Naming Cell Ranges" in this chapter.)
- It's a good idea to display the formula bar while constructing or editing formulas that reference other sheets. Doing so ensures that you can always see the current state of the formula (**Figure 9.44**). Choose View > Formula Bar.

Figure 9.44 The formula bar shows references to other sheets.

Consolidating worksheets

When various sheets of a workbook contain data that you want to summarize, you can total or perform other calculations across those sheets, placing the results in a *consolidation sheet.* Record keeping workbooks are often organized in a way that makes them amenable to such calculations. For example, a bookkeeping workbook might have a separate worksheet for each month of the year, followed by a single sheet in which totals and averages across all sheets are displayed.

Depending on how the data on your sheets is organized, you can consolidate manually (by position) or using the Consolidate dialog box:

- ▲ **Manually (by position).** The data to be consolidated must be identically organized on each sheet. That is, to consolidate a monthly sales total, it must be located in the same cell (B72, for example) on *every* sheet. You must create the formula for each cell or range that you want to consolidate.
- ▲ **Consolidate dialog box.** There is no requirement that the sheets be identically organized. Rather than creating the formulas manually, you select a function (such as Average) and the specific cell or range to be used from each sheet.

The following examples show how these two consolidation techniques work.

To manually consolidate (by position):

1. Create or select a sheet for the consolidation. On that sheet, click the destination cell for the formula. Type an equal sign (=) to begin the formula.
2. Enter a supported function, followed by an open parenthesis (**Figure 9.45**).
   Supported functions include AVERAGE, AVERAGEA, COUNT, COUNTA, MAX, MAXA, MIN, MINA, PRODUCT, STDEV, STDEVA, STDEVP, STDEVPA, SUM, VAR, VARA, VARP, and VARPA.
3. Click the tab of the first sheet in the consecutive set of sheets. Select the cell or range to include in the formula.
4. Hold down Shift and click the tab of the last consecutive sheet that you want to include in the calculation.
   This assumes, of course, that each sheet in the set contains the same data in the selected cell or range.
5. Press Return or Enter to complete the formula.
   Click the formula cell in the consolidation sheet to view the formula (**Figure 9.46**) or examine it in the formula bar.

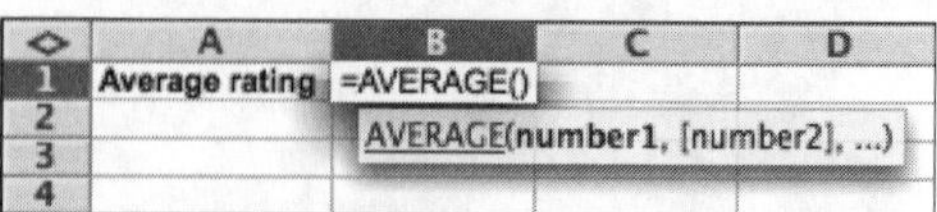

Figure 9.45 Start the formula as you normally do, but be sure to restrict it to the supported functions.

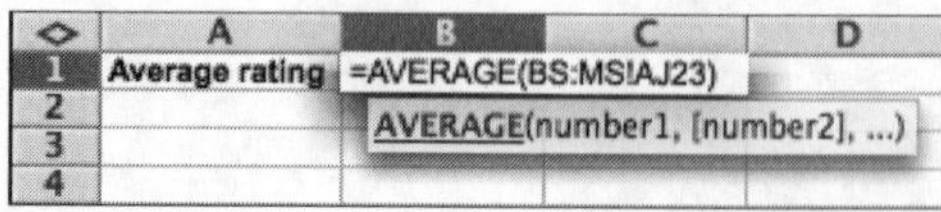

Figure 9.46 Double-click the cell to see the formula. (Or to view it in the formula bar, single-click the cell.)

WORKING WITH WORKBOOKS

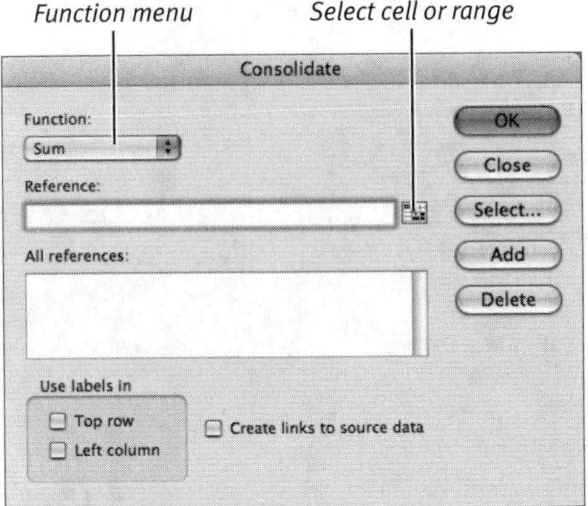

Figure 9.47 You can use the Consolidate dialog box to guide the creation of the necessary formulas.

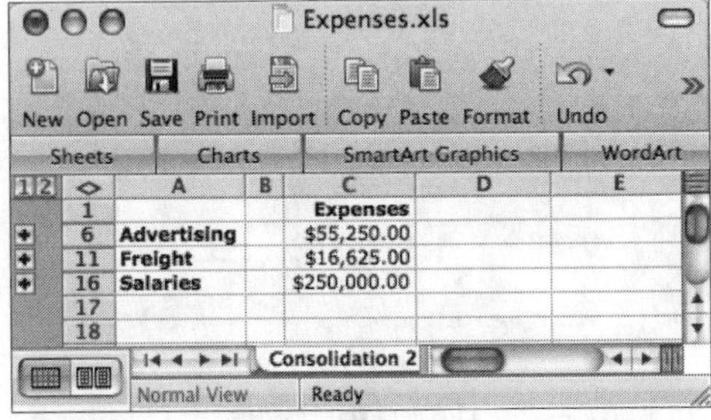

Figure 9.48 This sheet uses a SUM consolidation formula to total expenses across monthly worksheets.

To create a consolidation formula using the Consolidate dialog box:

1. Click the upper-left cell of the range in the worksheet where you want to consolidate the data.
2. Choose Data > Consolidate.

   The Consolidate dialog box appears (**Figure 9.47**).
3. Choose a function from the drop-down Function menu.
4. For each sheet that you want to include in the consolidation, enter a reference to the pertinent cell(s) in the Reference text box.

   You can type the reference (or a range name), manually click the cell(s), or click the selection icon.
5. After entering each reference, click Add.

   The new reference is added to the list in the All references box.
6. *Optional:* If you're identifying ranges by column or row headings, click the appropriate radio button in the Use labels in section of the dialog box.
7. *Optional:* To maintain a link between the referenced cells and the consolidation formula, click the Create links to source data check box.

   Doing so will cause the consolidation formula to automatically update if any of the referenced cells change. Do *not* check this box if you want the current result to remain unchanged.
8. Click OK.

   The consolidated data appears in the destination cell of the consolidation sheet (**Figure 9.48**).

✔ Tips

- The Consolidate dialog box retains the most recently used references. To create additional formulas that reference *other* cells, you'll have to delete or edit the entries in the All references box.
- To apply a different function to the *same* references, select a new destination cell, choose the new function, and click OK.

Printing Worksheets and Workbooks

Excel provides tools and options to ensure that you can print exactly what you want. For example, page breaks for each sheet are always visible onscreen. In Page Layout View, breaks are shown as new pages. In Normal View, they're indicated by dashed lines.

Printing is a two-step process: setting Page Setup options and printing the material.

To view or set Page Setup options:

1. Choose File > Page Setup.
   Excel's Page Setup dialog box appears.
2. On the Page tab of the Page Setup dialog box (**Figure 9.49**), *do any of the following:*
   - ▲ **Printer.** Click the Options button to specify a printer to use in the Mac OS X Page Setup dialog box (**Figure 9.50**).
   - ▲ **Orientation.** Click the Portrait or Landscape radio button. Changing the orientation changes the amount of material that will fit per page, as well as where page breaks will occur.
   - ▲ **Scaling.** To make the printout easier to read or to squeeze additional data onto each page, change one of these settings (**Figure 9.51**).
   - ▲ **First page number.** If this printout is the continuation of another printout or it will be inserted into another numbered publication, enter a starting number.
   - ▲ **Print quality.** You can choose a quality setting from this drop-down menu.
3. On the Margins tab of the Page Setup dialog box, you can change the page margins and indicate whether you want to center the output on each printed page.

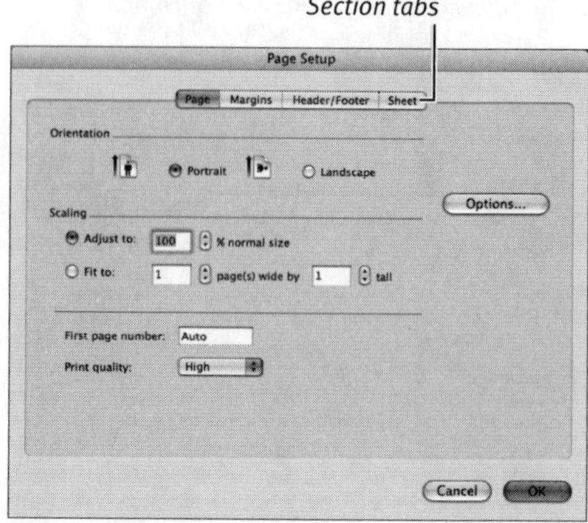

Figure 9.49 The Page tab of Excel's Page Setup dialog box.

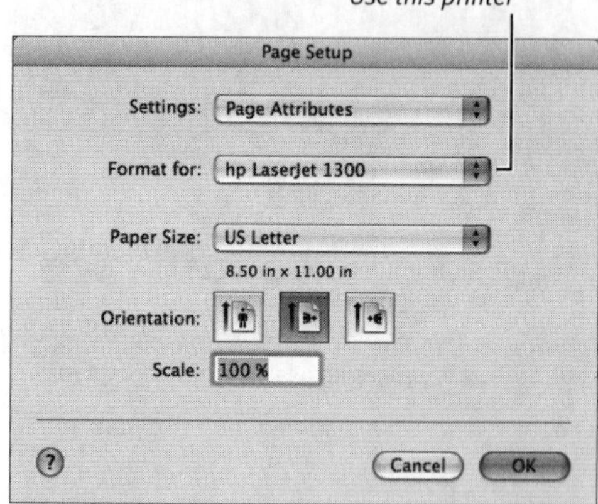

Figure 9.50 The printer you choose can affect other print settings, such as margins and quality.

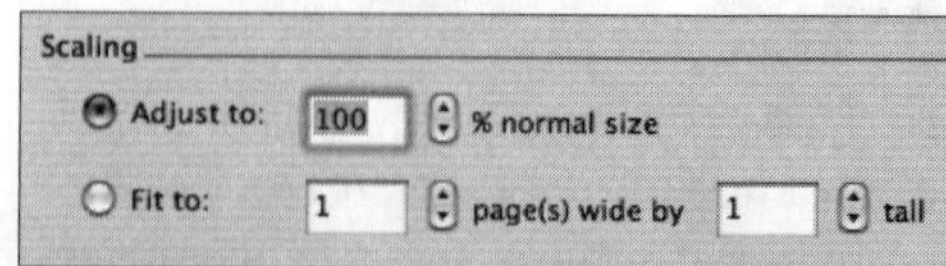

Figure 9.51 You can set a magnification/reduction percentage (top) or force the printout to scale as needed to fit a specific number of pages (bottom).

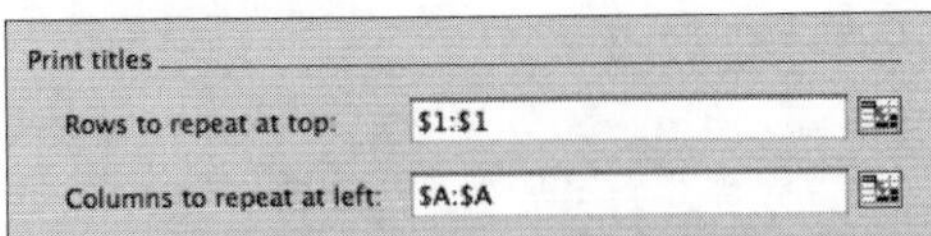

Figure 9.52 On the worksheet, select the row and column headings that will repeat on each page. In this example, material in row 1 and column A will repeat.

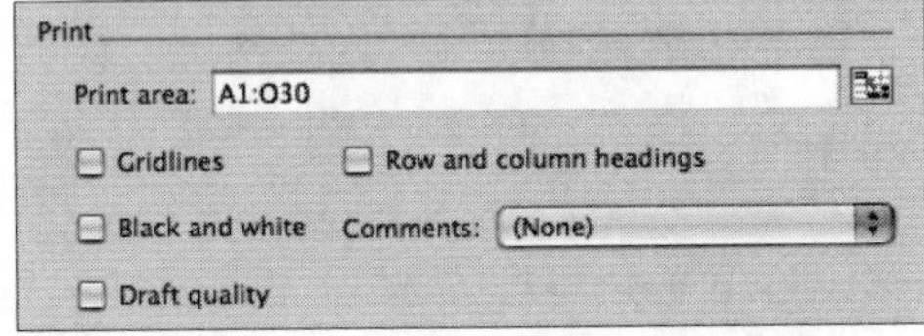

Figure 9.53 To customize the printout, set and select options in the Print section of the Sheet tab.

4. To specify a header or footer to print on each page, click the Header/Footer tab of the Page Setup dialog box. Select options from the Header and/or Footer drop-down lists.
5. To set display options for the printout, click the Sheet tab. *Do any of the following:*
   - ▲ **Print titles.** To repeat row and/or column headings on each page of the printout (making it easier to interpret), specify the rows and/or columns that contain headings (**Figure 9.52**).
   - ▲ **Print.** You can set these display options (**Figure 9.53**): *Print area* (select or type the range to print), *Gridlines* (print the dotted lines that surround cells), *Black and white* (ignore color), *Draft quality* (print at reduced quality and ignore graphics, such as charts), *Row and column headings* (print the row numbers and column letters), *Comments* (include cell comments in the printout).
6. When you're done examining and changing Page Setup settings, click OK.

To print a selected range, worksheet, or workbook:

1. *Optional:* To print only part of the active worksheet, select the area. If you intend to print an entire worksheet, the whole workbook, or a saved print area, you can skip this step.

   If you want to save the selection as the sheet's new *print area* (so it will be remembered the next time you print), choose File > Print Area > Set Print Area.
2. Choose File > Print (⌘P).

   The Print dialog box appears, open to the Copies & Pages section.

continues on next page

Printing Worksheets and Workbooks

3. Select a printer from the Printer drop-down list (**Figure 9.54**).
4. Specify the number of copies and range of pages to print.
5. Click a radio button (Selection, Active Sheets, or Entire Workbook) to specify the Print What setting.
6. *Optional:* The Quick Preview area shows the pages that will be printed, given the current printer and the Print and Page Setup settings. Click the arrow icons beneath the Quick Preview to view the pages, margins, and page breaks.
7. Ensure that the chosen printer is on. Click Print.

   The print job is routed to the printer.

✔ Tips

- To print immediately using the current settings (bypassing the Print dialog box), click the Print toolbar icon.
- Some Print and Page Setup options can be set in more than one place. For example, you can select a printer by clicking Options in the Page Setup dialog box or by choosing it in the Print dialog box. You can preselect the print range or set it on the Sheet tab of the Page Setup dialog box.
- The File and View menus no longer contain Print Preview-related commands. To preview your output, you can do any of the following:
  - ▲ Switch to Page Layout View.
  - ▲ In the Print dialog box, examine the Quick Preview box.
  - ▲ In the Print dialog box, click the Preview button to create a PDF preview that will open in Apple's Preview.

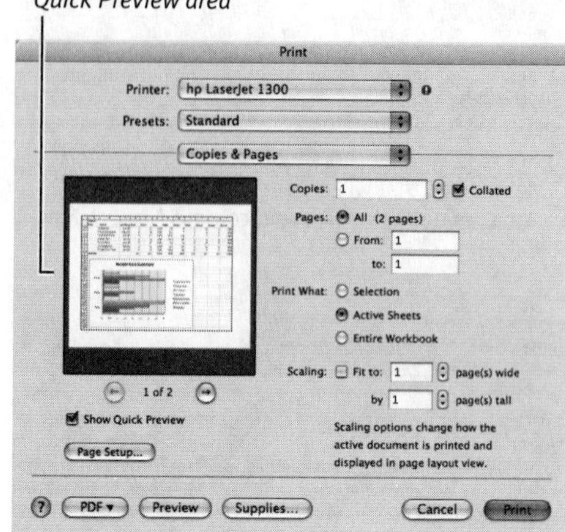

Figure 9.54 Set options in the Print dialog box.

10

MODIFYING WORKSHEETS

Raw data typed in a monospaced font into fixed-width columns is satisfactory for many worksheets, but it isn't fine for *all* worksheets. Excel provides a variety of formatting tools and procedures that you can apply to dress up any worksheet. With minimal effort, you can turn the ordinary into presentation-quality material.

In addition to formatting a sheet, you can alter its structure by changing the widths and heights of selected columns and rows; adding or deleting rows, columns, and cells; and moving or copying data to different areas of the sheet.

Setting Column and Row Sizes

You can change the width of selected columns and the height of selected rows as your data dictates. This is particularly useful when a lengthy text string spills into the adjacent columns (column width), for instance.

To manually adjust a column's width:

1. Move the pointer over the right edge of the column's heading.

   The pointer changes to a double arrow (**Figure 10.1**).

2. Click and drag to the right or left (**Figure 10.2**).

   As you drag, a ScreenTip appears, showing the current width of the column in characters (approximate) and in the default unit of measurement.

3. Release the mouse button to complete the resizing.

4. Repeat Steps 1–3 until the column is the desired width.

To manually adjust a row's height:

1. Move the pointer over the bottom edge of the row.

   The pointer changes to a double arrow.

2. Click and drag up or down.

   As you drag, a ScreenTip appears, showing the current height of the row in points and the default unit of measurement. (There are 72 points per inch.)

3. Release the mouse button to complete the procedure.

4. Repeat Steps 1–3 until the row is the desired height.

Pointer

C	D
Payee	Amount
St. Vincent dePa	$450.00
US Treasury	$852.00
Girl Scouts	$6.00
AZ Dept. of Rev	$415.00
US Treasury	$2,715.00
US Treasury	$1,576.00
U. of Minnesota	$19.73
US Treasury	$1,576.00
WAHS	$95.00
WAHS	$60.00
US Treasury	$1,576.00
US Treasury	$1,576.00

Figure 10.1 Move the pointer over the right edge of the column header. It changes to a double arrow.

Resizing column C

Width: 14.14 (1.44 inches) Charts

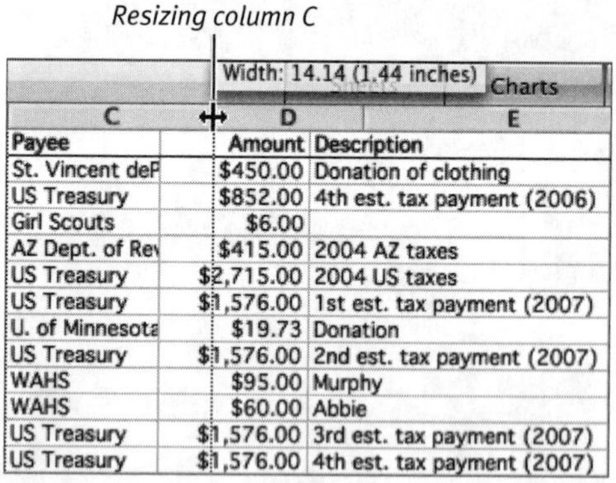

C	D	E
Payee	Amount	Description
St. Vincent deP	$450.00	Donation of clothing
US Treasury	$852.00	4th est. tax payment (2006)
Girl Scouts	$6.00	
AZ Dept. of Rev	$415.00	2004 AZ taxes
US Treasury	$2,715.00	2004 US taxes
US Treasury	$1,576.00	1st est. tax payment (2007)
U. of Minnesota	$19.73	Donation
US Treasury	$1,576.00	2nd est. tax payment (2007)
WAHS	$95.00	Murphy
WAHS	$60.00	Abbie
US Treasury	$1,576.00	3rd est. tax payment (2007)
US Treasury	$1,576.00	4th est. tax payment (2007)

Figure 10.2 Drag to the right or left to set a new column width.

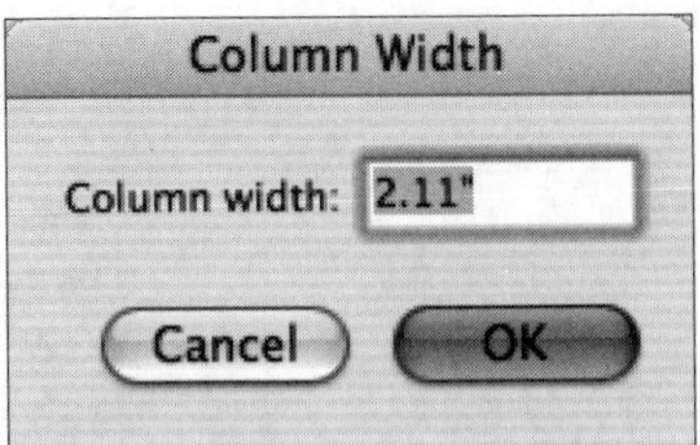

Figure 10.3 Use the Column Width (or Row Height) dialog box to enter a precise width or height.

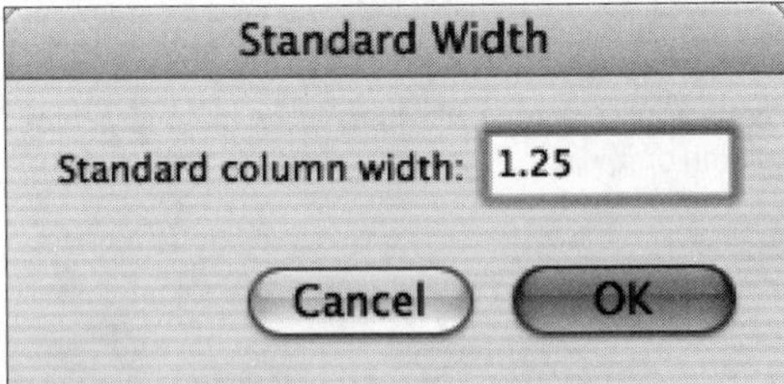

Figure 10.4 You can define a new default column width that will automatically be applied to blank and new columns.

✔ Tips

- To adjust a column width or row height to automatically accommodate the contents (the widest or highest entry, respectively), double-click the column heading's right border or the row heading's bottom border.
- To set *multiple* columns or rows to the same width or height, select the columns or rows by dragging across their headings. Then drag the edge of any selected column or row heading. All selected columns or rows will change uniformly.
- You can also set width or height by choosing commands from the Format menu:
  - To set a column width to the width required to fully display the longest text string, click the column heading and choose Format > Column > AutoFit Selection. To set the column width to that of a specific cell, select the cell and choose the same command.
  - To set the width or height for selected columns or rows, choose Format > Column > Width or Format > Row > Height. In the dialog box that appears (**Figure 10.3**), enter the new size (in the default measurement unit), and click OK.
  - To set a new default column width for the worksheet, choose Format > Column > Standard Width, enter the new width (**Figure 10.4**), and click OK.

Reorganizing a Worksheet

You can insert and delete rows, columns, and cells, as well as copy or move data from one area of a worksheet to another.

Inserting and deleting columns and rows

With a single command, you can insert or delete one or more multiple rows or columns.

To insert new rows or columns:

1. *Do one of the following:*
   - ▲ To insert a single row or column, select any cell in the row or column where you'd like the new row or column to appear (**Figure 10.5**).
   - ▲ To insert multiple rows or columns, select contiguous cells where you'd like the new rows or columns to appear.
2. Choose Insert > Rows or Insert > Columns.

   The new rows or columns appear. The worksheet adjusts to accommodate them.

To delete rows or columns:

1. *Do one of the following:*
   - ▲ To delete a single row or column, select any cell in the row or column you want to delete.
   - ▲ To delete multiple rows or columns, select contiguous cells in the rows or columns you want to delete.
2. Choose Edit > Delete.

   The Delete dialog box appears (**Figure 10.6**).
3. As appropriate, select Entire row or Entire column.
4. Click OK.

   The worksheet adjusts to accommodate the deleted row(s) or column(s).

Selected cell

◇	A	B
1	Date	Check #
2	1/20/04	Disc
3	1/20/04	Disc
4	2/12/04	Cash
5	2/12/04	3033
6	4/11/04	3051
7	4/11/04	
8	4/11/04	3052
9	6/14/04	
10		

Figure 10.5 Click the cell where you want to insert the column or row.

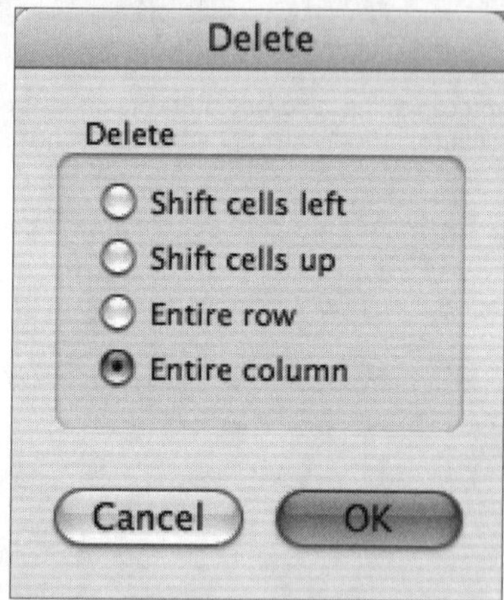

Figure 10.6 Indicate whether you'd like to delete the entire row or the entire column.

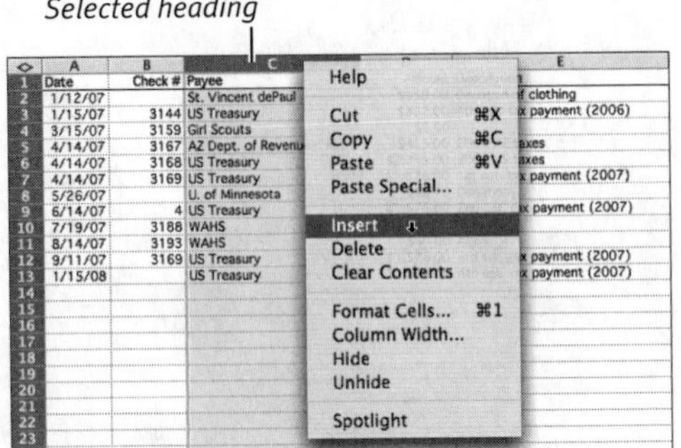

Figure 10.7 Another way to insert or delete rows or columns is to select one or more headings, Control-click one, and choose Insert or Delete from the pop-up menu that appears.

✔ Tips

- Rather than selecting one or more cells prior to inserting rows or columns, you may find it less confusing to select row or column *headings*.
- Although it's sufficient to select only cells prior to deleting rows or columns, it's more expedient to select *entire* rows or columns by clicking their heading. When you choose Edit > Delete, the selected rows or columns are instantly deleted—without displaying the Delete dialog box.
- You can also Control-click a column or row heading, and choose Insert or Delete from the pop-up menu (**Figure 10.7**). You can use this technique for multiple insertions and deletions, too. Simply select more than one row or column before you Control-click one of them.

Inserting and deleting cells

When you insert or delete one or more cells, Excel needs to know how to adjust the data in adjacent cells. You indicate your choice in either the Insert or Delete dialog box.

To insert blank cells:

1. Select a cell or a contiguous group of cells where you want to insert empty cells.
2. *Do one of the following:*
   - Choose Insert > Cells.
   - Control-click one of the selected cells, and choose Insert from the pop-up menu that appears.

   The Insert dialog box appears (**Figure 10.8**).
3. Select either Shift cells right or Shift cells down (referring to how the worksheet will be adjusted following the insertion).
4. Click OK.

   New, blank cells appear to replace the selected cells. Existing affected cells are shifted down or to the right, as directed.

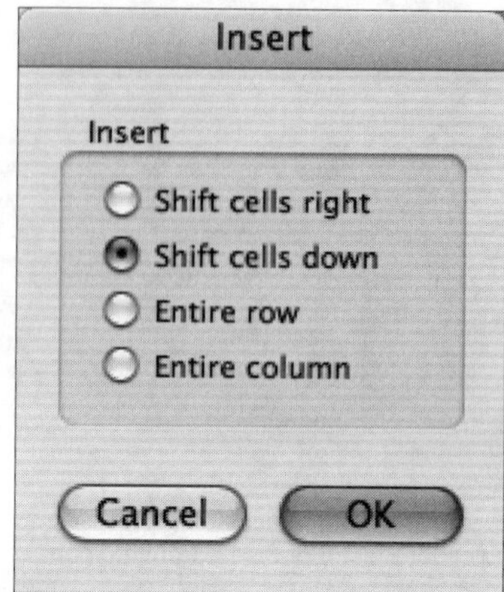

Figure 10.8 Select a Shift option to apply to affected areas of the worksheet following a cell insertion.

To delete selected cells:

1. Select a cell or a contiguous group of cells that you want to delete.
2. *Do one of the following:*
   - Choose Edit > Delete.
   - Control-click one of the selected cells, and choose Delete from the pop-up menu that appears.

   The Delete dialog box appears (see Figure 10.6).
3. Select Shift cells left or Shift cells up.
4. Click OK.

   The worksheet adjusts to fill in the hole left by the deleted cell(s).

✔ Tips

- The need to insert or delete individual cells is a rare occurrence for most users. One situation in which you may need to do this is when you notice you've left out a single piece of data in a lengthy record (row) or that you've accidentally duplicated a cell's data in the next cell.
- To clear a cell's contents rather than deleting the cell, press Delete or choose a command from the Edit > Clear submenu.

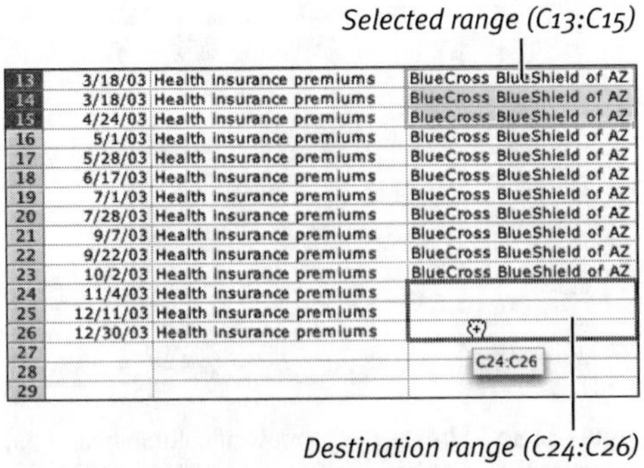

Selected range (C13:C15)

Destination range (C24:C26)

Figure 10.9 A plus appears in the hand pointer to show that Excel is copying rather than moving the range.

Copying and moving data

Excel's support of *drag and drop* makes it especially easy to move or copy data.

A drag-and-drop copy is a nondestructive procedure; the original cells remain unaltered. A drag-and-drop move, on the other hand, *is* a destructive procedure. It is the same as performing a Cut and then a Paste; that is, the contents of the original cells are deleted.

To move or copy a cell range:

1. Select a cell range to move or copy.
2. Move the pointer over the edge of the range. It becomes an open hand.
3. *Do one of the following:*
   - ▲ To move the cells, drag them to the destination.
   - ▲ To copy the cells, press Option while dragging to the destination. A plus sign (+) appears inside the hand pointer to indicate that you're copying the data rather than moving it (**Figure 10.9**).

   A yellow ScreenTip appears to show the destination range.
4. Release the mouse button to copy or move the cell range to the new location.

✔ Tip

- When copying or moving data, make sure that the destination range is empty. Copied or moved data always replaces the data (if any) in the destination range.

Working with Large Sheets

To simplify the process of working with large worksheets, you can freeze columns and/or rows, as well as split a sheet into multiple panes. Freezing columns and rows prevents their data from moving offscreen when you scroll. For example, you could freeze row 1 to ensure that its column headings are always visible. Splitting a sheet into multiple panes enables you to display and independently scroll through two or four worksheet regions. You can split a sheet horizontally, vertically, or in both directions.

To freeze column and/or row headings:

1. *Do one of the following* (**Figure 10.10**):
   - ▲ To freeze only rows, click the row heading that is immediately beneath the rows you want to freeze.
   - ▲ To freeze only columns, click the column heading that is immediately to the right of the columns you want to freeze.
   - ▲ To freeze both rows and columns, select the cell immediately below and to the right of the rows and columns you want to freeze.
2. Choose Window > Freeze Panes.

   Gray lines appear in the worksheet to mark the frozen areas (**Figure 10.11**).

✓ Tips

- To unfreeze the panes, choose Window > Unfreeze Panes.
- You cannot freeze panes when in Page Layout View. If they're currently frozen, they will be unfrozen if you switch to Page Layout View.
- When working with frozen panes, pressing Control Home selects the cell in the upper-left corner of the unfrozen data range rather than cell A1.

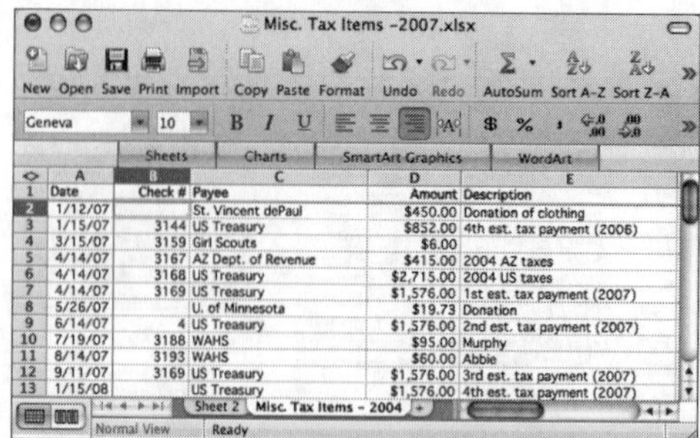

Figure 10.10 To freeze the top row of column headings, select row 2. To freeze the Date column (A), select column B. To freeze both, select cell B2.

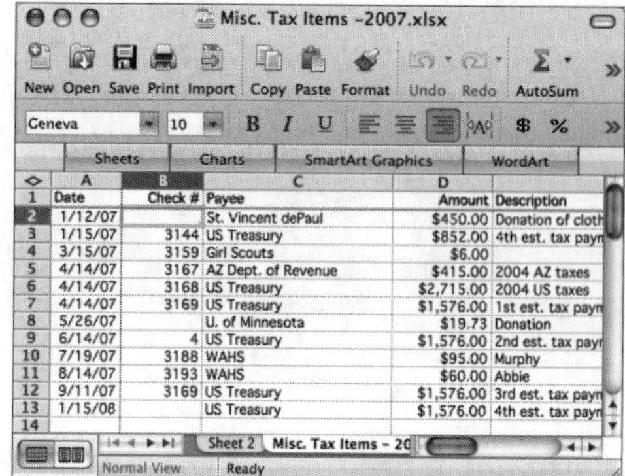

Figure 10.11 Both row 1 and column A are frozen. No matter which direction you scroll, row 1 and column A will remain onscreen.

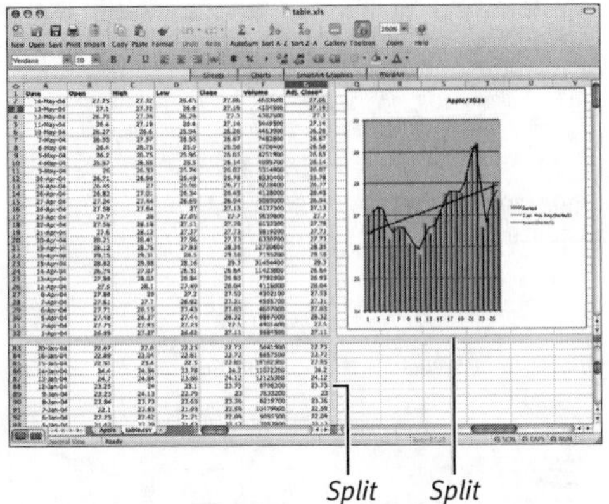

Figure 10.12 A worksheet can be split into two or four panes.

WordArt

F	G
Volume	Adj. Close*
4603600	27.06
4104500	27.19
4382500	27.3
5449500	27.14
4463900	26.28
7482800	26.67
4706400	26.58
4251900	26.65
4999700	26.14
5314900	26.07
8330400	25.78
8228400	26.77
4128000	26.45
5069000	26.94
4127300	27.13
5639800	27.7
6153300	27.78
5819200	27.73

Horizontal split box

Vertical split box

Figure 10.13 To manually create a split, click and drag a split box to the desired position.

To automatically split a worksheet into four panes:

1. Click the cell that you want to become the upper-left corner of the bottom-right pane.
2. Choose Window > Split.
   The worksheet is split into four panes (**Figure 10.12**).

To manually split a worksheet into multiple panes:

1. Decide whether you want to split the worksheet into two vertical panes, two horizontal panes, or four panes.
2. Each sheet has two split boxes—found at the top of the vertical scroll bar and the right end of the horizontal scroll bar (**Figure 10.13**). *Do any of the following:*
   - ▲ Drag the horizontal split box downward to split the worksheet into two horizontal panes.
   - ▲ Drag the vertical split box to the left to split the worksheet into two vertical panes.

   A ghost of the split bar appears as you drag.
3. Release the mouse button when the split bar is positioned correctly.

✔ Tips

- To adjust any split, click and drag its split bar or split box to a new position.
- To remove all splits, choose Window > Remove Split. To remove an individual split, drag its split bar or box off the right edge or top edge of the worksheet.

Worksheet Formatting

The remainder of this chapter discusses ways that you can make your worksheets more attractive and readable by applying formatting and adding objects and pictures.

Automatic range formatting

The easiest way to make a sheet presentable is to apply an AutoFormat. An AutoFormat creates a complete look for a range of cells by setting the font, text alignment, number formatting, borders, patterns, colors, and so on. Excel offers a variety of AutoFormat styles, each with a different look.

To AutoFormat a range of cells:

1. Select the cell range that you want to format (**Figure 10.14**).
2. Choose Format > AutoFormat.
   The AutoFormat dialog box appears (**Figure 10.15**).
3. Select an AutoFormat style from the scrolling list.
   A sample of the selected format appears in the center of the dialog box.
4. *Optional:* To select the specific formatting attributes that will be applied, click the Options button.
5. Click OK.
   The AutoFormat style is applied to the selected range (**Figure 10.16**).

✔ Tips

- To remove an AutoFormat style immediately after applying it, choose Edit > Undo (⌘Z) or click the Undo toolbar icon.
- To remove an AutoFormat style later, select the range, follow Steps 2 and 3, and select None as the AutoFormat style.

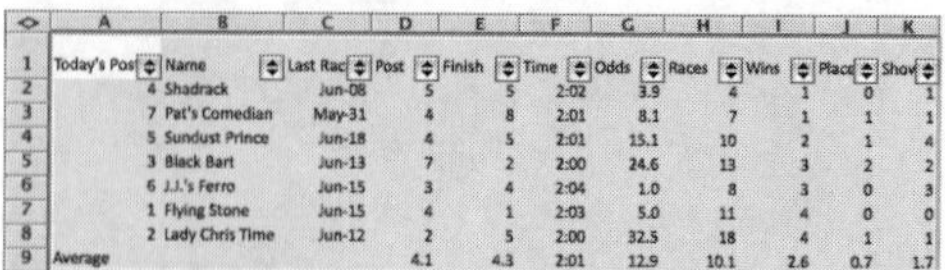

	A	B	C	D	E	F	G	H	I	J	K
1	Today's Pos	Name	Last Rac	Post	Finish	Time	Odds	Races	Wins	Plac	Sho
2	4	Shadrack	Jun-08	5	5	2:02	3.9	4	1	0	1
3	7	Pat's Comedian	May-31	4	8	2:01	8.1	7	1	1	1
4	5	Sundust Prince	Jun-18	4	5	2:01	15.1	10	2	1	4
5	3	Black Bart	Jun-13	7	2	2:00	24.6	13	3	2	2
6	6	J.J.'s Ferro	Jun-15	3	4	2:04	1.0	8	3	0	3
7	1	Flying Stone	Jun-15	4	1	2:03	5.0	11	4	0	0
8	2	Lady Chris Time	Jun-12	2	5	2:00	32.5	18	4	1	1
9	Average			4.1	4.3	2:01	12.9	10.1	2.6	0.7	1.7

Figure 10.14 Select the range to be formatted (in this instance, a list).

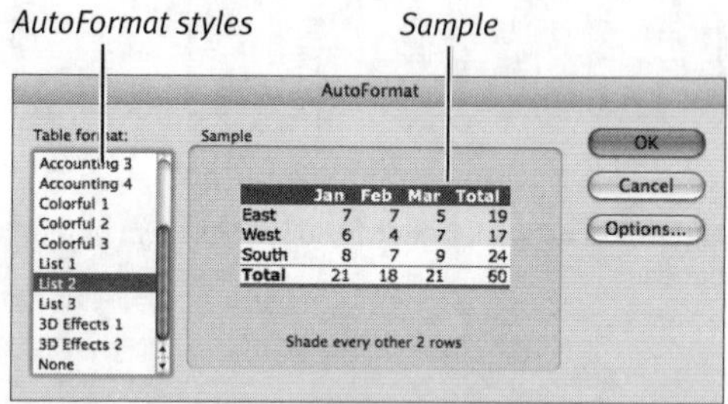

Figure 10.15 Select an AutoFormat style from the scrolling list.

	A	B	C	D	E
1	Today's Pos	Name	Last Race	Post	Finish
2	4	Shadrack	Jun-08	5	5
3	7	Pat's Comedian	May-31	4	8
4	5	Sundust Prince	Jun-18	4	5
5	3	Black Bart	Jun-13	7	2
6	6	J.J.'s Ferro	Jun-15	3	4
7	1	Flying Stone	Jun-15	4	1
8	2	Lady Chris Time	Jun-12	2	5
9	Average			4.1	4.3

Figure 10.16 This is the list after the AutoFormat style has been applied to it.

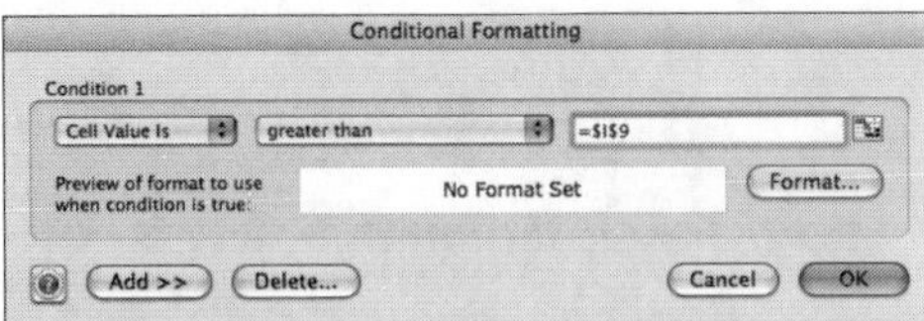

Figure 10.17 Specify a criterion to be satisfied. Click Format to specify the formatting that will be applied.

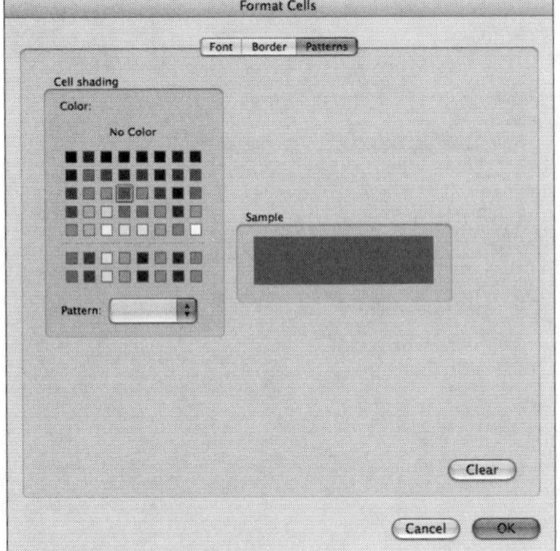

Figure 10.18 Select formatting options from the tabs of the Format Cells dialog box.

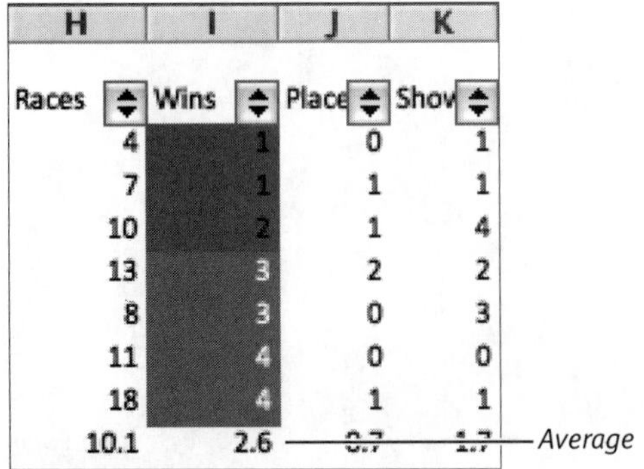

H	I	J	K
Races	Wins	Place	Show
4	1	0	1
7	1	1	1
10	2	1	4
13	3	2	2
8	3	0	3
11	4	0	0
18	4	1	1
10.1	2.6	0.7	1.7

Figure 10.19 In this two-criteria example, numbers above and below the average are formatted with different colored patterns.

Conditional formatting

Using *conditional formatting*, you can apply different formats to selected cells, depending on their value or whether they meet some other criteria. For example, you could specify that sales figures above a certain dollar amount should be colored blue to make them easy to spot.

To apply conditional formatting to cells:

1. Select the cells that you want to format.
2. Choose Format > Conditional Formatting.

   The Conditional Formatting dialog box appears (**Figure 10.17**).
3. From the first drop-down menu, choose one of the following:
   - ▲ **Cell value is.** Create a criterion based on the values in the selected cells.
   - ▲ **Formula is.** Base the criterion on a formula that references other cells and evaluates as true or false, such as =$B2 >= 18. (For information on formulas, see Chapter 11.)

   Complete the criterion by specifying a cell value or formula.
4. Click the Format button.

   The Format Cells dialog box appears (**Figure 10.18**).
5. Click the tabs at the top of the dialog box, and select the combination of font, border, and pattern formats that you want to apply to cells that meet the criterion. Click OK when you are done.
6. Click OK to close the Conditional Formatting dialog box.

   The cells are evaluated and formatted accordingly (**Figure 10.19**).

✔ Tips

- You can set additional criteria (up to a total of four) by clicking the Add button. If more than one criterion is satisfied by a given cell, the formatting specified by the first criterion satisfied is applied.
- You can copy conditional formats—like any other format—to other cells using the Format Painter tool (**Figure 10.20**).

Figure 10.20 Select a conditionally formatted cell, click the Format Painter icon, and paint the cells to which the format should be applied.

Formatting text

Excel offers a wide range of formatting options that you can apply to text. You can specify a font, color, effects (such as boldface or italic), and an alignment to selected cells.

To format text:

1. Select the cell or cells you want to format.
2. *Do any of the following:*
   - ▲ Choose Format > Cells, press ⌘1, or Control-click one of the selected cells and choose Format Cells from the pop-up menu. In the Format Cells dialog box (**Figure 10.21**), set formatting options on the Alignment and Font tabs, and click OK.
   - ▲ Set formatting options by clicking icons on the Formatting toolbar (**Figure 10.22**). If the toolbar isn't visible, you can display it by choosing View > Toolbars > Formatting.

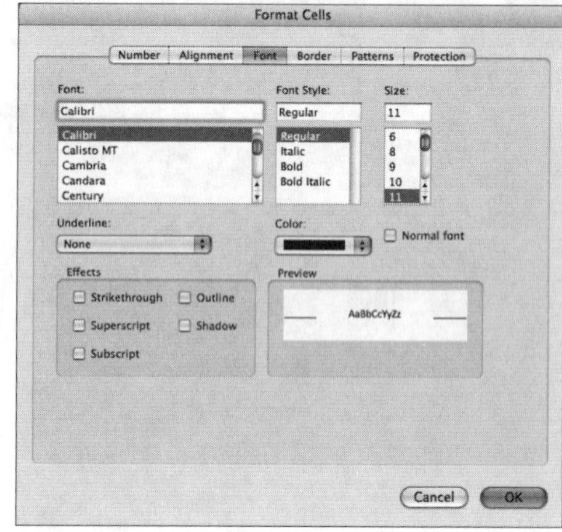

Figure 10.21 Select font and alignment settings from the tabs of the Format Cells dialog box.

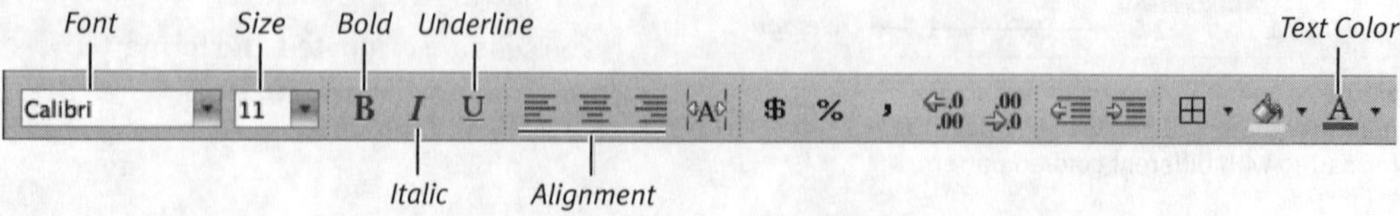

Figure 10.22 Text formatting options can be selected from the Formatting toolbar.

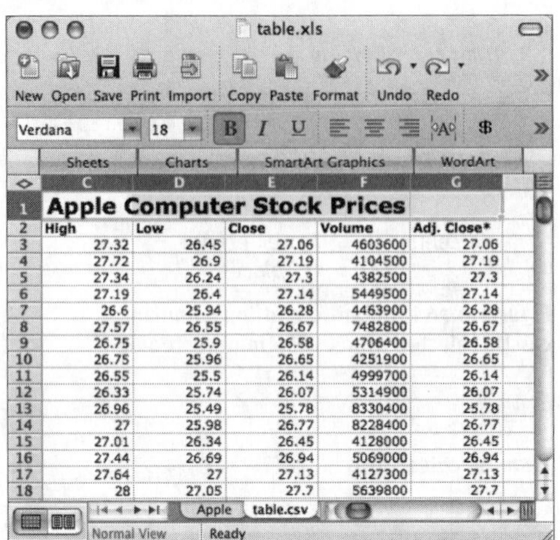

	C	D	E	F	G
1	Apple Computer Stock Prices				
2	High	Low	Close	Volume	Adj. Close*
3	27.32	26.45	27.06	4603600	27.06
4	27.72	26.9	27.19	4104500	27.19
5	27.34	26.24	27.3	4382500	27.3
6	27.19	26.4	27.14	5449500	27.14
7	26.6	25.94	26.28	4463900	26.28
8	27.57	26.55	26.67	7482800	26.67
9	26.75	25.9	26.58	4706400	26.58
10	26.75	25.96	26.65	4251900	26.65
11	26.55	25.5	26.14	4999700	26.14
12	26.33	25.74	26.07	5314900	26.07
13	26.96	25.49	25.78	8330400	25.78
14	27	25.98	26.77	8228400	26.77
15	27.01	26.34	26.45	4128000	26.45
16	27.44	26.69	26.94	5069000	26.94
17	27.64	27	27.13	4127300	27.13
18	28	27.05	27.7	5639800	27.7

Figure 10.23 Select the group of cells within which the text will be centered—in this case, A1:G1.

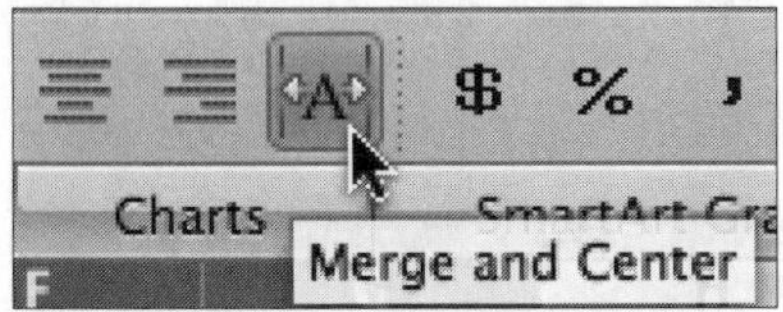

Figure 10.24 After selecting the cells, click the Merge and Center toolbar icon.

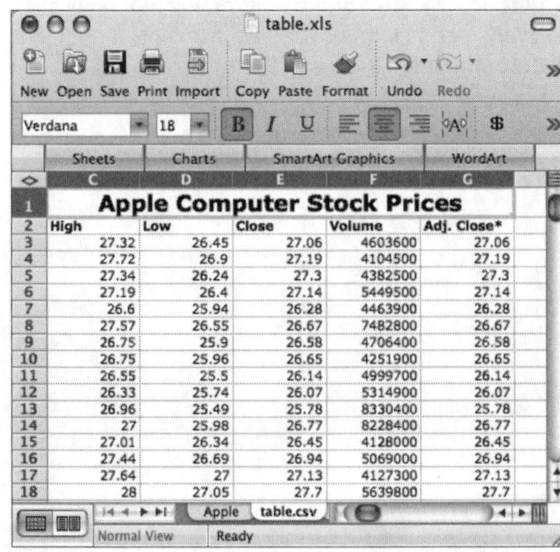

	C	D	E	F	G
1	Apple Computer Stock Prices				
2	High	Low	Close	Volume	Adj. Close*
3	27.32	26.45	27.06	4603600	27.06
4	27.72	26.9	27.19	4104500	27.19
5	27.34	26.24	27.3	4382500	27.3
6	27.19	26.4	27.14	5449500	27.14
7	26.6	25.94	26.28	4463900	26.28
8	27.57	26.55	26.67	7482800	26.67
9	26.75	25.9	26.58	4706400	26.58
10	26.75	25.96	26.65	4251900	26.65
11	26.55	25.5	26.14	4999700	26.14
12	26.33	25.74	26.07	5314900	26.07
13	26.96	25.49	25.78	8330400	25.78
14	27	25.98	26.77	8228400	26.77
15	27.01	26.34	26.45	4128000	26.45
16	27.44	26.69	26.94	5069000	26.94
17	27.64	27	27.13	4127300	27.13
18	28	27.05	27.7	5639800	27.7

Figure 10.25 The Merge and Center results in a single cell containing the centered text string.

To center text across a group of cells:

1. Type a title or other text into the leftmost cell of the cell group.
2. Select the cell group; that is, the cells within which you want to center the text string (**Figure 10.23**).
3. Click the Merge and Center icon on the Formatting toolbar (**Figure 10.24**).

   The selected cells are merged into a single cell and the text is centered within it (**Figure 10.25**).

Formatting numbers, dates, and times

Worksheets often contain columns of numbers, dates, and times. While the default formatting that Excel applies will occasionally suffice, you can also apply *specific* number, date, or time formatting to such cells.

To format numbers, dates, or times:

1. Select cells that contain a number, date, or time.
2. *Do one of the following:*
   - ▲ Click a number-formatting icon on the Formatting toolbar (**Figure 10.26**).
   - ▲ Choose Format > Cells (⌘1). On the Number tab of the Format Cells dialog box (**Figure 10.27**), select a Category and set formatting options.

✔ Tips

- Number formatting is in *addition* to any text formatting applied to the cells, such as font, color, and effects.
- Unless you select a special number format, Excel formats numbers with the General format.
- If you enter a number preceded by a dollar sign ($), Excel automatically applies Currency formatting. If you enter a number followed by a percent sign (%), Excel applies Percentage formatting.
- You can save number formatting as a *style*. See "Using Styles," at the end of this chapter.

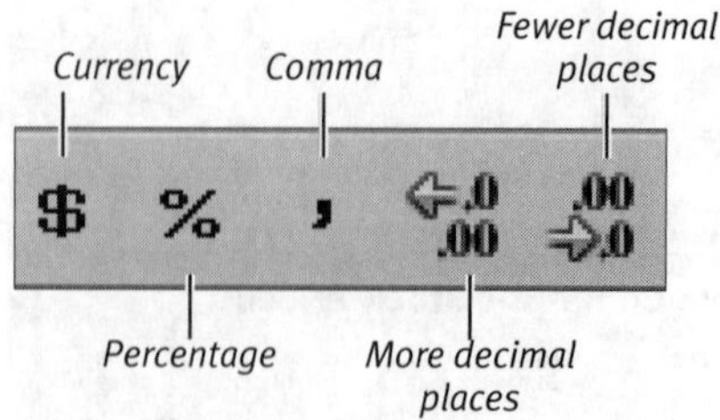

Figure 10.26 Number-formatting commands can be selected from the Formatting toolbar.

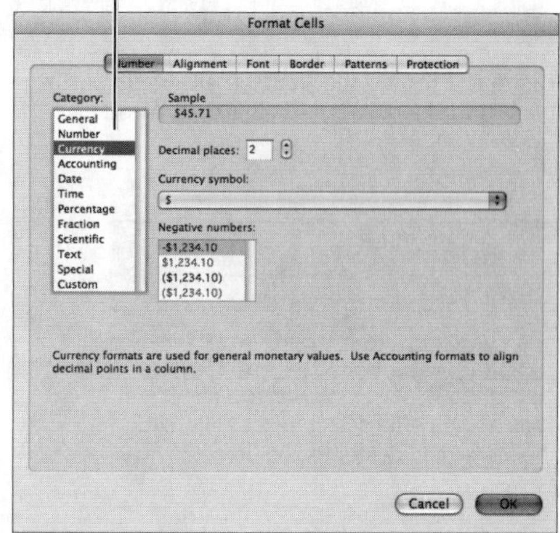

Figure 10.27 In the Format Cells dialog box, you can set very precise formats for cells that contain numbers, dates, or times.

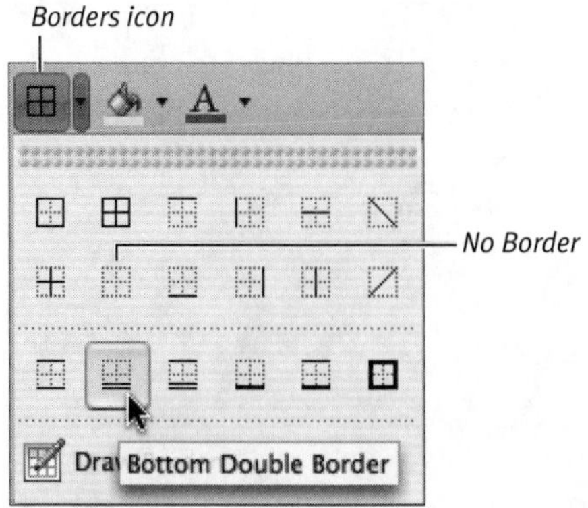

Figure 10.28 You can quickly select a border style from the Borders icon on the Formatting toolbar.

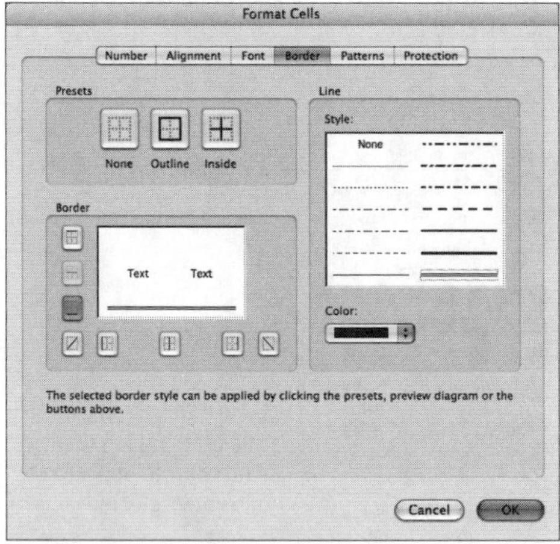

Figure 10.29 Select one or more borders by clicking icons, specify a line style, and choose a border color.

Figure 10.30 Borders and Shading area.

Cell borders and shading

A *border* is a line (or lines) at the edge of a cell. You can use borders to divide information on the sheet into logical regions. *Shading* is a pattern or color used to fill selected cells.

To apply a border to a cell or range:

1. Select the cell or range to which you'd like to apply a border.
2. *Do one of the following:*
   - ▲ To apply the most recently used border to the selected cell(s), click the Borders icon on the Formatting toolbar.
   - ▲ Click the down arrow beside the Borders icon on the Formatting toolbar and select a border (**Figure 10.28**).
   - ▲ Choose Format > Cells (⌘1). On the Border tab of the Format Cells dialog box, select borders, a line style, and a color (**Figure 10.29**). Click OK to apply the border(s) to the cells.
   - ▲ In the Toolbox, select border options from the Borders and Shading section of the Formatting Palette (**Figure 10.30**).

✔ Tip

- To remove borders from a selected range, *do one of the following:*
  - ▲ Click the down arrow beside the Borders icon on the Formatting toolbar and select the No Border icon (Figure 10.28).
  - ▲ In the Format Cells dialog box (Figure 10.29), click the None preset.
  - ▲ In the Borders and Shading section of the Formatting Palette (Figure 10.30). click the Style icon and choose No Border from the drop-down menu.

To apply shading to a cell or range:

1. Select the cell or range to which you'd like to add shading.
2. Choose Format > Cells (⌘1), or Control-click one of the selected cells and choose Format Cells from the pop-up menu.

   The Format Cells dialog box appears.
3. Click the Patterns tab (**Figure 10.31**).
4. *Do one or both of the following:*
   - ▲ To apply a solid color to the selected cells, click a color or gray swatch.
   - ▲ To apply a pattern to the selected cells, open the Pattern palette and select a pattern.

   The color and/or pattern are applied to the selected cell range.

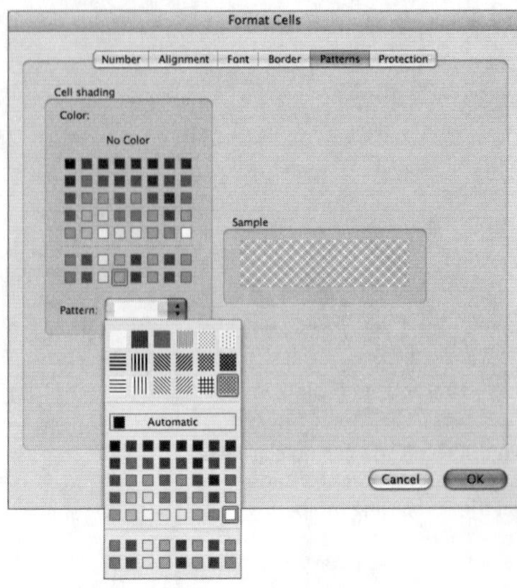

Figure 10.31 Select a color and/or pattern to apply to the selected cells.

✔ Tips

- You can quickly select a solid color shading from the Fill Color drop-down menu on the Formatting toolbar (**Figure 10.32**).
- Shading settings can also be selected from the Borders and Shading section of the Formatting Palette (see Figure 10.30).
- Note that you can also select a *color* from the Pattern palette. The colored pattern will be blended with the primary color chosen (if any).
- AutoFormat styles often include shading as part of their definition.
- If shading makes it difficult to read a cell's contents, you can correct this by choosing a text color that contrasts with the shading. For example, against a dark shading, white or a light-colored text works well (**Figure 10.33**).

Figure 10.32 You can click this toolbar icon to pick a fill color to apply to the currently selected cells.

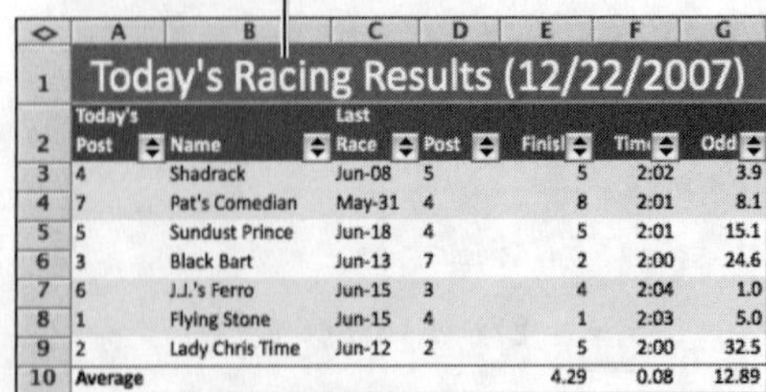

	A	B	C	D	E	F	G
1	Today's Racing Results (12/22/2007)						
2	Today's Post	Name	Last Race	Post	Finis	Tim	Odd
3	4	Shadrack	Jun-08	5	5	2:02	3.9
4	7	Pat's Comedian	May-31	4	8	2:01	8.1
5	5	Sundust Prince	Jun-18	4	5	2:01	15.1
6	3	Black Bart	Jun-13	7	2	2:00	24.6
7	6	J.J.'s Ferro	Jun-15	3	4	2:04	1.0
8	1	Flying Stone	Jun-15	4	1	2:03	5.0
9	2	Lady Chris Time	Jun-12	2	5	2:00	32.5
10	Average				4.29	0.08	12.89

Figure 10.33 Light-colored text is easiest to read against solid, dark shading.

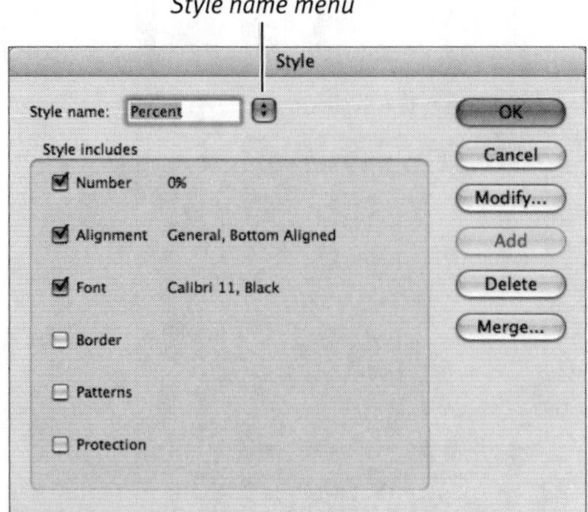

Figure 10.34 Choose an existing style from the Style name menu.

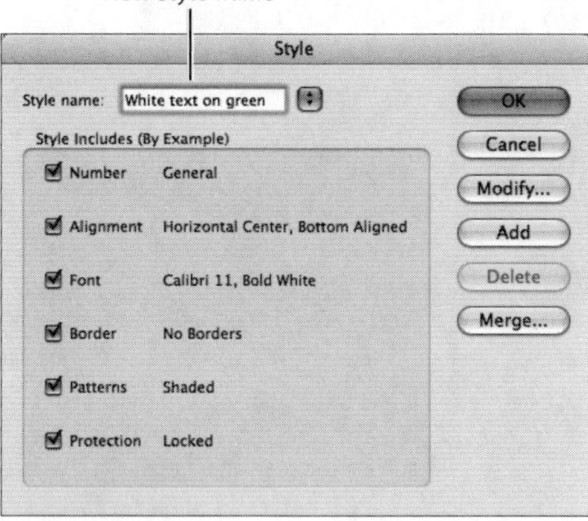

Figure 10.35 When you enter a new style name, Excel automatically displays the formatting attributes that will be part of the style based on the selected cell's formatting.

Using styles

A *style* is a preset formatting combination that you can apply to cells. In addition to the Excel built-in styles, you can create your own.

To apply an existing style:

1. Select the cell or range to which you want to apply formatting.
2. Choose Format > Style.

   The Style dialog box appears.
3. Select a style from the Style name list. Click check boxes to specify elements to include in the formatting (**Figure 10.34**).
4. Click OK to apply the style.

✔ Tips

- When a [0] follows a style name in the Style name menu, Excel formats the data with zero decimal places.
- By default, Excel assigns cells the Normal style unless you specify a different style. To change the default cell formatting, modify the Normal style.

To create a new style:

1. Format a cell as desired and then select it.
2. Choose Format > Style.
3. Type a new style name in the Style name box (**Figure 10.35**).

   Excel displays the attributes with which the current cell is formatted.
4. To remove attributes from the new style definition, clear their check marks.
5. Click OK to save the new style definition.

✔ Tips

- You can import the styles from another open workbook into the current one. Click the Merge button in the Style dialog box, select the other workbook in the Merge Styles dialog box (**Figure 10.36**), and click OK.
- To modify an existing style, select the style from the Style name list and click the Modify button. In the Format Cells dialog box, specify new formatting and click OK.
- You can delete styles that you no longer need by selecting them in the Style dialog box and clicking Delete. Note, however, that you can't delete the Normal style. And if you delete the Comma, Currency, or Percent style, they will no longer be available on the Formatting toolbar. (In general, it's best to restrict style deletions to the ones you've created.)
- If you delete a style that's currently in use in the worksheet, style-related formatting will be removed from any affected cells.

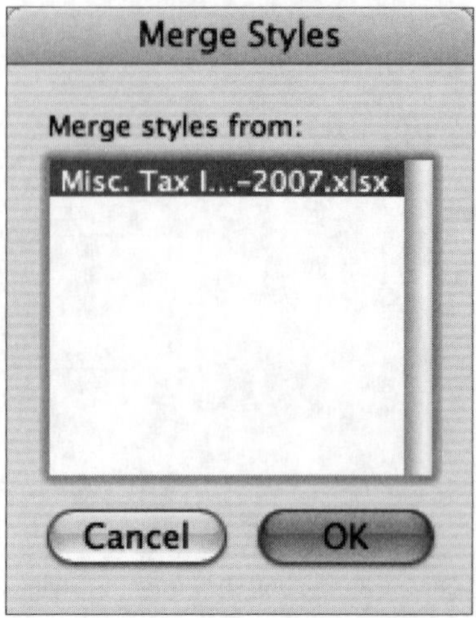

Figure 10.36 Select the open workbook whose styles you want to merge into the current worksheet.

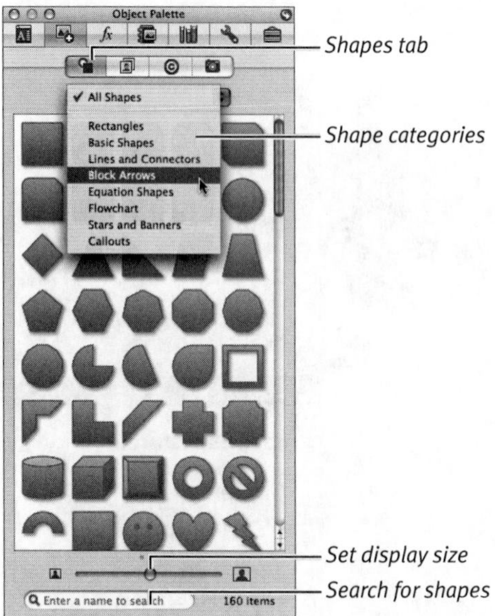

Figure 10.37 Pick an AutoShape to add to the sheet.

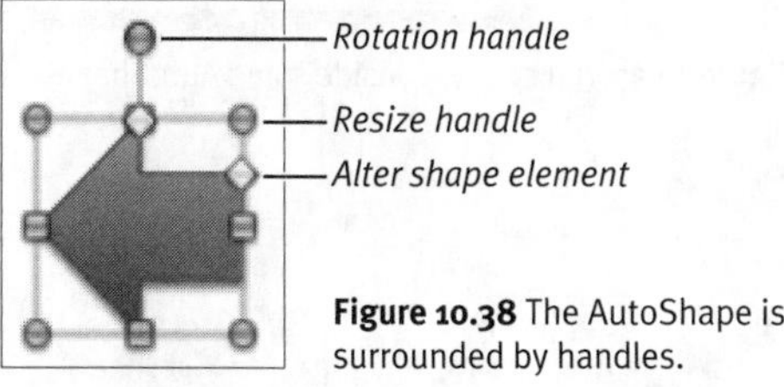

Figure 10.38 The AutoShape is surrounded by handles.

Shapes and Pictures

Although it doesn't come up often in most worksheets, Excel provides many ways for you to liven up worksheets for inclusion in presentations or reports, for example. You can add any of the following items to a sheet:

- AutoShapes (colored shape textholders)
- Clip art and photos
- SmartArt objects
- WordArt (decorative text)
- Organization charts
- Movies
- Special symbols, such as fractions and ©

In this and the following section, you'll learn how to insert shapes, pictures, and special characters into your worksheets. SmartArt, WordArt, organization charts, and movies are discussed in other chapters.

AutoShapes

An *AutoShape* is a defined Office object that you can move, resize, and rotate. After placing an AutoShape, you can change its formatting by choosing a new color or gradient fill, altering its 3D properties, or setting a transparency level. Some AutoShapes can also accept text.

To add an AutoShape to a worksheet:

1. If the Toolbox isn't open, choose Insert > Picture > Shape. Otherwise, click the Object Palette tab in the Toolbox.
2. Click the Shapes tab, and choose All Shapes or a specific shape category from the drop-down menu (**Figure 10.37**).
3. Drag the shape from the Object Palette onto the worksheet (**Figure 10.38**).

continues on next page

4. If desired, *do any of the following:*
   - ▲ Click inside the shape and drag it to a new location on the worksheet.
   - ▲ Press Shift as you drag a corner handle to resize the shape proportionately. Press Option as you drag to resize from the shape's center.
   - ▲ To flip the shape, drag a side, top, or bottom handle across the shape.
   - ▲ Drag the green rotation handle to change the shape's angle on the page.
   - ▲ Drag a yellow handle to alter that single element of the shape.
   - ▲ Choose Format > Shape, press ⌘1, or double-click the shape to change the formatting. You can also choose formatting options from the Formatting Palette.
   - ▲ If the AutoShape can accept text, Control-click it and choose Edit Text from the pop-up menu (**Figure 10.39**). A text insertion mark appears in the object. (If the shape can't accept text, the text insertion mark won't appear.) Type the text. To format the text, select the text and choose options from the Formatting toolbar.
   - ▲ If the AutoShape will be placed in a stack with other shapes or graphics, you can change its layering by Control-clicking the AutoShape and choosing an option from the Arrange submenu (Figure 10.39), such as Send to Back.
   - ▲ To perform more selective modifications on an AutoShape, choose Convert to Freeform from the Control-click menu (Figure 10.39), and then choose Edit Points from the same menu (**Figure 10.40**).
   - ▲ To remove the AutoShape from the worksheet, select the shape and press Delete.

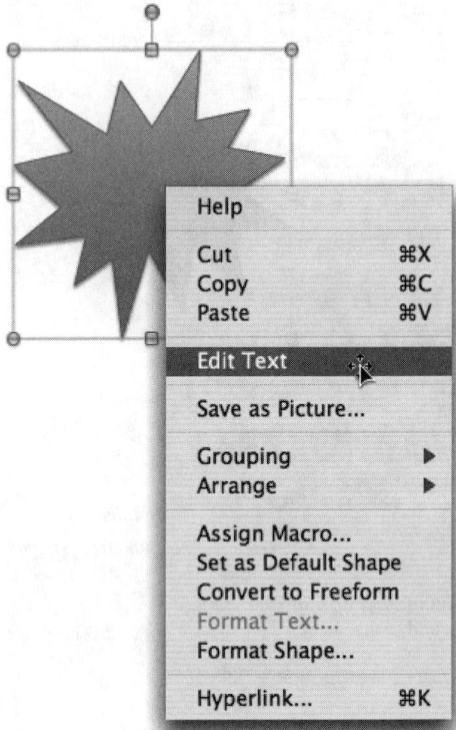

Figure 10.39 You can type inside some AutoShapes.

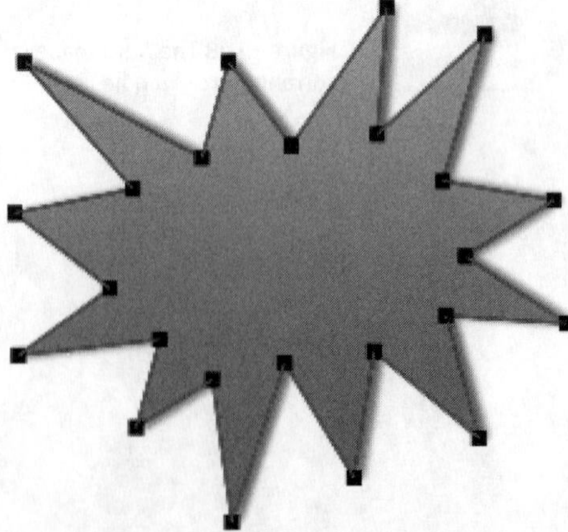

Figure 10.40 After converting an AutoShape to a free-form object, you can change any aspect by dragging individual points (represented by black dots).

SHAPES AND PICTURES

Categories

Figure 10.41 Microsoft Clip Gallery application.

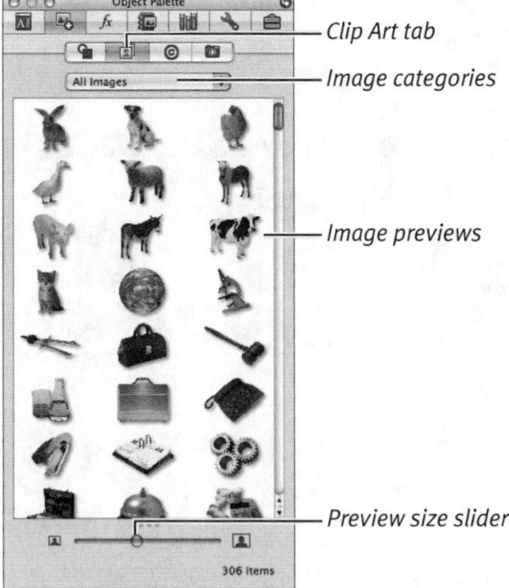

Figure 10.42 Select an image from the clip art gallery.

Figure 10.43 Inserted clip art is surrounded by handles—just like any other object.

Clip art and photos

You can also dress up worksheets by inserting Office clip art images or your own photos.

To insert a clip art image from the Microsoft Clip Gallery:

1. Choose Insert > Picture > Clip Art.
   Clip Gallery launches (**Figure 10.41**).
2. Locate the desired clip art image by selecting a category, scrolling through the thumbnails, and/or entering a text string in the Search box and clicking Search.
   To preview images in a separate window, click the Preview check box.
3. To add the selected clip art image to your worksheet, click Insert.

✔ Tip

- To view additional free clip art images at Office Online, click the Online button. Your default Web browser launches and opens to the site.

To insert a clip art image from the Object Gallery:

1. *Do one of the following:*
   - ▲ If the Toolbox isn't open, choose View > Object Palette.
   - ▲ If the Toolbox is open, click the Object Palette tab.
2. Click the Clip Art tab to display the stored clip art images (**Figure 10.42**).
3. Choose an image category from the drop-down menu.
4. Drag a clip art image onto the worksheet (**Figure 10.43**).

To insert a photo from your iPhoto library:

1. *Do one of the following:*
   - ▲ If the Toolbox isn't open, choose View > Object Palette.
   - ▲ If the Toolbox is open, click the Object Palette tab.
2. Click the Photos tab to display the images stored in iPhoto (**Figure 10.44**).
3. Find the desired image by doing any combination of the following:
   - ▲ Choose a library, album, or roll from the drop-down menu.
   - ▲ Enter a search string in the box to display images with matching filenames.
   - ▲ Scroll through the thumbnail list.
4. Drag a photo onto the worksheet.

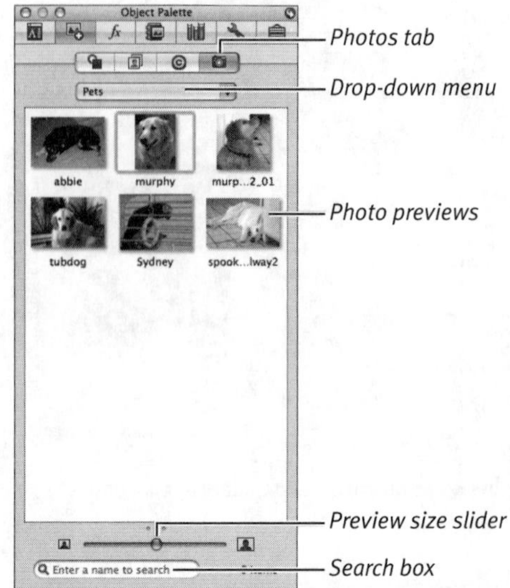

Figure 10.44 iPhoto images.

To insert other photos and pictures:

1. Choose Insert > Picture > From File.
   The Choose a Picture dialog box appears (**Figure 10.45**).
2. Navigate to the drive/folder that contains the file you want to insert and select the image's filename.
3. *Optional:* To maintain a link to the image file (allowing Excel to automatically show edits), click the Link to File check box.
4. Click Insert.
   The image appears on the worksheet, surrounded by normal object handles.

Figure 10.45 Select an image to insert (OS X 10.5/ Leopard shown).

✔ Tips

- Clip art and photos can be moved and manipulated like other objects. Refer to Step 4 of "To add an AutoShape to a worksheet" for some methods of working with clip art images and photos.
- To proportionately resize a placed clip art image or photo, drag any corner handle.
- To replace placed clip art or a picture with another one, you don't have to delete the original image. Simply Control-click the image on the worksheet, and choose Change Picture from the pop-up menu that appears.

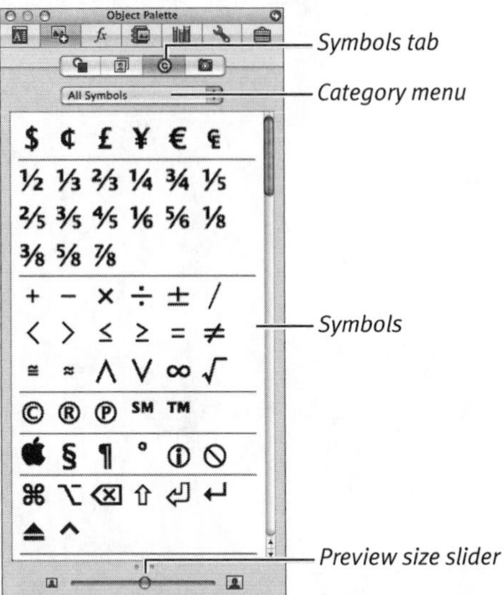

Figure 10.46 Symbols and special characters.

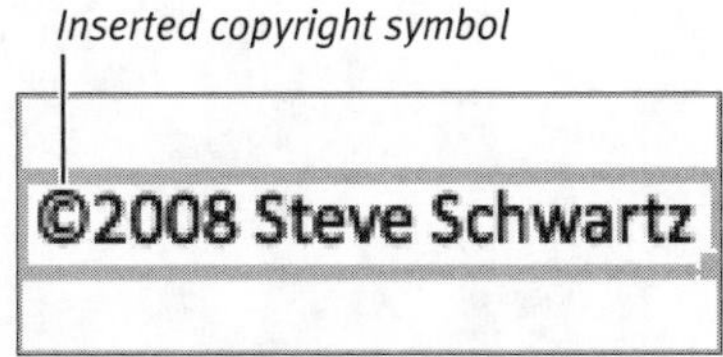

Figure 10.47 You can insert special characters into cell text.

Inserting Other Items

In addition to the item types described in the previous section, you can insert the following items into a worksheet. Rather than describe the required steps here, refer to the chapters listed below for explanations:

- WordArt decorative text (Chapter 5)
- SmartArt objects (Chapter 17)
- Organization charts (Chapter 18)
- Movies (Chapter 19)

Special characters

Excel makes it easy to insert special characters into cell text. Rather than hunting for "magic" key combinations that will enable you to type a copyright symbol, a fraction, or a foreign language character, you can select the character from the Symbols tab on the Object Palette.

To insert a special character:

1. *Do one of the following:*
   - If the Toolbox isn't open, choose View > Object Palette.
   - If the Toolbox is open, click the Object Palette tab.
2. Click the Symbols tab to view the list of supported symbol characters (**Figure 10.46**).
3. Set the text insertion mark at the spot within the cell where you want to add the symbol or special character.
4. Choose a symbol category from the drop-down menu.
5. Click the character or symbol you want to insert.

   The character or symbol appears in the current cell at the text insertion mark (**Figure 10.47**).

✔ Tip

- Resist the temptation to add currency symbols by selecting them from the Symbols tab. If you intend to treat the currency as a number (using it in a formula), choose Format > Cells and select the currency type on the Number tab of the Format Cells dialog box.

11

Formulas and Functions

Calculations are the way Excel "does the math." Even if you're only using Excel to keep lists, you may have numbers on which you'd like to perform some calculations (for example, totaling the number of items sold or computing bowling averages). Excel excels at calculations of this sort and provides tools to save you time and effort.

For instance, suppose you want to calculate the total of a column of numbers. You would create a *formula* in the cell beneath the column. The formula might look like this: `=SUM(B2:B12)`

All formulas begin with an equal sign (=), which enables Excel to distinguish them from text or a number. When you've finished entering the formula and move to another cell, Excel evaluates the formula based on any *functions* used (such as SUM) and the data to which it refers (cells B2 through B12). What's now shown in the cell is no longer the formula but its *result;* in this case, the total of the numbers in the specified cells.

Formula Basics

To add two numbers, you could select a cell and type =23+43. To add the contents of two cells, you use their *addresses* in the formula, as in =B3+B4. (The addresses are referred to as *cell references;* that is, you're referring to the cells by their addresses.) The cell into which you type the formula displays the result of the calculation as soon as you move to a different cell.

If data in any referenced cell changes, the result instantly changes. This quick recalculation lets you perform what-if analyses. Just change any of the numbers in the referenced cells to see how the changes affect the results.

Formulas can consist of any combination of data, cell references, functions, and operators (such as +, -, and /). The following steps show how to create a basic formula.

To create a simple formula:

1. *Optional:* You can create or edit formulas in the cell or in the formula bar, whichever you find convenient. To use the formula bar, choose View > Formula Bar.
2. Select the cell in which you want to create the formula and type an equal sign (=), either in the cell or in the formula bar (**Figure 11.1**).
3. *Do one of the following:*
   - Type the first number or cell reference to include in the formula.
   - Click the first cell you want to reference in the formula. (When creating or editing a formula, clicking a cell results in the cell's address being inserted into the formula.)
4. Type an operator, such as + or /.
   See **Table 11.1** for a list of common arithmetic operators.

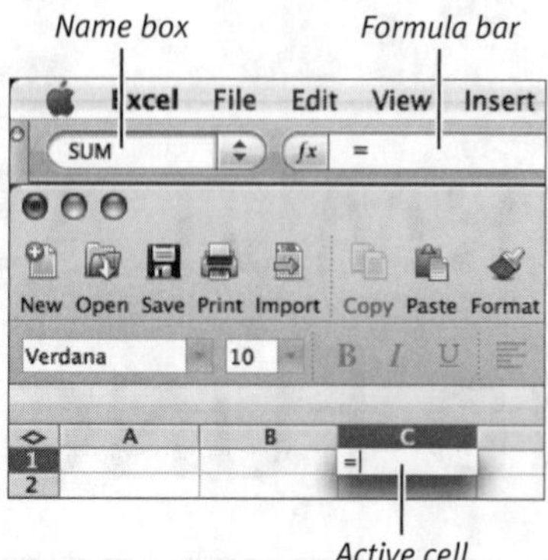

Figure 11.1 You can create or edit a formula in the cell or in the formula bar.

Table 11.1

Arithmetic Operators

Operator	Action
+	Addition
-	Subtraction
*	Multiplication
/	Division
%	Percentage
^	Exponentiation

Entering Formulas

When entering a formula, you can use any combination of these techniques:

- Type the formula, including cell references, range references, and names,
- Add a cell or range reference by clicking the cell or drag-selecting the range.
- Choose functions from the Name box or Formula AutoComplete lists. To dismiss a Formula AutoComplete list, continue typing rather than selecting a function name.
- Design the formula in the Formula Builder or Calculator window.

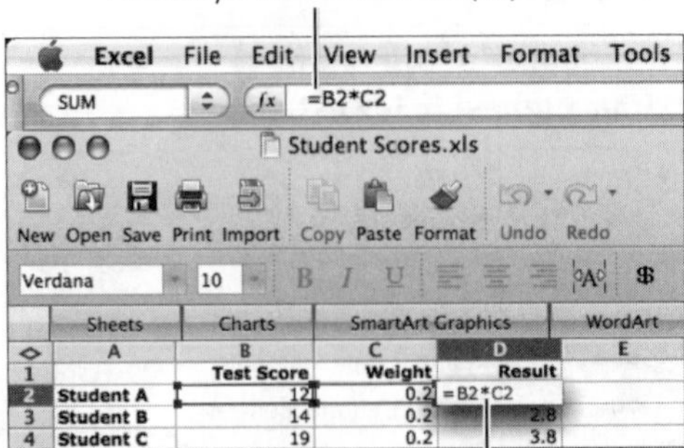

Figure 11.2 A cell normally displays the result rather than the formula. To view the formula, double-click the cell or select the cell and check the formula bar.

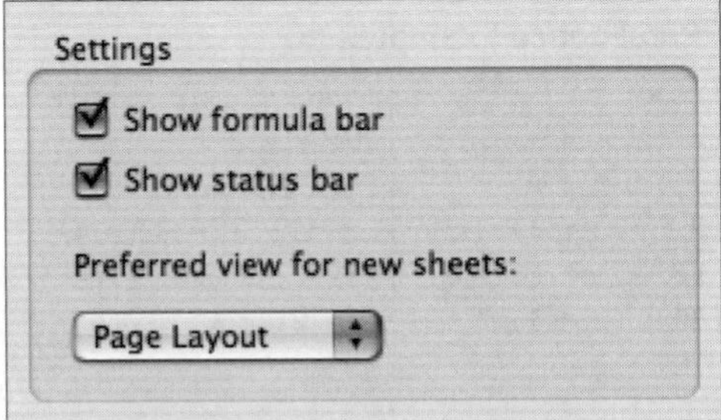

Figure 11.3 You can make the formula bar appear automatically whenever you create a new or open an existing workbook.

5. *Do one of the following:*
   - ▲ Type the final number or cell reference you want to include in the formula.
   - ▲ Click the final cell that you want to reference in the formula.
6. Press Return or Enter to complete the formula and view the result.

✔ Tips

- You can combine numbers (constants) and cell references in a formula, such as =C2*2.5 (the contents of cell C2 multiplied by 2.5).
- After the initial element in a formula has been typed or inserted, clicking a cell automatically adds the contents of the cell to the current formula. For example, if a formula currently contains =17 and you click cell A4, the formula becomes =17+A4.
- To view a cell's formula rather than its result, double-click the cell or check the formula bar (**Figure 11.2**). When you're done examining the formula, press Esc to restore the cell to its normal state.
- If adjacent cells require a similar formula, you can copy the formula from cell to cell. See "Copying a Formula to Adjacent Cells," later in this chapter.
- By default, the formula bar is not shown. To make it automatically appear, choose Excel > Preferences, click the View icon in the Excel Preferences window, click the Show formula bar check box in the Settings section (**Figure 11.3**), and click OK.

About Precedence

Here's a fact of spreadsheet life. Few formulas consist only of two cell references or numbers separated by an operator. They're often considerably more complex. And while it might make your life simpler if formulas were evaluated from left to right, that isn't necessarily the case. Instead, spreadsheets follow established rules of *precedence* when evaluating formulas. These strict rules determine the order in which a formula's components are combined.

For example, suppose you see the following formula:

```
= 3 + 7 * 2
```

If evaluated from left to right, the result would be 20. The *actual* result, however, is 17. This is because operators with a higher precedence (such as multiplication) are always evaluated before operators with a lower precedence (such as addition). Thus, our example is calculated by multiplying 7 times 2 and then adding 3, resulting in 17. **Table 11.2** shows the precedence of the various operators.

To avoid forcing you to rearrange numbers, cell references, and operators, Excel lets you alter the evaluation order for a formula by enclosing items in parentheses. Such items are automatically given higher precedence. If you use multiple sets of nested parentheses, they are evaluated from innermost to the outermost set.

By adding parentheses to our simple formula, as in = (3 + 7) * 2, we can now force it to be evaluated from left to right. Although addition is of lower precedence than multiplication, the parentheses will make it be evaluated by first adding 3 and 7 and then multiplying that result by 2, yielding 20. See **Table 11.3** for some additional examples.

Table 11.2

Precedence of Operators (from highest to lowest)

Operator	Meaning
-	Negation (-5)
%	Percentage
^	Exponentiation
* and /	Multiplication, division
+ and -	Addition, subtraction
&	Concatenation (for combining text strings)
=, <, >, <=, >=, <>	Comparison (equal, less than, greater than, less than or equal, greater than or equal, not equal)

Table 11.3

Precedence Examples

Example	Evaluation	Result
2 * 3 + 4	(6) + 4	10
2 + 3 * 4	2 + (12)	14
2 * (3 + 4)	2 * (7)	14
(7 - 2) * (3 * 4)	(5) * (12)	60
30 - (2 * 3) * 4	30 - (6 * 4)	6

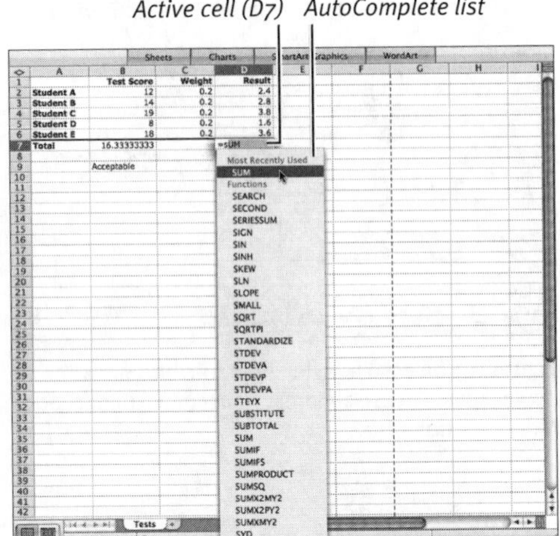

Figure 11.4 Select the cell, type =, and then begin entering the formula. The AutoComplete list appears, showing all functions that start with the typed letters.

Selected cells

C	D	E
Weight	Result	
0.2	2.4	
0.2	2.8	
0.2	3.8	
0.2	1.6	
0.2	3.6	
	=SUM(D2:D6)	
	SUM(number1, [number2], ...)	

Figure 11.5 Drag to select the cells you want to total with the Sum function; in this case, D2 through D6.

D
Result
2.4
2.8
3.8
1.6
3.6
14.2

Figure 11.6 After finishing the formula, the total of cells D2 through D6 (14.2) is displayed in cell D7.

Using Functions

Functions are shortcuts for calculations that would be difficult to create with a basic formula. Excel 2008's 300+ built-in functions can be included in formulas to enable you to easily perform financial, statistical, engineering, logical, and text-based computations.

Functions accept values called *arguments*, perform an operation on them, and then return one or more values. See **Table 11.4** at the end of this chapter for a list of common functions.

Totaling a column with SUM

Perhaps the simplest function-based calculation one can perform—and certainly the most common—is to total a column of numbers using the Sum function. (Sum can also be used to total rows or a combination of adjacent and nonadjacent cells.)

To total a column using Sum:

1. Click the cell in which you want the sum to appear.

   Although this will generally be the cell immediately beneath the column of numbers, you can choose *any* cell.

2. Enter =s to begin the formula. Excel displays a Formula AutoComplete list of functions that begin with s (**Figure 11.4**). Choose SUM from the list.

   Excel adds parentheses, displaying =SUM() and placing the insertion mark between the parentheses.

3. Drag down the column of numbers you want to total (**Figure 11.5**).

4. Press Return or Enter to complete the formula.

   The formula is evaluated. The result is displayed in the cell (**Figure 11.6**) and the formula is shown in the formula bar.

Using AutoSum

To make it easier to perform the most common computations on a column or row, Excel provides the AutoSum feature. When used directly beneath a column or to the right of a row, AutoSum determines the cell range by examining the data.

To perform a column or row calculation using AutoSum:

1. Click the empty cell directly beneath a column or to the right of a row.
2. *Do one of the following:*
   - ▲ To calculate a column or row total using the Sum function, click the AutoSum icon on the Standard toolbar.
   - ▲ Click the down arrow beside the AutoSum icon. Choose a function (such as Average or Max) from the drop-down menu (**Figure 11.7**).

   The complete formula is shown (**Figure 11.8**).
3. *Do one of the following:*
   - ▲ Press Return or Enter to accept the selected range and display the result.
   - ▲ Edit the formula (changing the range, for example). Then press Return or Enter to display the result.

✔ Tips

- AutoSum defaults to operating on columns. If it finds suitable data above the destination cell, it performs a column calculation. If not, it attempts to operate on a row.
- To quickly perform a calculation for a set of adjacent columns, select the empty cell beneath each of the columns before choosing an AutoSum function. Excel will insert a formula in each selected cell.

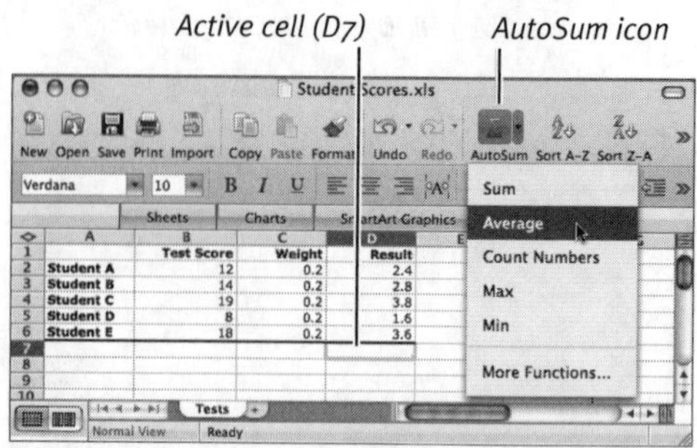

Figure 11.7 Select a function from the AutoSum drop-down menu. (To use a more advanced function, choose More Functions.)

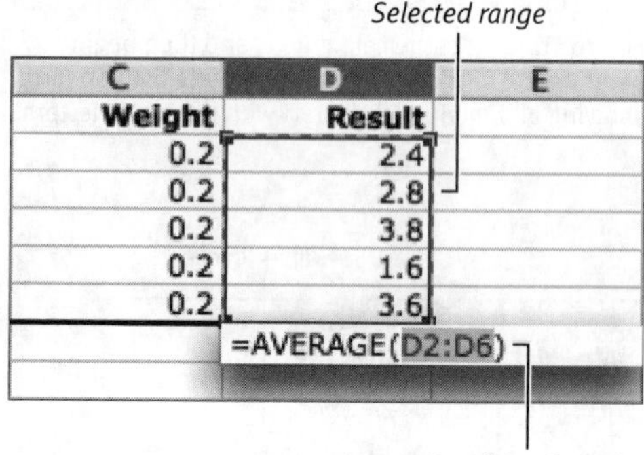

Figure 11.8 The formula (including the range selected by AutoSum) is displayed in the cell.

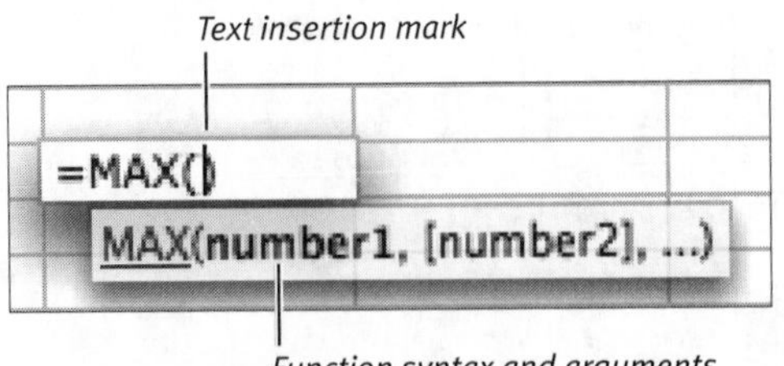

Figure 11.9 When you select a function from a Formula AutoComplete list, the opening and closing parentheses are automatically provided for you.

Nonadjacent references as function arguments

While column- and row-base calculations are commonplace, there's no requirement that a formula operate on adjacent cells. Referenced cells can be scattered all over a worksheet or workbook. The following example shows how to enter nonadjacent references as arguments to a function, such as `=MAX(A3,A5,D12:D17)`. Note that each reference is separated from its neighbor by a comma (,).

To include nonadjacent references as arguments to a function:

1. Click the cell in which you want to place the formula.
2. Type an equal sign (=), followed by the first letter or two of the function name.
3. Select the function name from the Formula AutoComplete drop-down list that appears (see Figure 11.4).
   The function appears in the cell. The text insertion mark is positioned between the provided parentheses (**Figure 11.9**).
4. Click the cell or select the range that will serve as the first argument to the function. If you prefer, you can type the cell or range reference, such as `G17` or `B12:B16`.
5. Type a comma (,).
6. Click the next cell or select the next range whose values you want to include in the formula. As before, you can also type this cell or range reference.
7. Repeat Steps 5 and 6 until you've included the necessary references.
8. Press Return or Enter to complete the formula.

Formula Builder

The Formula Builder is a new Toolbox utility designed to help you construct and edit formulas. It's especially useful if you're uncertain of a function's syntax or are unfamiliar with the process of creating formulas.

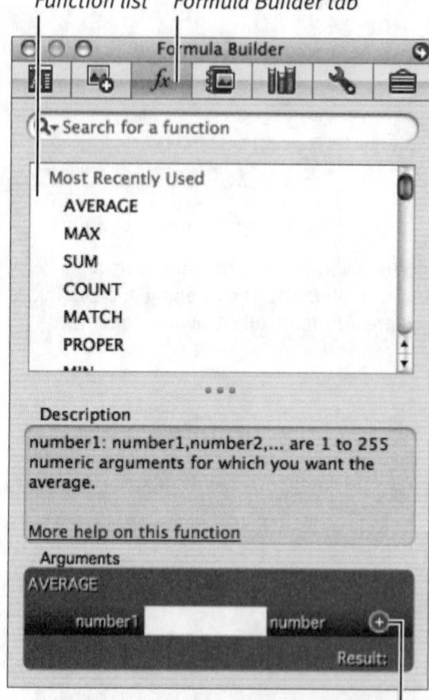

Figure 11.10 The Formula Builder tab of the Toolbox.

To create a formula using Formula Builder:

1. Select a cell to contain the formula.
2. If the Toolbox is currently open, click the Formula Builder tab. Otherwise, choose View > Formula Builder.
3. *Do one of the following:*
   - ▲ If the reference begins with a function, double-click its name in the Formula Builder (**Figure 11.10**). The equal sign, function name, and parentheses are inserted into the cell.
   - ▲ If the formula begins with data or a cell/range reference, start the formula by typing =, the data or reference, and the first operator, such as =A17+.
4. *Do one of the following:*
   - ▲ When following an operator, such as +, –, or *, type the data, type the reference, or select the reference on the sheet.
   - ▲ To add an argument to the current function, click the plus (+) icon or type a comma. A box for the new argument appears. Select a reference on the worksheet, or type the data or reference.

   As you add arguments and elements, Formula Builder evaluates the data and displays the current result (**Figure 11.11**).
5. Add the functions, arguments, and/or elements needed to finish the formula.
6. Press Return or Enter to complete the formula.

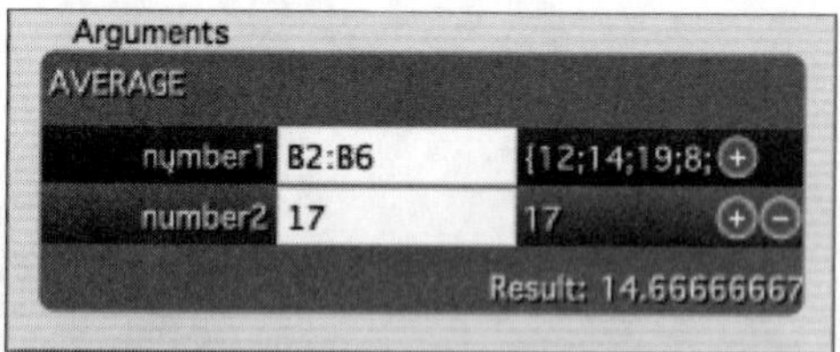

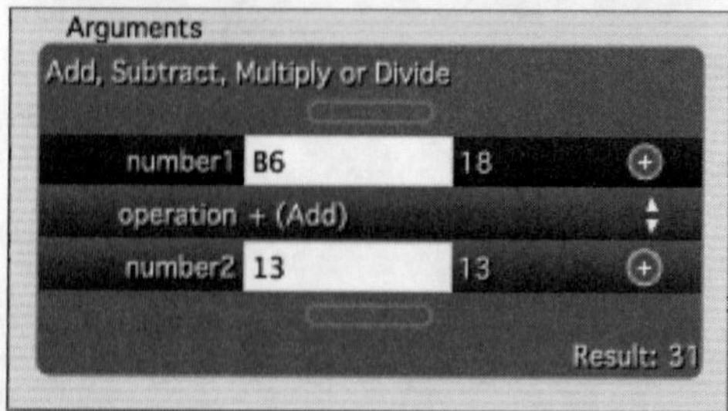

Figure 11.11 Formula Builder displays each argument and calculates the result so far. These examples show a function (top) and a simple calculation (bottom).

FORMULA BUILDER

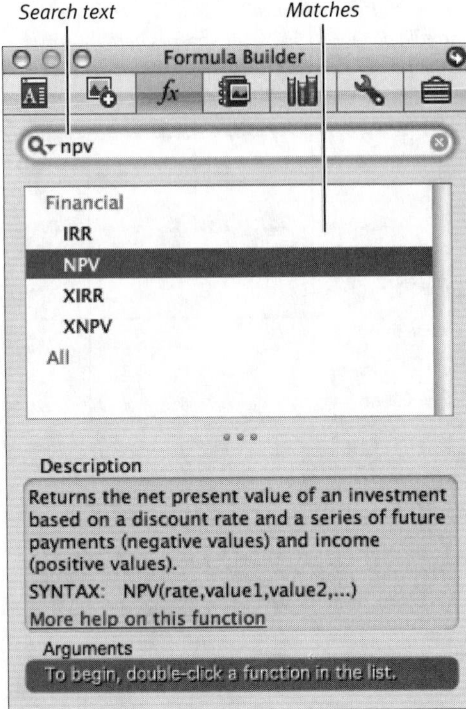

Figure 11.12 To find a function, type all or part of its name (npv) or some descriptive text (net present).

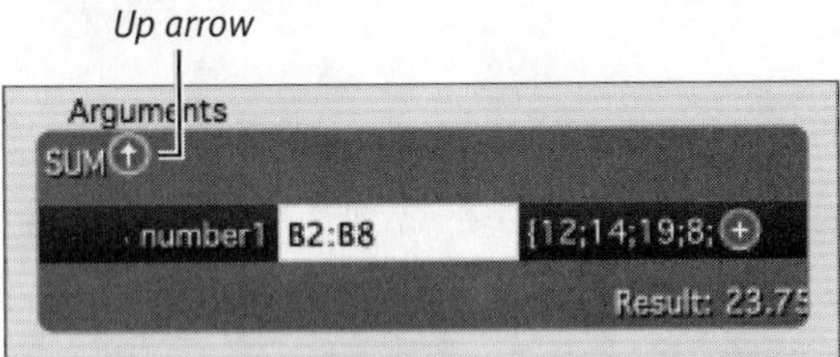

Figure 11.13 In this formula, a SUM function is an argument to the main function (AVERAGE). Click the up arrow to resume editing the AVERAGE function.

✔ Tips

- You can also use Formula Builder to aid in editing existing formulas.
- If the formula cell is near the end of a row or bottom of a column and the formula is function-based, Formula Builder may treat it as an AutoSum and insert the range for you. If the range is incorrect, you can change it.
- Rather than scroll through the entire function list, you can enter search text in the box at the top of Formula Builder. As you type, potential matches are listed (**Figure 11.12**).
- To insert a function as an argument to the current function (known as a *nested function*), double-click the function's name in the list. When a formula contains multiple functions, you work with each function separately. To switch between the functions, click the up arrow icon (**Figure 11.13**).

The Calculator

Excel also provides a special Calculator that you can use to create and edit formulas.

To create or edit a formula using the Calculator:

1. Click the cell where you want to insert the formula.

   If you want to edit an existing formula, select the cell that contains the formula.

2. Choose Tools > Calculator.

   The Calculator appears (**Figure 11.14**). An equal sign (=) is automatically inserted to begin the formula.

3. Click buttons to build the formula. As you add elements to the formula, they appear in the Calculator's formula pane.

   You can also type directly into the formula pane, adding the necessary elements and performing edits.

4. While creating or editing the formula, *do any of the following:*
   - ▲ Click buttons to build the formula.
   - ▲ To insert a cell reference, click the cell or range in the worksheet.
   - ▲ Click Sum to add a Sum function to the formula. A pane opens to the right, containing a text box in which to list the cells or range to be summed. Click, ⌘-click, or drag through the cells to be totalled. Click Insert to transfer the Sum function into the formula pane.
   - ▲ Click If to add a conditional test to the formula. Specify the conditional test, a true result, and a false result (**Figure 11.15**). Click Insert to transfer the If function into the formula pane (**Figure 11.16**).
   - ▲ To create or edit the formula in Formula Builder, click the More button.

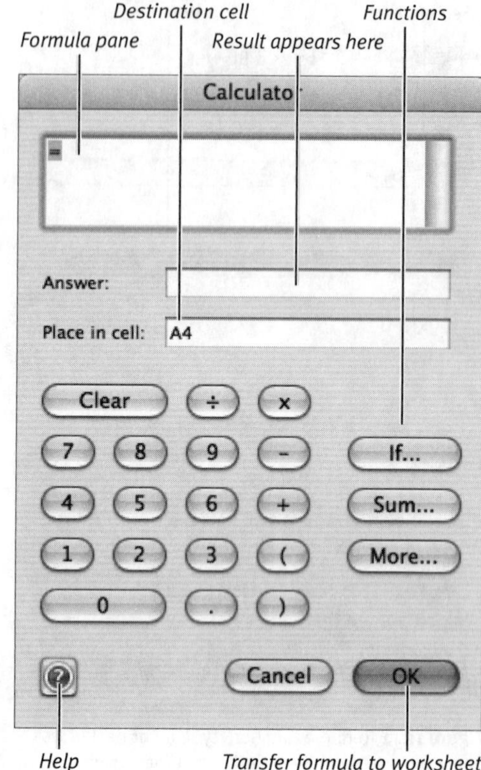

Figure 11.14 You can create and edit formulas using the Calculator.

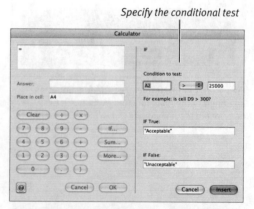

Specify the conditional test

Figure 11.15 Specify the If test by typing or selecting cells and choosing a condition from the drop-down menu. You must also specify what will happen in the event of a true or false test result.

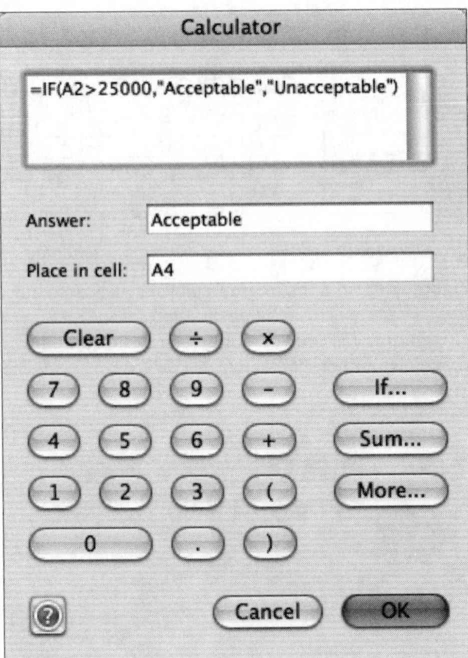

Figure 11.16 Creating a formula based on an If function is simple when using the Calculator.

5. When the formula is complete, click OK to transfer it into the destination cell on the worksheet (denoted by the Place in cell box).

✔ Tips

- When Calculator can convert the formula into a number, the result appears in the Answer box.
- When entering a text result for an If function (see Figure 11.15), it isn't necessary to surround the text with quotation marks. Excel will automatically add them.

Copying a Formula to Adjacent Cells

You'll occasionally want to perform the same calculation for several columns or rows. For example, in a worksheet that shows sales by region, you may want to display a total for every column of sales figures. Rather than rebuild the formula from scratch, you can copy it to adjacent cells. Excel changes the formula automatically to refer to the data in each destination column or row.

To copy a formula to adjacent cells:

1. Click the cell containing the formula.
2. Drag the fill handle at the lower-right corner of the cell across the adjacent cells to which you want to copy the formula (**Figure 11.17**).

   The formula's results appear in the cells, and the Auto Fill Options button appears (**Figure 11.18**).
3. *Optional:* To change the format of the destination cells, click the Auto Fill Options button and choose a formatting option from the drop-down menu.

✔ Tips

- Check copied formulas for accuracy if they reference cells in columns or rows other than the ones containing the formula. Excel sometimes guesses incorrectly about your intentions.
- The operation described above can also be accomplished by using a Fill command. Select the first cell and drag to select the destination cells. Then choose Edit > Fill > Right or Edit > Fill > Down, as appropriate.

	A	B	C	D	E
1		Sales Report: Second Quarter			
2					
3		Region 1	Region 2	Region 3	Region 4
4	Envelopes	0.75	0.4	1.1	0.27
5	Paper Clips	0.11	0.17	0.18	0.15
6	Blank CDs	1.15	2.03	1.58	0.99
7	Blank DVDs	2.78	3.04	1.96	4.17
8	Total	4.79			
9					

Original cell (B8) | Fill handle

Figure 11.17 From the original cell (B8), click and drag the fill handle across the destination cells (C8:E8). (To perform this copy operation on rows, you would drag down rather than across.)

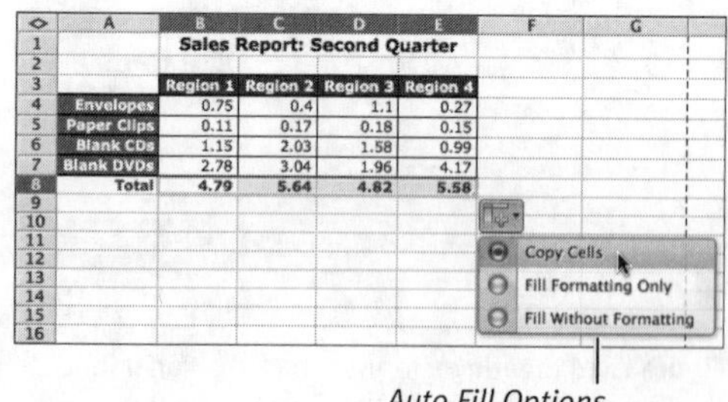

Figure 11.18 The results appear in the destination cells (C8:E8). Click the Auto Fill Options button to review formatting options.

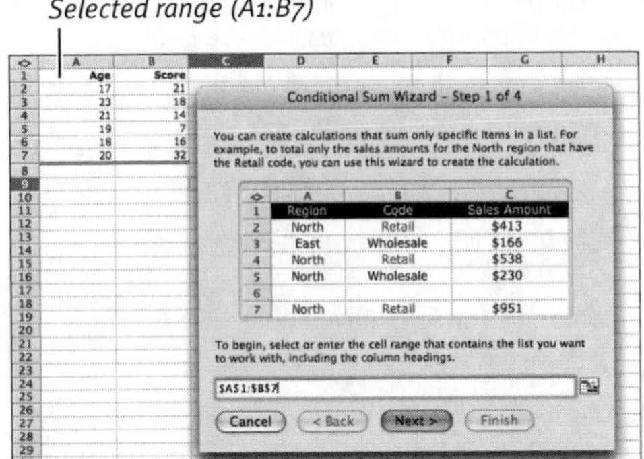

Figure 11.19 Select the range (including the column to total, any additional columns that contain criteria, and the column headings).

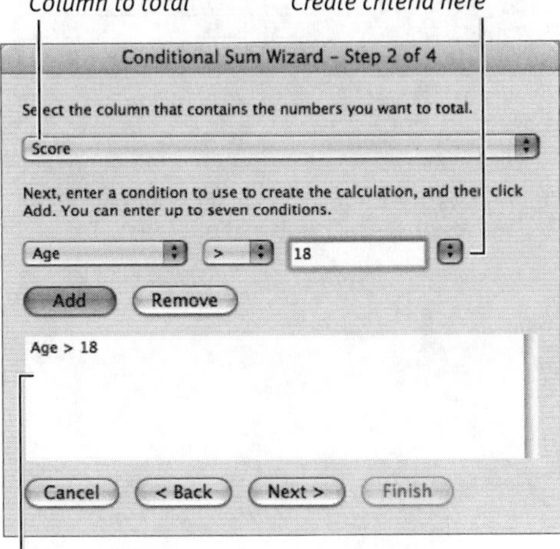

Figure 11.20 In Step 2, specify the column to total and the criteria that must be satisfied.

Select the way you want the results displayed on your sheet.

Calculate and display the total

71

Calculate and display the total and the conditions

18 | 71

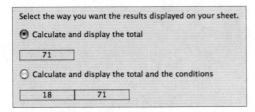

Figure 11.21 Indicate whether you want to display only the total or the criteria *and* the total.

Conditional Sums

Unlike an AutoSum, a *conditional sum* totals only numbers in a given column that match your criteria. For instance, if you had an art gallery that sold expensive prints and greeting cards, you could create a conditional sum that—based on a dollar value—totaled only the inexpensive greeting card sales or only expensive print sales.

To insert a conditional sum:

1. Choose Tools > Conditional Sum.
   The Conditional Sum Wizard appears.
2. Select the range—including the column to total, the column(s) containing the criteria, and the column headings (**Figure 11.19**). Click Next.
   Note that the column to total can also contain the criteria. In that case, select only that single column and its heading.
3. From the top drop-down list in Step 2, select the heading of the column to total. Specify the first criterion by selecting a column heading and a conditional test, and type or select a value in the text box. Click Add to record the criterion.
   In the example (**Figure 11.20**), the column to total is Score. The first criterion is individuals older than 18, based on each person's value in the Age column.
4. *Optional:* To specify more criteria, change the information in the center of the Wizard and click Add. When you are done specifying criteria, click Next.
5. In Step 3, indicate whether you want to display only the total or the total and the criteria (**Figure 11.21**). Click Next.
6. In the remaining Wizard step(s), select a cell in which to display the total and, optionally, the criteria. Click Finish.
   The result appears on the worksheet.

Correcting Formula Errors

To avoid erroneous results from incorrect formulas, Excel supplies a comprehensive set of auditing commands and troubleshooting tools. For instance, you can do the following:

- **Worksheet auditing.** By selecting a cell and then choosing the appropriate command, you can locate the following in a worksheet:
  - *Precedents.* Cells that provide data to the selected formula.
  - *Dependents.* Formulas that draw data from the selected cell.
  - *Errors.* To identify the source of a marked error (such as #N/A), you can find all cells that provide data to the selected formula.
- **Finding invalid data.** Excel can circle values that violate validation settings.
- **Error checking.** Automatically scan a worksheet and step through the process of correcting each identified error.

To audit a worksheet:

1. *Optional:* Choose View > Toolbars > Formula Auditing to display the Formula Auditing toolbar (**Figure 11.22**).
2. *Do any of the following:*
   - To locate precedents, select the cell containing the formula. Choose Tools > Auditing > Trace Precedents or click the Trace Precedents toolbar icon. Arrows appear on the sheet, showing formula dependencies (**Figure 11.23**). Perform Trace Precedents again to see if another level of precedents exists.

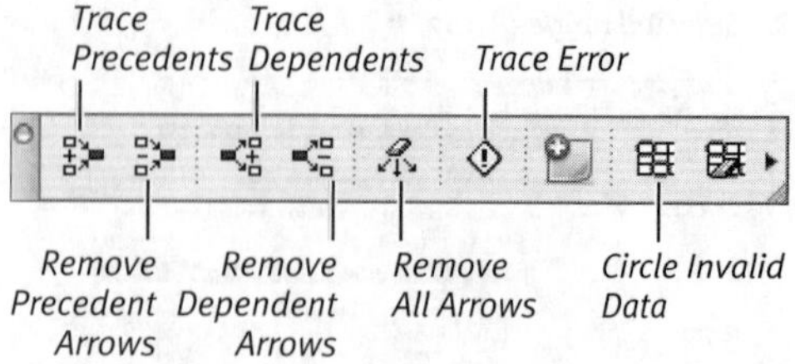

Figure 11.22 The Formula Auditing toolbar.

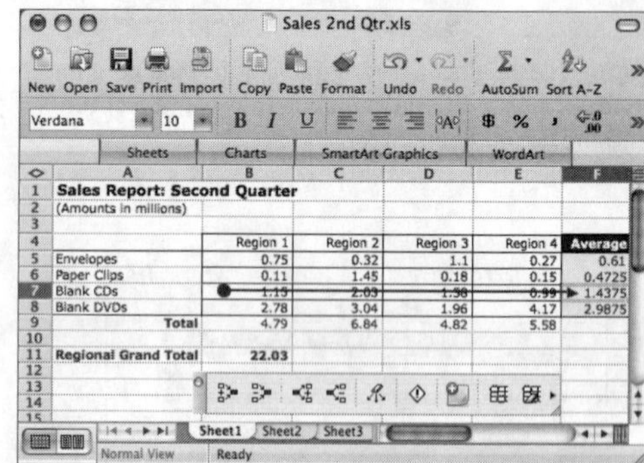

Figure 11.23 The arrow shows that the formula in cell F7 depends on the four cells in the range B7:E7.

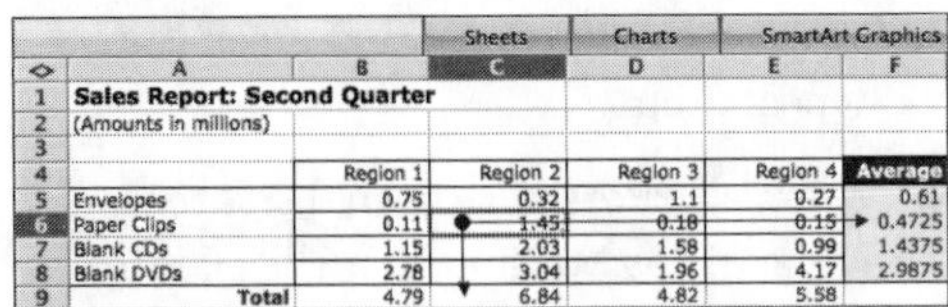

	A	B	C	D	E	F
1	**Sales Report: Second Quarter**					
2	(Amounts in millions)					
3						
4		Region 1	Region 2	Region 3	Region 4	Average
5	Envelopes	0.75	0.32	1.1	0.27	0.61
6	Paper Clips	0.11	1.45	0.18	0.15	0.4725
7	Blank CDs	1.15	2.03	1.58	0.99	1.4375
8	Blank DVDs	2.78	3.04	1.96	4.17	2.9875
9	Total	4.79	6.84	4.82	5.58	

Figure 11.24 The arrows show that cell C6 is used in two formulas, found in cells C9 and F6.

	A	B	C
1	**Sales Report: Second Quarter**		
2	(Amounts in millions)		
3			
4		Region 1	Region 2
5	Envelopes	0.75	0.32
6	Paper Clips	0.11	1.45
7	Blank CDs	1.15	2.03
8	Blank DVDs	2.78	3.04
9	Total	4.79	6.84

Figure 11.25 This cell is circled because numbers for the column must be between 0 and 2.

✔ Tips

- You can remove invalid data circles by clicking the Clear Validation Circles icon on the Formula Auditing toolbar.
- Validation criteria ensure that only certain data can be entered in a cell, range, or list column. For instance, you could specify that dates must fall between two values or that numbers must be larger than a particular value.

- ▲ To locate dependents, select the data cell. Choose Tools > Auditing > Trace Dependents or click the Trace Dependents toolbar icon. Arrows appear in the sheet, showing all formulas in which the selected cell is referenced (**Figure 11.24**).
- ▲ To trace an error, select the cell that contains an error indicator. An Error button appears. To identify the error type, rest the cursor on the Error button. To identify the cell(s) involved in the error, select the error cell and choose Tools > Auditing > Trace Error, click the Trace Error toolbar icon, or click the Error button and choose Trace *error condition.*

3. To remove arrows, *do the following:*
   - ▲ **All arrows.** Click the Remove All Arrows icon on the Formula Auditing toolbar or choose Tools > Auditing > Remove All Arrows.
   - ▲ **A dependent or precedent arrow.** Select the appropriate cell. Click the Remove Precedent Arrows or Remove Dependent Arrows icon on the Formula Auditing toolbar.

To identify invalid data:

1. Click the Circle Invalid Data icon on the Formula Auditing toolbar (see Figure 11.22).

   Any cell containing data that violates applied validation criteria is circled (**Figure 11.25**).

2. *Optional:* Correct the errors by editing the cells, changing the validation criterion, or removing the validation criterion.

   To view the criterion that a circled cell is violating, select the cell and choose Data > Validation.

To perform an error check:

1. Choose Tools > Error Checking.

   If no errors are found, a notification box appears. Click OK to dismiss it. Otherwise, the Error Checking dialog box appears, highlighting the first error (**Figure 11.26**).

2. For each identified error, *do any of the following:*
   - ▲ Click Help on this error to consult Excel Help for an explanation.
   - ▲ Click Trace Error to display arrows on the sheet that identify the other cells (if any) that are related to the error.
   - ▲ Click Ignore error to skip this error.
   - ▲ Click Edit in Formula Bar to correct the error.

3. Click Next to view the next error, if any. Repeat Step 2.

4. When all errors have been displayed, a final dialog box appears. Click OK to dismiss it.

Error description *Formula containing the error*

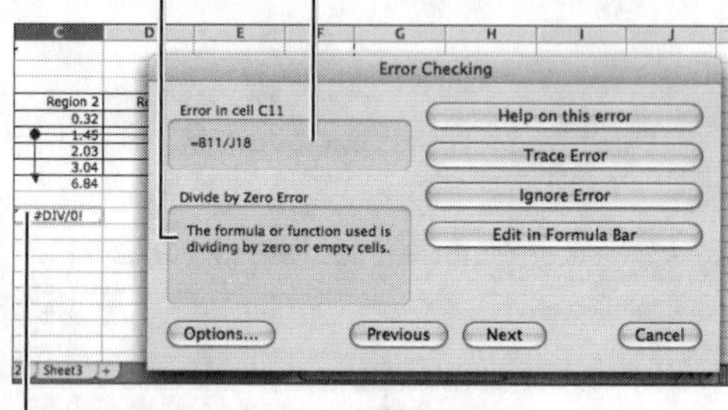

Cell containing the error (C11)

Figure 11.26 The Error Checking dialog box lists the first error. The erroneous cell is selected on the sheet.

Table 11.4

Common Excel Functions

Syntax	Description
AVERAGE(number1, number2, ...)*	Calculates the average (arithmetic mean) of the arguments
DAYS360(start_date, end_date, method)	Calculates the number of days between two dates based on a 360-day year (used in some accounting functions)
DDB(cost, salvage, life, period, factor)	Provides the depreciation of an asset for a specified period using the double-declining balance method or another specified method
FV(rate, nper, pmt, pv, type)	Calculates the future value of an investment
IRR(values, guess)	Provides the internal rate of return for a series of cash flows
MAX(number1, number2, ...)	Calculates the maximum value in a list of arguments
MEDIAN(number1, number2, ...)	Calculates the median (the middle value) of the given numbers
MIN(number1, number2, ...)	Calculates the smallest number in the list of arguments
NOW()	Provides the serial number of the current date and time
NPV(rate, value1, value2, ...)	Calculates the net present value of an investment based on a series of periodic cash flows and a discount rate
PMT(rate, nper, pv, fv, type)	Calculates the periodic payment for an annuity or loan
PV(rate, nper, pmt, fv, type)	Calculates the present value of an investment
ROUND(number, num_digits)	Rounds a number to a specified number of digits
SUM(number1, number2, ...)	Calculates the sum of all numbers in the list of arguments
STDEV(number1, number2, ...)	Estimates standard deviation based on a sample
TODAY()	Provides the serial number of today's date
VALUE(text)	Converts text to a number

*The expression (number1, number2,..) can also be specified as a range, such as C25:C47.

12

WORKING WITH LISTS

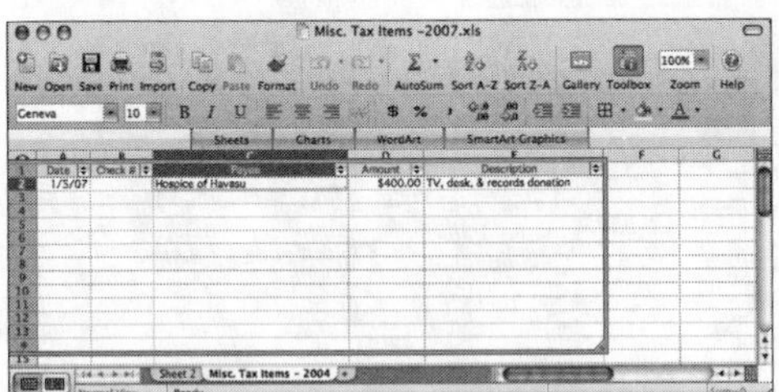

Figure 12.1 When you transform a data range into a list or create a list from scratch, Excel displays it with a special frame and attaches a drop-down menu to each column heading.

Many worksheets are simply lists of information, such as address data and club membership rosters. Such lists typically include few calculations, if any. A spreadsheet program is very adept at managing lists—considerably more so than a word processing program (the formerly preferred program for list management).

In recognition of the fact that people use spreadsheets to create and manage lists, Microsoft introduced the List Manager in Excel 2001. By creating a list (**Figure 12.1**), you can simplify cumbersome tasks such as sorting, filtering, and totaling data. This chapter explains how to use the List Manager to create and maintain lists.

Excel lists are essentially databases. If you intend to create lists in Excel, you'll also want to learn about Excel's database features, discussed in Chapter 14. Note that in Office 2007 (Windows), lists are called *tables*.

Creating a List

You can create a list by converting an existing data range or by using the List Manager to guide the list's creation.

To create a list:

1. *Do one of the following:*
   - ▲ To create a list in a new worksheet, choose File > Project Gallery, select the Blank Documents group, click the List Wizard icon, and click Open.
   - ▲ To create a new list in an existing worksheet, click the cell where you want the list to begin and choose Insert > List.
   - ▲ To convert an existing data range into a list, click any cell within the range and choose Insert > List.
   - ▲ Display the List toolbar (**Figure 12.2**) by choosing View > Toolbars > List. To convert an existing data range into a list, click any cell within the range. To create a list from scratch, click the starting cell. Then click the List Wizard icon on the List toolbar.

   The List Wizard appears (**Figure 12.3**).

2. In Step 1, select one of these options for the data source:
   - ▲ **None.** The list will be created from scratch.
   - ▲ **In an open workbook.** Use existing data from the specified range, converting it into a list. If the data already has column labels, be sure to check My list has headers.
   - ▲ **External data source.** Select this option and click the Get Data button to import the list data from an external file. (This option requires installed ODBC drivers.)

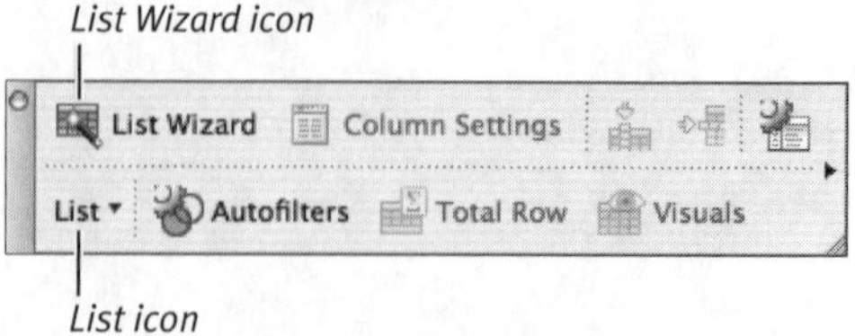

Figure 12.2 To create a list using the List toolbar, you can click the List Wizard icon or click the List icon's drop-down menu and choose List Wizard.

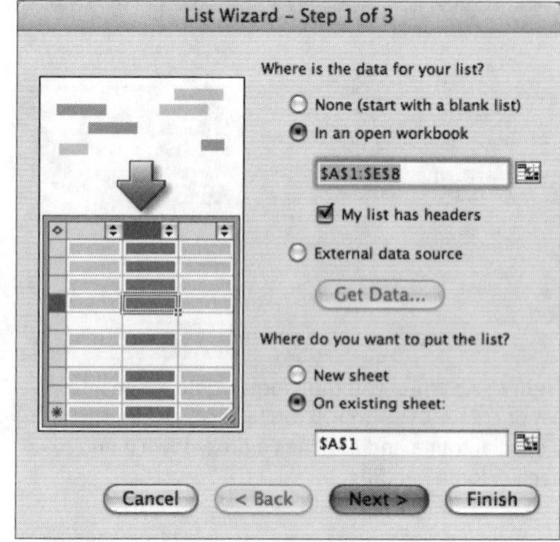

Figure 12.3 In Step 1, tell the List Manager where the data (if any) resides and where to create the list.

Moving a List

You can relocate any list. Move the cursor over any edge of the list. When it turns into an open hand, click and drag the list to its new location.

You can also use cut-and-paste to move a list—to another workbook or sheet, for example. Move the cursor over any edge of the list. When it turns into an open hand, click to select the list, and choose Edit > Cut (⌘X). Select a destination cell for the list, and choose Edit > Paste (⌘V).

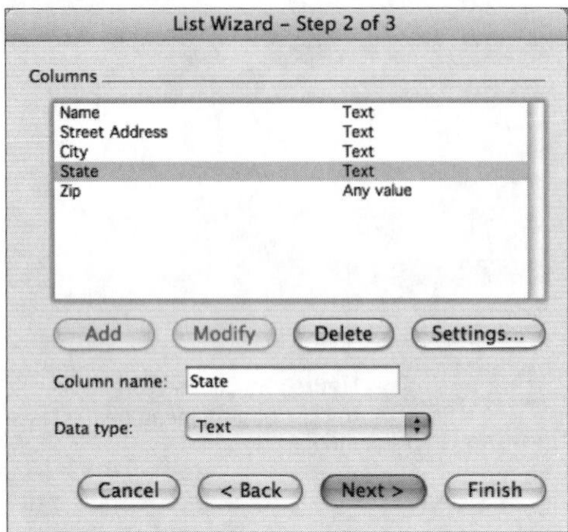

Figure 12.4 Specify column names and data types.

Figure 12.5 Name the list, indicate whether to add a totals row, and pick an AutoFormat style.

Name	Street Address	City	Stat	Zip
James Anderson	18 Birchmont Dr.	Bemidji	MN	56601
Mary Morton	273 Cedar Lane	Crookston	MN	58902
Simon Bolivar	453 Johns Rd.	Jamestown	NY	1702
Mark Abrams	67 Henderson Lane	Las Vegas	NV	70994
Julie Johnson	3456 Jones Dr.	Fredericks	WV	20338
Sarah Kendricks	237 Indian School	Phoenix	AZ	85022
Joan Thompson	786 Lian Street	San Francisco	CA	90023

Figure 12.6 This is an example of an existing data range converted to a named, formatted list.

3. Indicate where the list should be placed:
   - ▲ **New sheet.** Create the list in a new, blank worksheet.
   - ▲ **On existing sheet.** The upper-left corner of the list will begin at the specified cell.

   Click Next. Step 2 appears (**Figure 12.4**).
4. *Do one of the following:*
   - ▲ If the list is based on existing data, select each column, select a data type from the drop-down Data type list, edit the column name (optional), and click Modify after each column change.
   - ▲ If the list is being created from scratch, enter each column name, select a data type from the drop-down Data type list, and click Add. (The order in which columns are added will match their order in the list.)
5. *Optional:* To set formatting, conditional formatting, or validation options for the currently selected field, click Settings. Repeat for other fields as necessary. Click Next to continue.
6. In Step 3 (**Figure 12.5**), name the list and indicate whether you want a totals row. You can also choose an AutoFormat style.
7. Click Finish.

   The list appears on the worksheet, starting at the designated cell (**Figure 12.6**).

✔ Tips

- When your list appears, the List toolbar also appears (see Figure 12.2). You can use it to modify any list element.
- When converting existing data to a list, you can still add, delete, and modify columns (Figure 12.4).
- To convert a list back to normal data, click the List icon on the List toolbar and choose Remove List Manager.

Entering and Editing Data

Cells in a list are the same as other worksheet cells. You can use normal editing techniques to enter, delete, and modify list cell contents. In addition, you may find the following editing procedures useful.

To edit list data:

- To add new data to a list, you can use any of the following techniques:
  - Type data into each cell as you would in any worksheet. Press Tab or Shift Tab to move to the next or previous cell.
  - Choose Data > Form, or click the List icon on the List toolbar and choose Form (**Figure 12.7**). Use the Form dialog box to edit existing records, enter new records, or delete records (**Figure 12.8**).
  - To create a new *record* (list row), enter data in the row marked with an asterisk (*) at the bottom of the list.
- To delete a list row, select a cell in the row and *do one of the following:*
  - Choose Edit > Delete Row.
  - Click the List icon in the List toolbar and choose List > Delete > Row.

✔ Tips

- As you begin typing a cell entry, a list of previous entries for the column that begin with the same characters appears. You can select one of these items as a data-entry shortcut.
- To clear the contents of a row without deleting it, select the entire row. Choose Edit > Clear > Contents, or click the List toolbar icon and choose Clear Contents.
- See Chapter 14 for information on using forms for data entry and editing.

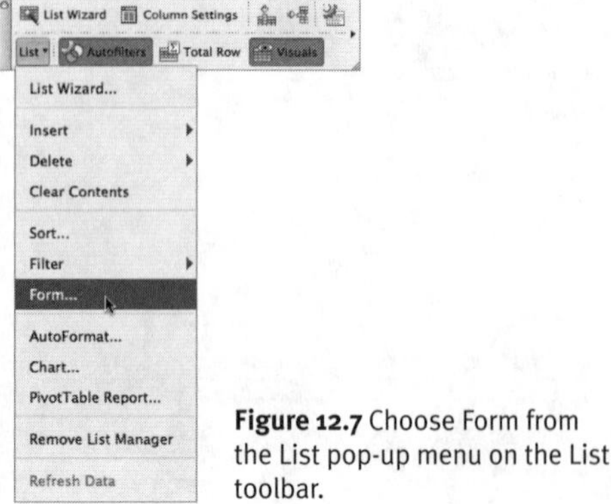

Figure 12.7 Choose Form from the List pop-up menu on the List toolbar.

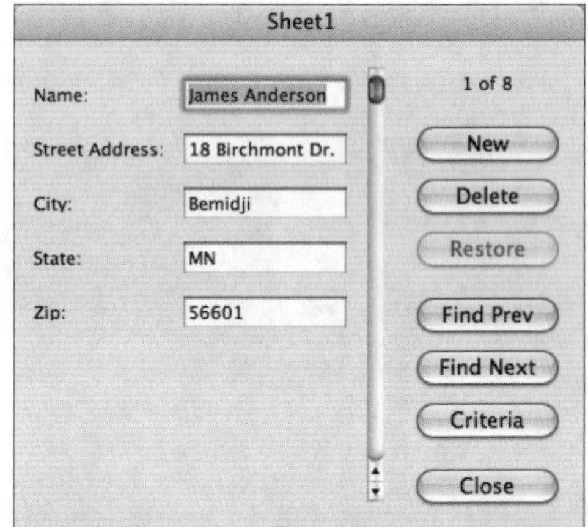

Figure 12.8 You can optionally use a form to enter new records, edit existing records, or delete records.

Adding New Columns

To add a new column to an existing list, click a cell where you want to insert the column. Then click the Insert Column icon on the List toolbar or choose Insert > Columns. To complete the process, edit the column name.

To add a blank column to the end of a list, widen the list frame by dragging its lower-right corner. A blank, gray area appears. Click the (New Column) text and name the new column.

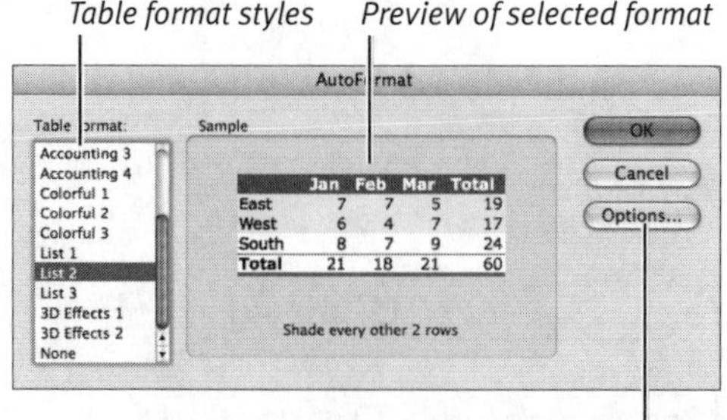

Figure 12.9 Select a format to apply to the list.

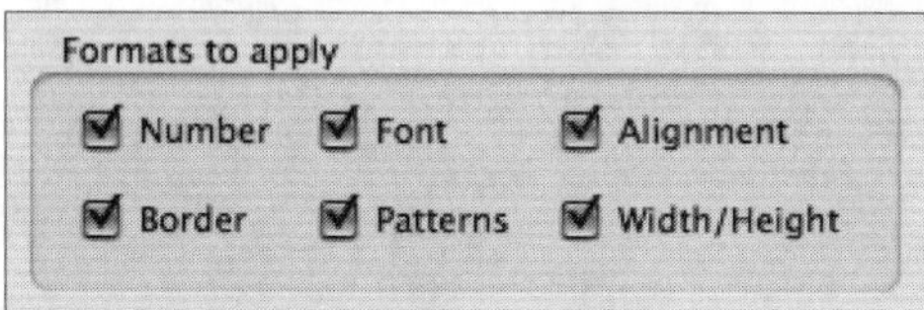

Figure 12.10 Click Options to reveal this section at the bottom of the AutoFormat dialog box, enabling you to specify formatting options to apply to the list.

Formatting a List

After you've entered the list data (or at least several records), you may want to format the list. In addition to standard cell-formatting options (such as bold, italic, font, size, borders, and shading), there are formats that you can apply to the entire list.

To format an entire list:

1. Click any cell in the list.
2. *Do either of the following:*
   - ▲ Choose Format > AutoFormat.
   - ▲ Click the List icon on the List toolbar and choose AutoFormat.

   The AutoFormat dialog box appears (**Figure 12.9**).
3. Select any of the Table format styles in the left pane to see a preview of the format. To apply the selected format to the list (see Figure 12.6), click OK.

✔ Tips

- If you click the Options button in the AutoFormat dialog box, you can selectively enable or disable AutoFormat elements, such as borders and cell patterns (**Figure 12.10**).
- After formatting a list with AutoFormat, you can still apply normal cell and text formatting.
- To get the full effect of your list's new appearance, click the Visuals icon on the List toolbar to hide the frame. Click the icon again to restore the list frame.
- To learn how to format individual cells, cell ranges, and particular columns or rows, see Chapter 10.

Filtering a List

As your list grows, you may occasionally want to view only rows that match certain criteria. You can *filter* a list in this manner to generate a data subset for printing, charting, or record deletion, for example.

To apply an AutoFilter to a list:

1. Set the list for AutoFilter by choosing Data > Filter > AutoFilter or by clicking the Autofilters icon on the List toolbar.

   When enabled, every column title is accompanied by a pair of arrows and the Autofilters toolbar icon is darkened.
2. Click the AutoFilter arrows beside the column on which you want to filter and choose a filtering option from the drop-down menu (**Figure 12.11**).

   Only records that match the criterion are shown. The others are temporarily hidden.
3. *Optional:* To further filter the list, choose additional criteria from other columns.
4. To restore all or some of the currently hidden records, *do one of the following:*
   - ▲ To show all list records, choose Data > Filter > Show All or choose Filter > Show All from the List toolbar icon.
   - ▲ If you've applied multiple filters, click the AutoFilter arrows for the filter you wish to remove and choose Show All.

✔ Tips

- If you want to edit records with missing data for a given column, choose Show Blanks.
- Any column to which a filter has been applied displays blue AutoFilter arrows.
- For additional filtering techniques and tips, see Chapter 14.

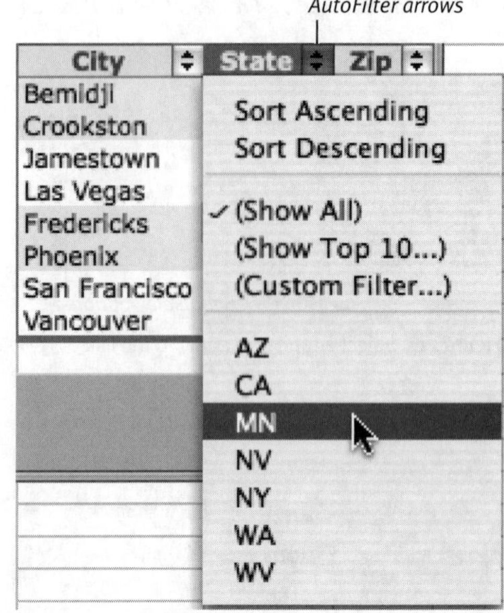

Figure 12.11 To apply or remove a filter, click a column's AutoFilter arrows and choose an option from the drop-down menu that appears.

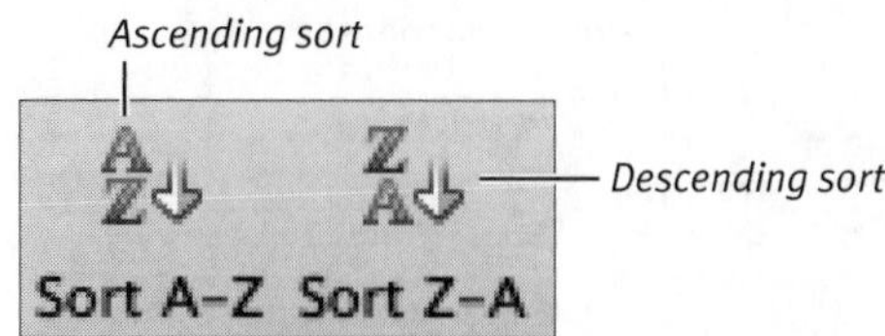

Figure 12.12 The Standard toolbar has icons for ascending and descending sorts.

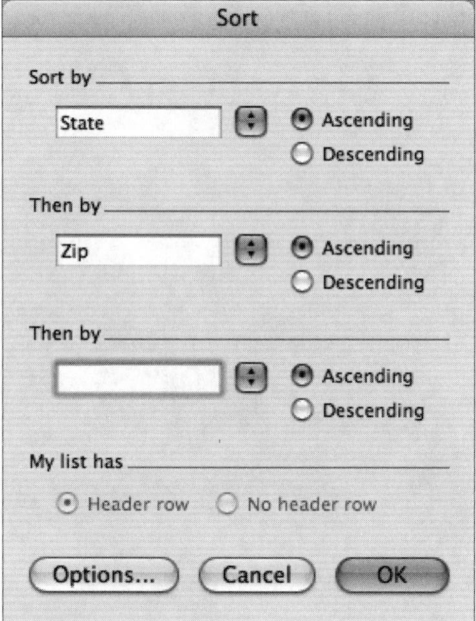

Figure 12.13 Specify fields by which you want to sort, and whether each one is ascending or descending.

Sorting a List

You can sort a list by the values in one or more columns. When sorting on multiple columns, each additional column serves as a tie-breaker. For instance, you could sort on State and on Zip Code. This would group each state's records together, while breaking them into subgroups for each Zip Code.

To perform a simple sort:

- *Do one of the following:*
  - Click any cell within the column on which you want to sort. Click the Sort A-Z or Sort Z-A icon on the Standard toolbar (**Figure 12.12**).
  - With AutoFilter enabled, click the AutoFilter arrows of the column on which you want to sort. Choose Sort Ascending or Sort Descending from the drop-down menu (see Figure 12.11).

  The list rows are reordered.

To perform a complex sort:

1. Click any cell in the list.
2. Choose Data > Sort, or click the List toolbar icon and choose Sort.

   The Sort dialog box appears (**Figure 12.13**).
3. Select the primary sort field from the Sort by drop-down list and click the Ascending or Descending radio button.
4. Select additional sort columns from the Then by drop-down lists, and set each one to Ascending or Descending.
5. Click OK to perform the specified sorts.

✔ Tips

- When sorting by day or month, you can sort in calendar order instead of alphabetically. Click Options in the Sort dialog box. In the Sort Options dialog box that appears (**Figure 12.14**), select a day or month format from the First key sort order drop-down list. (Note that such a custom sort can only be applied to the *primary* sort field.)
- The Sort Options dialog box is also where you can specify column sorts (rather than the usual row sorts). In the Orientation section of the dialog box (Figure 12.14), select Sort left to right and then click OK. In the Sort dialog box, the Sort by and Then by drop-down lists will now contain row identifiers.

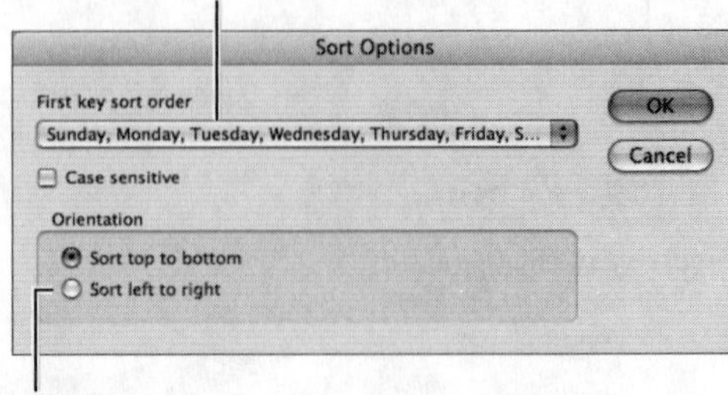

Figure 12.14 Use the Sort Options dialog box to specify a custom sort or to execute a column-based sort.

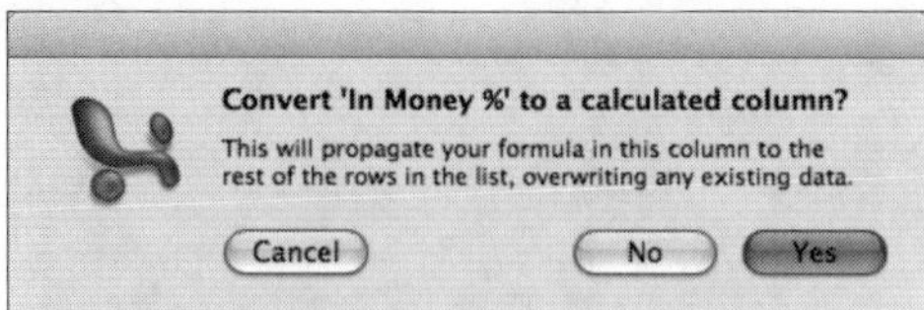

Figure 12.15 This dialog box appears whenever you enter a formula in a list cell.

H	I	J	K	L	M	N	O
Races	Wins	Places	Shows	Win %	Place %	Show %	In Money %
11	4	0	0	36%	0%	0%	36%
18	4	1	1	22%	6%	6%	33%
13	3	2	2	23%	15%	15%	54%
4	1	0	1	25%	0%	25%	50%
10	2	1	4	20%	10%	40%	70%
8	3	0	3	38%	0%	38%	75%
7	1	1	1	14%	14%	14%	43%

Figure 12.16 The last four columns in this list are calculated columns.

Calculated Columns

Formulas in a list work differently than ones elsewhere in the worksheet. Any column can contain a mixture of formulas and data. However, you also can insert the *same* formula into every cell of a column. This is known as a *calculated column*. If you later add rows to the list, the formula is automatically copied to the new cells in the column.

To create a calculated column:

1. If necessary, insert a new column in the list in which to place the formula.

   A calculated column can be defined in a column that contains data, but the column's cells will be overwritten by the formula results. It's usually more desirable to start with a new or empty column.

2. Select a cell in the column, and type or paste the formula into the cell. Complete the formula by pressing Return.

   A dialog box appears (**Figure 12.15**).

3. *Do one of the following:*
   - ▲ Click Yes to create a calculated column. The formula is copied to all other cells in the column (**Figure 12.16**).
   - ▲ Click No to apply the formula only to the current cell.
   - ▲ Click Cancel to resume editing the cell.

✔ Tips

- You can replace the formula in a calculated column with a new one. Click Yes in the dialog box that appears (Figure 12.15). Like the original formula, the new formula will propagate to every cell in the column.
- You can also create calculated columns using the List Wizard. Select Calculated Column as the data type for the column (see Figure 12.4), and enter the formula.

Adding a Total Row

A list can optionally have a single *total row* at its bottom, enabling you to calculate summary statistics across all records in the list. Each column can display a different statistic or none at all. In a donations list, for example, you could compute total donations, the average of the most recent donations, and a count of the number of donor records.

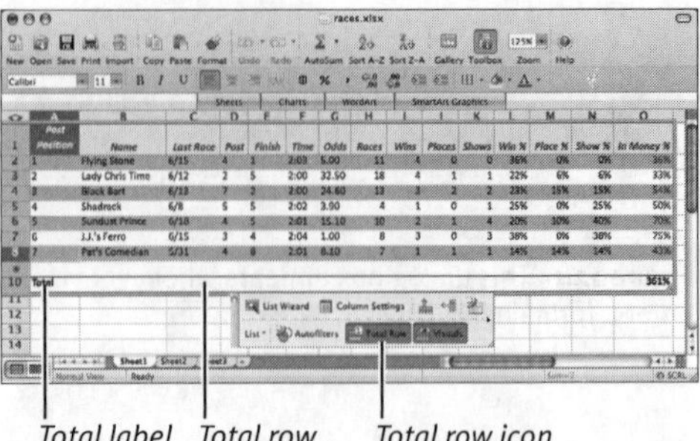

Figure 12.17 When enabled, the total row appears at the bottom of the list.

To add a total row to a list:

1. Select a cell in the list to make the list active.
2. Click the Total Row icon on the List toolbar.
   The total row appears at the bottom of the list (**Figure 12.17**).
3. *Optional:* Edit or delete the *Total* label in the left-most cell of the total row.
4. To display a summary statistic for a column, click the total row cell beneath the column. Click the arrows that appear beside the cell, and choose a statistic from the drop-down menu (**Figure 12.18**).
5. Repeat Step 4 for each additional column you want to summarize (**Figure 12.19**).
6. Format the total row cells as desired.

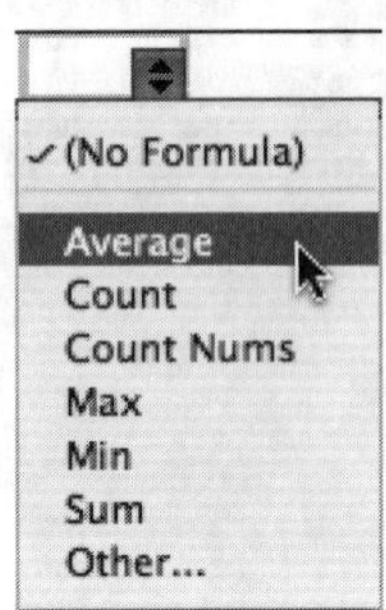

Figure 12.18 Each cell in the total row has a drop-down menu from which you can choose a statistical function.

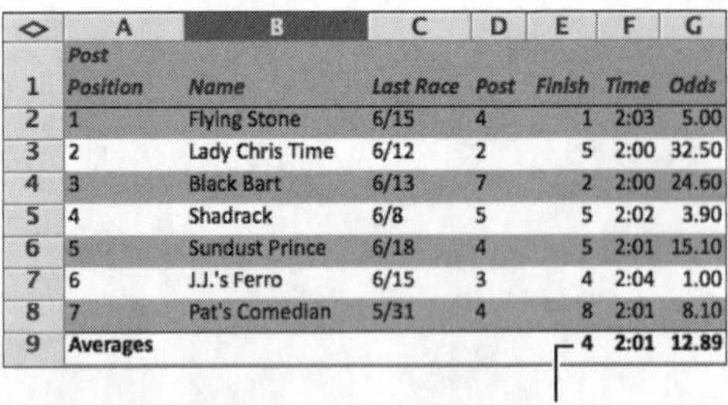

	A	B	C	D	E	F	G
1	Post Position	Name	Last Race	Post	Finish	Time	Odds
2	1	Flying Stone	6/15	4	1	2:03	5.00
3	2	Lady Chris Time	6/12	2	5	2:00	32.50
4	3	Black Bart	6/13	7	2	2:00	24.60
5	4	Shadrack	6/8	5	5	2:02	3.90
6	5	Sundust Prince	6/18	4	5	2:01	15.10
7	6	J.J.'s Ferro	6/15	3	4	2:04	1.00
8	7	Pat's Comedian	5/31	4	8	2:01	8.10
9	Averages				4	2:01	12.89

Figure 12.19 In this harness racing list, the total row displays averages for all appropriate columns.

✓ Tips

- If the function you need isn't listed in the drop-down menu, choose Other.
- To eliminate the summary statistic for a column, choose (No Formula) from the drop-down menu.
- If you disable the total row by clicking the Total Row icon again, all assigned summary statistics will be removed. Clicking the icon again will *not* restore them (as it does in Office 2007).

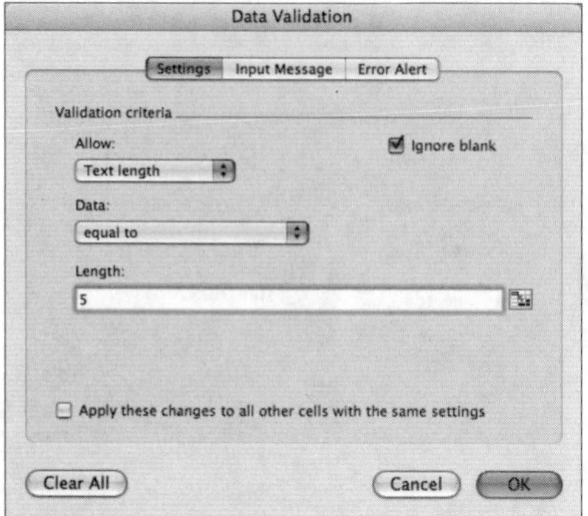

Figure 12.20 Specify a validation criterion on the Settings tab of the dialog box.

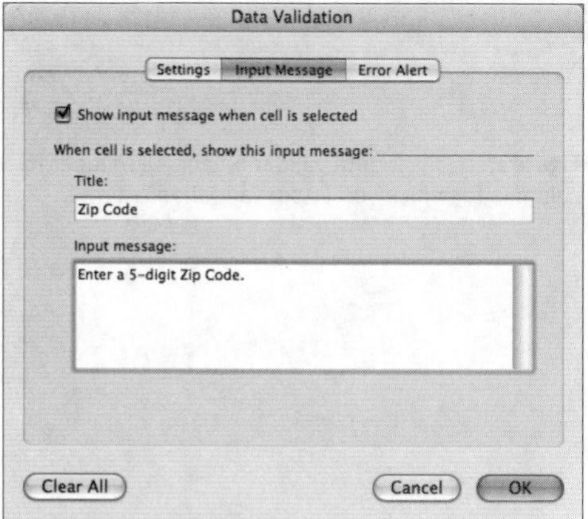

Figure 12.21 Enter an optional pop-up message for users who tab or click into a cell in this column.

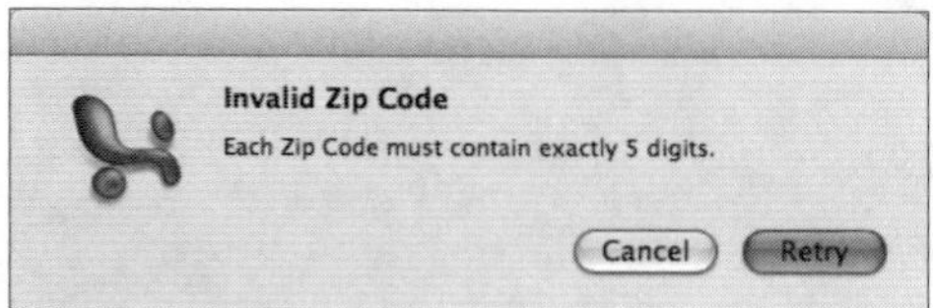

Figure 12.22 When a Stop error message appears, the user can click Retry to correct the error or Cancel to delete the errant cell entry.

Data Validation

Excel allows you to set a validation criterion for any column to ensure that only valid data is entered. For example, a Zip Code column could be restricted to entries of exactly five digits. Validation tests are automatically applied as you add items to the list. You can set validation options when creating a list or afterwards (described in the following steps).

To set validation options:

1. Click a cell in the column for which you'd like to set a validation criterion.
2. Choose Data > Validation.

   The Data Validation dialog box appears (**Figure 12.20**).
3. On the Settings tab, set a validation criterion by making choices from the drop-down lists and typing in the text box(es).
4. *Optional:* To prevent blank entries in the column, remove the check mark from Ignore blank.
5. *Optional:* If you want a pop-up box to appear whenever you select a cell in the column, click the Input Message tab. Enter a title and message text (**Figure 12.21**).
6. *Optional:* To enter an error message that will appear whenever validation fails, click the Error Alert tab. Enter a title and message text, and choose a message style from the Style drop-down menu:
   - **Stop.** Prevent further work until the error is corrected.
   - **Warning.** Offer a choice of correcting or accepting the entered data.
   - **Information.** Display only explanatory text.

   Click OK when you're done. If an incorrect value is later entered into a cell in this column, the error message appears (**Figure 12.22**).

✔ Tips

- You can also set validation criteria in the List Wizard.
- If you can't remember which columns have validation criteria, choose Edit > Go To. In the Go To dialog box, click Special. In the Go To Special dialog box that appears (**Figure 12.23**), select Data Validation and All. Click OK. Excel highlights the letters of all columns for which a data validation criterion has been set.

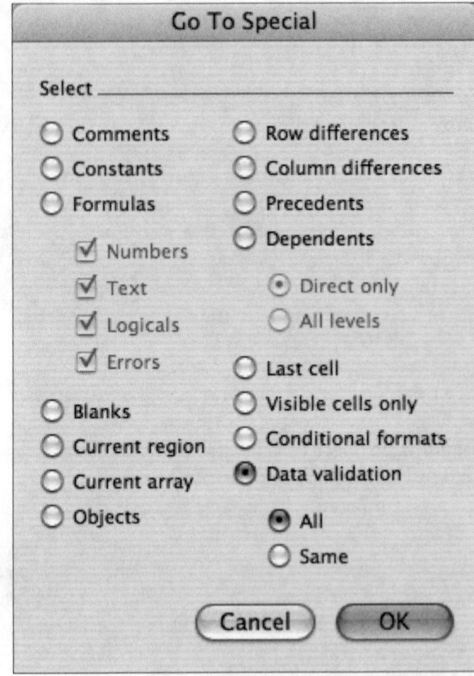

Figure 12.23 Click Data Validation and All to identify columns for which you've set validation criteria.

13

Charts and Graphs

Numeric information is often easiest to understand when presented graphically. In Excel 2008, you can create 73 different styles of charts, including bar, column, line, area, pie, scatter, bubble, radar, and stock charts—and many of them can be 3-D.

After Excel has generated a chart, you can tailor it to suit your needs. You can add, edit, or delete titles, labels, legends, and gridlines. You can also add, change, or remove color, patterns, or shading, as well as change the scale, labeling, and look of the axes. If you later edit a chart's source data, the chart will automatically reflect the new values.

In this chapter, you'll learn to create charts from existing data and display them in the current worksheet. Chapter 18 explains the process of creating charts to embellish a PowerPoint presentation. (These same techniques apply equally to adding a chart to a Word document.) Chapter 29 offers assistance in pasting, embedding, and linking existing Excel charts into Word documents and PowerPoint presentations.

✔ **Tips**

- Don't be afraid to experiment with options you don't completely understand. You can undo almost any modification by choosing Edit > Undo or by clicking the Undo icon on the Standard toolbar.
- The Chart Wizard is no longer a part of Office. It has been replaced by the chart thumbnails in the Elements Gallery. Creating charts in all Office applications requires the use of Excel. In fact, if Excel 2008 isn't installed on your Mac, you won't be able to create charts.

Creating Charts

As in former versions of Excel, you can easily create a clustered column chart (the default chart type) from selected data. In most cases, though, you'll begin by selecting a specific chart style from the Elements Gallery.

To create a default column chart:

1. Select the data from which you want to create the chart.
2. Choose Insert > Sheet > Chart Sheet.

   The clustered column chart appears on a new Chart Sheet (**Figure 13.1**).
3. Modify and customize the chart by following the instructions in the next section ("Modifying Charts").

✔ Tips

- You can also generate this type of chart by pressing F11.
- If they're relevant, be sure to include labels in the selected data. They're used when generating the chart.

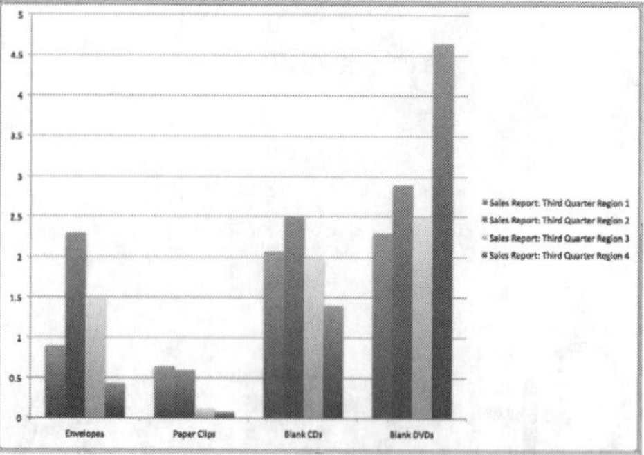

Figure 13.1 An attractive column chart is generated, complete with colored bars, axis labels, and a legend.

Fixing the F11 Shortcut

In Mac OS X 10.3 and later, F11 is a Mac OS X keyboard shortcut that you press to reveal the Desktop. To allow F11 to perform its charting function in Excel, you'll have to associate the Desktop shortcut with a different key. *Do the following:*

1. Click the System Preferences icon in the Dock or choose System Preferences from the Apple menu.
2. In the System Preferences window, click the Dashboard & Exposé (Tiger) or Exposé & Spaces (Leopard) icon.
3. Choose another shortcut for Desktop (**Figure 13.2**).
4. Close the System Preferences window.

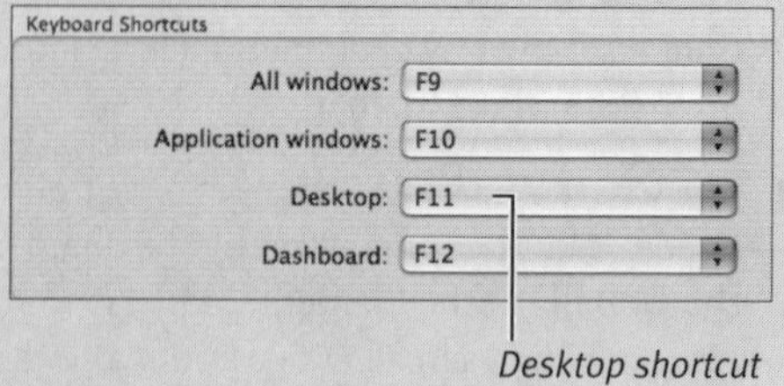

Figure 13.2 Choose a new keyboard shortcut for Desktop (OS X 10.4.11/Tiger shown).

◇	A	B	C	D	E
1		Sales Report: Second Quarter			
2					
3		Region 1	Region 2	Region 3	Region 4
4	Envelopes	0.75	0.4	1.1	0.27
5	Paper Clips	0.11	0.17	0.18	0.15
6	Blank CDs	1.15	2.03	1.58	0.99
7	Blank DVDs	2.78	3.04	1.96	4.17
8	Total	**4.79**	**5.64**	**4.82**	**5.58**

Figure 13.3 Select the data to be charted. In this case, the selections are A3:E4 and A6:E7 (skipping the data for paper clip sales).

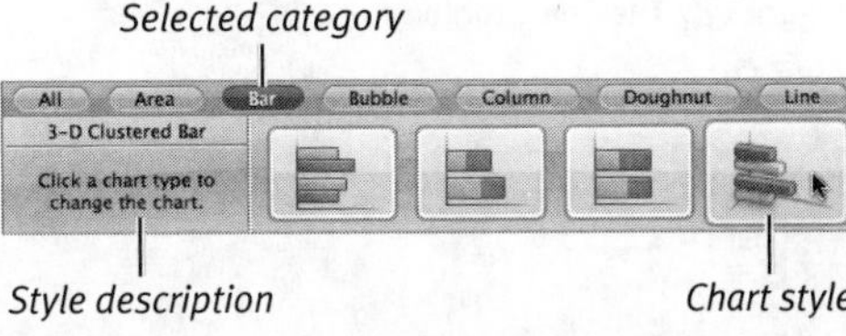

Figure 13.4 Select a chart category by clicking its button, and then select a style by clicking its thumbnail.

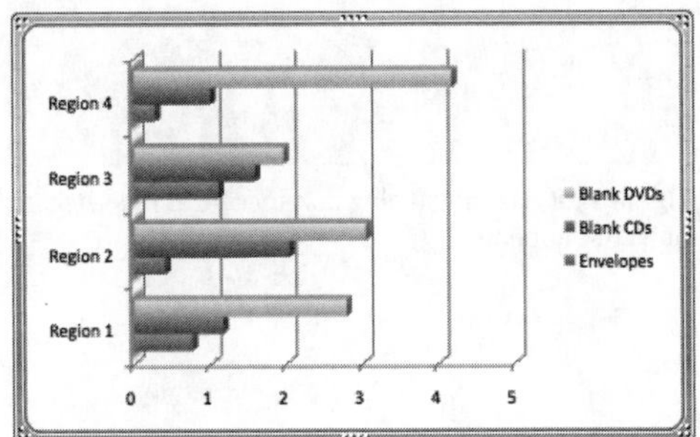

Figure 13.5 The initial chart appears (with default formatting and options).

To create a chart using the Elements Gallery:

1. Select the data from which you want to create the chart (**Figure 13.3**).
2. *Do one of the following:*
   - ▲ Click the Charts tab in the Elements Gallery.
   - ▲ Choose Insert > Chart.

   The chart category buttons and style thumbnails appear (**Figure 13.4**).
3. Select a chart category by clicking its button (beneath the Elements Gallery tabs).
4. Scroll through the chart styles thumbnails. Click a thumbnail to apply the chart style to your data, creating the initial chart.

   You can view a description for any chart style by resting the cursor on its thumbnail.

   The completed chart appears as a floating object on the same sheet as the source data (**Figure 13.5**).

✔ Tips

- If they're relevant, be sure to include labels in the selected data. They're used when generating the chart (see Figures 13.3 and 13.5, for example).
- To chart nonadjacent data as shown in Figure 13.3, press ⌘ while drag-selecting cell ranges.
- To change a Chart Sheet chart to a floating chart (or vice versa), choose Chart > Move Chart. In the Chart Location dialog box, you can move a Chart Sheet chart onto a designated worksheet as a new floating object or move a floating chart onto a new Chart Sheet.

Modifying Charts

Although the initial chart may be perfect for your needs, you can also modify or embellish it as you like. Using a variety of techniques, you can change virtually any chart element, the data series, or even the chart type/style.

To modify a chart element:

1. To open a formatting dialog box for a given chart object, *do any of the following:*
   - Double-click the chart object.
   - Select the chart object. Choose the first command in the Format menu or press ⌘1 (**Figure 13.6**).
   - Control-click the chart object, and choose Format *object type* from the pop-up menu that appears.
   - Display the Chart toolbar (**Figure 13.7**) by choosing View > Toolbars > Chart. Select the object you want to modify from the Chart Objects drop-down list, and then click the Format Selected Object toolbar icon.
2. In the Format *object* dialog box (**Figure 13.8**), make the changes and click OK.

✔ Tips

- You can resize or move some chart elements, such as the legend and title. To resize a selected element or the chart, drag one of its handles. To move most elements, click an edge and drag.
- To add a title, expand the Chart Options section of the Formatting Palette, select Chart Title from the drop-down menu in the Titles sub-section, and enter the title in the text box. You can edit a title in the same text box or on the chart.
- You can make many changes by setting options in the Formatting Palette. For instance, you can apply Quick Styles and effects to the legend or chart background.

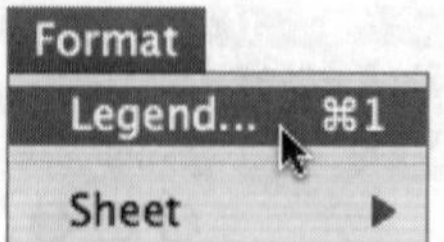

Figure 13.6 The wording of the first Format command changes to reflect the currently selected object(s).

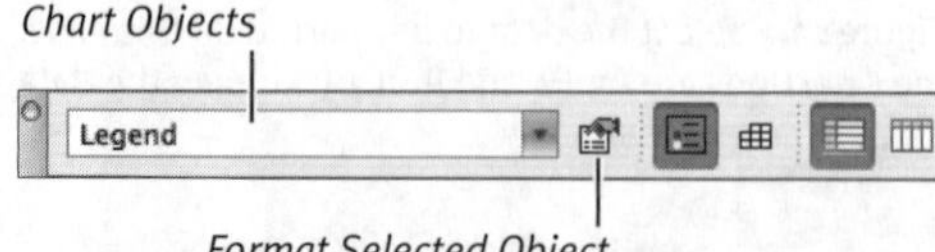

Figure 13.7 The Chart toolbar.

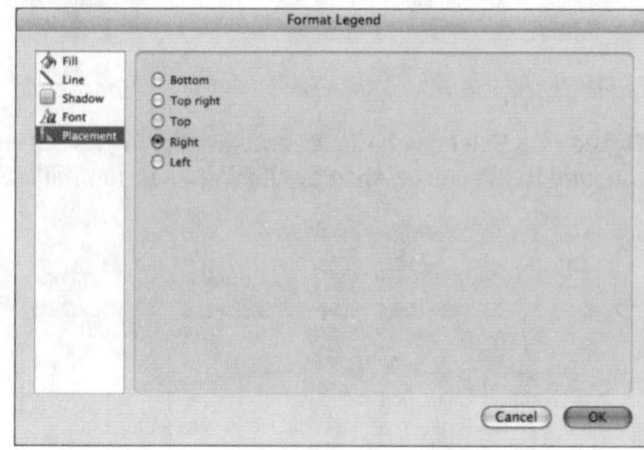

Figure 13.8 A Format dialog box specific to the selected object(s) appears.

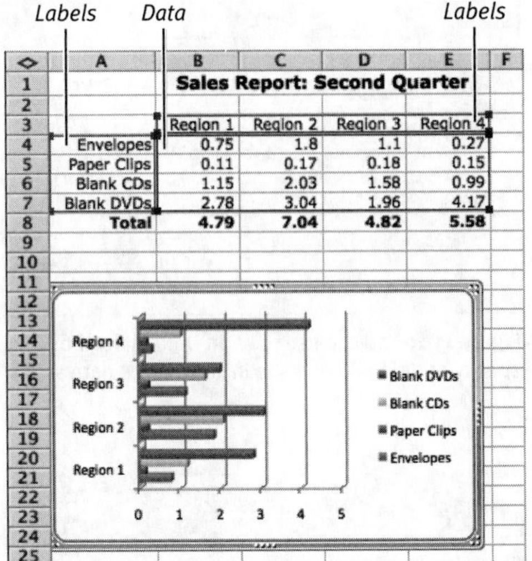

	A	B	C	D	E	F
1		Sales Report: Second Quarter				
2						
3		Region 1	Region 2	Region 3	Region 4	
4	Envelopes	0.75	1.8	1.1	0.27	
5	Paper Clips	0.11	0.17	0.18	0.15	
6	Blank CDs	1.15	2.03	1.58	0.99	
7	Blank DVDs	2.78	3.04	1.96	4.17	
8	**Total**	**4.79**	**7.04**	**4.82**	**5.58**	

Figure 13.9 When you select a chart that's on the same sheet as the source data, the source data and labels are surrounded by colored rectangles.

To change the chart type or style:

1. Make the chart active by selecting it or one of its elements.
2. Select a new chart type/style from the Charts tab of the Elements Gallery (see Figure 13.4).

   The chart is transformed as specified.

✔ Tip

- You can choose Chart > Chart Type to open the Charts tab of the Elements Gallery. Control-clicking the chart and choosing Change Chart Type from the pop-up menu has the same effect.

To change the data series for a chart on the same sheet as its data:

- To change any of the values in the current data series so they are reflected in the chart, edit the source data.
- To remove a data series from the chart, select the series in the chart and press Delete.
- To change the data series range, start by selecting the chart. (Click in the blank area around the chart or choose Chart Area from the Chart Objects menu on the Chart toolbar.) The current source data and labels are indicated by colored selection rectangles (**Figure 13.9**).

  Do any of the following:

  - To select a different contiguous series of the same size, move the cursor over any edge of the blue source data rectangle. When the cursor changes to a hand, drag the rectangle to select a new data range of the same size.
  - To change the size of the data range, move the cursor over a corner of the blue data selection rectangle and drag.

continues on next page

- To add another range to the data set, select the chart and choose Chart > Add Data. In the Add Data dialog box (**Figure 13.10**), select or type the additional range, and click OK.
- You can also change the data range for a selected chart in the Select Data Source dialog box. Choose Chart > Source Data or click the Edit icon in the Chart Data section of the Formatting Palette.

  Do any of the following:
  - Enter a new range or select the range in the worksheet (**Figure 13.11**).
  - To edit a single data series, select the series in the chart. References to the cells that contain data for the series appear in the formula bar, and the data range on the sheet is surrounded by a colored selection rectangle. Edit the references or alter the selection rectangle.
  - To remove a series, select it in the Series list box and click Remove (**Figure 13.12**).
  - To add a series to the chart, click the Add button. Click the icon beside the Y values box, select the new data values in the sheet, and click the icon again to record the values. Finally, to name the new series, type a name in the Name box or click the icon to the right of the box and select the name or label in the worksheet.
  - Click the Switch Row/Column button to reverse how the data is graphed. For example, when reversed, the chart in Figure 13.9 would group bars by item (**Figure 13.13**) instead of by region.

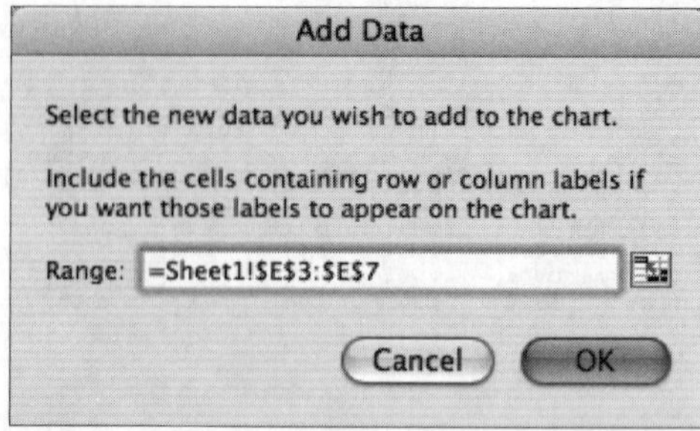

Figure 13.10 You can use the Add Data dialog box to specify additional ranges to include in the data set.

Figure 13.11 Select or type a new source data range in the top section of the Select Data Source dialog box.

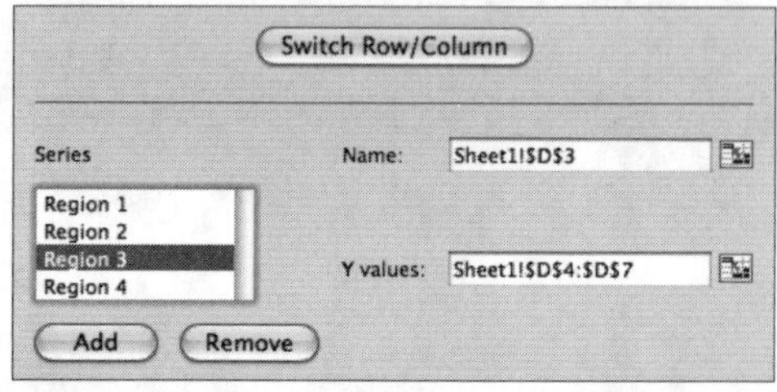

Figure 13.12 Use the bottom part of the Select Data Source dialog box to add and remove data series, as well as to swap rows and columns.

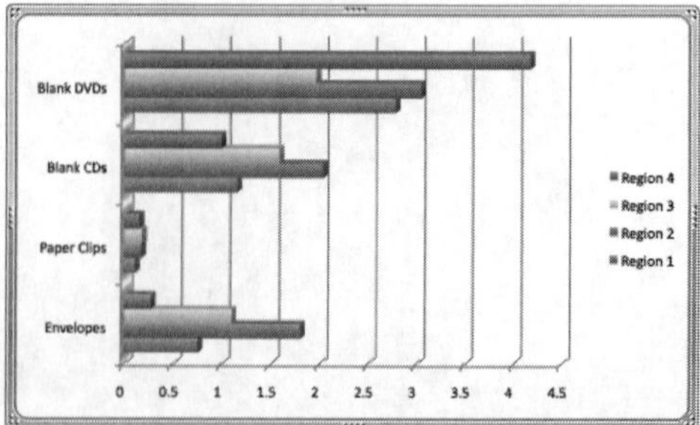

Figure 13.13 You can swap rows and columns to view your data in a different way.

To change the data series for a Chart Sheet chart:

- To change any of the values in the current data series so they are reflected in the chart, edit the source data.
- To remove a data series from the chart, select the series in the chart and press Delete.
- To edit a single data series, select the series in the chart. References to the cells that contain data for the series appear in the formula bar (**Figure 13.14**). Edit the references to change the data source.
- To use the Select Data Source dialog box to change the source data for a series, edit the data for the entire chart, or add or remove a series, select any part of the chart and *do one of the following:*
  - ▲ Choose Chart > Source Data.
  - ▲ Click the Edit icon in the Chart Data section of the Formatting Palette.

  Make the desired changes in the Select Data Source dialog box (see Figures 13.11 and 13.12), as explained in the previous step list.

✔ Tip

- ■ If the Chart toolbar is displayed, you can select any data series or chart element from the Chart Objects drop-down list.

=SERIES(Sheet1!$A$7,Sheet1!$B$3:$E$3,Sheet1!$B$7:$E$7,4)

Figure 13.14 You can edit the data range for a selected series in the formula bar.

To format all or a selected data series:

- To change the color of *all data series,* select the chart or any object on it and then select a new color scheme from the Chart Style section of the Formatting Palette (**Figure 13.15**).
- To format a *single data series*, select the series on the chart or by name from the Chart Objects list on the Chart toolbar. *Do any of the following:*
  - ▲ On the Formatting Palette, select a new fill color from the Colors, Weights, and Fills section.
  - ▲ Select new settings in the Format Data Series dialog box (**Figure 13.16**), and click OK.

    To open the Format Data Series dialog box, double-click an element in the data series, select a series element and choose Format > Data Series (⌘1), select a series element and click the Format Selected Object icon on the Chart toolbar, or Control-click an element in the data series and choose Format Data Series from the pop-up menu.

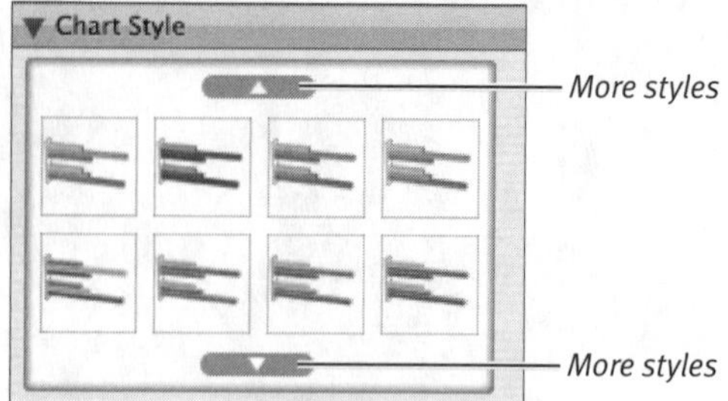

Figure 13.15 You can pick a new color scheme from the Chart Style section of the Formatting Palette.

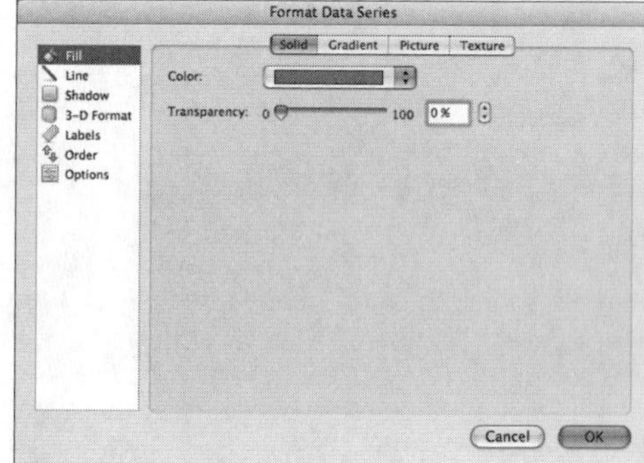

Figure 13.16 To format a single data series, you can set options in the Format Data Series dialog box.

Chart Element Definitions

The *chart area* is the chart's background. The *plot area* varies, depending on the chart style. In some, it is the background of the chart itself; in others, it refers only to the area immediately around the axis labels. (3-D column charts refer to the background areas as *walls.*) *Gridlines* are lines in the plot area denoting axis values. The *title, axes,* and *legend* are text identifiers used to label parts of the chart.

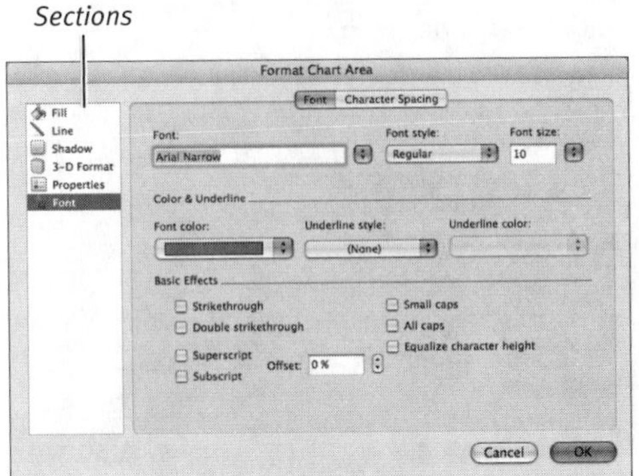

Figure 13.17 You can alter the formatting of the chart area (background) in Format Chart Area dialog box.

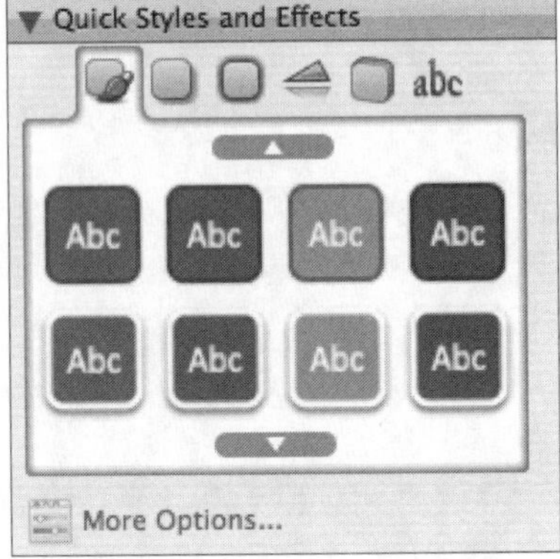

Figure 13.18 You can add a colorful background by applying a Quick Style.

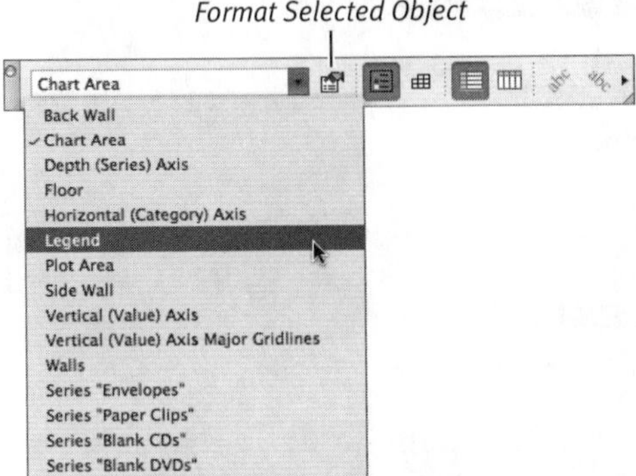

Figure 13.19 You can select chart elements by name from the Chart Objects list on the Chart toolbar.

To format the chart area (background):

◆ You can format the chart area using the Format Chart Area dialog box or the Formatting Palette:

- ▲ Open the Format Chart Area dialog box by double-clicking the chart area, selecting the chart area and choosing Format > Chart Area (⌘1), or selecting the chart area and clicking the Format Selected Object icon on the Chart toolbar.

  In the Fill section, set the fill color and transparency for the area surrounding the chart. Options chosen from the Line section apply to the border around the chart. Select the Font section (**Figure 13.17**) to pick a font for the axis labels, legend, and chart title.

- ▲ Additional options are available on the Formatting Palette. You can select an attractive, 3-D background from the Quick Styles and Effects section (**Figure 13.18**). You can also choose settings from the Font section and the Colors, Weights, and Fills section.

✔ Tips

- As you'll quickly discover, you can use the same techniques to format *any* chart element. Click the element or select it from the Chart Objects drop-down list on the Chart toolbar (**Figure 13.19**). Then click the Format Selected Object toolbar icon or select options from the Formatting Palette.

- Format the most general elements (such as the chart area) first and then the individual elements within that area (such as the axis labels).

To add or remove other chart elements:

◆ *Do any of the following:*

- ▲ You can delete any chart element (even a data series) by selecting it on the chart and pressing Delete.
- ▲ To add or remove the legend, click the Legend icon on the Chart toolbar. (If the legend has been manually moved, the first click restores it to the default position; the second click removes it.)

  You can also choose a legend option from the Legend drop-down menu in the Chart Options section of the Formatting Palette (**Figure 13.20**).
- ▲ To label the data points, choose an option from the Labels drop-down menu (Figure 13.20).
- ▲ To add or remove major or minor gridlines, click icons in the Gridlines subsection of the Chart Options section of the Formatting Palette.
- ▲ To display the source data with the chart (**Figure 13.21**), click the Data Table icon on the Chart toolbar or choose an option from the Chart Data section of the Formatting Palette.

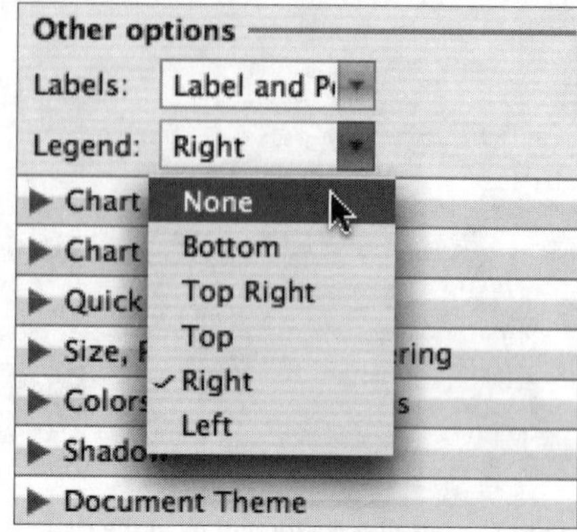

Figure 13.20 You can add, remove, or move the legend by choosing a command from this drop-down menu on the Formatting Palette.

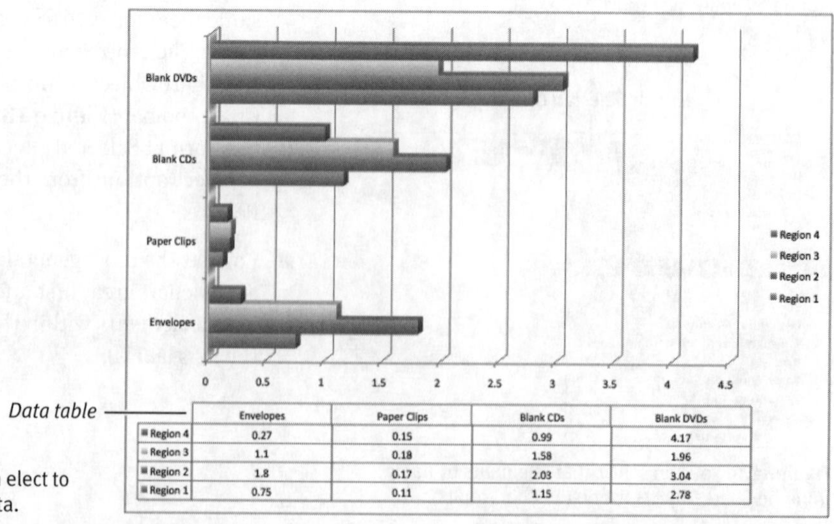

	Envelopes	Paper Clips	Blank CDs	Blank DVDs
Region 4	0.27	0.15	0.99	4.17
Region 3	1.1	0.18	1.58	1.96
Region 2	1.8	0.17	2.03	3.04
Region 1	0.75	0.11	1.15	2.78

Figure 13.21 You can elect to display the chart data.

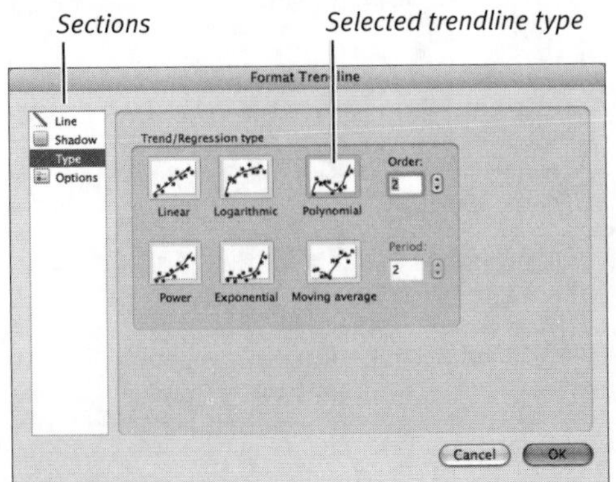

Figure 13.22 Specify a trendline type, line characteristics, and other settings.

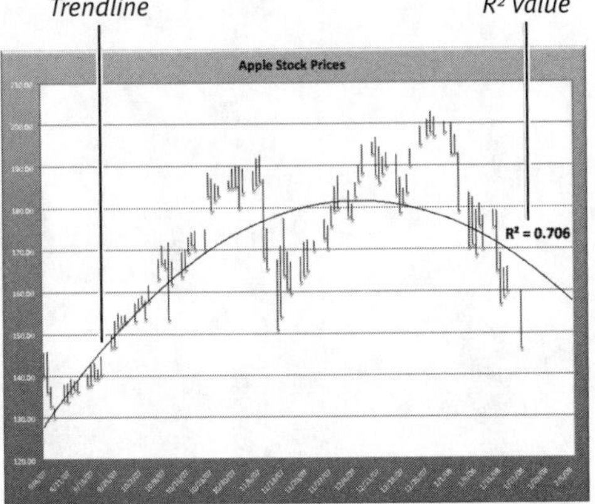

Figure 13.23 You can add a variety of trendline types and options to charts. In this example, a polynomial trendline is used to show a stock price trend.

Adding Trendlines

A *trendline* is a straight line or curve drawn through the points of a data series to show a trend. In order to provide additional information and make it easier to interpret the data, you can add a trendline to any chart in which the data changes over time.

To display a trendline for a data series:

1. Select a data series to which you want to add a trendline.

   Select the series by clicking one of its data points or by selecting the series name from the Chart Objects drop-down list on the Chart toolbar (see Figure 13.19).

2. Choose Chart > Add Trendline.

   The Format Trendline dialog box appears (**Figure 13.22**).

3. Select a section from the left side of the dialog box. Specify a trendline type, line type and characteristics, and other options, and then click OK.

   The trendline appears (**Figure 13.23**).

✔ Tips

- You can plot *multiple* trendlines, if you wish.
- To remove a trendline, select it on the chart and press Delete.
- To change the settings for an existing trendline, double-click it. Make changes in the Format Trendline dialog box and click OK.

14 Database Techniques

Office 2008 doesn't include a database application. However, unless you work with extremely large data sets or need a complex or relational database, Excel can probably provide all the database power you'll need.

In Excel, you enter data in rows. Each row is a *record* (one complete set of information). Each column is a *field* that contains one type of information for the record (**Figure 14.1**), such as a last name, Social Security number, or annual salary, for example. Rather than enter information directly into the worksheet cells, you can use an Excel "fill-in-the-blanks" form to make it easier to enter, edit, delete, and search for data. You can also import data from other programs, such as FileMaker Pro.

After you enter the data, you can sort it, view only the information that matches certain criteria, and calculate group totals and other summary statistics.

◇	A	B	C	D
1	Date	Service	Description	Amount
2	8/7/08	Eyeglasses and contact lenses	Visions	365.00
3	7/21/08	Eyeglasses and contact lenses	Repair	5.00
4	7/7/08	Doctors, dentists	Patty Stanton	20.00
5	3/11/08	Doctors, dentists	Dr. Lundin	290.00
6	5/1/08	Doctors, dentists	Dr. Lundin	67.00
7	6/11/08	Doctors, dentists	Dr. Lundin	10.00

Figure 14.1 In Excel, each row is a record; each column is a field.

Creating a Database

There are two ways to create a database in a worksheet. First, as explained in Chapter 12, you can use the List Manager. Second, you can manually create a database by entering the data in contiguous rows and columns, as explained below.

Note that *any* area of a worksheet can be considered a database as long as every data column has a label (which is treated as the field name) and the rows and columns are contiguous. A single blank row or column—even in the middle of an extensive data set—marks the edge of the database. Records beneath a blank row or fields to the right of a blank column aren't treated as part of the database.

To manually create a database:

1. In either a new or an existing worksheet, enter the field names at the top of a group of adjacent columns.
2. Enter the data into the rows below the field names (see Figure 14.1).

✔ Tips

- Create each new record directly beneath the last data row (**Figure 14.2**).
- You can speed data entry by preselecting a range—click and drag to make the selection. Press Tab after each cell entry to move through the range from left to right. When you reach the end of a row, you'll move to the start of the next row.
- If you *don't* preselect a range, the cell you initially select is treated as the beginning of your data-entry range. Press Tab after each cell entry to move to the cell to the right. When you complete the entry in the last cell of a row, press Return to move to the beginning of the next row (directly beneath the starting cell).

18	6/17/08	BlueCross BlueShield of AZ	237.00
19	7/1/08	BlueCross BlueShield of AZ	209.00
20			

Next record goes here

Figure 14.2 You add a new record in the blank row immediately beneath the last record.

- You don't have to dedicate an entire worksheet to a database. You can create a database as a separate area within any worksheet or include multiple databases in a single worksheet.

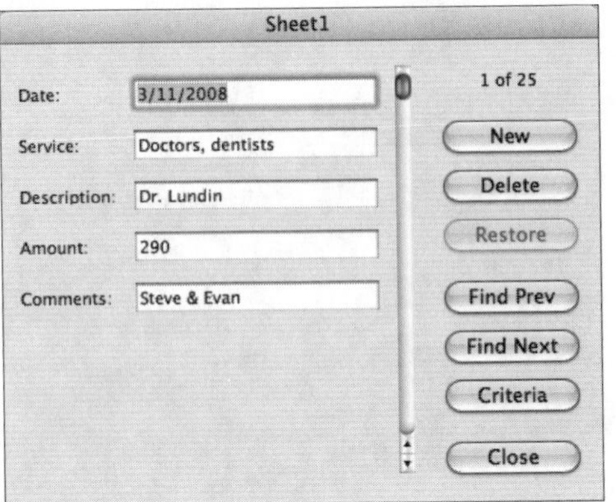

Figure 14.3 You can use a form to view records, create new records, edit data in existing records, and delete unwanted records.

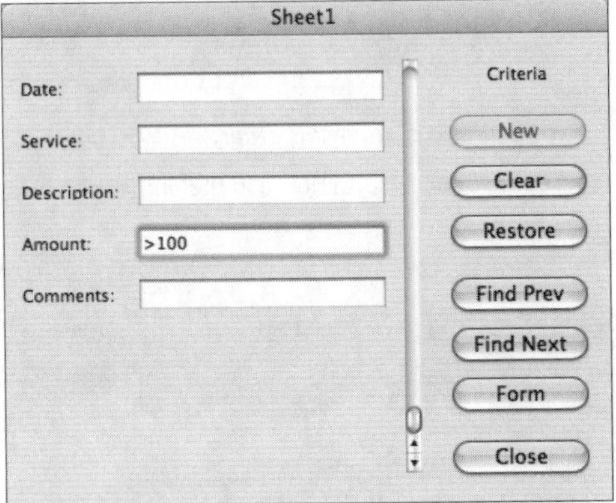

Figure 14.4 Enter search criteria in one or more fields. In this example, records in which the Amount field is greater than $100 will be identified as matches.

✔ Tips

- A form always opens to the first record in the database, regardless of the record that is selected when you choose Data > Form.
- A form can display up to 32 fields.

Using a Form for Data Entry

As explained in the previous section, you can manually create new records by adding rows at the bottom of the database. You can also use forms to speed data entry and make the process more like working with a traditional database application.

To use a form for data entry:

1. Click any cell in the database.
2. Choose Data > Form.
   A data-entry form appears (**Figure 14.3**).
3. With the form displayed, *do any of the following:*
   - To flip through the records in their current sort order, click Find Next, Find Prev, or the up and down arrows at the bottom of the scroll bar. To go directly to a record of interest, drag the scroll box/slider.
   - To create a new record, click the New button or drag the scroll box down to the blank record at the end of the database (labeled *New Record*). Enter the new data by typing and tabbing from field to field. When you're done, press Return or Enter to add the record.
   - To edit a record, display it, make the desired changes, and press Return or Enter.
   - Click Delete to delete the current record. Confirm the deletion.
   - To view only specific records, click Criteria. In the form that appears, enter search criteria (**Figure 14.4**). Repeatedly click Find Next and Find Prev to view the matching records. To resume working with the entire database, click Criteria, Clear, and Form.
4. To dismiss the form and record any changes you've made, click Close.

Database Operations

In any database, you can sort the records, *filter* (display only records that match certain criteria), and calculate subtotals.

To sort a database on a single field:

1. Select a cell in the column on which you want to sort the database.
2. Click the Sort A-Z or Sort Z-A toolbar icon.

To sort a database on one or more fields:

1. Click any cell in the database, and then choose Data > Sort.
2. In the Sort dialog box (**Figure 14.5**), set the primary sort field by selecting its field name from the Sort by drop-down list.
3. To sort from smallest to largest or earliest to latest, click the Ascending radio button. To sort from largest to smallest or latest to earliest, click Descending.
4. To perform additional sorts on the data, select fields from the Then by drop-down lists. Specify an Ascending or Descending sort for each field.
5. Select the Header row radio button to prevent Excel from treating the field labels as a data row that should also be included in the sort.
6. Click OK to sort the database.

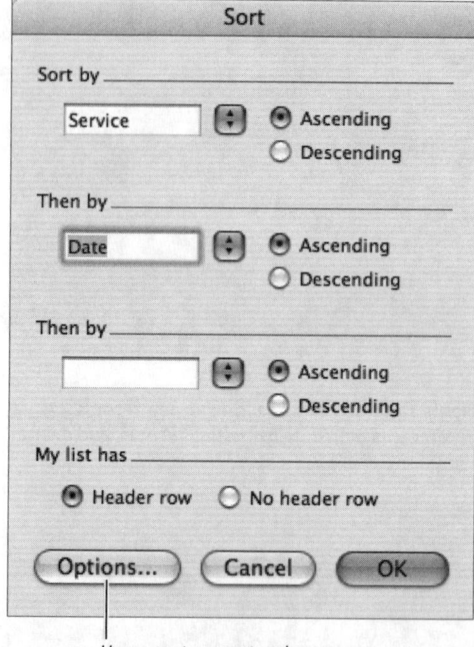

Figure 14.5 Specify sort criteria in the Sort dialog box.

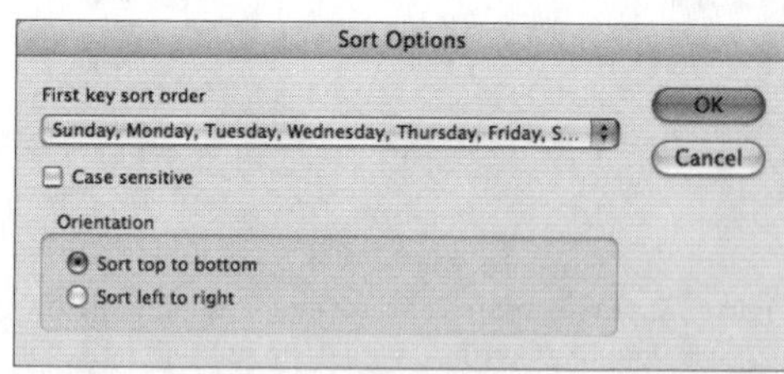

Figure 14.6 Select a custom sort order from the drop-down list. A custom sort can only be set for the primary sort field.

✔ Tips

- When sorting on multiple fields, specify fields in order of their importance. The second and third fields are tie breakers. For example, if you sort on Last Name, you could use First Name as the second sort field. If you sorted only on Last Name, all Johnsons would be grouped together, but their first names wouldn't be in a useful order.
- To sort by day or month name or to perform a column sort, click Options to display the Sort Options dialog box (**Figure 14.6**). Custom sorts are also discussed in Chapter 12.
- You can create your own custom sort order lists in the Custom Lists section of the Excel Preferences dialog box.

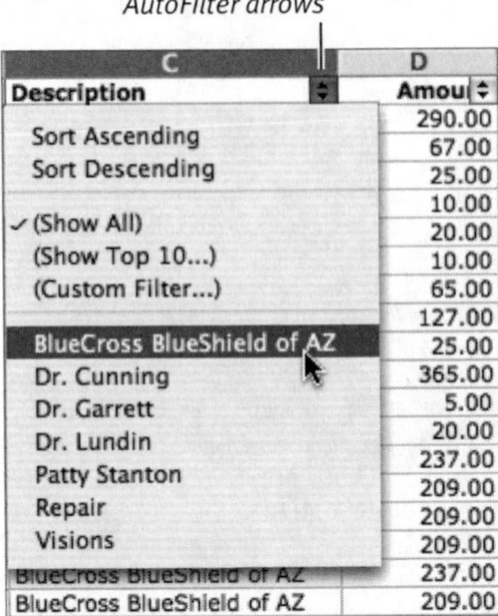

Figure 14.7 Select a filter criterion from a field's drop-down list.

	A	B	C
1	Da	Service	Description
2	3/18/08	Health insurance premiums	BlueCross BlueShield
3	3/18/08	Health insurance premiums	BlueCross BlueShield
4	4/24/08	Health insurance premiums	BlueCross BlueShield
5	5/1/08	Health insurance premiums	BlueCross BlueShield
6	5/28/08	Health insurance premiums	BlueCross BlueShield
7	6/17/08	Health insurance premiums	BlueCross BlueShield
8	7/1/08	Health insurance premiums	BlueCross BlueShield
9	7/28/08	Health insurance premiums	BlueCross BlueShield
10	9/7/08	Health insurance premiums	BlueCross BlueShield
11	9/22/08	Health insurance premiums	BlueCross BlueShield
12	10/2/08	Health insurance premiums	BlueCross BlueShield
13	11/4/08	Health insurance premiums	BlueCross BlueShield
14	12/11/08	Health insurance premiums	BlueCross BlueShield
15	12/30/08	Health insurance premiums	BlueCross BlueShield

Figure 14.8 The database is filtered to show only the records that match the selected criterion.

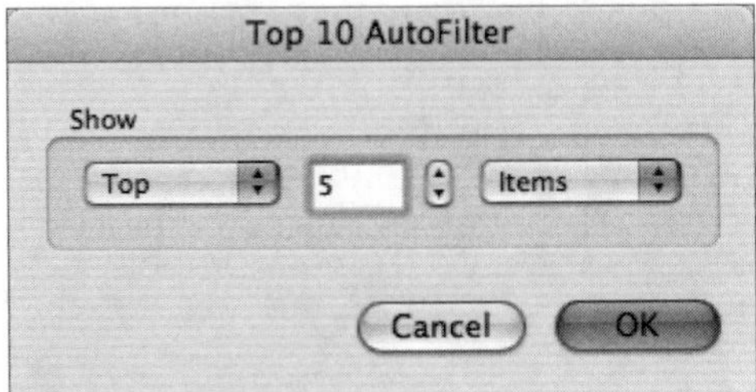

Figure 14.9 You can display the top (highest/most recent) or bottom (lowest/oldest) numeric or date values in a field by setting options in this dialog box.

To filter a database:

1. Click any cell in the database, and then choose Data > Filter > AutoFilter.
2. Click the AutoFilter arrows to the right of any field, and choose a filter criterion (**Figure 14.7**).

   The database is filtered to display only those records that match the criterion (**Figure 14.8**).
3. *Optional:* Select additional criteria by clicking the AutoFilter arrows beside other fields.

   Effects of filtering criteria are cumulative.
4. *Do one of the following:*
   - ▲ To remove the effects of a single filter, choose Show All from the field's AutoFilter drop-down menu
   - ▲ To remove the effects of all currently applied filters but continue filtering, choose Data > Filter > Show All.
   - ▲ To end filtering and show all records, choose Data > Filter > AutoFilter.

✓ Tips

- In a filtered database, row numbers of extracted records appear in blue, as do the AutoFilter arrows of criterion fields.
- In addition to filtering, you can sort by a field by selecting Sort Ascending or Sort Descending from the field's AutoFilter list.
- To display a specific number or percentage of the highest or lowest values in a field, choose Show Top 10 from the AutoFilter drop-down list. Set options in the Top 10 AutoFilter dialog box (**Figure 14.9**) and click OK.
- To create a complex filter, choose Custom Filter from the field's AutoFilter drop-down menu. Filtering is also discussed in Chapter 12.

To display subtotals or other grouping statistics:

1. Sort the database by the appropriate field(s) to create the groups of data on which to calculate subtotals or another statistic.
2. Select any cell in the database, and then choose Data > Subtotals.

   The Subtotal dialog box appears (**Figure 14.10**).
3. Select a break field from the At each change in drop-down list.

   A subtotal or other statistic will appear each time this field's value changes.
4. Select the mathematical or statistical function to calculate from the Use function drop-down list.
5. From the list box, click the check box for each field to which the function will be applied.
6. Make any desired changes in the remaining options and click OK.

   The function is applied to each subgroup in the database (**Figure 14.11**).

✔ Tips

- You can click the level controls to the left of the database to show only the grand total, only subtotals, or a mixture of subtotals and data (**Figure 14.12**). You can also selectively collapse/expand groups.
- To eliminate the subtotals, choose Data > Subtotals, click Remove All (Figure 14.10), and click OK.

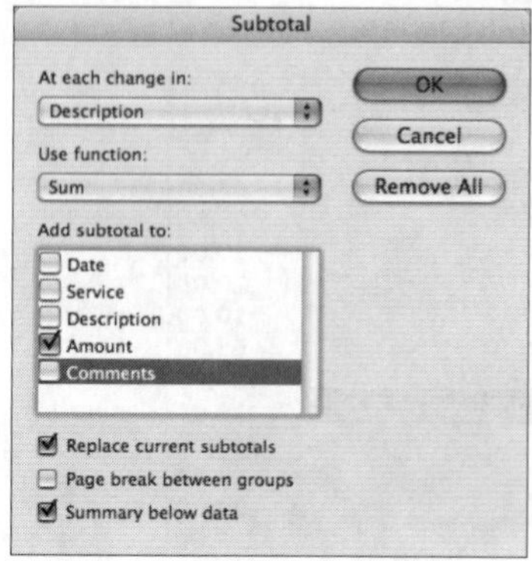

Figure 14.10 Set subtotal options.

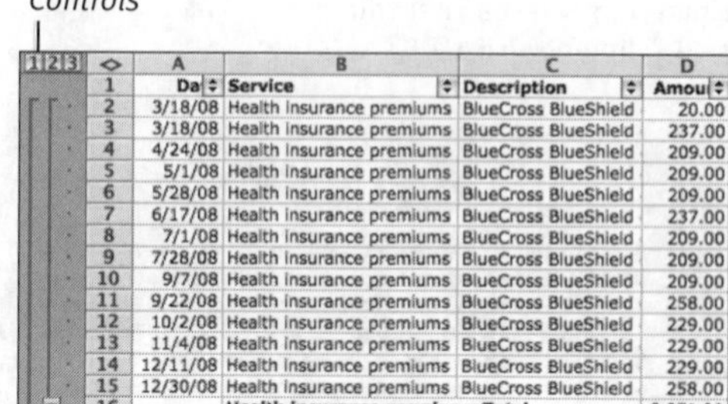

	A	B	C	D
1	Date	Service	Description	Amount
2	3/18/08	Health insurance premiums	BlueCross BlueShield	20.00
3	3/18/08	Health insurance premiums	BlueCross BlueShield	237.00
4	4/24/08	Health insurance premiums	BlueCross BlueShield	209.00
5	5/1/08	Health insurance premiums	BlueCross BlueShield	209.00
6	5/28/08	Health insurance premiums	BlueCross BlueShield	209.00
7	6/17/08	Health insurance premiums	BlueCross BlueShield	237.00
8	7/1/08	Health insurance premiums	BlueCross BlueShield	209.00
9	7/28/08	Health insurance premiums	BlueCross BlueShield	209.00
10	9/7/08	Health insurance premiums	BlueCross BlueShield	209.00
11	9/22/08	Health insurance premiums	BlueCross BlueShield	258.00
12	10/2/08	Health insurance premiums	BlueCross BlueShield	229.00
13	11/4/08	Health insurance premiums	BlueCross BlueShield	229.00
14	12/11/08	Health insurance premiums	BlueCross BlueShield	229.00
15	12/30/08	Health insurance premiums	BlueCross BlueShield	258.00
16		**Health insurance premiums Total**		2,951.00

Figure 14.11 The function is calculated and displayed in bold for each data group.

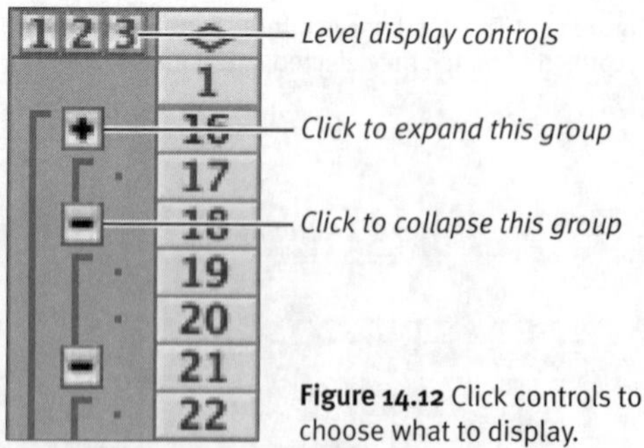

Figure 14.12 Click controls to choose what to display.

Working with External Databases

As you learned in Chapter 9, you can open or import text files into Excel. Excel also provides tools to import data directly from FileMaker Pro 5 through 9, as well as retrieve data from the Web.

Importing from FileMaker Pro

Keep the following in mind when importing FileMaker Pro data into Excel 2008:

- Files from FileMaker Pro 5.0 and higher can be imported. In addition to the database file, you must also have a working copy of an appropriate version of FileMaker Pro installed on the same computer as Excel 2008, as follows:
  - To import a FileMaker .fp5 file, you must have FileMaker Pro 5.0–6.0.
  - To import a FileMaker .fp7 file, you must have FileMaker Pro 7.0–9.0.
- If the FileMaker database doesn't permit exporting data from some user accounts, you must first open the database using an account that allows exporting.
- Only the *results* of FileMaker calculations are imported, not the actual formulas.
- The worksheet will probably need to be sorted following the import because Excel doesn't recognize the current FileMaker sort order, if any.
- If the number of records or fields in the FileMaker database exceeds Excel's maximum rows or columns, the additional records or fields will be discarded.
- If any cell contains more than 35,767 characters, the additional characters will be truncated.

To import a FileMaker Pro database:

1. *Do one of the following:*
   - ▲ Choose File > Open (⌘O). Select the database in the Open dialog box.
   - ▲ Choose File > Import, select FileMaker Pro database in the Import dialog box, click Import, and select the database in the Choose a Database dialog box.
   - ▲ Choose Data > Get External Data > Import from FileMaker Pro. Select the database in the Choose a Database dialog box. (This procedure can only be used if a workbook is already open.)

   FileMaker launches, the database opens, and the FileMaker Pro Import Wizard appears (**Figure 14.13**).
2. Specify fields to import by moving them into the Import these fields list. From the Layouts or Tables drop-down list, select a layout or table in which the fields appear. Add each field to the Import these fields list by clicking the Add button. To simultaneously move *all* fields from a layout or table, click the Add All button.
3. Fields are imported in the order in which they are listed. To change the position of a field in the Import these fields list, select the field and click the up or down button.
4. Click Next to continue.
5. In the Step 2 screen (**Figure 14.14**), you can specify up to three criteria for record selection (if you don't want to import the entire database). Click Finish.

   If you used File > Open to import the data, a new worksheet is automatically created. If you used File > Import or the Get External Data procedure, a dialog box appears (**Figure 14.15**). You can create a new worksheet or add the imported data to the current worksheet starting in a cell of your choice.

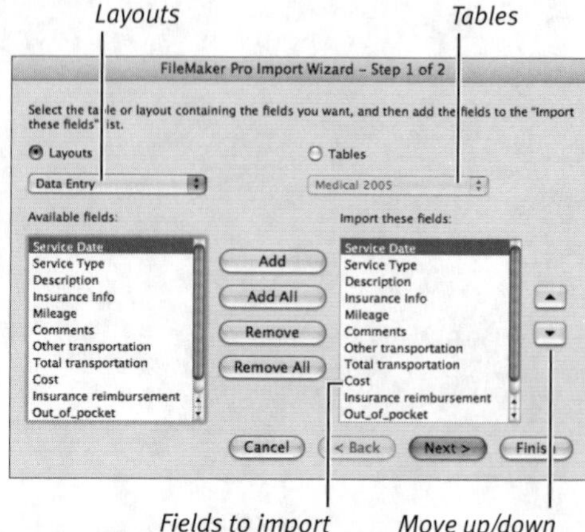

Figure 14.13 In the wizard's first screen, specify the fields to import and their order.

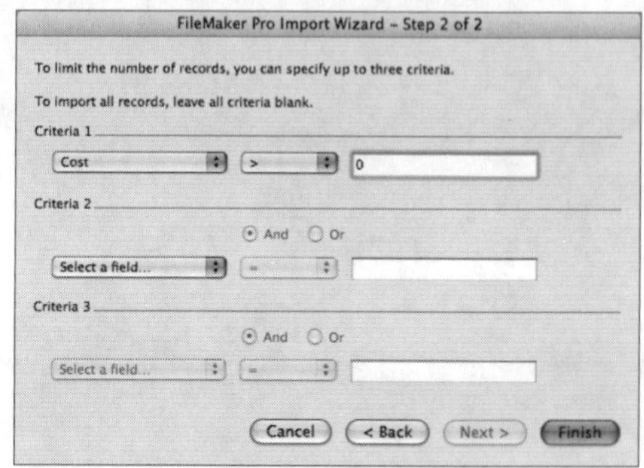

Figure 14.14 If you don't want to import the entire database, you can enter record-selection criteria.

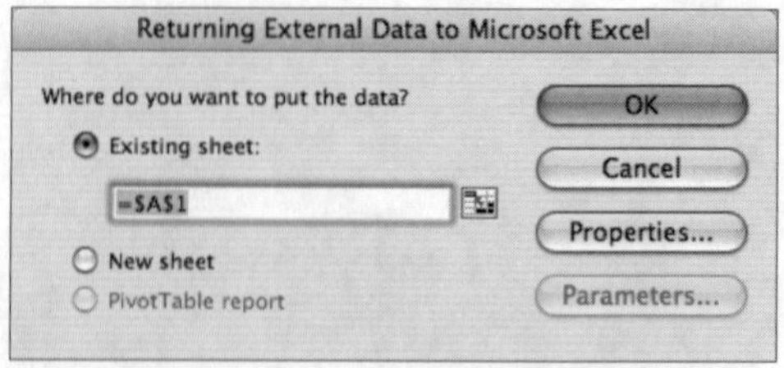

Figure 14.15 Specify where to place the imported FileMaker data.

Working with External Databases

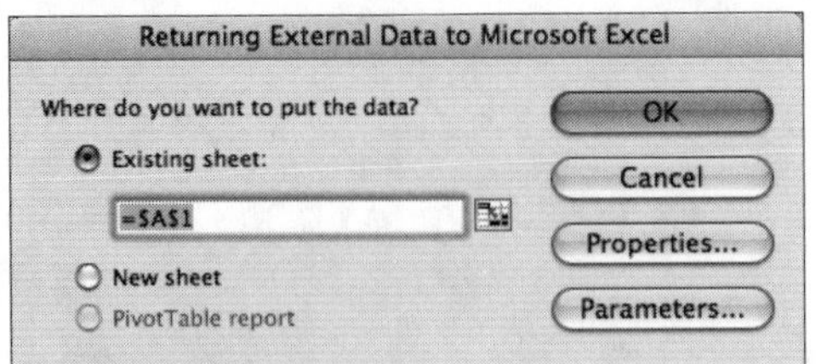

Figure 14.16 You can import query results into a new worksheet or the current one.

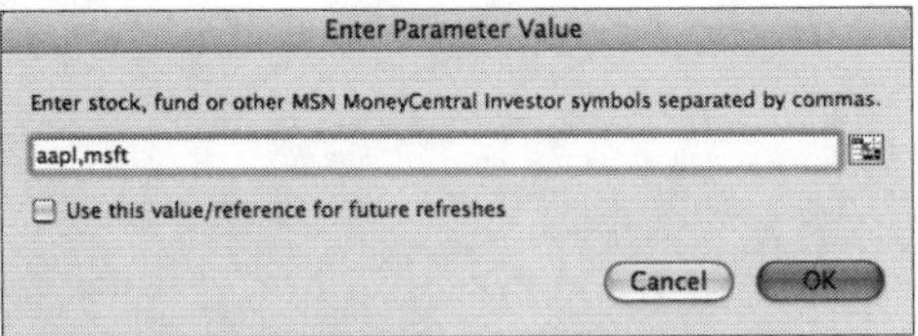

Figure 14.17 Enter symbols for the stocks and mutual funds, separated by commas.

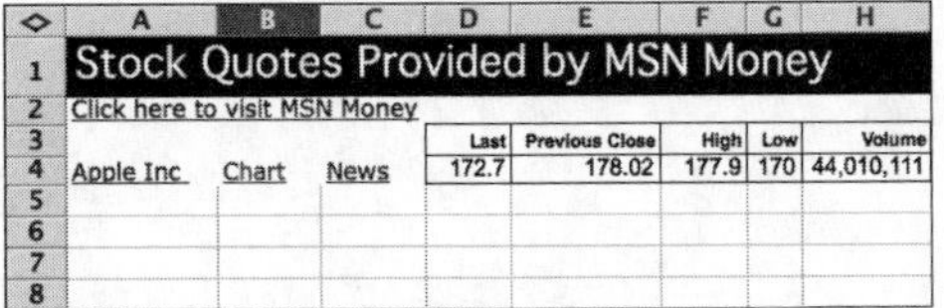

Figure 14.18 Excel connects to the Web site, downloads the data, and adds it to the worksheet.

Importing data from the Web

You can copy selected data from a table on a Web page and paste it into an Excel worksheet, but it doesn't always work as expected. A more precise method of retrieving data from the Web is to create a *Web query* using HTML forms.

Office includes several sample queries you can use. They're found in the `Microsoft Office 2008:Office:Queries` folder. The following example shows how to use one of the sample queries to retrieve stock data from the Web.

To retrieve Web data using a query:

1. Choose Data > Get External Data > Run Saved Query.

   The Choose a Query dialog box appears, open to the Queries folder.

2. Select the `MSN MoneyCentral Stock Quotes` query. Click Get Data.

   The Returning External Data to Microsoft Excel dialog box appears (**Figure 14.16**).

3. *Do one of the following:*
   - To import the data into the current worksheet, click the Existing sheet radio button. Type or click the starting cell address that will receive the import data.
   - To import the data into a new, empty worksheet, click New sheet.

4. Click OK to continue.

   The Enter Parameter Value dialog box appears (**Figure 14.17**).

5. Enter one or more stock or mutual fund symbols. (To enter multiple symbols, separate them with commas.) Click OK.

   The query report appears in the worksheet (**Figure 14.18**).

✔ Tip

- To create your own database query, choose Data > Get External Data > New Database Query. Note that you must first install the required ODBC (Open Database Connectivity) driver. For additional information, review "Import data from a database" in Excel Help.

15

DATA ANALYSIS

Excel provides several excellent tools to help you analyze worksheet data. In this chapter, you'll be introduced to the following data analysis tools:

- **PivotTables.** Examine relationships between variables using an interactive table.
- **Goal seeking.** Use goal seeking to force a particular result in a calculation by changing one of its elements.
- **What-if analyses.** Calculate equations with one or two unknown variables by substituting user-provided test values called *scenarios*.

✔ Note

- Much of the functionality of the add-ins provided with previous versions of Excel is now built into Excel 2008.

Working with PivotTables

A *PivotTable* is an interactive table that helps you summarize and analyze data from existing lists and tables. PivotTables enable you to easily examine large amounts of data in different ways.

Starting with a long list or database, you can create a PivotTable summary of the data. By taking advantage of the PivotTable features, you can easily change columns into rows, drill down from the summary numbers to the data elements, and find the presentation format that best reveals the information you want to see.

PivotTables are rich with functionality. A complete discussion of how to use them is beyond the scope of this book. However, we'll cover the essentials here, and you can explore them further on your own.

To create a PivotTable:

1. Open the worksheet that contains the data source you want to analyze. Choose Data > PivotTable Report.

   The PivotTable Wizard appears (**Figure 15.1**).

2. Click a radio button to specify the data source. Click Next to continue.

3. Specify the cell range within the data source (**Figure 15.2**). Click Next.

4. Indicate whether to place the PivotTable report in a new worksheet or an existing one (**Figure 15.3**).

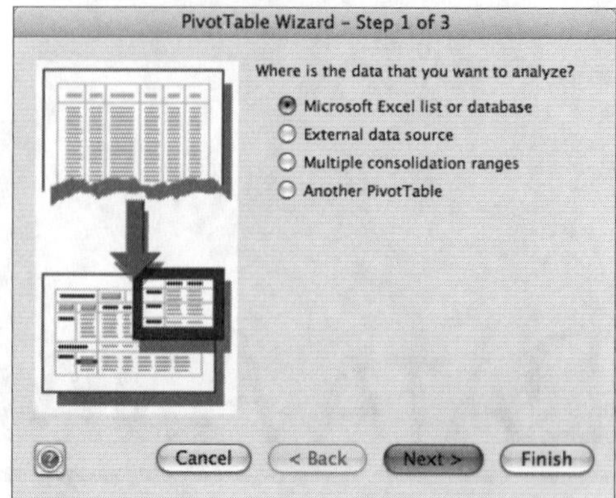

Figure 15.1 Click a radio button to indicate the type of data source.

Figure 15.2 Type or paste the data range into this text box. You can also specify the range by selecting it in the worksheet.

Figure 15.3 Indicate where you'd like the PivotTable to be placed.

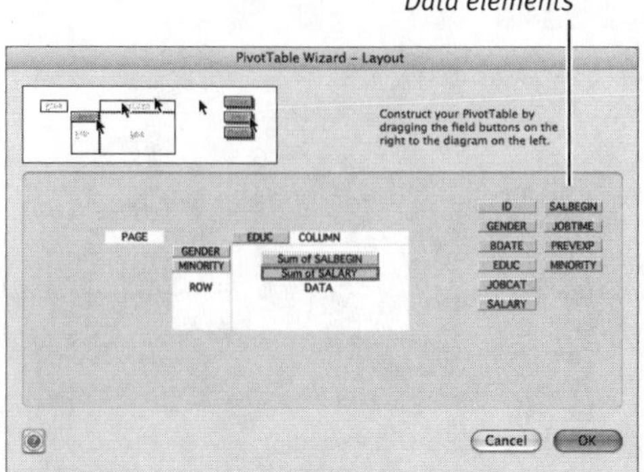

Figure 15.4 Create the initial PivotTable layout by dragging fields into position in the diagram.

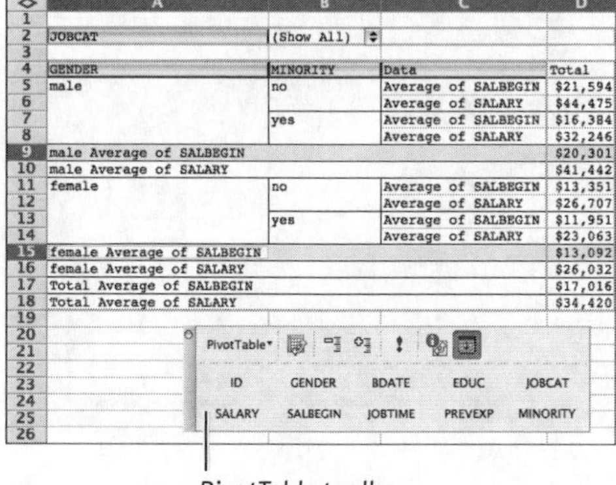

Figure 15.5 After the PivotTable appears, you can modify and experiment with it (as I've done here).

5. *Optional:* Rather than start with an empty layout, you can specify the initial PivotTable layout by clicking the Layout button (see Figure 15.3). The PivotTable Wizard – Layout dialog box appears.

   Drag data elements into the desired spots on the layout (**Figure 15.4**). (Note that numeric items normally go into the Data area.) Click OK when you're done.

6. *Optional:* To set data and formatting options, click the Options button (see Figure 15.3). Click OK when you're done.

7. Click Finish on the final wizard screen.

   The PivotTable report and PivotTable toolbar appear (**Figure 15.5**). See the following page for assistance in using the PivotTable.

✔ Tips

- Select a categorical field with few categories as a *page field*. (The more categories, the harder it will be to make sense of the data.) In Figure 15.5, the Jobcat page field has only three categories: line staff, middle management, and upper management. By selecting a category other than Show All from the page field's drop-down list, you are electing to show only the data for that specific category.
- When a PivotTable is generated, Excel ignores any filters you've applied to the data. If you are only interested in examining a subset of your data, filter the data as desired, copy the resulting records, and paste them into another area of the sheet. Then create the PivotTable based on the pasted range.
- If you've enabled *drilldown* in the Table Options dialog box (see Step 6), you can double-click any cell in the Total column to view only the data that relates to that number.

To customize a PivotTable:

- *Do any of the following:*
  - ▲ To add a field to the PivotTable, drag it into position from the PivotTable toolbar. (If the field list isn't visible, click the Display Fields toolbar icon.)
  - ▲ To remove a field, drag it into an unused portion of the worksheet.
  - ▲ To reorganize currently used fields in a PivotTable, drag each one to the desired area. You can move a column field to the rows area, for instance.
  - ▲ To change the summary statistic used for a field, select the summary label in the PivotTable (such as `Sum of Salary`) and click the Field Settings toolbar icon. In the PivotTable Field dialog box (**Figure 15.6**), select a new Summarize by statistic and click OK. To set a display format for the statistic (**Figure 15.7**), click the Number button.
  - ▲ If you've modified the original Excel list by adding fields, you can display them in the field list on the PivotTable toolbar by clicking the Refresh icon. Once displayed, you can then add them to the PivotTable.

✔ Tips

- If you make *any* modifications to the data on which the PivotTable is based, such as editing data or changing numerical data to text, click the Refresh icon on the PivotTable toolbar to reflect the changes in your PivotTable.
- To delete a PivotTable report, select a cell in the PivotTable report, choose Select > Entire Table from the PivotTable icon's drop-down menu, and then choose Edit > Clear > All.

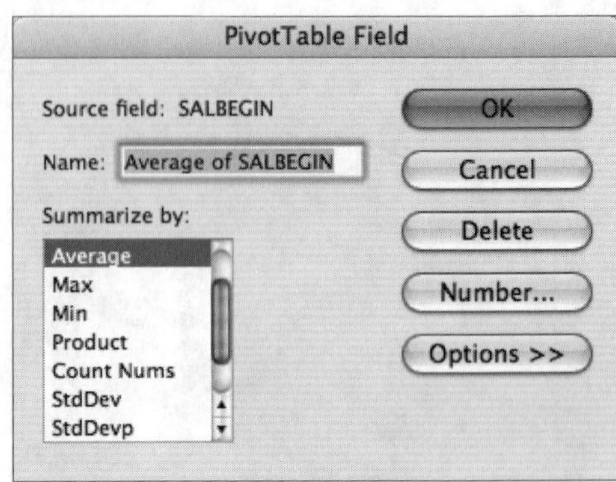

Figure 15.6 You can change the summary statistics used. In the example, an average is considerably more useful than a sum.

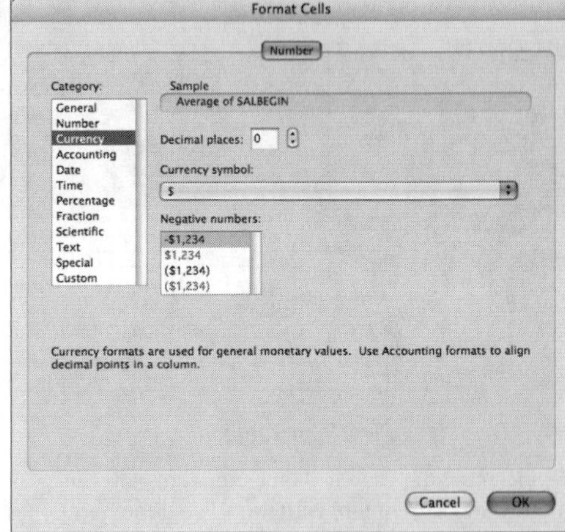

Figure 15.7 It can be a lot easier reading the data in the PivotTable if you specify an optimal format for it.

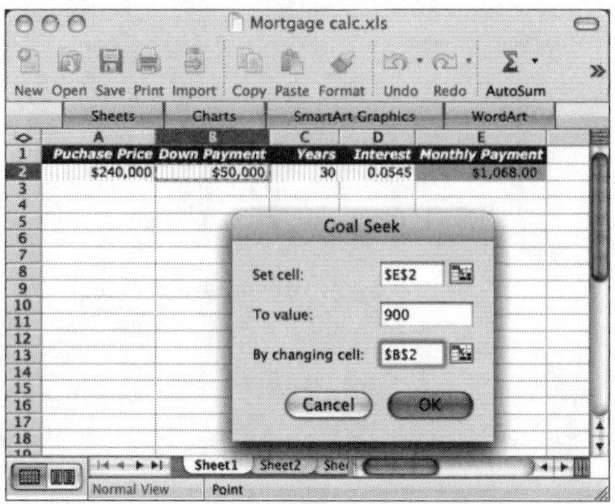

Figure 15.8 Fill in the Goal Seek text boxes.

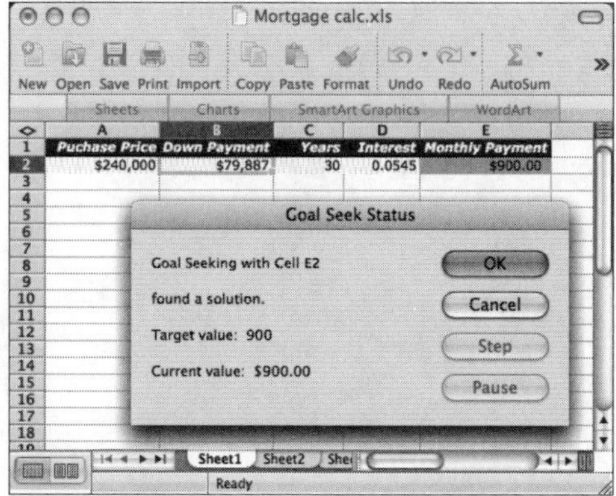

Figure 15.9 The Goal Seek Status dialog box indicates whether a solution was found. If so, the worksheet is changed as specified.

Goal Seeking

Use *goal seeking* to force a particular result in a calculation by changing one of its elements. For example, if you know how much you can afford for a monthly payment on a loan, you can use goal seeking to find the down payment necessary to produce that monthly payment.

To use goal seeking:

1. Display the cell range you want to examine. Choose Tools > Goal Seek.

   The Goal Seek dialog box appears (**Figure 15.8**).

2. Enter the following:
   - **Set cell.** The cell whose value you want to set (Monthly Payment or `E2`, in this example).
   - **To value.** The value you want the Set cell to become (`$900`, in this example).
   - **By changing cell.** The cell whose value will change in order to make the Set cell result (`E2`) equal the To value (`$900`). In this example, the By changing cell is Down Payment (`B2`).

3. Click OK to perform the calculation.

   The Goal Seek Status dialog box appears (**Figure 15.9**) and displays the result. The By changing cell is altered, as specified.

✔ Tips

- You can click cells rather than typing their addresses in the Goal Seek dialog box.
- To prevent Goal Seek from modifying the worksheet with the found result, click Cancel in the Goal Seek Status dialog box.
- The same Goal Seek dialog box can easily be modified to answer other questions. You could find out what the interest rate would have to be in the event that you had a fixed amount available as a down payment, for instance.

What-If Analyses

If you're uncertain of some elements in your calculations, Excel provides tools you can use to play "what if?"

- *Data tables* calculate equations with either one or two unknown variables. You provide the test values for each unknown variable. Excel then calculates the result(s) by substituting the test value(s).
- *Scenarios* are saved sets of input values for one or more variables that can be substituted into an equation. For example, when calculating profit, you can see what happens if sales exceed expectations or if advertising costs rise dramatically.

The first example below (**Figure 15.10**) uses a one-variable, column-oriented data table to calculate monthly mortgage payments at various interest rates (the test values) when the loan amount and term are known. (In a *column-oriented data table,* test values are arranged in a column. In a *row-oriented data table,* test values are arranged in a row.)

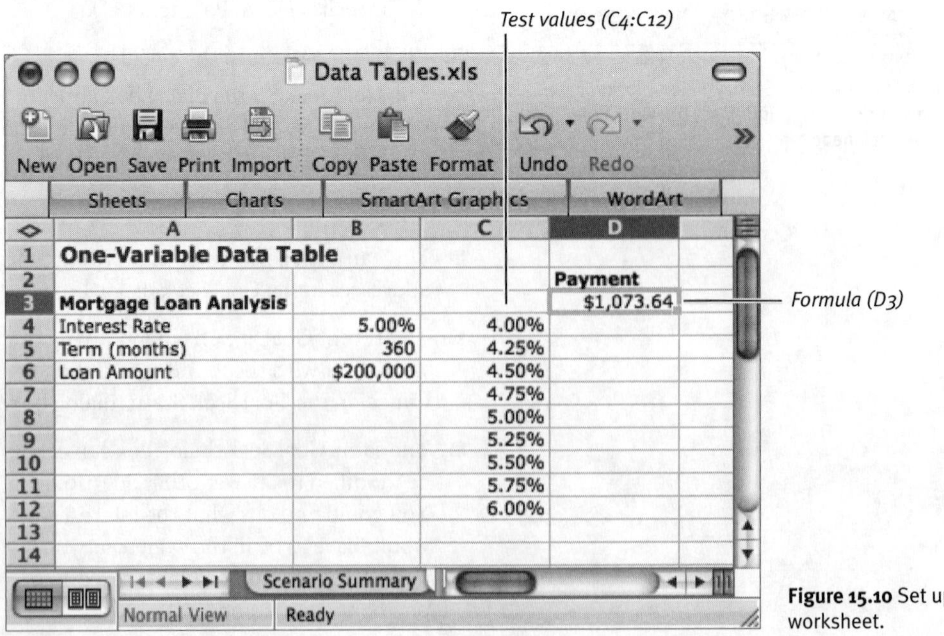

Figure 15.10 Set up the worksheet.

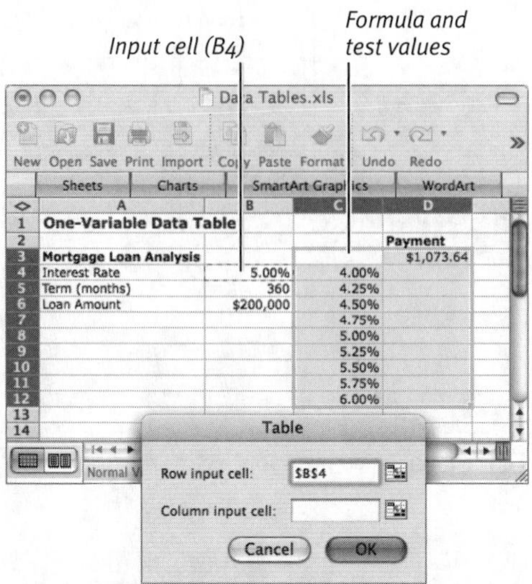

Figure 15.11 Select the test values and formula cell, choose Data > Table, and specify the single input cell in the Table dialog box.

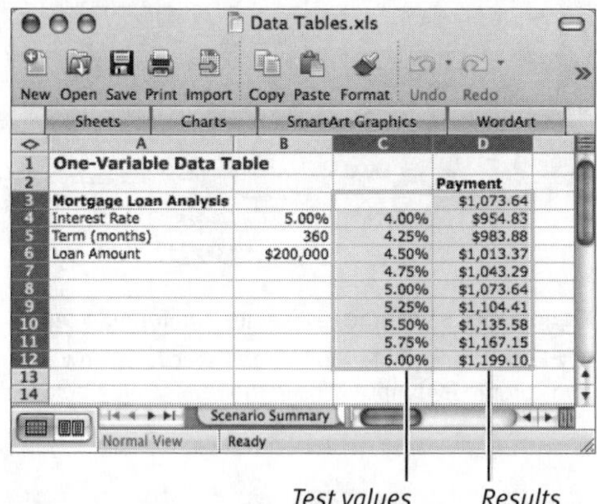

Figure 15.12 The results are displayed. (Each result appears to the right of its corresponding test value.)

The second example illustrates the creation of a two-variable, row- and column-oriented data table. In that example, only the loan amount is known; the interest rate and term are unknown. Finally, this section concludes with an example of scenarios involving several different loan amounts..

To create a one-variable data table:

1. Set up the worksheet as shown in Figure 15.10 (previous page).

   The set of test values (in this case, interest rates) extends down a column one cell below and to the left of the cell that contains the formula.

2. Select the cell range that includes the formula and the test values.

   In this example, the range is C3:D12.

3. Choose Data > Table.

   The Table dialog box appears (**Figure 15.11**).

4. *Do one of the following:*
   - ▲ **Column-oriented data table.** Click in the Column input cell text box. Enter or point to the input cell.
   - ▲ **Row-oriented data table.** Click in the Row input cell text box. Enter or point to the input cell.

   The *input cell* is the initial value referred to in the formula for which the test values will be substituted. In our column-oriented example, the input cell is the initial interest rate (B4).

5. Click OK.

   The cells beneath the formula are filled with the results of substituting the test values (**Figure 15.12**).

To create a two-variable data table:

1. Set up the worksheet (**Figure 15.13**).
   The two sets of test values (in this case, interest rates and loan term) are entered as follows:
   - ▲ *Interest rates* (C4:C12) extend down a column directly below the cell that contains the formula (C3).
   - ▲ *Loan term values* (D3:E3) are entered in the same row as the formula, beginning one cell to the right.
2. Select the range of cells that covers the formula and the test values.
   In this example, the range is C3:E12.
3. Choose Data > Table.
   The Table dialog box appears.
4. Enter or point to the Row input cell and the Column input cell (**Figure 15.14**).
   In this example, the Row input cell is B5 and the Column input cell is B4. (These are the original cells referred to in the formula.)
5. Click OK to display the results in the worksheet (**Figure 15.15**).

✔ Note

- The same formula was used in both the one- and two-variable examples (found in cell D3 and C3, respectively):

```
=PMT(B4/12,B5,-B6)
```

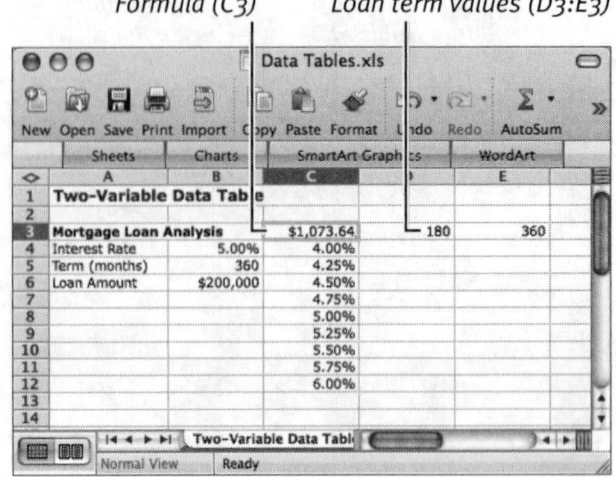

Figure 15.13 Set up the worksheet.

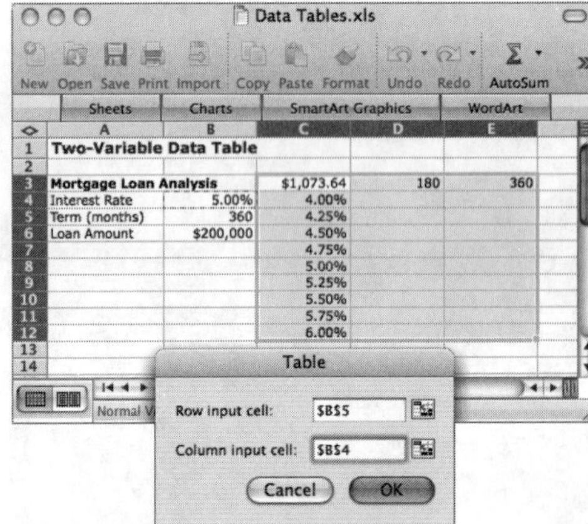

Figure 15.14 Select the test values and formula cell (C3:E12), choose Data > Table, and specify the row (B5) and column (B4) input cells in the Table dialog box.

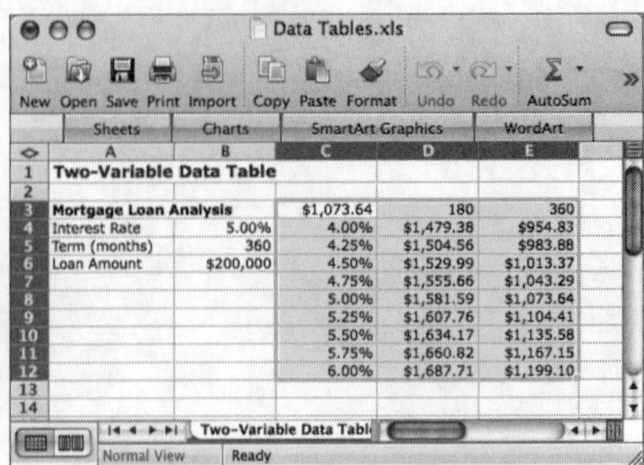

Figure 15.15 The results appear (D4:E12).

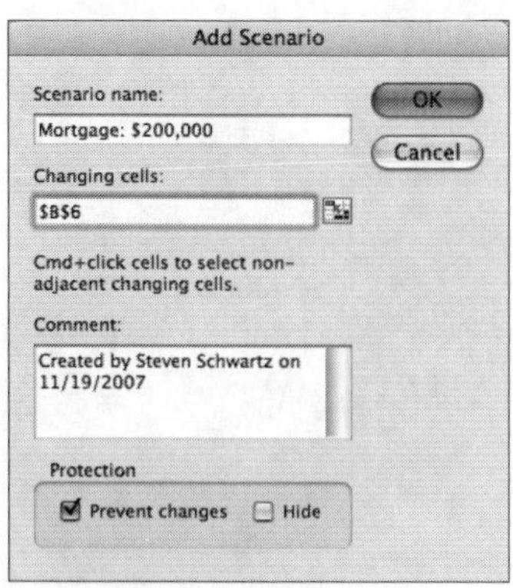

Figure 15.16 Name the scenario, specify the cells in which new data will be substituted, and edit the comment text (if desired).

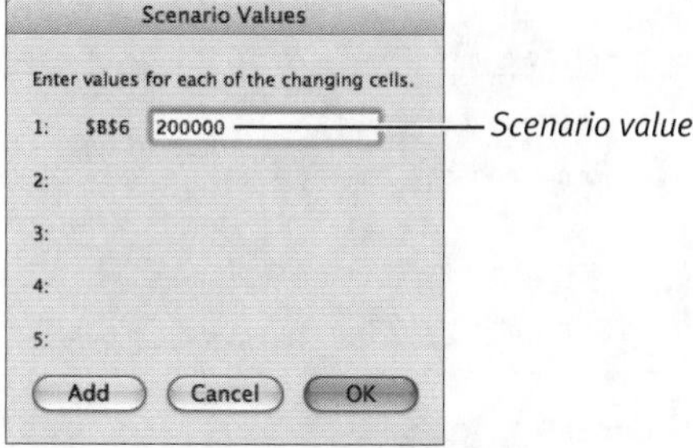

Figure 15.17 Specify value(s) to substitute in this scenario.

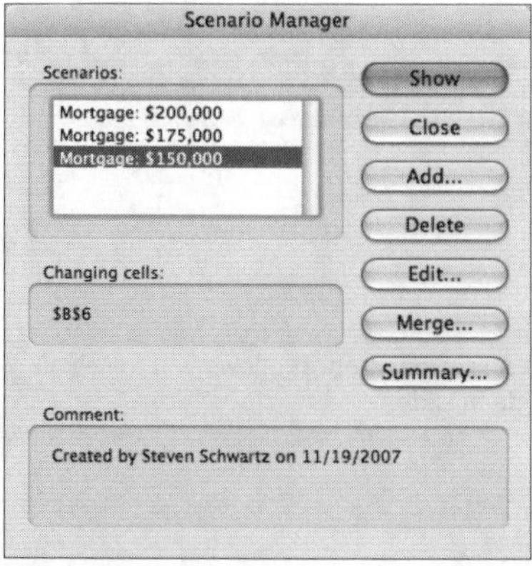

Figure 15.18 The Scenario Manager lists the defined scenarios.

To create scenarios:

1. Open the worksheet containing the data for which you want to create scenarios.

   For this example, we'll use the one-variable data table shown in Figure 15.10.

2. Choose Tools > Scenarios.

   The Scenario Manager dialog box appears.

3. Click Add to create the first scenario.

   The Add Scenario dialog box appears (**Figure 15.16**).

4. Name the scenario. Click in the Changing cells text box and select the cell(s) that will change with this scenario. Edit the default comment, if you like. Click OK.

   The Scenario Values dialog box appears (**Figure 15.17**).

5. Specify the new values for the changing variables in the current scenario. Click Add to create another scenario.

6. Repeat Steps 3 and 4 until all scenarios have been defined. After defining the final scenario, click OK (rather than Add).

   The Scenario Manager dialog box appears (**Figure 15.18**). All defined scenarios are shown in the scrolling list box.

7. To dismiss the Scenario Manager, click the Close button.

To view scenarios:

1. If the Scenario Manager isn't open, choose Tools > Scenarios.
2. To view the results of any scenario, select its name in the Scenario Manager dialog box (see Figure 15.18) and click Show.

   Excel substitutes the scenario value(s) for the specified worksheet cell(s) and shows the results (**Figure 15.19**). Repeat as desired to view other scenarios.
3. To see a summary of *all* scenarios, click Summary.

   The Scenario Summary dialog box appears (**Figure 15.20**).
4. Click the Scenario summary or Scenario PivotTable radio button. Specify the *result cells* (the ones that will change as a result of the scenario data) to include in the report. Click OK.

   The chosen report appears in a new sheet in the current workbook (**Figure 15.21**).

✔ Tip

- After generating the report, you are free to edit it to make it more readable. For example, in the report in Figure 15.21, you could copy and paste the mortgage rates from column C of the original worksheet rather than show result cell addresses in column C.

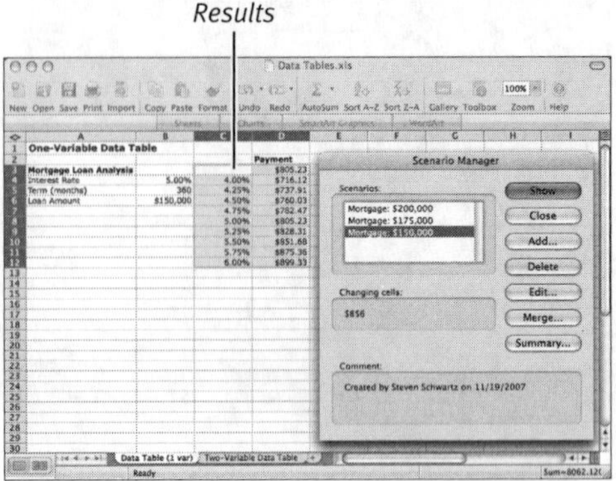

Figure 15.19 Select a scenario, click Show, and examine the changed data on the worksheet.

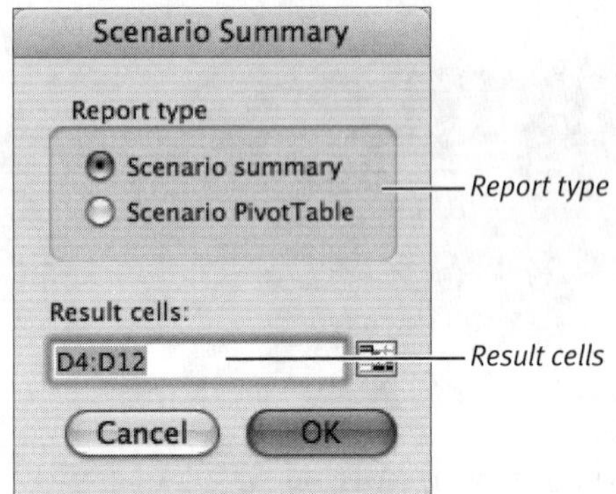

Figure 15.20 Request a summary report of all scenarios.

Scenario Summary				
	Current Values:	Mortgage: $200,000	Mortgage: $175,000	Mortgage: $150,000
Changing Cells:				
$B$6	$150,000	$200,000	$175,000	$150,000
Result Cells:				
$D$4	$716.12	$954.83	$835.48	$716.12
$D$5	$737.91	$983.88	$860.89	$737.91
$D$6	$760.03	$1,013.37	$886.70	$760.03
$D$7	$782.47	$1,043.29	$912.88	$782.47
$D$8	$805.23	$1,073.64	$939.44	$805.23
$D$9	$828.31	$1,104.41	$966.36	$828.31
$D$10	$851.68	$1,135.58	$993.63	$851.68
$D$11	$875.36	$1,167.15	$1,021.25	$875.36
$D$12	$899.33	$1,199.10	$1,049.21	$899.33

Notes: Current Values column represents values of changing cells at time Scenario Summary Report was created. Changing cells for each scenario are highlighted in gray.

Figure 15.21 A summary report allows you to see all scenarios side by side.

WHAT-IF ANALYSES

16

Sharing Workbooks

Individuals in workgroups often need to share workbooks. Excel provides tools to distribute workbooks on the Web or a network, protect parts of workbooks that shouldn't be changed, and track and review the changes that have been made.

Publishing Excel Data on the Web

Excel makes it easy to save workbooks or worksheets for display on the Web. One advantage of publishing in this manner is that those who only need to view the contents don't need Excel to open the file. All they need is a browser. You can also *preview* any Excel file as it will look if saved as a Web page.

To preview a file's Web appearance:

1. Open the workbook in Excel (**Figure 16.1**).
2. Choose File > Web Page Preview.
   The active worksheet opens in your Web browser as it would appear on the Web (**Figure 16.2**).

✔ Tips

- To avoid surprises, it's a good idea to use Web Page Preview until you're satisfied with the file's appearance and formatting. *Then* save it as a Web page. (Note, however, that a Web page preview doesn't always produce identical results to saving the file as a Web page.)
- Comment indicators are displayed in a Web preview as bracketed numbers. Click a comment indicator to go to the spot on the Web page where the comment is explained (see Figure 16.2).

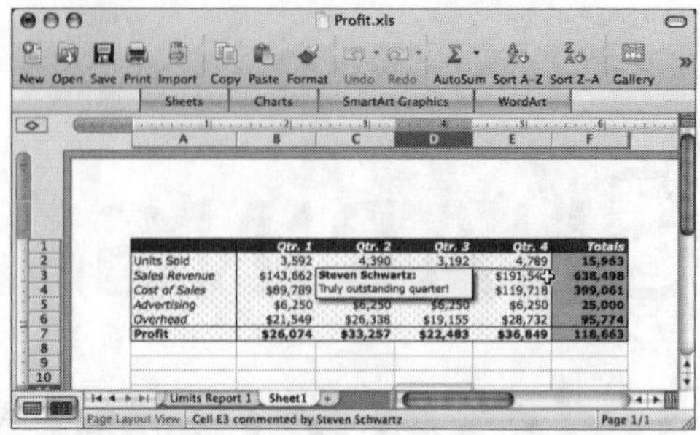

Figure 16.1 Create or open a workbook.

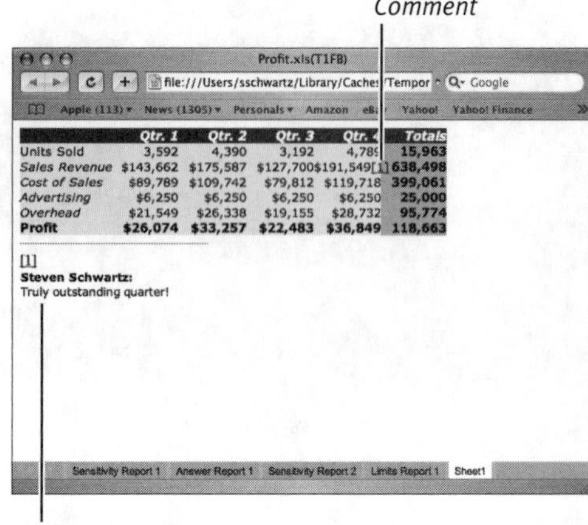

Figure 16.2 When you choose Web Page Preview, a temporary HTML file is created and opens in your default browser.

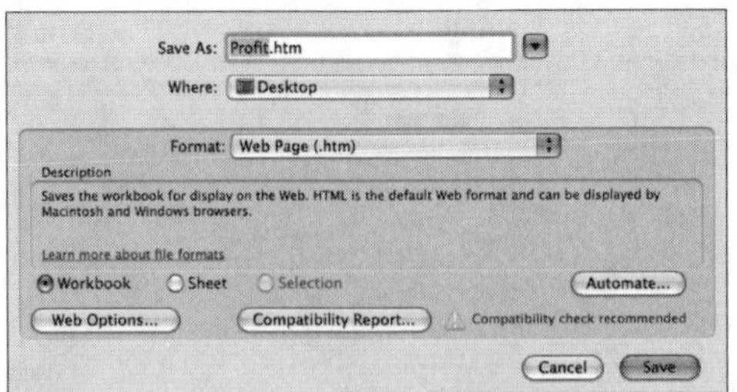

Figure 16.3 Specify the filename, destination, and options.

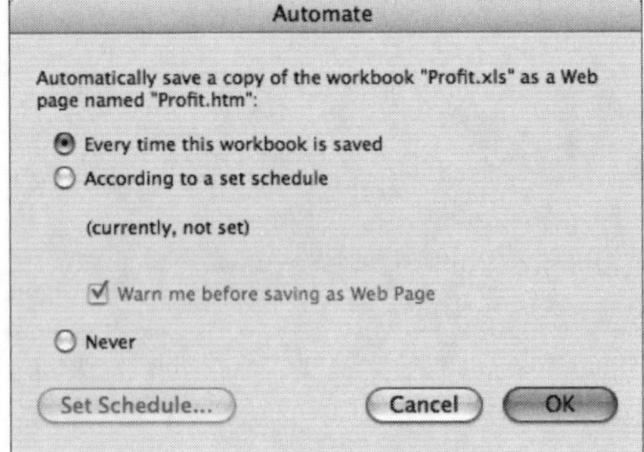

Figure 16.4 Indicate the condition under which a new HTML file will automatically be generated.

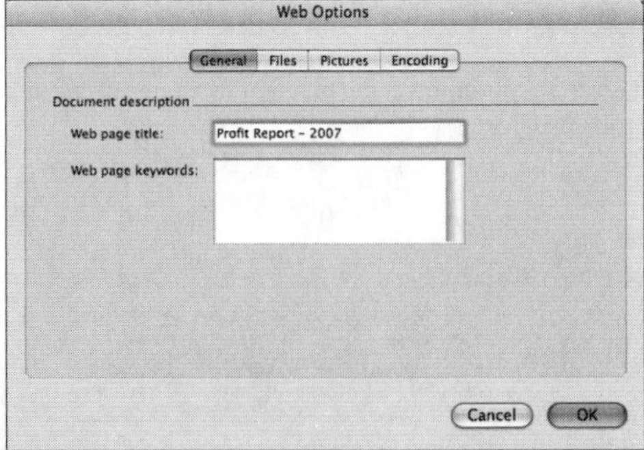

Figure 16.5 Click the Web Options button to enter a title for the generated Web page and to set other options.

To save a file as a Web page:

1. *Optional:* To save a specific worksheet or only a range of a worksheet as a Web page, select the worksheet and/or range.
2. Choose File > Save as Web Page.

   A Save As panel appears (**Figure 16.3**). The Web Page (.htm) format is automatically selected.
3. Click a radio button to indicate whether you want to save the entire workbook, only the active worksheet, or only the currently selected cell range.
4. *Optional:* If this workbook, sheet, or range is updated regularly, you can instruct Excel to automatically create a new HTML file whenever you save the workbook or according to a particular schedule. Click the Automate button.

   The Automate dialog box appears (**Figure 16.4**). *Select one of the following:*
   - ▲ **Every time this workbook is saved.** Automatically generate a new HTML file whenever you save the workbook.
   - ▲ **According to a set schedule.** Generate a new HTML file daily, weekly, or on some other schedule. Click the Set Schedule button to set the schedule.
   - ▲ **Never.** Disable the automatic generation of new HTML files.

   Click OK to close the Automate dialog box.
5. *Optional:* Click the Web Options button to set Web-specific settings, such as the page title and keywords that will be used by search engines (**Figure 16.5**). Review the information on the various tabs and click OK.
6. *Optional:* Click Compatibility Report to check for potential problems.
7. Click Save to create the HTML file and the folder of supporting files.

Sharing Workbooks on a Network

When *sharing* has been enabled for an Excel workbook, other network users can simultaneously view and edit the workbook.

To enable sharing for a workbook:

1. Choose Tools > Share Workbook.
   The Share Workbook dialog box appears (**Figure 16.6**).
2. On the Editing tab, click Allow changes by more than one user at the same time.
3. Click the Advanced tab to review or set options for managing changes by multiple users.
4. Click OK to dismiss the dialog box.
   A confirmation dialog box appears (**Figure 16.7**).
5. Click OK to save the workbook and enable sharing.
6. Save or copy the workbook file to a shared network folder so it can be accessed by authorized users. For assistance, contact your network administrator.

✔ Tips

- To later disable sharing for a workbook, choose Tools > Share Workbook, remove the check mark from Allow changes by more than one user at the same time, click OK to close the dialog box, and then click Yes in the confirmation dialog box that appears (**Figure 16.8**).
- Sharing is primarily intended for viewing and working with workbook data. While a workbook is being shared, you can't add certain elements, such as pictures, charts, PivotTable reports, or subtotals. Such items must be added *before* you elect to share the workbook.

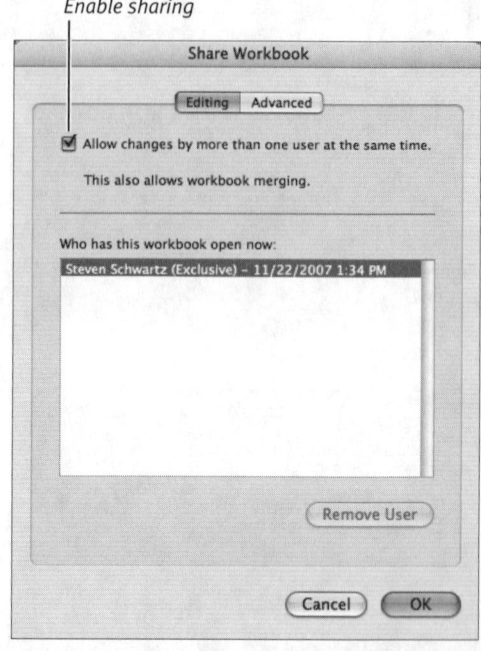

Figure 16.6 Enable sharing by clicking this check box.

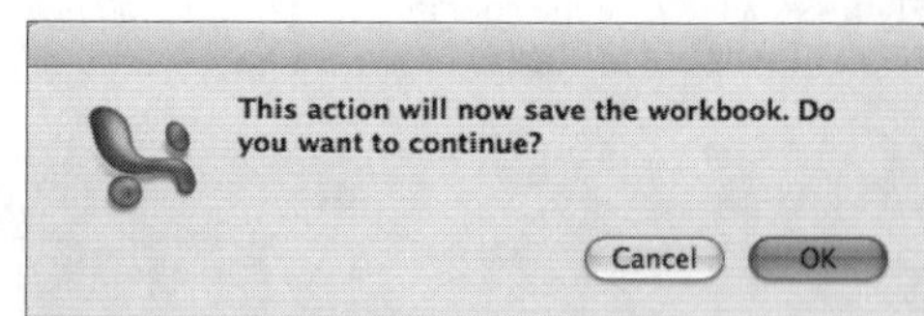

Figure 16.7 Confirm that you want to share the workbook by clicking OK.

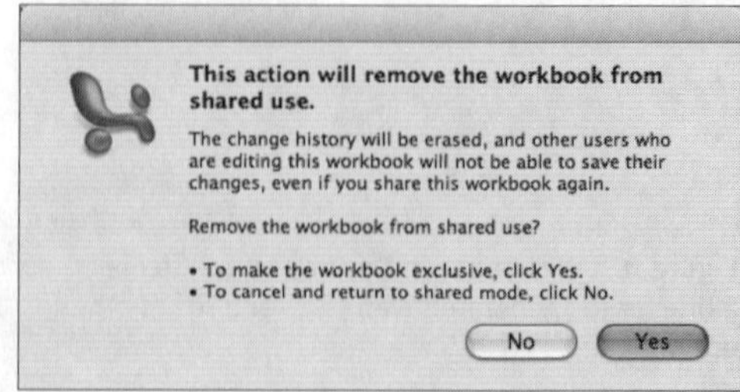

Figure 16.8 To disable sharing for the workbook, click the Yes button.

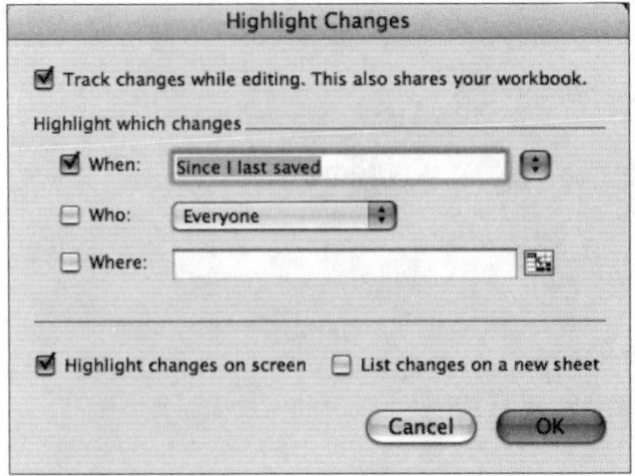

Figure 16.9 Specify criteria for tracking and displaying changes.

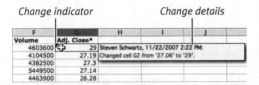

Change indicator *Change details*

F	G	H	I	J
Volume	Adj. Close*			
4603600	29	Steven Schwartz, 11/22/2007 2:22 PM:		
4104500	27.19	Changed cell G2 from '27.06' to '29'.		
4382500	27.3			
5449500	27.14			
4463900	26.28			

Figure 16.10 To view the details for a given change, move the cursor over the changed cell.

Tracking Changes

When sharing an Excel workbook, changes made by the various users are tracked and recorded in a *change history*. (View the Advanced tab of the Share Workbook dialog box for change history options.) When you enable the option to highlight changes, Excel marks each modified cell with an indicator and provides an explanation of the change. You can then review and accept or reject each change.

To enable change highlighting:

1. Choose Tools > Track Changes > Highlight Changes.

   The Highlight Changes dialog box appears (**Figure 16.9**).

2. Click the Track changes while editing check box.

   Doing so enables both change tracking and sharing of the workbook.

3. Set any of these tracking options:
   - ▲ **When.** Specify which changes to track, based on a time period or a save.
   - ▲ **Who.** Indicate whose changes to track.
   - ▲ **Where.** If you're interested in only a particular cell range, click this check box and drag-select the range.

4. Click OK.

   Modified cells will have a colored triangle added to their upper-left corner. To view a change explanation, move the pointer over the changed cell (**Figure 16.10**).

✔ Tips

- Workbook sharing and change tracking go hand in hand. Enabling one automatically enables the other. When you elect to share a workbook, you should also review the Highlight Changes settings in Step 3.
- You can also track and highlight changes when you're the sole user of a workbook. Although the workbook will automatically be shared, you don't have to store it in a location that's accessible to others.

To review changes:

1. Choose Tools > Track Changes > Accept or Reject Changes. If necessary, you will be prompted to save the workbook before proceeding.

   The Select Changes to Accept or Reject dialog box appears (**Figure 16.11**).

2. Use the When, Who, and Where criteria to specify the changes you want to review. Click OK.

   The Accept or Reject Changes dialog box appears (**Figure 16.12**).

3. Excel displays each change, while simultaneously selecting the affected cell in the worksheet. For each proposed change, click Accept, Reject, Accept All, or Reject All.

   To end the review process immediately (even if there are still unreviewed changes), click Close.

✔ Tip

- To indicate a cell range for the Where criterion (Figure 16.11), you can drag-select the desired cells in the workbook.

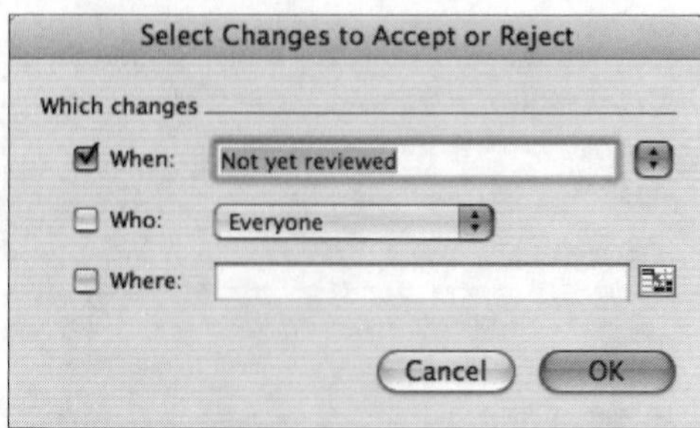

Figure 16.11 Select the changes you want to review.

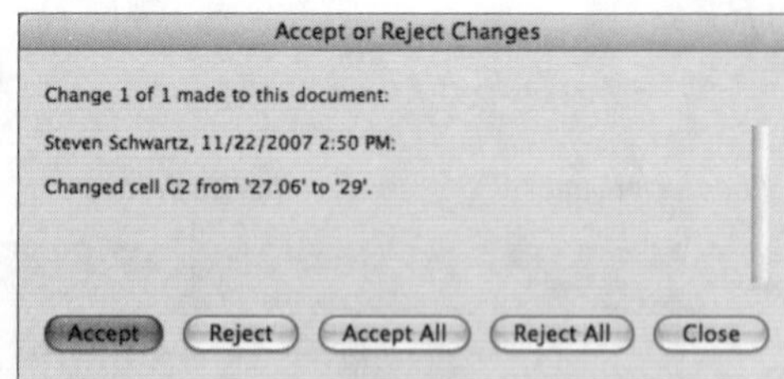

Figure 16.12 For each change, click a button to indicate how you want to handle it.

Figure 16.13 The Protect Sheet dialog box.

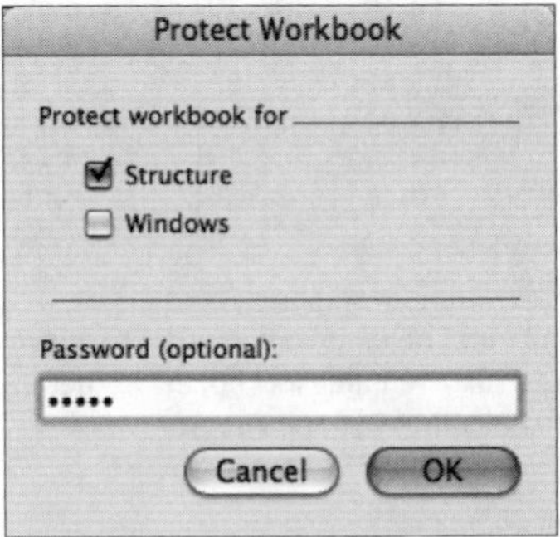

Figure 16.14 The Protect Workbook dialog box.

Figure 16.15 The Protect Shared Workbook dialog box.

Protecting Your Data

When working in a sharing environment or if you're afraid others might be able to view your data without permission, you can prevent certain types of changes and optionally require a password for entire workbooks or individual worksheets.

To protect a workbook or worksheet:

1. If the workbook is currently open in shared mode, temporarily disable sharing by following the tip at the end of "Sharing Workbooks on a Network," earlier in this chapter.

2. *Do one of the following:*
   - ▲ To protect only the current sheet, choose Tools > Protection > Protect Sheet (**Figure 16.13**).
   - ▲ To protect an entire workbook, choose Tools > Protection > Protect Workbook (**Figure 16.14**).
   - ▲ To simultaneously protect a workbook and enable sharing, choose Tools > Protection > Protect and Share Workbook (**Figure 16.15**). Click the Sharing with track changes check box.

3. Click the check boxes of the elements you want to protect.

4. *Optional:* To add password protection to the worksheet or workbook, enter a password in the text box.

   A password is an additional layer of protection. In addition to preventing the changes specified in Step 3, each user must supply the password whenever accessing the worksheet or workbook.

5. Click OK to dismiss the dialog box and enact the new protection settings.

6. If you assigned a password, you'll be prompted to re-enter it.

✔ Tips

- Protecting a worksheet or workbook is more about preventing inadvertent or malicious changes than security. Use protection to keep critical data from being altered. To prevent others from opening and viewing a workbook or sheet, assign a password.

- By default, every worksheet cell is *locked*. This locked status has no effect unless you also protect the sheet or workbook. To allow some cells to be modified in a protected sheet or workbook, you must unlock them.

  Unprotect the sheet (if it's currently protected), select the cells to unlock, and choose Format > Cells. In the Format Cells dialog box, click the Protection tab, remove the check mark from Locked (**Figure 16.16**), and click OK. Finish by protecting the sheet (**Figure 16.17**).

- To remove protection, choose Tools > Protection, followed by Unprotect Sheet, Unprotect Workbook, or Unprotect Shared Workbook, as appropriate. If you assigned a password to the worksheet or workbook, you'll be prompted to supply it (**Figure 16.18**). Otherwise, unprotection will occur immediately.

- Unprotecting a shared workbook does *not* disable sharing. If you wish to do this, too, choose Tools > Share Workbook. In the Share Workbook dialog box (see Figure 16.6), remove the check mark from Allow changes by more than one user at the same time, click OK to close the dialog box, and then click Yes in the confirmation dialog box that appears (see Figure 16.8).

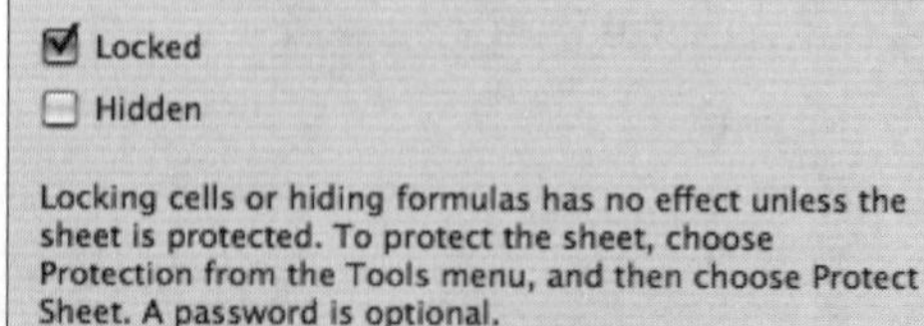

Figure 16.16 To make selected cells modifiable, clear the check mark from Locked.

Sales Tax %	Sale Amt.	Tax	Total
0.0775	$66.00	$5.12	**$71.12**
	$17.23	$1.34	**$18.57**
	$6.45	$0.50	**$6.95**
	$12.00	$0.93	**$12.93**
	$8.75	$0.68	**$9.43**
	$125.00	$9.69	**$134.69**
	$3.72	$0.29	**$4.01**
	$9.99	$0.77	**$10.76**
	$15.70	$1.22	**$16.92**
	$23.65	$1.83	**$25.48**
	$87.00	$6.74	**$93.74**
	$164.23	$12.73	**$176.96**
	$8.33	$0.65	**$8.98**
	$15.25	$1.18	**$16.43**

Figure 16.17 In this simple worksheet, cells in the `Sale Amt.` column must be unlocked in order to allow editing. The `Sales Tax %` remains locked, as do the formulas used to calculate `Tax` and `Total`.

Figure 16.18 To unprotect a worksheet or workbook that has a password associated with it, you must supply the password.

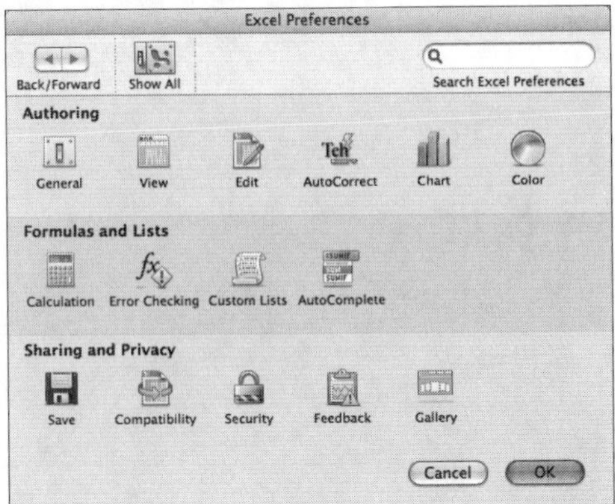

Figure 16.19 Set security and other preferences by clicking icons in the Excel Preferences dialog box.

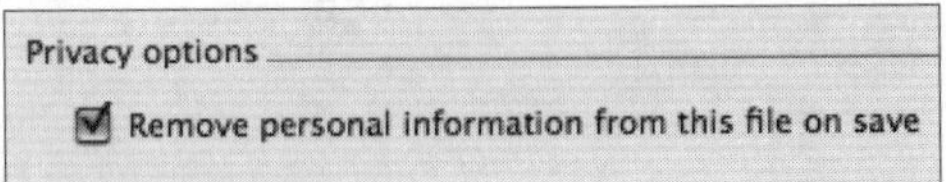

Figure 16.20 Click this check box to remove identifying information from the open workbook.

Removing Personal Information

When you save a new workbook, identifying information is also saved with the file. At a minimum, this includes your user name (as specified in the General dialog box). To protect your privacy, you can remove the user name and other types of identifying information from selected workbooks.

To remove identifying information:

1. Open the workbook.
2. Choose Excel > Preferences.

   The Excel Preferences dialog box appears (**Figure 16.19**).
3. Click the Security icon in the Sharing and Privacy section of the dialog box.

   The Security dialog box appears.
4. Click the check box in the Privacy options section of the Security dialog box (**Figure 16.20**), click OK, and save the workbook.

   Your user name and other identifying information (such as names of reviewers and comment authors, and data on the Summary and Statistics tabs of the Properties dialog box) are removed from the workbook file.

✔ Tip

- To set or change your user name, click the General icon in the Authoring section of the Excel Preferences dialog box (Figure 16.19).

Document Properties

To add identifying information to a workbook (such as the workbook name, author, company name, and custom identifiers), choose File > Properties. Make the desired additions and changes on the tabs of the Properties dialog box, and then click OK. To record this information, save the workbook.

Part IV: Microsoft PowerPoint

17 Creating a Presentation

PowerPoint provides you with the tools necessary to create impressive onscreen, Web-based, and traditional slide presentations. You can choose from a variety of professional themes designed to help you create a presentation with a compelling visual message.

The first part of this chapter explains the essentials of creating a new presentation, working in different views, adding and deleting slides, and working with text and graphics. The second part shows how to use slide masters to add a background design, static images, and color to your presentation. You'll find that customizing presentations in PowerPoint is as straightforward as it has always been.

New features introduced in PowerPoint 2008 include the following:

- The Elements Gallery provides ready access to major slide design tools and features, such as themes, layouts, transitions, charts, tables, and SmartArt.
- You can send slide shows to iPhoto, saving them as a series of pictures that can be viewed on a video iPod.
- Dynamic guides make it easier to position slide objects in relation to one another.
- You can use an Apple Remote to control presentations.

Starting a Presentation

A theme, template, or a blank document can serve as the starting point for a presentation.

To create a new presentation:

1. Open the Project Gallery by choosing File > Project Gallery, pressing Shift⌘P, or clicking the Microsoft Project Gallery icon in the Dock. Click the New tab.
2. *Do one of the following:*
   - ▲ To create a presentation without a *theme* (background, colors, and fonts), select the Blank Documents category and click the PowerPoint Presentation thumbnail (**Figure 17.1**).
   - ▲ To create a presentation with a theme, choose PowerPoint Documents from the Show drop-down menu, select the Office Themes category, and select a theme thumbnail (**Figure 17.2**).
   - ▲ To open a template, select Presentations in the Category list and click a template.
3. Click the Open button.

   The presentation appears. If you picked a template, the presentation contains explanatory slides. If you selected a blank or theme-based presentation, it contains a single slide (**Figure 17.3**).

✔ Tips

- You can also start a blank presentation by choosing File > New Presentation (⌘N). (If you've removed the check mark from Show Project Gallery at Startup in General Preferences, a blank presentation is created automatically at PowerPoint startup.)
- You can set or change the theme at any time by selecting one from the Slide Themes tab of the Elements Gallery (see "Slide Backgrounds," later in this chapter).

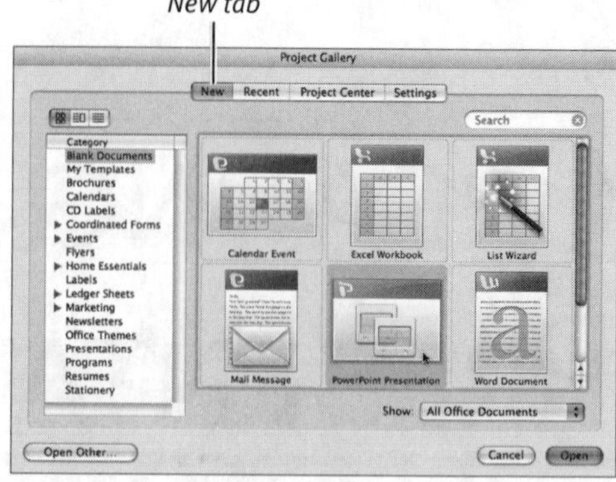

Figure 17.1 Click the PowerPoint Presentation thumbnail to create a themeless presentation from scratch.

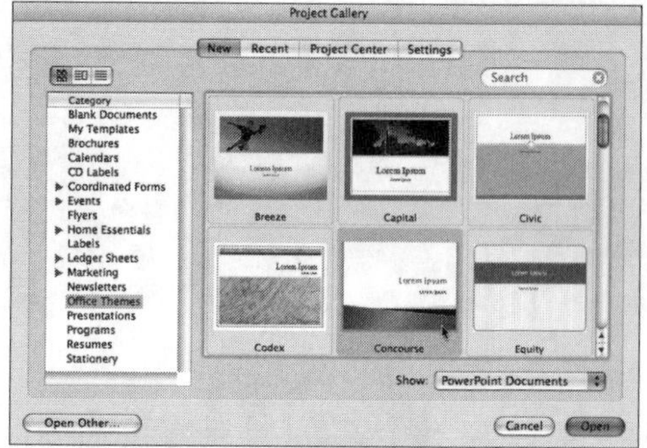

Figure 17.2 To create a presentation from scratch but *with* a theme, select a thumbnail from the Office Themes category.

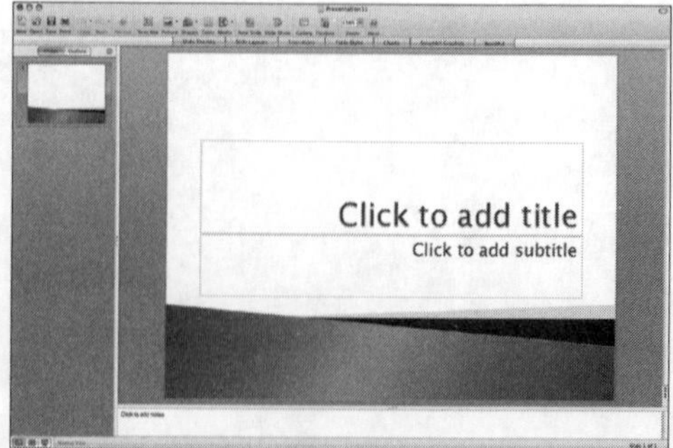

Figure 17.3 The new presentation appears.

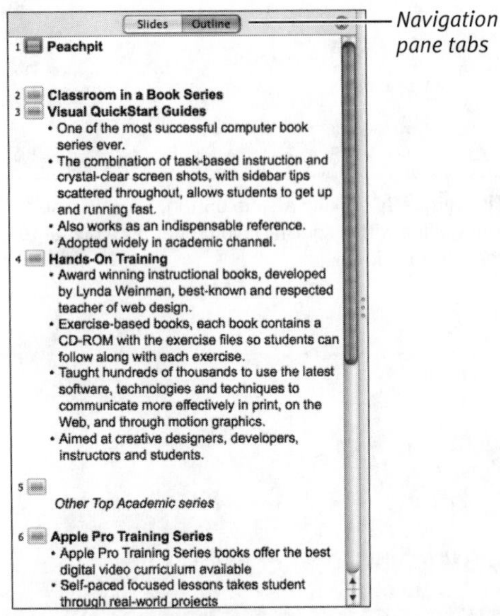

Figure 17.4 In Normal View, you can click a slide thumbnail or outline element to display its slide.

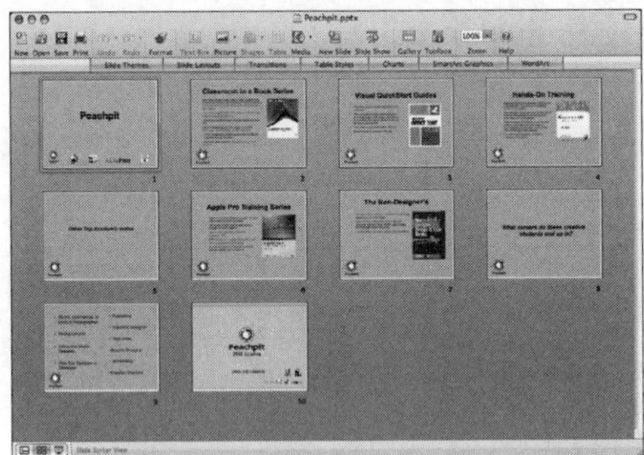

Figure 17.5 Slide Sorter View.

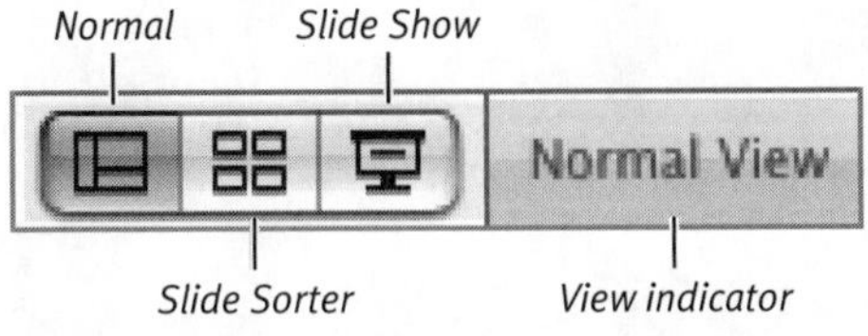

Figure 17.6 You can switch views by clicking an icon. The name of the current view is displayed.

About Views

PowerPoint provides five *views* that you'll use while creating, preparing for, and giving a presentation. Each view has a particular purpose. For instance, if you need to rearrange the slides, you can use Slide Sorter View.

- *Normal View* (see Figure 17.3) displays the text, slide, and notes, enabling you to work on all parts of your presentation in one window. The navigation pane in Normal View can display slide thumbnails or an outline of the slides' key points (**Figure 17.4**).
- *Slide Sorter View* (**Figure 17.5**) displays slide thumbnails. You can reorganize the slides by clicking and dragging or go directly to any slide by double-clicking a thumbnail. You can also use this view to add and edit effects within and between slides.
- *Notes Page View* lets you conveniently enter and edit the speaker notes that will accompany the slides.
- *Presenter Tools View* contains tools to help you prepare to give the presentation.
- *Slide Show View* displays the presentation as an onscreen slide show.

You'll learn more about each view in the next two chapters.

To switch views:

- Click an icon in the lower-left corner of the presentation window (**Figure 17.6**) or choose a command from the View menu.

Adding and Deleting Slides

Designing presentations is seldom a linear process. Along the way, you'll have many occasions where you'll need to add or delete slides. You can do so in any view other than Slide Show View or Presenter Tools View.

To add a slide:

1. A new slide is always inserted after the currently active slide. Select or display the slide after which you want the new slide to appear.
2. *Do one of the following:*
   - ▲ To insert a slide of the same type as the selected slide, click the New Slide icon on the Standard toolbar, choose Insert > New Slide, or press Shift⌘N.
   - ▲ To insert a slide with a different layout, click the Slide Layouts tab of the Elements Gallery, click the Insert new slide radio button, and click a layout thumbnail (**Figure 17.7**).

To delete a slide:

1. Select or display the slide that you want to delete.
2. Choose Edit > Delete Slide or press Delete. The active slide is immediately deleted.

✔ Tips

- To recover a slide you mistakenly deleted, choose Edit > Undo Delete Slide, choose Edit > Undo Clear, or press ⌘Z.
- You can go directly to the Slide Layouts tab by choosing Format > Slide Layout or Insert > Slides From > Slide Layout.
- Rather than selecting a slide, you can Control-click a slide and choose New Slide or Delete Slide from the pop-up menu that appears (**Figure 17.8**).

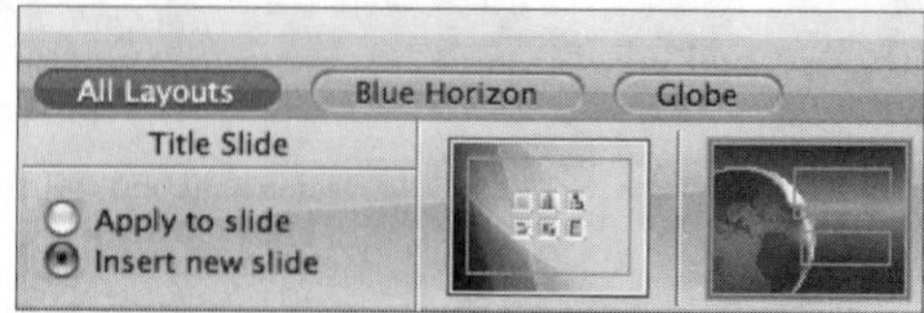

Figure 17.7 By clicking a radio button, you can insert a new slide with a specific layout or apply a layout to the current slide.

Figure 17.8 You can choose many useful commands when you Control-click a slide.

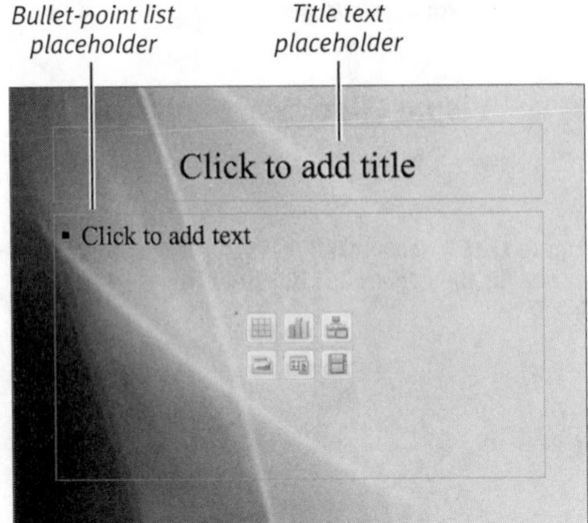

Figure 17.9 The new slide appears, ready for you to enter text into the placeholders.

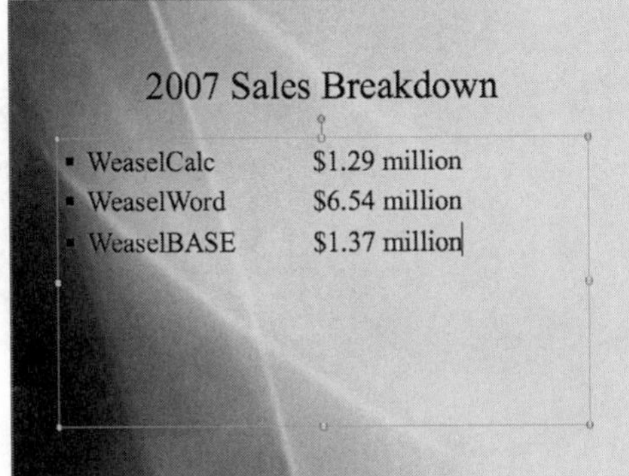

Figure 17.10 Click each text placeholder and type or paste your text.

Adding Text to Slides

Most slide layouts contain text placeholders into which you can enter a title or other text.

To create a new text slide:

1. A new slide is always inserted after the currently active slide. Select or display the slide after which you want the new slide to appear.
2. *Do one of the following:*
   - ▲ To insert a slide of the same type as the selected slide (assuming it has text placeholders), click the New Slide icon on the Standard toolbar, choose Insert > New Slide, or press Shift⌘N.
   - ▲ To insert a slide with a different layout, select the Slide Layouts tab of the Elements Gallery, click the Insert new slide radio button, and click a layout thumbnail (see Figure 17.7).

   The new slide appears (**Figure 17.9**).
3. Click the "Click to add title" or "Click to add text" placeholder and type the text (**Figure 17.10**).

✔ Tips

- When you finish typing text in a placeholder, you can press Option Return to jump to the next text placeholder. When you finish typing the text in the lowest placeholder, you can press Option Return to automatically create another slide of the same type.
- To format text, set paragraph alignment, or create additional bulleted or numbered lists, you can choose commands from the Format menu, the Formatting toolbar, or the Formatting Palette.
- If you don't need a particular text placeholder, you can leave it blank or delete it.

Working with Text Boxes

You can select characters, words, or paragraphs within a text box the same way you do in a Word document (see "Working with Text" in Chapter 1). However, PowerPoint differs a bit in the manner in which you move and format text boxes.

To select a text box:

- Click its edge or inside the text box.

  The text box is surrounded by handles (**Figure 17.11**), enabling you to move and resize it as necessary.

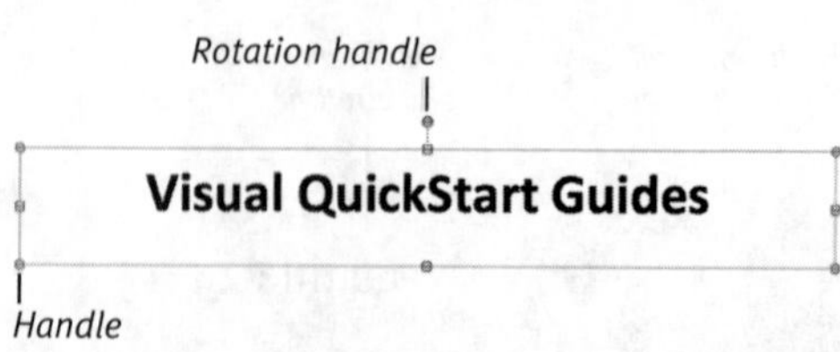

Figure 17.11 When a text box is selected, handles appear as they do around any other selected object in Office.

To move or resize a text box:

- To move a selected text box, move the cursor over any edge until it changes to a cross (**Figure 17.12**), and then drag the box to a new position on the slide.
- Drag a handle to resize a text box.

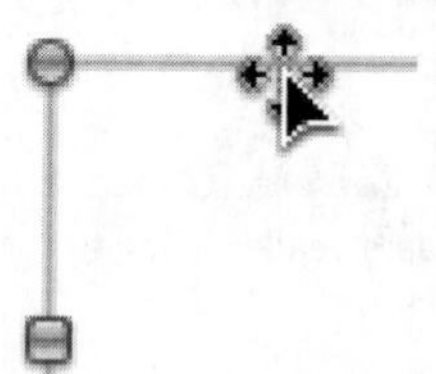

Figure 17.12 The cursor takes this shape when it's moved over the edge of a text box.

✔ Tips

- To resize a text box proportionately, hold down Shift as you drag a corner handle. To resize a text box from its center, hold down Option as you drag a corner handle. (If the box was originally centered on the slide, this will keep it centered.)
- Text inside a resized text box automatically rewraps to fit the box's new size.
- To edit text within a text box, you can simply click in it to set the text insertion mark. You can select text within a text box using normal editing procedures.
- You can drag a text box's rotation handle to change its angle.
- In addition to the text placeholders, you can add your own text boxes to any slide. Choose Insert > Text Box or click the Text Box toolbar icon, and then draw the text box on the slide.

Figure 17.13 Icons indicate the types of objects a placeholder can accept. The top row denotes a table, chart, and SmartArt graphic. The bottom row icons are for a picture, clip art, and movie.

Figure 17.14 Insert an image from the Clip Gallery.

Adding Shapes and Lines

In addition to adding a variety of images, you can embellish your slides by adding lines and shapes from the Drawing toolbar (View > Toolbars > Drawing) or from the Toolbox's Object Palette tab. Many shapes, such as callout balloons, can accept text.

Adding Images to Slides

You can make your slides more interesting by adding clip art from the Clip Gallery or photos and other image files stored on disk. As an example, the steps below explain how to add clip art to a slide. Information on adding other types of graphic elements can be found in these chapters:

- **SmartArt graphics.** See the next section ("Adding SmartArt Graphics").
- **Charts and tables.** Chapter 18.
- **Organization charts.** Chapter 18.
- **Movies.** Chapter 19.
- **WordArt.** Chapter 5.

To add clip art to a slide:

1. Create a new slide, selecting a layout that includes a clip art placeholder (**Figure 17.13**).
   The new slide appears.
2. Click the clip art placeholder.
   The Clip Gallery window appears.
3. Select a category from the list on the left or perform a search by entering a keyword in the Search box and clicking Search.
   Clip art is displayed in the panel on the right (**Figure 17.14**).
4. Select an image and click Insert.
   The clip art image is inserted into the placeholder.

✔ Tips

- Another way to insert clip art is to drag it from the Object Palette tab (Clip Art section) of the Toolbox onto a placeholder (**Figure 17.15**). iPhoto pictures can also be placed this way by dragging them from the Photos section of the Object Palette tab.
- Even if you haven't created a slide with a clip art placeholder, you can manually add clip art to *any* slide by choosing Insert > Clip Art. You can also insert clip art into a graphic placeholder by selecting the placeholder and choosing the same command.
- To insert a *different* type of image (such as a photo), follow the same procedure but create a new slide that contains a picture placeholder. When you double-click the placeholder, the Choose a Picture dialog box appears (**Figure 17.16**), allowing you to select a picture from your hard disk.
- You can insert any compatible image by dragging its file icon onto a placeholder.
- If you want to edit a picture, you can select options in the Formatting Palette or choose Format > Picture to open the Format Picture dialog box.
- You can also open the Format Picture dialog box by double-clicking a placed picture.
- Don't import or drag *multiple* pictures into the same placeholder. Rather than replacing the previous image, the new image is placed atop the old one. Delete the original image first.
- You can substitute one photo for another by Control-clicking it on the slide and choosing Change Picture from the pop-up menu that appears.

Figure 17.15 You can insert a clip art image or photo by dragging it from the Object Palette onto a slide.

Figure 17.16 You can insert an image file from your hard disk by selecting it in the Choose a Picture dialog box (OS X 10.4.11/Tiger shown).

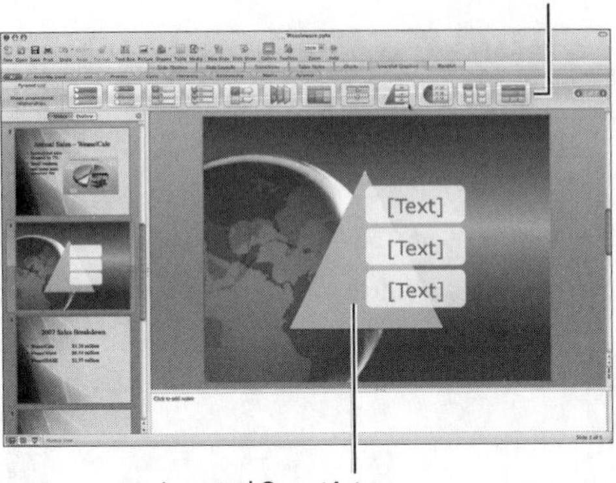

Figure 17.17 Click a thumbnail to add the SmartArt to the current slide.

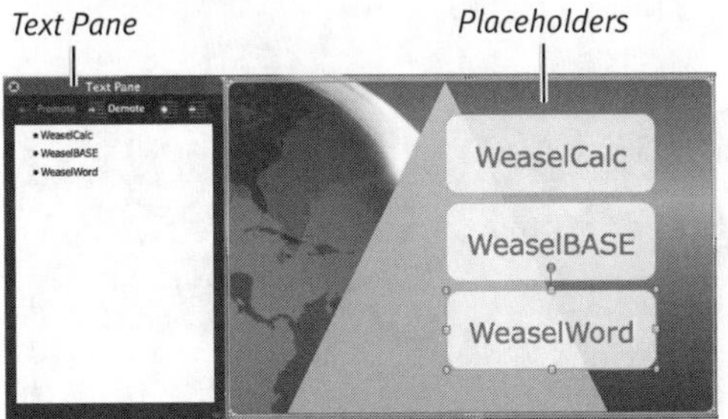

Figure 17.18 Enter text into the placeholders.

Figure 17.19 Some SmartArt also has placeholders for pictures or photos.

Adding SmartArt Graphics

Available on a tab in the Elements Gallery, *SmartArt graphics* are colorful combinations of graphics and text that you can insert to create eye-catching bullet lists, processes, hierarchies, and so on. Although SmartArt is also available in Word and Excel, it's more commonly used in presentations.

To insert a Smart art graphic:

1. *Do either of the following:*
   - ▲ To add SmartArt to an existing slide, select a placeholder on the slide.
   - ▲ To add SmartArt to a new slide, click the Slide Layouts tab of the Elements Gallery, select the Insert new slide radio button, and select the layout onto which you'll add the SmartArt. On the new slide, select a placeholder.
2. To view the SmartArt thumbnails, *do one of the following:*
   - ▲ Choose Insert > SmartArt Graphic.
   - ▲ Click the SmartArt Graphics tab in the Elements Gallery.
3. Click a SmartArt thumbnail.

   The SmartArt graphic is added to the slide. (**Figure 17.17**).
4. Enter text into the placeholders.

   You can type directly into the placeholders or into the Text Pane (**Figure 17.18**).
5. If the SmartArt contains picture placeholders (**Figure 17.19**), click each icon and select a photo or other picture.

✔ Tips

- You aren't *required* to select a placeholder before inserting SmartArt. If you fail to do so, the Smart Art will be placed as a floating graphic.
- The Text Pane (**Figure 17.20**) contains additional controls for managing a SmartArt graphic's text blocks. You can do the following:
  - ▲ Drag the title bar to move the Text Pane to a different location.
  - ▲ Drag the resize corner to change the size of the Text Pane.
  - ▲ Select a text box and click the plus (+) icon to insert an additional text placeholder beneath the selected one.
  - ▲ To delete the currently selected text box, click the minus (-) icon.
  - ▲ Click the Demote icon to change the current text item into a sub-item of the item above it. Click Promote to change a sub-item into a normal item.
  - ▲ Click the close (X) button to close the Text Pane.
- If the Text Pane isn't visible, click the icon in the upper-left corner of the SmartArt.
- When working on SmartArt, a new section appears in the Formatting Palette (**Figure 17.21**). You can modify the SmartArt by selecting a new style or color. If you don't like the changes, you can click Reset Graphic to restore the SmartArt to its original style and color.

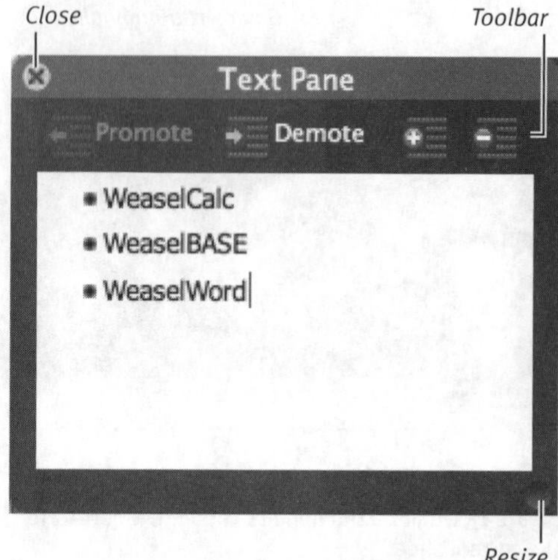

Figure 17.20 The Text Pane has a toolbar and other controls for managing a SmartArt graphic's text.

Figure 17.21 Use the SmartArt Graphic Styles section of the Formatting Palette to change the style or color of a SmartArt graphic.

Working with Placeholders

In the previous sections, you saw that almost all slide layouts have placeholders for some combination of text, photos, charts, tables, clip art, and the like. Placeholders have two purposes. First, clicking an icon in a placeholder enables you to easily add that type of material to the layout. Second, designers can format text within a placeholder, ensuring consistency among the slides.

Since you'll be spending a lot of time working with placeholders, here are a few additional facts and tips that may be helpful:

- Like other layout objects, you can resize, move, or delete placeholders:
  - To change a placeholder's size or shape, drag a handle.
  - To move a selected placeholder, position the cursor over any edge, click, and then drag.
  - To delete a selected placeholder, press Delete.
- You can selectively set formatting within a text placeholder or apply the formating to *all* of the placeholder's text. To do the latter (such as changing the bullet symbol, paragraph alignment, or font, for example), select the placeholder by clicking one of its edges and then apply the formatting.
- Most built-in themes contain a layout without placeholders. If you want more control over slide layouts in your presentation, you can add your own text boxes, photos, and SmartArt to the blank layout.

Slide Backgrounds

Rather than selecting a presentation theme from the Slide Themes tab of the Elements Gallery, you can create your own theme by judiciously choosing background graphics and colors.

Creating a picture background

There are two ways to quickly add a background image to the slides in your presentation. First, you can place the image on a slide master. Second, you can use the Format > Background command. In either case, you can choose graphics from the art collections included with Office or use your own images.

To add an image to a slide master:

1. Choose View > Master > Slide Master or press Shift as you click the Normal View icon at the bottom of the document.
   The Slide Master window appears (**Figure 17.22**).
2. In the navigation pane on the left, select a slide layout as follows:
   - ▲ To apply the image to a specific slide layout, select that layout.
   - ▲ To apply the image to *all* layouts, select the first layout (Office Theme Slide Master).
3. Choose Insert > Picture or Insert > Clip Art, or click the Picture toolbar icon and choose an Insert command.
   The Choose a Picture or Clip Gallery dialog box appears.
4. Select an image and click Insert.
   The picture appears on the slide master.
5. As necessary, modify, resize, or move the image (**Figure 17.23**).
6. To leave Slide Master View, click a View icon or choose a View menu command.

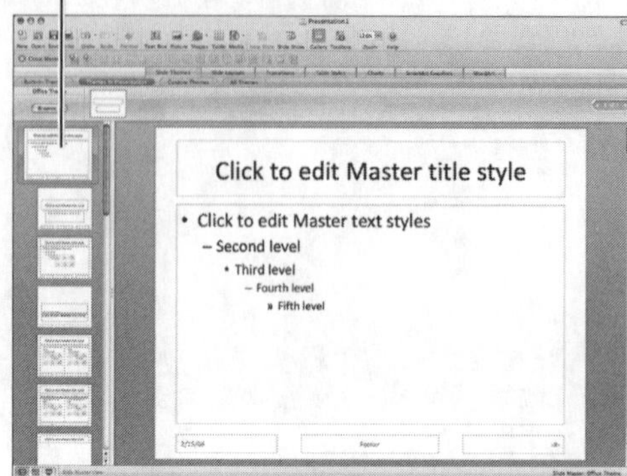

Figure 17.22 Graphics and text added to a slide master can appear on every slide in the presentation.

Figure 17.23 When resized, this image from the Clip Gallery fills the background.

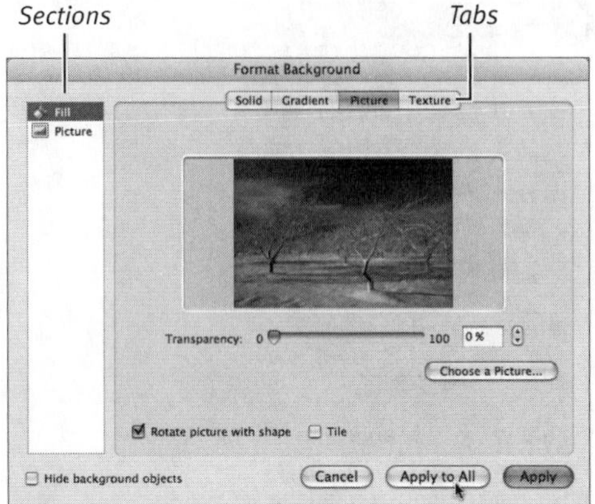

Figure 17.24 The selected image file is displayed. To apply it to the background of all slides in the presentation, click Apply to All. To apply it only to the current slide, click Apply.

To use a picture as the background:

1. Choose Format > Slide Background.
   The Format Background dialog appears.
2. With Fill selected in the pane on the left, click the Picture tab.
3. Click the Choose a Picture button.
   The Choose a Picture dialog box appears.
4. Select an image file and click Insert.
   The image appears in the dialog box (**Figure 17.24**) and on the current slide.
5. *Optional:* Make the image transparent by dragging the Transparency slider or by typing a percentage in the text box.
6. *Optional:* If the selected image doesn't fill the slide as you'd like, click the Tile check box to repeat the original image as many times as necessary to fill the slide.
7. To add the image to the background of all slides in the presentation, click Apply to All.

✔ Tips

- Graphics already on the slide master as part of a template background may need to be ungrouped before you can alter them.
- You can copy and paste a graphic image from another program onto the slide master, as well as copy and paste graphics from the slide master of another presentation onto the slide master of the current presentation.
- The Office 2008 clip art can be found in `Applications: Microsoft Office 2008: Office: Media: Clipart`.
- The Fill section of the Format Background dialog box has tabs that enable you to set the background to a solid color, gradient, picture, or texture. Although you can't *remove* a background, you can select a different one or apply a solid white fill.

Applying a background color, gradient, or texture

The Format Background dialog box also can be used to apply a solid color, gradient, or texture to the background. The background formattting can vary from slide to slide or be applied to all slides in the presentation.

To set a background color, gradient, or texture:

1. *Optional:* To set the background for only one slide, select that slide.

   When you're applying a background to *all* slides in a presentation, the selected slide doesn't matter.

2. *Do one of the following:*
   - ▲ Choose Format > Slide Background.
   - ▲ Click the Format Background button in the Slide Background section of the Formatting Palette (**Figure 17.25**).

   The Format Background dialog box appears. Ensure that the Fill section is selected in the pane on the left.

3. Click one of these tabs:
   - ▲ **Solid.** Select a color from the drop-down menu. If you don't see the color you want, choose More Colors to set a color using a color picker.
   - ▲ **Gradient.** Select a gradient style from the Style drop-down menu. Alter the other controls as desired to create the gradient (**Figure 17.26**).
   - ▲ **Texture.** Select a texture thumbnail from the scrolling list.

   A preview of the chosen effect is applied to the current slide.

4. *Do one of the following:*
   - ▲ To apply the new background to only the current slide, click Apply.
   - ▲ To apply the background to all slides in the presentation, click Apply to All.

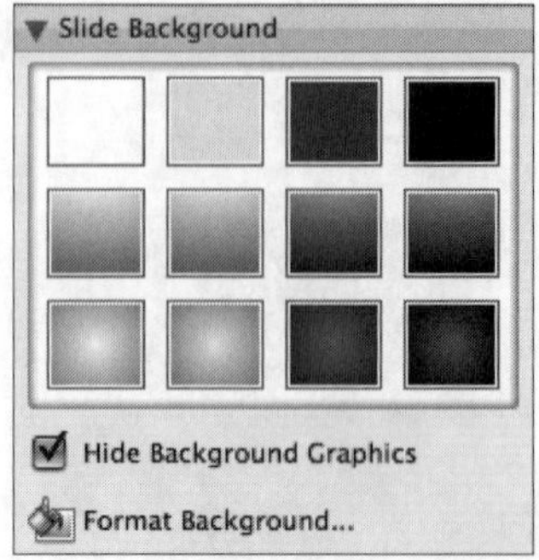

Figure 17.25 You can use the Slide Background section to select a basic background or open the Format Background dialog box.

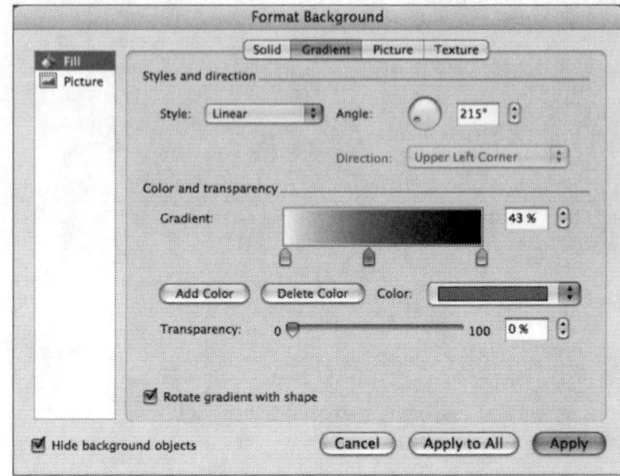

Figure 17.26 On the Gradient tab, choose a style, color, angle, and other settings to create the gradient. The interactive preview on the current slide shows the settings' effects.

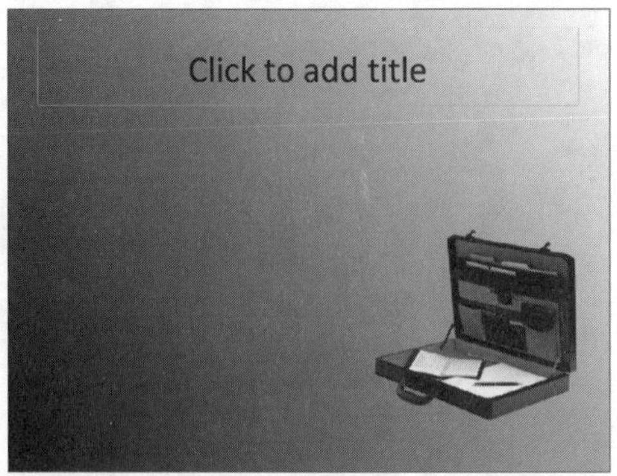

Figure 17.27 If graphics inserted onto a slide master don't cover the slide, you can combine them with a background format, such as this gradient.

✔ Tips

- When formatting the background, you can apply a solid color, gradient, *or* a texture; they're mutually exclusive. If you set a new background, it replaces the current background.
- If you preselect a color on the Solid tab before creating a gradient, the gradient is based on the selected color. Otherwise, a grayscale gradient is initially used.
- As seen in Figure 17.25, you can set the background to any of a dozen gradients by clicking a Formatting Palette icon.
- The Format Background dialog box and the Formatting Palette each contain a check box that enables you to hide background objects/graphics. If the current slide theme contains graphics that have been inserted onto a slide master, click this check box to enable your color, gradient, or texture background to be seen, while hiding the slide master graphic(s). As an alternative, you can edit the slide master and delete the graphic(s).
- Even if a slide master contains inserted graphics, you can still use the Format Background dialog box to specify a background color, gradient, or texture—but *only* if the inserted graphics don't completely cover the slide (**Figure 17.27**).

Changing Theme Colors

You can also add consistency to a presentation by specifying a color scheme (theme colors). The eight colors of a color scheme are applied to all elements on slides in the presentation. You can select a provided color scheme or create one of your own.

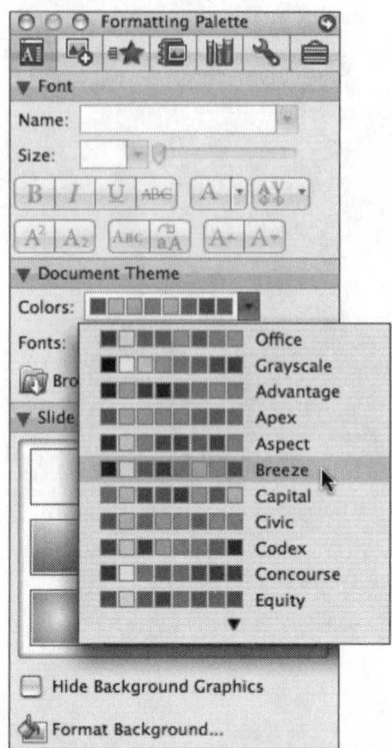

Figure 17.28 You can choose a new color scheme.

To specify a new color scheme (theme colors):

- In the Document Scheme section of the Formatting Palette, choose a color scheme from the Colors drop-down menu (**Figure 17.28**).

  The new color scheme is immediately applied to the presentation.

✔ Tips

- To customize the current color scheme, choose Format > Theme Colors. In the Create Theme Colors dialog box (**Figure 17.29**), select new colors by clicking an element's color box and then clicking the Change Color button. The effects (if any) are shown in the preview area. When you're finished, name the color scheme and click Apply to All.
- If you choose a different theme from the Slide Themes tab of the Elements Gallery, the color scheme and font set automatically change, too.
- In addition to a color scheme, each theme selected from the Slide Themes tab of the Elements Gallery also uses a particular set of fonts for placeholder text. You can choose a different font set from the Fonts drop-down menu in the Document Scheme section of the Formatting Palette.
- To replace one or more fonts in the current font set, choose Format > Replace Fonts, make the change(s) in the Replace Font dialog box, and click Close.

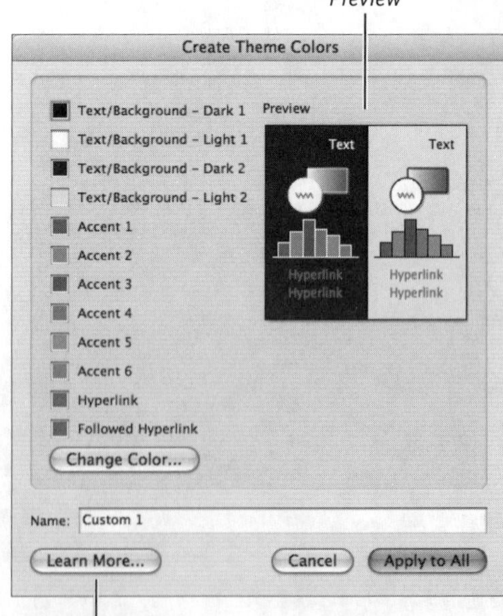

Figure 17.29 You can customize the current color scheme by choosing new colors for the elements.

Saving and Reusing a Custom Design

After spending hours modifying a PowerPoint template or creating a presentation from scratch, you can optionally save its design as a custom template or theme that you can use as the basis for future presentations.

To save a presentation as a template or theme:

1. Choose File > Save As.
   The Save As panel appears (**Figure 17.30**).
2. Choose PowerPoint Template (.potx) or Office Theme (.thmx) from the Format drop-down menu.
3. Name the template or theme, and click the Save button.
   Templates are stored in the My Templates folder and can later be selected from the Project Gallery. Custom themes are stored in the My Themes folder. They can be selected for use in other presentations from the Custom Themes section of the Slide Themes tab of the Elements Gallery.

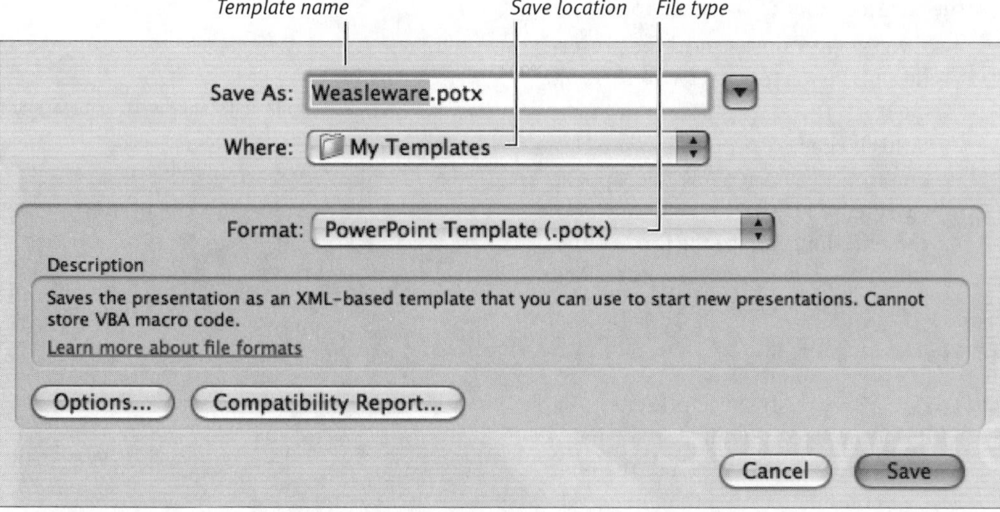

Figure 17.30 You can save the current presentation as a reusable PowerPoint Template or custom theme.

Saving Presentations

Don't forget to save the presentation on which you're working. In addition to saving it as a standard presentation that can be opened, viewed, and edited in PowerPoint 2008, you can save in a variety of formats for different purposes and audiences, such as:

- **HTML.** Using a Web browser, anyone can view the presentation on a Web page or their own computer desktop.
- **QuickTime movie.** This option enables people to view the presentation as it might appear during a live presentation.
- **PDF.** This output can be viewed in Adobe Reader, Preview, and similar utilities.
- **Pictures.** You can save a presentation as a series of iPhoto pictures, enabling it to be shown on an iPod.

Figure 17.31 shows the supported save formats. See Chapter 19 for an in-depth discussion of some useful Save options.

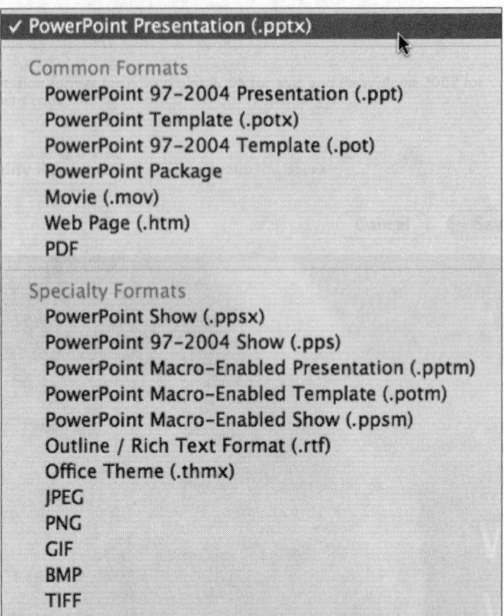

Figure 17.31 When saving a presentation for the first time or when using Save As, these file formats can be chosen from the Format drop-down menu.

To save a presentation:

- Choose File > Save, press ⌘S, or click the Save icon on the Standard toolbar.
  - ▲ If you've previously saved the presentation, this version overwrites the old one.
  - ▲ If this is the first time you've saved the presentation, a Save As panel appears (see Figure 17.30). Enter a name for the presentation, choose the format in which you'd like to save, select a location on disk, and click Save.

✔ Tip

- To save a previously saved presentation with a new name, in a different format, or in another location on disk, use the File > Save As command rather than File > Save.

18

CHARTS AND TABLES

A chart or graph can make complex numerical information easier to interpret by expressing it visually. To create or edit a chart, PowerPoint and Word 2008 use Excel. (In earlier versions of Office, charts were made using an application called Graph.) When creating a new chart or editing an existing one, you temporarily leave PowerPoint and work in Excel.

✔ Tips

- Information in this chapter concerning the process of creating charts in PowerPoint is also applicable to creating them in Word.
- See Chapter 13 for additional information about creating, editing, and formatting charts.
- If you've already created and formatted a chart in Excel, you don't need to follow the instructions in this chapter. See "Copying, Linking, and Embedding" in Chapter 29 for help transferring the chart into PowerPoint.

Creating a Chart

You can add a chart to an existing slide or to a new slide.

Figure 18.1 Some placeholders have a chart icon.

To add a chart to a slide:

1. *Optional:* Create a new slide by choosing Insert > New Slide, clicking the New Slide icon on the Standard toolbar, or pressing Shift ⌘ N.

   The new slide's layout duplicates that of the initially selected slide. To change the layout, select the Slide Layouts tab of the Elements Gallery, click the Apply to slide radio button, and click a layout thumbnail.

2. *Do one of the following:*
   - ▲ If the slide contains a chart placeholder (**Figure 18.1**), click the chart icon.
   - ▲ If the slide contains a placeholder for another type of object (such as a picture), select the placeholder.
   - ▲ If the slide has no suitable placeholder but has a blank area large enough to receive the chart, do nothing.

3. If the Charts tab of the Elements Gallery isn't displayed, click the tab or choose Insert > Chart.

   Chart thumbnails appear (**Figure 18.2**).

4. Click a chart category button, and then click the thumbnail of the chart you want to create.

   Excel launches and displays a worksheet with sample data (**Figure 18.3**).

5. Replace the sample data with your own data by typing or pasting. Drag the lower-right corner to match your data range.

6. Click the worksheet's close button (X).

   The chart appears on the slide as a new floating object (**Figure 18.4**).

Figure 18.2 Click a button to choose a chart category, and then click a chart style thumbnail.

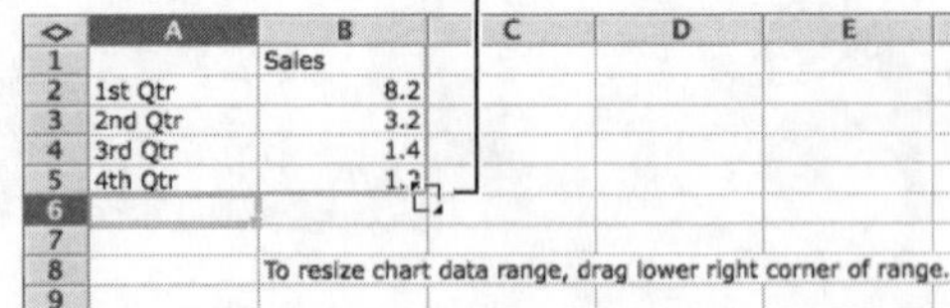

Figure 18.3 Replace the sample labels and data with your own data.

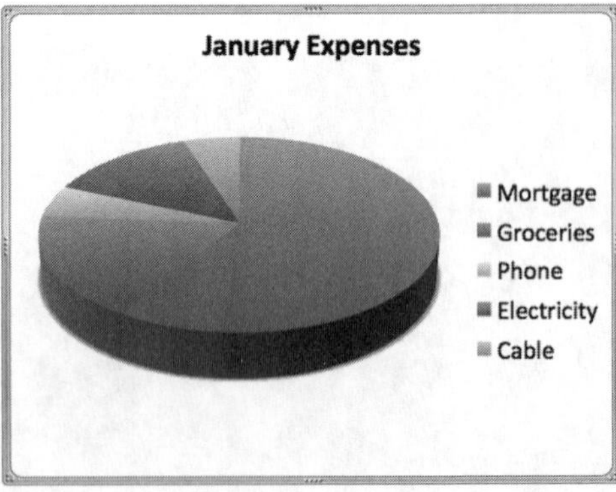

Figure 18.4 The new chart appears on the slide.

Figure 18.5 In the Chart Data section of the Formatting Palette, you can edit the data, transpose the data array, or choose a data table display option.

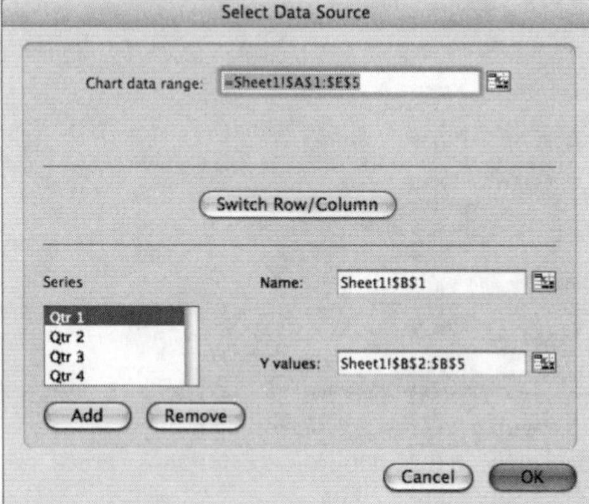

Figure 18.6 Before editing the chart data, you must respond to the Select Data Source dialog box. You can change the data series used in the chart, transpose the data, or accept the current settings.

✔ Tips

- If your data is in another worksheet, copy it, select cell A1 in the sample worksheet, and paste over the sample data.
- If you want to "play" with the chart labels and data arrangement before committing to the chart, it isn't necessary to close the Excel worksheet. As long as it stays open, you can switch back and forth between it and the chart to see the effects of your edits.
- After creating a chart, you can change its type or style by selecting the chart (or any part of it) on the slide and then clicking a new thumbnail on the Charts tab of the Elements Gallery.
- Not every chart type is appropriate for every data set. It's important to select a suitable chart type when creating a chart or changing chart types. For example, a column or bar chart is typically created from multiple data series. If you later convert such a chart to a pie chart (which is created from a *single* data series), unexpected results will likely ensue.
- After creating a chart, you can modify its data or labels. Select the chart, and choose Edit > Edit in Excel or click the Edit in Excel button in the Chart Data section of the Formatting Palette (**Figure 18.5**). The Select Data Source dialog box appears (**Figure 18.6**). You can transpose the data by clicking Switch Rows/Columns or remove selected series from the chart. Click OK when you're ready to edit the worksheet data.
- You can also transpose the data by clicking the other Sort by icon in the Chart Data section of the Formatting Palette (Figure 18.5).

Chart Appearance Options

You can embellish charts and make them easier to interpret by adding a legend, gridlines, data point labels, chart data, and chart or axis titles.

Legends

A *legend* graphically allows you to differentiate the various data series on a chart.

To show or hide the legend:

- With the chart or any part of it selected, choose a legend position from the Legend menu in the Chart Options section of the Formatting Palette (**Figure 18.7**).

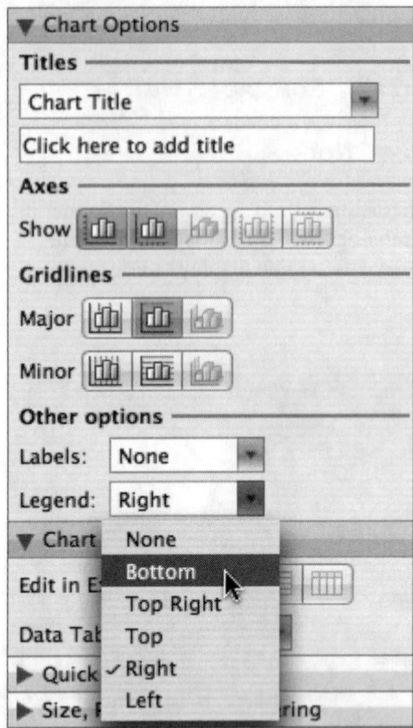

Figure 18.7 You can position or remove the legend in the Chart Options section of the Formatting Palette.

✓ Tips

- You can also change the legend's position and formatting in the Format Legend dialog box (**Figure 18.8**). To open the dialog box, double-click the legend or select it and choose Format > Legend.
- You can remove the legend by choosing None from the Legend drop-down menu (Figure 18.7) or by selecting the legend on the chart and pressing Delete.
- As is the case with other objects in Office, you can modify the legend in many ways. Select it, and *do any of the following:*
  - ▲ To move the legend, click in its center and drag it to a new position.
  - ▲ To change the legend size or shape, drag a handle.
  - ▲ To change the legend text, edit it in the worksheet.
  - ▲ You can set a new font, size, and style for the legend text on the Formatting toolbar, in the Font section of the Formatting Palette, or on the Font tab of the Format Legend dialog box.

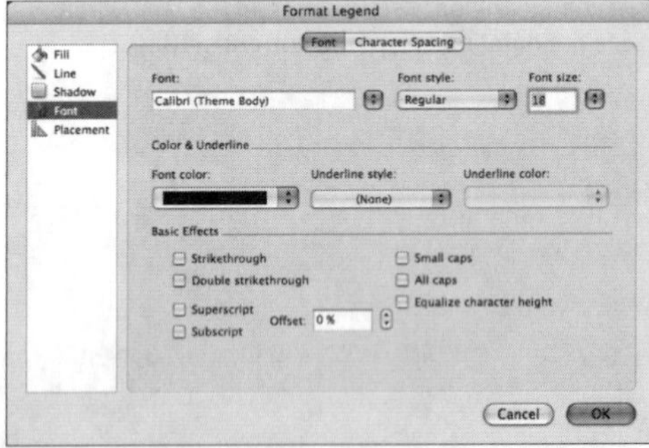

Figure 18.8 You can also set position and formatting for the legend in the Format Legend dialog box.

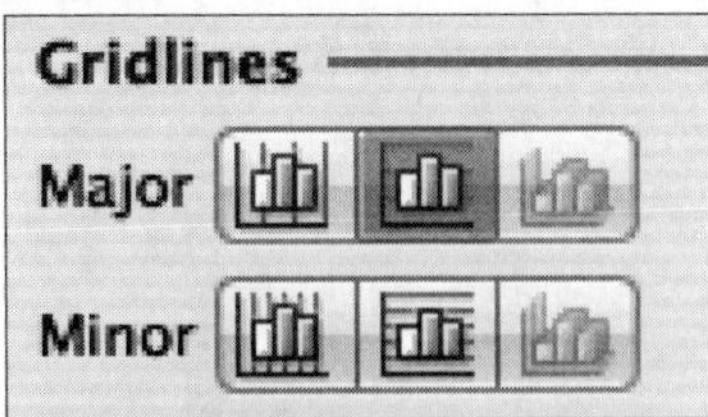

Figure 18.9 Click icons to show or hide the different types of gridlines.

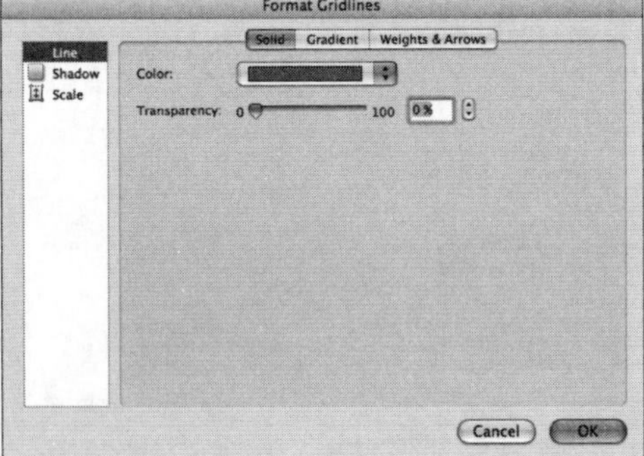

Figure 18.10 On the Solid tab of the Format Gridlines dialog box, you can set line color and transparency.

Gridlines

Gridlines can help viewers interpret the data, since they make it easier to see the approximate size or value of each data point. You can add gridlines to most chart types.

To show or hide gridlines:

- Click icons in the Chart Options section of the Formatting Palette (**Figure 18.9**). You can display any combination of major, minor, vertical, and horizontal gridlines. The gridline icons work as toggles, showing or hiding the gridlines with each click. When a gridline option is displayed on the chart, its icon is dark.

✔ Tip

- To format a gridline set (changing its style, color, or weight), select a gridline on the chart and choose Format > Gridlines. Alternately, you can double-click a gridline. Set formatting options in the Format Gridlines dialog box (**Figure 18.10**). You can change the gridline increments on the Scale tab of the dialog box.

Data point labels

You can label the data values in your chart to highlight the differences between them or to make it easier for viewers to interpret the chart (**Figure 18.11**).

To label every data point:

- With the chart or any part of it selected, choose a data label option (Value or Label) from the Labels drop-down menu in the Chart Options section of the Formatting Palette (see Figure 18.7).

To label a single data series:

1. Select a data series on the chart.
   In a bar or column chart, for example, you can click any colored bar to select all members of that data series.
2. Choose Format > Data Series.
   The Format Data Series dialog box appears.
3. In the Labels section (**Figure 18.12**), select a label option and click OK.

✔ Tips

- You can also specify a label for a single data *point*, labeling only the highest and lowest values, for example. After clicking once to select the series, click the specific data element within the series and choose Format > Data Point.
- To remove all data labels from a chart, choose None from the Labels drop-down menu tab in the Chart Options section of the Formatting Palette (see Figure 18.7). To remove data labels from only one series, choose None in the Labels section of the Format Data Series dialog box.
- Data labels take on the formatting of other chart text. To change the font, size, or color of the labels, you must format them one series at a time.
- The numeric format of the labels (such as the number of decimal places) is determined by cell formatting in the worksheet.

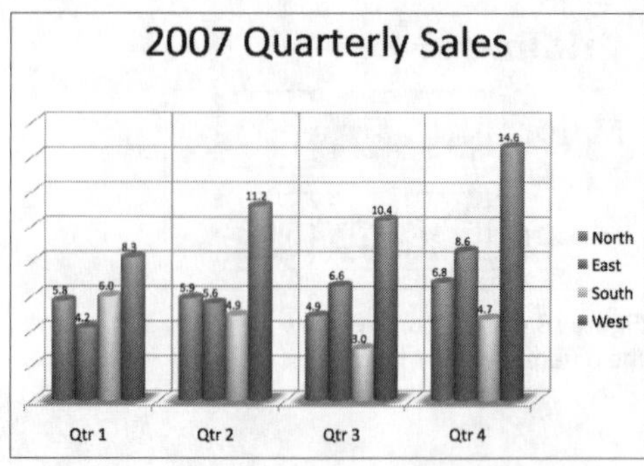

Figure 18.11 If exact numbers are important to the presentation, you can label the data points.

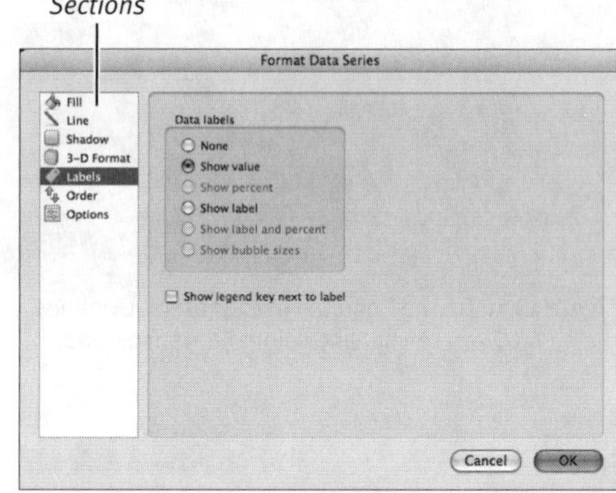

Figure 18.12 After selecting a data series on the chart, you can selectively label and format the data points in the series.

Figure 18.13 Choose a display option from the Data Table drop-down menu.

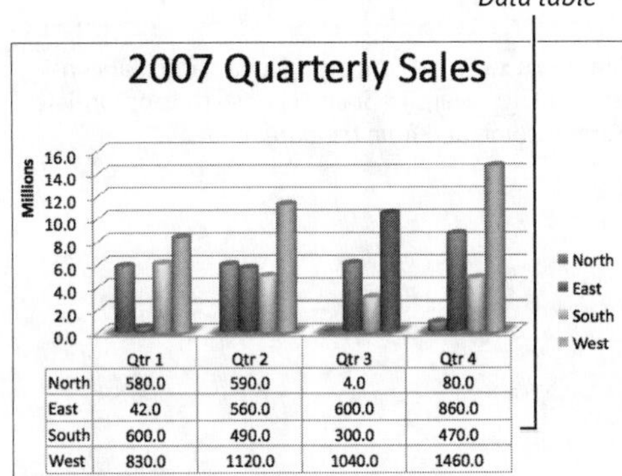

Figure 18.14 Chart with a data table.

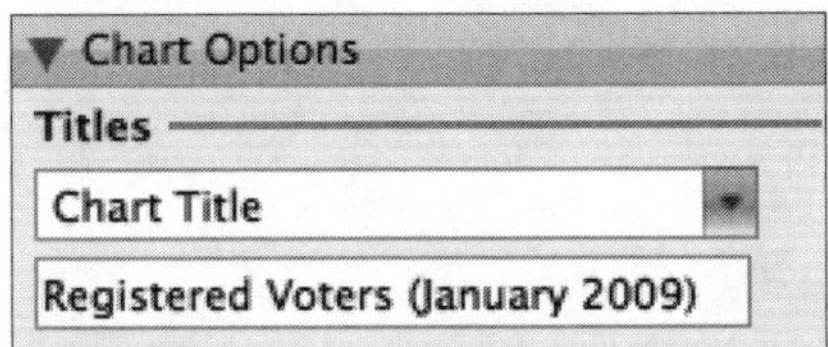

Figure 18.15 You can insert a chart title and axis titles.

✔ Tips

- You can also add a vertical or horizontal axis title to any chart. Choose an Axis option from the Titles drop-down menu and then type the title in the text box.
- After creating a title, you can edit it on the chart or in the Formatting Palette text box.

Chart data

In many types of charts, it's impractical—and ugly—to label the data points. As an alternative, you can display the chart data below the chart.

To display the chart data:

- With the chart or any part of it selected, choose an option (Data Table or Data Table with Legend Keys) from the Data Table drop-down menu in the Chart Options section of the Formatting Palette (**Figure 18.13**).

  The data table appears beneath the chart (**Figure 18.14**).

✔ Tips

- If the effect isn't what you had in mind, remove the data table by choosing None from the Data Table drop-down menu.
- If you choose the Data Table with Legend Keys option, the normal legend becomes superfluous. You can remove the legend by selecting it and pressing Delete. Or you can choose None from the Legend drop-down menu on the Formatting Palette.

Chart titles

In general, a chart should have a title that clearly explains what's being shown. If the chart slide doesn't have a title placeholder, you can add a title to the chart itself.

To add a chart title:

1. Select the chart or any part of it.
2. In the Chart Options section of the Formatting Palette, choose Chart Title from the Titles drop-down menu.
3. Type or paste the chart title in the text box (**Figure 18.15**).

   The title appears at the top of the chart.

Formatting Chart Elements

You can change the appearance of any chart element, such as a single set of bars, a line, or an axis. You can also change the style of any data series in the chart by formatting the series.

To format a chart element:

1. Select the chart element that you want to format and then double-click it.

   The dialog box for that element appears, such as Format Chart Area (with the entire chart selected), Format Axis, Format Data Series, or Format Legend.

2. Set formatting options, and click OK.

✔ Tip

■ To avoid opening the *wrong* dialog box, [Control]-click an element and choose the command from the pop-up menu that appears (**Figure 18.16**).

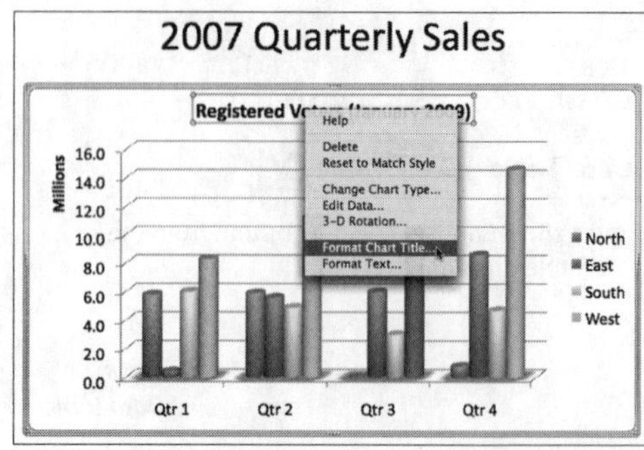

Figure 18.16 To set formatting for a particular chart element, [Control]-click it and choose the appropriate Format command from the pop-up menu.

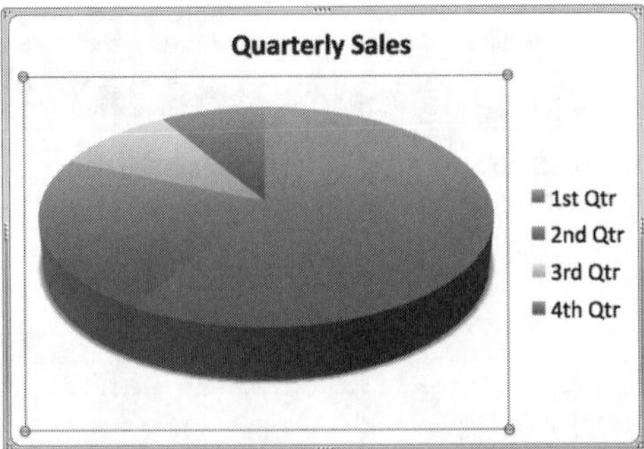

Figure 18.17 Select the plot area. A rectangle appears around the pie.

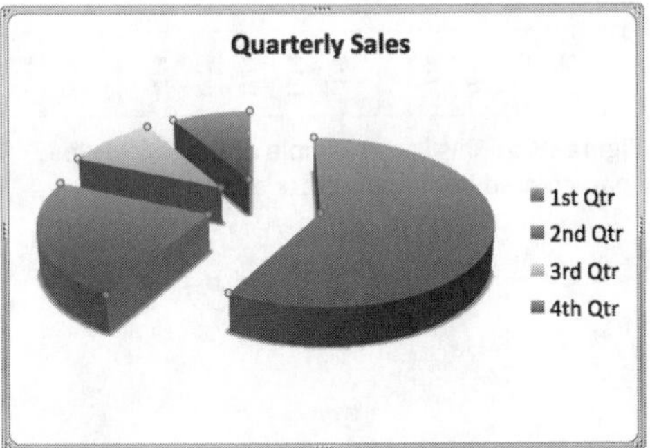

Figure 18.18 Drag outward to explode the entire pie.

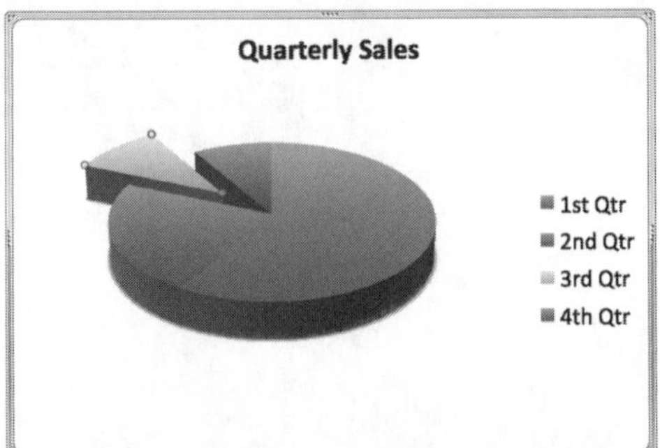

Figure 18.19 If you select and drag a single slice, you can separate the slice from the rest of the pie.

Exploding a Pie Chart

If you've created a pie chart, you can *explode* the chart (pull all pieces out from the center to make it more visually interesting) or pull out an individual piece (to emphasize a data value).

To explode or cut a normal pie chart:

1. Click the chart to make it active.
2. To explode a pie, *do either of the following:*
   - ▲ Choose the Exploded Pie or 3D Exploded Pie thumbnail from the Charts tab of the Elements Gallery. The original pie chart is replaced by an exploded pie chart.
   - ▲ Click once to select the plot area (**Figure 18.17**) and then drag a slice outward (**Figure 18.18**).
3. To cut a slice, click once to select the plot area (Figure 18.17), and then click a second time to select only the slice that you want to cut. Drag the selected slice outward (**Figure 18.19**).

✔ Tips

- The distance you drag when exploding or cutting *does* make a difference.
- To rejoin a cut slice with the pie, drag the slice back to the center of the pie. To rejoin an exploded pie, drag *any* slice back to the center of the pie.

Creating Stock Charts

Stock charts (also known as *high-low-close charts*) can display daily prices and, optionally, the opening price and daily volume for a given stock. Stock charts can also be used to present other types of numeric data, such as temperatures or barometric pressure readings.

To create a stock chart:

1. In an Excel worksheet, arrange the stock data in columns. Depending on the type of chart you intend to create, arrange the columns to match one of the following:
   - ▲ Date, High, Low, Close
   - ▲ Date, Open, High, Low, Close
   - ▲ Date, Volume, High, Low, Close
   - ▲ Date, Volume, Open, High, Low
2. In the Excel worksheet or other source document, copy (Edit > Copy or ⌘C) the data from which the chart will be created.

   The data is stored on the OS X Clipboard.
3. In PowerPoint, switch to or create the slide on which you'll insert the stock chart.
4. Follow the instructions in "Creating a Chart" (earlier in this chapter) to create the chart. On the Charts tab of the Elements Gallery, click the Stock button and select a stock chart thumbnail (**Figure 18.20**).

   Excel launches and displays a worksheet with sample data.
5. Paste (Edit > Paste or ⌘V) the stock data into cell A1 and resize the range to encompass the pasted data.
6. Close the worksheet.

   The stock chart appears on the slide.
7. Format the chart (**Figure 18.21**).

   You can remove the legend and change the vertical axis to display a more appropriate range, for example.

Figure 18.20 Select a stock chart thumbnail that matches the data fields you intend to use.

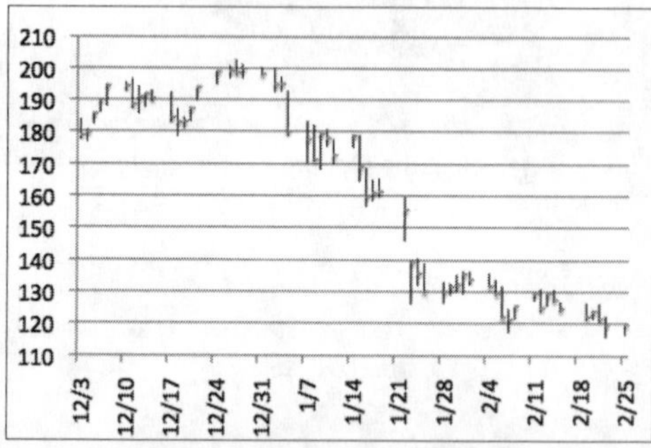

Figure 18.21 This is an example of a high-low-close chart created from Apple stock data.

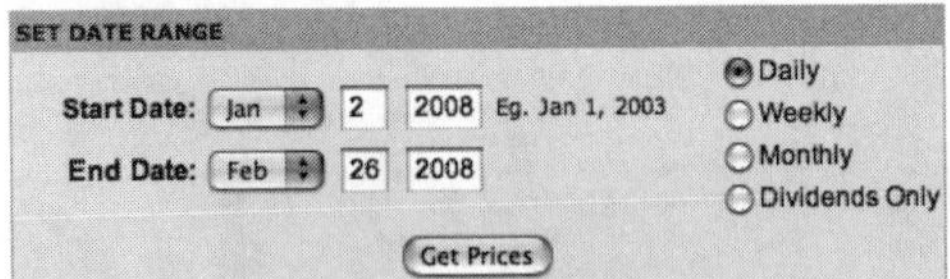

Figure 18.22 Specify a date range for the quotes.

	A	B	C	D
1	Date	High	Low	Close
2	1/3/07	86.58	81.9	83.8
3	1/4/07	85.95	83.82	85.66
4	1/5/07	86.2	84.4	85.05
5	1/8/07	86.53	85.28	85.47
6	1/9/07	92.98	85.15	92.57
7	1/10/07	97.8	93.45	97
8	1/11/07	96.78	95.1	95.8
9	1/12/07	95.06	93.23	94.62
10	1/16/07	97.25	95.45	97.1
11	1/17/07	97.6	94.82	94.95
12	1/18/07	92.11	89.05	89.07

Figure 18.23 This worksheet contains daily prices, sorted in ascending order.

Gathering stock data

You can download historical stock data from many of the bigger financial Web sites. As an example, the following steps explain how to get data from `http://finance.yahoo.com`.

To download stock data from Yahoo!:

1. Go to `http://finance.yahoo.com` in your Web browser.
2. Request a quote for the company in which you're interested. Click the Historical Prices link on the new page that appears.
3. In the Set Date Range area of the page (**Figure 18.22**), specify a date range and interval, and click Get Prices.
4. At the bottom of the page, click the Download to Spreadsheet link. A new page appears that contains the quotes.
5. In the browser, choose File > Save to save the page as a .csv file.
6. Open the file in Excel and rearrange the data to match the requirements of the chart you'll create. Sort the data array by Date in ascending order (**Figure 18.23**).
7. Select, copy, and paste the data into cell A1 of the sample worksheet. Drag the lower-right corner of the chart range to encompass the pasted data.

✔ Tips

- The more data you plot, the more difficult it becomes to see the data points. You can improve the chart's readability by dragging its lower-right corner to resize it.
- Another approach to this problem is to reduce the amount of data. For instance, you could use weekly quotes rather than daily ones. Or you might consider charting data over a shorter time period.

Organization Charts

Organization charts (*org charts*) can be a useful part of a business presentation. You create them with Organization Chart, an application included as part of Office 2008. You launch Organization Chart from within PowerPoint and then create the org chart as a new object.

To add an org chart to a slide:

1. *Do either of the following:*
   - ▲ Create a new slide by clicking the Slide Layouts tab in the Elements Gallery, clicking the Insert new slide radio button, and clicking a layout thumbnail. You might select a blank layout or one with only a title, for example.
   - ▲ Switch to an existing slide on which you want to insert the org chart.
2. Choose Insert > Object.

   The Insert Object dialog box appears.
3. Click the Create new radio button, select Microsoft Organization Chart as the Object type, and click OK (**Figure 18.24**).

   Organization Chart loads (**Figure 18.25**).

✔ Tip

■ While you're working on an org chart, Organization Chart adds its icon to the Dock (**Figure 18.26**). To switch between PowerPoint and Organization Chart, click the appropriate Dock icon.

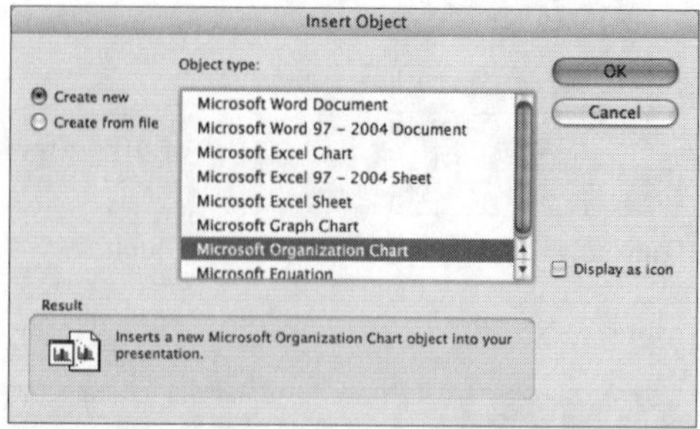

Figure 18.24 Create a new Microsoft Organization Chart in the Insert Object dialog box.

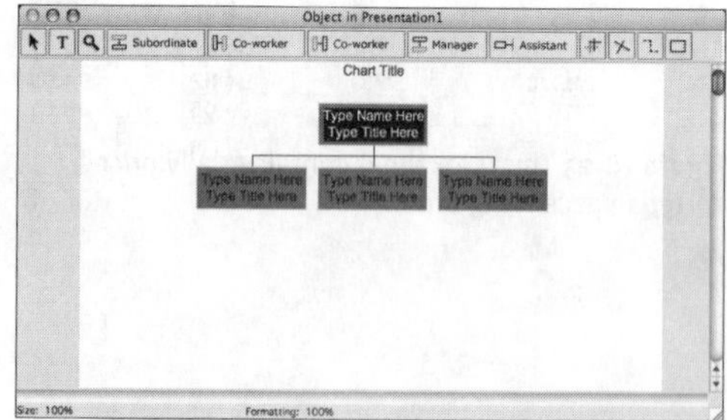

Figure 18.25 Organization Chart launches and displays the framework of a new org chart.

Figure 18.26 You can switch back to Organization Chart by clicking its Dock icon.

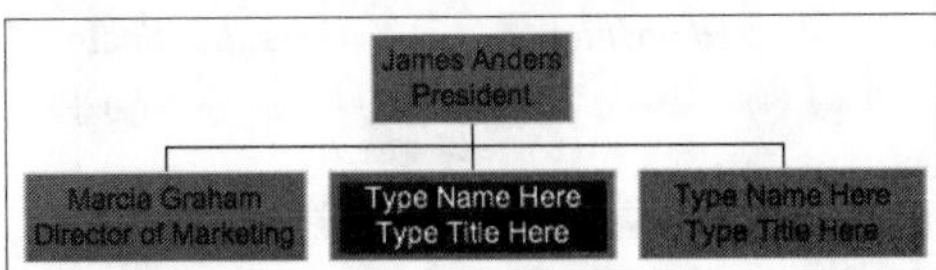

Figure 18.27 Click any box and type a person's information.

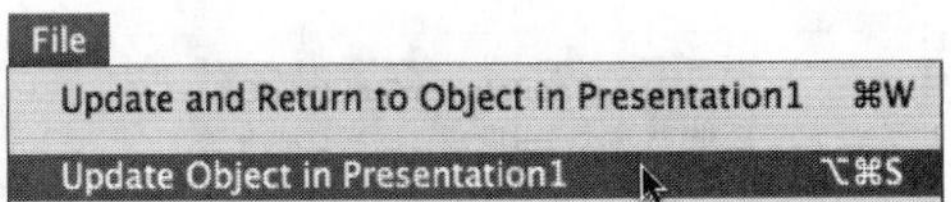

Figure 18.28 To transfer the org chart to your slide, choose Update Object.

Entering people

Recording information about people on an organization chart is straightforward. Each person's name and title appear in a separate box. A person's placement in the org chart depends on his or her position in the organizational hierarchy.

To add people:

1. Type the name of the organization's head in the text box that is preselected when Organization Chart launches.
2. Press Tab, Return, or Enter to highlight the next line within the same box and then type the person's title or position.
3. Click a different box. Enter that person's name and title (**Figure 18.27**).

✔ Tips

- When you are done entering the names and titles for the initial positions, you can transfer the information to the slide by choosing File > Update Object in *presentation* (**Figure 18.28**).
- To edit the information in a box, click the box, pause briefly, and then click again to set the text insertion mark. If you double-click too quickly, the program may think you want to select the current box and all others at the same level.

Adding subordinates

The initial org chart structure contains only a manager and three *subordinates*, but you can add other subordinates as needed.

To add a subordinate:

1. Click the Subordinate icon on the toolbar (**Figure 18.29**, page bottom).
2. Click the box of the position that needs a new subordinate.
   A subordinate box appears (**Figure 18.30**).

✔ Tips

- To add multiple subordinates beneath a position, click the Subordinate icon once for each subordinate, and then click the box of the position to which you are adding the subordinates (**Figure 18.31**).
- To add a coworker box beside a box, click one of the Co-worker icons on the toolbar (depending on whether you want to show the coworker to the left or right), and then click the box of the position to which the coworker will be added.
- To move a subordinate box beneath another member's box, drag the subordinate box on top of the other member's box, and then release the mouse button.

  Whether a moved person will be added as a subordinate, left coworker, or right coworker depends on which *edge* of the box you drag him or her onto. Drag onto the left edge of the box to add the person as a left coworker, onto the right edge to add the person as a right coworker, or onto the bottom edge to add the person as a subordinate.

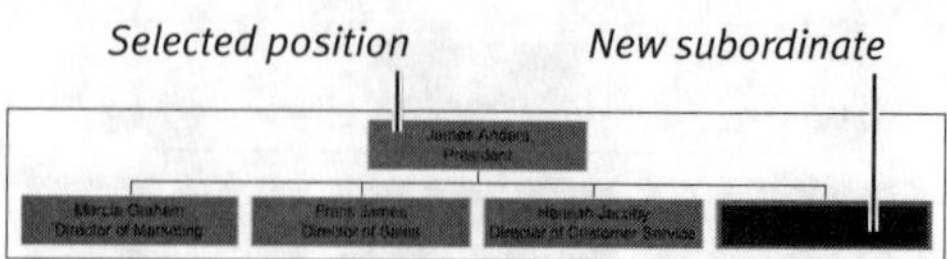

Figure 18.30 A new subordinate box appears.

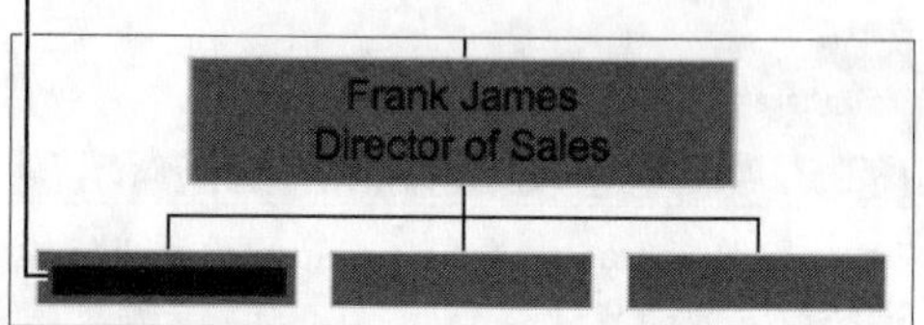

Figure 18.31 Click the Subordinate icon three times and then click the superior's box to simultaneously create three subordinate boxes. The number to be created is shown on the status bar.

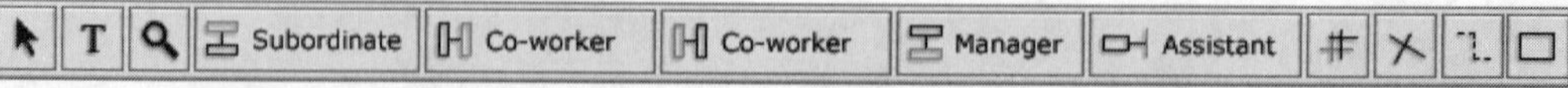

Figure 18.29 To create a new subordinate, coworker, manager, or assistant, click a toolbar icon and then click the box with which the person is associated.

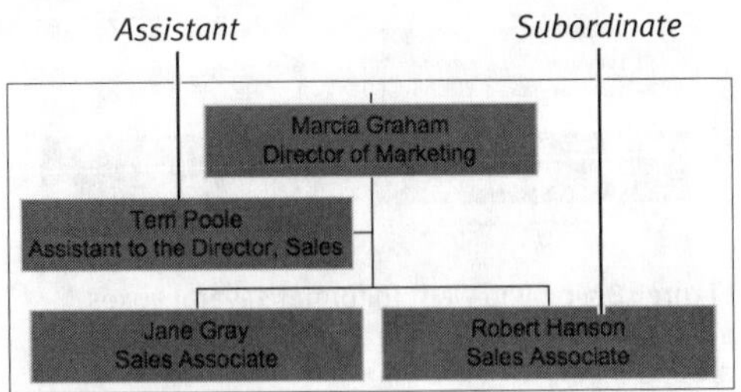

Figure 18.32 An assistant is denoted by a different connecting line (from the side) than a subordinate (from the top).

Adding assistants

Adding assistants is like adding subordinates. There is no limit to the number of assistants you can add.

To add an assistant:

1. Click the Assistant toolbar icon (see Figure 18.29).
2. Click the box of the person who will receive the assistant.

   An assistant box appears (**Figure 18.32**).

✔ Tips

- You can assign several assistants to a member in the same manner as creating multiple subordinates. Click the Assistant icon once for every assistant you want to add, and then click the box of the member who will receive the assistants.
- To delete an assistant box (or any other box on the org chart), click the box and press Delete.
- If you delete the box of someone who isn't one of the lowest members in a group (a supervisor, for instance), the program will do its best to reorganize the remaining boxes. You may have to make some additional corrections.

Formatting an org chart

You can change the look of an organization chart to suit your taste. If the chart will be an important part of the presentation, you may want to spend some extra time formatting its boxes, lines, and text.

To format boxes:

1. *Do one of the following:*
   - ▲ Click to select a box.
   - ▲ Shift-click to select multiple boxes.
   - ▲ Drag a selection rectangle to enclose multiple boxes (**Figure 18.33**).

   The selected boxes are blackened.
2. Choose formatting commands from the Boxes menu (**Figure 18.34**).

To format selected text:

1. Select the text that you want to format.
2. Choose formatting commands from the Text menu.

   The new formatting is applied to the selected text.

To format connecting lines:

◆ Select one or more connecting lines and then choose options from the Lines menu.

✔ Tips

- To apply the same formatting to all text in a box, simply select the box and then choose formatting commands. You can also apply text formatting to selected text within a box, such as only a person's name or title.
- To select multiple line segments, draw a selection rectangle around them or Shift-click the segments.
- To save the formatted org chart and transfer it to the slide, choose one of the File > Update commands.

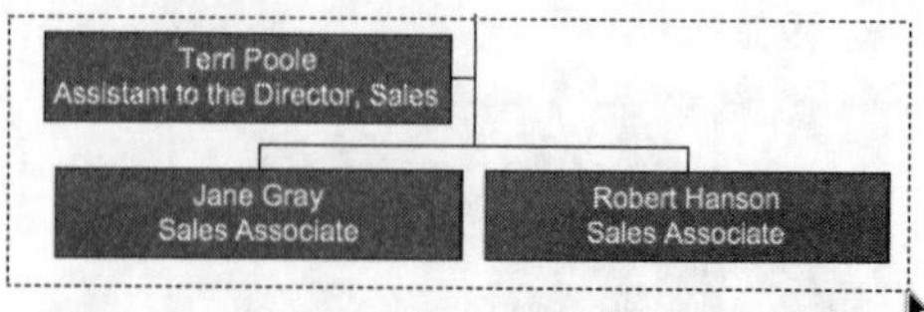

Figure 18.33 If you want to format several boxes simultaneously, you can drag a selection rectangle around them.

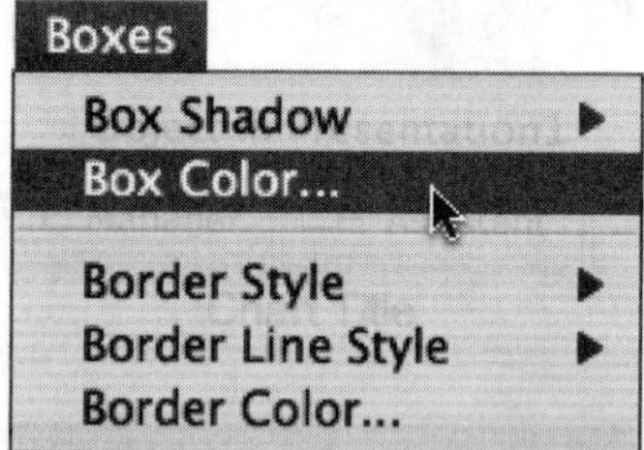

Figure 18.34 Choose commands from the Boxes menu to set the shadow, fill color, and border characteristics.

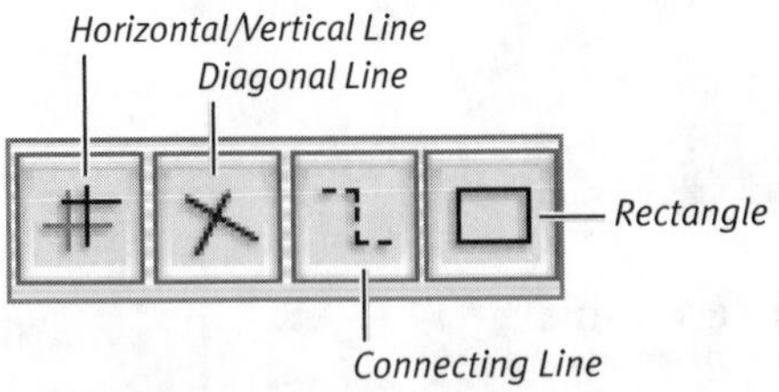

Figure 18.35 The toolbar also has several useful drawing tools.

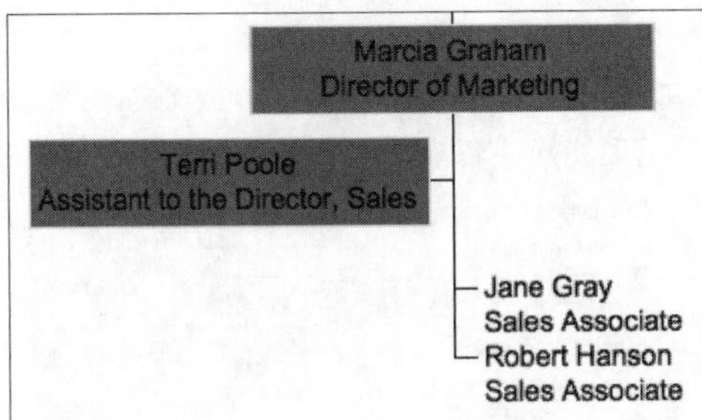

Figure 18.36 You can choose alternate ways to show groups in the org chart, such as Stacked Group No Boxes (assigned to the two sales associates).

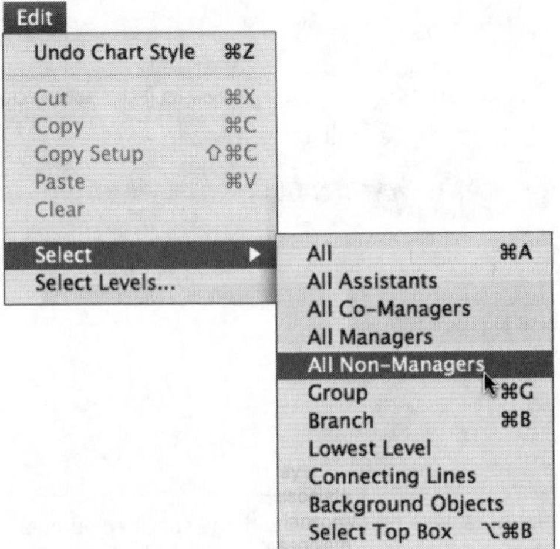

Figure 18.37 Another way to select objects for simultaneous formatting is to choose a command from the Edit >Select submenu.

More org chart tips

Organization Chart has many capabilities the preceding pages didn't touch on. Here are some more tips and areas for you to explore:

- You can add text anywhere on an org chart—to include comments, titles, and so forth. Select the Text tool (T) on the toolbar, click an empty space on the chart, and begin typing. The resulting text is an object that you can format and move as you wish.
- The right end of the toolbar contains a set of drawing tools you can use to embellish your org chart (**Figure 18.35**). In order, they are the Horizontal/Vertical Line tool, Diagonal Line tool, Connecting Line tool, and Rectangle tool.
  All but the Connecting Line tool are for drawing additional objects on the org chart. The Connecting Line tool is used to draw additional connections between member boxes (showing shared subordinates, for example). To use it, click one box and then drag to the second box.
- You can change a chart's background color by choosing Chart > Background Color.
- You might also want to experiment with different chart styles using options in the Style menu. For example, you can select the boxes of several people in a department and display them using one of the alternate "group" styles, such as Style > Stacked Group No Boxes (**Figure 18.36**).
- In addition to Shift-clicking or dragging a selection rectangle to select multiple boxes, you can select specific *classes* of boxes and objects by choosing commands from the Edit > Select submenu (**Figure 18.37**).
- You can launch Organization Chart at any time by double-clicking the org chart on your slide.

Adding a Table to a Slide

Tables help present information efficiently. Creating and formatting a table in PowerPoint is similar to working with tables in Word. See Chapter 6 for more details.

To add a table to a new slide:

1. Create a new slide or select an existing slide on which to insert the table.
   Several slide layouts include an Insert Table placeholder icon (**Figure 18.38**).
2. *Do one of the following:*
   - ▲ If the slide has a placeholder that contains an Insert Table icon, click the icon.
   - ▲ To place a table manually (on a blank slide, for example), choose Insert > Table.

   The Insert Table dialog box appears (**Figure 18.39**).
3. Specify the number of columns and rows, and then click OK.
   The table appears on the slide (**Figure 18.40**).
4. *Optional:* To aid in formatting the table and its contents, you can display additional toolbars. From the View > Toolbars submenu, choose Tables and Borders and/or Formatting.
   You can also choose commands from the Format menu and the Formatting Palette.
5. Enter the table's text. Format the cells and table as desired.

Figure 18.38 Although it isn't essential, you may want to select a slide layout that contains an Insert Table placeholder icon.

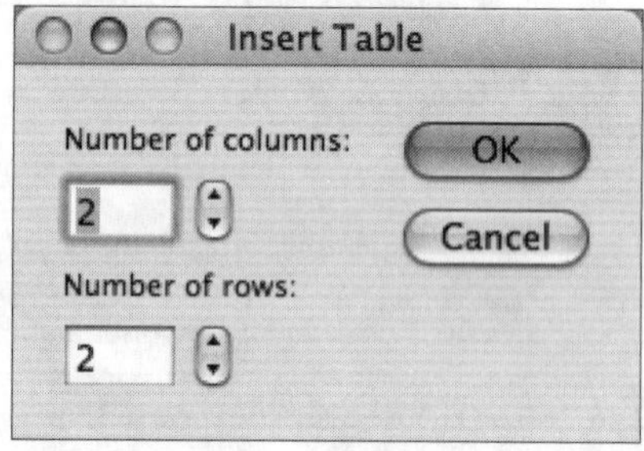

Figure 18.39 Set the number of columns and rows for the new table.

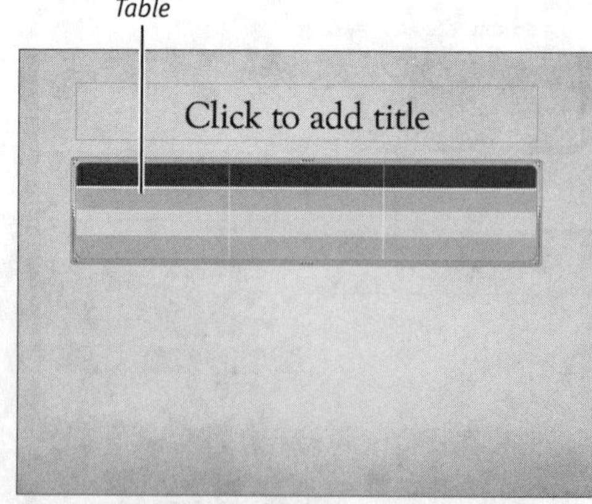

Figure 18.40 A blank table with the specified number of columns and rows appears on the slide. Enter the text, format the cells, and modify the table.

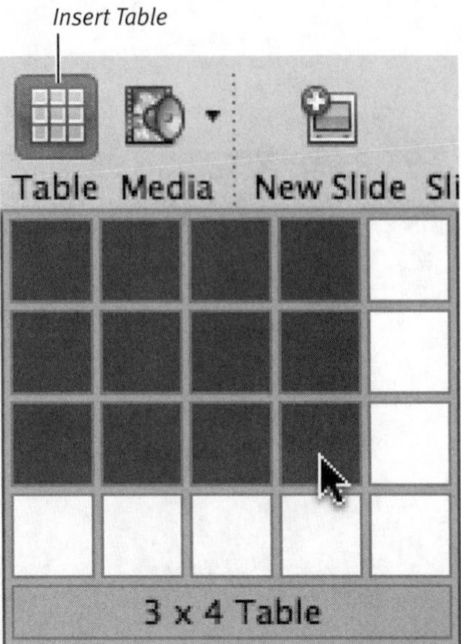

Figure 18.41 You can add a table to *any* slide by clicking the Table toolbar icon and dragging to set the table dimensions.

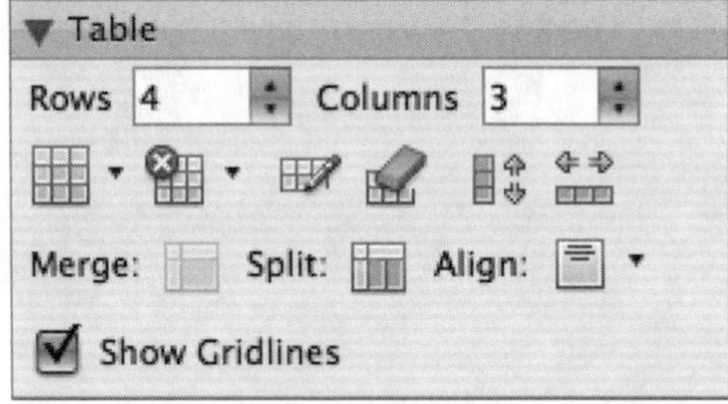

Figure 18.42 You can modify a table by choosing commands from the Table section of the Formatting Palette. For instance, you can change the number of rows or columns, merge cells, or delete the table.

✔ Tips

- Additional table formatting commands can be found in the Format Table dialog box. Choose Format > Table to open the dialog box.
- Another way to quickly add a table to a slide is to click the Table icon on the Standard toolbar and drag to set the desired number of rows and columns (**Figure 18.41**).
- To remove a table, select its frame and press Delete. If you prefer, you can click the Delete Table icon in the Table section of the Formatting Palette (**Figure 18.42**) and choose Delete Table from the drop-down menu.

19

THE PRESENTATION

When you've finished constructing a presentation, it's time to get it ready to be viewed by an audience. This is when you make final decisions about details such as slide order and design, and whether to also save the presentation as a QuickTime movie or for viewing on the Web.

The first part of the chapter discusses preparing the presentation. The second part covers some options and tools for giving and sharing the presentation.

Using the Slide Sorter

Use Slide Sorter View to get an overview of your presentation. It's similar to viewing 35mm slides on a light table. You can reorder the slides, switch templates to change the presentation's look, and delete or duplicate slides.

To switch to Slide Sorter View:

◆ Choose View > Slide Sorter or click the Slide Sorter View icon in the bottom-left corner of the PowerPoint document window (**Figure 19.1**).

✔ Tip

- To revert to viewing a single slide, double-click the slide in Slide Sorter View or select the slide and click the Normal View icon (Figure 19.1).

To reorder slides:

1. Click the slide you want to move and drag it to a new position.
2. A faint vertical line appears, indicating where the slide will be inserted when you release the mouse button (**Figure 19.2**).
3. Release the mouse button to drop the slide into its new position.

✔ Tips

- To move a contiguous group of slides, click and drag the mouse across the slides to select them (**Figure 19.3**), and then drag the group to the new position. If you find it easier, you can also Shift-click the first and last slide in the contiguous group.
- To move a noncontiguous group, ⌘-click each slide and drag the group to the new position. All selected slides will appear in sequence and in the same relative order.

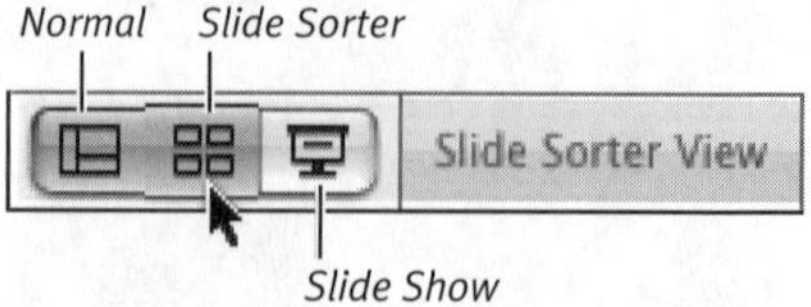

Figure 19.1 One way to switch to Slide Sorter View is to click this icon at the bottom of the document window.

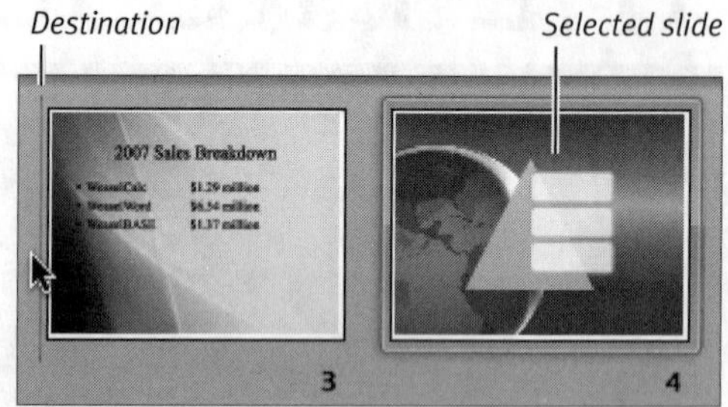

Figure 19.2 When rearranging slides, a line indicates where the slide(s) will be moved when you release the mouse button.

Figure 19.3 You can click and drag the mouse across multiple slides and then move them as a group. In this example, slides 2, 3, and 4 are selected.

Theme sets

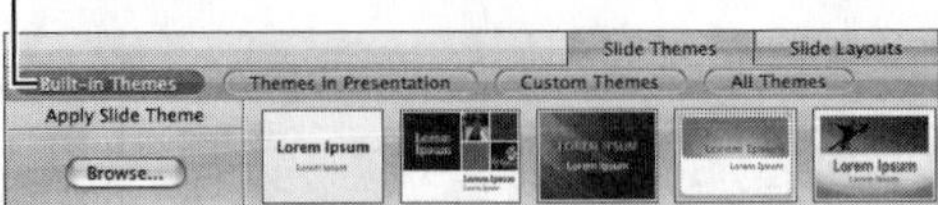

Figure 19.4 Click a thumbnail to apply the new theme to the presentation.

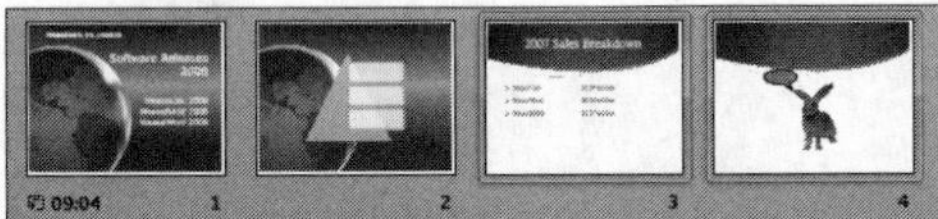

Figure 19.5 The new theme is applied to the selected slides (in this instance, the two slides on the right).

To delete or duplicate slides:

1. Select the slide(s) that you want to delete or duplicate.
2. *Do one of the following:*
   - ▲ To delete the slide(s), choose Edit > Delete Slide or press Delete.
   - ▲ To duplicate the slide(s), choose Edit > Duplicate, press ⌘D, or press Shift⌘D.
   - ▲ Control-click a slide, and choose Delete Slide or Duplicate Slide from the pop-up menu that appears.

✔ Tip

- You can reverse the effects of a slide deletion or duplication by immediately choosing Edit > Undo or pressing ⌘Z.

To apply a new theme to selected slides:

1. Select the slides to which you want to apply the new theme.

   Select slides by clicking, ⌘-clicking, Shift-clicking, or dragging through them.
2. In the Elements Gallery, click the Slide Themes tab or choose Format > Slide Theme > From Gallery.

   Theme thumbnails appear (**Figure 19.4**).
3. *Optional:* To view a particular theme set, click a button.
4. Click the thumbnail of the theme you want to apply to the selected slides.

   The slides adapt the theme (**Figure 19.5**).

✔ Tips

- To quickly select all slides in the presentation, choose Edit > Select All or press ⌘A.
- This technique can also be applied to selected slides in Normal View.

Adding Transition Effects

Transition effects are visual effects, such as dissolves, splits, and wipes, used to transition between slides. You can apply different transitions to different slides. Note that an applied transition appears as you switch *to* the slide—not *from* it.

1. In Normal View, select the slide to which you want to add a transition.
2. Click the Transitions tab in the Elements Gallery or choose Slide Show > Transitions.

   Transition thumbnails are displayed (**Figure 19.6**, page bottom).
3. Click a category tab to indicate the type of transitions you want to consider.
4. Click a transition thumbnail.

   A preview of the transition is shown on the current slide. Repeat until you find the transition you want to use.
5. Click the Options button.

   The Transition Options dialog box appears (**Figure 19.7**).
6. Review and set options.
7. *Do one of the following:*
   - ▲ To apply the transition to only the selected slide(s), click Apply.
   - ▲ To apply the transition to *all* slides in the presentation, click Apply to All.

Figure 19.7 Set options and indicate whether the transition will be applied to the selected slides (Apply) or to all slides in the presentation (Apply to All).

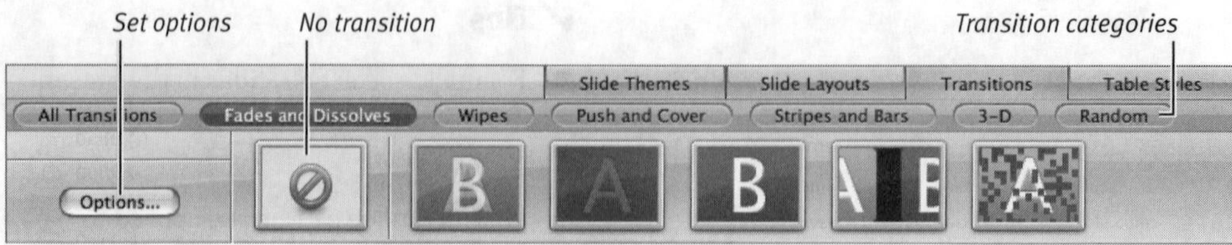

Figure 19.6 Select a transition by clicking its thumbnail.

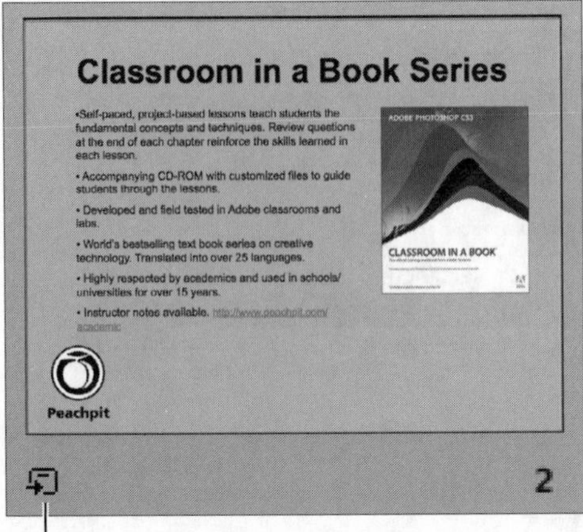

Figure 19.8 In Slide Sorter View, a slide with a transition displays this icon under its left edge. Click the icon to see the transition.

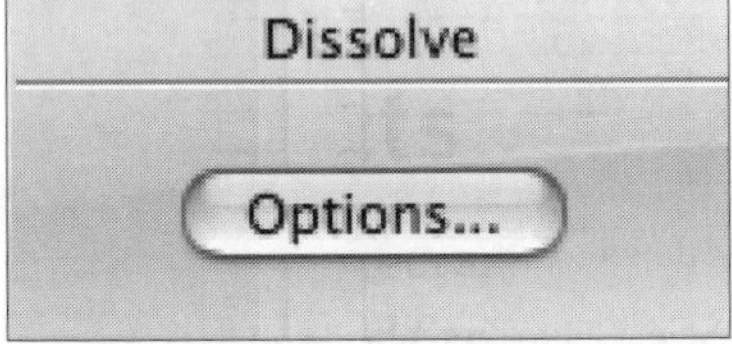

Figure 19.9 This transition is assigned to the selected slide.

✔ Tips

- To apply the same transition to multiple slides, ⌘-click the slides and select a transition.
- A slide can have only one transition. Any new transition that you select replaces the current transition, if any. To remove the transition from selected slides, select No Transition (see Figure 19.6).
- If you create a presentation from a template, slides may already have transitions.
- In Slide Sorter View, you can view a slide's transition by clicking the transition icon beneath the slide (**Figure 19.8**). You can also set transitions in this view.
- To determine *which* transition, if any, has been applied to the currently selected slide, select the All Transitions tab. The name of the transition (or No Transition) will be shown above the Options button (**Figure 19.9**). Otherwise, the transition name will appear only if the correct category tab is selected. This procedure can be used in Slide Sorter or Normal View.
- Supported transition types change from one version of PowerPoint to the next. For instance, PowerPoint 2001 and v.X supported QuickTime transitions, but they were *not* supported in PowerPoint 2004. If you open an earlier presentation in PowerPoint 2008, be sure to check the transitions to ensure that they still work or that undesired ones haven't been substituted for any unsupported transitions.
- PowerPoint 2008 adds 17 new transitions. (For the list, see "I can't see my slide transitions" in PowerPoint Help.) If you intend to play the presentation in an earlier version of PowerPoint, you should avoid using the new transitions.

Animation Within Slides

Motion within a slide is known as *animation*. An animation can be applied to text, objects, or charts, as well as applied selectively or to all material on a slide. You can apply multiple animations to an object, if desired. Animations are set on the Custom Animations tab of the Toolbox.

To add animation to a slide:

1. In Normal View, select a slide to which you want to add animation.
2. Open the Toolbox and click the Custom Animation tab (**Figure 19.10**).
3. Select the text box or object on the slide that you want to animate.

   You can also apply an animation to multiple selected objects, if you wish.
4. *Do one of the following:*
   - ▲ Click the Entrance, Emphasis, or Exit Effect icon to choose an effect. The effect is immediately added to the Animation order list.
   - ▲ Choose More Effects from any Add Effect icon's drop-down menu. The Animation Effects dialog box appears (**Figure 19.11**). Click an effects type tab, select an animation, and watch the preview. If you're satisfied with the effect, click OK to add it to the Animation order list.
5. Choose options for the selected effect from the pop-up menus at the bottom of the Custom Animation tab.
6. If desired, repeat Steps 3 and 4 to animate other objects or to add additional effects to an object.
7. To view all animations applied to the slide, click the Play button (Figure 19.10).

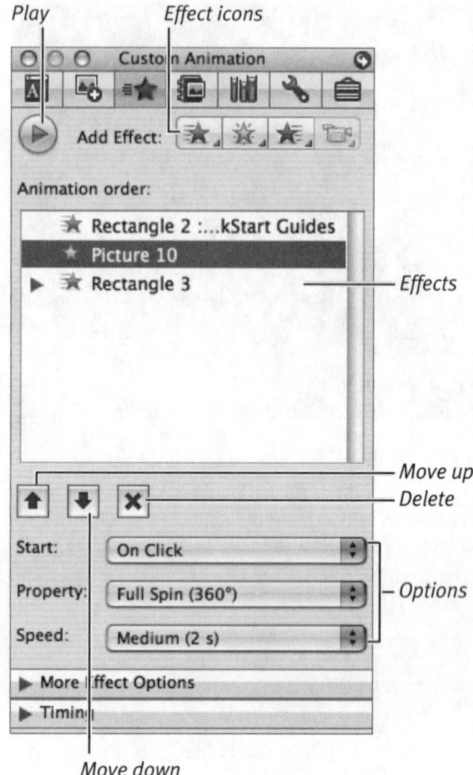

Figure 19.10 Select animation effects and settings on the Custom Animation tab.

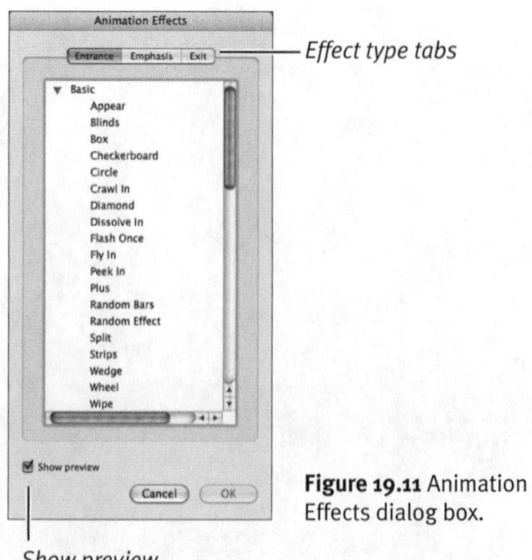

Figure 19.11 Animation Effects dialog box.

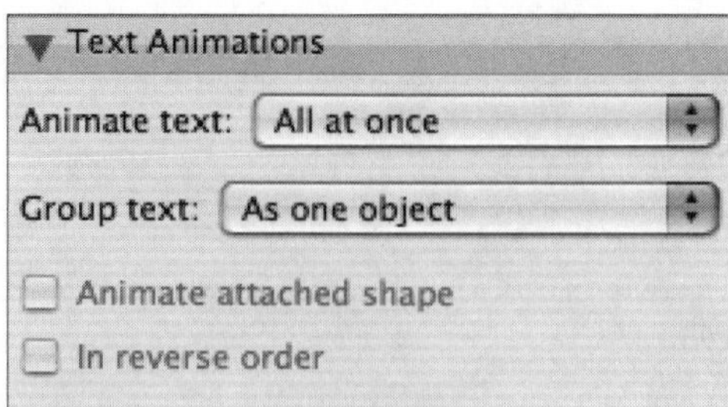

Figure 19.12 Rather than accepting an effect's default settings, you can easily customize it by exploring other Custom Animation sections.

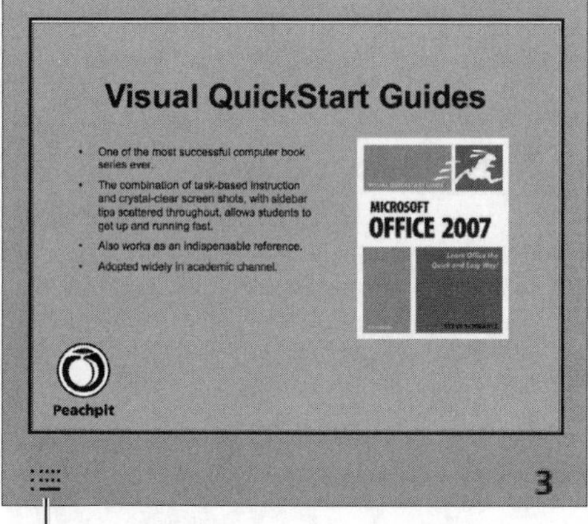

Figure 19.13 In Slide Sorter View, a slide with one or more animations displays this icon under its left edge. Click the icon to play the animations.

✔ Tips

- You can go directly to the Custom Animation tab by choosing Slide Show > Custom Animation.
- Unless you know what specific effect you want to apply to an object, choose More Effects from any Add Effect drop-down menu. Doing so ensures that you can see an effect preview before committing to it.
- *Entrance effects* play when you transition to the slide; *exit effects* play as you transition to the next slide.
- In Normal View, you can play a single animation by Control-clicking it in the Animation order list and choosing Play from the pop-up menu that appears.
- Each object in the Animation order list is uniquely identified by its type (such as Rectangle or Picture) and a number. If multiple effects have been applied to an object, its name will be preceded by a triangle. Click it to see the individual effects.
- To remove an unwanted effect, select it in the Animation order list and click the Delete icon.
- Effects play in the order listed. To change the order, select an effect and click the Move up or Move down icon.
- Be sure to explore all options offered for a particular animation. For instance, if you're animating a text block or series of bullet points, you can set options in the Text Animations section (**Figure 19.12**), animating the text by letter, word, or all at once, for example.
- In Slide Sorter View, a slide that contains an animation displays a bulleted text icon beneath it (**Figure 19.13**). To preview the applied effect(s), click the icon.

Adding Sound and Movies

To enliven a presentation, you can add audio, music, or movies to selected slides.

To insert a sound file:

1. In Normal View, select the slide on which you'd like a sound file to play.
2. Choose Insert > Sound and Music > From File or choose Insert Sound and Music from the Media toolbar icon.

   The Insert Sound dialog box appears.
3. Select the sound clip that you want to add to the slide and click Insert.

   A tiny speaker icon is added to the slide. A dialog box appears (**Figure 19.14**).
4. Click a button to specify when the sound will play:
   - ▲ **When Clicked.** The sound will only play when/if you click its speaker icon while giving the presentation.
   - ▲ **Automatically.** The sound is added to the Animation order list for the slide (see Figure 19.10). To specify when the sound will play, move it up or down in the list.

To play audio/music from a CD:

1. In Normal View, select the slide on which you'd like to play CD tracks.
2. Put the audio/music CD into your Mac.
3. Choose Insert > Sound and Music > Play CD Audio Track.

   The Play Options dialog box appears (**Figure 19.15**).
4. Specify numbers for the starting and ending tracks. Click OK.

   A tiny CD icon is added to the slide and a dialog box appears (Figure 19.14). See "To insert a sound file" for an explanation of the dialog box buttons.

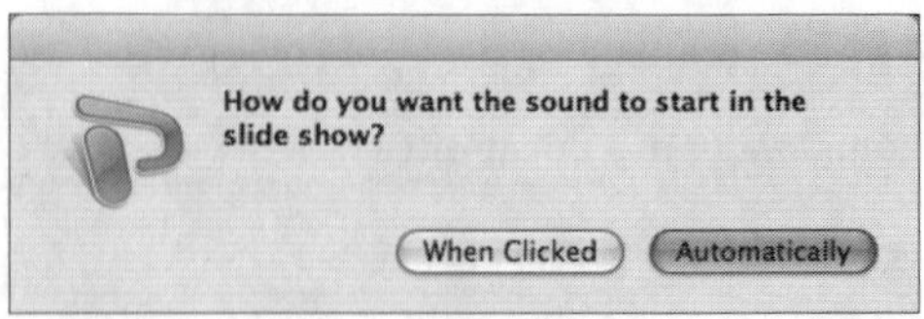

Figure 19.14 Click a button to indicate when the sound will play.

Figure 19.15 Indicate a starting and ending track to play. (To play only a single track, enter its number as both the Start and End track.) Tracks must be played in order.

Figure 19.16 Create and listen to your recording in the Record Sound dialog box.

Figure 19.17 You can control playback by clicking the controls on the movie controller.

To record audio:

1. In Normal View, select the slide that will include recorded audio.
2. Choose Insert > Sound and Music > Record Sound.

   The Record Sound dialog box appears (**Figure 19.16**).
3. Ensure that the choices for Sound input device and Input source are correct, click Record, and speak into your internal or connected microphone. When you're done recording, click Stop.
4. Click Play to listen to the recording, and *do one of the following:*
   - ▲ If the recording isn't satisfactory, repeat Step 3. The new recording will replace the previous one.
   - ▲ If you're satisfied with the recording, enter name for the recording, and click Save. The dialog box closes and a tiny speaker icon appears on the slide.

To insert a movie:

1. In Normal View, select the slide on which you'd like to insert a movie clip.
2. Choose Insert > Movie, choose Insert Movie from the Media toolbar icon, or click a movie placeholder on the slide.

   The Insert Movie dialog box appears.
3. Select the movie clip that you want to add to the slide and click Choose.

   A black frame representing the movie appears on the slide.
4. Resize and reposition the frame, if desired.
5. To test the movie, click the movie icon in its lower-left corner. A movie controller appears beneath the movie frame. Click the Play button (**Figure 19.17**).

✔ Tips

- You can view or change playback settings for inserted audio or movies in the Sound or Movie section of the Formatting Palette (**Figure 19.18**).
- A From File item can also be a music file, such as an MP3 or AIFF.
- The `System: Library: Sounds` folder contains a selection of simple sound effects (normally used for the system beep).
- If you use the Play CD Audio Track option to add music to a presentation, the CD must be in the Mac's drive when you give the presentation.
- You can record slide narration in a manner similar to recording an audio clip. Choose Slide Show > Record Narration.
- In addition to traditional movie file types, such as QuickTime and MPEG-4, you can use the Insert > Movie command to insert any file type supported by QuickTime. For instance, you can insert a multipage PDF file and flip through its pages using the movie controller.

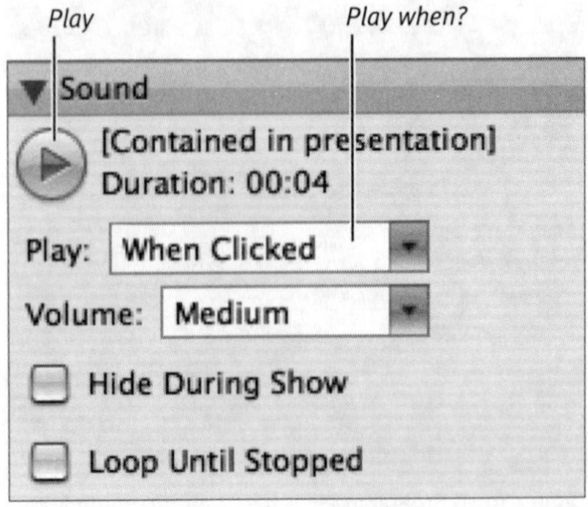

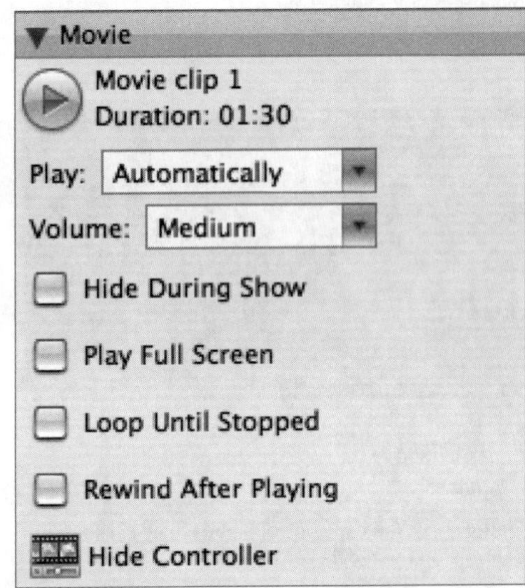

Figure 19.18 To set playback options for inserted audio or a movie, select the item's icon on the slide and make changes in the Sound (top) or Movie (bottom) section of the Formatting Palette.

Figure 19.19 In Handout Master View, you can specify the number of slides per page and optionally edit the header and footer.

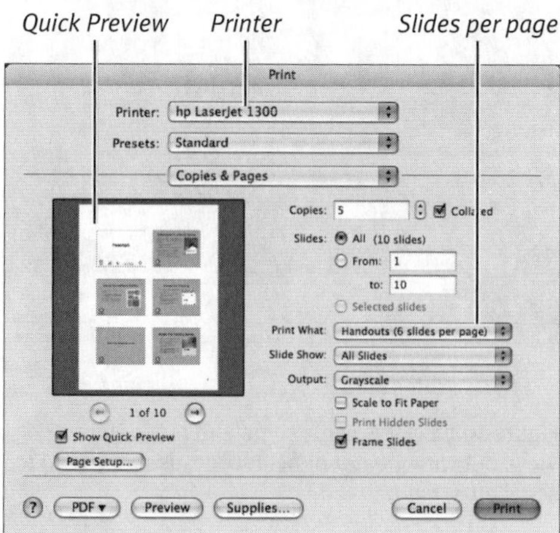

Figure 19.20 To print handouts, set options in the Print dialog box.

Creating Handouts and Speaker Notes

From within PowerPoint, you can prepare *handouts* (slide printouts to give to the audience) and *speaker notes* to assist you during the presentation.

To create handouts:

1. Choose View > Master > Handout Master.

   The Handout Master and Handout Master View toolbar appear (**Figure 19.19**).

2. Click a toolbar icon to set the number of slides per page that you want to display.
3. *Optional:* Edit the header or footer text.
4. Click the Close Master toolbar icon.
5. Choose File > Print.

   The Print dialog box appears (**Figure 19.20**).

6. From the Printer drop-down list, select a printer on which to print the handouts.
7. From the Print What drop-down menu, choose Handouts (*x* slides per page). Review the other settings.

   View a preview of the handout pages in the Quick Preview box. The preview reflects the current print settings.

8. *Do one of the following:*
   - ▲ Click Print to print the handouts on the specified printer.
   - ▲ Click the PDF button and choose Save as PDF to create an Adobe Acrobat file that you can view in Apple's Preview or Adobe Reader.

To create speaker notes:

- *Do one of the following:*
  - Choose View > Notes Page. Click in the notes placeholder to type speaker notes for a given slide (**Figure 19.21**).
  - Switch to Normal View and enter notes in the text window beneath each slide (**Figure 19.22**).

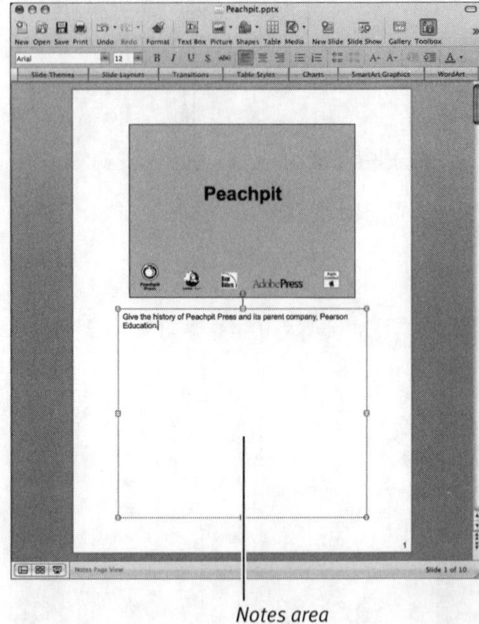

Figure 19.21 Speaker notes are easy to create in Notes Page View.

✔ Tips

- Your notes will *not* appear on the slides during the presentation.
- If you're working in Normal View and need to enter copious notes for a slide, you can enlarge the notes area by dragging the divider between the slide and notes panes (Figure 19.22).
- To print each slide along with its associated notes, choose Notes from the Print What drop-down menu in the Print dialog box (see Figure 19.20). Be sure to check the settings for Copies, Collated, and Slides.

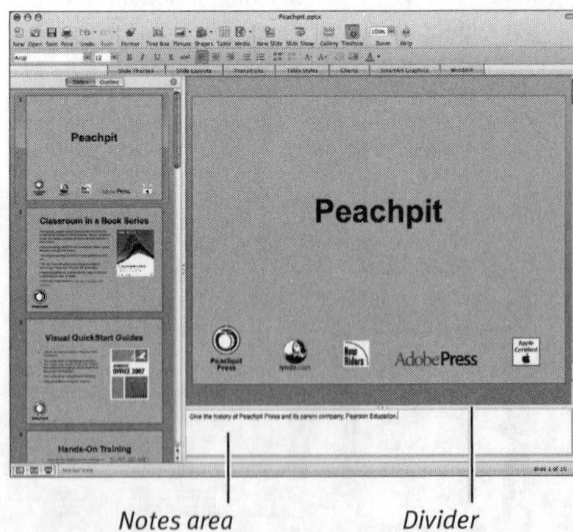

Figure 19.22 Notes can also be entered in Normal View, but with greater difficulty because they tend to scroll off-screen.

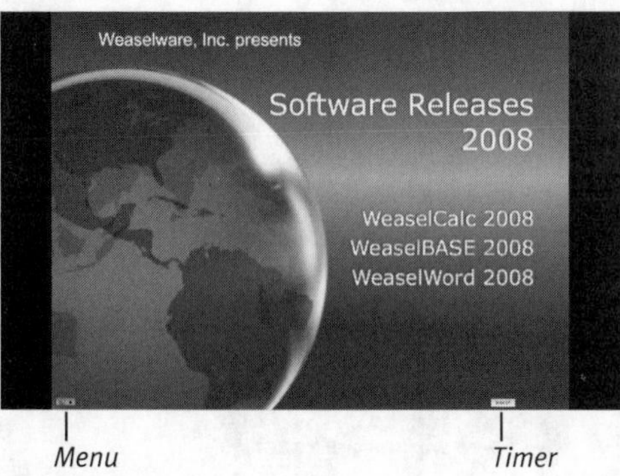

Figure 19.23 When rehearsing a presentation, a timer is displayed at the bottom of each slide.

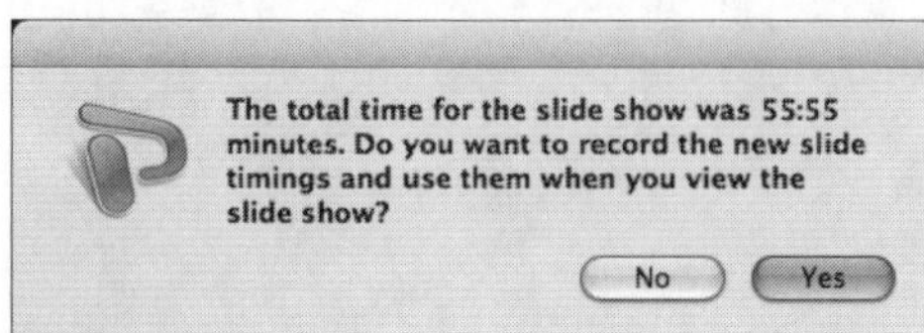

Figure 19.24 Choose whether to record slide timings for use in future presentations of the slide show.

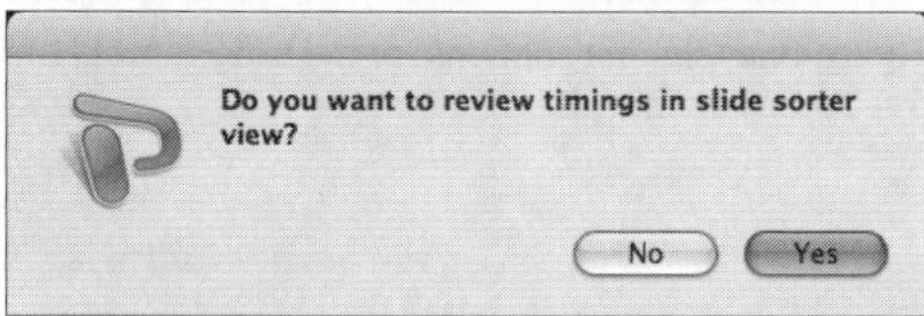

Figure 19.25 You can switch to Slide Sorter View to review the saved slide timings.

Figure 19.26 Click this icon to reveal a menu of helpful options.

Rehearsing a Presentation

It's always a good idea to rehearse a presentation, especially if there's a time limit. When you've finished assembling the presentation, you can rehearse it and time how long each slide needs to remain onscreen.

To rehearse a presentation:

1. Choose Slide Show > Rehearse Timings.

   The first slide in the presentation appears. A timer is in the bottom-right corner (**Figure 19.23**).

2. Perform the presentation exactly as you would in front of the audience.

3. Click the mouse, press Spacebar, or press → to advance from one action to the next within a slide, as well as to move from slide to slide.

4. At the end of the slide show, a dialog box appears, showing the presentation's total time (**Figure 19.24**). Click Yes or No to indicate whether you want to record the time for each slide (for later use in playing the slide show on automatic).

5. If you click Yes, a second dialog box appears (**Figure 19.25**). Click Yes if you'd like to switch to Slide Sorter View to review the slide timings.

✔ Tips

- You can immediately stop a rehearsal or slide show by pressing Esc.
- You can also halt a show by moving the cursor to the lower-left corner of the screen, clicking the icon, and choosing End Show from the pop-up menu (**Figure 19.26**). There are other useful options in the menu, such as a pen cursor you can use to write or draw onscreen during the presentation.

Running a Slide Show

You can view your show at any time to get an idea of how it will look to an audience. Before finalizing it, however, you should consider the available play options. For example, you can manually control when slides change or allow the show to run automatically.

To set options for a slide show:

1. Choose Slide Show > Set Up Show.
   The Set Up Show dialog box appears (**Figure 19.27**).
2. Specify the type of show, display options, the slides to be used, and the method used to advance slides.
   You can advance each slide manually by clicking the mouse, clicking an Apple Remote, or pressing keys. Or you can show each slide for a specific amount of time before advancing to the next one (using the timings set in the rehearsal).
3. Click OK.

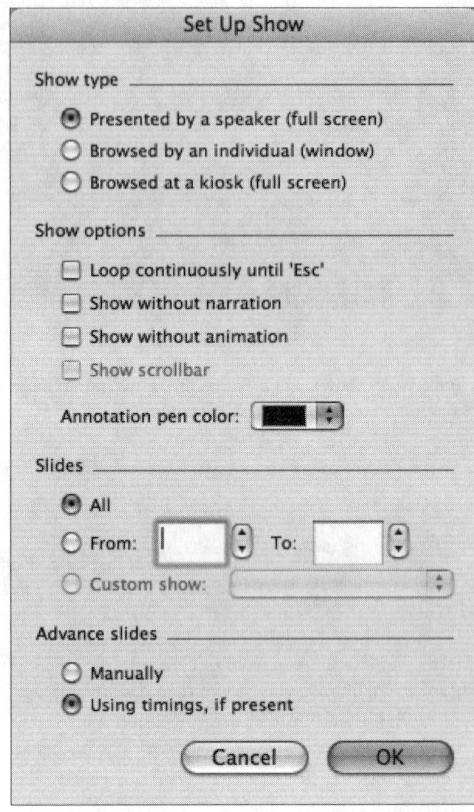

Figure 19.27 Set play options for the slide show in the Set Up Show dialog box.

To view a slide show:

1. *Do one of the following:*
   - ▲ To view the show from the beginning, choose Slide Show > View Slide Show or View > Slide Show.
   - ▲ To view the slide show starting with some slide other than the first, switch to Normal or Slide Sorter View, select the first slide to view, and click the Slide Show View icon in the bottom-left corner of the window.
2. Press Esc to end the show.

Using the Apple Remote

When presented on a Mac, a PowerPoint 2008 presentation can optionally be controlled with an Apple Remote—stepping through animations and slides, as well as changing the volume.

After *pairing* a remote with the playback computer (preventing your show from being hijacked by someone else's Apple Remote), you simply press buttons to step through the presentation. For more information, see "Give a presentation by using an Apple Remote" in PowerPoint Help.

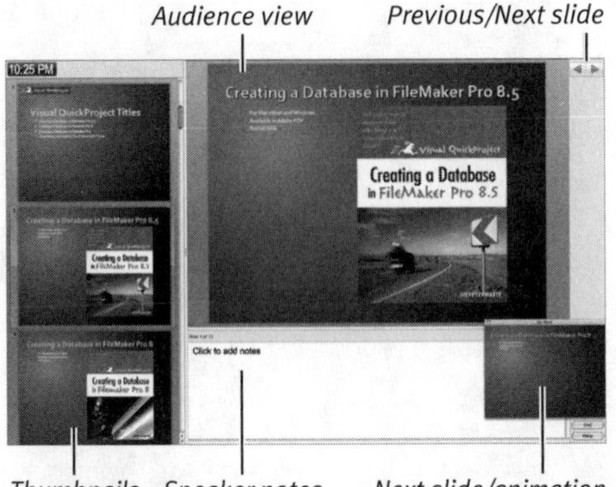

Figure 19.28 The presenter tools show the presenter information that isn't seen by the audience, such as the notes and a preview of the next slide.

Using the Presenter Tools

If you have a dual-monitor system, you can use the presenter tools to assist with your presentation. The presentation appears on the audience's monitor, while the tools appear on only your monitor. You can also use the Presenter Tools to *rehearse* a presentation. While practicing, one monitor will suffice.

To use the presenter tools:

1. *Optional:* In Displays System Preferences, set up your Mac so it can address two monitors by clearing the Mirror Displays check box on the Arrangement tab.
2. Turn on the presenter tools (**Figure 19.28**) by choosing Slide Show > View Presenter Tools or by pressing Shift as you click the Slide Show View icon in the bottom-left corner of the document window.
3. Use normal slide show navigation methods to move from one slide to the next. You can also do the following:
   - ▲ Click an arrow icon in the upper-right corner to move forward or backward one slide.
   - ▲ Click a slide thumbnail to move directly to that slide.
4. To end the slide show, click the End button, or press Esc, ⌘., or -.

✔ Tips

- Click the Help button to view keyboard shortcuts for the presenter tools.
- To change the notes magnification, select a percentage from the pop-up menu above the notes area.
- To time a manual show, click the stopwatch in the lower-right corner. The clock at the top of the screen becomes a stopwatch. Record slide times in the notes.

Publishing a Presentation on the Web

One way to share your presentation with a large audience is to publish it in HTML format, enabling it to be viewed with any current Mac or PC browser.

To create a presentation for the Web:

1. Choose File > Save As Web Page.

   A Save As panel appears (**Figure 19.29**).
2. Select a folder in which to save the presentation and name the output file.
3. *Optional:* If compatibility problems are noted, click the Compatibility Report button and examine the list of problems.

   In many cases, the problems will be related to opening the presentation in other versions of PowerPoint rather than displaying it on the Web.
4. Click the Web Options button.

   The Web Options dialog box appears (**Figure 19.30**).
5. On the General tab, type a title for the Web page. (This title will appear in the upper-left corner of the browser window.) You can also enter keywords for the page, enabling Internet search engines to find and index it.
6. Click the Appearance tab and choose settings from the drop-down menus (**Figure 19.31**).
7. On the Pictures tab, pick a target monitor size and indicate whether you want to support PNG as a picture file type.
8. When you are through changing settings, click OK to close the Web Options dialog box.

   The Save As dialog box reappears.

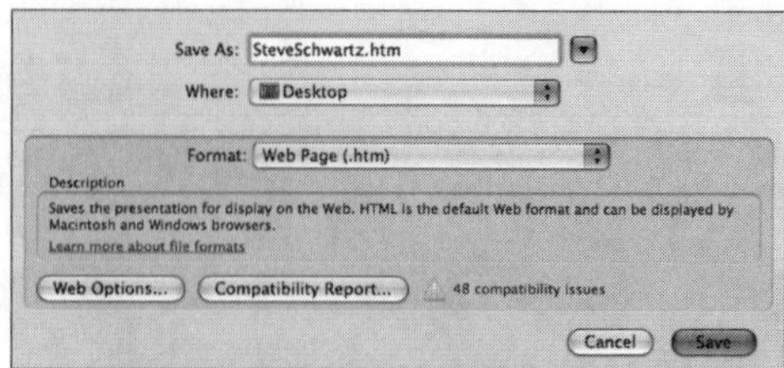

Figure 19.29 Saving a presentation for display on the Web.

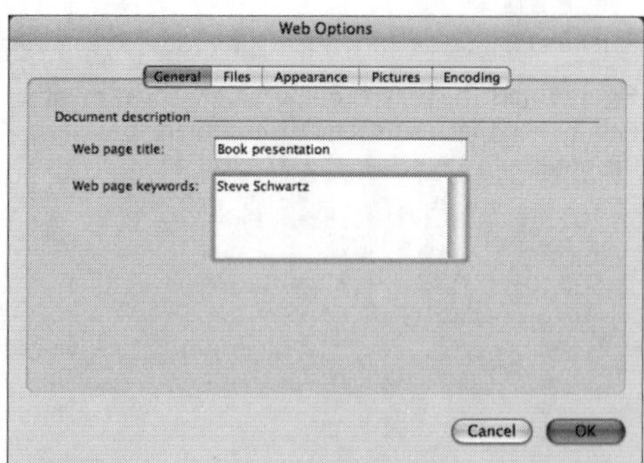

Figure 19.30 Enter a title and keywords for your Web presentation on the General tab of the Web Options dialog box.

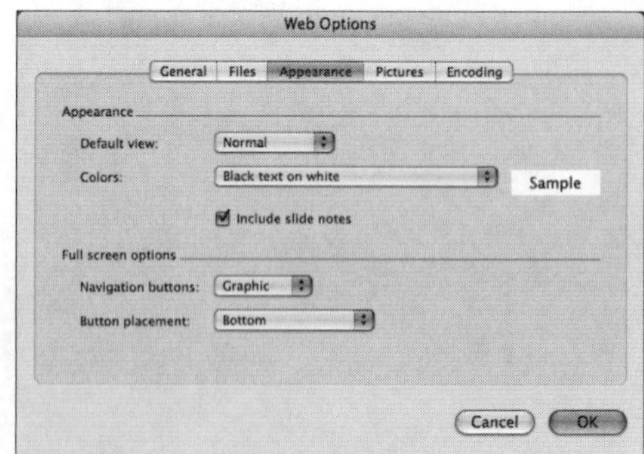

Figure 19.31 Set Appearance options, such as the text color, style of navigation buttons, and whether your notes will be displayed.

PUBLISHING A PRESENTATION ON THE WEB

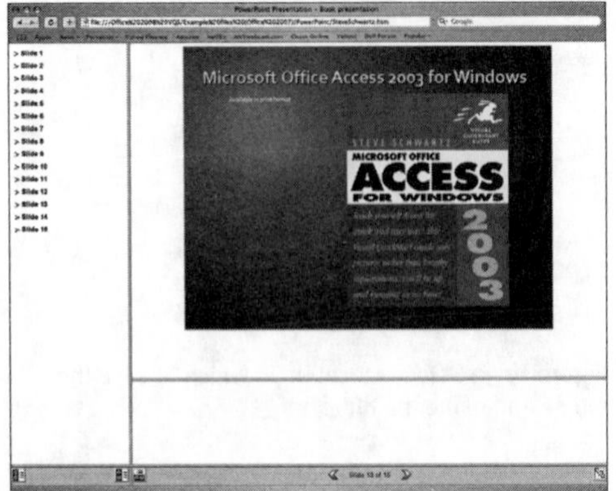

Figure 19.32 The presentation can be viewed and navigated in any current Web browser.

9. Click Save.

   The presentation is saved as an HTML file (with an .htm extension), along with a folder containing the graphics and additional pages.

10. Double-click the HTML file to view and test the presentation in your browser (**Figure 19.32**).

✔ Tips

- A Web (HTML) version of a presentation doesn't include transitions or animations.
- As you can see, you can view a Web-based presentation directly from your hard disk. This means if you want *others* to view it, all you have to do is send them the .htm file and the associated folder.
- Of course, the *real* destination of a Web presentation is typically the Internet or a corporate intranet. For instructions on publishing your presentation to the Web or to an intranet, ask your Internet Service Provider (ISP) or your network administrator, respectively.
- Unless you want to make the actual PowerPoint presentation file available to a recipient, you should remove the check mark from this option on the Files tab of the Web Options dialog box.
- Certain text characters, such as curved (curly) quotation marks, will not display properly in a Web browser. To scan for these and other problems before committing your presentation to the Web or intranet, choose File > Web Page Preview.
- If you intend to publish a presentation on the Web, you may want to design it (or a version of it) with that output in mind. For instance, see "Apply Web-safe colors to your presentation" in PowerPoint Help.

Saving a Presentation as a Movie

Another way to make a presentation easily transportable is to save it as a PowerPoint (QuickTime) movie. The movie can be viewed in any QuickTime-compatible player program, such as Apple's QuickTime Player.

To save a presentation as a PowerPoint movie:

1. Choose File > Save as Movie.
   A Save As panel appears (**Figure 19.33**).
2. Enter a filename for the movie in the Save As text box.
3. In the Where section of the dialog box, select a location in which to save the movie.
4. To view or change the default movie settings, click the Movie Options button.
   The Movie Options dialog box appears (**Figure 19.34**).
5. On the Movie Settings tab, set the movie size and quality. You can also select a sound track, if desired. On the Credits tab, record details about the presentation's creators. When you've finished, click OK.
6. In the Save As panel, click Save to create the movie.

✔ Tips

- Not all PowerPoint features are supported in movies. Animations are ignored and transitions may play differently, for example.
- Only certain file formats, such as WAV, can be used for the sound track. When selecting a sound track, files with unsupported formats are grayed out.

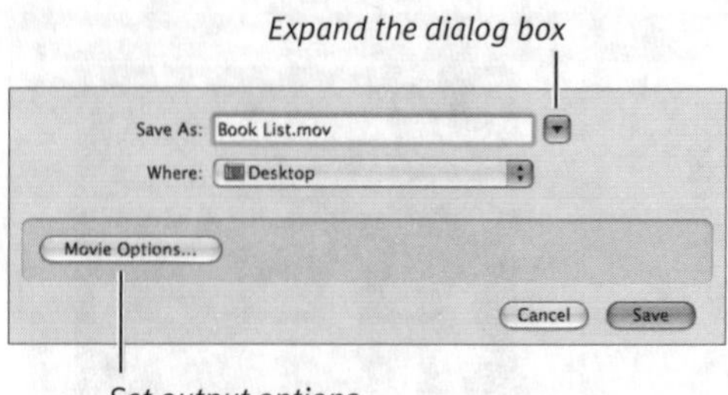

Figure 19.33 Select a location in which to save the movie and name the file.

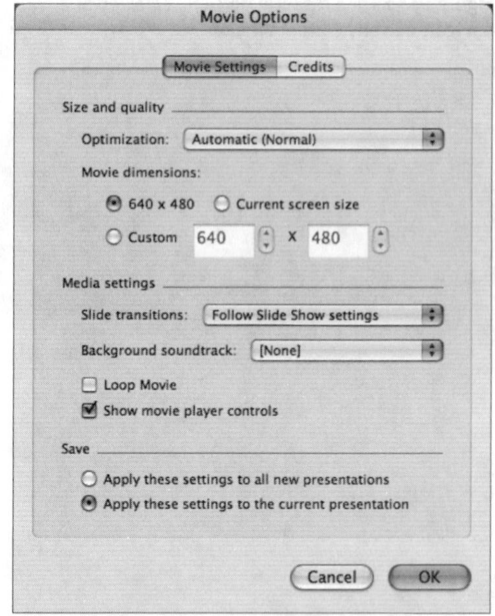

Figure 19.34 Review and set movie options.

- A movie can include clickable navigation buttons. On a slide master, add a Next Slide action button. See "Insert a navigation button" and "Save and run a presentation as a movie" in PowerPoint Help.

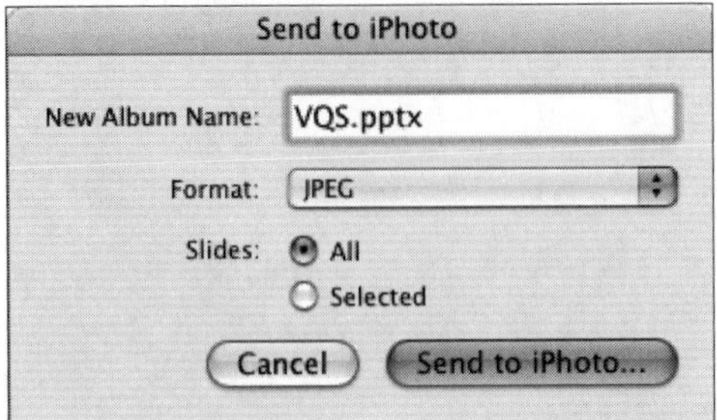

Figure 19.35 Set output options, and then click Send to iPhoto.

Saving a Presentation to iPhoto

New in PowerPoint 2008, you can save a presentation as a series of iPhoto still images and then transfer the resulting output to a video iPod for playback. To use the following step list, you must have iPhoto 6.0 or higher.

To save a presentation to iPhoto:

1. Open the presentation that you want to transfer to iPhoto.
2. *Optional:* If you only want to include certain slides, switch to Slide Sorter View and select the slides.
3. Choose File > Send to > iPhoto.
   The Send to iPhoto dialog box appears (**Figure 19.35**).
4. Enter a name for the new album in which the slide pictures will be stored. Choose a file format from the Format drop-down menu.
5. Click a Slides radio button to indicate whether you want to include all slides from the presentation or only those that are currently selected.
6. Click Send to iPhoto.
   Each slide is converted to a graphic and stored in the new album.
7. Sync your video iPod as you normally do. If iTunes isn't set to automatically sync All photos and albums, add the new album to the sync list on the Photos tab.

✔ Tip

- If you have a version of iPhoto older than 6.0, you can transfer your slides by choosing File > Save as Pictures. After converting the slides to image files, create a new album in iPhoto and then import the files by dragging them onto the album.

Part V: Microsoft Entourage

20 Introducing Entourage

Users new to Office for Mac may think of Entourage as an email application. But while mail handling is certainly Entourage's *main* function, it does much more than that.

Personal organizer. You can add personal and business contacts to the Address Book, schedule appointments and other events in the Calendar, record to-do and follow-up items in Tasks, and store important bits of information in Notes.

Newsgroup reader. If your *ISP* (Internet Service Provider) offers newsgroup support or you want to read posts concerning major hardware and software manufacturers, you don't need to hunt for a newsgroup reader. Entourage is more than up to the task.

Project management. You can track and manage multiple projects in the Project Center. A project can coordinate the data from many parts of Entourage (email, contacts, events, and notes) and can also include links to files from Office and non-Office applications.

In this chapter, you'll learn about many of the tools and techniques that are used throughout Entourage. The remaining chapters in Part V are dedicated to specific parts of Entourage.

The Entourage Interface

Entourage has six components (or *views*). Although there are differences between the views, the most important interface elements (**Figure 20.1**, page bottom) are available in all views.

Views. Click an icon (**Figure 20.2**) to display that Entourage view. Although you can also change views by choosing a View > Go To command or by pressing a keyboard shortcut, many users rely heavily on these navigation icons.

Figure 20.2 Click an icon to go to that Entourage view.

Folder list Views Favorites Bar Message list Toolbar Preview pane Quick Filter Search box

Show/hide mini calendar Mini calendar Status bar

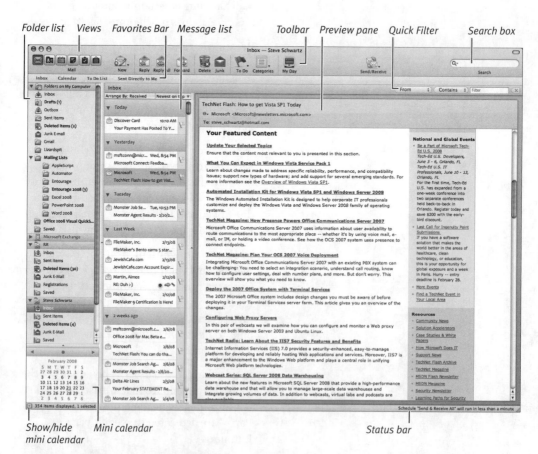

Figure 20.1 The Entourage interface (Mail view).

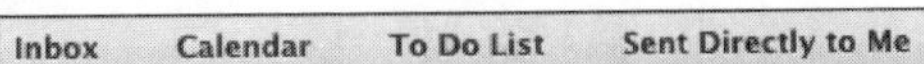

Figure 20.3 The Favorites Bar contains text buttons. You may find it more direct to click one of these buttons than to click a View icon (Figure 20.2).

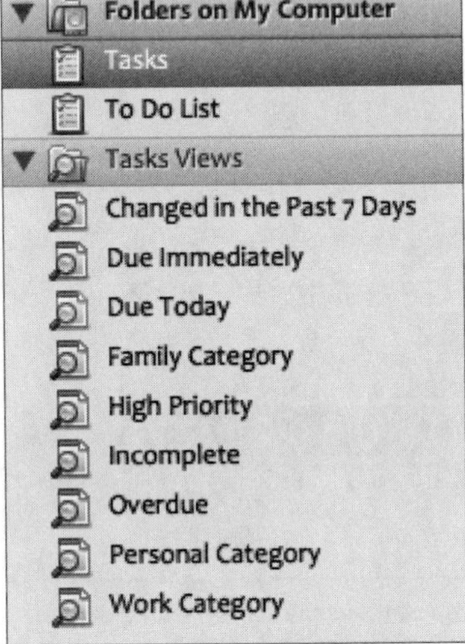

Figure 20.4 Click a view name to see only items that match the view's criteria. To examine the criteria, Control-click the name and choose Edit Custom View.

Toolbar. The toolbar contains icons for frequently used commands, enabling you to perform tasks such as classifying email as junk or launching My Day without having to hunt through menus. You can customize any window toolbar by adding or removing buttons, as explained in "Customizing Toolbars" at the end of this chapter.

Favorites Bar. New in Office 2008, the Favorites Bar (**Figure 20.3**) provides button shortcuts to your favorite parts of Entourage. If you click the Inbox button, for example, you go to Mail view and the Inbox folder of your main email account is automatically selected. As explained later in this chapter, you can customize items on the Favorites Bar.

Folder list. In Mail view, the Folder list contains folders for each of your email accounts, as well as subfolders in which account mail is organized, such as Inbox and Sent Items. To view messages, the first step is to select a folder in the folder list.

At the bottom of the each folder list is a special folder that contains *custom views* (**Figure 20.4**). The folder is named for the current view, such as Notes Views or Address Book Views. Select an item in this folder to see only material that matches the custom view's criteria, such as High Priority or Created in Past 7 Days.

Message list. In Mail view, the message list displays message headers for the mail folder that's selected in the folder list. You can set a new sort order for any folder's message list by clicking the Arrange By text above the list.

Preview pane. After selecting an email or newsgroup message header in the message list, you can read it in the Preview pane. If you'd like a larger reading window, you can double-click either type of message to open it in its own window.

Quick Filter. By setting options and typing, you can filter the list in any view to show only items that match the filter criterion. Filtering options, however, are limited.

Search box. More powerful than filtering, you can type a text string into the Search box and then specify the folders to be searched. Using the Spotlight search engine, matches are returned as you type.

Entourage also supports advanced searches in which you can supply multiple criteria. For more information about displaying only select items, see "Filtering and Searching" in this chapter.

Status bar. Entourage status, progress, and error messages are displayed in the status bar (**Figure 20.5**). Messages indicate when you're working offline and the amount of time until the next scheduled send/receive, for instance.

Mini calendar. You can click a date on the mini calendar to view the schedule for that date in Calendar view. To see the schedule for a longer period of time, drag-select the dates (**Figure 20.6**). To hide or show the mini calendar, click the button in the lower-left corner of the Entourage window. To display multiple mini calendar pages, you can widen the folder list area by dragging the section divider to its right.

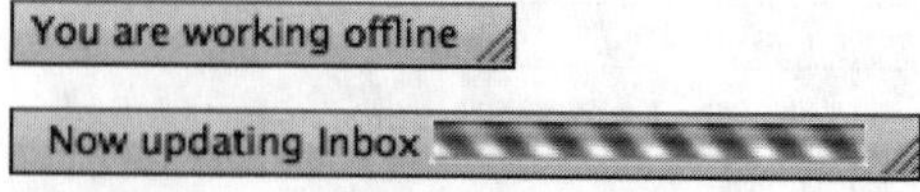

Figure 20.5 Status messages (mainly related to mail) are shown in the status bar.

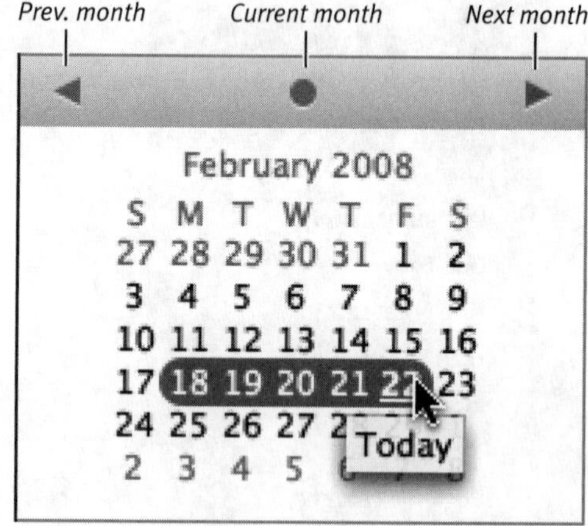

Figure 20.6 You can view the schedule for a date or range by selecting it in the mini calendar.

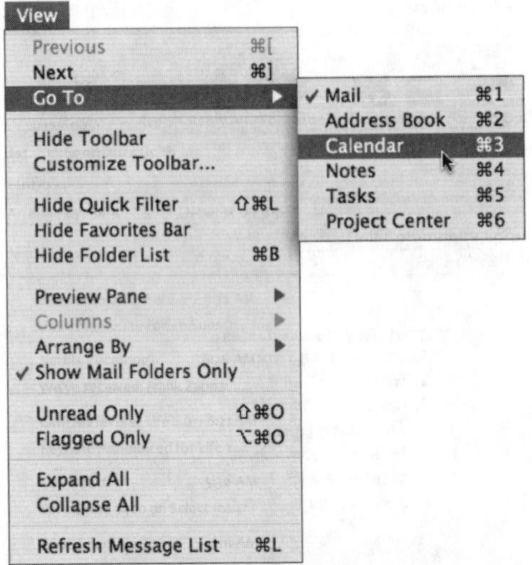

Figure 20.7 Although less convenient than clicking a view icon, choosing a command from the Go To submenu is also less confusing.

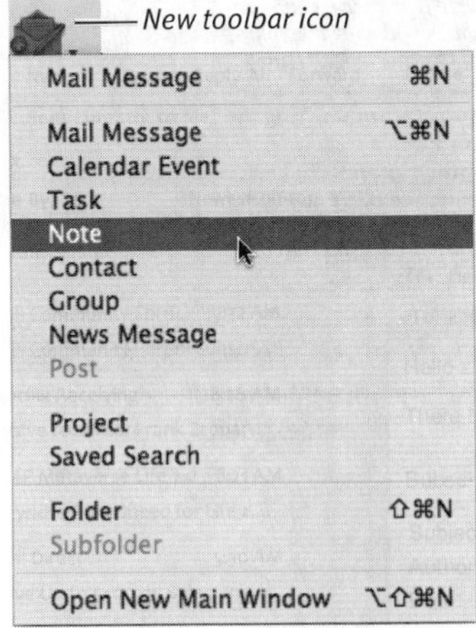

Figure 20.8 You can create a new item of any type by clicking the New icon on the Entourage window's toolbar.

Navigating Entourage

As mentioned in the previous section, Entourage has six components called *views*. To examine, open, or change items in a view, you begin by switching to the view.

To switch to a different view:

- *Do one of the following:*
  - Click a view icon in the upper-left corner of the Entourage window (see Figure 20.2).
  - Choose a command from the View > Go To submenu (**Figure 20.7**).
  - Press the view's keyboard shortcut (between ⌘1 and ⌘6, as shown in Figure 20.7).
  - Click a button in the Favorites Bar (see Figure 20.3).

✓ Tips

- If you aren't certain which icon represents which view, rest the cursor on an icon without clicking it. The view's name is shown under the row of view icons.
- If all you want to do is *create* a new item, it isn't necessary to switch to the appropriate view. You can choose a command from the File > New submenu or from the New drop-down menu on the Standard toolbar (**Figure 20.8**).

Entourage and the Toolbox

Although used less frequently and containing fewer tabs than in Word, Excel, or PowerPoint, the Toolbox (**Figure 20.9**) is also available in Entourage. You can use it to accomplish the following tasks:

- **Scrapbook.** Paste stored material into email messages and notes, as well as store Entourage material for pasting into future items (such as email) or into other Office documents.
- **Reference Tools.** Improve your writing by looking up definitions and synonyms, translating terms and phrases, and performing Web searches. Enter a term or phrase in the search box, press Return, and then expand the panes that you want to consult (Figure 20.9).
- **Object Palette.** By clicking the three tabs on the Object Palette, you can insert clip art, symbol and foreign language characters, or photos into Entourage items.

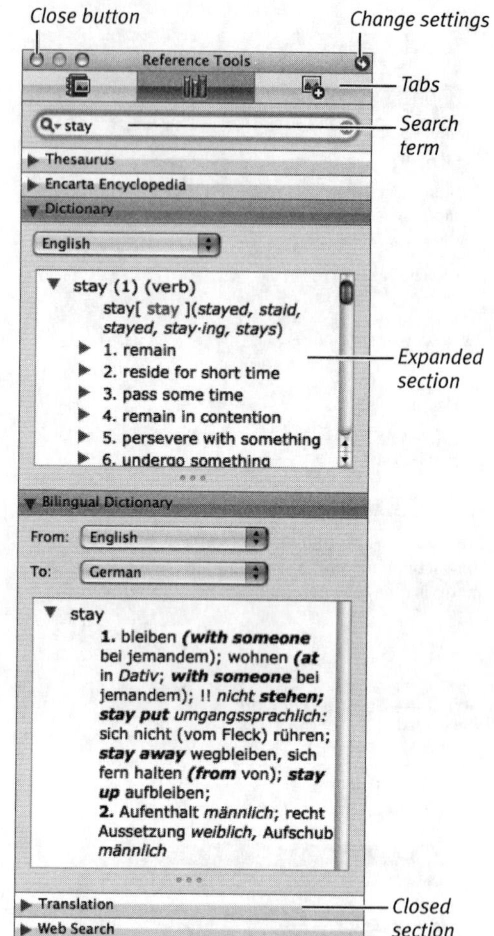

Figure 20.9 To see reference information for the search term or phrase, expand the appropriate sections.

To open the Toolbox:

- Choose a tab/palette from the Tools > Toolbox submenu. The following occurs:
  - If the Toolbox is closed, it opens and displays the chosen tab/palette.
  - If the Toolbox is open and another tab is active, the chosen tab is displayed.
  - If the Toolbox is open and you chose the current tab, the Toolbox closes.

✔ Tips

- To insert an image into the body of an email message (rather than including it as an attachment), you must set the message format to HTML.
- These Toolbox tabs, as well as others available only in Word, PowerPoint, or Excel, are discussed throughout the book.

Figure 20.10 Create the filter criterion by choosing from drop-down menus and typing. In this example, the email message list is filtered to show only received messages from people with an AOL account.

Filtering and Searching

To simplify the process of finding an email message, event, task, or other Entourage item, you can search or filter in a variety of ways. The techniques described in this section can be used in any view. However, their usefulness is greater in views in which you've amassed a lot of data or items, such as Mail, Address Book, or Calendar view.

Filtering a list

Think of filtering as a convenient, single-criterion search. After applying a filter, only items that match the criterion are shown; all others are hidden. In every view, the filter controls can be found near the top of the Entourage window.

To filter a list:

1. Switch to the view that shows the items you want to filter. Select a folder in the folder list.
2. Select a filter type from the first drop-down menu (**Figure 20.10**).
   Depending on your choice, additional drop-down menus or a text box appears.
3. To complete the filter criterion, choose an option from the additional drop-down menu (if present) and/or type a text string in the text box (if present).
   When you're done, the item list or display is automatically filtered to match the specified criterion.
4. When you're ready to restore the complete list, click the Clear button, delete text in the text box, or choose All from the final drop-down menu.

✔ Tips

- Be creative when typing a filter text string. The string doesn't have to be found at the beginning of items, and you don't have to enter a complete word.
- In some views, such as Calendar, Address Book, and Notes, the default folder is automatically selected for you. In Mail view, however, it's *essential* to first select the message folder or subfolder that you want to filter.

Performing a Find

The familiar Find dialog box from previous versions of Entourage is gone. You now perform a Find by typing a string in the Search box at the top of the Entourage window. You can't specify which item fields are searched; all parts of every item are considered.

To perform a Find:

1. Click in the Search box, choose Edit > Find, or press ⌘F.

   The Search box (**Figure 20.11**) is selected.

2. If the Search box contains text from the most recent search, delete it or click the Clear button (X).

3. *Do one of the following:*
   - ▲ Type or paste search text into the Search box.
   - ▲ To repeat a recent search, select the search string from the magnifying glass's drop-down menu.

   As you type, Entourage finds and displays all matching items (**Figure 20.12**).

4. *Optional:* To restrict or expand the search, click a button at the top of the search pane.

5. When you've finished examining the matches, click either Clear (X) button.

   The Search area is cleared and the item list is restored.

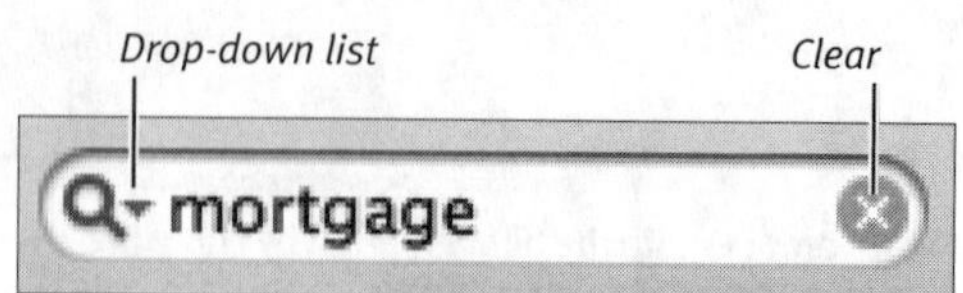

Figure 20.11 Type, paste, or select a search string.

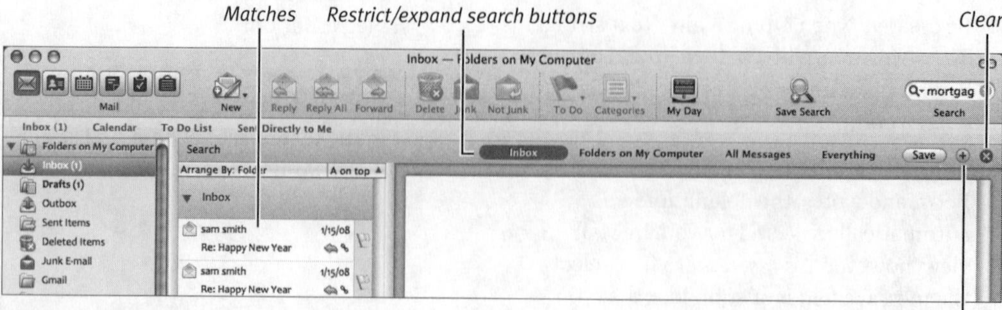

Figure 20.12 Displaying the results of a Find.

Performing an Advanced Search

A Find identifies matches by considering every element and field. If you want to set specific criteria, perform an Advanced Search.

To perform an Advanced Search:

1. *Optional:* If you're searching for mail and want to restrict the search to a folder or subfolder, select the folder or subfolder in the Folder list.
2. Choose Edit > Advanced Search (Option ⌘ F).

   A search pane appears (**Figure 20.13**), similar to the one used to perform a Find.
3. Specify the first criterion by selecting options from drop-down menus and, if presented, typing a string in the text box.
4. *Optional:* To add another criterion, click the plus (+) icon. As needed, repeat Steps 3 and 4 to add additional criteria.
5. Choose a match option from the top drop-down menu:
   - **Match if all criteria are met.** To be considered a match, an item must satisfy all specified criteria.
   - **Match if any criteria are met.** To be considered a match, an item must satisfy at least one criterion.

   As you set criteria and make choices, the match list is continuously updated.
6. When you've finished examining the found items, click the Clear (X) button to restore the item list.

✔ Tips

- If you are only specifying a single criterion, the match option is irrelevant.
- As in a Find, you can change the search's scope by clicking a button at the top of the search pane.
- To remove a criterion, click the minus (-) icon to its right.
- You can switch from a Find to an Advanced Search by clicking the plus (+) icon (Figure 20.12).

Figure 20.13 Perform Advanced Search in this pane.

Searching within an item

You can also search within an individual email message or note.

To search within an item:

1. Open the email message or note in its own window by double-clicking the item in the message or note list.
2. Click to set the text insertion mark in the message or note.

   The search will begin at the text insertion mark.
3. Choose Edit > Find (⌘F).

   The Find dialog box appears (**Figure 20.14**).
4. Enter a search string and click Find.
   - ▲ If the string is found, the first instance is highlighted (**Figure 20.15**).
   - ▲ If the string is not found, you'll hear a beep sound.

   Repeat this step to locate additional instances of the search string. Each Find repetition searches further down the message or note. When the bottom of the item is reached, the search wraps around.
5. To dismiss the Find dialog box, click its close button (X) or click Cancel.

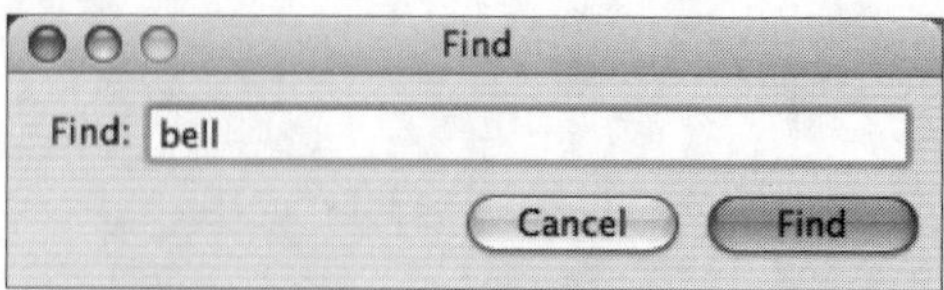

Figure 20.14 You use the Find dialog box to search for matching text within an item, such as a mail message or note.

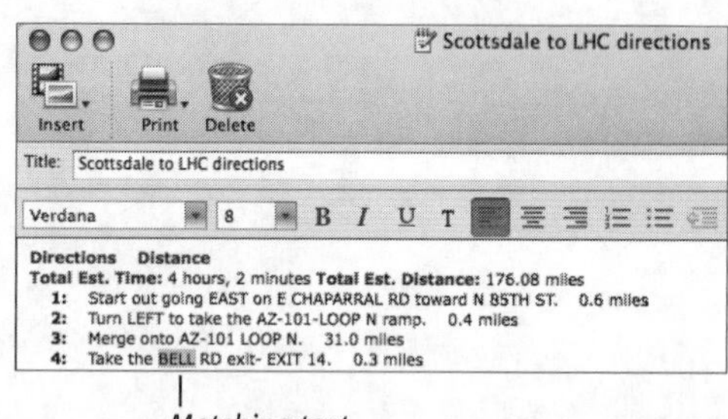

Figure 20.15 If found, the first match is highlighted.

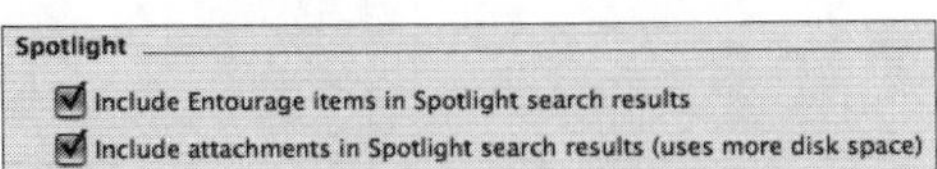

Figure 20.16 This pair of options instructs Spotlight to index and display Entourage items in searches.

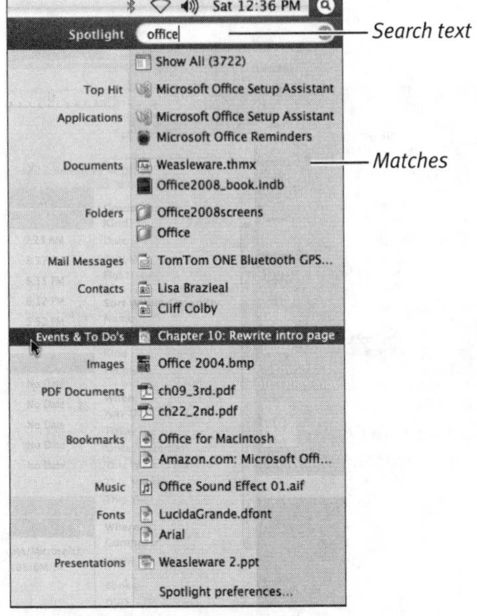

Figure 20.17 A Spotlight search.

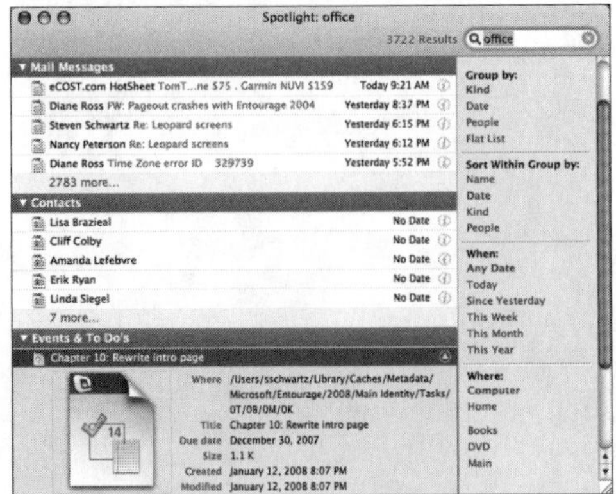

Figure 20.18 Show All displays all matches. To get more information about an item, click its tiny *i* icon.

Performing a Spotlight search

If you've enabled the Spotlight preferences in Entourage, you can perform searches from the Desktop and file dialog boxes to locate email, Calendar events, tasks, Address Book records, and other Entourage items. By default, the Spotlight preferences are enabled.

To view or set Spotlight preferences:

1. Choose Entourage > Preferences (⌘,).
2. In the left pane of the Preferences dialog box, select Spotlight in the General Preferences group.
3. Set Spotlight preferences by checking or clearing the check boxes (**Figure 20.16**).
4. Click OK to save the changes.

To perform a Spotlight search:

1. Type the search string in any Spotlight search box.

   Spotlight lists matches as you type (**Figure 20.17**).

2. *Do one of the following:*
   - ▲ If you see the desired Entourage item, double-click it to open it in Entourage.
   - ▲ Click Show All to display all matches in a new window (**Figure 20.18**). As needed, expand sections to see the matches. Double-click any item to open it.

✔ Tips

- You can perform Spotlight searches even when Entourage isn't running. If you double-click an Entourage item, Entourage will automatically launch to display the item.
- Each Spotlight match is preceded by a file icon. The Entourage item icons are purple and white.

Synchronizing Entourage with an iPod

Using *Sync Services* (a central database on your Mac for sharing data among applications and hardware), you can synchronize your Entourage Address Book and Calendar events with data in the Apple Address Book and iCal. Using iTunes, you can then sync these items with your iPod or iPhone.

To enable Sync Services for Entourage:

1. Choose Entourage > Preferences (⌘,).
2. In the left pane of the Preferences dialog box, select Sync Services in the General Preferences group.
3. Click check boxes (**Figure 20.19**) to enable Entourage data to be synchronized with Address Book, iCal, or both.

   If you've added an Exchange Server account to Entourage, you can synchronize with that account's Contacts and/or Calendar by choosing the Microsoft Exchange option from the drop-down menus.
4. Click OK.

   The Synchronization Options dialog box appears (**Figure 20.20**).
5. Click a radio button to indicate how you want data from the applications to be handled. Click OK.

   You can merge the Entourage data with Address Book and iCal data, replace the Entourage data with the Address Book and iCal data, or replace the Address Book and iCal data with the Entourage data.

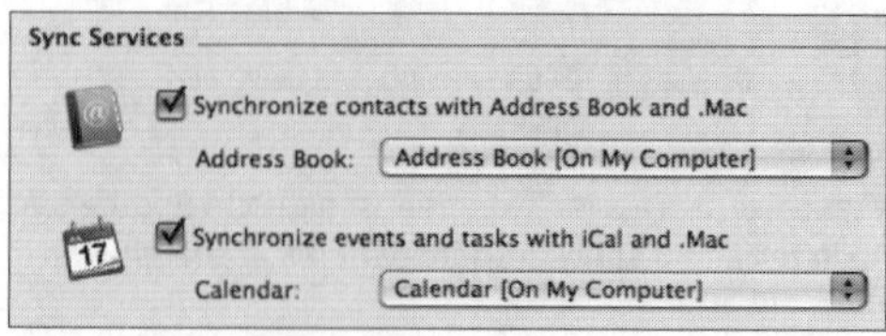

Figure 20.19 To enable Sync Services, click one or both of these check boxes.

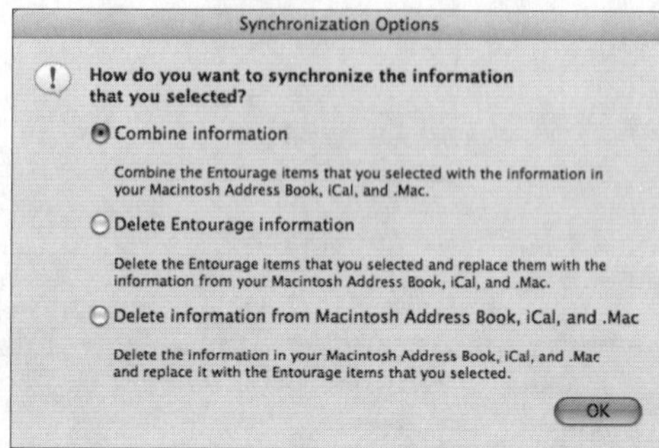

Figure 20.20 Click a radio button to specify how data in the applications should be handled or merged.

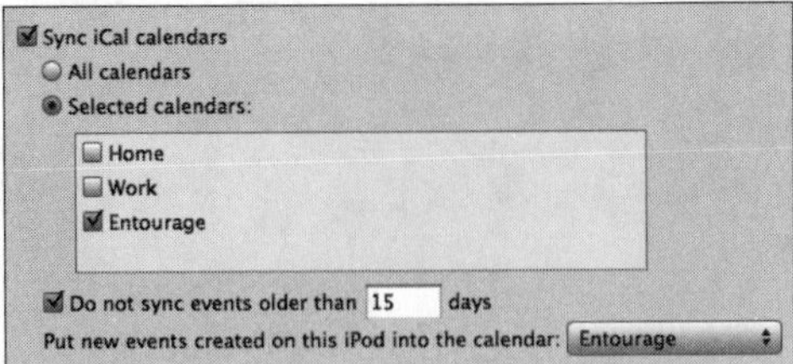

Figure 20.21 Set calendar synchronization options.

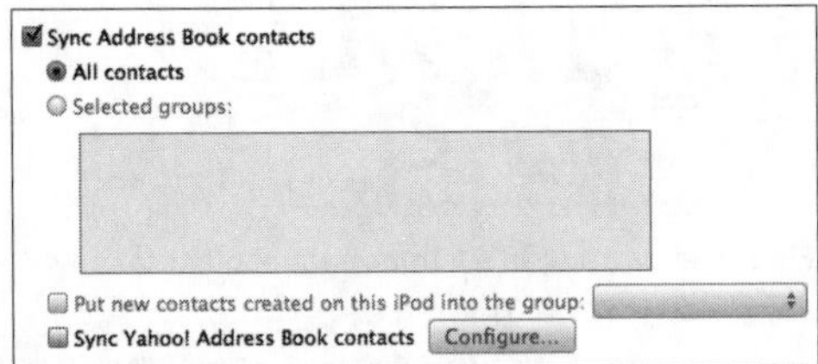

Figure 20.22 Set contacts synchronization options.

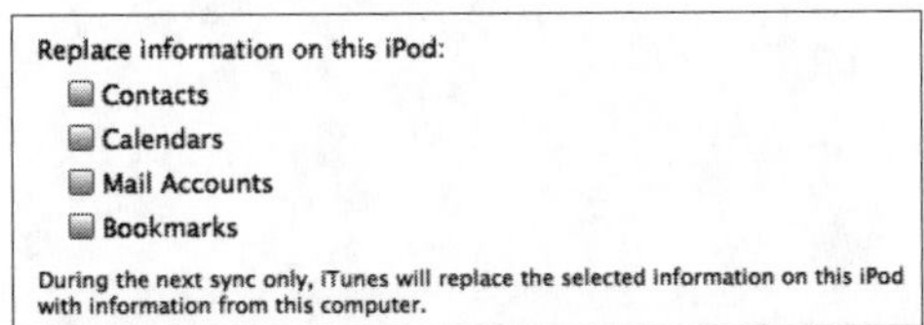

Figure 20.23 Click check boxes in the Advanced section to replace data on your iPod or iPhone with data from your Mac.

To synchronize Entourage data with an iPod, iPod Touch, or iPhone:

1. Connect your iPod or iPhone to your Mac.

   iTunes launches and a synchronization is performed.

2. Select your device in the Devices list (in the lefthand pane) and click the Info or Contacts tab (at the top of the window).

   The tab name depends on whether you have an iPod or an iPod Touch/iPhone.

3. In the Calendars section (**Figure 20.21**), click Sync iCal calendars and specify the calendars to sync.

   If you have an iPod Touch or iPhone, you can also specify that new events created on the device will be recorded in Entourage.

4. In the Contacts section (**Figure 20.22**), click Sync Address Book contacts and specify the contacts to sync.

5. Click Apply.

   A new synchronization is performed. In future sessions, these syncs will continue until you change options in iTunes or disable Entourage support in Sync Services.

✔ Tip

- In the Advanced section of the Info or Contacts tab (**Figure 20.23**), you can perform a one-time synchronization to replace selected types of data on your iPod, iPod Touch, or iPhone with data from your Mac.

Customizing Toolbars

As you've learned in this chapter, one way to customize Entourage is to change settings in Preferences. To further customize Entourage, you can change the toolbar above any type of window (such as the main window, outgoing mail window, or new Calendar event window) by adding or removing icons.

To customize a toolbar:

1. Open the type of window that you want to customize. The window must have a toolbar, and it must be displayed.
   If you want to customize the Entourage toolbar, you don't need to open a window.
2. Choose View > Customize Toolbar.
   A special pane appears directly beneath the toolbar (**Figure 20.24**).
3. *Do any of the following:*
   - ▲ **Add icons.** Drag an icon from the pane into position on the toolbar.
   - ▲ **Rearrange icons.** Drag icons to new positions to change their order.
   - ▲ **Remove icons.** Drag any icon off the toolbar to remove it from the set.
   - ▲ **Restore the default toolbar.** Drag the default set onto a customized toolbar to restore the original icon set.
4. When you're finished, click Done.
   All windows of the same type will now display the new toolbar icon set.

✔ Tips

- If you like, you can restore icons that were present in Entourage 2004 but are absent in Entourage 2008, such as Save. Similarly, you can remove icons that you never use, such as Links.
- If you choose new options from the Show section of the pane, they apply to *all* Entourage toolbars.

Figure 20.24 You can customize the toolbar for any Entourage window type.

Customizing the Favorites Bar

Like toolbars, you can change the buttons on the Favorites Bar (located beneath the toolbar in the main Entourage window).

- ◆ To add a button, drag any folder from the folder list onto the Favorites Bar.
- ◆ To remove a button, drag it off the Favorites Bar.
- ◆ To change the button order, click any button and drag it to a new position on the Favorites Bar.

The Favorites Bar buttons and their order are identical in all Entourage views.

21

Email

Since electronic mail (*email*) first became available, it has been the centerpiece of most people's Internet use. Entourage is the Office 2008 program that handles your email needs. Using Entourage, you can exchange messages with anyone who has an email address, attach files to messages, organize incoming and outgoing mail, and link email to other items.

In addition to email, Entourage can manage your contacts (Chapter 22), schedule (Chapter 23), to-do list (Chapter 24), and notes (Chapter 25). Entourage is also a capable newsgroup reader (Chapter 26) and Office's command central for project tracking (Chapter 30).

Although the general information in this chapter applies to every account type, see Chapter 28 for additional instructions on setting up and using a Microsoft Exchange Server account.

Setting Up an Account

In order to use email, you need an account with an Internet service provider (ISP). The literature you received with your account or the ISP's tech support staff can tell you whether the service uses Post Office Protocol (POP) or Internet Message Access Protocol (IMAP) for email. There are also two other types of accounts that Entourage supports: Hotmail (Web-based email from Microsoft) and Microsoft Exchange Server (an email server used by many corporations).

Your first step in setting up Entourage as an email client is to import information from your current email accounts or to create a new Entourage account for each one. If your old accounts weren't imported when you first ran Entourage or you've just opened a new ISP, corporate, or Hotmail account, follow the steps below to record the account.

To set up an account:

1. Choose Tools > Accounts.
   The Accounts dialog box appears.
2. On the Mail tab, click the New toolbar icon.
   The Account Setup Assistant appears (**Figure 21.1**).
3. Enter your full email address in the form:
   `username@domain`
   (such as `bob723@msn.com`). If this is an Exchange server account, click the check box, too. Click the right-arrow icon to continue.
4. Entourage should now display a screen indicating that it has determined the account type. Click the right-arrow icon to continue.
   If Entourage fails to detect your account type, you will have to enter and select the appropriate information on the screens that follow.

Figure 21.1 Enter your email address. Click the check box if an Exchange server is being used.

Figure 21.2 Enter the account password and verify (or enter) the other requested information. (If your account type was detected, the bottom part of this dialog box may be empty.)

Figure 21.3 To ensure that Entourage can both send and receive using your supplied account information, click Verify My Settings. (This test occurs online.)

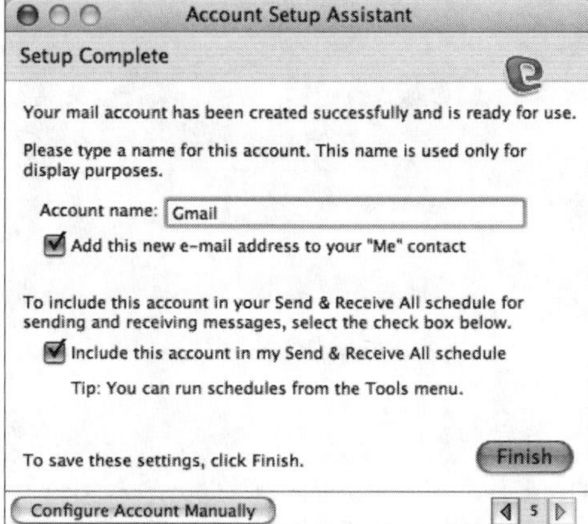

Figure 21.4 Name the account, and then click Finish.

- To review or change an account's settings, double-click its name in the Accounts window.
- To delete an account (one that no longer exists or which you don't want to track with Entourage), select its name in the Accounts window and click Delete.

5. The information requested on the Verify and Complete Settings screen (**Figure 21.2**, previous page) depends on whether Entourage detected your account type in the previous step. *Do the following:*
   - ▲ Enter your name (or how you want your messages identified to recipients) and your email password.
   - ▲ To save your password, click Save password in Mac OS X Keychain. (If you don't save the password, you'll be prompted for it each time you connect to the mail server.)
   - ▲ If shown, verify/enter the incoming and outgoing mail server names. Choose a server type from the Incoming mail server type drop-down menu. (You can get this information from your ISP, company, or institution.)

   Click the right-arrow icon to continue.
6. To ensure that the settings are correct, click Verify My Settings (**Figure 21.3**). The test results will appear in the text box. When the test is successful, click the right-arrow icon to continue.
7. On the final screen (**Figure 21.4**), name the account, review the options, and click Finish. (The account name isn't critical. Its purpose is only to identify the account to you—not to others.)

   The new account is added to the Accounts list. Close the Accounts window.

✔ Tips

- If you have multiple accounts, make one the *default* (primary) account. Select the account name in the Accounts dialog box and click the Make Default icon. When you create a new email message, it's assumed that you want to send it using the default account.

Creating and Sending Mail

One of the most basic functions of email is that of creating and sending messages.

To send email:

1. *Do one of the following:*
   - ▲ From the Mail section of Entourage, click the New toolbar icon or press ⌘N.
   - ▲ From any Entourage section, choose File > New > Mail Message, click the arrow beside the New toolbar icon and choose Mail Message from the drop-down menu (**Figure 21.5**), or press Option⌘N.

   A new message form appears with the address window on top (**Figure 21.6**).

2. In the To box, specify the email address to which you want to send the message by doing one of the following:
   - ▲ Type or paste a complete email address.
   - ▲ Click the Address Book icon to display the contact records you've created. Double-click or drag a contact record into the To box.
   - ▲ If the individual is in your Address Book or you've recently received mail from him/her, begin typing the name or email address. As you type, Entourage lists matching names and addresses from which you can select (**Figure 21.7**).

3. *Optional:* To enter more To addresses, click beneath the last address and repeat Step 2.

4. *Optional:* You can also include recipients in the Cc (carbon copy) or Bcc (blind carbon copy) boxes. Click in the appropriate box and follow Steps 2–3.

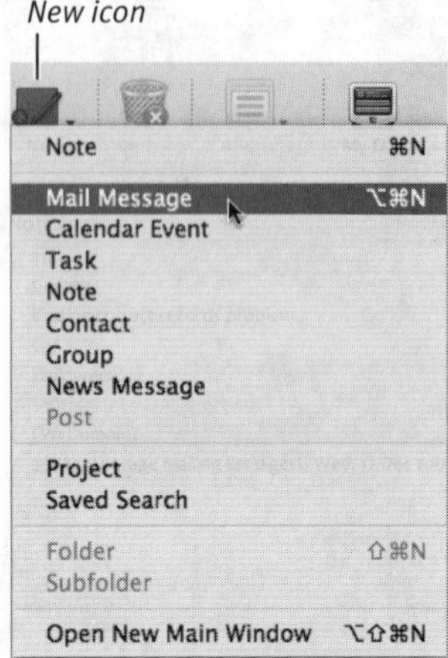

Figure 21.5 Choose Mail Message from the New icon's menu.

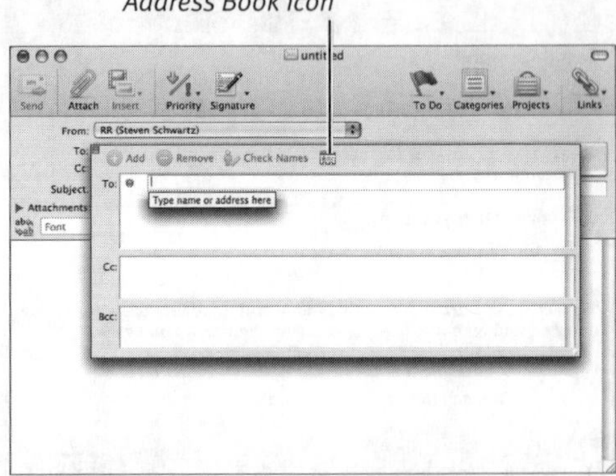

Figure 21.6 Type the recipient's address, or click the Address Book icon and select the person or company from the Address Book pane.

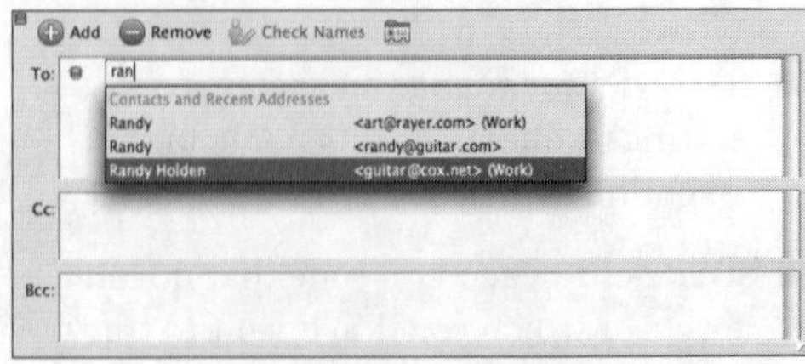

Figure 21.7 You can often select a recipient's address from the list of matches that Entourage presents.

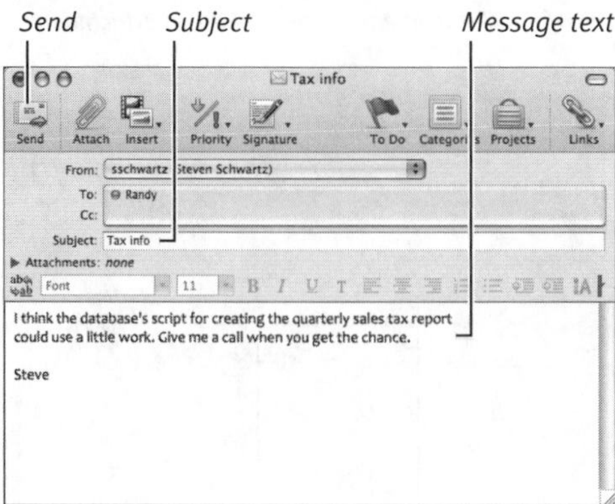

Figure 21.8 Enter the message text.

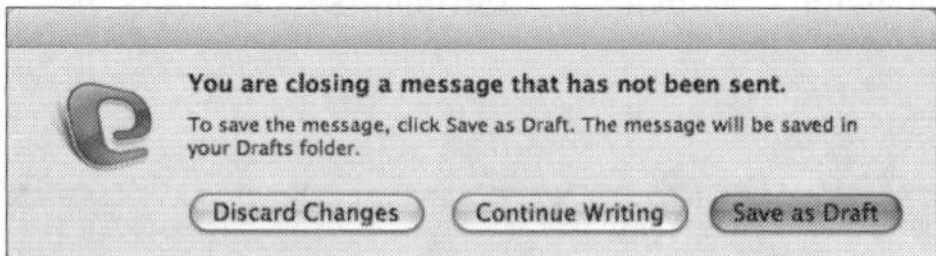

Figure 21.9 If you close a new message without sending or saving it, this dialog box appears.

5. When you've finished entering recipient addresses, click outside the address box, press Return, or press Enter.

   The message window appears, and the insertion text mark is in the Subject field.

6. Enter a subject to identify the message.

7. Move the text insertion mark into the message box by clicking in the box, pressing Return, or pressing Tab. Type the message (**Figure 21.8**).

8. *Do one of the following:*
   - ▲ **Send Now.** If you want to send the message immediately, click the Send toolbar icon, choose Message > Send Message Now, or press ⌘Return.
   - ▲ **Send Later.** To store the message in your Outbox where it will wait for the next Send/Receive, choose Message > Send Message Later (Shift⌘Return).
   - ▲ **Save as Draft.** If you want to edit the message before sending it or delay its sending, close the message. Click Save as Draft in the dialog box that appears (**Figure 21.9**). The message will be stored in the Drafts folder until you open, edit, and send it.

✔ Tips

- Entries in the Cc box represent secondary recipients—people who you want to receive a copy of the message. Bcc people are "invisible" recipients; that is, no other recipient will know that a Bcc recipient also received the message.
- Sent messages are automatically stored in the Sent Items folder. To store an outgoing message in a different folder, choose Message > After Sending, Move To > *folder name*.
- Another way to save the current message as a draft is to choose File > Save (⌘S) and then close the message window.
- Most messages are sent as plain text (single font, no formatting). To create a formatted message, choose Format > HTML (Shift⌘T) or click the Use HTML toolbar icon above the message body.
- Depending on the settings in Spelling Preferences, Entourage may automatically mark potential spelling errors as you type and/or initiate a spell check prior to transmitting each message. To learn about spell checking options, see "Checking Spelling," later in this chapter.

Sending Attachments

In addition to sending text messages, you can optionally attach files to any email message. The files can be any type, such as pictures, word processing documents, worksheets, or even programs. When sent with email, these files are called *attachments*.

To attach a file to a message:

1. Click the triangle beside the word Attachments (between the Subject field and the message body) to open the Attachments pane (**Figure 21.10**).
2. *Do any of the following:*
   - ▲ Click the Add button. In the Choose Attachment dialog box that appears, select a file and click Choose.
   - ▲ Drag file icons into the Attachments pane.
3. Click the bar beneath the Attachments pane to open the options window (**Figure 21.11**). *Do the following:*
   - ▲ Set Encode for to Any computer (AppleDouble), unless you're sure the recipient requires another setting.
   - ▲ If the attachments are large, you can reduce their size by clicking the Compress in ZIP format check box.
4. Send the message by clicking Send.

✔ Tips

- You can add attachments at any point during the message-creation process.
- You can also add an attachment by clicking the Attach toolbar icon at the top of the message window.
- To remove an attachment, select it in the Attachments pane and click the Remove button.

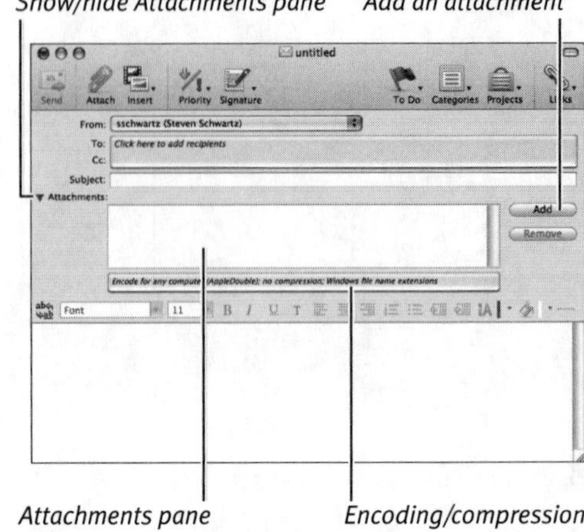

Figure 21.10 When working with attachments, it can be helpful to open the Attachments pane.

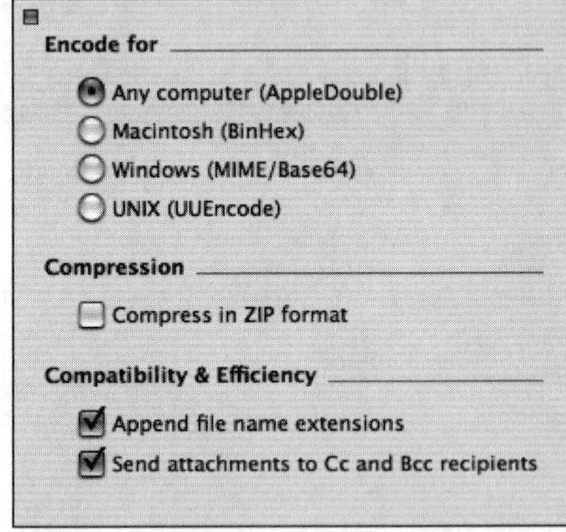

Figure 21.11 You can change the encoding and compression settings for files attached to the message.

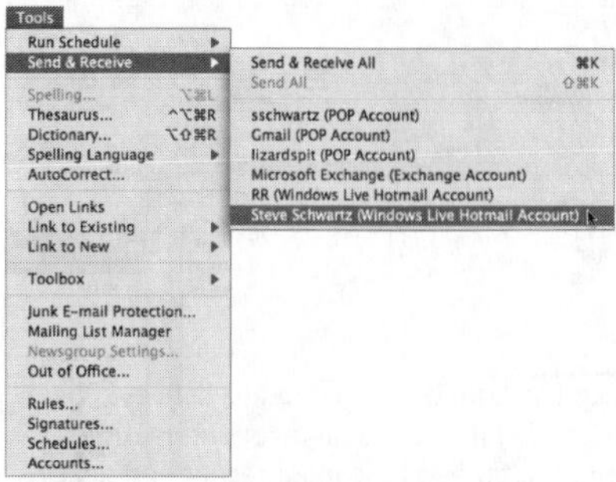

Figure 21.12 To retrieve email from a specific account, choose its name from the Send & Receive submenu.

Incoming Email

You can check for new email manually or automatically. To check automatically, you need to define one or more schedules. A *schedule* specifies the circumstances under which Entourage will check for new email, accounts that will be checked, and when the checks will occur. In this section, you'll learn how to manually check for new mail and on an automatic, repeating schedule.

To check for new email manually:

- *Do any of the following:*
  - Click the Send/Receive toolbar icon to perform a send and receive for all email accounts that you've associated with the Send & Receive All schedule.
  - Click the down arrow beside the Send/Receive icon. Choose Send & Receive All or the name of a specific account. If you choose an account, the send/receive is performed only for that account.
  - Choose Tools > Send & Receive > Send & Receive All (⌘K) to perform a send/receive for all email accounts that you've associated with the Send & Receive All schedule or choose the name of a specific email account to check (**Figure 21.12**).

  Enter requested passwords, if prompted.

✔ Tips

- Send & Receive All is a built-in schedule that is provided to help you check for new mail in your primary email accounts.
- It isn't necessary to add Exchange accounts to schedules or to perform manual Send/Receives for them. As long as you're connected to the Exchange Server, these accounts are automatically updated once every minute.

Working with Identities

If several people use Office on your Mac, you can create multiple *identities* so you can share Office while keeping your email and Office documents separate from theirs. You can create additional identities for family members or to distinguish home and business email activities, for example.

You create new identities and switch among them by choosing Entourage > Switch Identities. As long as every user remembers to switch to their identity at the beginning of every session and has a separate email account, only that user's new mail will be retrieved by the Send & Receive All command.

To check for new mail on a repeating schedule:

1. Choose Tools > Schedules.

   The Schedules dialog box appears (**Figure 21.13**).

2. Click the New toolbar icon.

   The Edit Schedule dialog box appears (**Figure 21.14**).

3. Name this schedule in the Name text box.

4. Choose Repeating Schedule from the pop-up menu in the When section, and specify a time interval and increment unit (**Figure 21.15**).

5. If you want this schedule to run only when you're connected to the Internet, click the Only if connected check box.

6. Choose Receive Mail and an account from the pop-up menus in the Action section.

7. If you have additional email accounts you'd like to check on the same schedule, click Add Action and set this action to Receive Mail, as you did for the email account specified in Step 6.

8. In the Dial-up options section, select Stay connected—unless you want to immediately disconnect after each receive.

9. Be sure that Enabled is checked, and then click OK.

   The Schedules dialog box reappears and includes the new schedule. Whenever Entourage is running, it will check for and receive messages for the specified email accounts at the designated interval. (Note that you can still perform manual send/receives.)

✔ Tip

- To edit a schedule, double-click its name in the Schedules dialog box. To remove a schedule, select it and click Delete.

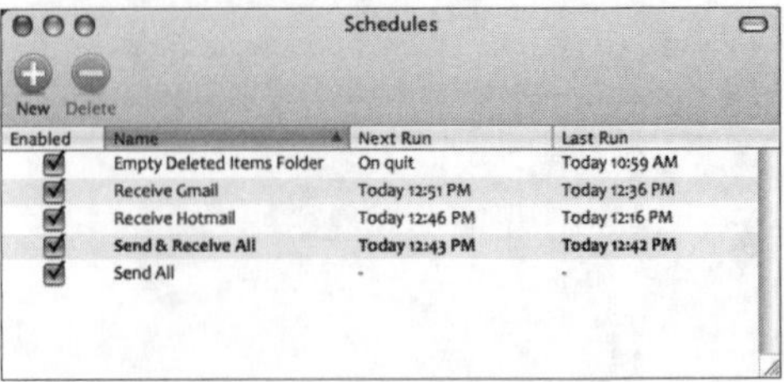

Figure 21.13 The Schedules dialog box lists every defined schedule. If a schedule is repeating, timed, or recurring, the times of the most recent and next scheduled runs are shown.

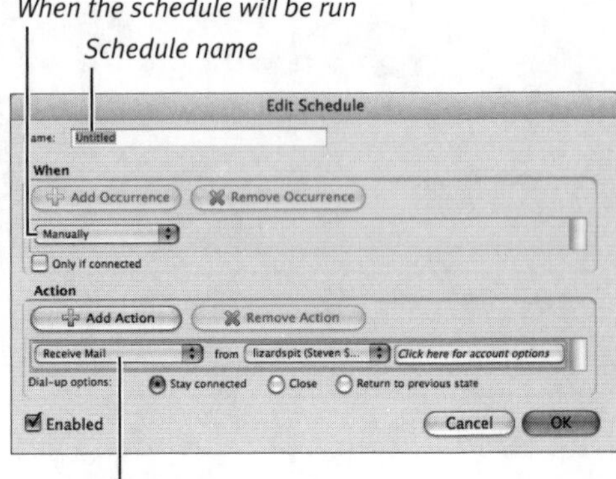

Figure 21.14 You create and edit schedules in the Edit Schedule dialog box.

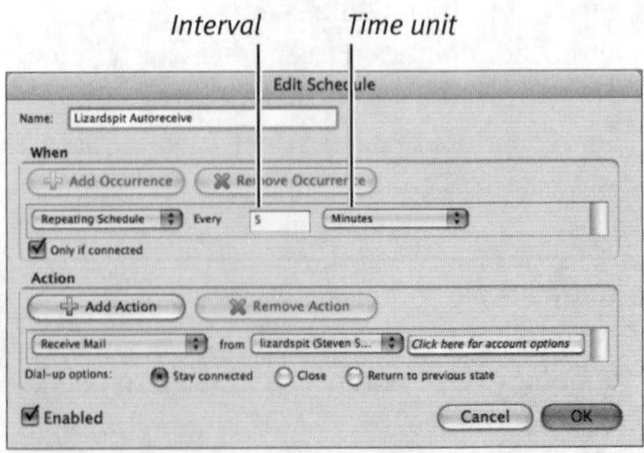

Figure 21.15 When creating a repeating schedule, you must choose a time interval and unit.

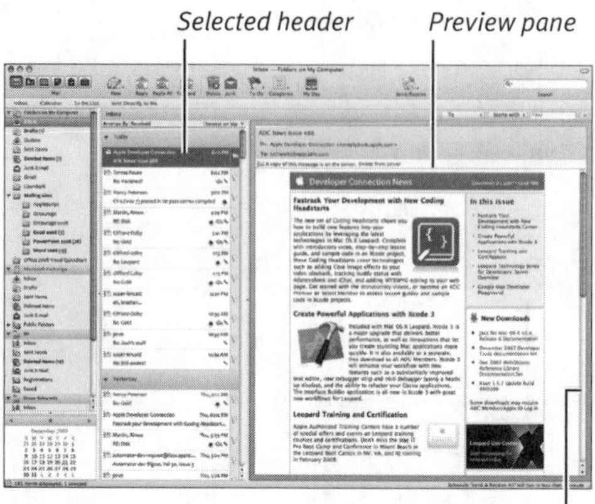

Figure 21.16 Select a header in the message list to read the message in the Preview Pane.

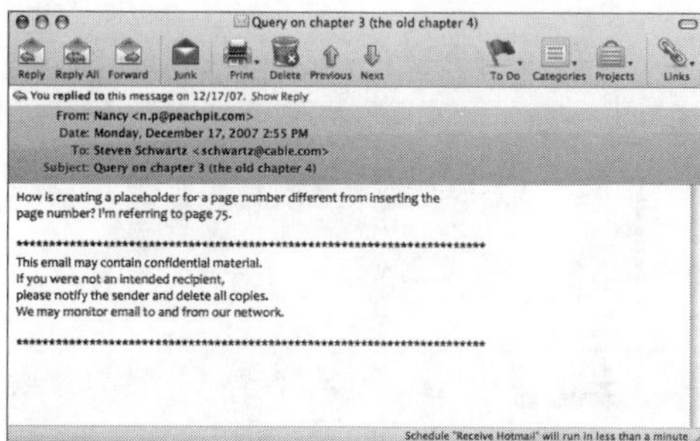

Figure 21.17 You can open a message in its own window. To read additional messages in this same window, click the Previous and Next toolbar icons.

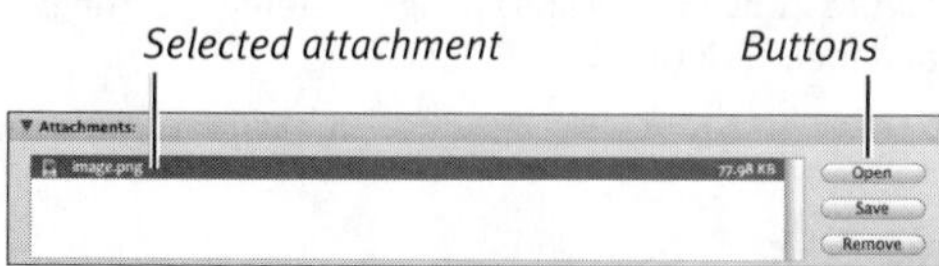

Figure 21.18 Click a button to perform an action on the selected attachment(s).

To read a message:

1. *Do either of the following:*
   - ▲ Select a message header in the message list. The message appears in the Preview pane (**Figure 21.16**).
   - ▲ Double-click a message header in the message list. The message opens in its own window (**Figure 21.17**). Toolbar icons across the top provide message-handling options.
2. Scroll through the message using the vertical scroll bar or by pressing Spacebar.

✔ Tips

- The Preview pane can be placed below or to the right of the message list. Choose a position from the View > Preview Pane submenu.

To manage received attachments:

1. When you open or preview a message that contains an attachment (indicated by a paper clip icon), the Attachments pane opens.
2. Select an attachment and click one of the buttons on the right to open the file, save it to disk, or delete it (**Figure 21.18**).

✔ Tips

- You can also open an attachment by double-clicking it in the Attachments pane. And you can save an attachment by dragging its file icon onto the Desktop.
- If a message has multiple attachments, you can remove or save them all with a single command. From the Message menu, choose Remove All Attachments or Save All Attachments.
- Entourage can display certain types of attachments (such as PDF and JPEG files) in the Preview pane. Thus, it's not necessary to open all files just to view them.

Replying to Email

There are several ways to reply to received email. This section explains the options.

To reply to a message:

1. Select the header in the message list or open the message in its own window.
2. Click the Reply toolbar icon, choose Message > Reply, or press ⌘R.

   A message window opens, addressed to the author (**Figure 21.19**). The Subject is the original one preceded by RE (for *reply*).
3. Type your reply text, and send the message.

✔ Tips

- By default, the entire original message is quoted when a reply is generated. However, it's polite to quote only relevant parts. Delete any unnecessary text from the original message.
- Another option is to select the text that you want to quote and *then* issue the Reply command. Only the selected text will be quoted in the reply.
- There are *three* Reply commands:
  - **Reply.** Use when replying only to the person who sent the message to you.
  - **Reply to All.** Reply to the message author, as well as to all others listed in the To and Cc lines.
  - **Reply to Sender.** When replying to a message from a mailing list, this command allows you to address the reply to the message author rather than to the list.
- To specify default behaviors to use when replying to messages, choose Entourage > Preferences, and select the Reply and Forward category (**Figure 21.20**).

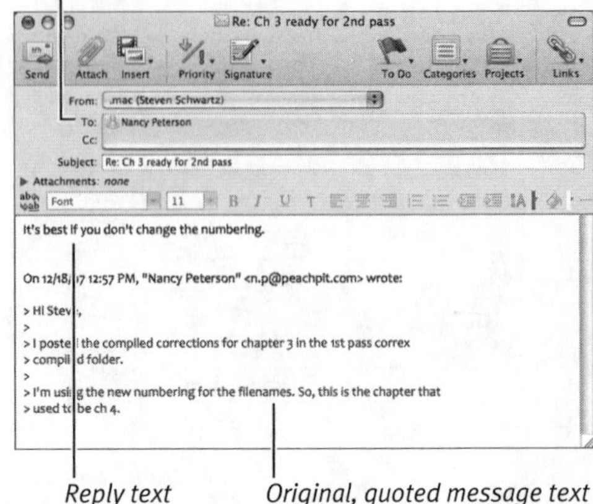

Figure 21.19 Edit the original, quoted text (if desired), add your reply, and send the message.

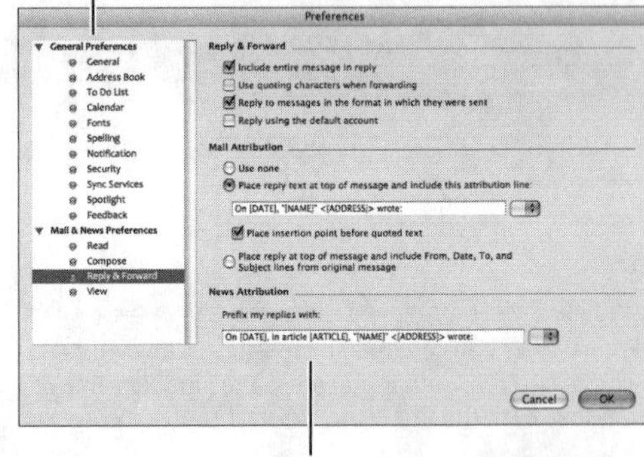

Figure 21.20 Review and change preference settings, and then click OK.

The Progress Window

The Progress window (Window > Progress or ⌘7) shows the progress of each email account send/receive. When the Progress window is closed, send/receive progress is displayed in the status bar.

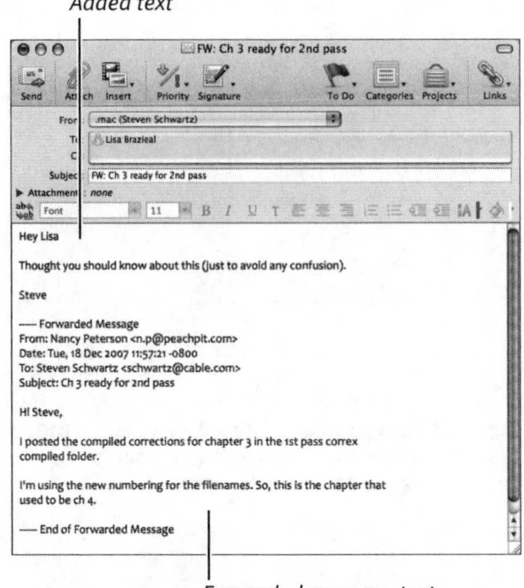

Figure 21.21 A forwarded message can include new text that you've added, as well as new attachments.

Forwarding and Redirecting

If you receive mail that you want to send to others, you can forward or redirect it. When you *forward* mail, you can add your own comments, the recipients see a message that came from you, and any replies will go to you.

If you *redirect* email, on the other hand, you cannot alter or add to the message, the email appears to have come from the original sender, and any replies go to that sender. As a result, redirection is generally used to pass on email that was mistakenly sent to you or when there's a more suitable recipient.

To forward email:

1. With the message selected in the message list or opened in its own window, click the Forward toolbar icon, choose Message > Forward, or press ⌘J.
2. Enter the address or addresses to which you want to forward the message.
3. By default, the Subject is the original subject preceded by FW (such as, `FW:Today's Joke`). You can edit the Subject, if you like.
4. *Optional:* Add an introductory note to the message body, edit the forwarded text, and/or add attachments (**Figure 21.21**).
5. Click the Send toolbar icon or choose Message > Send Message Now (⌘Return) to forward the message to the recipients.

To redirect email:

1. With the message selected in the message list or opened in its own window, choose Message > Redirect (Option⌘J).
2. Enter or select the addresses to which you want to redirect the message.

   You may not edit the Subject or message text, nor can you add attachments.
3. Send the message.

✔ Tips

- You can also forward a message as an attachment. Select the header in the message list and choose Message > Forward as Attachment. A new message window appears. Instead of quoting the original message text, it's included as an attached file (**Figure 21.22**).
- Think carefully before choosing to redirect a message rather than forwarding it. Redirected messages always appear to have been sent by the original author—not you.
- You can also forward and redirect email to *yourself*. For instance, if I receive an important message in one of my secondary email accounts (such as Hotmail, Gmail, or Yahoo! Mail), I can forward or redirect it to my ISP account. If I ever need to refer to the message again, I won't have to guess the account in which it's stored.

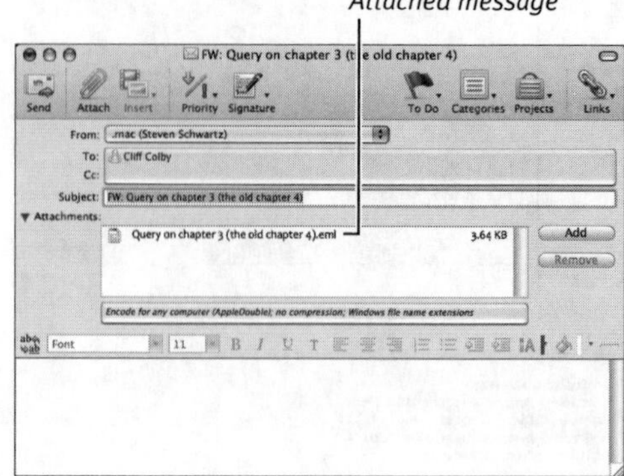

Figure 21.22 You can also forward a message as an attached file. Doing so allows you to separate your own message text from the forwarded material.

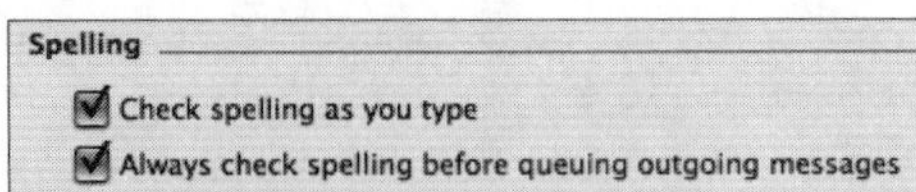

Figure 21.23 Choose Entourage > Preferences, and select the Spelling category. The settings for the first two options determine the automatic spell-checking actions that Entourage will perform.

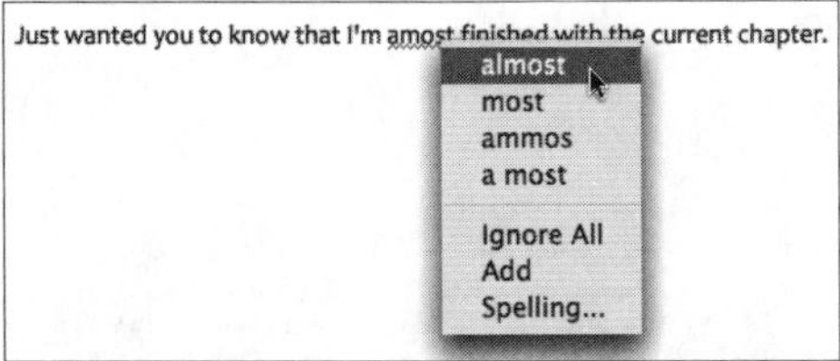

Figure 21.24 In many cases, you can select the correct spelling from a pop-up menu.

Checking Spelling

Because Office's spelling checker is available to all Office applications, even the poorest spellers can avoid embarrassing misspellings and typos in their messages. Depending on settings in Spelling Preferences (**Figure 21.23**), Entourage will automatically flag errors as you type each message and/or perform a spell check immediately before each new message is sent.

To fix an "as you type" spelling error:

- An "as you type" error is marked with a wavy red underline. You can correct such an error by doing one of the following:
  - **Ignore.** If you're sure that the word is spelled correctly, you can ignore it.
  - **Edit.** If you know the correct spelling, edit the word. If the revised word is in Office's spelling dictionaries, the wavy red underline will disappear.
  - **Spell check.** You can Control-click a flagged word to display spelling options (**Figure 21.24**). Click a suggested replacement (if one is listed), choose Ignore All to instruct the spelling checker to ignore all instances of the word in this message, choose Add to accept the word's spelling and add it to your custom dictionary, or choose Spelling to use the full spelling checker to examine the word.

Using the Dictionary and Thesaurus

Office includes a dictionary and thesaurus among its tools. If you want to improve your writing by ensuring that you're using the correct word or by substituting a different word or phrase for the current one, you can use the dictionary and thesaurus, respectively.

To look up a word or phrase, Control-click it and choose Look Up > Definition or Look Up > Synonyms from the pop-up menu. If the Toolbox isn't currently open, it appears and the Reference Tools tab is selected. To learn more about using the Toolbox in Entourage, refer to Chapter 20.

To perform a routine spelling check:

1. Initiate the spelling check (**Figure 21.25**) in one of these ways:
   - ▲ If Always check spelling before queuing outgoing messages (Figure 21.23) is enabled and the message contains at least one suspected error, a spelling check will automatically be initiated when you click Send.
   - ▲ Choose Tools > Spelling (Option ⌘ L). (If you only want to check a single word or part of the message, select it before choosing Tools > Spelling.)

   If at least one suspect word is identified, the Spelling dialog box appears (Figure 21.25). The suspect word is shown in the dialog box and selected in the message.

2. *Do one of the following:*
   - ▲ If the correct spelling is shown in the Suggestions list, select it and click Change. (Or click Change All to substitute the replacement word for all instances of this misspelling found in the message.)
   - ▲ Correct the spelling by editing the word in the top box and clicking Change. (Or click Change All to substitute the edited word for all instances of this misspelling found in the message.)
   - ▲ Click Ignore to skip this instance of the word. (Or click Ignore All to skip all instances of the word in the message.)
   - ▲ If the word is spelled correctly, click Add to add it to Office's custom dictionary so it will be ignored in future spelling checks.
   - ▲ If you often misspell this word the same way, select a replacement or edit the word. Click AutoCorrect to add the misspelling to the AutoCorrect list. If you make the error in future messages or documents, AutoCorrect will instantly correct it.

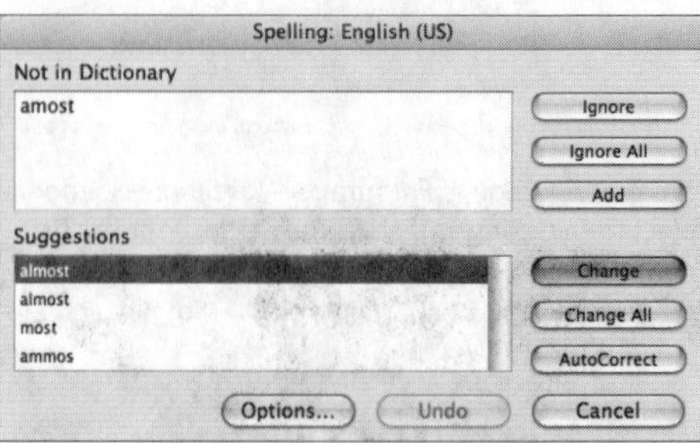

Figure 21.25 The Spelling dialog box.

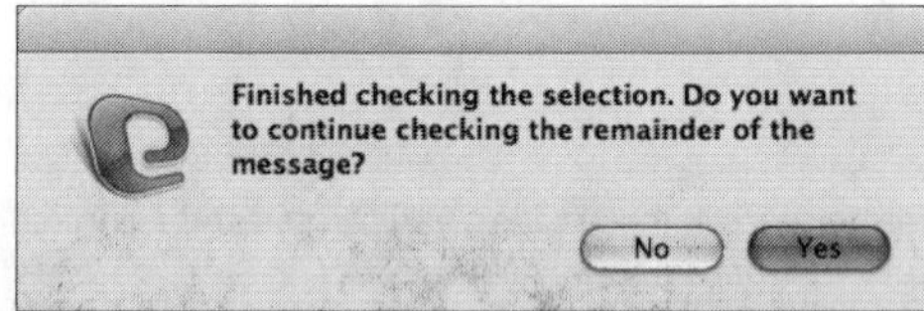

Figure 21.26 This dialog box appears after a spelling check is performed on selected text.

   The next suspected mistake (if any) is displayed in the Not in Dictionary box and is highlighted in the document.

3. Repeat Step 2 for each additional error. When you've dealt with the final error, the Spelling dialog box will close.

✔ Tips

- You can click Cancel at any time to immediately end the spelling check.
- If you performed the spelling check on selected text, a dialog box appears after the text is checked (**Figure 21.26**). Click Yes to check the rest of the message or click No to end the spelling check.

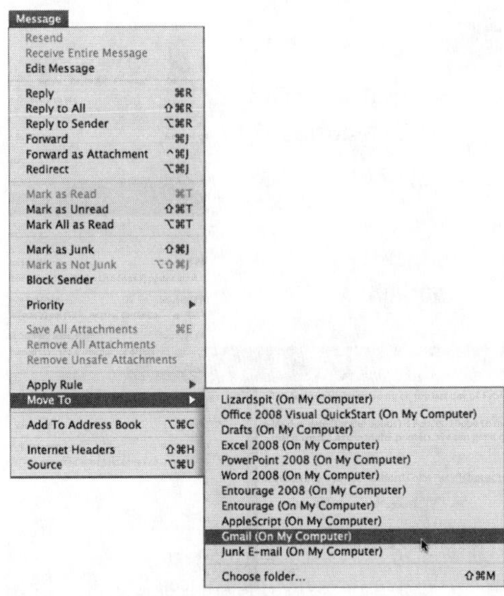

Figure 21.27 You can choose any recently used folder from the Move To submenu.

Figure 21.28 Select the destination folder and click Move. (To create a folder, click the New Folder button.)

Organizing the Mail

When you start receiving a significant amount of email, you'll want to organize it. Entourage provides several tools for this purpose:

- You can organize mail in folders you've created. (To create a folder, choose File > New > Folder, choose Folder from the New toolbar icon's drop-down menu, or press Shift ⌘ N. To create a folder within another folder, select the main folder in the Folders list and choose File > New > Subfolder.)
- You can categorize messages, and then sort or filter the message list based on assigned categories.
- After reading messages, you can delete those that aren't important.
- You can define rules that take specific actions when messages matching your criteria are received.

To move mail to another folder:

1. In the Folders list, select the folder that contains the message you want to move.
2. Select the message(s) you want to move.
3. *Do one of the following:*
   - Drag the selected message header(s) onto the destination folder in the Folders list.
   - Choose a destination folder from the Message > Move To submenu (**Figure 21.27**).
   - To pick the destination folder from a dialog box, choose Message > Move To > Choose folder, press Shift ⌘ M, or Control-click a message header and choose Move To > Choose folder.

   The Move dialog box appears (**Figure 21.28**). Select a destination folder and click Move.

✔ Tip

- To *copy* a message rather than move it, press Option as you drag the message onto the destination folder.

To assign categories to messages:

- To assign a single category to a selected or open message, *do one of the following:*
  - Click the down arrow beside the Categories toolbar icon and choose a category (**Figure 21.29**).
  - Choose a category from the Edit > Categories submenu.
  - Control-click the message header, and choose a category from the Categories submenu of the pop-up menu.
- To assign multiple categories to a selected or open message, *do one of the following:*
  - Click the down arrow beside the Categories toolbar icon and choose Assign Categories (Figure 21.29).
  - Choose Edit > Categories > Assign Categories (⌘;).

  In the Assign Categories dialog box that appears (**Figure 21.30**), click the check box beside each category that you want to assign to the message. Then click OK.

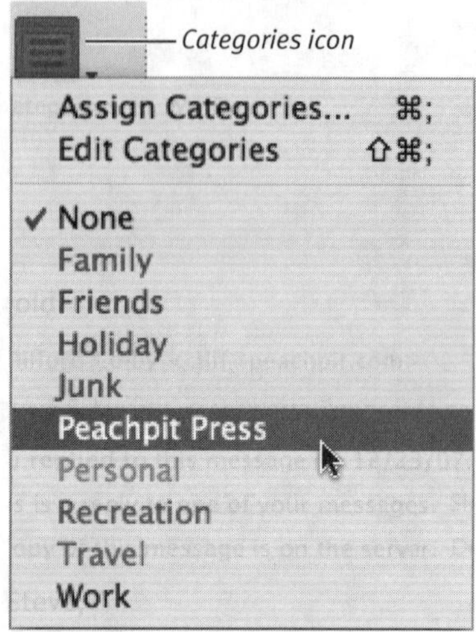

Figure 21.29 You can choose a category by clicking the Categories toolbar icon.

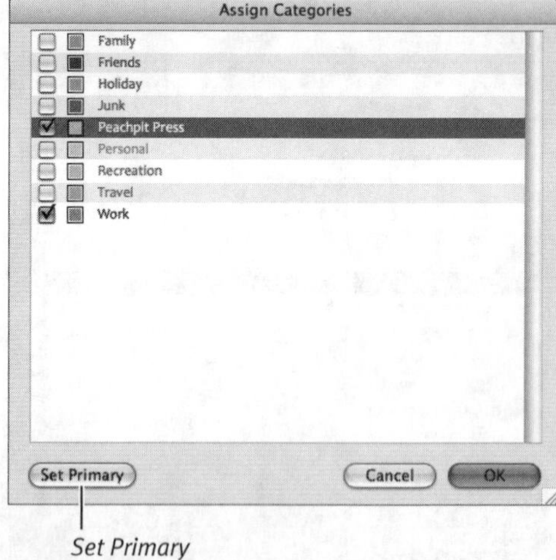

Figure 21.30 Select categories to assign to the message and (optionally) set one of them as primary.

✔ Tips

- When you assign multiple categories to a message, you can specify which category is most important by making it the *primary category*. In Entourage lists, the primary category is always listed first for each item. To set or change the primary category for a selected message, select the category in the Assign Categories dialog box (Figure 21.30) and click the Set Primary button.
- To clear all categories assigned to an item, select None (Figure 21.29). To clear individual categories for the item, select those categories again.
- If you assign a category to a contact in the Address Book, future email from or to the contact will automatically be assigned that category.

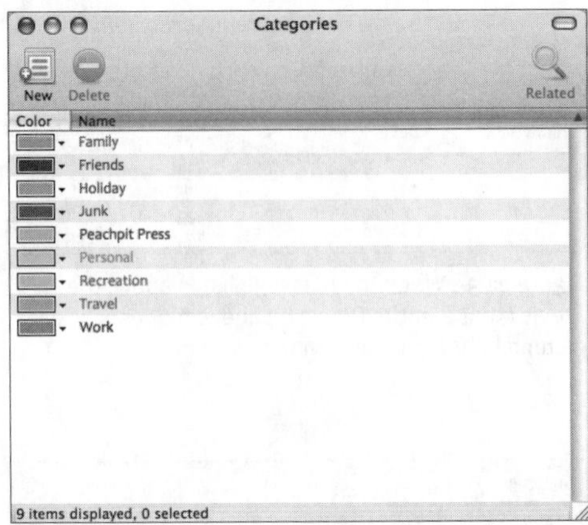

Figure 21.31 You can edit existing categories and create new ones in the Categories dialog box.

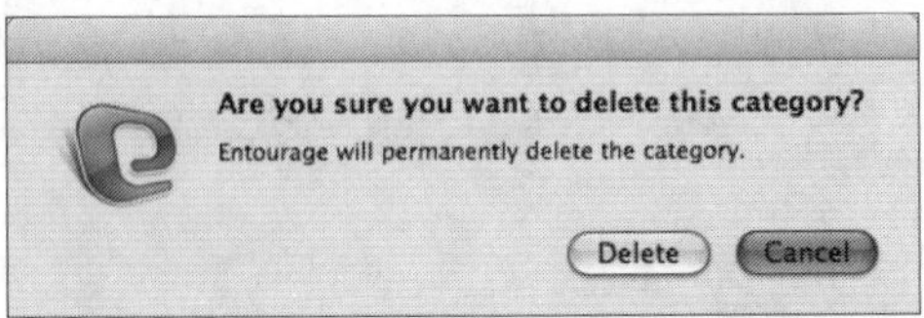

Figure 21.32 You must confirm a category deletion by clicking the Delete button.

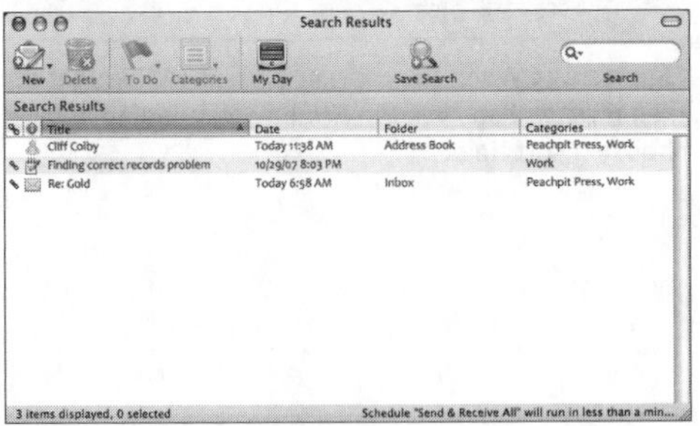

Figure 21.33 All items associated with the category are listed in a Search Results window. To view a found item, double-click it. When you're done, close the Search Results window.

To edit the category list:

1. *Do either of the following:*
   - ▲ Click the down arrow beside the Categories toolbar icon and choose Edit Categories (see Figure 21.29).
   - ▲ Choose Edit > Categories > Edit Categories (Shift⌘;).

   The Categories dialog box appears (**Figure 21.31**).
2. To create a new category, click the New toolbar icon. An Untitled category appears. Name the category, and select a color to associate with the category by clicking the Color icon beside its name.
3. To rename a category, click its name. Doing so makes the name editable.
4. To change a category's color, choose a color from the Color pop-up menu beside its name.
5. To delete a category, select it, click the Delete toolbar icon, and confirm the deletion in the dialog box that appears (**Figure 21.32**).
6. When you're done making changes, close the Categories dialog box.

✔ Tips

- Try not to duplicate category colors. To assign a custom color to a category, choose Other from the Color pop-up menu.
- You can assign categories to *any* type of Entourage item, such as contact records, notes, and calendar events. To view a list of all items that have been assigned a given category (**Figure 21.33**), select the category name in the Categories dialog box and click the Related toolbar icon.

To sort the messages in a folder:

1. Select a folder in the Folders list.
2. *Do one of the following:*
   - ▲ If the Preview pane is below the message list or is hidden (**Figure 21.34**), click a column heading to sort by that column. (The current sort column is displayed in blue.)

     To toggle between an ascending and descending sort, click the column heading again.
   - ▲ If the Preview pane is to the right of the message list, click the Arrange By heading above the message list and specify the data on which you want to sort (**Figure 21.35**).

     To toggle between an ascending and descending sort, click the text to the right of Arrange By, such as Newest on top.

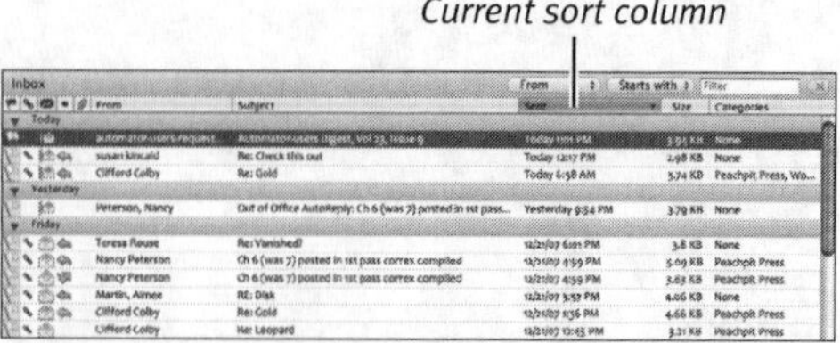

Figure 21.34 When the message list is above the Preview pane or the Preview pane is hidden, click a column heading to sort on that column.

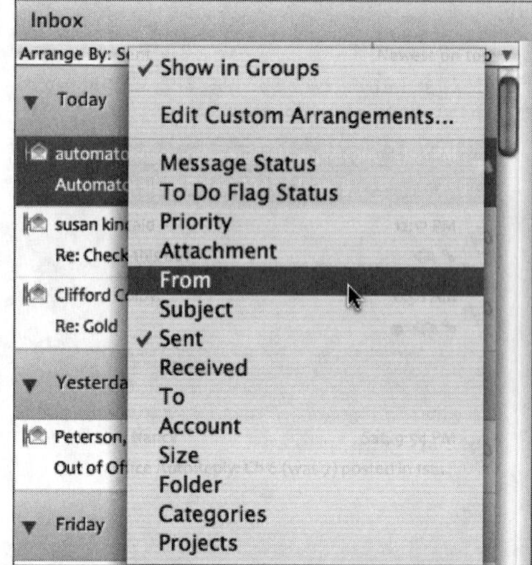

Figure 21.35 When the Preview pane is to the right of the message list, click the Arrange By heading and choose a sort field.

✔ Tips

- Every folder can have a different sort field.
- Long a feature of newsgroup readers, the ability to *group* email messages in any way that's convenient is also an Entourage feature. For instance, if you group messages by Subject, you can view all related messages together rather than scattered throughout the message list.

  Enable Show in Groups by choosing View > Arrange By > Show in Groups or by choosing Show in Groups from the Arrange By drop-down menu (Figure 21.35). Then choose a grouping method (such as From, Date, or Subject) from the View > Arrange By submenu or from the Arrange By heading above the message list (Figure 21.35).
- You can also *filter* any message list to make it easier to find certain messages. See Chapter 20 for filtering information.

Create a new rule

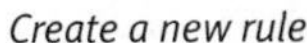

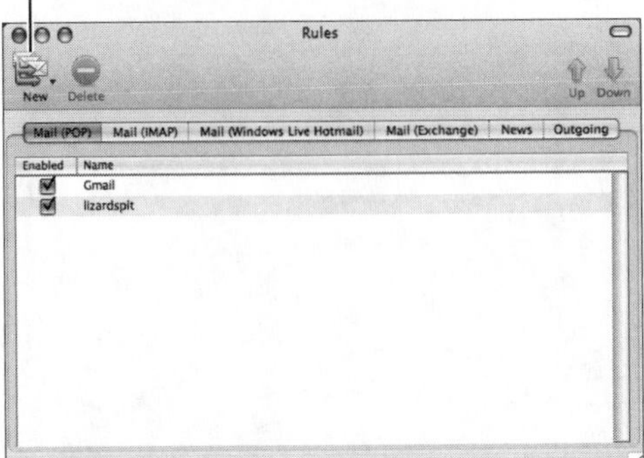

Figure 21.36 To create a new message rule, click the appropriate Mail tab and then click New.

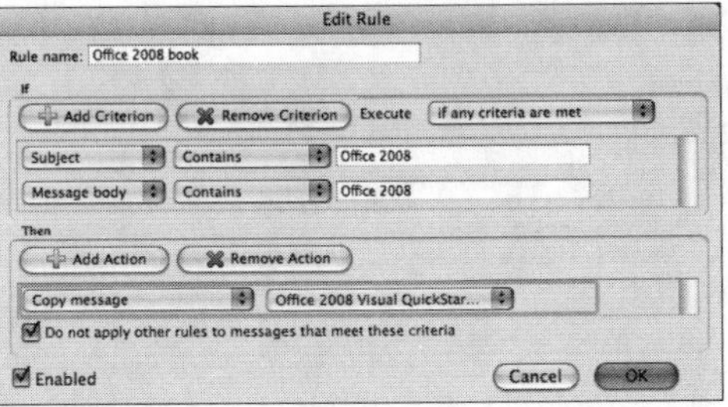

Figure 21.37 Name the message rule, specify criteria, and set actions. This rule scans each message's Subject and text for the phrase `Office 2008`. If found, the message is copied into the designated folder.

- Although rules are automatically applied to new messages, you can also apply a rule to *existing* messages. Select a folder in the Folders list. Choose Message > Apply Rule, followed by the rule you want to run.

To delete unwanted messages:

- Select the message(s) in the message list, and *do one of the following:*
  - Press Delete or ⌘ Delete.
  - Choose Edit > Delete Message.
  - Control-click the message header, and choose Delete Message from the pop-up menu that appears.
  - Drag the message header onto the account's Deleted items folder.

  Deleted messages are stored in the Deleted items folder until it is emptied.

To create rules for processing email:

1. Choose Tools > Rules.

   The Rules dialog box appears (**Figure 21.36**).
2. Click a Mail tab for the type of email to which you want the rule to apply, and then click the New toolbar icon.

   The Edit Rule dialog box appears.
3. Name the rule, specify the criteria that will trigger the rule, and specify the actions that will be taken (**Figure 21.37**).
4. Ensure that Enabled is checked. (Only enabled rules will be processed.)
5. Click OK.

   The Rules dialog box reappears, and the new rule is added to the list.
6. Close the Rules dialog box.

✔ Tips

- Click toolbar icons in the Rules dialog box to delete a selected rule or move it up or down in the processing order. (Higher rules are processed first.)
- You can temporarily disable a rule by clearing its Enabled check mark in the Rules dialog box.

Managing Mailing Lists

Internet mailing lists allow people with a common interest to connect. They provide subscribers with an email-based forum for conducting discussions, asking questions, and sharing experiences. When you're a member of a mailing list, you receive copies of all messages sent to the list. And when you post a message, everyone who subscribes to the list will receive a copy of your message. You can use the Mailing List Manager to handle your list subscriptions.

To manage a mailing list subscription:

1. Select a received message from the list and choose Tools > Mailing List Manager.
   The Mailing List Manager dialog box appears (**Figure 21.38**).
2. Click the New toolbar icon.
   The Edit Mailing List Rule dialog box appears (**Figure 21.39**).
3. Name the mailing list, type or paste the list address (if it isn't already filled in), and specify where messages to and from the list should be stored.
4. *Optional:* Review options on the Advanced tab and make any desired changes, such as marking all new messages as read.
5. Click OK.
   The new mailing list is recorded in the Mailing List Manager dialog box.

✔ Tips

- To change the settings for a mailing list, double-click its name in the Mailing List Manager dialog box.
- A mailing list subscription can flood your Inbox with dozens of individual messages per day. If the list allows it, subscribe in *digest mode* to request that each day's messages be combined into one message.

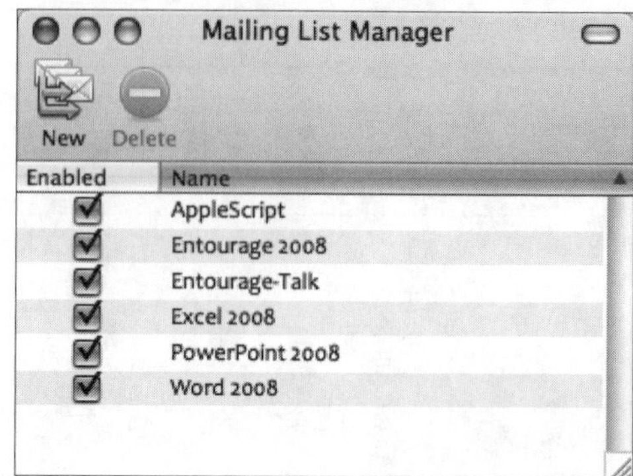

Figure 21.38 In the Mailing List Manager dialog box, you can add new mailing list subscriptions, edit existing ones, and delete others.

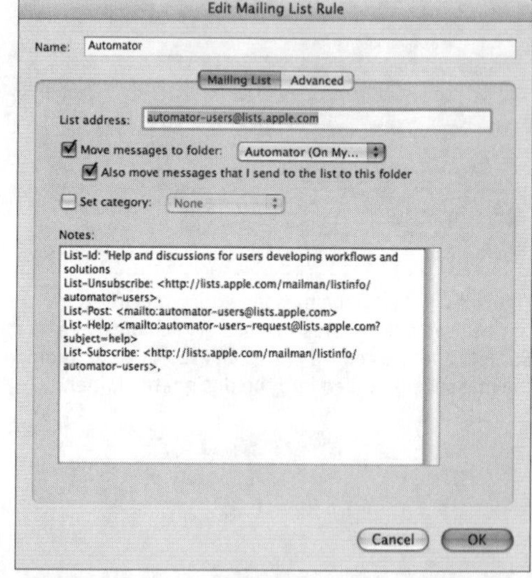

Figure 21.39 Specify the list address and actions to be taken on list messages.

- To make it easier to find list messages, you can create a separate folder for each list. For example, I created a Mailing Lists folder and—within it—a subfolder for each list. Then in each list's rule, I specified that all messages to and from the list should be moved into the list folder.

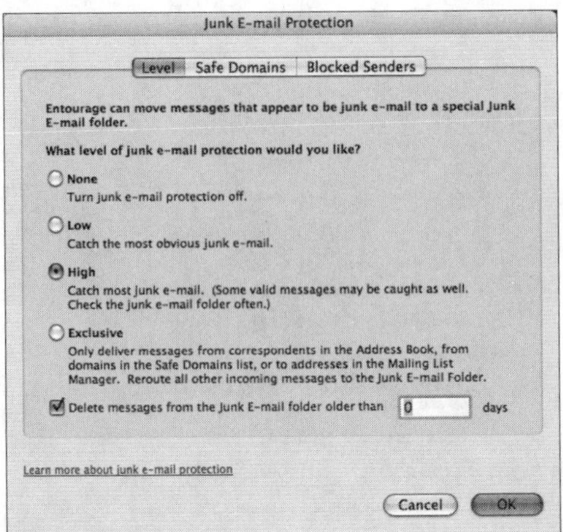

Figure 21.40 On the Level tab, specify a filtering level to use to identify incoming junk mail.

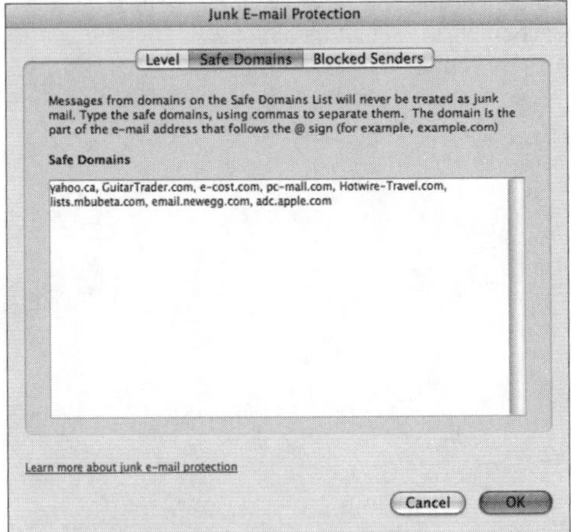

Figure 21.41 On the Safe Domains tab, enter a comma-delimited list of trusted domains. Doing so prevents their messages from being classified as junk.

- To classify a received message as junk, select or open it and click the Junk toolbar icon.
- If a message is mistakenly classified as junk, select or open it, click the Not Junk icon or This is not junk e-mail (at the top of the message), and select a handling option from the dialog box that appears.

Handling Junk Mail

Anyone with an email account will eventually receive junk mail (*spam*). If you use your regular email address to register on Web sites or if you send email to corporations, newsgroups, or mailing lists, your volume of received junk mail is liable to increase. Using the Junk E-mail Protection feature, you can filter out much of this time-wasting mail.

To filter out suspected junk mail:

1. Choose Tools > Junk E-mail Protection.
   The Junk E-mail Protection dialog box appears.
2. On the Level tab (**Figure 21.40**), select the desired protection level.
   When received, suspected junk email is automatically assigned the Junk category and is moved into the Junk E-mail folder.
3. To instruct Entourage to automatically delete junk mail after a period of time, click the Delete messages from the Junk E-mail folder older than *X* days check box and enter a number in the text box.
4. *Optional:* On the Safe Domains tab (**Figure 21.41**), list the *domains* (the part of an email address after the @ sign) whose mail should never be classified as junk. Separate entries with commas.
   On the Blocked Senders tabs, enter the list of domains and email addresses that should *always* be treated as junk.
5. Click OK to save the new settings.

✔ Tips

- You can specify other actions for junk mail by creating message rules.
- To prevent Entourage from classifying mail from certain individuals as junk, create Address Book records for them (see Chapter 22).

Email Security

Entourage 2008 offers two types of security for your messages. First, you can *digitally sign* messages, assuring recipients that they actually came from you. Second, messages can be *encrypted*, allowing only recipients with the proper software key to decode and read them. While most users won't bother with either of these features, corporate and government employees are likely to find them useful.

Before you can employ either feature, you must obtain a *digital ID* from an authorized issuer, such as VeriSign (`www.verisign.com`). The digital ID can be used for both encryption and digital signing.

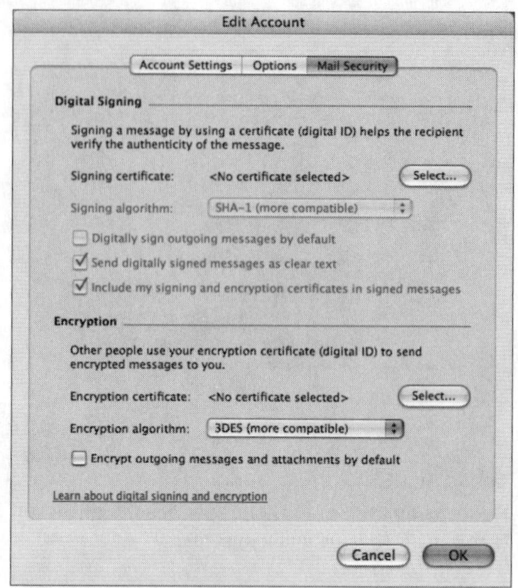

Figure 21.42 On the Mail Security tab of the Edit Account dialog box, record your digital ID and set encryption and signature options.

To enable encryption and/or a digital signature for an email account:

1. Choose Tools > Accounts.
   The Accounts dialog box appears.
2. On the Mail tab of the Accounts dialog box, double-click the account for which you want to enable encryption or a digital signature.
   The Edit Account dialog box for the account appears.
3. Click the Mail Security tab (**Figure 21.42**).
4. To specify a certificate for digital signing, click the top Select button.
5. To select a certificate to use for encryption, click the bottom Select button.
6. Set encryption and digital signing options by clicking check boxes and making selections from the drop-down lists.
7. Click OK to close the Edit Account dialog box.
8. Close the Accounts dialog box.

✔ Tip

- To manually enable a digital signature or encryption for an outgoing message, choose Message > Security > Digitally Sign Message or Encrypt Message, respectively.

Figure 21.43 A message folder in MBOX format.

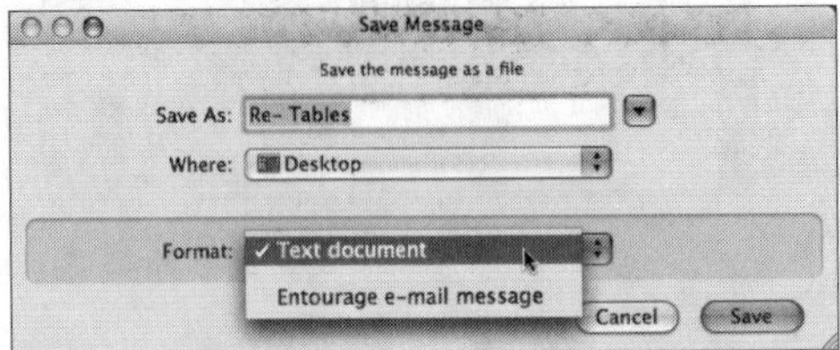

Figure 21.44 In the Save Message dialog box, choose a message format and a location in which to save the message.

- You can also back up a single message by selecting its message header and choosing File > Save As (**Figure 21.44**).
- When dragging an MBOX file into the Folders list, you *must* drag it onto an existing folder, such as the Inbox. After the move is finished, you can move the folder to the same level as the Inbox by dragging it onto Folders on My Computer in the Folders list.

Backing Up Email

Entourage provides an extraordinarily easy way to back up any message folder. If necessary, the backed-up folder can later be imported into the same copy of Entourage, into a different copy (when copying messages to your laptop, for example), or into any other Mac or Windows program that supports the MBOX text format.

To back up a message folder:

◆ Select a folder in the Folders list (such as the Inbox, for example) and drag it onto the Desktop.

  Entourage creates a backup of all messages in the folder using the MBOX text format (**Figure 21.43**). If the dragged folder also contains subfolders that you want to back up, they must be dragged separately onto the Desktop.

To import an MBOX message folder:

◆ *Do one of the following:*
  - ▲ Drag the MBOX file onto a folder in Entourage's Folders list. The imported folder is created as a subfolder within the destination folder.
  - ▲ Choose File > Import. In the Import wizard, choose Contacts or messages from a text file, and then choose Import messages from an MBOX-format text file. In the Import Mail dialog box, select the MBOX file and click Import. A new email folder appears in the Folders list.

✔ Tips

- You can also use the File > Export command to export email messages from a selected folder.
- To back up only selected messages, drag their message headers onto the Desktop.

Printing Messages

As is the case with other Entourage components, printing messages is accomplished using a nonstandard Print dialog box (**Figure 21.45**). The Quick Preview box reflects the selected print options and settings.

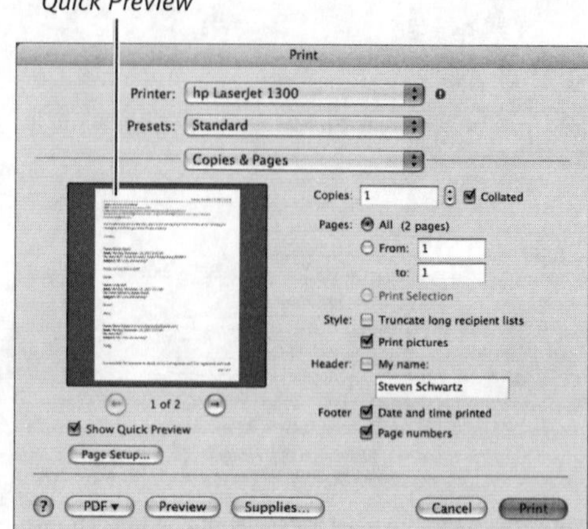

Figure 21.45 Specify print options in the Print dialog box, and then click Print.

To print a message:

1. Switch to the Mail section of Entourage.
2. Select the header of the message you want to print or open the message in its own window.
3. *Optional:* To print only selected text from the message, select the text.
4. Choose File > Print (⌘P).
   The Print dialog box appears.
5. Select a printer to use from the Printer drop-down list.
6. Indicate the number of copies to print, whether copies should be collated (when printing multiple copies), and whether to print all pages or a page range.
   If you preselected message text in Step 3, Print Selection will automatically be chosen rather than a page range.
7. Set options in the Style, Header, and Footer sections.
8. If you need to specify a different paper size or orientation, click Page Setup.
9. Click Print to generate the printout.

✔ Tips

- To decide which pages to print, flip through the pages in the Quick Preview.
- If a message is open in its own window and you click the Print toolbar icon, the Print dialog box is bypassed. The message is immediately printed using the default print settings.

22

Address Book

The Entourage Address Book is the repository of your contact information for people, companies, and organizations. In addition to the standard information normally stored in an address book (such as name, home and work addresses, phone numbers, and email addresses), an Address Book record can hold a birth date, picture, anniversary date, spouse's name, children's names, and notes. If you feel that an important bit of data is missing, you can even define custom fields.

✔ Tips

- While you'll probably create and edit most of your contact records from within Entourage, the contact information is also available to you from Word's Contact toolbar. Using the toolbar, you can create new records, insert contact data into documents (to address letters, for example), and perform mail merges. For more information, see Chapter 8.
- Office 2008 supports multiple users (called *identities*). In addition to having separate email, each user who shares a copy of Office on a Mac has a separate Address Book. To learn how to switch from one user to another, see the tip at the end of "Emailing Office Documents" in Chapter 31.
- In addition to the Address Book that's stored on your Mac, Exchange Server users can create additional address books that are kept on the server. Those address books can be shared with or delegated to other users. For information about these capabilities, see Chapter 28.

Adding Contacts

If you're currently using another program to manage your address data, Entourage can import address information from two popular programs and exported text files.

You can also add contact records manually or create them from received email. (Note that if an earlier version of Entourage is installed on your Mac, your existing data will be imported on Entourage's first run.)

Importing an address book

There's nothing more painful than having to re-create an address book simply because you've changed programs or upgraded to a new version. Happily, Entourage can import contact data from many programs.

To import an existing address book:

1. Choose File > Import.
   The Import wizard appears, displaying the Begin Import screen (**Figure 22.1**).
2. *Select one of these options:*
   - ▲ **Entourage information from an archive or earlier version.** If you decided not to import data from an existing version of Entourage during the Office 2008 setup, you can do so now. This option is also useful if you've created an archive on another computer (such as a laptop) that you want to import into this copy of Entourage.
   - ▲ **Information from another application.** Select this option to import data from Apple Mail or Qualcomm Eudora.

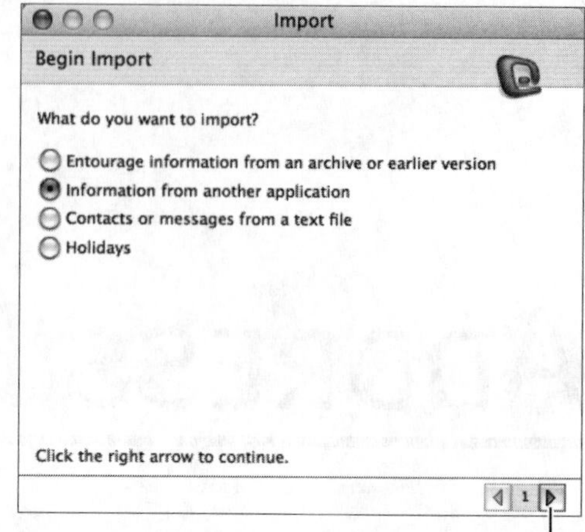

Figure 22.1 In the Import wizard's first screen, select an import option and then click the right arrow icon.

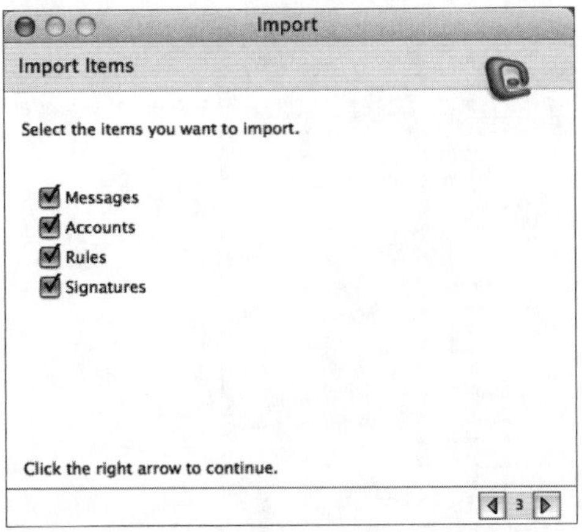

Figure 22.2 If you import data from Mail or Eudora, you can specify the types of data to import.

- ▲ **Contacts or messages from a text file.** For any other email, utility, or database application in which you've stored contact records, select this option if you're able to export the data as a tab- or comma-delimited text file or as an MBOX file.

Click the right-arrow icon to continue.

3. Depending on the option chosen in Step 2, you will be asked to select a program from which to import, select a data file to import, and/or specify the types of data to import (**Figure 22.2**). Follow the directions in the remaining screens.

✔ Tips

- If you're asked which items you want to import, make sure that Contacts is checked—this is your address data. Depending on the import method you select, you may also be able to import other Entourage-compatible data, such as calendar events and mail.
- Programs and utilities can sometimes export in multiple formats. Some formats may be easier to import into Entourage than others.
- MBOX is the file format in which Entourage stores its data. When electing to import another program's data in this format, you should note that not all MBOX files are created equal. If the data doesn't import correctly, try exporting it to one of the delimited text formats.
- Be very careful not to import ant type of data twice. Eliminating the hundreds or thousands of *duplicate* messages and contact records that can result is a major chore. (If you do end up with duplicates, one tactic is to simply remove Office 2008 and then reinstall.)

Creating contact records from email messages

You can extract email addresses from received messages and use them as the basis for new contact records.

To create a contact record from a received message:

1. *Do one of the following:*
   - ▲ Select the message header in the message list and choose Message > Add to Address Book (Option ⌘ C).
   - ▲ Control-click the message header in the message list, and choose Add Sender To Address Book from the pop-up menu that appears (**Figure 22.3**).
   - ▲ Select the message header in the message list. At the top of the Preview pane, Control-click any email address in the header section of the message. Choose Add to Address Book from the pop-up menu that appears (**Figure 22.4**). You can also select other recipients—not just the sender. (If a contact record for the selected address already exists, Add to Address Book won't be shown in the pop-up menu.)

   The contact record for the new address book entry appears.
2. Fill in as much additional contact information for the person, company, or organization as you like (**Figure 22.5**). Click tabs to move from one section to another.
3. *Do one of the following:*
   - ▲ **No edits.** Click the close box (red *X*).
   - ▲ **Edits.** Save your changes by choosing File > Save (⌘ S). If you simply close an edited record, a dialog box prompting you to save will appear.

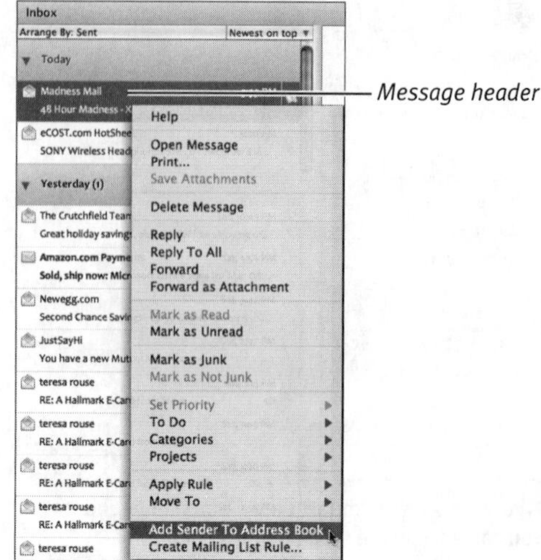

Figure 22.3 You can Control-click a message header and choose Add Sender To Address Book.

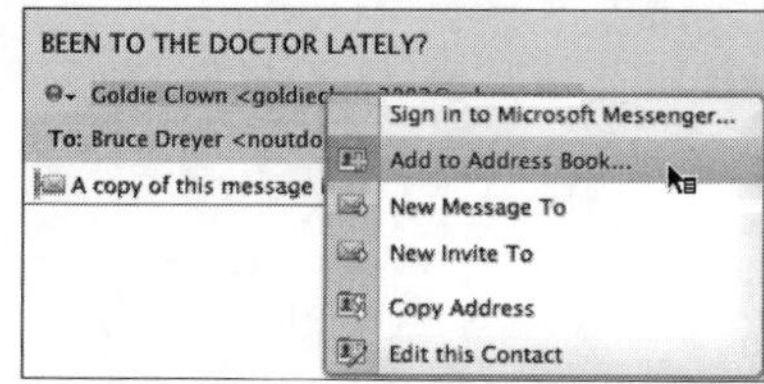

Figure 22.4 You can Control-click any new address displayed at the top of the Preview Pane and choose Add to Address Book.

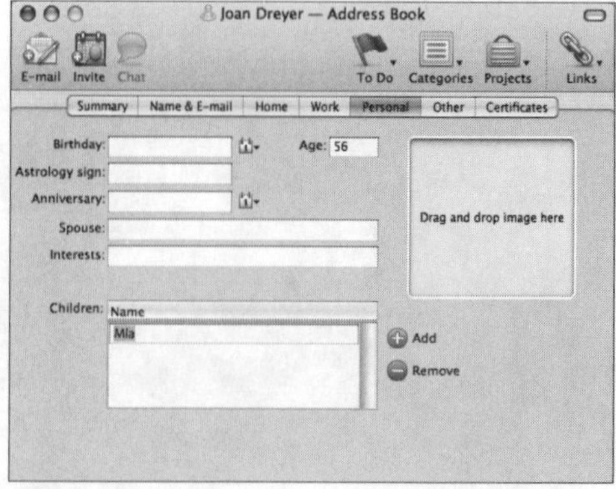

Figure 22.5 Enter additional information for the new contact record.

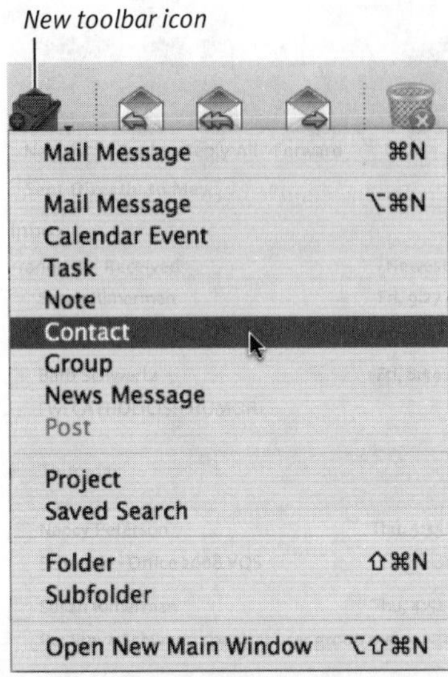

Figure 22.6 You can create a contact record by clicking the down arrow beside the New icon and choosing Contact.

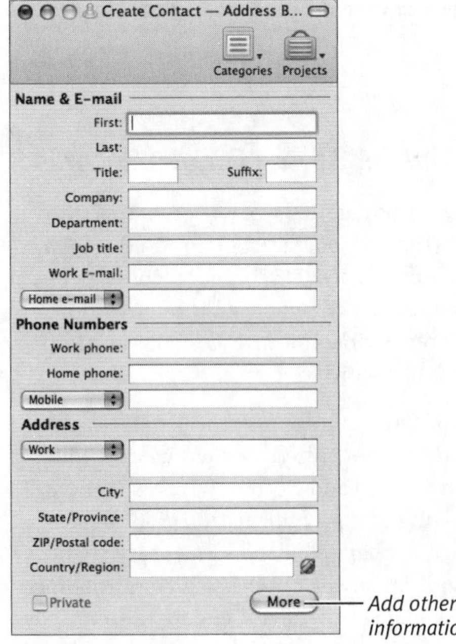

Figure 22.7 Enter essential contact information in the Create Contact dialog box.

Manually creating new records

You can also create new contact records from scratch.

To create a new contact record:

1. *Do one of the following:*
   - ▲ If the Address Book window is currently displayed, click the New toolbar icon or press ⌘N.
   - ▲ Regardless of the part of Entourage that is displayed, you can choose File > New > Contact or click the down arrow beside the New toolbar icon and choose Contact (**Figure 22.6**).

   The Create Contact dialog box appears (**Figure 22.7**).
2. Enter the basic information for the contact.
3. *Do one of the following:*
   - ▲ If you're done entering information, choose File > Save (⌘S). If you simply close the new record, a dialog box prompting you to save will appear.
   - ▲ If you want to enter additional information, click the More button. The individual's full record appears (see Figure 22.5). Enter any information that you want, clicking tabs to view other sections of the record.

     When you're finished, choose File > Save (⌘S). If you simply close the new record, a dialog box prompting you to save will appear.

Deleting Contacts

There are several ways to permanently remove contact records from the Entourage Address Book.

To delete contacts:

1. Switch to the Address Book by clicking the Address Book icon in the upper-left corner of the Entourage window (**Figure 22.8**), choosing View > Go To > Address Book, or pressing ⌘2.
2. In the contact list, select one or more contact records to delete. (You can Shift-click to select contiguous records or ⌘-click to select noncontiguous records.)
3. Click the Delete toolbar icon (**Figure 22.9**), choose Edit > Delete Contact (or Delete Selected Items), press Delete, or press ⌘Delete.
   A confirmation dialog box appears (**Figure 22.10**).
4. *Do one of the following:*
   - ▲ To delete the selected contact(s), click the Delete button.
   - ▲ If you've changed your mind, click the Cancel button.

Figure 22.8 Click the second icon to work with the Address Book.

Figure 22.9 Click the Delete toolbar icon to delete the selected record(s).

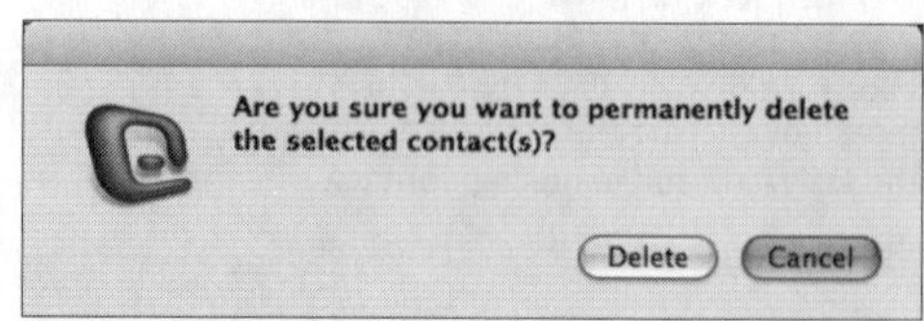

Figure 22.10 Record deletions must be confirmed.

✔ Tips

- If a contact record is open in its own window, you can delete it by choosing Edit > Delete Contact or pressing ⌘Delete.
- You can also Control-click selected records in a contact list, and choose Delete Contact (or Delete Selected Items) from the pop-up menu that appears.
- Deleting a contact record is immediate and permanent. Deleted records are *not* moved to the Deleted Items folder.

Tips for Saving Contact Records

In Entourage 2004, open contact records had a Save toolbar icon. To add this icon to Entourage 2008 contact records, open a contact record, choose View > Customize Toolbar, drag the Save icon into position on the record toolbar, and click Done.

To instruct Entourage to automatically save new or edited contact records, edit any record and close its window without saving. In the confirmation dialog box that appears, click the Always save changes without asking check box. (To restore the original Save behavior, choose Entourage > Preferences, select Notification in the General Preferences section, and click the Reset Confirmation Dialogs button.)

Figure 22.11 Click the various tabs to display and edit the contact data.

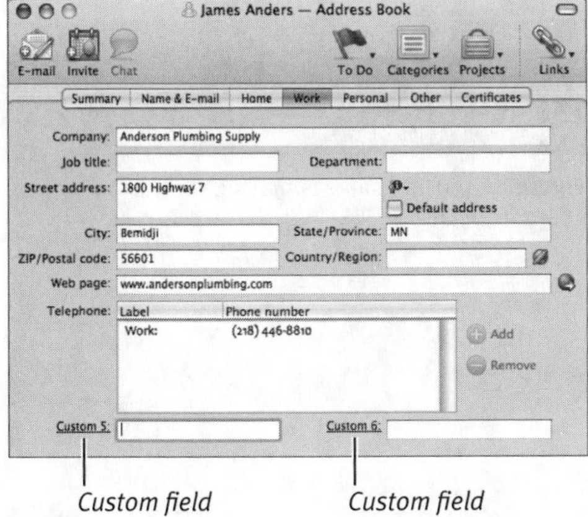

Figure 22.12 Click a Custom field's label to rename it.

Figure 22.13 Rename the custom field and click OK.

Editing Contact Records

People occasionally move, change jobs, or get new email addresses. You're free to make additions and changes to your contact records.

To edit contact information:

1. Switch to the Address Book.
2. In the contact list, double-click the contact you want to edit.

   The selected contact record opens in its own window.
3. Click a tab at the top of the window to select the type of information you want to edit (**Figure 22.11**) and then make the desired changes.
4. If desired, click other tabs to make additional changes. When you're done editing, choose File > Save (⌘S).

✔ Tips

- You can synchronize your contacts and calendar events with an iPod, iPod Touch, or iPhone using iTunes or Sync Services. For instructions, see "Synchronizing Entourage with an iPod" in Chapter 20.
- To help you better identify people, you can store a picture as part of any contact record (Figure 22.11). Open the record, click the Personal tab, and drag the icon of any image file into the gray square. To remove a picture, drag it to the Trash.
- Several tabs contain Custom fields. You can rename a Custom field by clicking the underlined *Custom* label (**Figure 22.12**). Name the field in the Edit Custom Label dialog box (**Figure 22.13**). The new field name will appear on *all* contact records.

Electronic Business Cards (vCards)

You may occasionally receive electronic business cards (*vCards*) as attachments to email. You can recognize them by the .vcf filename extension. Entourage can read and create new contact records from vCards. You can also email contact records to others as vCard attachments.

To add a received vCard to the Address Book:

1. Select the message header in the message list. If necessary, click the Attachments triangle to open the Attachments pane and display the vCard (**Figure 22.14**).
2. Double-click the vCard attachment.
   A warning message may appear. If so, click the Open button. A new contact record containing the vCard data opens.
3. Make any necessary changes to the contact data, and choose File > Save (⌘S).
   The vCard is added to your Address Book as a new contact record.

✔ Tips

- There's another way to add a received vCard to your Address Book. Open the email message in its own window, switch to the Address Book section of Entourage, and drag the vCard attachment into the contact list.
- You may also receive vCards as files on disk (**Figure 22.15**) rather than as email attachments. To create a new record from such a vCard, open Entourage, switch to the Address Book section, and drag the vCard file icon into the address list.

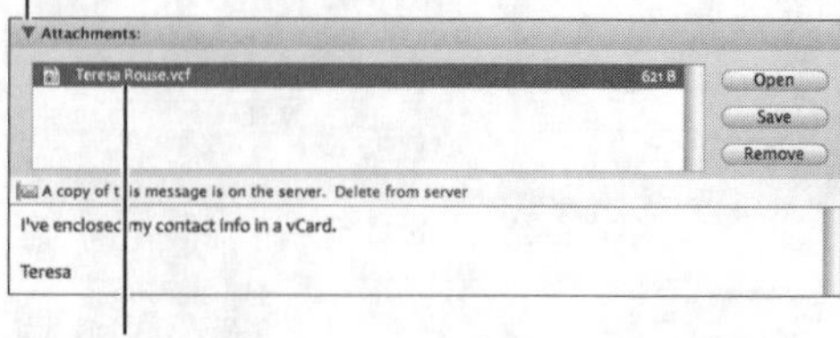

Figure 22.14 A vCard (.vcf) attachment in an incoming message is listed in the Attachments pane like any other attachment.

Figure 22.15 This is an example of a vCard file icon.

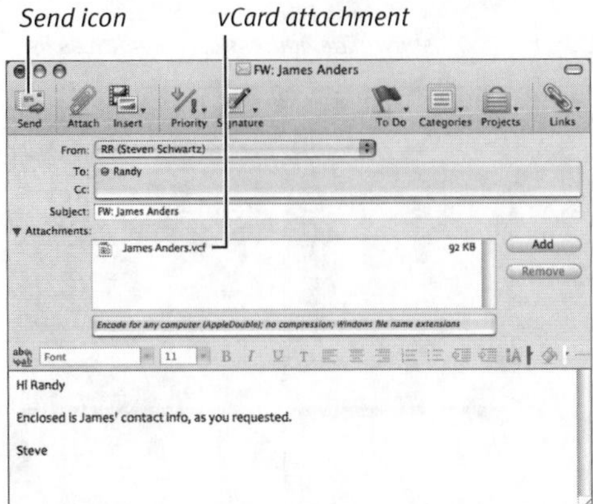

Figure 22.16 The selected contact record is added as a vCard attachment to a new message.

To email a vCard:

1. Switch to the Address Book section of Entourage. In the contact list, select the contact record you want to send as a vCard.

   You can select your own record or any other record in the Address Book.

2. Choose Contact > Forward as vCard (⌘J).

   A new email message opens that contains the vCard file as an attachment.

3. Fill in the address information and body of the message. (The Subject is already filled in for you, although you are free to change it.) You can add other attachments, if you wish.

   The selected address record is included in the Attachments pane as a vCard file (**Figure 22.16**).

4. To send the message, click the Send icon at the top of the message window.

✔ Tips

- To send *multiple* contact records as vCards, simply select all the desired records from the contact list before choosing Contact > Forward as vCard.
- You can also send a contact record as a vCard by dragging the record from the contact list into an open email message. (Note that *any* file dragged into an email message is automatically treated as an attachment.)

Addressing Email from the Address Book

In Chapter 21, you learned the most common methods of addressing email. You can also address email directly from the Address Book.

To address email from the Address Book:

1. Switch to the Address Book section of Entourage.
2. In the contact list, select the person or people to whom you want to send the message.
3. *Do one of the following:*
   - ▲ Choose Contact > New Message To (⌘R).
   - ▲ Control-click any selected contact record and choose New Message To from the pop-up menu that appears.

   A new message window opens, addressed to the selected contact(s).

Address Book icon (show/hide address list)

Address list

Open an Address Book on an Exchange Server

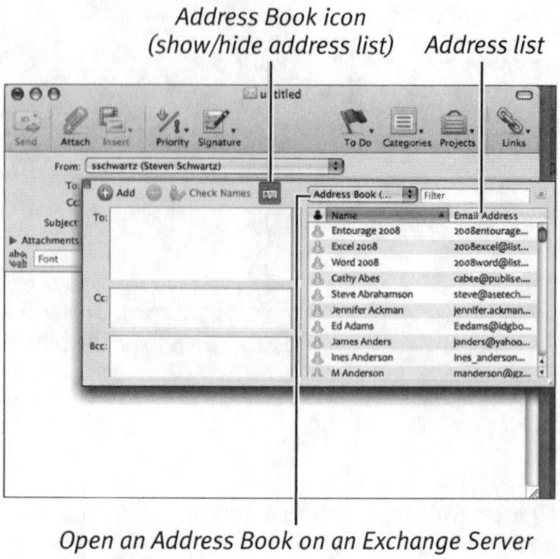

Figure 22.17 When addressing email, you can optionally display your address list.

✔ Tips

- To rearrange contacts in the To, Cc, and Bcc sections of the address pane, drag the contacts to where you want them.
- You can also address messages by dragging contact records from the address list into the To, Cc, or Bcc area of an outgoing message's address pane.
- Regardless of how you're creating a message, it can be convenient to have the address list displayed when selecting recipients. Open the address pane of an outgoing message and click the Address Book icon (**Figure 22.17**). To add a new recipient, click in the To, Cc, or Bcc area, and double-click the name in the address list. You can also drag names from the address list into the address pane.
- If you have a Microsoft Exchange Server account, you can also open Address Books that you've created on the server, as well as the address books of other Exchange users. Select the Address Book you want to use from the drop-down list (Figure 22.17).

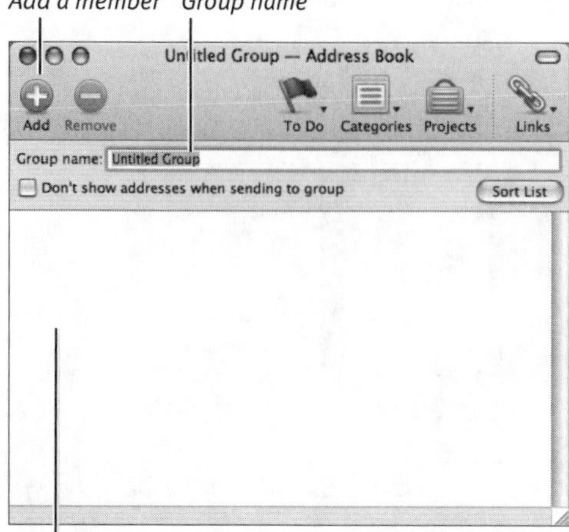

Figure 22.18 Specify the group's membership in the Group window.

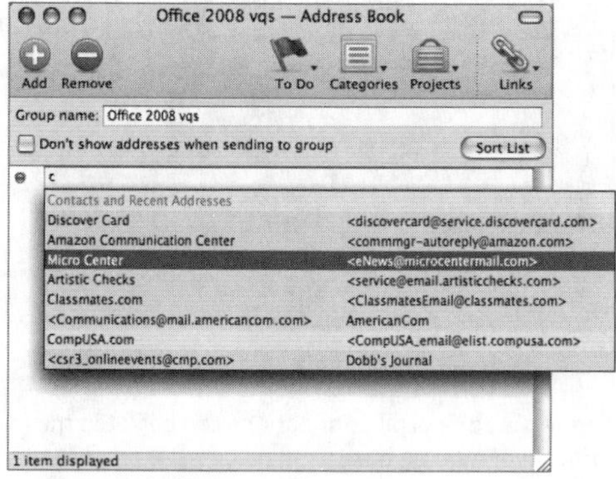

Figure 22.19 Many group members can be added by selecting names from a drop-down list.

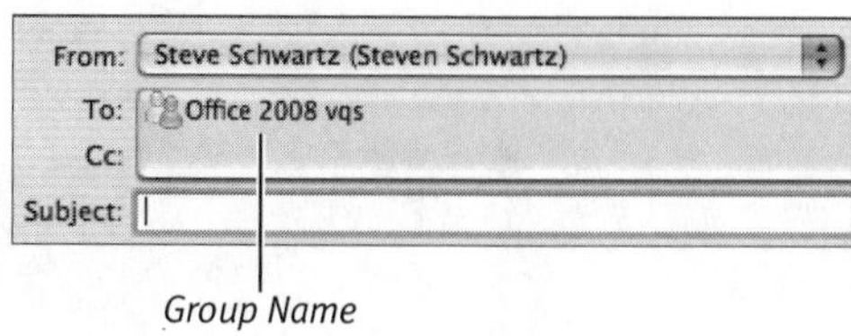

Figure 22.20 Addressing a message to the group name is the equivalent of specifying its members as recipients.

Creating Contact Groups

If you regularly send email to the same set of people, you can define a *group* for them. New emails can then be sent to the group name rather than to the individual email addresses.

To create a contact group:

1. Choose File > New > Group, or click the New toolbar icon and choose Group.

   An Untitled Group window appears (**Figure 22.18**).
2. Enter a name for the group in the Group name box.
3. To add a member to the group, click the Add button or click in the member list box.
4. Begin typing the person's name or email address. A drop-down list of matching contacts appears (**Figure 22.19**), drawn from Address Book records and people with whom you've recently exchanged email.
5. *Do one of the following:*
   - ▲ Select a listed person or company.
   - ▲ To add a person who is not in your Address Book, type the complete email address.
6. To add more members to the group, repeat Steps 3–5.
7. *Optional:* To prevent the display of the group members' email addresses, click Don't show addresses when sending to the group.
8. Click the close button (red *X*). If a confirmation dialog box appears, click Save.

   The group is added as a new contact record. To address mail to the group, enter the group name in the To, Cc, or Bcc box of the message's address pane (**Figure 22.20**).

Printing the Address Book

Using the Print command, you can print one contact record, selected records, or all records (in phone list or address book format).

To print contact records:

1. Switch to the Address Book section.
2. *Optional:* To print only certain records, select the records in the contact list.

   Select a single record, or you can ⌘-click or Shift-click to select multiple records.
3. Choose File > Print (⌘P).

   The Print dialog box appears (**Figure 22.21**).
4. Select a printer to use from the Printer drop-down list.
5. From the Print drop-down menu, choose what you want to print: Selected Contacts, All Contacts, or Flagged Contacts.
6. Choose a print format (Address Book or Phone List) from the Style drop-down menu.
7. If the printout will be used in a personal organizer, such as a Day Runner, choose a style from the Form drop-down menu.
8. To review or change print options, click the Layout button. In the Print Layout dialog box (**Figure 22.22**), make any necessary changes and click OK.
9. Indicate the number of copies to print, whether copies should be collated (when printing multiple copies), and whether to print all pages or a page range.
10. If you need to specify a different paper size or orientation, click Page Setup.
11. Click Print to generate the printout.

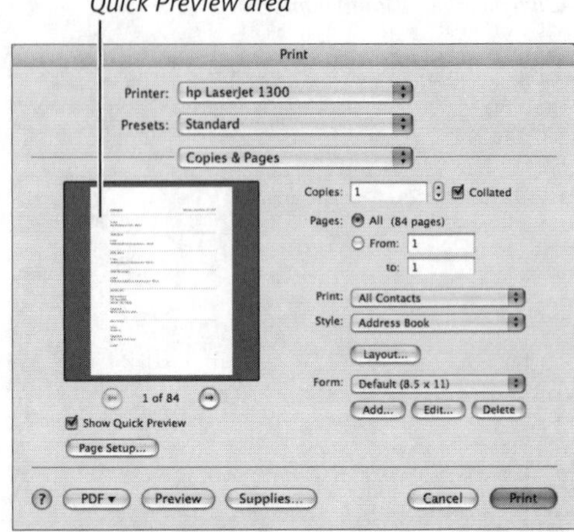

Figure 22.21 Select print settings and click Print.

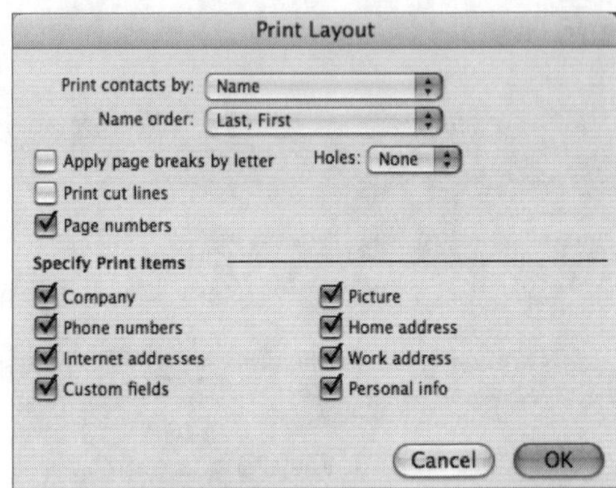

Figure 22.22 Special print options can be set in the Print Layout dialog box.

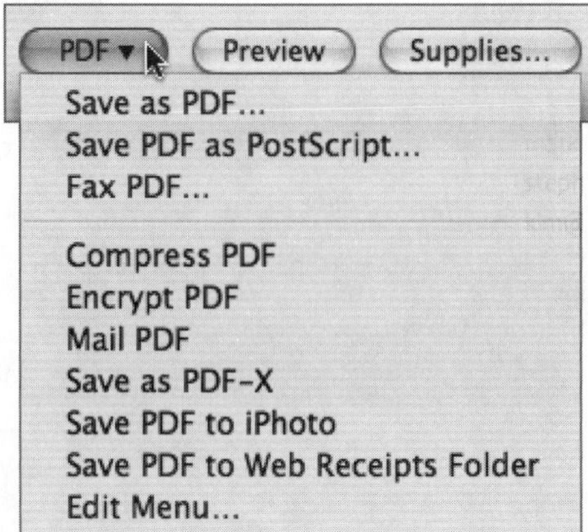

Figure 22.23 In addition to Save as PDF, many other PDF options are available in the Print dialog box (OS X 10.4.11/Tiger shown).

✔ Tips

- You can use these same Print procedures when a contact record is open in its own window.
- To get an idea of what the printout will look like, click the Show Quick Preview check box. The preview changes as you select different print options. Click the arrow buttons beneath the Quick Preview box to review other pages, if any.
- As with other OS X programs, you can create a PDF (Portable Document Format) file from a contacts printout. To save the printout as a PDF file, click the PDF button (**Figure 22.23**) and choose Save As PDF. Or click the Preview button to create a temporary PDF file that will open in the default viewer (Preview or Adobe Reader).

23

Calendar

Entourage provides a calendar you can use to record upcoming appointments and events, whether they occur only once or many times. You can schedule reminders for events, send and receive meeting invitations, and view your calendar in a variety of formats.

Upcoming events can also be viewed in My Day, a new utility program introduced in Office 2008 (see Chapter 27). And if you have an Exchange Server account, you can create and view additional calendars that are stored on the server (see Chapter 28).

Viewing the Calendar

You can change the calendar display in many ways: showing a day, work week, week, or month at a time; hiding or showing the To Do List pane; or displaying only a sequential event list rather than a calendar. In addition to setting a view, you can select the particular date or range of dates you want to see.

To change the calendar view:

1. Switch to the calendar by clicking its icon, clicking Calendar in the Favorites bar, choosing View > Go To > Calendar, or pressing ⌘3.
   The Views pane contains a list of custom calendar views. Below it is a mini calendar. To the right is the current calendar view (showing events for the day, work week, week, or month), and on the far right is the To Do List pane (**Figure 23.1**).

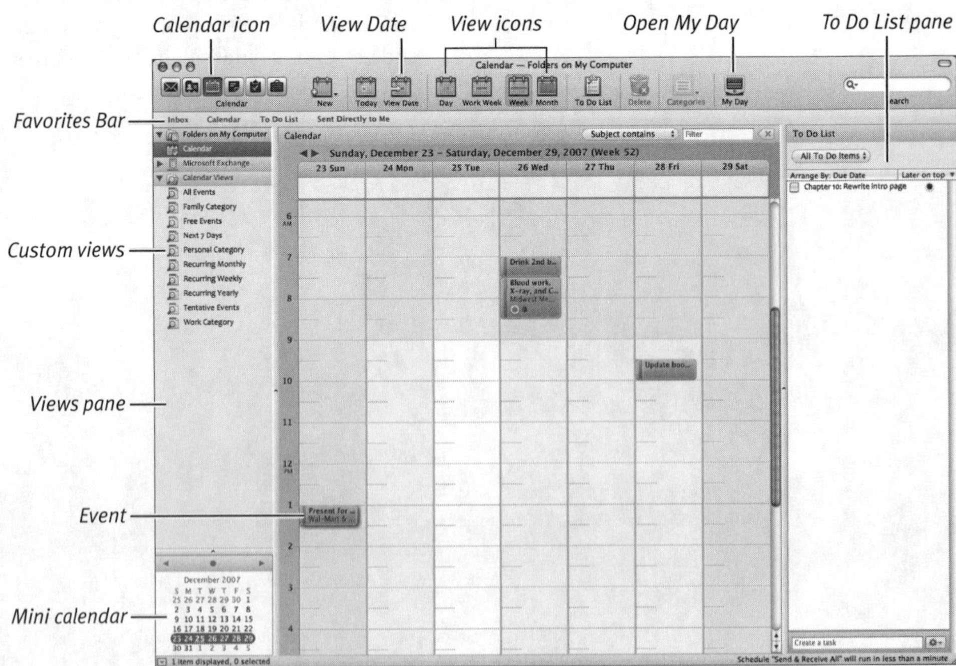

Figure 23.1 To view the calendar, you can click the Calendar icon.

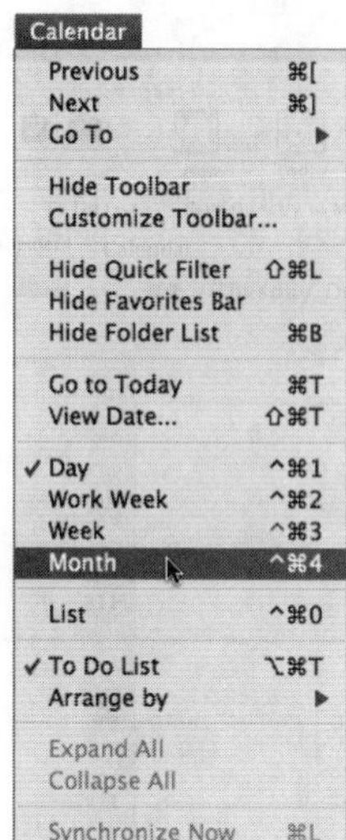

Figure 23.2 You can change the current view by choosing a command from the Calendar menu.

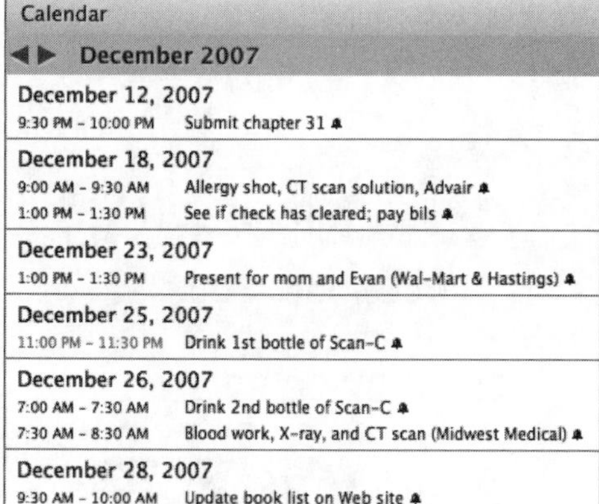

Figure 23.3 Choose Calendar > List to view the list of events for the selected time period.

2. To change the current view, *do either of the following:*
   - ▲ Click the Day, Work Week, Week, or Month toolbar icon.
   - ▲ Choose a command from the Calendar menu (**Figure 23.2**).

   The current date range is displayed using the new view. The active view is indicated by a darkened toolbar icon.

✔ Tips

- Displaying the To Do List pane is optional. To make it appear, click the To Do List toolbar icon or choose Calendar > To Do List (Option⌘T). Issue the command again to hide the pane.
- To display only the list of events for the current view (**Figure 23.3**), choose Calendar > List (Control⌘0). To return to a normal calendar view, click a toolbar icon or choose a Calendar command.
- You can also display a *custom view* in list form (**Figure 23.4**) by selecting it from the Views pane on the left side of the window. To return to a normal view, click Calendar in the Folders list or in the Favorites Bar.
- In some cases, you may not be able to read the full text of an event by just glancing at the calendar. However, if you rest the cursor on the event for a couple of seconds, the full text will be displayed.

Next 7 Days

Title	Date	Folder	Categories	Projects
Drink 1st bottle of Scan-C	Today 11:00 PM	Calendar	None	None
Drink 2nd bottle of Scan-C	Tomorrow 7:00 AM	Calendar	None	None
Blood work, X-ray, and CT scan	Tomorrow 7:30 AM	Calendar	None	None
Update book list on Web site	12/28/07 9:30 AM	Calendar	None	None
Pay mortgage	1/1/08 12:00 AM	Calendar	None	None

Figure 23.4 To see a list of upcoming events, select a custom view. Here is the Next 7 Days custom view.

To view a specific date:

- To select a date to view, *do any of the following:*
  - Click the left and right arrows above the calendar view to scroll until the desired date is visible (**Figure 23.5**).
  - Click the left and right arrows above the mini calendar to scroll until the date you want is visible. (Holding down the mouse button over either arrow makes the calendar scroll quickly through the months.) Click the desired date.
  - Choose Calendar > Previous (⌘[) or Calendar > Next (⌘]) to view the previous or next day, work week, week, or month (depending on the current view).
  - To jump to a specific date, click the View Date toolbar icon or choose Calendar > View Date (Shift⌘T). In the View Date dialog box that appears (**Figure 23.6**), type a date or select it from the pop-up calendar. Click OK.
  - To display today's date, click the Today toolbar icon, choose Calendar > Go to Today, press ⌘T, or click the View Date icon and click OK in the View Date dialog box. (The default date is always today.)

  The selected date is displayed in the current view.

✔ Tips

- To restrict the calendar to showing a particular date range, you can drag-select from one to six weeks in the mini calendar (**Figure 23.7**). Unlike other date-selection methods, this one changes the view to match the number of weeks selected.
- You can widen the Views pane to display a pair of mini calendars. Drag the right edge of the Folders list pane.

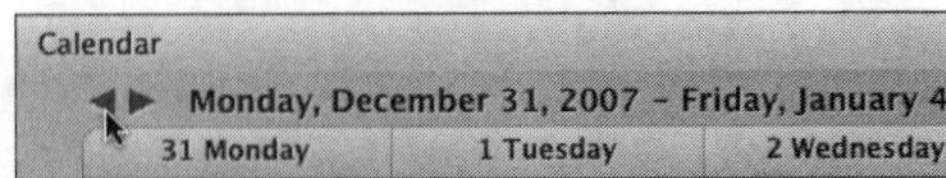

Figure 23.5 Click an arrow icon to move backward or forward. The amount moved (a day, week, or month) is determined by the calendar view in effect.

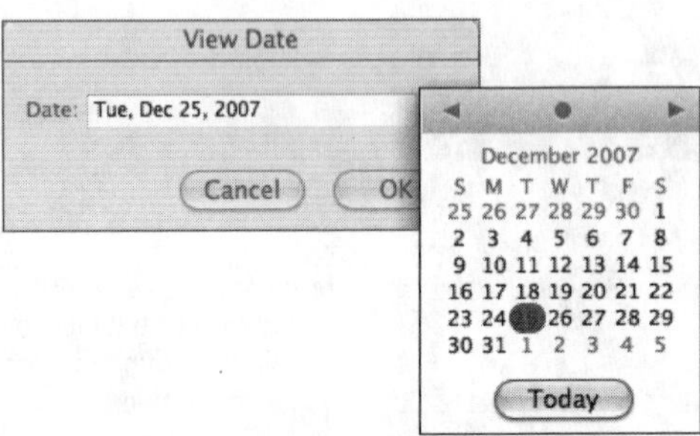

Figure 23.6 You can select a particular date to view by choosing it from the pop-up calendar in the View Date dialog box.

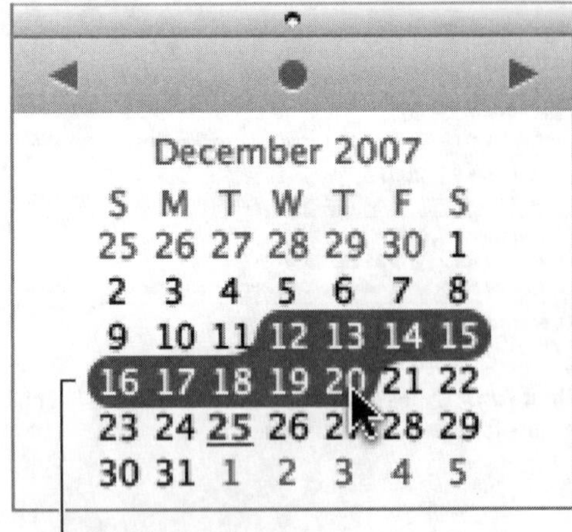

Selected date range

Figure 23.7 To view a specific range of dates (up to six weeks), drag-select the range in the mini calendar.

Viewing the Calendar

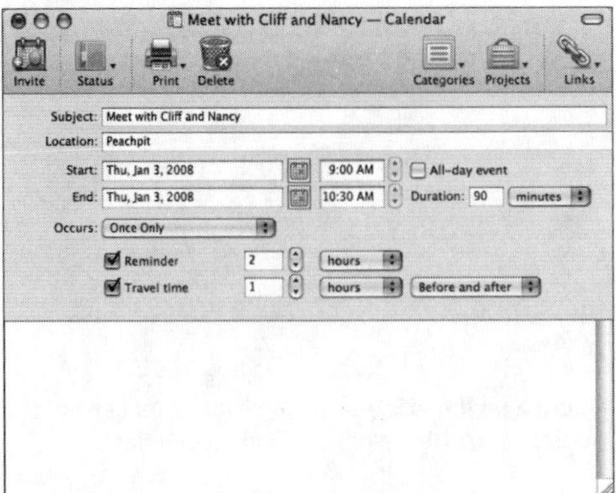

Figure 23.8 Enter the event information.

Adding Events

As you might expect, there are multiple ways to record new calendar events.

To create a standard Calendar event:

1. *Do one of the following:*
   - ▲ When viewing the Calendar, click the New toolbar icon or press ⌘N.
   - ▲ When viewing any part of Entourage, click the down arrow beside the New toolbar icon and choose Calendar Event from the drop-down menu.
   - ▲ Choose File > New > Calendar Event.
   - ▲ On the calendar, double-click the time or date of the event.

   If you first select the event's date in Month view, the event will default to that date.
2. In the event window that appears (**Figure 23.8**), enter the information for the event.
3. To assign a category to the event or associate it with a project:
   - ▲ Select a category or project from the Categories or Projects toolbar icon.
   - ▲ Choose Edit > Categories or Edit > Projects, and then choose a category or project from the submenu.
4. To set start and end dates, type dates in the appropriate fields. Or click the calendar icon to the right of each date field and select a date.
5. Depending on the event type, *do one of the following:*
   - ▲ **Timed event.** Set start and end times by typing or by clicking the up and down arrows. Or you can set the start time and then specify a duration.
   - ▲ **All-day event.** Click the All-day event check box.

continues on next page

Adding Events

6. If this event will occur more than once, choose a recurrence schedule from the Occurs drop-down menu. To set a different schedule, choose Custom, specify the schedule details in the Recurring Event dialog box (**Figure 23.9**), and click OK.
7. *Optional:* To include travel time in the event's schedule, click the Travel time check box, specify the amount of time, and choose an option from the rightmost drop-down menu.
8. *Optional:* To be reminded of the event prior to its occurrence, click the Reminder check box and specify the number of minutes, hours, or days before the event that you want to be reminded.

   At the designated time, the Office Reminders window will appear (**Figure 23.10**). For information about handling reminders, see "To respond to a reminder," later in this chapter.
9. Save the event by choosing File > Save or pressing ⌘S.

   The event is added to the calendar.

✔ Tip

■ To quickly create an all-day event, click in the area immediately below the date in the current calendar view (**Figure 23.11**).

To create a Calendar event from an Entourage item:

1. Select an item (such as a note or email message), and choose Tools > Link to New > Calendar Event.
2. Enter the event information (as described above).

✔ Tip

■ You can also link Entourage items to a currently scheduled event by choosing Tools > Link to Existing > Calendar Event.

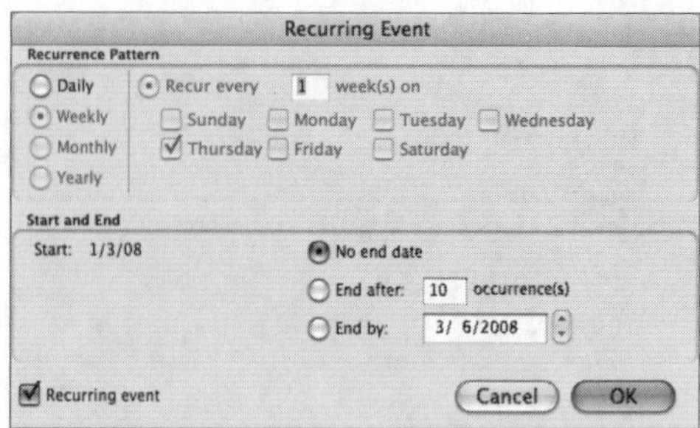

Figure 23.9 If this is a recurring event, you can specify a custom recurrence pattern and an end date.

Figure 23.10 Optionally, you can be reminded ahead of time about an upcoming event.

Figure 23.11 Create an all-day event by clicking directly under the date.

ADDING EVENTS

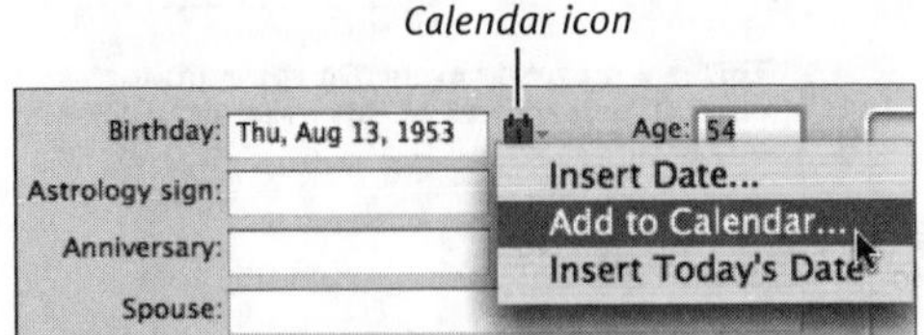

Figure 23.12 Add the date to the calendar.

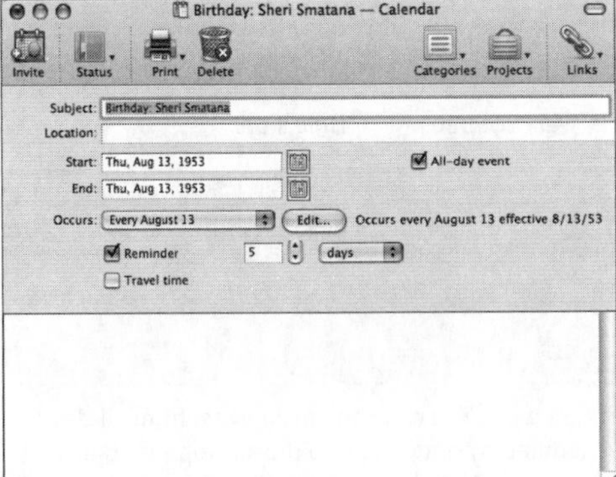

Figure 23.13 A new event is automatically created for the date. Edit it as necessary and save the event.

To create a Calendar event from a date on a contact record:

1. Switch to the Address Book by clicking its icon in the upper-left corner of the Entourage window, choosing View > Go To > Address Book, or pressing ⌘2.
2. Double-click the contact record to open it in its own window.
3. Click the Personal or Other tab (whichever one contains the date field you want to add to the calendar).
4. Click the calendar icon beside the date field and choose Add to Calendar from the pop-up menu (**Figure 23.12**). If prompted to do so, save the contact record.

   A new event window opens (**Figure 23.13**) that contains the information required to add the date as a new annual event.
5. Make any necessary changes, save the event by choosing File > Save (⌘S), and close the event window.

✔ Tip

- To view annual events created from contact records (such as birthdays and anniversaries), as well as other annual events you've added to the Calendar, click the Recurring Yearly custom view in the Views pane.

Modifying Events

You can edit any aspect of a saved event, such as changing its date, time, or location.

To edit an event:

1. Switch to a Calendar view that displays the event you want to change.
2. To open the event for editing, *do one of the following:*
   - ▲ Double-click the event.
   - ▲ Select the event, and choose File > Open Event (⌘O).
   - ▲ Control-click the event, and choose Open from the pop-up menu that appears.
3. If the event you are editing is part of a recurring series, a dialog box appears (**Figure 23.14**). Select an option and click OK.
4. In the event window, make any necessary changes.
5. Save the edited event by choosing File > Save (⌘S).

✔ Tips

- You can change the scheduled date or time of an event by dragging it to a new location on the calendar. You can also change an all-day event to a time-based event (or vice versa) by dragging it out of or into the all-day area (**Figure 23.15**).
- If you only need to edit an event's subject or location, click the event in any Calendar view and edit the text.

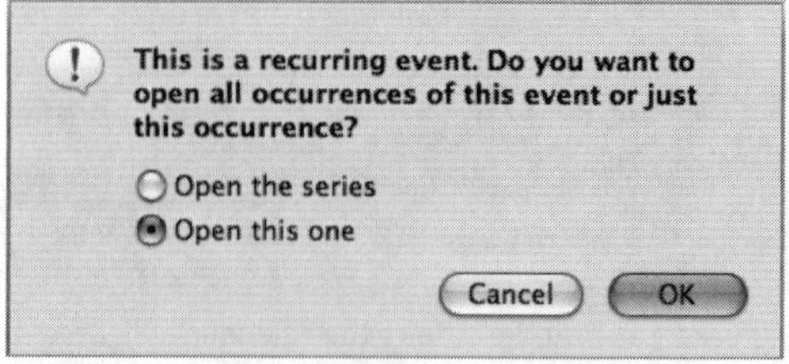

Figure 23.14 When editing a recurring event, you can edit just the selected occurrence or the entire event series.

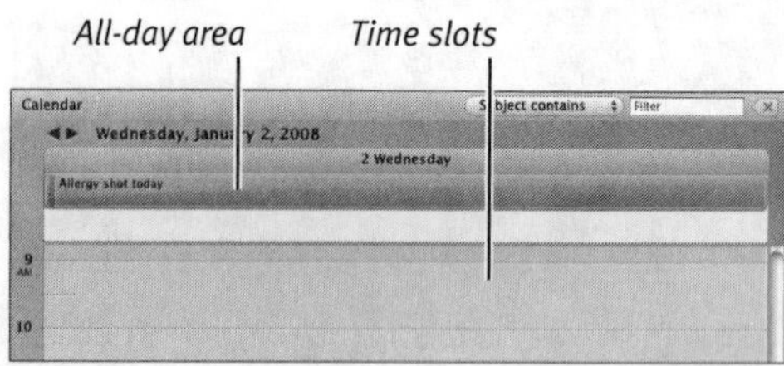

Figure 23.15 You can change an event from all-day to scheduled by dragging it to the appropriate time slot. To change a timed event into an all-day event, drag it into the all-day area.

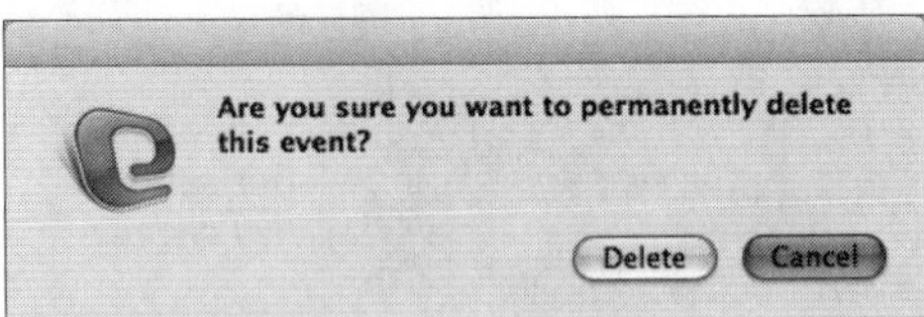

Figure 23.16 You must confirm the deletion of a normal, one-time event.

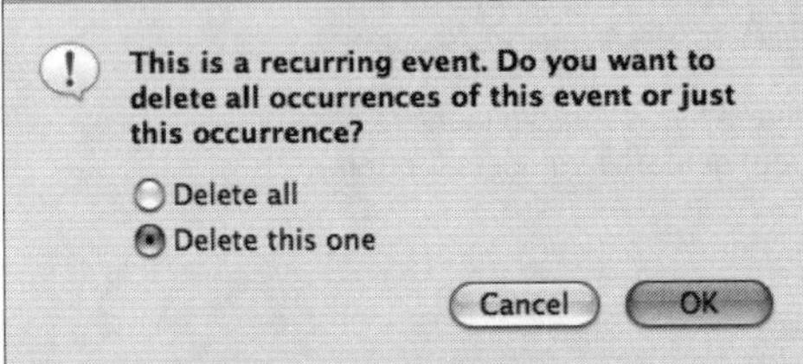

Figure 23.17 When deleting a recurring event, you can delete just the selected occurrence or the entire event series.

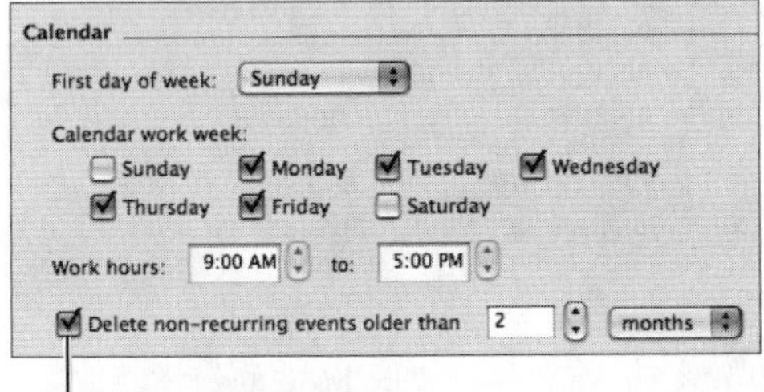

Figure 23.18 If you set this preference, Entourage will automatically delete expired events.

Deleting Events

You can delete events that have passed or that you no longer wish to track.

To delete a Calendar event:

1. In the Calendar window, switch to a view that displays the event you want to delete, and select the event.
2. *Do one of the following:*
   - ▲ Click the Delete toolbar icon.
   - ▲ Choose Edit > Delete Event.
   - ▲ Press ⌘Delete or Delete.
   - ▲ Control-click the event and choose Delete Event from the pop-up menu that appears.

   A confirmation dialog box appears. The specific dialog box displayed depends on whether this is a one-time or a recurring event.
3. *Do one of the following:*
   - ▲ If this is a one-time event (**Figure 23.16**), click the Delete button.
   - ▲ If this is a recurring event (**Figure 23.17**), click a radio button to indicate whether you want to delete all occurrences of the event or just this one, and then click OK.

✔ Tips

- If an event is open in its own window, you can delete it by clicking the Delete toolbar icon, choosing Edit > Delete Event, or pressing ⌘Delete.
- You can instruct Entourage to delete old calendar events automatically. Choose Entourage > Preferences (⌘,), select the Calendar category, and check the option to Delete non-recurring events older than *X* (**Figure 23.18**). Specify a time interval, and click OK to dismiss the dialog box.
- Be careful when deleting events. There is no Undo command to restore a deleted event.

Responding to Reminders

When one or more event reminders are due (or have passed without being handled), the Office Reminders window appears—even if Office isn't running. You can handle reminders in several ways.

To respond to a reminder:

1. In the Office Reminders window, select the reminder or reminders that you want to handle (**Figure 23.19**).

   You can Shift-click or ⌘-click to select multiple reminders.

2. *Do one of the following:*
   - ▲ **Dismiss.** To acknowledge a selected reminder and discontinue further notices, click Dismiss. The selected reminder is removed from the Office Reminders window.
   - ▲ **Dismiss All.** To simultaneously dismiss all listed reminders, hold down the mouse button as you click Dismiss and choose Dismiss All from the drop-down menu that appears. All reminders are removed and Office Reminders closes.
   - ▲ **Snooze.** To request that the reminder be presented again at a later time or date, click Snooze and choose a time period from the drop-down menu.
   - ▲ **Open the item.** To edit an event, double-click its reminder.
   - ▲ **Do nothing.** Close the Office Reminders window by clicking its close box or by choosing File > Close.

3. To handle other displayed reminders, repeat Steps 1 and 2.

✔ Tips

- Dismissing a reminder doesn't delete its event from the calendar. Follow the instructions in the previous section.

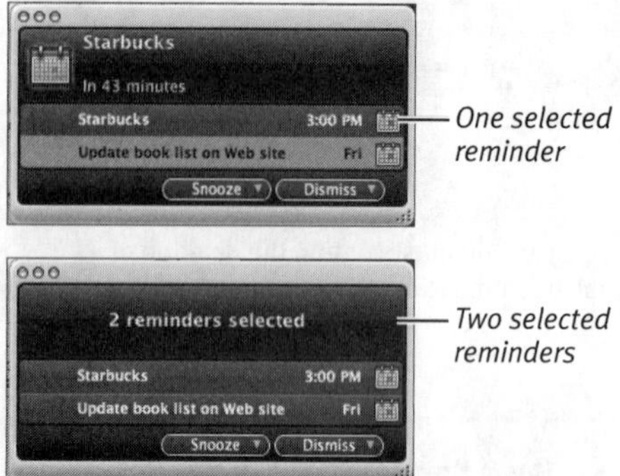

Figure 23.19 You can manage one (top) or more reminders (bottom).

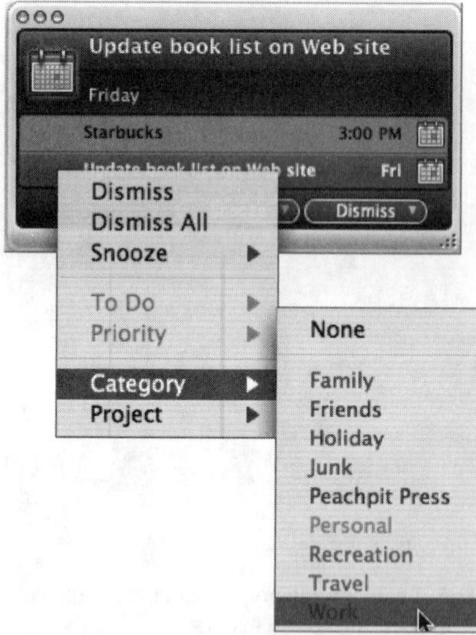

Figure 23.20 You can use the Office Reminders window to associate a project or category with a selected event.

- You can choose additional commands from Office Reminder's menus or by Control-clicking an item (**Figure 23.20**).
- If you merely want to get the Office Reminders window out of your way, it isn't necessary to close it. You can click its minimize (yellow) button to minimize it to the Dock.

Invite icon

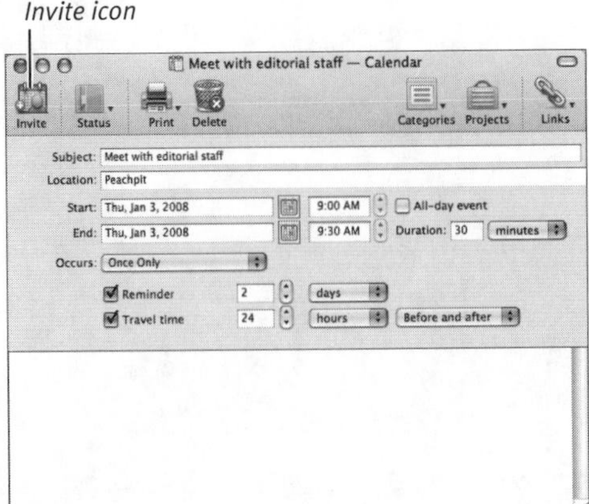

Figure 23.21 To invite others to attend the event, click the Invite toolbar icon.

Display Address Book

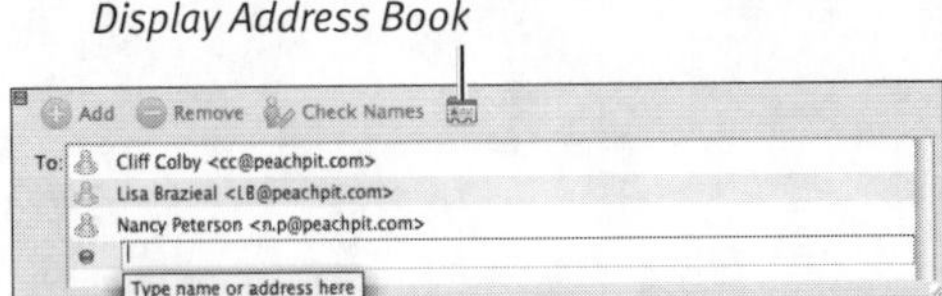

Figure 23.22 Add invitation recipients as you do email recipients. To select people from your address book, click the Address Book icon.

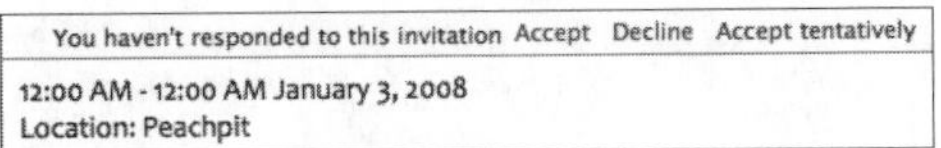
You haven't responded to this invitation Accept Decline Accept tentatively
12:00 AM - 12:00 AM January 3, 2008
Location: Peachpit

Figure 23.23 Recipients who use Entourage can respond to an invitation by clicking a text link.

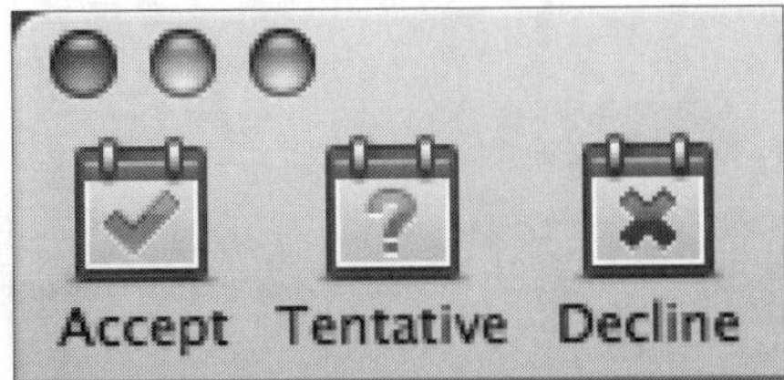

Figure 23.24 If an invitation is opened in its own window, an Entourage user can respond by clicking one of these toolbar icons.

Sending and Responding to Invitations

You can use Entourage to email invitations to events and to reply to invitations that you receive from others.

To invite others to an event:

1. Switch to the Calendar window. Double-click the event to open it in a separate window (**Figure 23.21**).

   If it's a repeating event, indicate in the dialog box that appears whether you're editing just this instance or the entire event series (see Figure 23.14).

2. Click the Invite toolbar icon.

3. In the address pane (**Figure 23.22**), specify the people to whom you wish to send an invitation. Close the pane.

   The full event invitation is displayed.

4. If you have multiple email accounts, click the From drop-down list to select the account from which you want to send the invitation.

5. Edit the invitation as necessary.

   To change the event from all day to a specific time span, for example, uncheck the All-day event check box. Note that you can also attach files, if you wish.

6. Click the Send Now toolbar icon to email the invitation to the designated people.

7. Recipients receive a message to which, if they are using Entourage, they can respond by clicking the Accept, Decline, or Accept tentatively text (**Figure 23.23**) or the equivalent toolbar icon (**Figure 23.24**). Entourage then relays the response to the person who sent the invitations.

   Recipients who don't use Entourage or a compatible email client, such as Outlook, can reply with a normal email message.

✔ Tips

- Invitation recipients can change their minds at any time by opening the invitation message again and clicking a different response icon.
- To cancel an invitation you've already sent, open the event and click the Cancel Invite toolbar icon. Participants will receive a cancellation email message.
- If you're the person who sent out the invitations, you can check the responses (**Figure 23.25**) by opening the event and clicking the View attendee status text beneath the toolbar.
- If your organization's email is managed by an Exchange Server, you can appoint a *delegate* to manage your messages, invitations, and Calendar events on the server. For details, see Chapter 28.

Attendee Status

Name	Response
Steven Schwartz lizardspit...	Accepted

Figure 23.25 You can review invitation responses in the Attendee Status window.

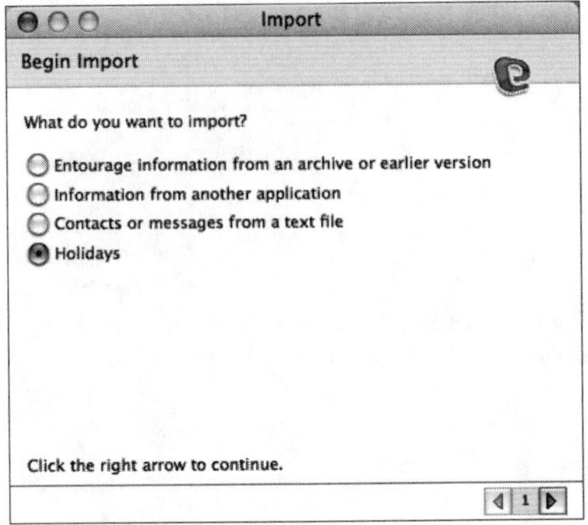

Figure 23.26 Select Holidays on the first screen of the Import wizard.

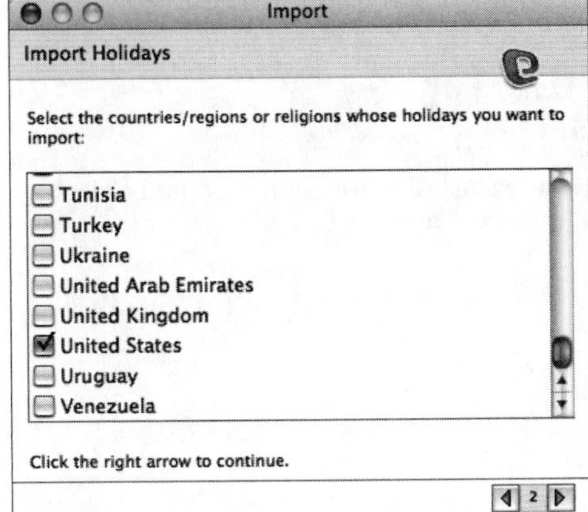

Figure 23.27 Click check boxes of the countries and religions whose holidays you want to import.

Adding and Removing Holidays

The default Calendar doesn't include holidays. If you like, you can import religious and/or country-specific holidays, adding them as new all-day events. You can also decide later to remove all or some of these holidays.

To add holidays to the Calendar:

1. Choose File > Import.

   The Import wizard appears (**Figure 23.26**).

2. Click the Holidays radio button. Click the right-arrow icon to continue.

3. After Entourage finishes building the list of available country and religious holiday sets, make your selections by entering check marks (**Figure 23.27**). Click the right arrow icon to continue.

   The chosen holidays are imported into the calendar.

4. Click Finish to dismiss the wizard.

To remove holidays from the Calendar:

1. Switch to the Calendar.
2. Choose Edit > Advanced Search or press Option ⌘ F.

   A Search area appears at the top of the Entourage window.
3. Using the drop-down menus (**Figure 23.28**), specify the holiday set you want to remove or edit. Choose Category Is, followed by Holiday or a holiday set.

   The list of holidays appears (**Figure 23.29**).
4. Select the holidays you want to delete. (Note that each holiday is listed multiple times, representing the different years for which it was added to the calendar.)
5. Click the Delete toolbar icon, choose Edit > Delete, or press Delete or ⌘ Delete.
6. Click the Delete button in the confirmation dialog box that appears.
7. To return to the normal Calendar window, click the close (*X*) button (Figure 23.29), the Calendar icon, or Calendar on the Favorites Bar.

✔ Tips

- If you want to delete *all* found holidays, select one of them, choose Edit > Select All (⌘ A), and then perform the deletion.
- You can remove individual holidays (marked in red on the calendar) by selecting and then deleting them as you would any other event.

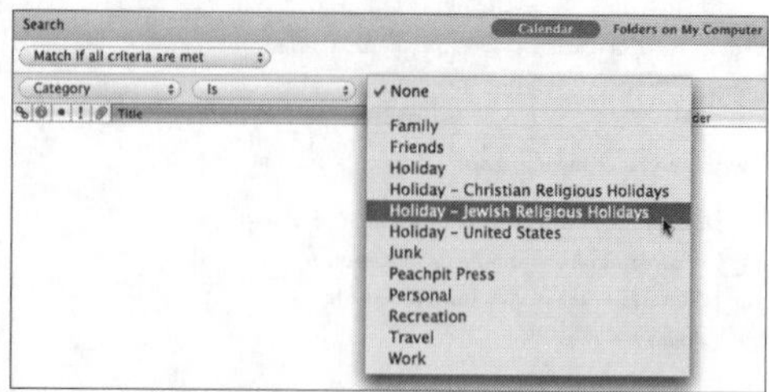

Figure 23.28 Set the search criterion to `Category Is`, followed by `Holiday` or a specific holiday set.

Close the search

Figure 23.29 In the results list, select the holidays you want to delete.

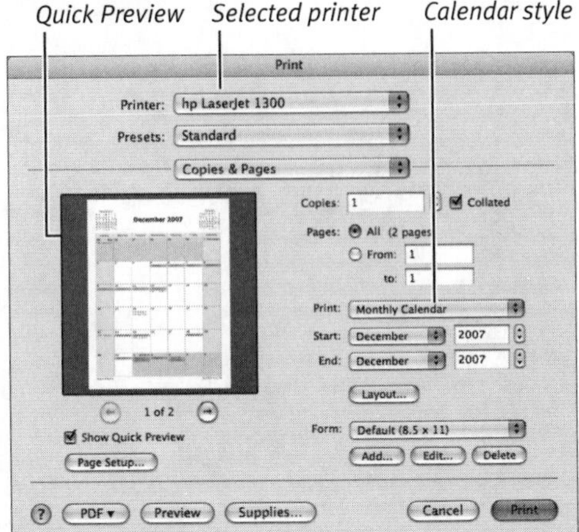

Figure 23.30 All setup options for printing a calendar are specified in the Print dialog box.

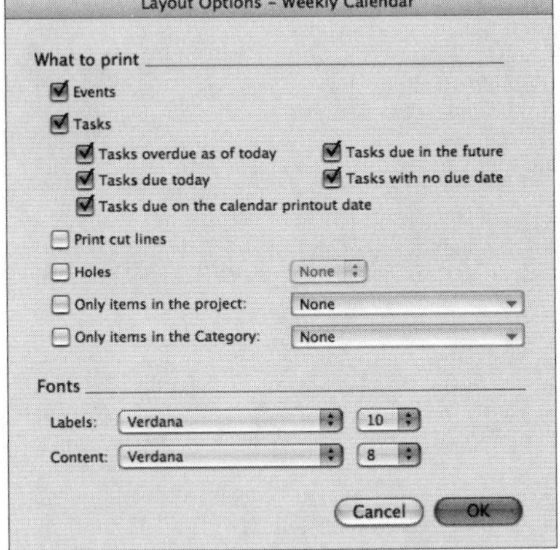

Figure 23.31 In the Layout Options dialog box, specify the types of information to include in the printout and special print options.

✔ Tip

- To generate a PDF file rather than a printout (so you can email your schedule to a colleague or friend, for example), click the PDF button (Figure 23.30) and choose Save as PDF or Mail PDF.

Printing a Calendar

As is the case with other Entourage components, printing a calendar is accomplished via a nonstandard Print dialog box (**Figure 23.30**). The Quick Preview box reflects the selected print settings.

To print a calendar:

1. Switch to the Calendar.
2. Choose File > Print (⌘P).

   The Print dialog box appears (**Figure 23.30**).
3. Select a printer to use from the Printer drop-down list.
4. From the Print drop-down menu, choose the form of calendar you want to print: Daily Calendar, Calendar List, Weekly Calendar, or Monthly Calendar.
5. Specify the date range to include.
6. If you intend to put the printout in a personal planner, choose a paper style from the Form drop-down menu. Otherwise, select Default (8.5 x 11).
7. To review print options, click the Layout button. In the Layout Options dialog box (**Figure 23.31**), make any necessary changes and click OK.

   For example, you can specify fonts to use, include/exclude tasks, and restrict events to those that meet certain criteria, such as belonging to a project.
8. Indicate the number of copies to print, whether copies should be collated (when printing multiple copies), and whether to print all pages or a page range.
9. If you need to specify a different paper size or orientation, click Page Setup.
10. Click Print to generate the printout.

Printing a Calendar

24

Tasks

You use the Tasks section of Entourage to track two kinds of items:

- **Tasks.** A *task* is an event or process, such as washing the car, painting the porch, or writing a budget proposal, that you either need to complete by a certain date or at some undetermined future time. Like Calendar events, some tasks are *repeating*. For example, a rent or mortgage payment could be scheduled at regular intervals.
- **To do items.** A *to do item* is either an email message or a contact record that you've marked with a To Do flag—signifying that you want to follow up at some future time. Like tasks, a to do item can have a proposed completion date.

You can mark tasks and to do items as completed, be reminded when they're due, and link them to other Entourage items and Office documents. Although some tasks and to-do items have specific due dates, neither are listed on the Calendar.

Creating Tasks

You can create new tasks by adding them directly to the Tasks list or by linking them to other events.

To create a new task:

1. *Do one of the following:*
   - ▲ To create a new task in Tasks view, click the New toolbar icon at the top of the Entourage window, choose File > New > Task, or press ⌘N.
   - ▲ To create a new task in any view, choose File > New > Task, or click the New toolbar icon's down arrow and choose Task (**Figure 24.1**).

   A new task window opens (**Figure 24.2**).
2. Enter a name for the task in the Task box.

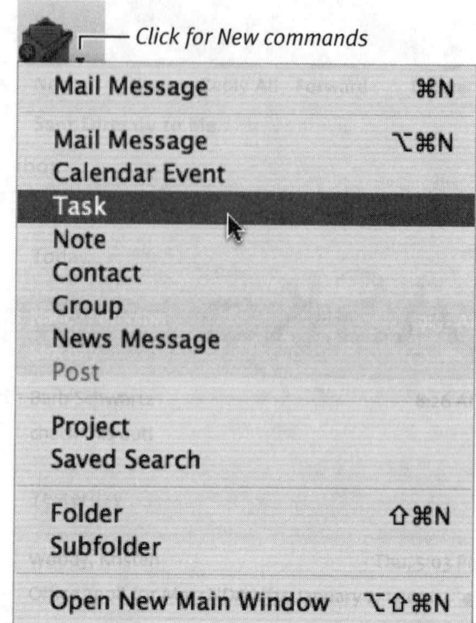

Figure 24.1 Regardless of the active Entourage component, you can create a new task by choosing this command from the New toolbar icon.

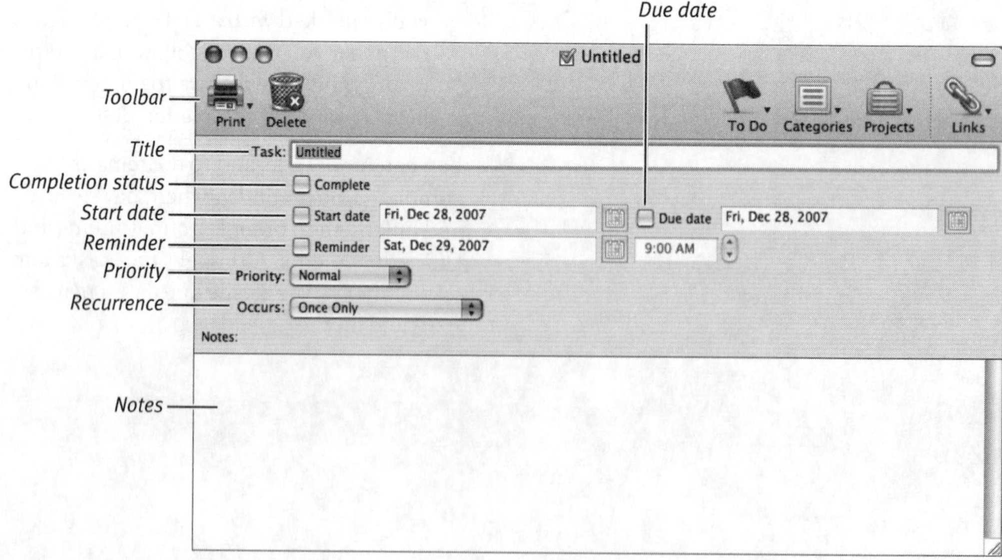

Figure 24.2 Enter a title and set options for the new task.

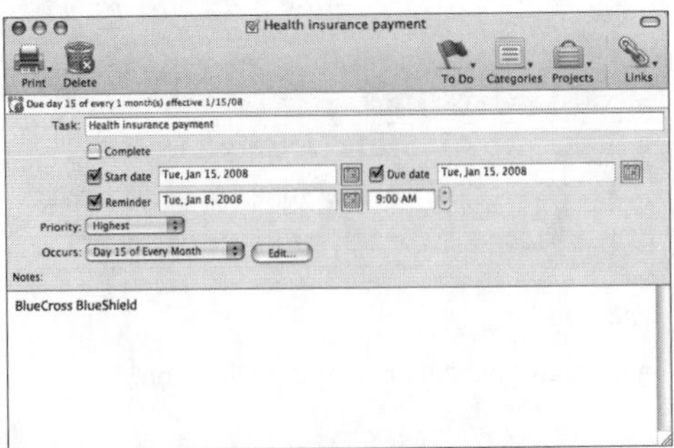

Figure 24.3 This task has a start date, due date, reminder, recurrence schedule, and notes.

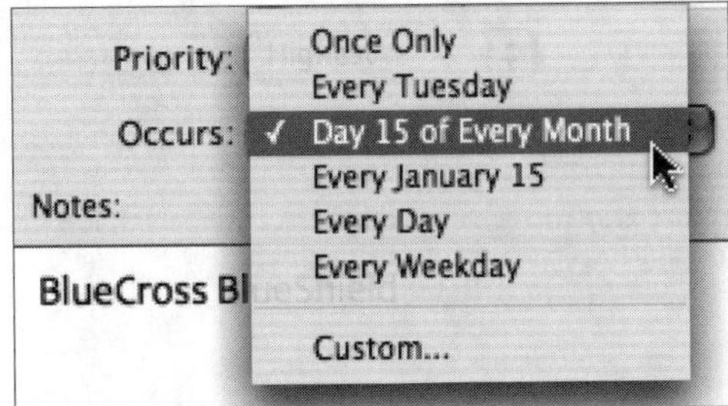

Figure 24.4 Choose common recurrence schedules from the Occurs pop-up menu. If no option is appropriate, choose Custom.

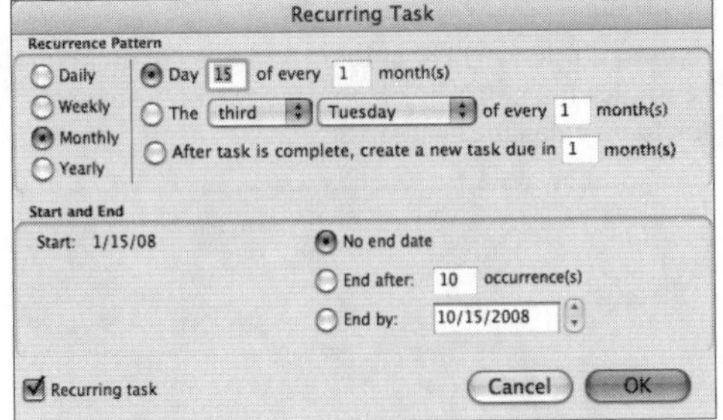

Figure 24.5 Specify more complex schedules in the Recurring Task dialog box.

3. *Optional:* Choose a category for the task, associate it with a project, assign a priority, specify a start date and/or due date, schedule a reminder, and/or add notes (**Figure 24.3**).
4. For a recurring task, *do one of the following:*
   - ▲ Choose a recurrence schedule from the Occurs pop-up menu (**Figure 24.4**).
   - ▲ To set a schedule other than the ones listed, choose Custom from the Occurs pop-up menu. The Recurring Task dialog box appears (**Figure 24.5**). Set a recurrence pattern and select an end criterion from the options in the Start and End section. Click OK.
5. To save the task, choose File > Save (⌘S). Close the task window.

   The task is inserted into the Tasks list in the current sort order.

✔ Tips

- For a task that doesn't have a specific due date and doesn't recur, it's often sufficient to enter only the task's name. Everything else (such as assigning a priority, reminder, or category) is optional.
- When creating a task that's similar to an existing one, it can be quicker to create a duplicate and edit the copy. Select the task, and choose Edit > Duplicate (⌘D).
- Reminders are discussed in greater detail later in this chapter.

To create a new task as a link to another Entourage item:

1. Select an Entourage item (an email message or note, for example) or open it in its own window.
2. Choose Tools > Link to New > Task.
   A new Task window opens.
3. Enter the task information.
4. Save the task by choosing File > Save (⌘S).
5. Close the task window.
   The new task is created, and a link is established between it and the item. The link is indicated by a link icon (**Figure 24.6**). For more information about linking Entourage items, see Chapter 29.

✔ Tips

- If an email message is already linked to at least one other item, you can create a new link for it by clicking the link icon to the right of the message header (**Figure 24.7**).
- To the left of each item in the Tasks list and Notes list is a Links column (Figure 24.6). You can create a new link for the item by clicking in the Links column and choosing an Entourage item from the Link to New submenu.
- To determine what links exist between an item and other Entourage items, click the item's link icon (**Figure 24.8**), choose Open Links, or choose Tools > Open Links.
- You can create a task from an email message by selecting its message header, opening the Scripts menu, and choosing Create Task from Message (Control T).

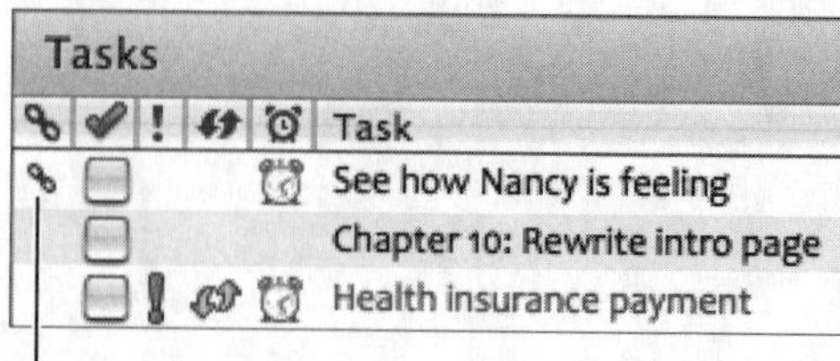

Figure 24.6 Linked items display a link icon.

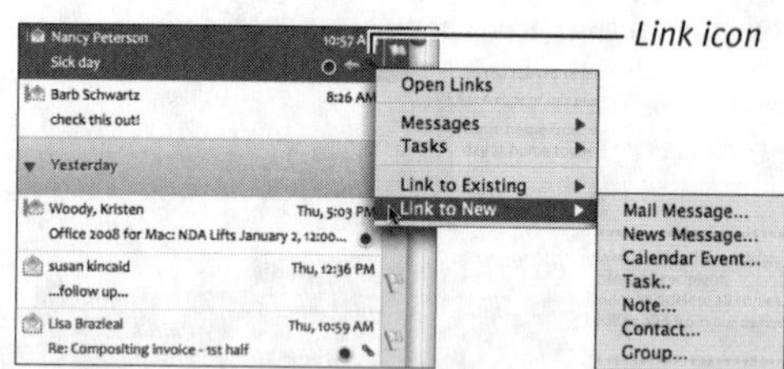

Figure 24.7 You can easily add links to items that already have at least one other link.

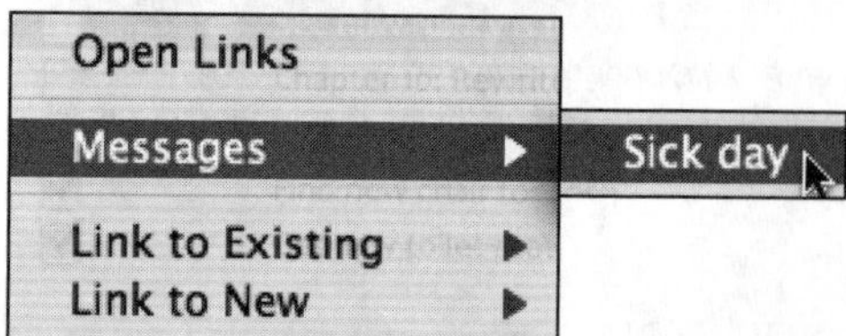

Figure 24.8 To view the Entourage items linked to an item, click the item's link icon. This example shows a link to an email message with Sick Day as its Subject.

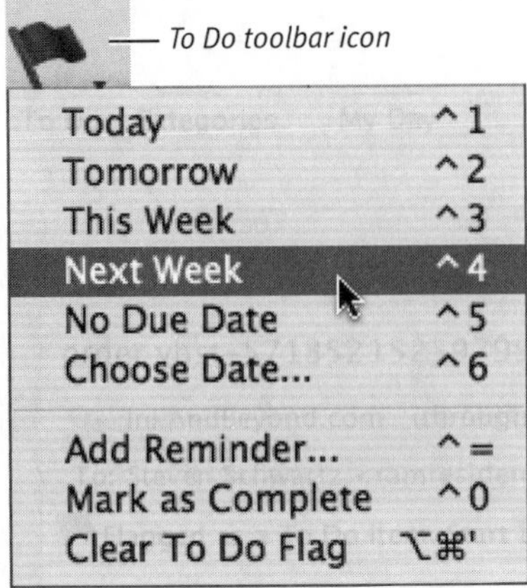

Figure 24.9 With the message or contact record selected or open, choose a command from the To Do toolbar icon.

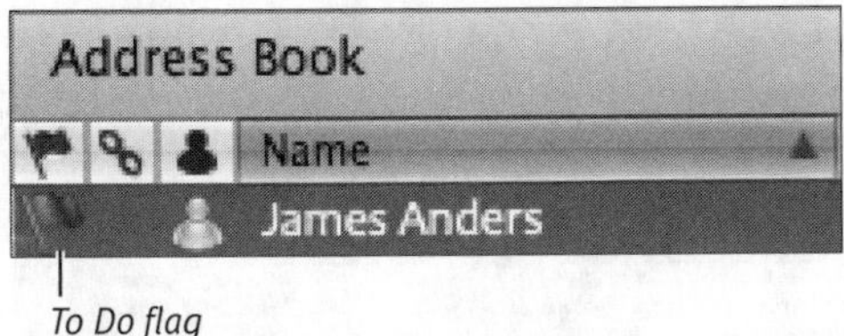

Figure 24.10 In a message list (top) or the Address Book (bottom), you can quickly mark an item for follow-up by clicking to set the flag icon.

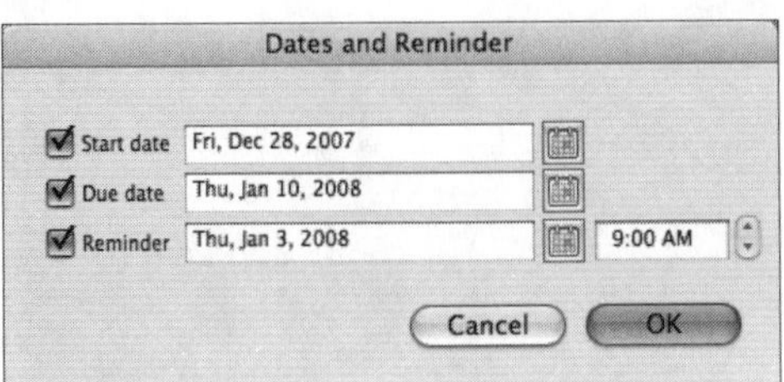

Figure 24.11 You can enter a start date, due date, and reminder in the Dates and Reminder dialog box. Only checked items are set.

Creating To Do List Items

As mentioned earlier, Entourage 2008 supports an additional type of task called a *to do item*. By setting a follow-up flag for an email message or contact record, you are creating a To Do List item.

To create a to do list item:

1. Select an email message or contact record in its list or open the item.
2. *Do one of the following:*
   - ▲ Click the To Do toolbar icon, and choose an option from the drop-down menu (**Figure 24.9**).
   - ▲ To flag the item for follow up but without specifying details, click in the flag area (email) or column (contact) until a flag appears (**Figure 24.10**).

   The item is added as a new to do.

✔ Tip

- The due date chosen from the To Do toolbar icon (Figure 24.9) automatically sets a Start date for the item. Choosing Today or This Week sets Start date to Today; choosing Tomorrow or Next Week sets it to Tomorrow. To set a different Start date, an unlisted Due date, or a reminder, choose Choose Date or Add Reminder. Make the desired changes in the Dates and Reminder dialog box (**Figure 24.11**).

Viewing the Tasks and To Do Lists

You can view your tasks and to do items in several ways, sort them by important characteristics, and filter the list of visible items to make it more manageable.

To view the Tasks or To Do List:

1. Click the Tasks icon in the upper-left corner of the Entourage window, choose View > Go To > Tasks, or press ⌘5.

   The Tasks section appears (**Figure 24.12**).

2. In the Folders list, select Tasks or To Do List.

   Tasks shows all items created as tasks; To Do List displays the combined list of to do (follow-up) items and tasks.

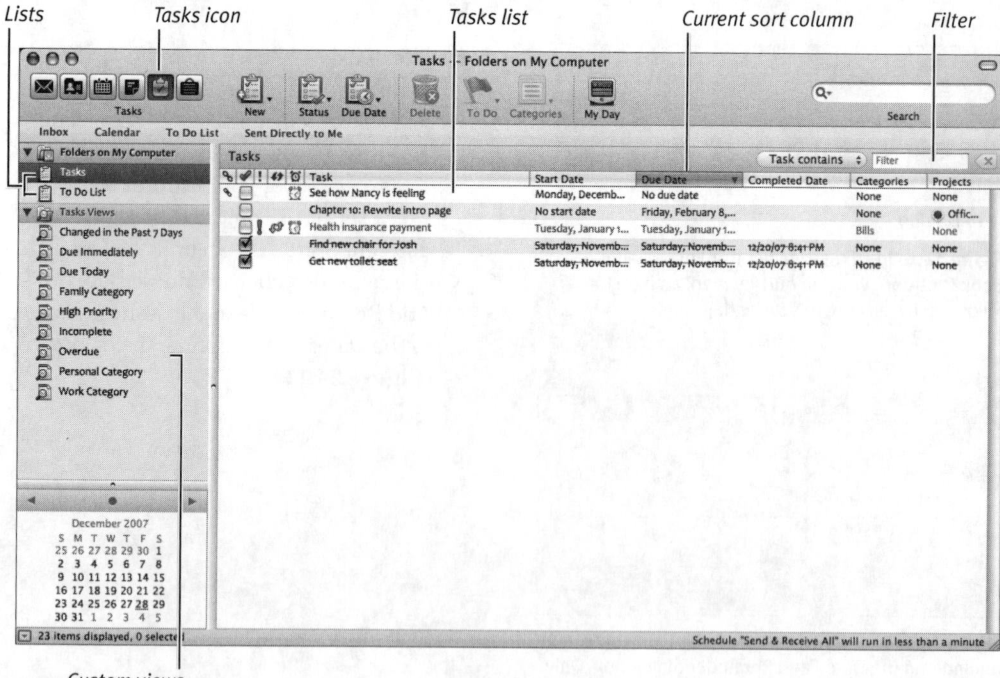

Figure 24.12 In Tasks, you can view the Tasks list or the To Do List.

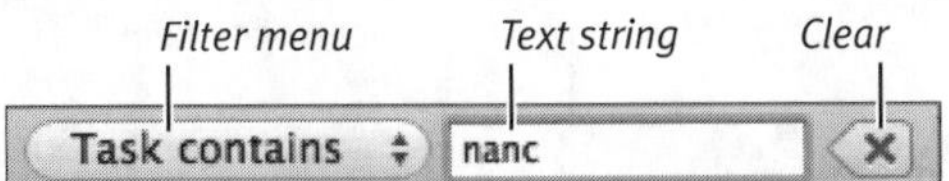

Figure 24.13 You can filter the Tasks or To Do List by entering a text string.

Figure 24.14 You can specify the tasks or to do items to show by choosing a View command.

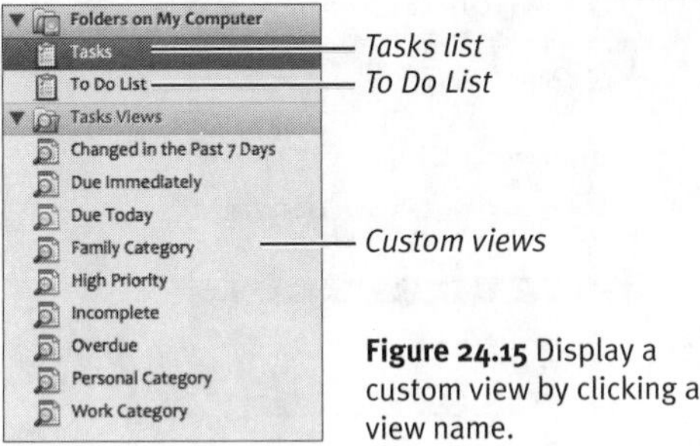

Figure 24.15 Display a custom view by clicking a view name.

✔ Tips

- To go directly to the To Do List, click To Do List in the Favorites Bar.
- When working in the Calendar, you can show or hide the To Do List by clicking the To Do List toolbar icon.

3. To sort the list, click any column heading except the first. To reverse the sort order, click the same column heading again.

   The sort column's heading is blue.

4. *Optional:* You can restrict list entries by choosing commands from the Status and Due Date toolbar icons. To restore the list, choose the same commands again.

5. You can filter the list to show only items that match a criterion: matching text, an assigned category, or an associated project. You can also filter the list by selecting a custom view, such as Overdue or Incomplete. *Do one of the following:*

   ▲ Choose Task contains from the drop-down menu above the list, and type a text string in the box (**Figure 24.13**). As you type, Entourage filters the list to show only items that contain the typed characters. To restore the list, click the Clear icon or delete the text.

   ▲ Choose Category is from the drop-down menu and choose a category from the second drop-down menu. To restore the Tasks list, click the Clear icon or set the category to All.

   ▲ Choose Project is from the drop-down menu and choose a project from the second drop-down menu. To restore the Tasks list, click the Clear icon or set the project to All.

   ▲ Choose a completion or due command from the View menu (**Figure 24.14**). To restore the list after choosing a completion command, choose All Tasks or All To Do Items (depending on the list you're viewing). To restore the list after choosing a due command, choose the same command again.

   ▲ In the Views pane, select a custom view from the Tasks Views folder (**Figure 24.15**). To restore the list, click the list name: Tasks or To Do List.

Editing Tasks/To Do Items

You can change task and to do item settings.

To edit a task or to do item:

1. In Tasks, open the Tasks or To Do List by clicking its name in the Folders list.
2. Double-click the item you wish to edit. If the item is a task, its task window opens. If the item is a to do, the original email message or contact record opens.
3. Make the changes (as described below).
4. Choose File > Save (⌘S).

To change an item's attributes:

- To change an item's completion status, click its check box in the list, My Day, or Office Reminders. Completed items are shown in strike-through text in the To Do List (**Figure 24.16**) and, if a task, are removed from the Tasks list.
- To change a tasks's title, select the task in either list. Click its title to select it for editing (**Figure 24.17**), make the change, and save the new title by pressing Return or clicking elsewhere in the window. (A to do item's title is taken from the message Subject or the contact name. It can't be changed in Tasks.)
- To change a to do item's schedule, select the item in the To Do List and choose an option from the To Do toolbar icon's drop-down menu (see Figure 24.9).
- To associate a category or project with a selected item, click its Categories or Projects entry, and choose an option from the pop-up menu (**Figure 24.18**). To remove an associated category or project, choose its name from the pop-up menu. To remove *all* categories or projects, choose None.

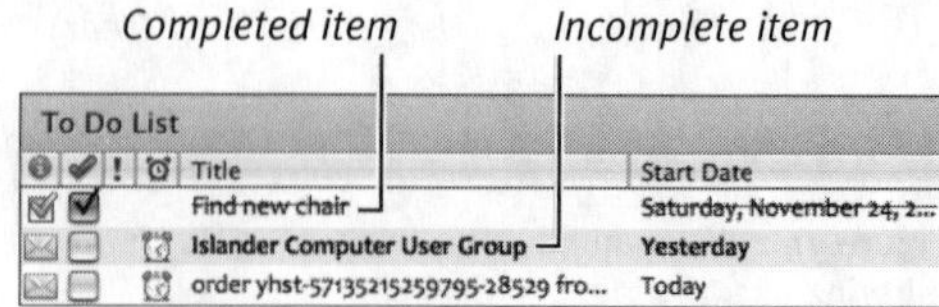

Figure 24.16 Completed items are displayed in the To Do List in strike-through type and have a check mark in their Status check box.

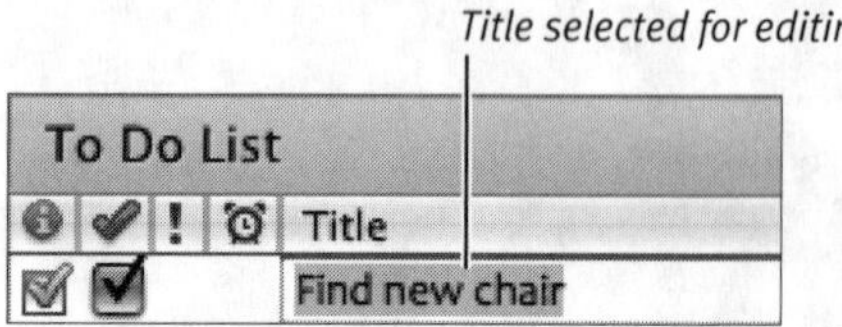

Figure 24.17 You can edit a task's title by clicking the title in the Tasks or To Do List.

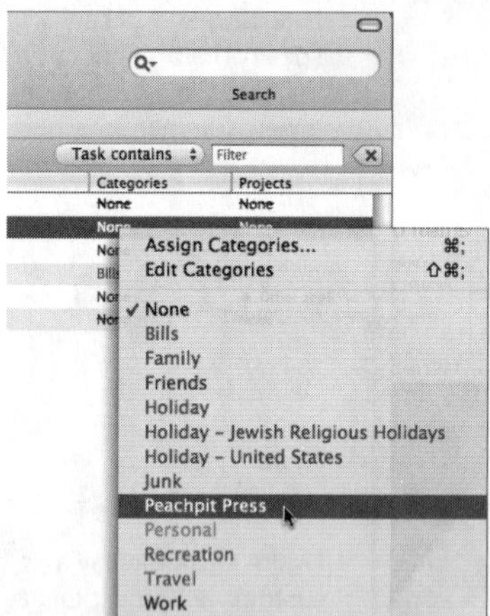

Figure 24.18 To assign a category or project to an item, click its Categories or Projects entry in the list and choose an option from the pop-up menu.

✔ Tip

- When you want to make several changes to a task, it may be more convenient to open it rather than editing it in the list.

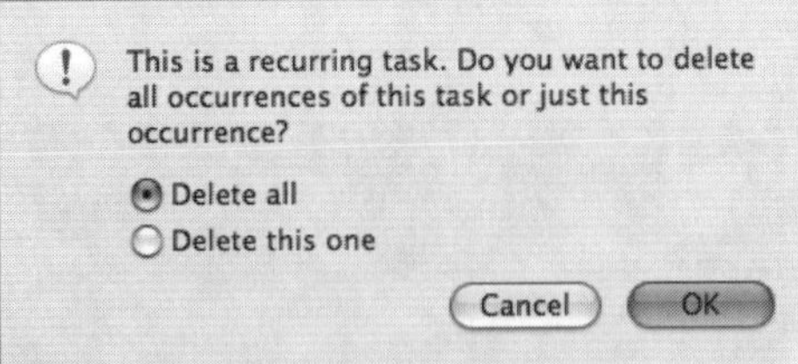

Figure 24.19 You can delete this occurrence only (Delete this one) or the entire task series (Delete all).

Confusing Logic (and Some Workarounds)

Entourage 2008 treats tasks as a subset of to do items rather than the other way around. When working in Tasks, you can view your items in either of two ways:

- The Tasks list displays only the items you've defined as tasks.
- The To Do List displays all of your to do (follow-up) items, *plus* your tasks.

The problem is that there's no easy way to view only to do items in the To Do List. You can't, for example, sort on Item Type or select only to do items. However, to distinguish to do/follow-up items from tasks, you *can* use these approaches:

- **By icon.** To do items have an envelope or person's head in the Item Type column; tasks have a checked box.
- **By category.** Create a category named *Follow-up* and apply it to each to do item. Then filter the To Do List to show only the Follow-up category.
- **Create a saved search.** Choose Edit > Advanced Search. Select Match if any criteria are met, specify two criteria: To Do Flag–Not Completed and To Do Flag–Completed, and save the search.

Deleting Tasks/To Do Items

When you've completed or are no longer interested in tracking a task or to do item, you can remove it from the Tasks and/or To Do List.

To delete a task or to do item:

1. Select one or more items in the Tasks or To Do List.
   To select multiple items, ⌘-click (for noncontiguous items) or Shift-click (for contiguous items).
2. *Do one of the following:*
   - Click the Delete toolbar icon, choose Edit > Delete (or Delete Task), press Delete, or press ⌘Delete.
   - With the task open in its own window, click the Delete toolbar icon, choose Edit > Delete Task, or press ⌘Delete.

   A confirmation dialog box appears.
3. Click Delete to delete the task(s) and/or to do item(s).
4. If a selected task is a recurring one, a second dialog box appears, offering the option to delete only this instance or the entire task series (**Figure 24.19**). Click a radio button to indicate your choice and then click OK. (To cancel the deletion, click Cancel.)
   The deleted items are removed from the Tasks and/or To Do List.

✔ Tips

- You cannot Undo a task or to do item deletion.
- *Caution!* Deleting a to do item from the To Do List deletes the actual message or contact record—*not* just its instance in the list. To remove a selected to do from the To Do List, choose Clear To Do Flag from the To Do toolbar icon's menu.

Managing Reminders

Task and to do item reminders aren't the same as Calendar event reminders. Rather than specifying how far in advance you want to be reminded, you select a specific time at which the task/to do reminder will appear.

Office 2008 presents reminders for tasks, to do items, and Calendar events using a separate program called Office Reminders. This enables reminders to appear any time your Mac is on, regardless of whether an Office application is running.

To respond to a reminder:

1. When the Office Reminders dialog box appears (**Figure 24.20**), select the item to which you want to respond.
2. *Do one of the following:*
   - ▲ If you've performed the task, click the Complete check box. Doing so dismisses the reminder and marks the task or to do item as complete in the list(s).
   - ▲ To dismiss the reminder so it doesn't reappear, click the Dismiss button.
   - ▲ If this is a recurring task, you can dismiss this and all future occurrences of the reminder by holding down the Dismiss button and choosing Dismiss All from the drop-down menu.
   - ▲ To delay the reminder for the default snooze time (when it will reappear onscreen), click the Snooze button.
   - ▲ If you want to be reminded later (from 5 minutes to 2 weeks from now), hold down the Snooze button and choose a delay interval (**Figure 24.21**).

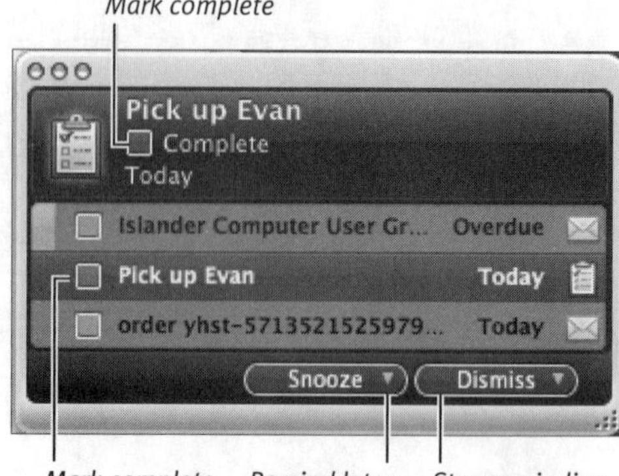

Figure 24.20 When a task or Calendar reminder is due, Office Reminders appears.

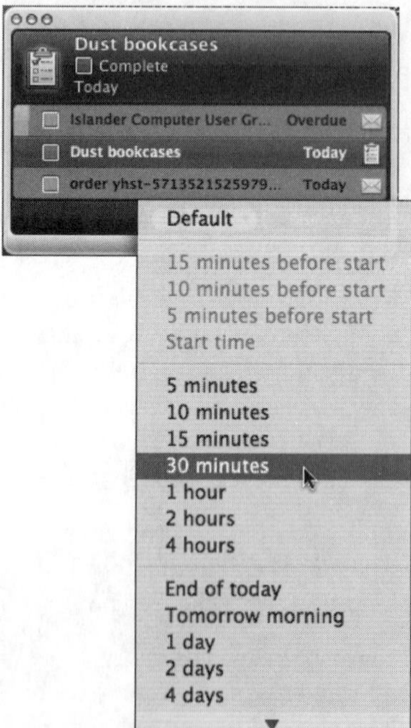

Figure 24.21 Click Snooze button to be reminded again in 5 minutes (the default period) or choose another Snooze period from the pop-up menu.

Figure 24.22 Office Reminders adds its icon to the Dock. The number is the current number of reminders.

Figure 24.23 The Calendar can also display the To Do List, but shows only incomplete tasks. You can restrict the list by choosing an option from the filter drop-down menu.

Figure 24.24 In Entourage Preferences, you can set the default due date, snooze time, and reminder time for tasks and to do items.

✔ Tips

- When Office Reminders opens, its Dock icon shows the number of unhandled reminders (**Figure 24.22**). Office Reminders remains open until you've responded to each reminder or until you close or quit it.
- If you want to open a task or to do item, double-click it in Office Reminders.
- You can also view all unfinished tasks and to do items in the Calendar window (**Figure 24.23**) by clicking the To Do List toolbar icon or by choosing Calendar > To Do List. To mark an item as complete, click its check box. To view the details for an item, double-click it.
- Although unfinished tasks and to do items can be viewed in the Calendar window and some may have due dates or reminders, tasks are *not* listed as events on the Calendar. This is why it's important to carefully decide which items should be tasks or to do items and which ones should be recorded as events.
- To change the default due date, snooze time, or reminder time for tasks and to do items, choose Entourage > Preferences and select the To Do List category (**Figure 24.24**). To change the default snooze time for Calendar events, select the Calendar category.
- You can turn Office Reminders off and on by choosing Entourage > Turn Off Office Reminders. They'll remain off until you later choose Entourage > Turn On Office Reminders.
- Upcoming tasks and to do items are also listed in My Day. You can mark these items as complete by clicking their My Day check boxes, if you like.

Printing Tasks/To Do Items

As is the case with other Entourage components, printing tasks is accomplished via a nonstandard Print dialog box (**Figure 24.25**). The Quick Preview box reflects your selections.

To print tasks:

1. Switch to Tasks, and select Tasks or To Do List in the Folders list.
2. *Optional:* To print only certain items, select their titles in the list. (You can Shift-click or ⌘-click to select multiple items.)
3. Choose File > Print (⌘P).
   The Print dialog box appears.
4. Select a printer to use from the Printer drop-down list.
5. From the Print drop-down list, indicate what you want to print, such as All Tasks, Selected Tasks, or Items Due Today.
6. If you intend to put the printout in a personal planner, select a paper style from the Form drop-down list.
7. To review print options, click the Layout button. In the Print Layout dialog box (**Figure 24.26**), make any desired changes and click OK.
8. Indicate the number of copies to print, whether copies should be collated (when printing multiple copies), and whether to print all pages or a page range.
9. If you need to specify a different paper size or orientation, click Page Setup.
10. Click Print to generate the printout.

✔ Tip

- You can also use these Print procedures when a task or to do item is open in its own window.

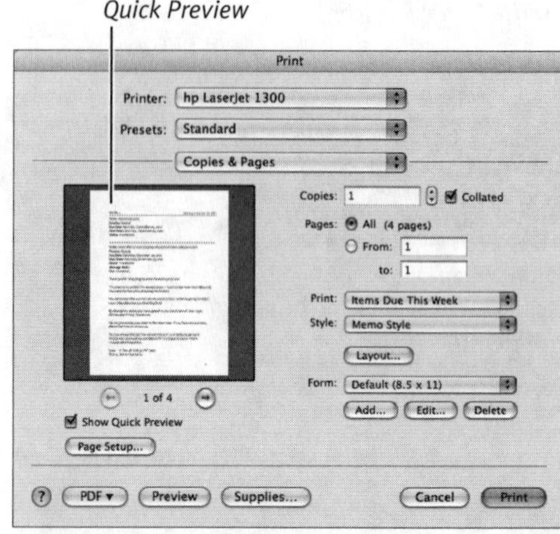

Figure 24.25 Select print settings, and click Print.

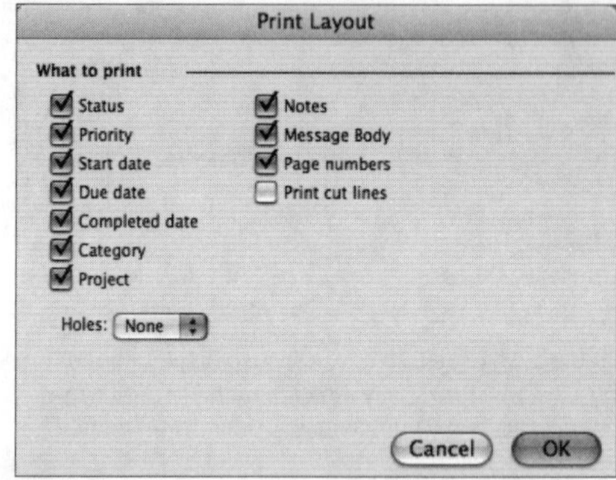

Figure 24.26 Special print options can be set in the Print Layout dialog box.

25

Notes

Figure 25.1 Click the Notes icon in the upper-left corner of the Entourage window to see your Notes list.

Entourage's Notes section is designed as a free-form note-taking utility. You can combine text, images, and sounds in notes. You can optionally assign categories to notes or associate notes with projects. Unlike most simple note-taking applications, Entourage creates formatted text notes. Any note can contain multiple fonts, sizes, styles, colors, and paragraph formatting.

To view or work with your notes, switch to Notes view by clicking the Notes icon (**Figure 25.1**), choosing View > Go To > Notes, or pressing ⌘4.

Note: If you have a Microsoft Exchange account, Entourage notes do not synchronize with it.

Creating and Deleting Notes

You can create as many notes as you like. And when notes cease to be useful, you can delete them.

To create a new note:

1. *Do one of the following:*
   - ▲ To create a new note from Notes view, click the New toolbar icon at the top of the Entourage window, choose File > New > Note, or press ⌘N.
   - ▲ To create a new note from any other view, click the down arrow beside the New toolbar icon and choose Note (**Figure 25.2**), or choose File > New > Note.

   A new note window appears (**Figure 25.3**).

2. Enter a title for the note. Fill in the body by typing, pasting, or dragging and dropping text.

   You can optionally assign categories to the note to classify it and/or associate it with a project. Choose options from the Categories and Projects toolbar icons.

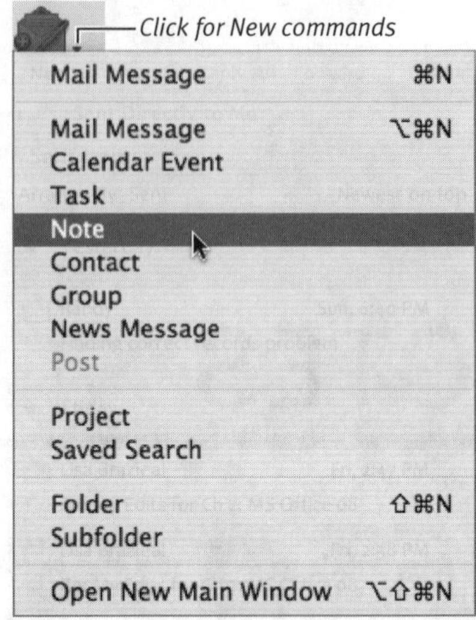

Figure 25.2 Regardless of the active Entourage component, you can create a new note by choosing the Note command from the New toolbar icon's drop-down menu.

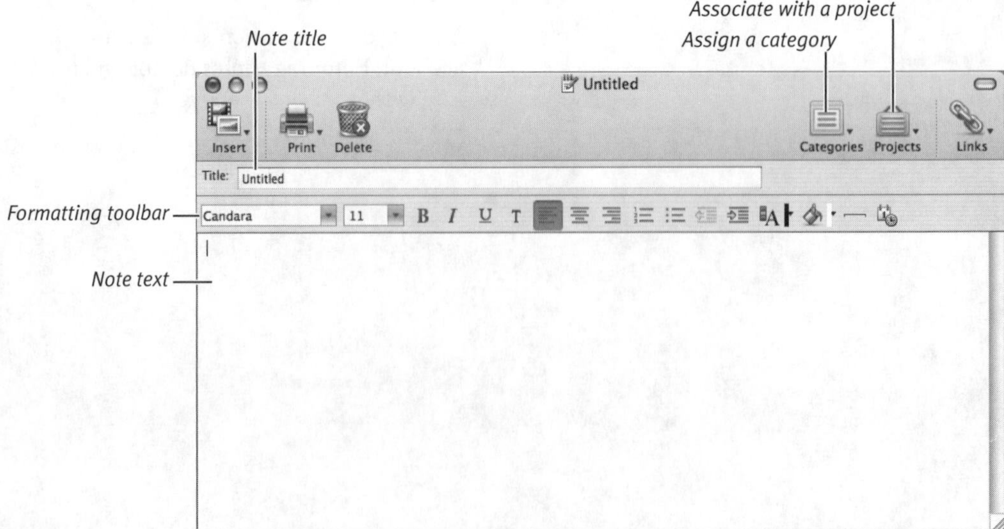

Figure 25.3 A new note window appears, ready to receive a title and the note text.

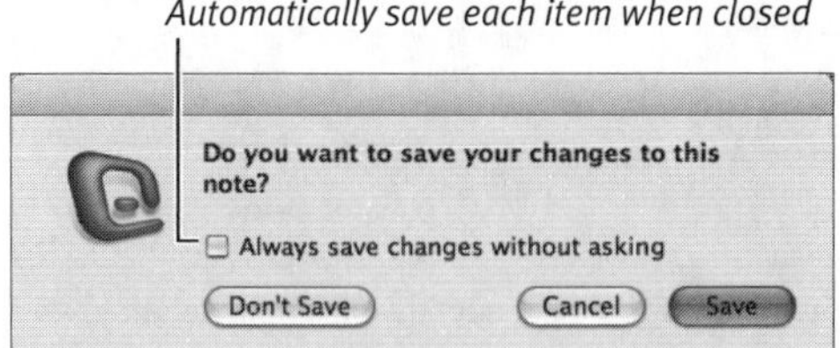

Figure 25.5 If your Entourage items aren't automatically saved when you close them, click Save.

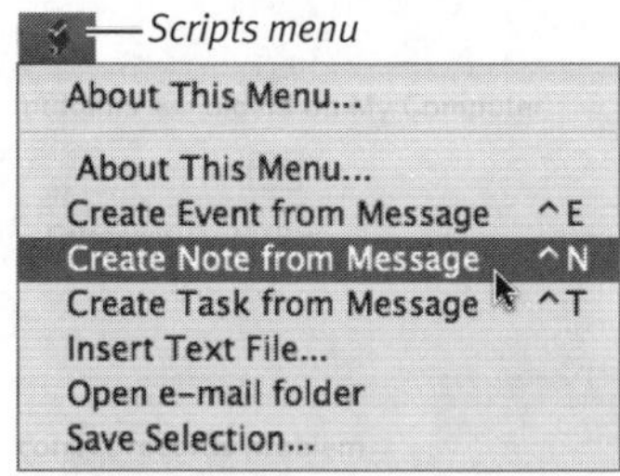

Figure 25.6 You can save the current email message as a note by choosing the Create Note from Message script.

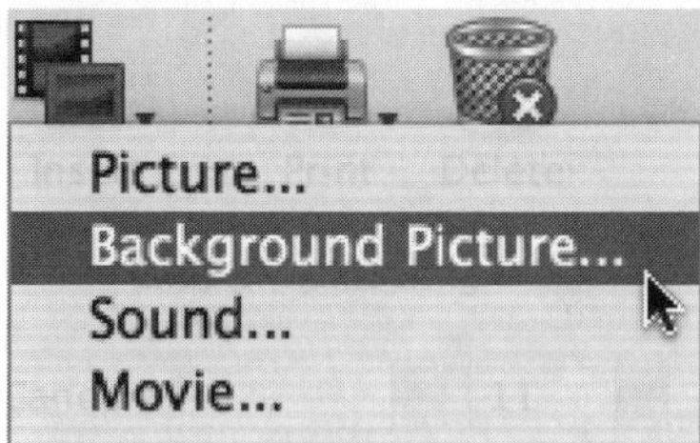

Figure 25.7 You can add pictures, sounds, movies, or a background picture to a note by choosing commands from the Insert toolbar icon.

3. You can use the Formatting toolbar (**Figure 25.4,** bottom) to format the note's text, or you can choose commands from the Format menu.
4. To save the note, choose File > Save, press ⌘S, or close the note window and confirm that you wish to save (**Figure 25.5**).

✔ Tips

- To save an email message for future reference, you can create a note from it. Select the email message's header in the message list, open the Scripts menu, and choose Create Note from Message (**Figure 25.6**) or press Control N. If desired, you can edit the message text.
- You can add a background color to a note by clicking the Background Color icon on the Formatting toolbar or by choosing a color from the Format > Background Color submenu.
- Notes can optionally contain images, sounds, movies, or a background picture. Position the text insertion mark and click the Insert icon on the note window's toolbar (**Figure 25.7**) to add one of these items to the current note.
- You can keep track of important Web site addresses by dragging them from Safari into a note. You can drag any link you find in the body of a Web page or the current Web page's address from the Address box.

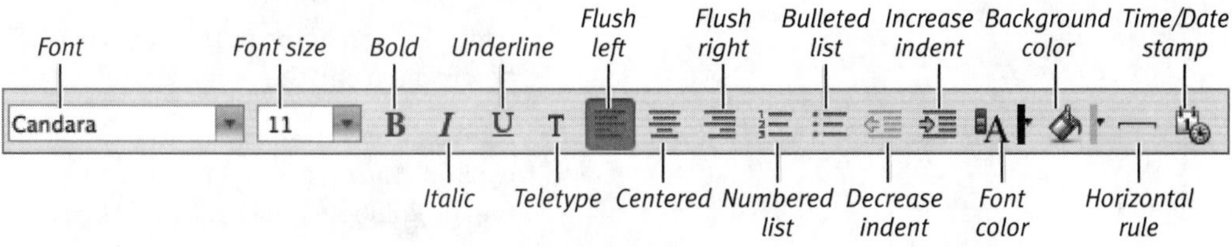

Figure 25.4 You can format note text by choosing commands and options from the Formatting toolbar.

To delete a note:

1. Switch to Notes view and select the note's heading in the Notes list.
2. Click the Delete toolbar icon, choose Edit > Delete Note, or press Delete or ⌘Delete.
3. In the dialog box that appears (**Figure 25.8**), confirm the deletion by clicking the Delete button.

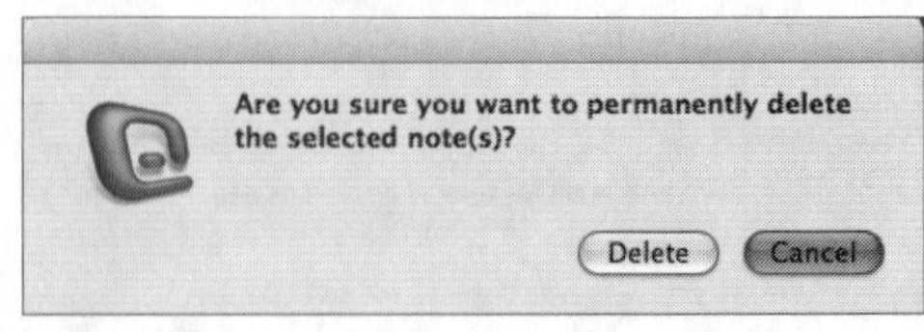

Figure 25.8 You must confirm each note deletion.

✔ Tips

- Another way to delete a note is to Control-click its heading in the Notes list and choose Delete Note from the pop-up menu that appears.
- You can also delete a note that's open in its own window. Click the Delete toolbar icon, choose Edit > Delete Note, or press ⌘Delete.
- To simultaneously delete multiple notes, hold down ⌘ to select the additional notes from the Notes list, and perform the deletion as you would for an individual note. (You can also press Shift to select multiple contiguous notes.)
- Note deletions can't be reversed. There is no Undo Delete command.

Customizing the Notes List

As you use the Notes component, you can customize it to better suit your needs and the way you work. *Do any of the following:*

- **Remove unwanted headings.** Choose column headings from the View > Columns submenu. Only the checked headings will appear above the message list.
- **Rearrange headings.** To change the order in which the column headings are displayed, you can drag any heading left or right to a new position.
- **Customize the toolbar.** To change the icons on the Notes toolbar, choose View > Customize Toolbar. To change the toolbar shown when creating, editing, and reading notes, open a note before choosing the same command.
- **Hiding unwanted elements.** You can hide the Quick Filter, Favorites Bar, or Folder List by choosing Hide commands from the View menu.

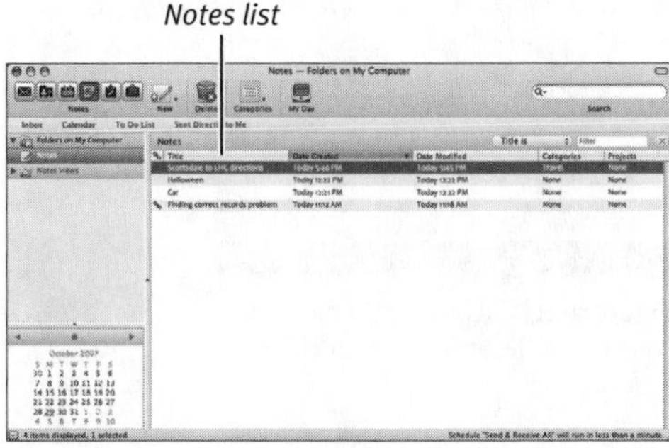

Figure 25.9 The Notes list is displayed in the main window. Double-click a note to view that note.

Reading Notes

You can read notes, sort the Notes list, and filter the list to display only notes that contain matching title text, have been assigned a particular category, or are associated with a given project.

To view notes:

1. Switch to Notes view.

   The Notes list appears in the main pane (**Figure 25.9**).

2. To view a note (**Figure 25.10**), double-click its title. Or you can select the note in the list, and then choose File > Open Note (⌘O).

continues on next page

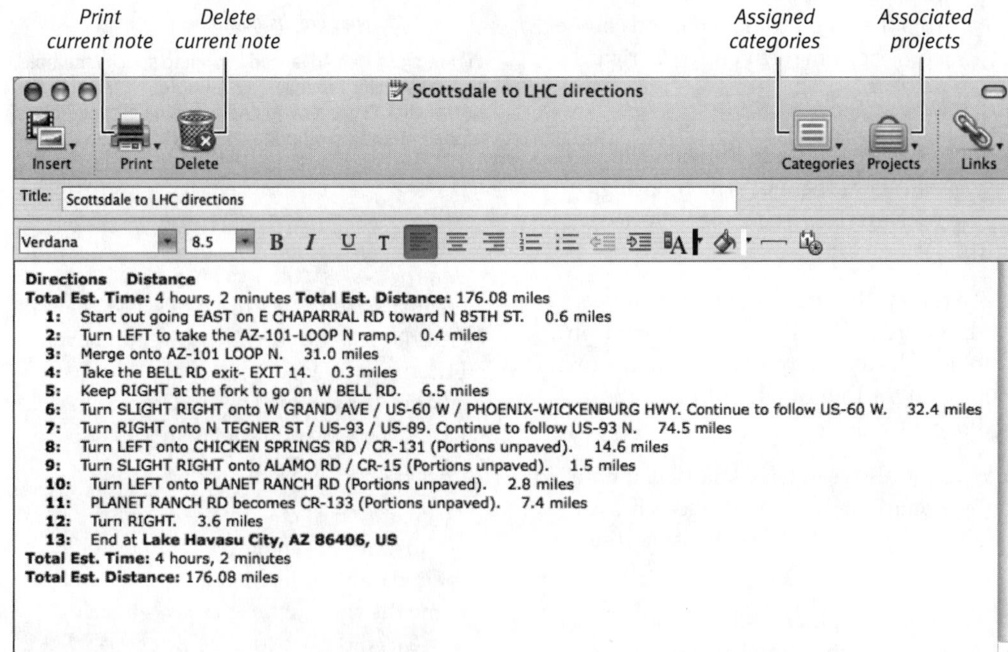

Figure 25.10 To read a note, you must first open it.

3. You can sort the Notes list by the contents of any column by clicking the column name. To reverse the sort order, click the column name again.

   The sort column is indicated by a blue column heading. The sort direction is indicated by the triangle following the column name (**Figure 25.11**).

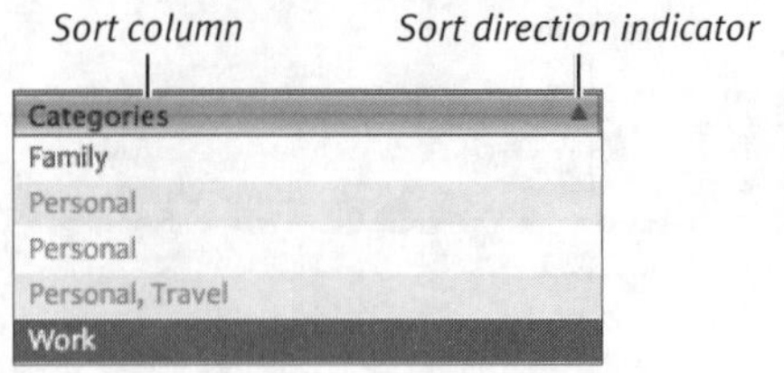

Figure 25.11 Click any column name to sort the Notes list by that column.

4. *Optional:* You can filter the Notes list to show only note titles that contain a particular text string or notes to which a specific category or project has been assigned (**Figure 25.12**).
   - ▲ To filter by title, choose Title is from the Quick Filter drop-down menu above the Notes list, and type a string in the text box.
   - ▲ To filter by category, choose Category is from the drop-down menu, and choose a category from the menu to its right.
   - ▲ To filter by project, choose Project is from the drop-down menu, and choose a project from the menu to its right.

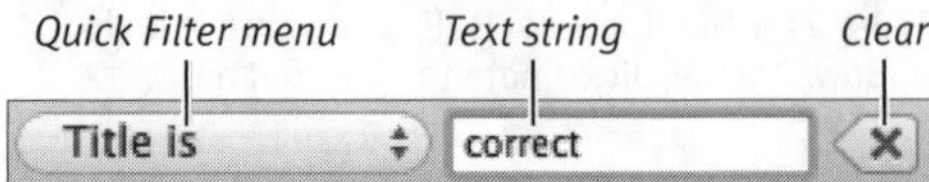

Figure 25.12 To restrict the Notes list, you can filter it by title, category, or project.

✔ Tips

- When a note is open in its own window, you can view other notes by choosing View > Next (⌘]) or View > Previous (⌘[).
- To reverse the effects of filtering (to see the entire Notes list), click the Clear icon beside the filter, delete the text in the text box, set the Category to All, or set the Project to All.
- You can also search for a particular note by typing search text in the Search box above the notes list. Search displays all matching notes as you type.
- For more complex searches, choose Edit > Advanced Search. Enter criteria by choosing options and typing (**Figure 25.13**).

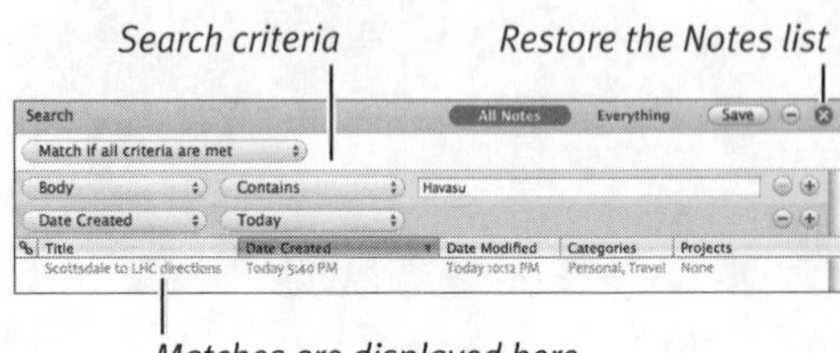

Figure 25.13 Use Advanced Search to specify multiple or field-specific criteria. Click All Notes to search only notes; click Everything to find every match, regardless of the Entourage component in which it's stored.

Custom Views

Another way to filter the Notes list is to create a *custom view* (a set of saved Search criteria that you can replay over and over). Entourage provides several ready-to-use custom Note views, such as Created in the Past 7 Days. Custom views are listed in the left pane of the Entourage window.

To create a new custom view, perform an Advanced Search that specifies the desired criteria, click the Save icon, and name the view in the Save Search dialog box. To edit an existing view, Control-click its name and choose Edit Custom View.

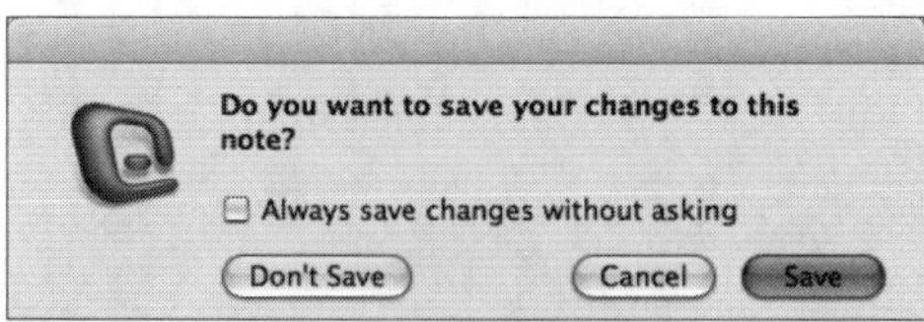

Figure 25.14 When you close an edited note without saving it, this dialog box appears.

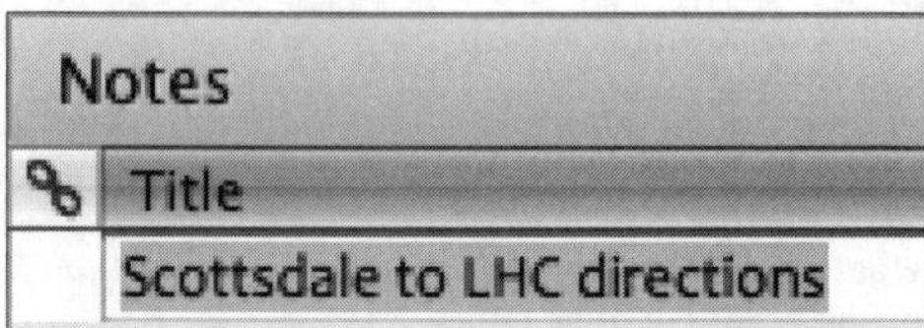

Figure 25.15 You can edit any note's title by clicking its title in the Notes list.

Editing Notes

You can easily change any aspect of a note—its text, formatting, assigned categories, or even its title.

To edit a note:

1. Switch to Notes view.
2. In the Notes list, open the note you want to edit.

   Double-click the note title. Or select the note title and choose File > Open Note (⌘O).
3. Make any desired changes.
4. Choose File > Save, press ⌘S, or close the note window and confirm that you want to save the changes (**Figure 25.14**).

To change a note's title:

1. Select the note in the Notes list.
2. Click the note's title.

   The title is selected and ready for editing (**Figure 25.15**).
3. Edit the title.
4. To save the revised title, press Return or Enter, or click elsewhere in the window.

✓ Tips

- If you edit a note and close its window without saving, a dialog box automatically appears (Figure 25.14).

  Do one of the following:

  - Click Save to save the note's changes.
  - Click Cancel if you want to continue editing the note.
  - Click Don't Save to close the note and discard the changes.

  To instruct Entourage to save all changed notes *automatically* (without forcing you to use the Save command), click the Always save changes without asking check box.
- You can also edit a note's title after opening the note (see Figure 25.3).
- If you miss Entourage 2004's Save toolbar icon, you can restore it by creating a new note or opening an existing one, choosing View > Customize Toolbar, and dragging the Save icon onto the message toolbar.

Printing Notes

As is the case with the other Entourage components, printing options abound. You can print individual notes or combine several into a single print job. You can even generate printouts designed to fit a personal planner, such as a Day Runner.

To print notes:

1. Switch to Notes view.

   The Notes list appears in the main pane (see Figure 25.9).

2. In the Note list, select the title of the note you want to print. To print multiple notes in one printout, ⌘-click each note title.

3. Choose File > Print (⌘P).

   The Print dialog box appears (**Figure 25.16**).

4. Select a printer to use from the Printer drop-down list.

5. From the Print drop-down menu, indicate what you want to print by choosing Selected Notes or All Notes.

6. *Optional:* To print on nonstandard paper, choose its style from the Form drop-down menu.

7. To review print options, click the Layout button. In the Print Layout dialog box (**Figure 25.17**), make any necessary changes and click OK.

8. Indicate the number of copies to print, whether copies should be collated (when printing multiple copies), and whether to print all pages or a page range.

9. If you need to specify a different paper size or orientation, click Page Setup.

10. Click Print to generate the printout.

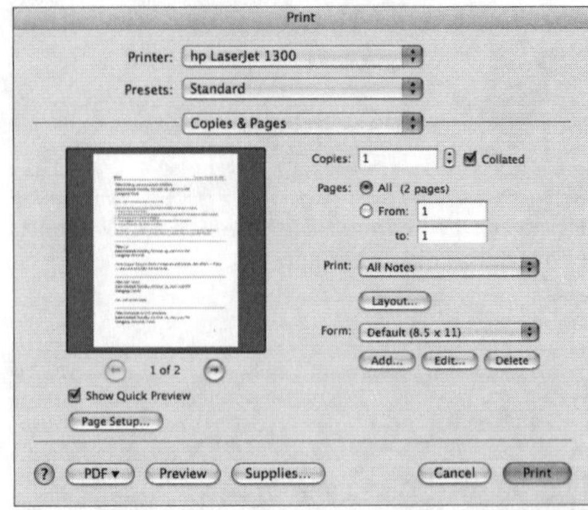

Figure 25.16 Entourage presents this modified Print dialog box for printing notes.

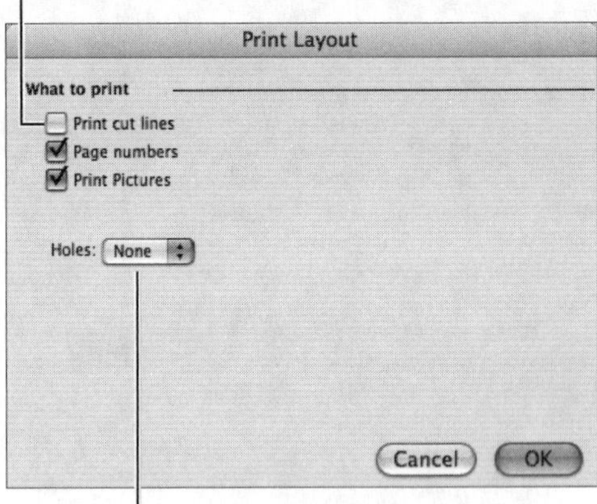

Figure 25.17 Several special print options can be set in the Print Layout dialog box.

✔ Tips

- You can use these same Print procedures when a note is open in its own window. Open note windows include a handy Print toolbar icon.
- Entourage also has a File > Print One Copy (Option⌘P) command. Use it to print the open note with the current print settings, bypassing the Print dialog box.
- To get an idea of what the printout will look like, click the Show Quick Preview check box (see Figure 25.16). The preview changes as you select different print options. Click the arrow buttons beneath the preview to review other pages, if any.
- As with other OS X applications, you can create a PDF (Portable Document Format) file from a notes printout. Click the PDF button and choose Save As PDF, or click Preview to create a temporary PDF file that will open in your default viewer (Preview or Adobe Reader, for example).
- When you choose All Notes from the Print drop-down list, all notes in the Note list are printed in a continuous list, separated by horizontal rules.

26

Newsgroups

Internet newsgroups (sometimes called Usenet newsgroups) are like computerized public bulletin boards. There are tens of thousands of newsgroups on the Internet, each focused on a particular topic. Messages (or *posts*)—resembling email messages—are posted to newsgroups. Anyone with access to the newsgroup can read them. If you respond to a message you've read, your reply is posted along with it. Like email messages, some newsgroup posts contain attachments that you can download.

Using Entourage 2008, you can subscribe to, read, and post to newsgroups. Just as you can manage multiple email accounts with Entourage, you can manage accounts on multiple news servers, too.

Creating a News Server Account

To use Entourage for working with newsgroups, you need access to a news server that uses Network News Transfer Protocol (NNTP). Your Internet service provider (ISP) may have one. Check its sign-up instructions for the name of its news server.

If your ISP doesn't offer newsgroups, you can use a search engine to locate one of the many free public news servers. Visit www.google.com, for example, and search for "public news servers." There are also Web-based news servers, such as groups.google.com, but you view them in a Web browser, not Entourage.

To set up a news server account in Entourage, you'll need the name or IP (Internet Protocol) address of a news server that you can access. You may also need a user name and password. Once you have the necessary information, you can set up Entourage as your newsreader.

To create a news server account:

1. Choose Tools > Accounts.

   The Accounts dialog box appears.
2. Click the News tab (**Figure 26.1**).
3. Click the New toolbar icon to create a new account.

   The Account Setup Assistant appears (**Figure 26.2**).
4. People who reply to your newsgroup posts can respond to your email address and/or post a public reply on the newsgroup. If you have multiple email accounts in Entourage, open the Mail account drop-down list and select the address you want to use for sending newsgroup posts and receiving replies.

   See "Use a Phoney Email Address" in the next section for a helpful tip.

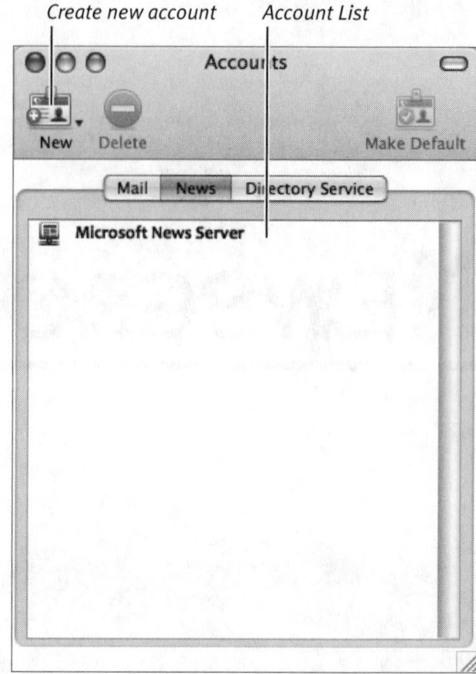

Figure 26.1 The News tab lists the names of all news servers that you've set up, plus those imported from previous versions of Office.

Figure 26.2 Select a reply-to email address from the Mail account list. If you like, you can also enter the name of your company or organization.

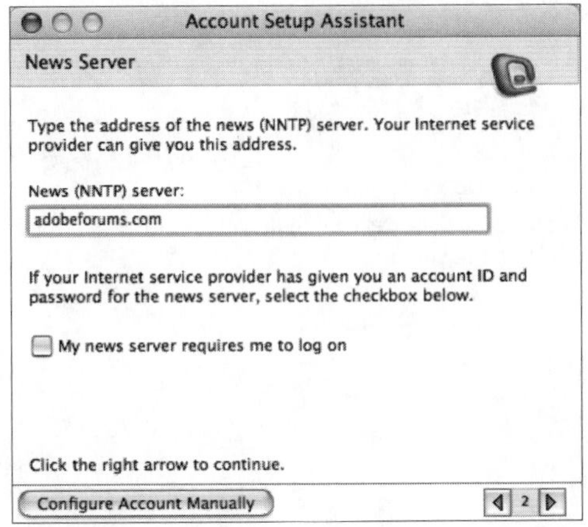

Figure 26.3 Enter the name or IP address of the news server.

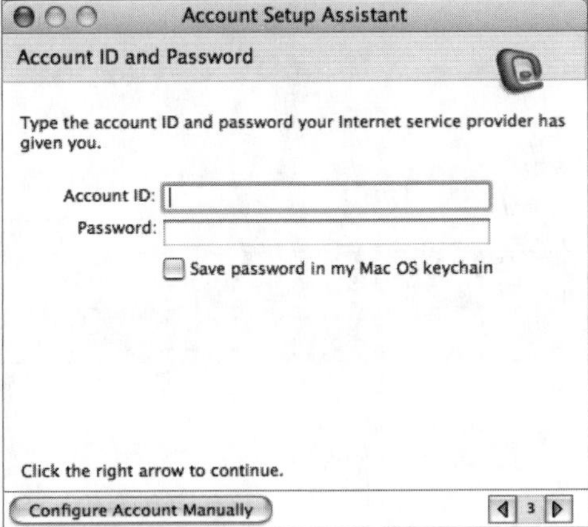

Figure 26.4 If this news server requires you to have an account, enter your account ID (user name) and password.

5. The header information included with your posts can include an organization with which you're affiliated. Enter its name in the Organization text box, if you like.
6. Click the right-arrow button to continue.
7. Enter the name or IP address of the news server to which you want to connect (**Figure 26.3**). If the server requires you to enter a user name and password, check My news server requires me to log on. Click the right-arrow button.
8. If you indicated that a user name and password are required, enter them here (**Figure 26.4**). To have the password automatically entered each time you access the news server, check Save password in my Mac OS keychain. Click the right-arrow button to continue.
9. In the final dialog box, enter a name for the news server account and click Finish.

   The news server account is added to the Accounts list and the Folders list. To add other news servers, repeat these steps for each account.

✔ Tips

- To get you started, you can configure Entourage to access the Microsoft News Server (`msnews.microsoft.com`) for Microsoft's product-related newsgroups.
- Your default news account is shown in bold in the Accounts list. To set a different default, select the account and click Make Default (see Figure 26.1). Note that you can also *delete* news server accounts here.
- People who send junk email (*spam*) often collect the addresses of people who post to newsgroups. To avoid receiving unwanted email in your primary account, consider using Hotmail or another free email account as your email address.
- Most news servers do *not* require a user name and password. Unless you're told otherwise, assume this is the case.

Managing Newsgroup Lists

Once you've set up at least one news server account, you can download the list of newsgroups available on that server. You can also specify the newsgroups you'd like to read on a regular basis.

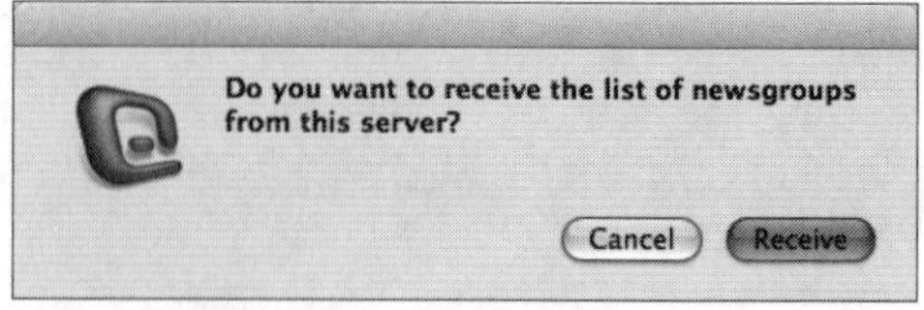

Figure 26.5 Click Receive to download the newsgroup list from the server.

To view the newsgroups on a server:

1. Select the news server in the Folders list.
2. If this is the first time you've selected this news server, Entourage will ask if you want to receive the list of the newsgroups carried on the server (**Figure 26.5**).
3. Click the Receive button.

   The list of available newsgroups will appear in Entourage's right pane (**Figure 26.6**). It may take a while to receive the entire list, depending on the speed of your Internet connection and the number of newsgroups the server offers.

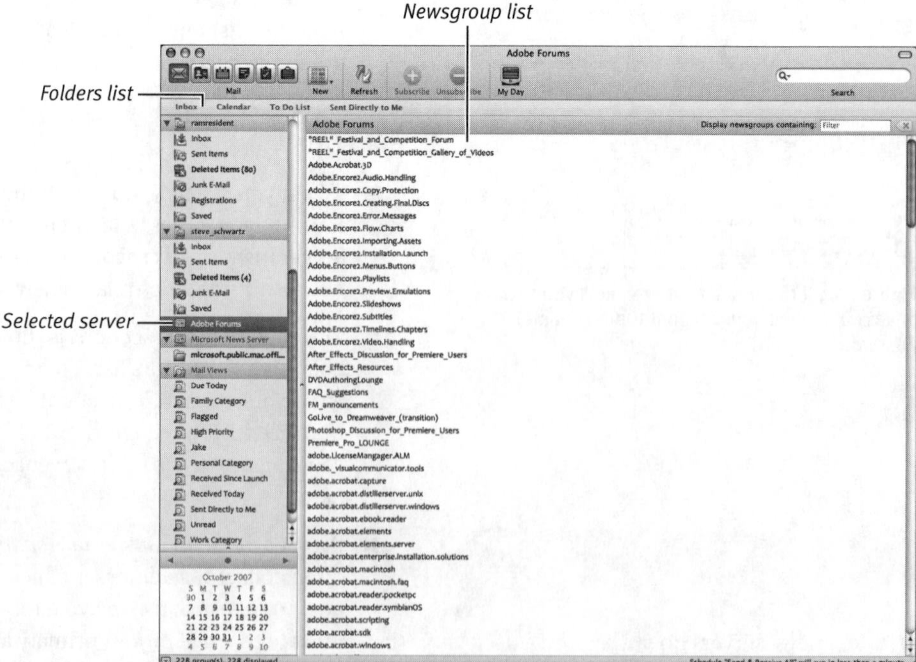

Figure 26.6 The list of newsgroups appears.

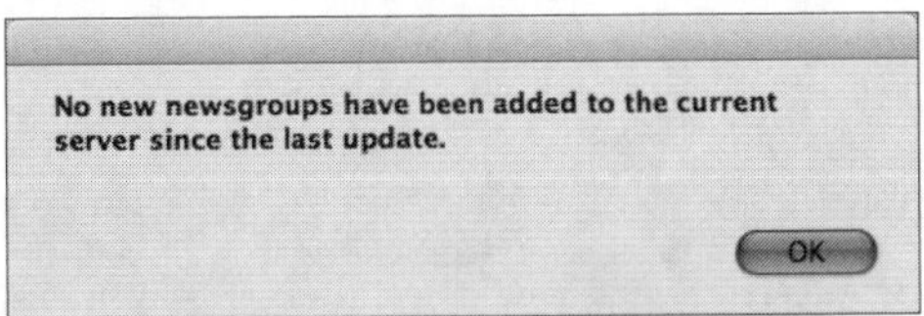

Figure 26.7 If you choose the Get New Newsgroups command but there are no new ones, this message appears. (If you click Refresh, no message appears if there are no new newsgroups.)

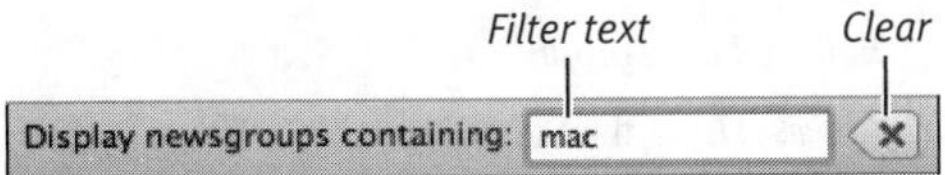

Figure 26.8 Type a text string to filter the newsgroup list to show only newsgroups that contain the string.

Updating the newsgroup list

The newsgroups available on any given news server can—and often do—change over time. If it's been awhile since you last downloaded the list of newsgroups on a server, you can refresh the list.

To update the list of newsgroups on a given server:

1. Click the name of the news server account in the Folders list.
2. *Do one of the following:*
   - ▲ Click the Refresh icon on the toolbar.
   - ▲ Choose View > Get New Newsgroups.

   If there are new newsgroups, they will appear in the list. If no new newsgroups have been added, you will be informed (**Figure 26.7**).

Filtering the newsgroup list

Many news servers carry thousands of newsgroups. It can be a daunting task to find a particular one that you may want to read. Entourage lets you *filter* the list of newsgroup names to show only the ones of interest.

To filter the list of newsgroup names:

1. Click the name of the news server account in the Folders list.
2. Type a search string (**Figure 26.8**) in the box labeled Display newsgroups containing (located above the newsgroup list).

   Like a Spotlight search, the filter is automatically applied to the list as you type. Only newsgroups that contain the search string in their titles are displayed; all others are temporarily hidden.
3. To restore the complete newsgroup list after filtering, click the Clear icon or delete the filter text.

Use a Phoney Email Address

Because supplying a real reply-to email address—even a Hotmail or Yahoo! one—can subject you to unwanted email, you might want to go a step further and use a *fake* address. Unfortunately, since you can only select a registered account for your newsgroup reply-to address (see Figure 26.2), you'll have to create the fake account in Entourage.

Subscribing to Newsgroups

If you find some newsgroups you'd like to read regularly, you can *subscribe* to them. This isn't the same as subscribing to a magazine; you don't receive anything automatically. And subscribing to a newsgroup doesn't add you to a list somewhere, as subscribing to an email mailing list does. Subscribing simply makes it easier to follow a newsgroup by adding its name to the Folders list beneath the news server and displaying its name in bold in the server's newsgroup list.

To subscribe to a newsgroup:

1. Click the name of the news server account in the Folders list.

   The newsgroup list for the selected news server appears in the pane on the right.

2. *Optional:* Filter the newsgroup list (as described on the previous page) to make it simpler to find newsgroups to which you want to subscribe.

3. Select a newsgroup to which you want to subscribe.

4. Click the Subscribe toolbar icon (**Figure 26.9**), choose Edit > Subscribe, or Control-click the newsgroup name and choose Subscribe from the pop-up menu that appears.

   The newsgroup name is added to the Folders list beneath the news server and is displayed in bold in the newsgroup list.

To view only subscribed-to newsgroups:

1. With a news server's newsgroup list displayed, choose View > Subscribed Only.

   Newsgroups to which you haven't subscribed are hidden (**Figure 26.10**).

2. To see the entire newsgroup list, choose View > Subscribed Only again.

   The command works as a toggle.

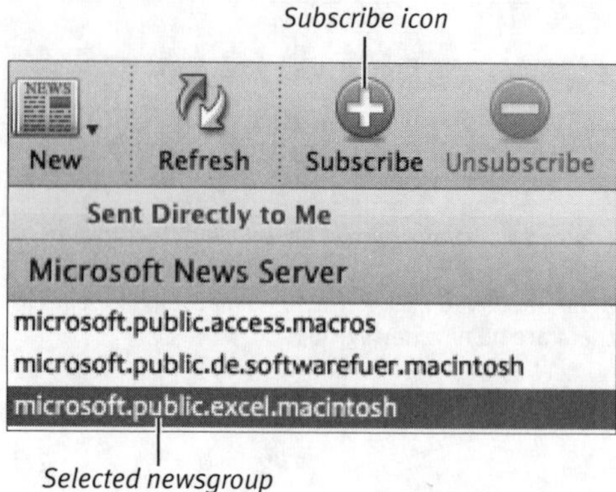

Figure 26.9 Click the Subscribe toolbar icon to subscribe to the selected newsgroup.

Microsoft News Server
microsoft.public.excel.macintosh
microsoft.public.mac.office.entourage

Figure 26.10 Only newsgroups to which you've subscribed remain visible. Their names are shown in bold.

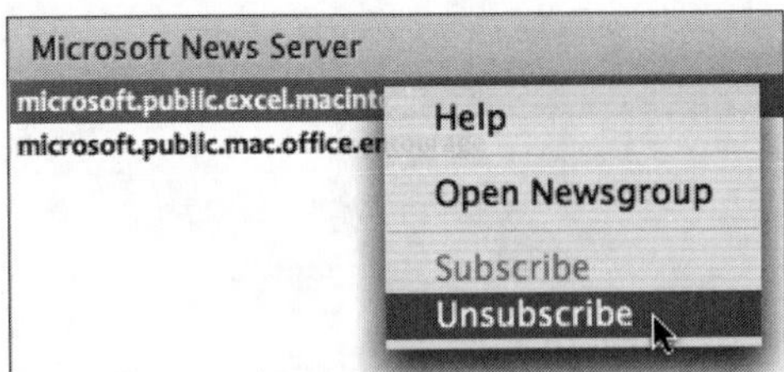

Figure 26.11 You can Control-click a newsgroup and choose Unsubscribe from the pop-up menu.

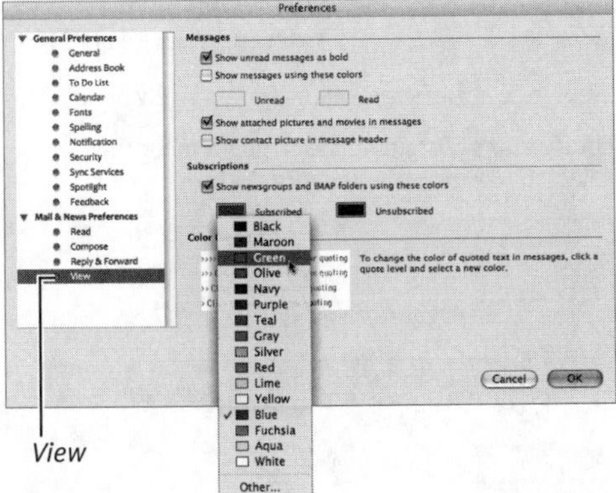

Figure 26.12 Click the Subscribed box to display this pop-up color list, and then select a new color.

To unsubscribe from a newsgroup:

1. Click the name of the news server account in the Folders list.
2. *Optional:* To easily find the newsgroup, choose View > Subscribed Only.
3. Select the newsgroup from the list in the right pane.

   The names of subscribed-to newsgroups are shown in bold text.
4. Click the Unsubscribe toolbar icon (see Figure 26.9), choose Edit > Unsubscribe, or Control-click the newsgroup name and choose Unsubscribe from the pop-up menu (**Figure 26.11**).

✔ Tip

- Names of newsgroups to which you have subscribed appear in bold in the newsgroup list. They can also appear in color, if you set a Preferences setting. To pick a color, choose Entourage > Preferences, click the View topic in the left pane, and ensure that Show newsgroups and IMAP folders using these colors is checked. Click the Subscribed color box, select a color from the pop-up list, and click OK (**Figure 26.12**).

Managing Newsgroup Messages

Once you've set up a news server account, retrieved the list of newsgroups, and found a newsgroup or two that you'd like to read, the next step is to retrieve the current list of posts and read the ones that interest you.

Older posts are periodically deleted from the news server to make room for new ones. Posts are usually updated several times a day.

To manage the current list of posts in a newsgroup:

1. *Do one of the following:*
   - ▲ If you subscribe to the newsgroup, click its name in the Folders list. The initial list of message headers for the newsgroup appears (**Figure 26.13**).
   - ▲ If you don't subscribe to the newsgroup, select the news server in the Folders list and then double-click the name of the desired newsgroup in the right pane. The list of message headers appears in a new window.
2. If additional posts for this newsgroup are available on the server, you can retrieve the next batch by clicking the More toolbar icon (Figure 26.13) or by choosing View > Get More News Messages.
3. You can sort the message list by clicking the Arrange By text above the list and choosing a sort field (**Figure 26.14**). To change the sort direction, click the text to the right of Arrange By (**Figure 26.15**).

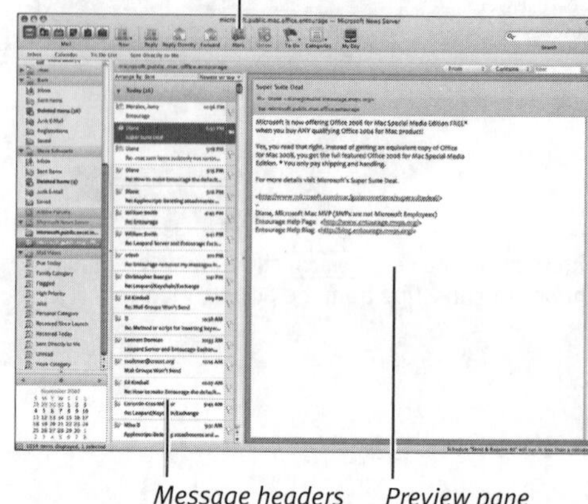

Figure 26.13 Current message headers for the selected newsgroup appear in the message list.

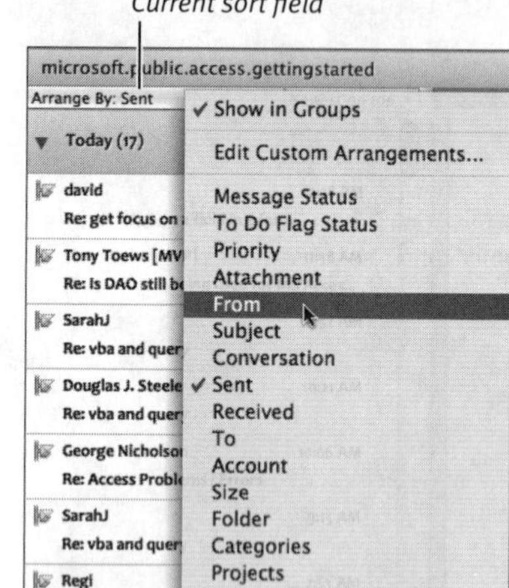

Figure 26.14 Click the Arrange By text to choose a sort field.

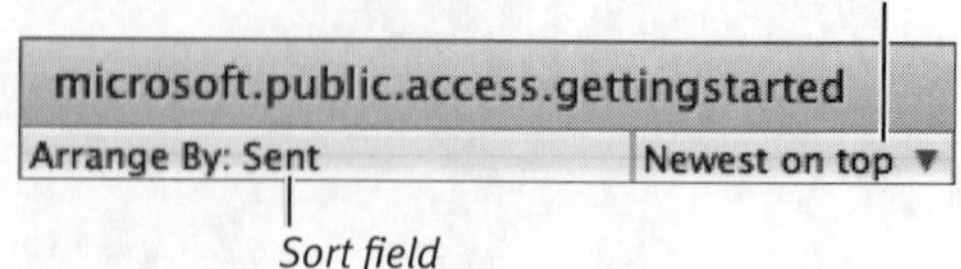

Figure 26.15 Each click on the sort direction text reverses the sort order.

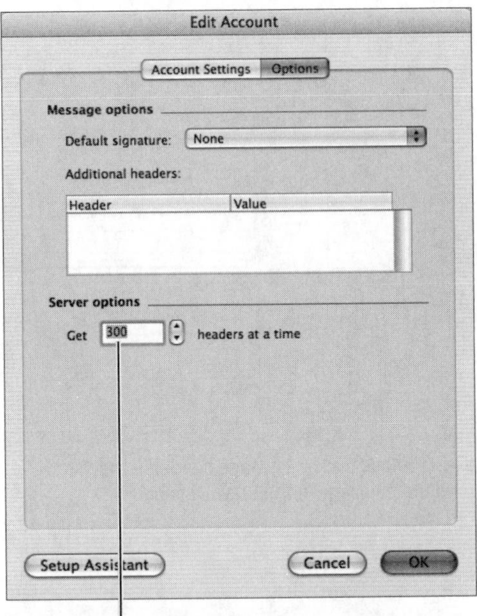

Figure 26.16 You can change the number of messages downloaded from a given news server in each pass.

Expand/collapse

[ANN] Office for Mac 2008 prices annou...

JE McGimpsey 10/20/07
Re: [ANN] Office for Mac 2008 prices a...

CCM 10/20/07
Re: [ANN] Office for Mac 2008 prices a...

John McGhie 10/13/07
Re: [ANN] Office for Mac 2008 prices a...

Mike Persell 10/13/07
Re: [ANN] Office for Mac 2008 prices a...

Diane 9/29/07
Re: [ANN] Office for Mac 2008 prices a...

Figure 26.17 When Show in Groups is enabled, you can group messages by Subject (shown here), Sent, or almost anything else you want.

✔ Tips

- The number of message headers downloaded in each pass is a news server-specific setting. The default is `300`. To increase or decrease the number, choose Tools > Accounts, click the News tab in the Accounts dialog box, and double-click the name of the news server. Click the Options tab, specify a new number for Server options (**Figure 26.16**), click OK, and then close the Accounts dialog box.
- To make it easier to follow a particular message conversation (called a *thread* or *group*), choose View > Arrange By > Subject and ensure that the View > Arrange By > Show in Groups command is checked. This groups every original message with all responses to it (**Figure 26.17**).
- Messages can be grouped by many other useful criteria, such as Sent (date posted) or From (message author).
- To simultaneously reveal or hide all grouped messages in the message list, select any message header and then choose View > Expand All or View > Collapse All.

  Choosing Collapse All results in a list of only groups, followed by a number in parentheses showing the number of messages in each group. To expand a group so you can read its messages, click the triangle icon to the left of the group's name (Figure 26.17).

Reading Messages

When Entourage displays the message list for a newsgroup or updates the list, it downloads only the message headers—not the message body or attachments. After you've selected one or more message headers, Entourage downloads their text.

To read a message:

1. *Do one of the following:*
   - ▲ Select a message header to view its text in the Preview pane (**Figure 26.18**).
   - ▲ Double-click a message header to open the message in its own window (**Figure 26.19**).

   The text of the selected message is downloaded to your Mac and then displayed.

2. To read additional messages, *do any of the following:*
   - ▲ Click another message header in the message list.
   - ▲ Choose View > Next (⌘]) or View > Previous (⌘[).
   - ▲ Click the Next or Previous toolbar icon. (You can only do this if reading messages in a separate window and you've customized the toolbar by adding these icons.)

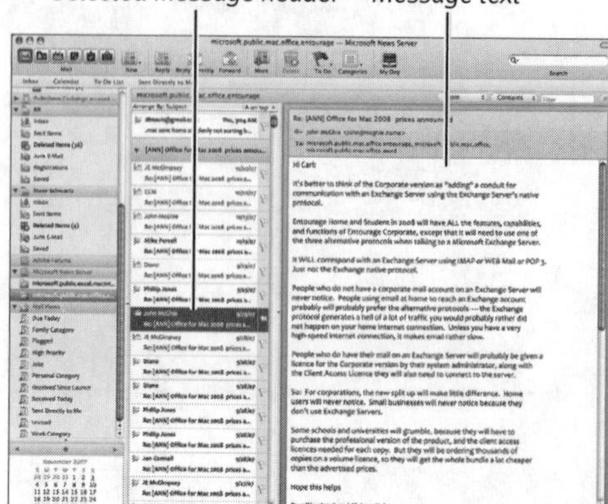

Figure 26.18 Click a message header in the list to read the message in the Preview pane.

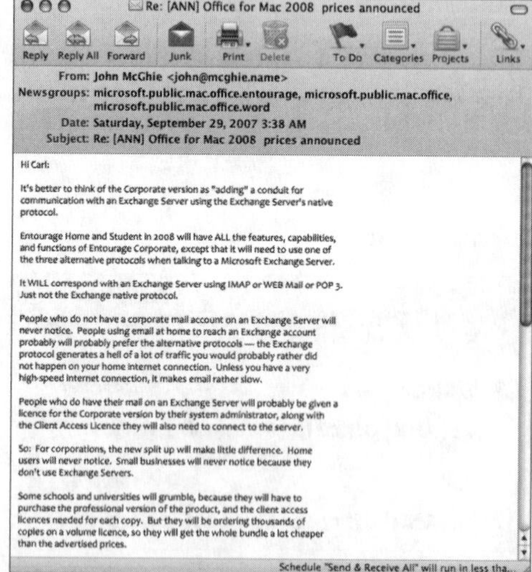

Figure 26.19 Double-click a message header to open the message in its own window.

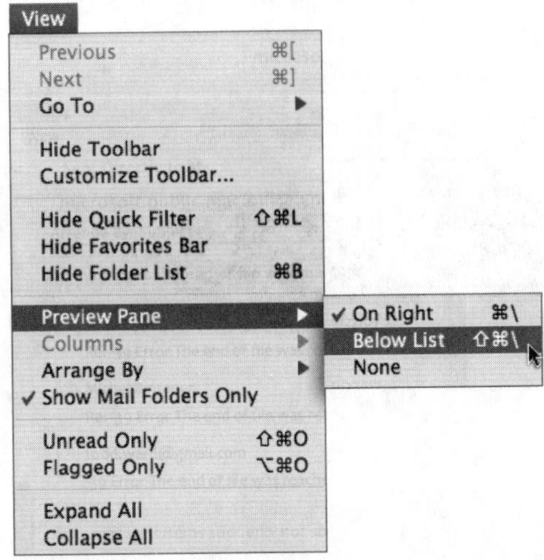

Figure 26.20 You can choose a location for the Preview pane or even opt to hide it.

✔ Tips

- You can also use the cursor keys to select messages to read. Press → and ← to expand or collapse a group, and press ↓ and ↑ to read the next or previous message. Note, however, that any message the cursor touches—even momentarily—will be downloaded.
- You can scroll through a lengthy message by holding down Spacebar or scroll up by pressing Shift Spacebar. When you reach the end of the message, press Spacebar to jump to the next unread message in the message list.
- You cannot *delete* newsgroup messages as you can email. However, you can set the message list to display only messages you haven't read by choosing View > Unread Only. To revert to seeing the entire list, choose the command again.
- You can select the headers of messages you want to ignore and mark them as read by choosing Message > Mark as Read (⌘T). Then set the view to Unread Only to hide these messages in the message list.
- In Entourage 2008, the location of the Preview pane is up to you. Choose a location from the View > Preview Pane submenu (**Figure 26.20**).

Posting to Newsgroups

You can post messages to newsgroups by either replying to an existing message or creating a new one.

It's common courtesy (and in your own best interest) to read the messages in the newsgroup for a while before posting. Also, be sure to read the FAQ for the newsgroup. The FAQ (if one exists) usually explains what constitutes an appropriate posting. Messages the group's regular participants deem inappropriate are likely to be on the receiving end of *flames* (attacking or insulting messages).

Figure 26.21 To send a reply to the newsgroup, click the Reply toolbar icon.

To reply to a message:

1. Click a header in the message list to view the message in the Preview pane, or double-click a header to open the message in its own window.
2. *Do one of the following:*
   - ▲ To post a reply to the newsgroup, click the Reply toolbar icon (**Figure 26.21**), choose Message > Reply, or press ⌘R.
   - ▲ To send an email message to the author of the newsgroup post, choose Message > Reply to Sender, click the Reply Directly toolbar icon (displayed at the top of the Entourage window), or press Option⌘R.
   - ▲ To post a reply to the newsgroup *and* send an email message to the author, click the Reply All toolbar icon (displayed at the top of an open message window), choose Message > Reply to All, or press Shift⌘R.

   A new message window opens, containing a copy of the message to which you are replying. The message is pre-addressed to the newsgroup, the author, or both, as appropriate.

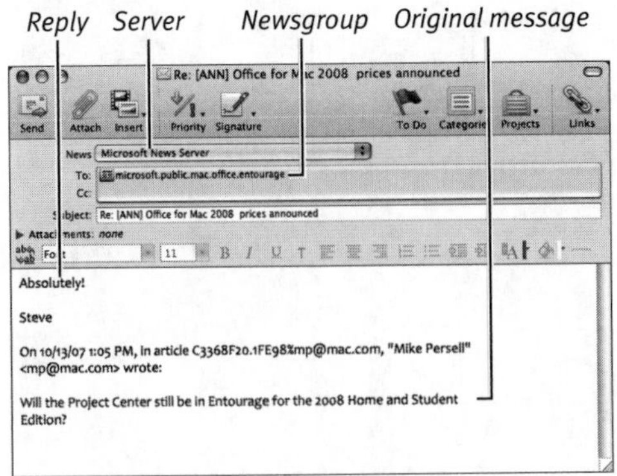

Figure 26.22 A pre-addressed reply message opens. Remove any unnecessary text and type your reply.

3. Delete any of the original message text that's irrelevant to your response, but quote the part of the message to which you're replying.

4. Add your comments in the body of the message (**Figure 26.22**).

5. *Do one of the following:*
   - ▲ Click the Send toolbar icon at the top of the message window.
   - ▲ Choose Message > Post Message Now (⌘Return) or Message > Post Message Later (Shift⌘Return). *Post Message Later* is the equivalent of the Send Message Later command for email. The message is stored in your Outbox and sent the next time you perform a Send/Receive for your newsgroup reply-to email account.

✔ Tips

- Different Reply icons are displayed above the Entourage window and at the top of an open message window. The former shows Reply and Reply Directly icons, while the latter shows Reply and Reply All icons (see Figure 26.21).
- Before sending a reply, carefully check the To line. If the original author sent the post to multiple newsgroups, you may want to respond to only the most popular or logical one rather than sending your reply to *all* the groups.

To post a new message to a newsgroup:

1. Open the newsgroup list to which you want to post a message by selecting it in the Folders list or by double-clicking it in the news server's newsgroup list.
2. Click the New toolbar icon, choose File > New > News Message, or press ⌘N.

   A new message window opens, addressed to the newsgroup (**Figure 26.23**).
3. Add other desired recipients to the address field (additional newsgroups go in the To line and email recipients go in the Cc line), enter a Subject, and type the body of the message as you would an email message.
4. *Optional:* You can add attachments as you would with an email message. Click the Attach icon, choose Message > Add Attachments, or press ⌘E.

   You may want to compress large attachments to reduce retrieval time for the recipients.
5. *Optional:* Click the Use HTML icon on the Formatting toolbar (Figure 26.23) to toggle between unformatted and formatted text. You can also choose Format > HTML.

   However, be aware that many people use text-only newsreaders and may find formatted text unreadable.
6. When you're through composing your message, *do one of the following:*
   - Click the Send toolbar icon.
   - Choose Message > Post Message Now (⌘Return) or Message > Post Message Later (Shift⌘Return).

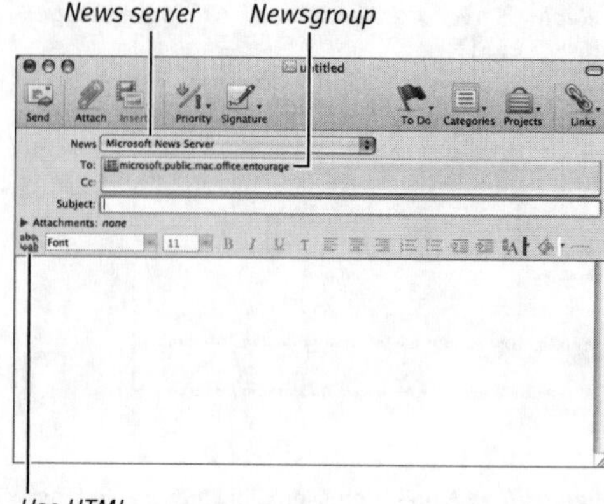

Figure 26.23 Compose your message in the new window that appears.

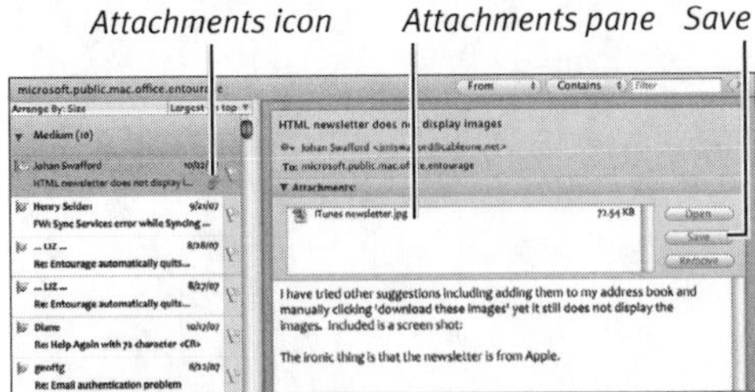

Figure 26.24 The Attachments icon and pane appear after the message is downloaded from the server.

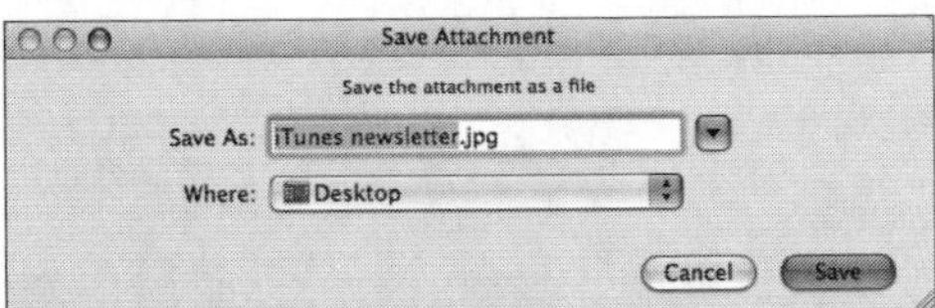

Figure 26.25 Select a destination drive and folder, and then click Save.

✔ Tips

- Picture attachments that are in a format Entourage supports (such as JPEG, GIF, and PDF) appear as pictures in the body of the message.
- Newsgroups that actively promote attachments (such as pictures, movies, or song files) may have the word *binaries* in their name.
- To find messages that contain attachments without first downloading them, sort the message list by size. Choose Size from the Arrange By pop-out menu above the message list (Figure 26.14).

Downloading Files from Newsgroups

Attached files are shown in newsgroup message headers as attachments, just as they are in email messages. However, the paper clip icon does not appear in the message header until you've downloaded the message.

You can usually tell if a message contains an attachment by its size—anything over a few kilobytes is almost certain to include an attachment. After you've previewed or opened the message, you can handle its attachments in the same way as you would in email (see Chapter 21).

To download a file from a newsgroup:

1. In the Folders list, select the newsgroup or double-click the newsgroup's name in the newsgroup list.
2. Select the header of a message that you believe contains an attachment.

   After your Mac downloads the message and attachment(s) from the news server, the Attachments pane appears (**Figure 26.24**).
3. Select the attachment and click the Save button beside the Attachments pane.

   The Save Attachment dialog box appears (**Figure 26.25**).
4. Navigate to the drive and folder in which you want to save the file, and then click the Save button.

27

My Day

New in Office 2008, My Day is a separate application that displays upcoming events and tasks—even when Entourage and other Office applications aren't running. Unlike Office Reminders, the My Day list of events and tasks isn't restricted to only those for which you've set reminders.

Launching My Day

You can launch My Day automatically or manually, depending on whether you always want it running or simply want it to be visible at certain times.

To launch My Day manually:

- *Do any of the following:*
  - ▲ Within Entourage, click the My Day toolbar icon.
  - ▲ Within Entourage, choose Window > My Day (⌘9).
  - ▲ Double-click the My Day file icon (found in the /Applications/Microsoft Office 2008/Office folder).
  - ▲ If My Day is running but its window is closed, choose Show My Day from the My Day menu (**Figure 27.1**), click the My Day icon on the Dock, or press Control M.

To launch My Day automatically:

1. Launch My Day manually by following one of the procedures listed above.
2. *Do either of the following:*
   - ▲ Click the Preferences icon at the bottom of the My Day window.
   - ▲ Choose Preferences from the My Day menu (Figure 27.1).

   The Preferences window appears.
3. If the General icon isn't automatically selected, click it now.
4. Check the option to Open after computer logon (**Figure 27.2**), and click OK.

   In future computing sessions, My Day will automatically run at startup—even if no other Office 2008 applications are running.

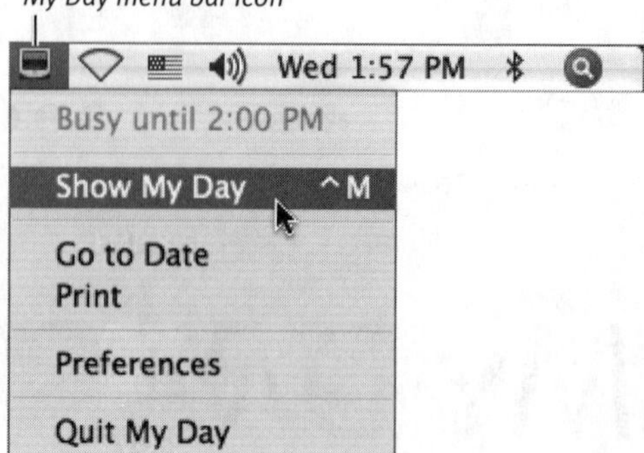

Figure 27.1 Depending on a General preferences setting (Figure 27.2), you can choose commands from this My Day icon or from the My Day menu.

Figure 27.2 You can set preferences for My Day, such as whether it automatically runs at startup.

✔ Tip

- Depending on the Show... option you select from General preferences (Figure 27.2), My Day will either display an icon menu on the right side of the menu bar (Show on Mac OS menu bar) or an application menu (Show in Dock).

Figure 27.3 Like other Mac applications, My Day provides the three standard buttons in its top left corner.

Figure 27.4 When rolled up (unzoomed), My Day displays only the date, time, time line, and icons.

Changing the Display

Like other applications, My Day offers several ways for you to change the way it's displayed

To change how My Day is displayed:

- *Do any of the following:*
  - **Hide/show.** To hide or show My Day, choose Hide My Day or Show My Day from the My Day menu (see Figure 27.1), or press Control M.
  - **Minimize/maximize.** To minimize My Day to the Dock, click the minimize button (**Figure 27.3**). To maximize My Day (moving it from the Dock back onto the Desktop), click its Dock icon.
  - **Unzoom/zoom.** Click this button (Figure 27.3) to roll up My Day (**Figure 27.4**) or restore the normal display.
  - **Keep on top.** My Day's layering can optionally be set to ensure that it always floats atop other windows. Click the Preferences icon at the bottom of the My Day window, click the General tab in the Preferences dialog box, and ensure that Keep on top of all other applications is checked (see Figure 27.2).

✔ Tip

- It isn't necessary to quit My Day before shutting down. However, if you'd like to do so, choose Quit My Day from the My Day menu (Figure 27.1) or choose Quit from the My Day icon in the Dock. To restart My Day after quitting it, use any of the methods described on the previous page.

The My Day Interface

Following are the important elements of the My Day interface (**Figure 27.5**), what they do, and how to use them.

Displayed date. This is the date for the events and tasks that you are currently viewing. If you click this date, the Go to Date dialog box appears (**Figure 27.6**). Type the date you want to view, and click OK.

View other dates. Use these icons to view the events and tasks for other dates. Click an arrow icon to go back (left) or forward (right) one day at a time. Click the center (bullet) icon to display today's information.

Time line. Click the arrow icons to review the displayed date's time slots. Each slot for which an event is scheduled is shaded blue.

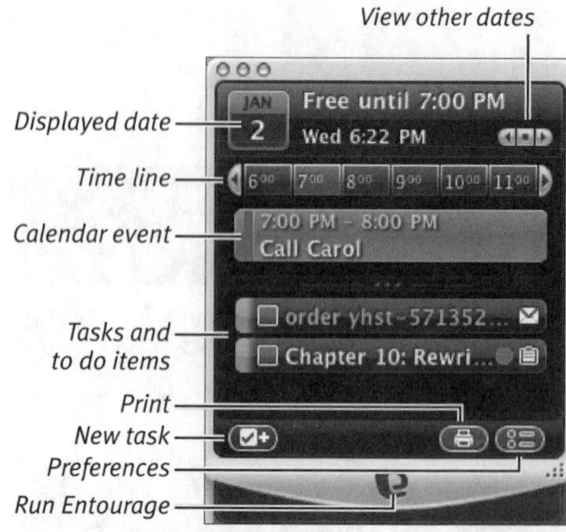

Figure 27.5 The My Day window.

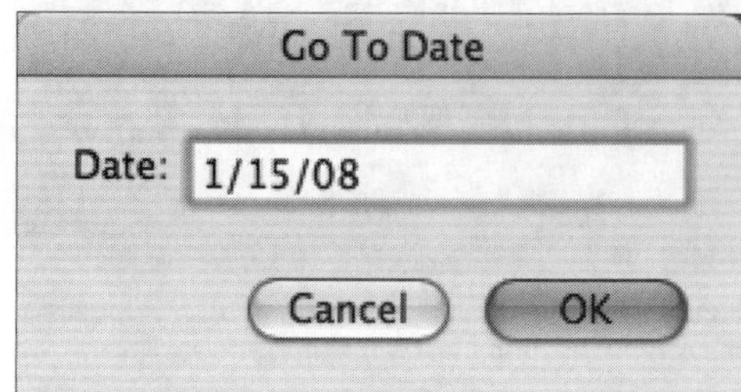

Figure 27.6 Use the Go to Date dialog box to display information for a specific date.

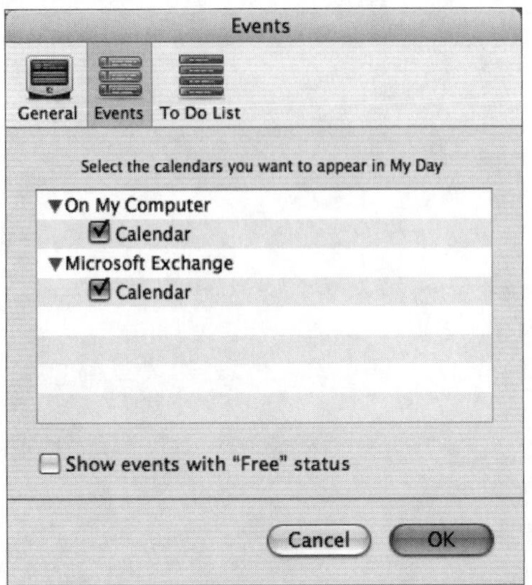

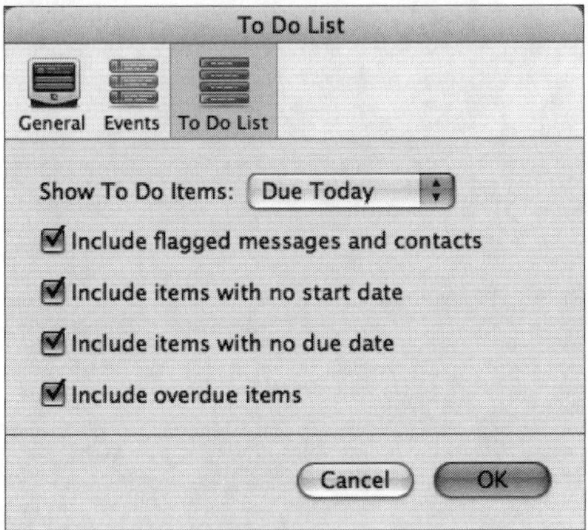

Figure 27.7 In addition to the General preferences (see Figure 27.2), there are others for Events (top) and To Do List items (bottom).

Calendar events, tasks, and to do items. All scheduled events, tasks, and to do items are listed in the main part of the window. You can open any item by double-clicking it. To mark a task or to do item as complete (removing it from the list), click its check box.

Print. Click this icon to print a list of the events, tasks, and to do items for the displayed date. You can also choose Print from the My Day menu (see Figure 27.1).

New task. To create a new Entourage task, click this icon.

Preferences. Click this icon to review or change My Day preference settings (**Figure 27.7**). You can also choose Preferences from the My Day menu (see Figure 27.1).

Launch Entourage. If Entourage isn't running, you can launch it by clicking this icon.

✔ Tips

- Events that have already passed in the current day are removed from My Day. However, they remain marked on the time line. Thus, although you can see that an event has passed, you'll have to view the Calendar to determine what the event was.
- You can also view items for a specific date by choosing Go to Date from the My Day menu (see Figure 27.1).
- Currently, all-day events are *not* shown in My Day. If you want to display an all-day event, change it to a scheduled event with an assigned time.

28 Microsoft Exchange Accounts

About Synchronization

Synchronization is the primary advantage of an Exchange account. As long as you have a network or Internet connection, changes that you make to your Exchange Address Books, Calendars, and mail are automatically synched with the server once per minute. This means that if you examine, modify, or create new items on any computer using Exchange-compliant software, the data will be identical on all of those computers.

If you compute in multiple locations, such as work, home, and on the road, you don't have to worry that you have the wrong set of messages, contacts, or appointments. As long as you use your Exchange email account, Address Books, and Calendars (rather than the ones in Entourage's On My Computer folder), you can access and use the data from anywhere it's convenient.

To learn how to synchronize account data with an iPod, iPhone, or iPod Touch, see "Synchronizing Entourage with an iPod" in Chapter 20.

If you're associated with or work for a large corporation or institution, your mail may be handled by Microsoft Exchange Server. With Office 2008 for Mac or Office 2008 for Mac: Special Media Edition (but *not* the Home & Student Edition), Entourage can manage your Exchange account email, as well as Exchange Calendars and Address Books.

When you use an Exchange account, certain items are continuously kept in sync in the application and on the server. The following Exchange account items can be synchronized using Entourage:

- Message folders and subfolders
- Exchange Address Book contacts
- Exchange Calendar and events
- Flagged (to-do) items

Only *Exchange* Address Books and Calendars are synched. (You can create *multiple* Exchange Address Books and Calendars.) Items in the standard Address Book and Calendar are visible and available for editing only in the copy of Entourage in which they're created.

Tasks, notes, and message rules created in Entourage are not synchronized. Message rules created in certain other email clients that *are* synchronized can be executed—but not edited—in Entourage.

Exchange Email

Mail sent from or received by your Exchange account is stored on the server and remains there until it's deleted. Entourage also stores a local copy of Exchange data on your Mac. As a result, you get the best of both worlds. You can connect to the server from any computer to read and create email, and you can review existing messages in Entourage even when you aren't connected to the corporate network or the Internet.

Setting up an Exchange account

Although more account data is required, setting up an Exchange account in Entourage follows the same basic steps as setting up other types of accounts (see "Setting Up an Account" in Chapter 21). At a minimum, you'll need your Exchange email address and password (**Figure 28.1**).

If automatic setup fails, you'll also need the names of the Exchange, LDAP (Lightweight Directory Access Protocol), and Public servers, as well as whether you must use SSL (Secure Sockets Layer) when connecting to the servers. If you have trouble registering the account, contact your network administrator or IT department for assistance.

To set up an Exchange account:

1. Choose Tools > Accounts.
   The Accounts dialog box appears.
2. On the Mail tab, click the New toolbar icon and choose Exchange or Mail from the drop-down menu.
   The Account Setup Assistant appears (Figure 28.1).
3. Enter your full Exchange email address, such as `steve@jmass.net`. Click the check box, and then click the right-arrow icon to continue.

Figure 28.1 Enter your Exchange email address, click the check box, and then click the right-arrow icon.

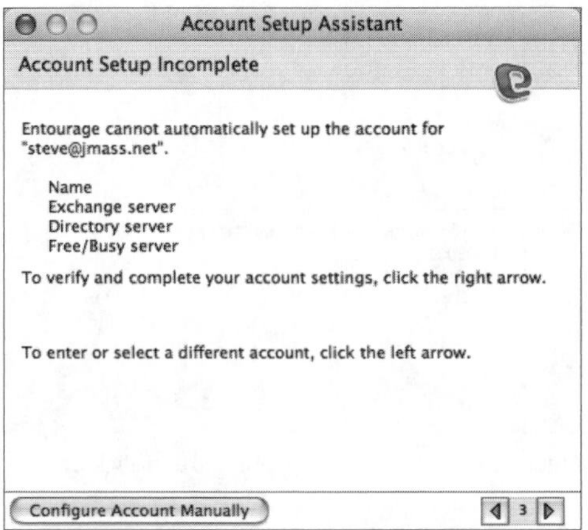

Figure 28.2 If Entourage can't set up your Exchange account automatically, this screen appears.

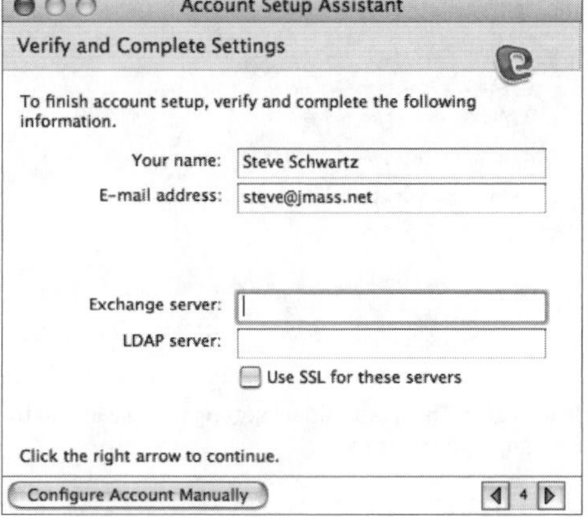

Figure 28.3 The Account Setup Assistant will guide you through the remaining steps. Be sure to test and verify the account settings in the final step.

4. *One of the following will occur:*
   - ▲ Entourage may indicate that it has determined the account settings, based on the email address entered.
   - ▲ Entourage can't determine the account settings (**Figure 28.2**). You can enter the necessary information on the Account Setup Assistant screens that follow (**Figure 28.3**).

✔ Tips

- If you have the required account information, you can also configure the account manually by clicking the Configure Account Manually button (Figure 28.2).
- You can add additional mail folders and subfolders and create message rules to automatically move relevant messages into the proper subfolder. For assistance, read the next section and "Organizing the Mail" in Chapter 21.

Sending and receiving mail

Unlike a POP or Hotmail account, there's no need to create a send/receive schedule for an Exchange account, add it to the Send/Receive All schedule, or ever click the Send/Receive toolbar icon. As long as you're connected to the Exchange server (over the network or Internet), the contents of your Exchange mail folders in Entourage are automatically synched with the server once per minute. Incoming messages simply arrive in your Inbox without requiring a schedule or action on your part.

✔ Tip

- In addition to your Exchange mail, contact records in your Exchange Address Books and events in your Exchange Calendars are also synched continuously.

Out of Office autoreplies

If you go on vacation or a business trip, you can configure Entourage to automatically send an out of office message in response to incoming mail that's addressed to your Exchange account. Because the autoreply is handled by the server, the out of office tool works even when Entourage isn't running.

To enable an out of office autoreply:

1. In the folder list, select the Exchange account for which you want to enable an out of office autoreply.
2. Choose Tools > Out of Office.

   The Out of Office Assistant appears (**Figure 28.4**).
3. Click the Send Out of Office messages radio button.
4. Type your reply text in the Reply to messages with text box.
5. If your company is running Microsoft Exchange Server 2007, click the More options icon to expand the dialog box (**Figure 28.5**). You can specify an out of office time frame and whether replies will be sent to email received from outside of your company.
6. Click OK.

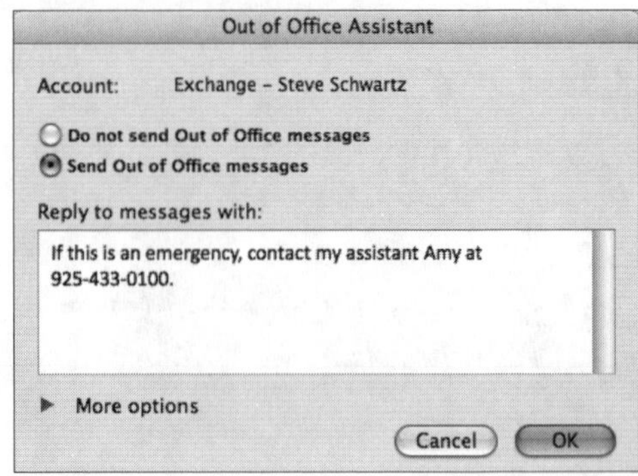

Figure 28.4 Set out of office options and click OK.

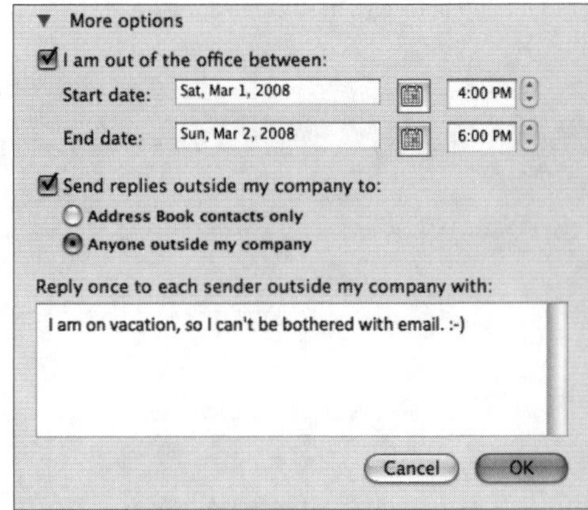

Figure 28.5 These additional settings are available to Exchange 2007 users.

✔ Tips

- Enabling an out of office autoreply affects only the selected Exchange account. Other Exchange accounts (if any) must be enabled separately.
- When you return to the office, be sure to disable the out of office autoreply for each of your Exchange accounts. Select the Do not send Out of Office messages radio button and then click OK.
- Although the Out of Office Assistant can only be used with Exchange accounts, you can generate a similar message for POP and IMAP accounts by creating a message rule (**Figure 28.6**). Specify messages to which the rule will apply and add a Reply action with a Reply Text message. Enable the rule as you're leaving; disable the rule when you return. (Note that you *must* leave your Mac and Entourage running while you're away.)

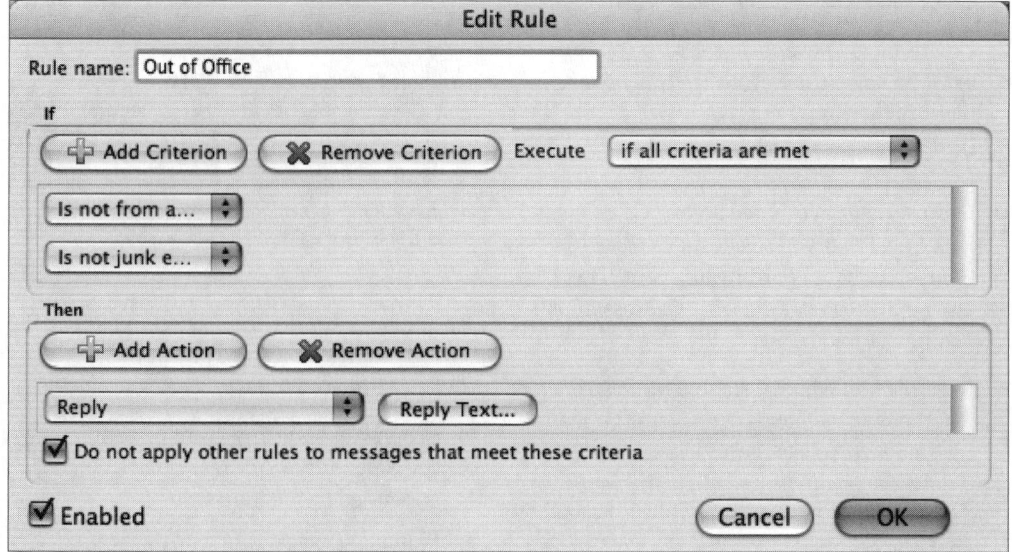

Figure 28.6 You can create a rule to send an out of office message from any non-Exchange account. In this example, an autoreply is sent to every incoming message except those received from a mailing list or classified as junk mail.

Exchange Calendars and Address Books

If you check the folder list, you'll note that your Exchange account includes Calendar and Contacts folders (**Figure 28.7**). They are the default *Exchange* Calendar and Contacts (Address Book)—one for each Exchange account. These folders are unrelated to the *Entourage* Calendar and Address Book that are stored on and accessible only from your Mac. Your Exchange Calendars and Contacts can be accessed from any Mac or PC using Exchange-compatible applications, such as Entourage or Outlook (Windows).

If desired, you can create additional Exchange Calendar and Contacts folders. For instance, you might want to separate business and personal data or create project-related folders.

To use an Exchange Calendar folder:

1. To create a new event for an Exchange Calendar, select the Exchange Calendar folder in the folder list (Figure 28.7).

   The selected calendar appears.

2. Create and edit events in the same manner as when using the Entourage Calendar (see Chapter 23).

✔ Tips

- Because data isn't shared among Calendars, it's critical that you select the *correct* Calendar when recording an event. This also applies to working with Address Book (Contacts) folders.
- Regardless of which Calendar you use or whether you decide to use several, Office Reminders displays reminders for *all* Calendars. If you double-click an event listed in Office Reminders, Entourage will open the event from the correct Calendar.

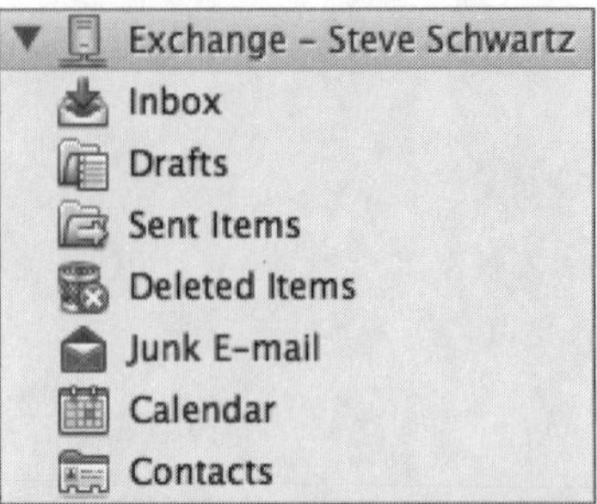

Figure 28.7 An Exchange account has its own Calendar and Contacts folders. These Exchange folders are synched with and accessible from any computer.

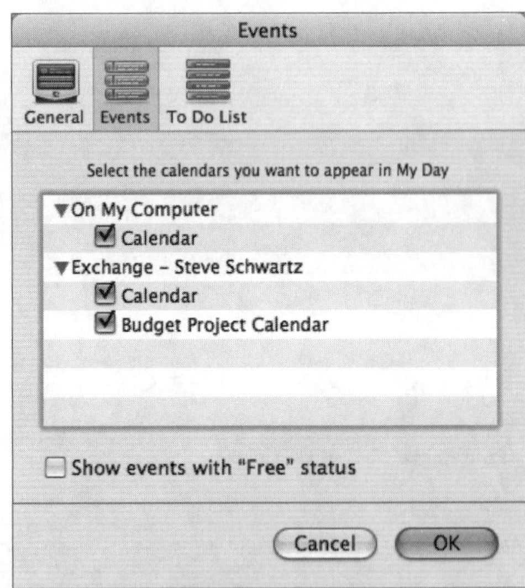

Figure 28.8 In My Day Preferences, click the Events tab and specify the Calendars you wish to display.

- Similarly, events from selected Exchange Calendars can also be presented in My Day (**Figure 28.8**).
- When you open any event or contact, the Calendar or Address Book's name is appended to the item title.
- Follow these same steps when creating or editing contact records in an Exchange Contacts folder.

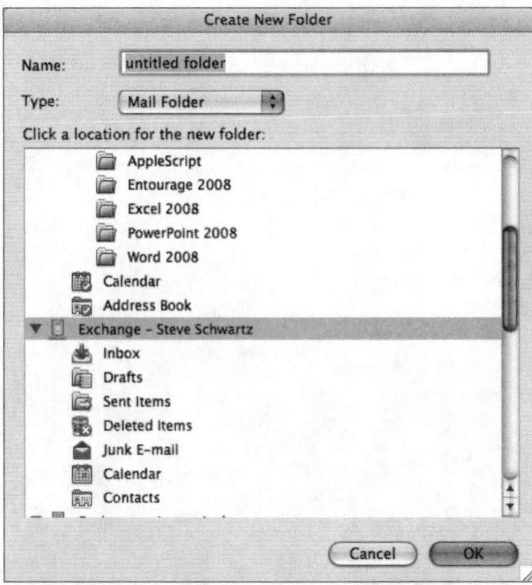

Figure 28.9 Specify the type and location of the new folder you're creating.

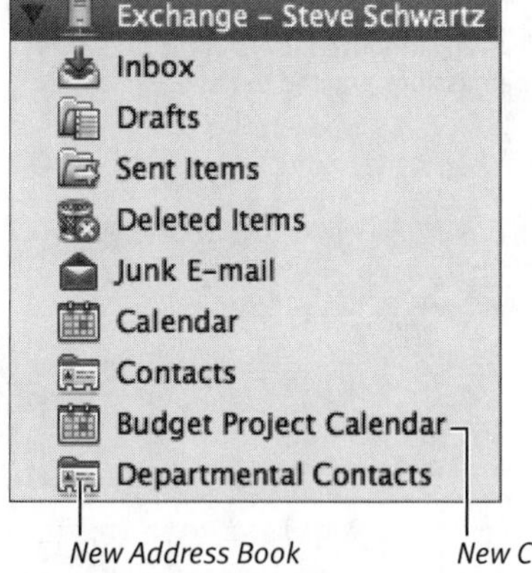

Figure 28.10 The Exchange account now has a new Calendar and Address Book.

- To change an Address Book or Calendar from a sub-item into a main item, drag it onto the Exchange account's name in the folder list. Conversely, you can change a main item into a sub-item by dragging it onto the appropriate main item or folder. (This tip applies to all sections of the folder list, such as On My Computer.)

To create a new Exchange Calendar or Address Book:

1. In the folder list, select the Exchange account (or any of its folders) in which you want to create an additional Calendar or Address Book (Contacts).
2. *Do one of the following:*
   - ▲ Choose File > New > Folder.
   - ▲ Click the New toolbar icon and choose Folder from the drop-down menu.
   - ▲ Press Shift⌘N.

   The Create New Folder dialog box appears (**Figure 28.9**).
3. From the Type drop-down menu, choose the type of item to create: Calendar or Address Book.
4. In the scrolling list, *do one of the following:*
   - ▲ To create the Calendar or Address Book at the same level as the other primary items and folders, select the account name.
   - ▲ To create the Calendar or Address Book as a subfolder of an existing folder in the account (such as Inbox, Calendar, or Contacts), select the folder within your Exchange account.
5. Type a descriptive name for the new item in the Name text box, such as `Work Contacts` or `School Calendar`.
6. Click OK to create the item.

   The new item appears in the folder list (**Figure 28.10**).

✔ Tips

- To delete an unwanted Address Book or Calendar, Control-click its name in the folder list and choose Delete Address Book or Delete Calendar from the pop-up menu that appears.

Sharing Exchange Folders

Data duplication among department members or within the corporation may represent a waste of time and energy, as well as a waste of storage space. As an Exchange user, you can designate Calendar, Contacts, or Mail folders as *shared*, making them available to other select users. If broader access is required, an administrator can created *public folders* that are accessible to all users or certain groups, depending on the permissions set for the folders.

Shared folders

Any user can elect to share an Exchange folder with other designated users. If you're a manager, for example, you could share your Exchange Calendar with an assistant or office manager to make it simpler for the person to schedule meetings.

To share a folder:

1. Switch to Mail view.
2. In the folder list, select the Exchange folder that you want to share.
3. *Do either of the following:*
   - ▲ Control-click the folder and choose Sharing from the pop-up menu.
   - ▲ Choose Edit > Folder Properties.

   The Folder Properties dialog box appears.
4. Click the Permissions tab (**Figure 28.11**).
5. To specify a user with whom you want to share the folder, click Add User.

   The Select User dialog box appears.
6. In the Find text box, type part of the user's name or email address, and click Find.

   A user list appears (**Figure 28.12**).
7. Select the desired person and click OK.

   The person is added to the user list on the Permission tab.

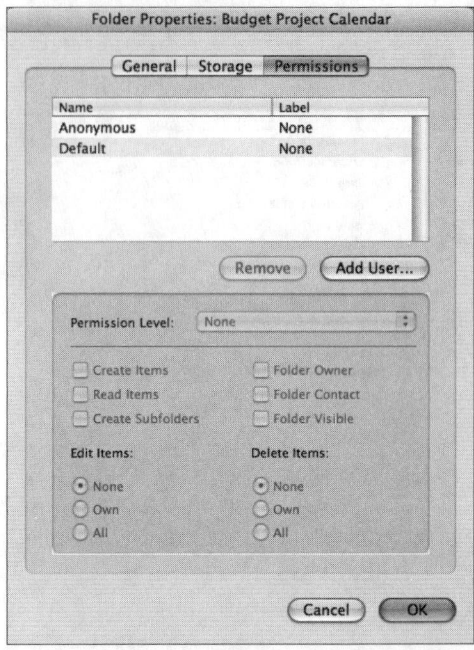

Figure 28.11 The Permissions tab of a Folder Properties dialog box lists all authorized users of the folder, as well as the permissions granted to them.

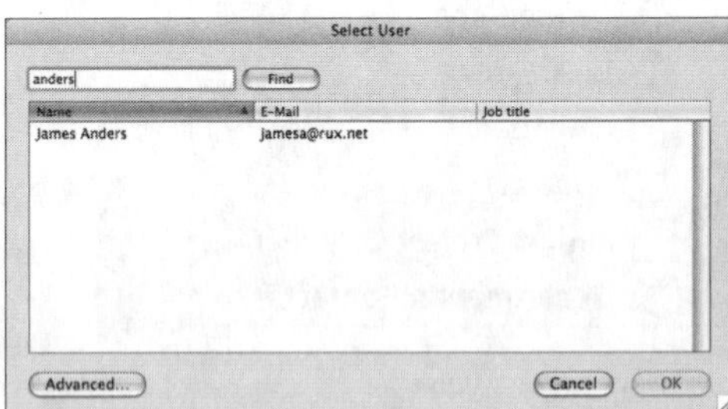

Figure 28.12 Find the person with whom you want to share the selected folder.

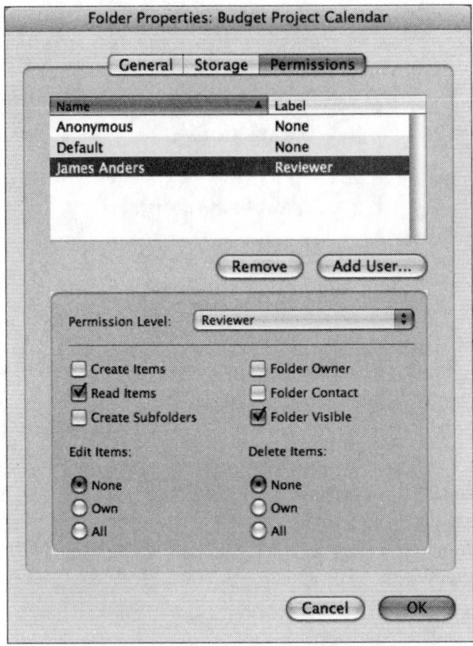

Figure 28.13 Set permissions for the new user.

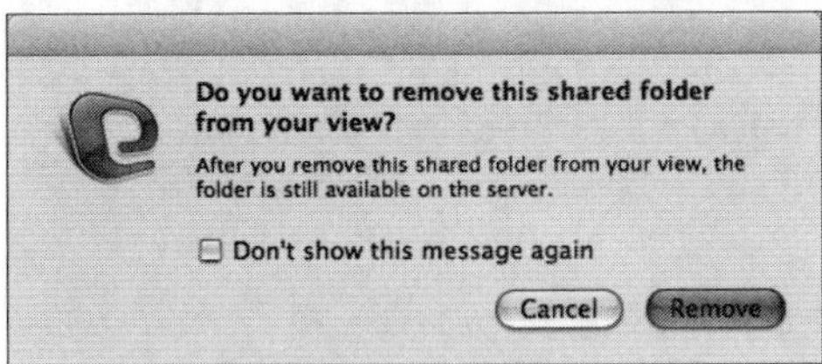

Figure 28.14 Confirm the removal of the shared folder.

8. To set folder permissions for the new user, select the person's name in the Folder Properties dialog box (**Figure 28.13**), and *do any of the following:*
   - ▲ Choose a permissions set from the Permission Level drop-down menu.
   - ▲ Click check boxes and radio buttons to set various permissions.
9. *Optional:* Repeat Steps 5–8 to specify other users that can share the folder.
10. Click OK to save the changes.

    The shared folder will appear in each user's folder list on the next sync.

✔ Tips

- Rather than create custom permissions by clicking check boxes and radio buttons, review the sets in the Permission Level drop-down menu. The Reviewer set (Figure 28.13), for example, allows a user to read items, but not to create, edit, or delete items.
- When a folder is shared, all items within it are accessible to the designated users. Rather than sharing an existing folder, it may be preferable to create a new folder, and then add or copy the items to be shared into the folder.
- To stop sharing a folder with a person, perform Steps 1–4 and select the person's name in the list on the Permissions tab (Figure 28.13). To *permanently* stop sharing the folder with the person, click Remove. To *temporarily* halt sharing, choose None from the Permission Level menu.
- If you no longer want to view a shared folder, select its name in the folder list and then choose Edit > Remove from View (**Figure 28.14**). If you later wish to restore the folder to the folder list, choose File > Open Other User's Folder.

Public folders

Exchange administrators can create *public folders*. For instance, a public Contacts folder might contain employee, vendor, or customer contact information that would be helpful to many employees. A public mail folder could serve as a company-wide forum where users can read and post messages. You can *subscribe* to those public folders that you regularly read or use, making it easier to find them.

Unless the administrator has set special permissions for a public folder, users can read items within the folder, as well as contribute new items. For obvious reasons, users are seldom granted permission to create or delete public folders.

To use a public folder:

1. Switch to Mail view. In the folder list, select a public folder in your Exchange account (**Figure 28.15**).
2. *Do any of the following:*
   - ▲ Examine messages, contact records, and events as you do in your other mail folders, Address Books, and Calendars.
   - ▲ Create a new item of the appropriate type (post, contact, or event) by clicking the New icon on the Standard toolbar (**Figure 28.16**).
   - ▲ Create a public reply to the currently selected message by clicking the Post Reply toolbar icon.
   - ▲ Click the Reply Directly toolbar icon to send an email message to the author of the selected message. (Your reply is *not* sent to the public folder.)

Figure 28.15 Select a public folder in the folder list.

Figure 28.16 When reading messages in a public folder, you can click these Standard toolbar icons to create new posts and replies.

Sharing Custom Folders

Sharing a custom Exchange folder that you've created is different from sharing the default Exchange folders. To share a custom folder, the individual with whom you'll be sharing must first agree to be your delegate by doing the following:

1. Choose Tools > Accounts.
2. In the Accounts dialog box, double-click the Exchange account.
3. In the Edit Account dialog box, click the Delegate tab.
4. In the Users I am a delegate for section, click the Add button.
5. In the Select User dialog box, enter part of the person's actual or Exchange user name. Click Find. Select the person from the list and click OK.
6. Close the Edit Account dialog box by clicking OK.

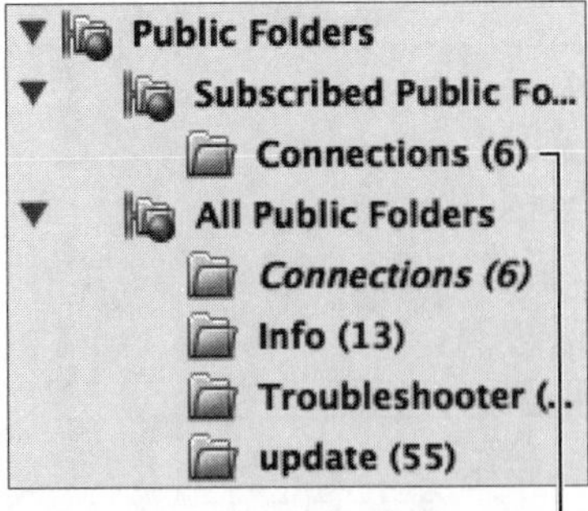

Figure 28.17 A subscribed folder's contents can be viewed by selecting the folder in Subscribed Public Folders or All Public Folders.

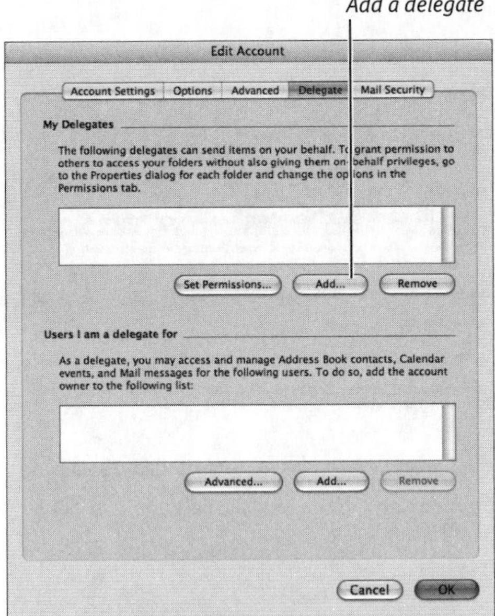

Figure 28.18 Add, remove, and manage delegates and permissions on the Delegate tab of the Edit Account dialog box.

To subscribe to a public folder:

1. Switch to Mail view. In All Public Folders (see Figure 28.15), select the folder to which you want to subscribe.
2. Choose Edit > Subscribe.

   The folder is added to the Subscribed Public Folders list (**Figure 28.17**). The folders to which you've subscribed are shown in italics in All Public Folders.

✔ Tips

- If you don't see a list of public folders in the folder list, it's likely you've forgotten to or incorrectly specified the Public Folders server's name. Make the necessary change by double-clicking the Exchange account's name in the Accounts dialog box and clicking the Advanced tab in the Edit Account dialog box (Figure 28.17).
- To unsubscribe from a folder, select its name in Subscribed Public Folders, and choose Edit > Unsubscribe.

Delegates

You can also share your data by naming *delegates* to your Exchange Inbox, Address Book, or Calendar. The setup process is similar to that of sharing a folder.

To designate a delegate:

1. Choose Tools > Accounts.

   The Accounts dialog box appears.
2. Double-click your Exchange account.

   The Edit Account window appears.
3. Click the Delegate tab (**Figure 28.18**). In the My Delegates section, click Add.

   The Select User dialog box appears (see Figure 28.12).

continues on next page

4. In the Find text box, type part of the user's name or email address, and click Find.

   A user list appears (see Figure 28.12).

5. Select the desired person and click OK.

   The Delegate Permissions dialog box appears (**Figure 28.19**).

6. Choose permission sets for your Exchange Calendar, Inbox, and/or Address Book from the drop-down menus.

7. *Optional:* To notify the person of their new delegate status, click the check box.

   A notification email (**Figure 28.20**) is sent to the individual.

8. Click OK to close the Delegate Permissions dialog box.

9. Click OK to close the Edit Account dialog box. Close the Accounts dialog box.

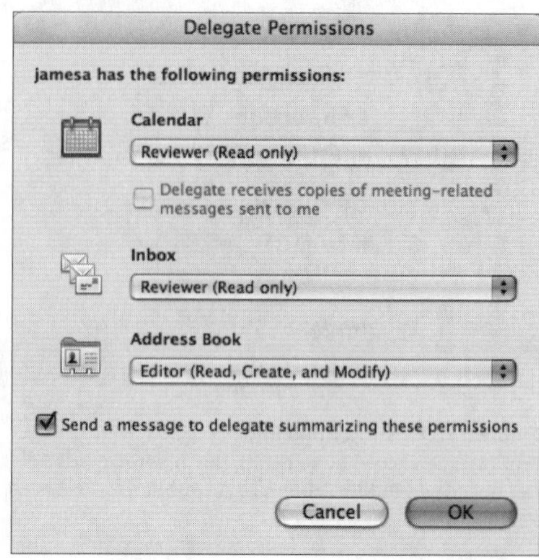

Figure 28.19 Set delegate permissions by choosing options from the drop-down menus.

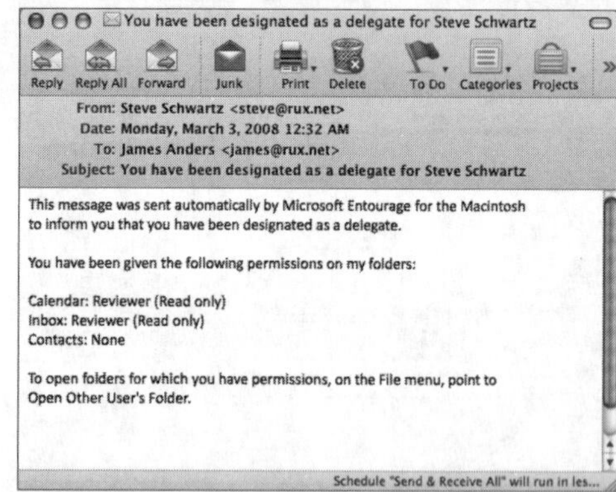

Figure 28.20 You can send the delegate a list of the permissions you've granted.

✔ Tips

- It's common to grant Author permissions for the Inbox and/or Calendar. The named delegate can respond to email and create appointments on your behalf, as well as read items in those folders. However, the delegate cannot modify existing items in those folders.
- To remove a delegate, select the person's name in the My Delegates section of the Edit Account dialog box (see Figure 28.18) and click Remove.
- To change a delegate's permissions, select the person's name in the My Delegates section of the Edit Account dialog box and click Set Permissions. Make the necessary changes in the Delegate Permissions dialog box (Figure 28.19).

Part VI: Integrating Applications

Combining Office Data

Separately, each Office application is impressive. But when combined, they form a powerful system for sharing information.

One simple way of combining information from different Office applications is by copying, embedding, or linking. You can copy a table of numeric data from Excel into a Word document to add some relevant numbers to a memo, for example. Or to ensure that later changes to the Excel data automatically flow to the table in the Word document, you can link the data between the documents.

In addition to explaining copying, linking, and embedding, this chapter provides some specific examples of ways to share data among Office applications. It also explains how to link Entourage items to each other and to Macintosh documents.

Copying, Linking, and Embedding

Office lets you easily share information among its applications. The three main methods are to copy, embed, or link information from one application to another.

The simplest method is to *copy and paste* or *drag and drop* material between programs. For example, you can copy a range in Excel and paste it into a Word document. Or you can simply drag the range into Word. The data becomes part of the Word document as an editable table. Similarly, after switching to Slide Sorter View in PowerPoint, you can drag a copy of a slide into a Word document. Data added via the copy-and-paste or drag and drop method becomes a part of—and is saved with—the destination document. This means that you can move the document to another machine or email it to someone secure in the knowledge that the copied or dropped data will be intact.

If you want to maintain a link between the original data or object and the new document, you can use *embedding* or *linking*. The difference between the two procedures lies in where the data is stored. Embedded data becomes part of the destination document, making it transportable. Linked data, on the other hand, is stored only in the original document and is *referenced* by the destination document. Thus, linking is an excellent choice for working with files on a network or when combining data from several members in a workgroup project.

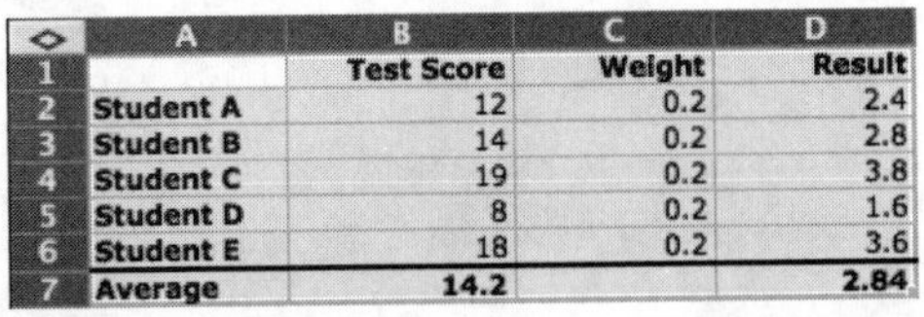

	A	B	C	D
1		Test Score	Weight	Result
2	Student A	12	0.2	2.4
3	Student B	14	0.2	2.8
4	Student C	19	0.2	3.8
5	Student D	8	0.2	1.6
6	Student E	18	0.2	3.6
7	Average	14.2		2.84

Figure 29.1 To duplicate this section of an Excel worksheet in a Word document, start by selecting the data range to be copied; in this case, A1:D7.

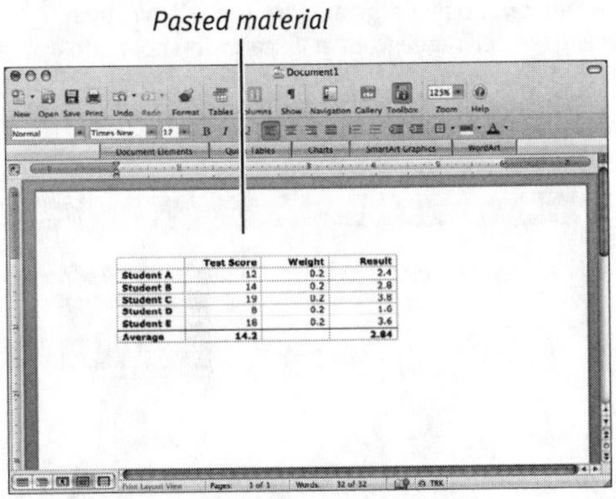

Pasted material

Figure 29.2 When pasted into a Word document, the Excel range becomes a Word table.

Using copy and paste

Copy and paste (and cut and paste) are the simplest, most familiar methods of duplicating data between two documents—even if documents are from different applications. Pasted material maintains no link with the original data or its document.

To copy and paste between documents:

1. In the first document, select the material you want to copy, such as a text block, cell range, slide, or one or more objects (**Figure 29.1**).
2. Choose Edit > Copy (⌘C).
   The material is copied to the Clipboard, a temporary area in memory that stores the most recent item you've copied or cut.
3. Switch to/open the destination document.
   Note that the document must be capable of accepting the type of data you're about to paste. Office 2008 applications can accept most types of material created in other Office applications.
4. In the destination document, specify the location in which you'll paste by setting the text insertion mark, selecting a cell, making a slide active, and so on.
5. Choose Edit > Paste (⌘V).
   The material is pasted from the Clipboard (**Figure 29.2**). The Clipboard contents remain unchanged until you copy or cut something else.

✔ Tip

- Every Office application has an Edit > Paste Special command. If you need to control the format when pasting certain material, be sure to check the options provided by this command.

Using drag and drop

Other than copy and paste (or cut and paste), the easiest way to move something from one application to another is to use drag and drop. The drag and drop process is the same whether it's *between* applications or *within* a single application. Arrange the document windows of the two applications so you can see them both. Then drag selected text or an object from one window to its destination in the other application's document window. **Table 29.1** lists some of the items you can drag and drop between applications.

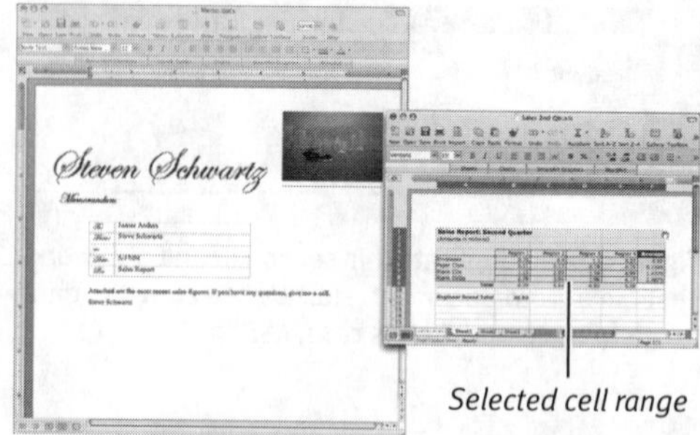

Figure 29.3 Using drag and drop, you can copy a selected cell range from an Excel worksheet into a Word document, for example.

To drag and drop an object:

1. Arrange the applications' document windows so you can see both the source object and its intended destination.
2. Select the object or text, such as a worksheet range (**Figure 29.3**).
3. Drag the border of the object or text to its destination in the other window.
4. Release the mouse button.

   The object or text appears in the destination document (**Figure 29.4**).

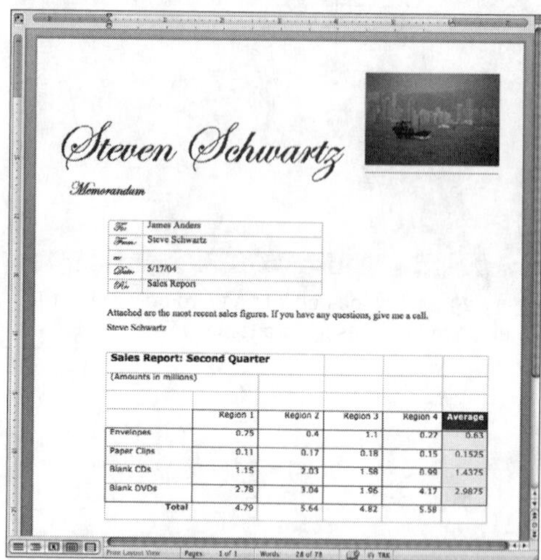

Figure 29.4 Release the mouse button when the Excel object is properly positioned in the Word document.

✔ Tips

- When you drag and drop an item, it becomes part of the destination document. The item will not reflect changes made to the original material unless you establish a link. See "Linking objects," later in this chapter.
- You are free to modify the object or text in the destination document.
- If you hold down Option ⌘ as you drag an object between applications, a pop-up menu allows you to either copy or move the object. (Moving deletes the original object.)

Table 29.1

Common Objects to Drag and Drop

Source Application	Object
Word	Selected text or table cells
Excel	A cell, range, graphic, or list
PowerPoint	A slide from Slide Sorter view

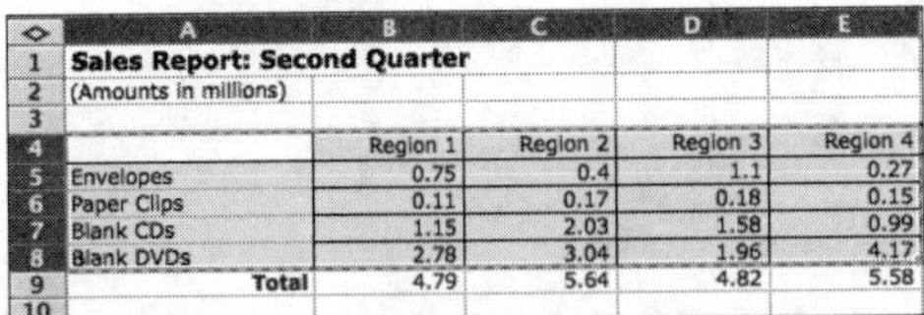

	A	B	C	D	E
1	Sales Report: Second Quarter				
2	(Amounts in millions)				
3					
4		Region 1	Region 2	Region 3	Region 4
5	Envelopes	0.75	0.4	1.1	0.27
6	Paper Clips	0.11	0.17	0.18	0.15
7	Blank CDs	1.15	2.03	1.58	0.99
8	Blank DVDs	2.78	3.04	1.96	4.17
9	Total	4.79	5.64	4.82	5.58
10					

Figure 29.5 Select and copy the material you want to embed, such as this Excel worksheet range.

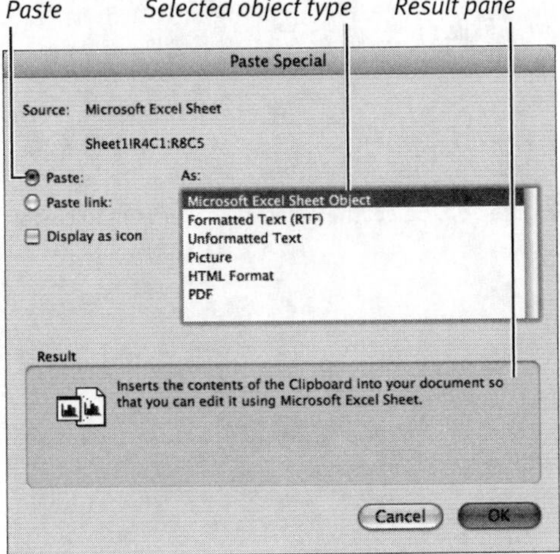

Figure 29.6 In the Paste Special dialog box, select the appropriate object type from the As list. The Result pane shows the type of object that will be inserted.

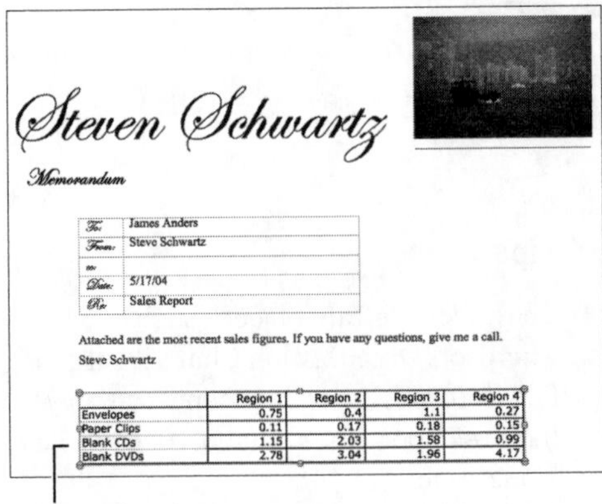

Steven Schwartz

Memorandum

To:	James Anders
From:	Steve Schwartz
cc:	
Date:	5/17/04
Re:	Sales Report

Attached are the most recent sales figures. If you have any questions, give me a call.

Steve Schwartz

	Region 1	Region 2	Region 3	Region 4
Envelopes	0.75	0.4	1.1	0.27
Paper Clips	0.11	0.17	0.18	0.15
Blank CDs	1.15	2.03	1.58	0.99
Blank DVDs	2.78	3.04	1.96	4.17

Figure 29.7 The embedded object appears in the Word document.

Embedding objects

An *embedded object* is material that is copied in its source application and pasted into the target application as a Microsoft Object. The advantage to embedding material rather than linking it (see the next section) is that the material resides entirely in the destination document. As a result, you can safely move the document to another computer.

Unlike a *linked object* (which is updated whenever the source data changes), an embedded object changes only when you initiate an edit from within the target document. This ensures that the object will change only when—or if—you want it to change.

This section explains how to embed an existing object in a target application, as well as how to create an embedded object from scratch.

To embed an existing object:

1. Select the object or text in its source application (**Figure 29.5**).
2. Choose Edit > Copy (⌘C).
3. Switch to the target application and click to set the destination for the object.
   The embedded object will appear at the text insertion mark.
4. Choose Edit > Paste Special.
   The Paste Special dialog box appears (**Figure 29.6**).
5. Select the item labeled as an *object* (such as Microsoft Excel Worksheet Object, for example). Ensure that the Paste radio button is selected, and click OK.
   The embedded object appears in the target document (**Figure 29.7**).

To create an embedded object:

1. Click to set the destination for the object.

   The embedded object will appear at the text insertion mark.

2. Choose Insert > Object.

   The Object dialog box appears (**Figure 29.8**).

3. Select the object type, and click OK.

   The appropriate Office application opens and a new document appears.

4. Create the object (**Figure 29.9**).

5. *Optional:* Save the object document by choosing File > Save Copy As.

6. Close the object document.

   The object appears in the document at the text insertion mark. (You may need to alter the text wrap setting in order for the object to display correctly.)

To edit an embedded object:

1. *Do either of the following:*
   - ▲ Double-click the object (a worksheet embedded in a Word document, for example).
   - ▲ Select the object and choose Edit > *object type* > Edit.

   The source application launches, and the object appears.

2. As you modify the object, the changes automatically appear in the embedded object, too. When you're finished editing, close the document window.

   It is *not* necessary to save changes when editing an object. Any changes you make to the object are automatically conveyed to the document in which the object is embedded.

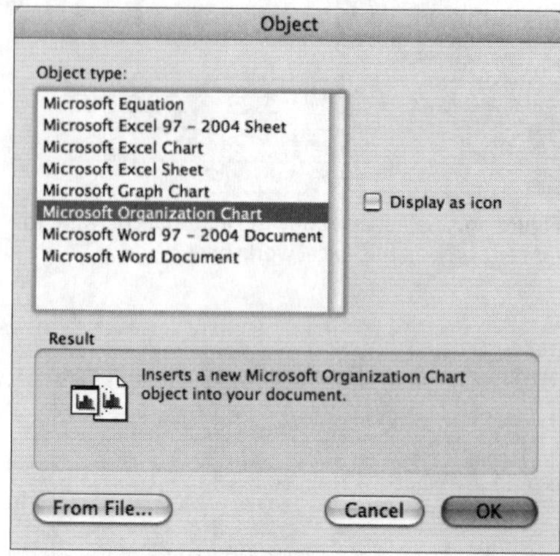

Figure 29.8 Select the object type you want to create.

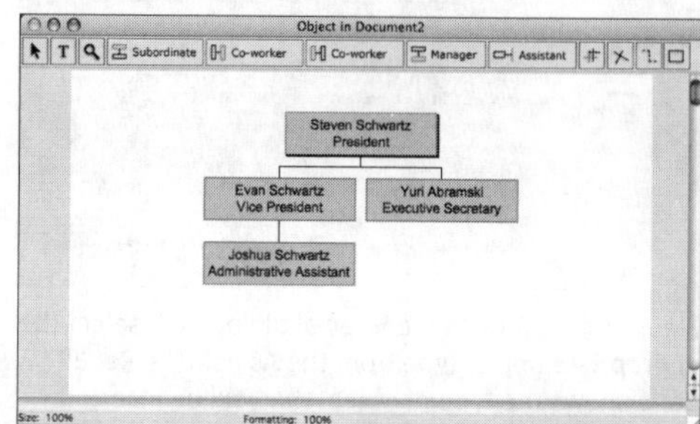

Figure 29.9 Create the new object. If sample data is presented, replace it with your own data.

✔ Tips

- To transfer certain objects, such as a Microsoft Organization Chart, it isn't sufficient to close the document. You may have to choose a command, such as File > Update Object.
- You can represent the embedded object as an icon by checking Display as icon in the Object dialog box (Figure 29.8).

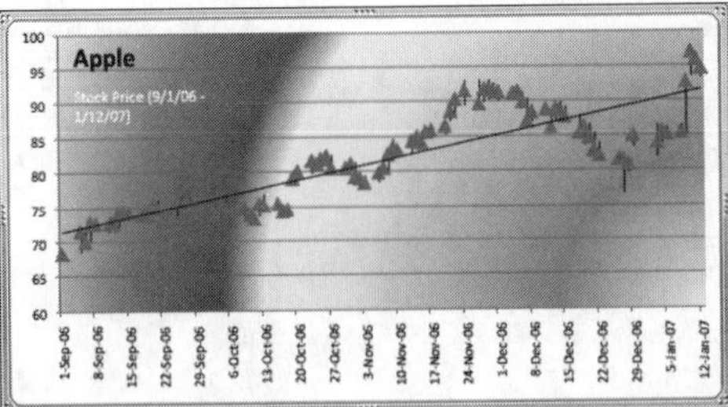

Figure 29.10 Select and copy the object or material to which you want to link, such as this Excel chart.

Paste link *Selected object*

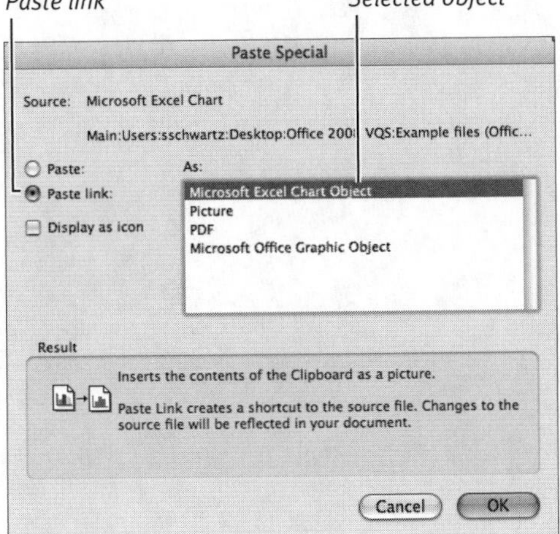

Figure 29.11 Click the Paste link radio button, select the specific object type, and click OK.

Linking objects

When you link rather than embed an object, the object remains in the original application's document. A *copy* of the object—linked to the original—is displayed in the second application's document. Think of the copy as representing the linked object. It is merely a reference to the original. Any changes that are made to the original object also appear in the linked copy.

You create linked objects using the Copy and Paste Special commands. The object is updated whenever you reopen the destination file, ensuring that the object is always current. Linking is ideal for any object whose data regularly changes or is being edited. In addition to (or instead of) updating a link automatically, you can update it manually.

To link an object:

1. In the source document, select the object you wish to link (**Figure 29.10**).
2. Choose Edit > Copy (⌘C).
3. Open the destination document, and click where you want the linked object to appear.
4. Choose Edit > Paste Special.

   The Paste Special dialog box appears (**Figure 29.11**).
5. Click the Paste link radio button, select the object to link, and click OK.

   The linked object appears in the destination document.

✔ Tips

- You can double-click a linked object in the destination document to edit the original object.
- When you open a document containing links that automatically update, the links are checked for any necessary updates.

To manually update a link:

1. Choose Edit > Links.

   The Links dialog box appears (**Figure 29.12**).

2. Select the link from the list and click Update Now.

   The linked object is updated.

3. Click OK to close the Links dialog box.

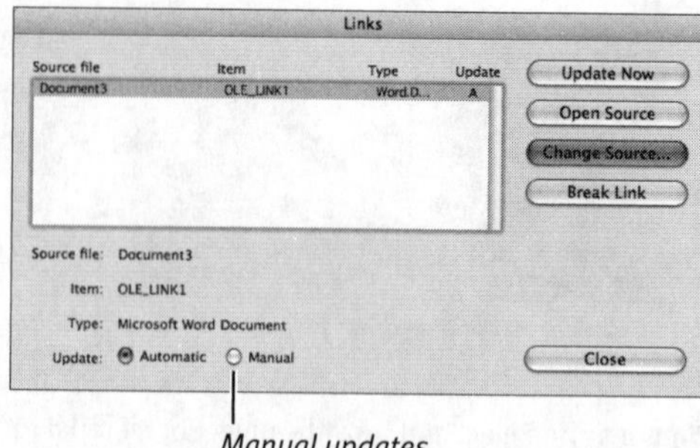

Figure 29.12 In the Links dialog box, click Update Now to update the selected link.

✔ Tips

- The linked object will appear in the target document at its original size. You can resize it as necessary.
- To set the link so that it updates *only* when you click Update Now, select Manual as the Update option.
- To change a linked object into an embedded object, select the link and click the Break Link button.

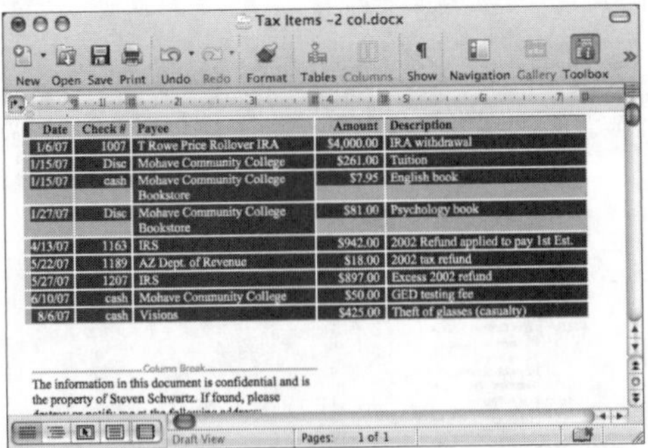

Figure 29.13 To select a table in Word, click any cell of the table and choose Table > Select > Table.

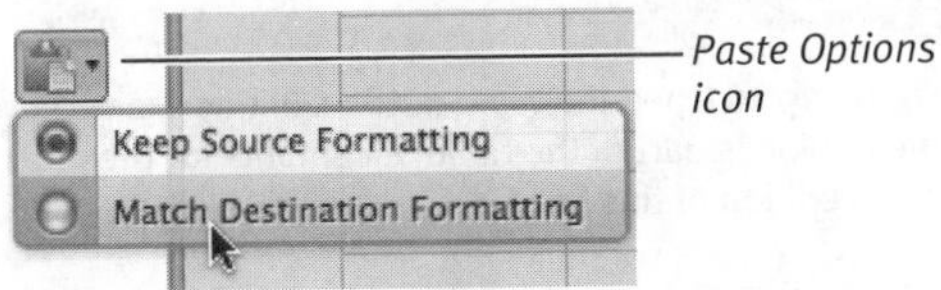

Figure 29.14 Specify formatting for the pasted material.

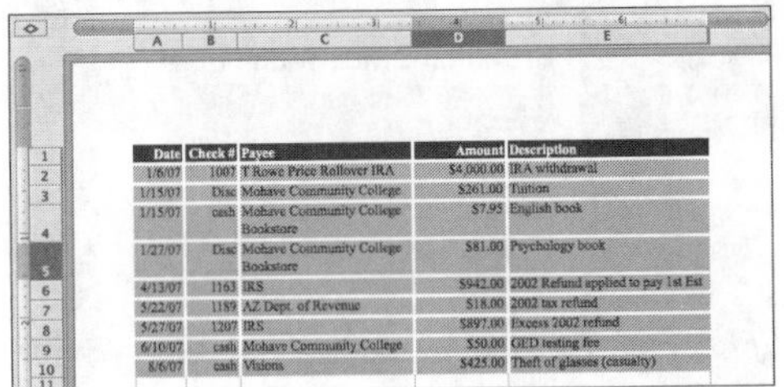

Figure 29.15 The formatted Word table appears in the Excel worksheet.

Word Table into Excel

Word and Excel work well together, especially when you're creating Word documents that display structured numerical data. The previous sections explained how to copy and link Excel data into Word documents. In this section, you'll learn to do the reverse—copy a Word table into an Excel worksheet. Later in this chapter, you'll see how to copy normal Word text into Excel or PowerPoint.

To copy a Word table into Excel:

1. In Word, click any cell within the table you want to copy.
2. Choose Table > Select > Table.
   The table is selected (**Figure 29.13**).
3. Choose Edit > Copy (⌘C).
4. Switch to Excel. Select the cell in which the Word table will begin.
5. Choose Edit > Paste (⌘V).
   The Word table appears in the worksheet.
6. *Optional:* By default, the original formatting is retained. To make the formatting of the pasted material match that of the target cells, click the Paste Options icon (**Figure 29.14**) and select Match Destination Formatting.
7. Adjust the column widths as necessary to fully display the contents of each column (**Figure 29.15**).

✔ Tips

- You can also select a table for copying by dragging through its cells.
- A table copied in this manner is fully editable within Excel. You can also change the formatting, if desired. The pasted data isn't linked to the Word document.

Sharing Outlines: Word and PowerPoint

You can use Word and PowerPoint together, too. This section explains how to move an outline from one application to the other.

To use a Word outline file in a PowerPoint presentation:

1. Open or create a presentation outline in Word (**Figure 29.16**).

   Each Heading 1 paragraph will become the title of a new slide. Heading 2 paragraphs will become first-level text.

2. Choose File > Send To > PowerPoint.

   PowerPoint launches and the Word outline appears as a new presentation. No link is maintained to the original Word outline.

3. Apply a slide theme and other formatting to the new presentation (**Figure 29.17**).

✔ Tips

- Starting a presentation in Word isn't outlandish. Most people find writing and editing easier to do in Word than in PowerPoint.
- If you use the first line of your Word outline as its title, this will result in only *one* PowerPoint slide (since only the title is a Heading 1 paragraph). To prepare such an outline for PowerPoint, select all the outline text after the first line, click the Promote toolbar icon to raise every point by one level, and then delete the title line.

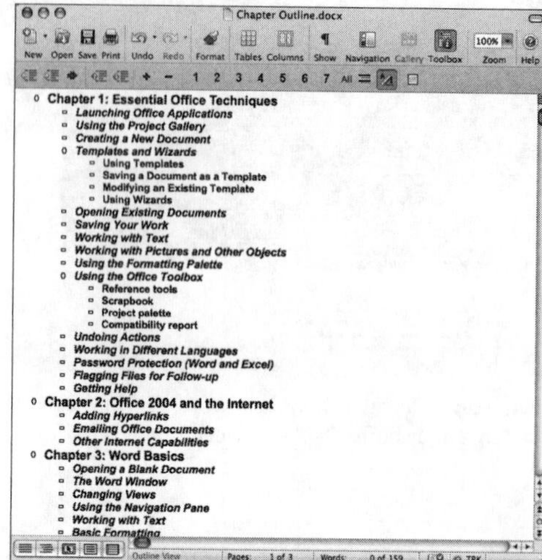

Figure 29.16 Open the Word outline. In this example, the outline is part of the table of contents for the previous edition of this book.

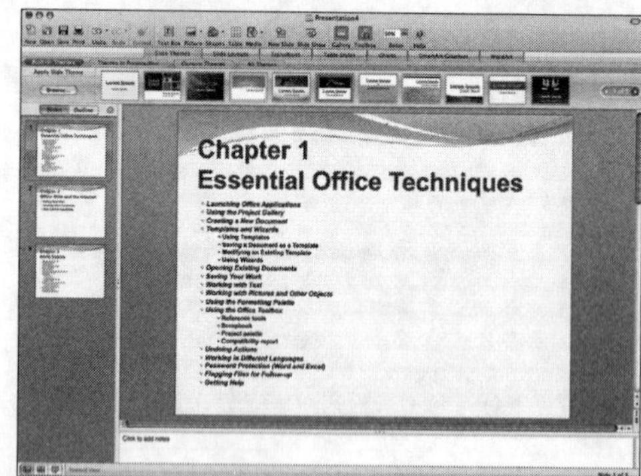

Figure 29.17 With minor work, a Word outline can be transformed into a presentation.

Outline tab

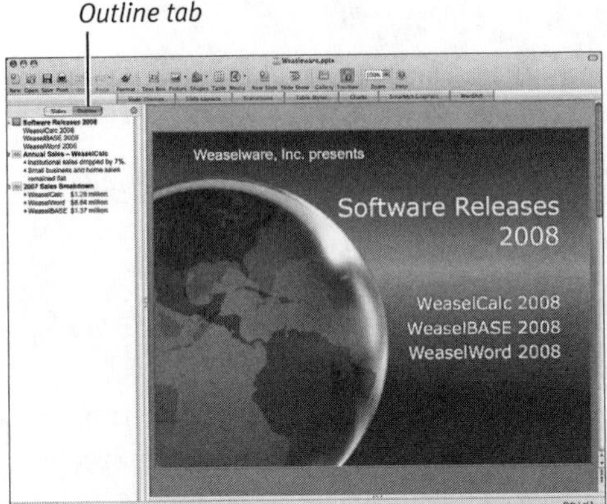

Figure 29.18 Create or open a PowerPoint presentation in Normal View. Click the Outline tab.

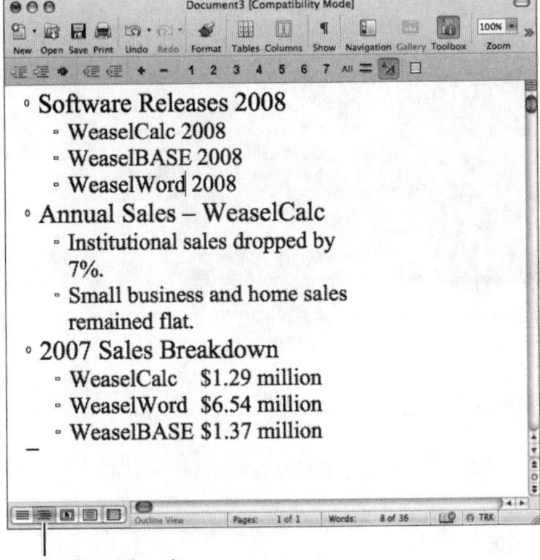

Outline View icon

Figure 29.19 This is the exported PowerPoint outline in Word.

To copy a PowerPoint presentation outline into a Word document:

1. In PowerPoint, switch to Normal View by choosing View > Normal or by clicking the Normal icon in the bottom-left corner of the document window.
2. Click the Outline tab to display the presentation outline rather than the slide thumbnails (**Figure 29.18**).
3. Choose File > Send To > Microsoft Word.

   The PowerPoint outline opens as a new Word document.
4. In Word, switch to Outline view by choosing View > Outline or by clicking the Outline View icon in the bottom-left corner of the document window.
5. Reformat the text as desired (**Figure 29.19**).

✔ Tip

- Rather than laboriously reformatting the text, you may find it simpler to reapply the appropriate Heading styles to the outline points.

Word Text into Excel or PowerPoint

You can transfer text from Word into Excel or PowerPoint using copy and paste or drag and drop.

To copy text from Word:

1. Arrange the Word document window so you can also see the Excel or PowerPoint document window.
2. In Word, select the text to be copied.
3. *Do one of the following:*
   - ▲ Choose Edit > Copy (⌘C). Paste the text into an Excel cell or a PowerPoint slide by choosing Edit > Paste (⌘V).
   - ▲ Drag the text to a destination range in Excel or onto a PowerPoint slide (**Figures 29.20** and **29.21**).

✔ Tips

- Text formatting, such as font, size, and style, is also copied and will appear in the Excel worksheet. In PowerPoint, however, the formatting of the destination placeholder text determines the initial font size.
- In Excel, pasted Word text frequently overflows the cells. If necessary, you can expand the column width or enable text wrapping for the affected cells.
- Excel mimics the paragraph formatting of copied Word text. A tab within a paragraph is treated as an instruction to place the text in the next cell; a return is treated as an instruction to move down to the next row.
- You can also paste Word text as a floating object. In Excel or PowerPoint, choose Edit > Paste Special and select Microsoft Word Document Object as the format (**Figure 29.22**). The result is an embedded text object that is editable in Word.

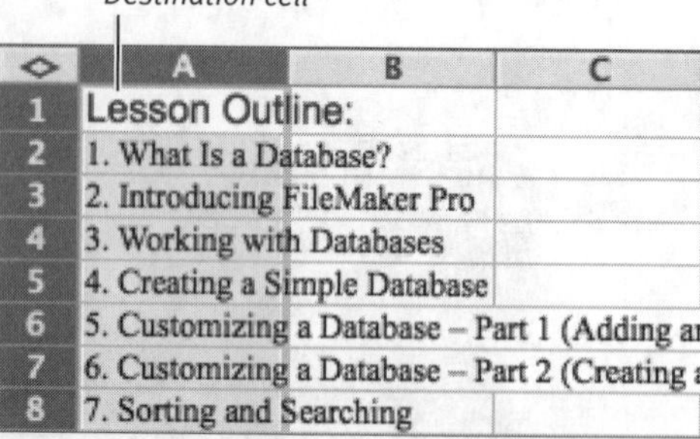

Figure 29.20 Drag or paste the text into a cell or range. Each line of pasted text becomes a new row.

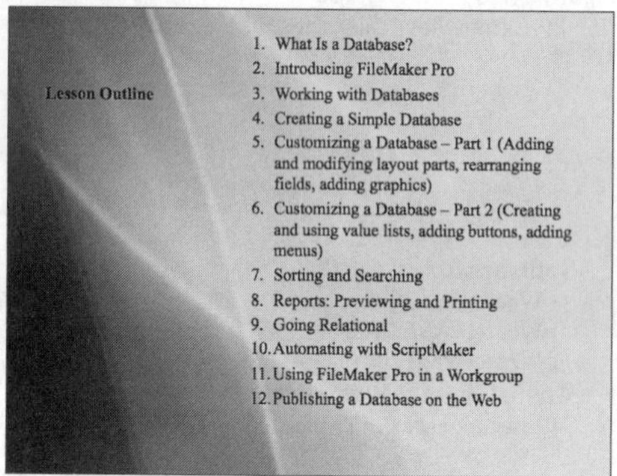

Figure 29.21 You can also drag or paste into a text placeholder on a PowerPoint slide.

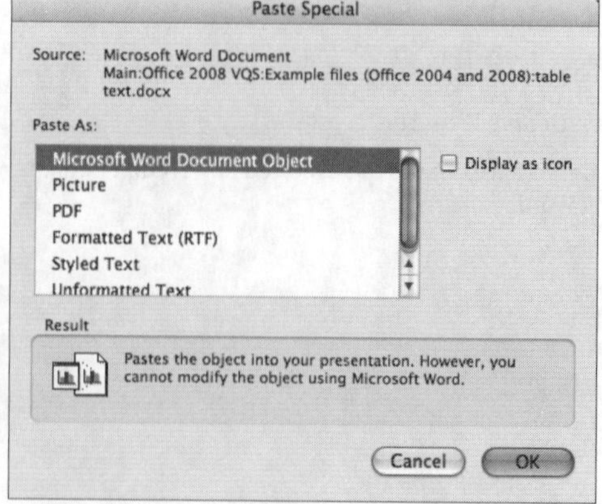

Figure 29.22 Using the Edit > Paste Special command, you can paste Word text as an object.

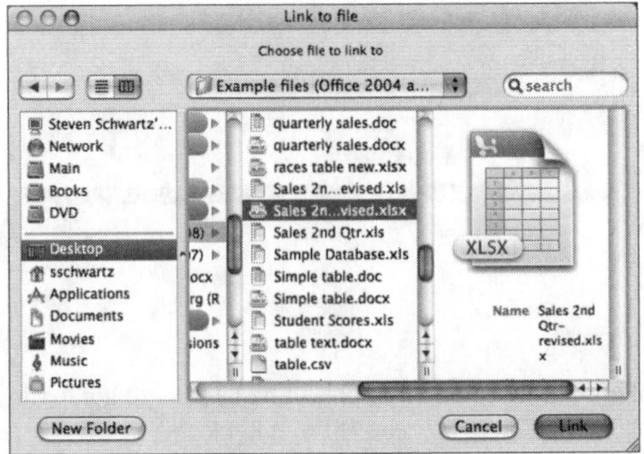

Figure 29.23 Select the document in the Link to file dialog box (OS X 10.4.11/Tiger shown).

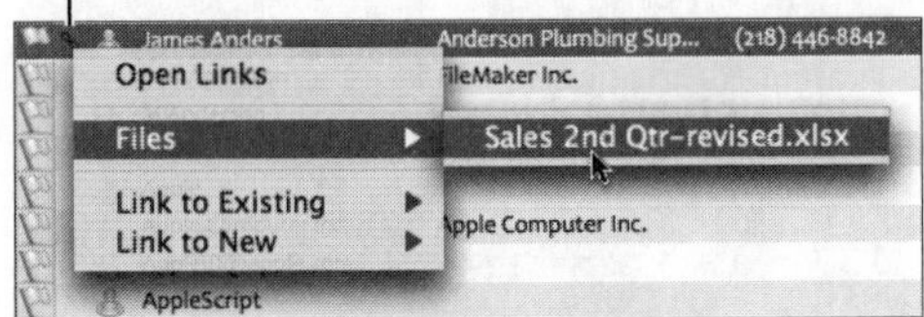

Figure 29.24 A link indicator appears beside the contact name in the Address Book. To open the linked document, click the link indicator and choose the file from the pop-up menu.

Entourage Linking

You can link an Entourage item to a Mac file or another Entourage item. Links are especially useful when planning a meeting, for example. You can link a document pertaining to the meeting to a contact record in your Address Book. This allows you to open the document directly from the Address Book, as shown in the following example.

To link an Entourage contact to an Office document:

1. In Entourage, switch to the Address Book by clicking its icon in the upper-left corner of the window, choosing View > Go To > Address Book, or pressing ⌘2.
2. Select the record in the contact list.
3. *Do either of the following:*
   - ▲ Choose Tools > Link to Existing > File.
   - ▲ Click in the contact record's Links column and choose Link to Existing > File from the pop-up menu.

   The Link to file dialog box appears.
4. Select the file that you want to link to the contact information (**Figure 29.23**). Click Link.

   A link indicator appears beside the contact name in the Address Book, showing that there's a link to a file or Entourage item. To later view the linked file, click the link indicator in the person's record and choose the linked file from the pop-up menu that appears (**Figure 29.24**).

✔ Tips

- You can create links with files created in *any* application—not just Office 2008.
- Use the Project Center (Chapter 30) to provide ready access to project materials, such as any related files, messages, notes, events, tasks, and contacts.
- When a link ceases to be useful, you can break it. Click the link icon and choose Open Links from the pop-up menu that appears (see Figure 29.24). The Links To dialog box appears, listing all links to the selected item (**Figure 29.25**). Select the link to break, click the Remove toolbar icon, and close the dialog box.

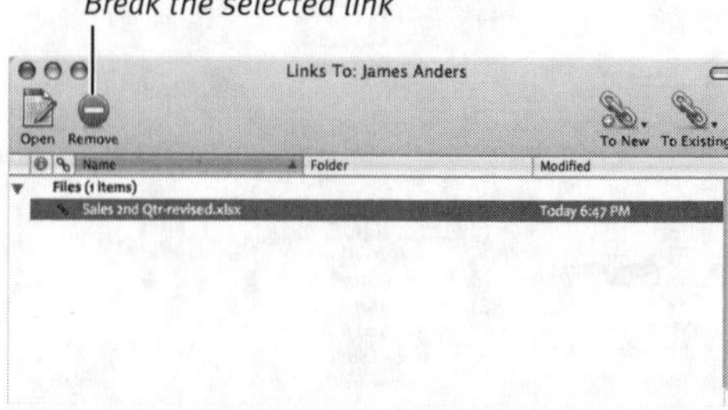

Figure 29.25 You can break a link by selecting it in the Links To dialog box and clicking Remove.

Adding Office Material to Email

In Entourage, HTML email messages can include Word tables, Excel charts and cell ranges, SmartArt layouts, WordArt, and other objects:

1. Create a new message, and choose Format > HTML.
2. Select an Excel chart or data range, Word table, SmartArt layout, WordArt, or other object.
3. Choose Edit > Copy (⌘C).
4. Set the text insertion mark in the email message.
5. Choose Edit > Paste Special > Paste As Picture.

✔ Tips

- Certain items, such as charts, SmartArt, and WordArt can be pasted using the normal Edit > Paste command. Excel data ranges and Word tables, on the other hand, lose their formatting when pasted this way.
- To add complex Scrapbook material to a message, select the item, click the down arrow beside the Paste icon, and choose Paste as Picture.

30

The Project Center

The Project Center helps you manage projects. It provides a convenient place in which to gather all project-related email, tasks, appointments, notes, and important Office and non-Office documents. A project can be something you're working on alone (such as a school paper or a trip plan) or shared with others (such as a business report or a product launch).

Although it's an Entourage component, the Project Center is accessible from any Office application via the Toolbox's Project Palette tab.

Creating a Project

Of course, the first step is to create a new project. All projects are created and managed in Entourage's Project Center.

To create a new project:

1. *Do one of the following:*
   - ▲ Switch to the Project Center by clicking its icon (**Figure 30.1**), choosing View > Go To > Project Center, or pressing ⌘6. Click the New toolbar icon, choose File > New > New Project, or press ⌘N.
   - ▲ From any other part of Entourage, click the down arrow beside the New toolbar icon and choose Project or choose File > New > Project.

   The New Project Wizard appears (**Figure 30.2**).
2. To identify the project, enter a name for it in the Name text box.
3. *Optional:* If there is a due date for project completion, select a date by clicking the calendar icon. Ensure that the Due Date check box is checked.
4. *Optional:* To associate a color with all project-related items, click the Color icon and select a color from the pop-up list. You can also add an identifying picture by dragging its file icon into the designated area. If you have general notes about the project which you'd like to record, enter them in the Notes to Self text box.
5. Click the right-arrow icon to continue. The next Wizard screen appears (**Figure 30.3**).
6. Every project has two *watch folders*. Their purpose is to enable Entourage to make note of documents and items that are part of the project.

Figure 30.1 Click the Project Center icon to view and manage your projects.

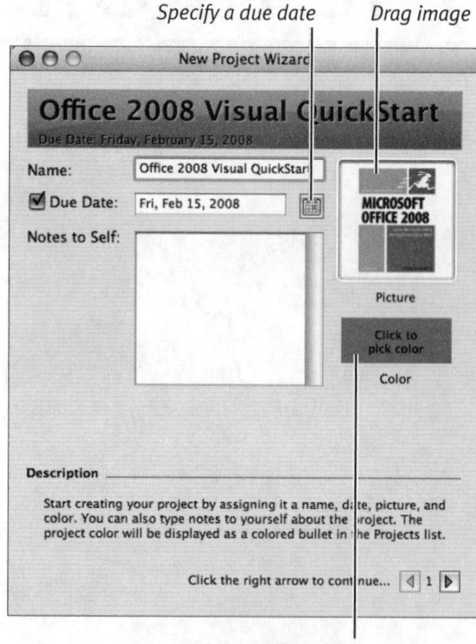

Figure 30.2 The New Project Wizard will step you through the process of setting up a new project.

Project Setup: The Aftermath

After a project has been created, you can revisit your settings whenever you like. You can do so to review the choices you made or to modify them. In the Project Center, click the Overview tab and then click the Properties button at the bottom of the window.

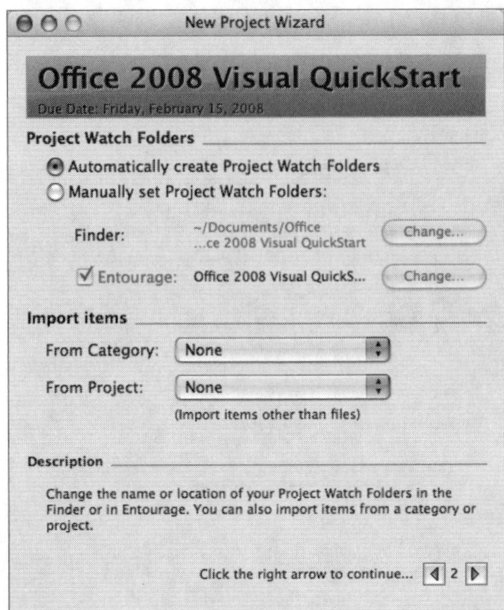

Figure 30.3 Create the two Watch folders and optionally import existing items into the new project.

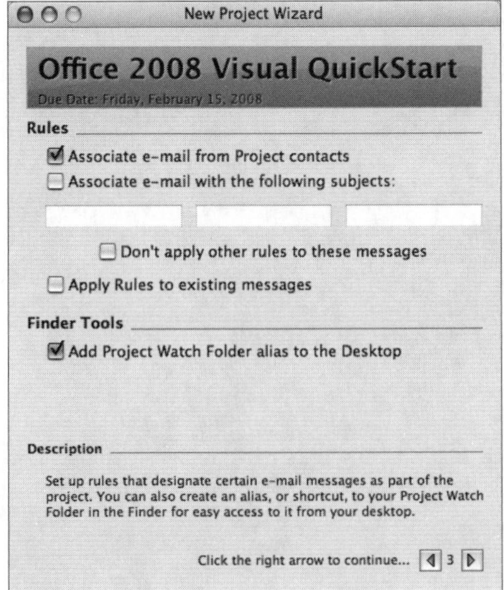

Figure 30.4 Set rules for associating email messages with the project.

- **Entourage Project Watch Folder.** When an email message is moved or copied to this folder in the Folders List, it is associated with the project.
- **Finder Project Watch Folder.** This folder contains the documents (or aliases to them) that you've associated with the project.

Click a radio button in the Project Watch Folders area to indicate whether the folders will be created for you or whether you want to create them. In the latter case, click each Change button to select an existing folder or to create a new one.

7. To import items that are already assigned to an existing category or project, select an Entourage category and/or project from the drop-down lists. Click the right-arrow icon to continue.

   The next Wizard screen appears.

8. Set rules for associating email messages with the project (**Figure 30.4**):
   - **Associate e-mail from Project contacts.** If you designate project contacts (see "Adding and Removing Project Contact"), email from them will automatically be associated with the project.
   - **Associate e-mail with the following subjects.** Enter up to three keywords that—if found in an incoming message's Subject—will be used to classify the message as project-related.
   - **Don't apply other rules to these messages.** When checked, this prevents other message rules you've created from being applied to project-related messages.
   - **Apply rules to existing messages.** Check this box if you want to use the specified rules to attempt to reclassify current Entourage messages as being project-related.

9. In the Finder Tools section, click the check box to place an alias to the Project Watch folder on the Desktop.

   Creating the folder alias will give you easy access to project documents. It will also enable you to add new documents to the project by simply dragging them or their aliases into the folder.

10. Click the right-arrow icon to continue.

    The final Wizard screen appears (**Figure 30.5**).

11. Read the information presented and click the right-arrow icon to create the project.

    The project is generated, and you are taken to the Project Center.

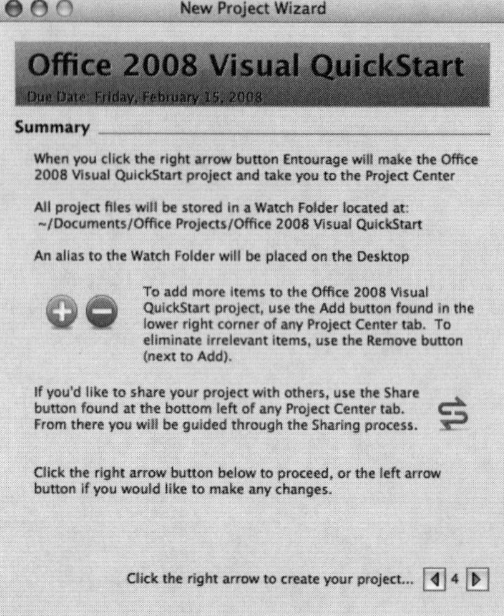

Figure 30.5 Review this material and then click the right-arrow icon to create the project.

Customizing the Overview Tab

At the bottom of a project's Overview tab (Figure 30.6) are two areas where you can view recent project-related messages, upcoming tasks, and so on. To specify what each section will display, click a triangle icon and choose an option from the drop-down menu. You can change the types of information displayed as often as you like.

The Project Center

In the Project Center (**Figure 30.6**), you can view the status of and components in your projects. Above each project is a series of tabs you can click to view, add, or remove project-related items.

To view a project:

1. In Entourage, click the Project Center icon to open the project Center.
2. Click the project name in the Folders list.
   The project appears, open to the most recently used tab.

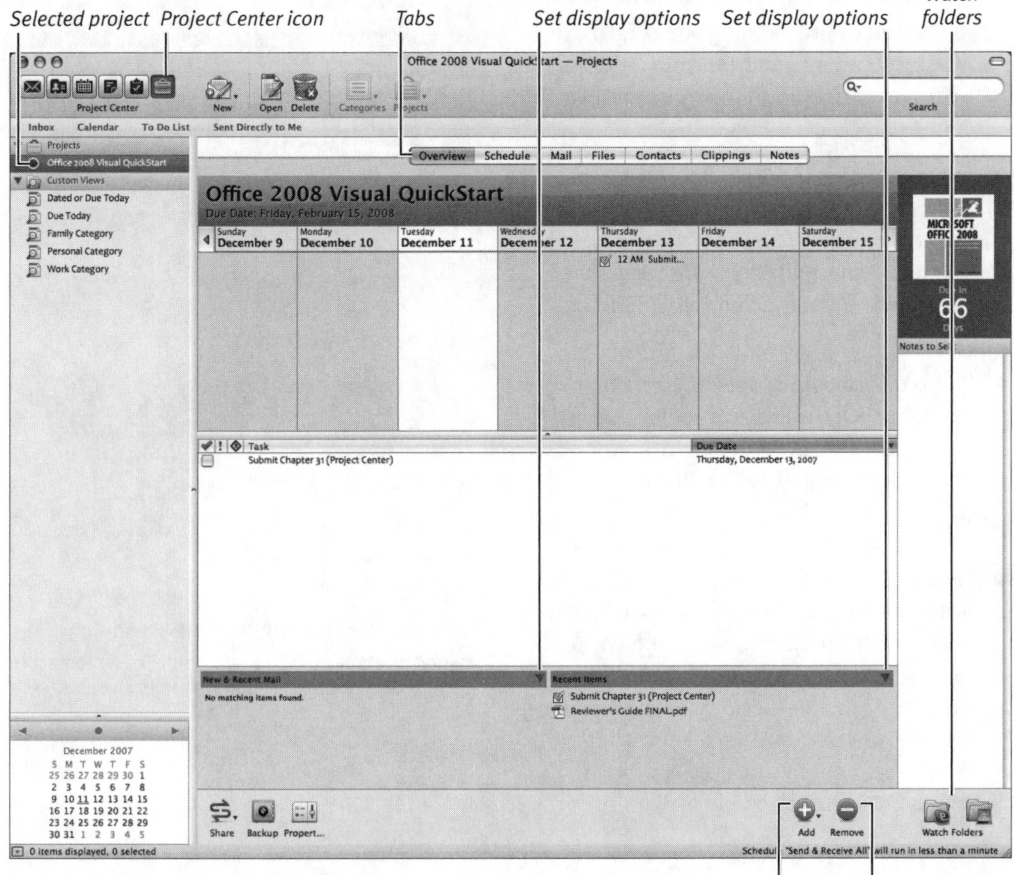

Figure 30.6 The Project Center, open to a project overview.

Adding and Removing Project Contacts

People are often—but not always—associated with a project. You can add any person from your Address Book to a project.

To add contacts to a project:

- In the Project Center, you can add new contacts to the currently selected project by doing either of the following:
  - ▲ On the Contacts tab, click the Add button.
  - ▲ On the Overview or Schedule tab, click the Add button and choose Contact from the pop-up menu (**Figure 30.7**).

  In the Add Contact dialog box (**Figure 30.8**), select contacts from your Address Book and click Add. (To select multiple contacts, ⌘-click each one.)
- In an Entourage Address Book, select a contact from the list and choose Edit > Projects > *project name*. Or Control-click a contact name and choose Projects > *project name* from the pop-up menu that appears.
- If a contact record is open in its own window, click the Projects toolbar icon and choose the project name from the drop-down menu (**Figure 30.9**).

✔ Tip

- Not every project participant will already be in your Address Book. To associate *new* people with a project, you'll first have to create contact records for them. See Chapter 22 for instructions. (You can also create a new contact from within the Project Center. Click the New icon on the Contacts or Schedule tab.)

Figure 30.7 You can add a project contact by clicking the Add button.

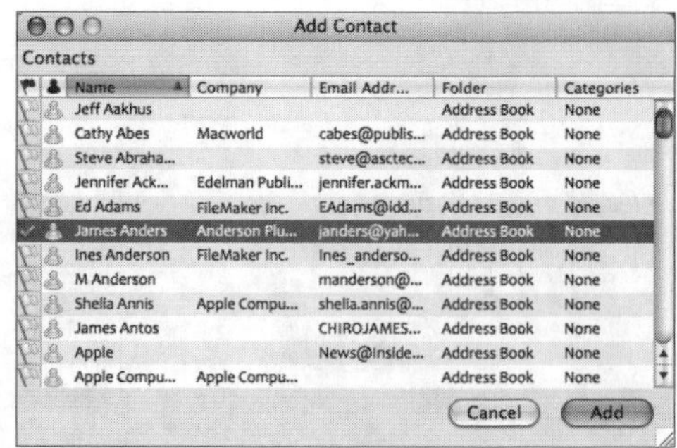

Figure 30.8 In the Add Contact dialog box, select contact records and click Add.

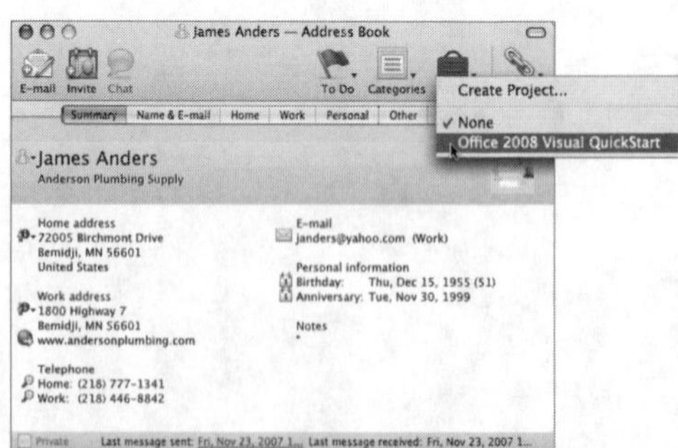

Figure 30.9 You can add a selected or open contact to a project by clicking the Projects toolbar icon.

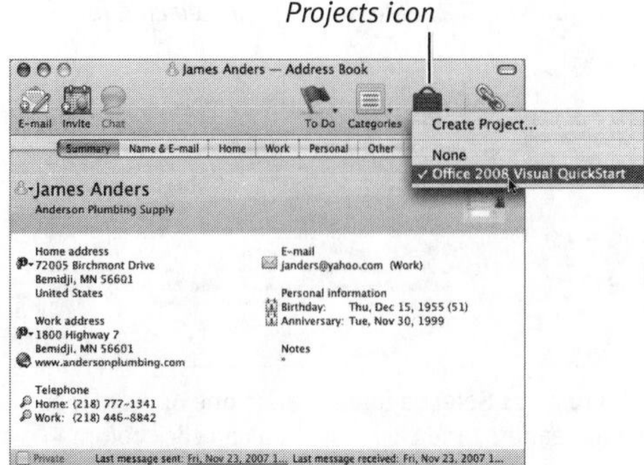

Figure 30.10 You can remove a contact from a project by choosing the project name from the Projects drop-down menu.

To remove a contact from a project:

◆ *Do one of the following:*

  ▲ In the Project Center, select the project in the Folders list and click the Contacts tab. Select the contact to be removed and click the Remove button, choose Edit > Projects > *current project*, or Control-click the contact name and choose Projects > *current project*. (The project name is a toggle; select it again to reverse its state.)

  ▲ In the Address Book, select the contact record and choose Edit > Projects > *current project*. Or Control-click the contact name and choose Projects > *current project*.

The contact is immediately removed from the project. No confirmation dialog box appears, and the removal can't be reversed by choosing Undo.

✔ Tips

- If you open a contact in its own window, you can choose the project name from the Projects toolbar icon (**Figure 30.10**).
- Use these same techniques to remove *any* project item, not just contacts.
- To simultaneously remove a contact from *all* projects, choose None. (If this is the only project with which the person is associated, choosing None has the same effect as choosing *current project*.)
- Do not *delete* a contact to remove the person from a project. Any of the various Delete commands deletes the person's contact record from the Address Book.
- You can also create a new project by clicking the Projects toolbar icon and choosing Create Project (Figure 30.10).

Adding Email Messages

Being able to see all project-related email messages in one place can vastly simplify your project management and tracking duties. When you created the project, Entourage made a new email folder in the Folders list for project message storage. You can store messages in it from or to your project contacts, as well as messages from other people that are related to the project.

To add an email message to a project:

- *Do any of the following:*
  - ▲ On the Mail tab of the Project Center, click the Add button. In the Add Mail dialog box (**Figure 30.11**), select an email folder from the list, select one or more messages from those displayed, and click Add. A copy of each message is added to the project's email folder.
  - ▲ In Mail view, switch to the folder that contains the messages you want to associate with the project. To move or copy a message, drag or Option-drag its header into the project folder in the Folders list.
  - ▲ Two other ways to copy a message from the message list into a project folder are to select the message and choose Edit > Projects > *project name*, or Control-click the header and choose Projects > *project name* from the pop-up menu that appears.

✔ Tips

- To remove messages from a project, switch to the project's Mail tab, select the message headers, and click the Remove button at the bottom of the window.
- You can add project-related messages that *you* wrote by including yourself as a contact or via selective message copying.

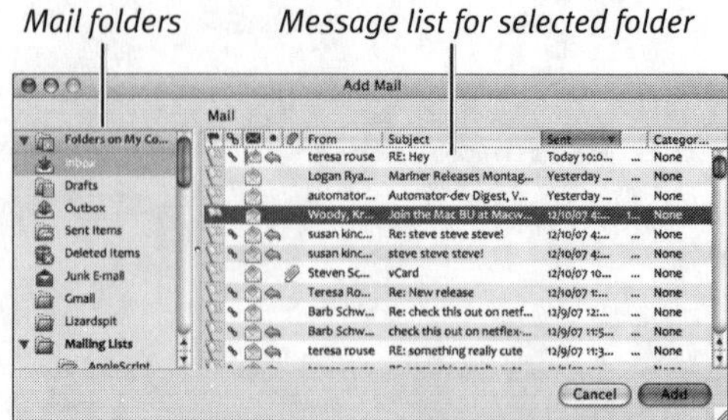

Figure 30.11 Select a folder, select one or more message headers, and click Add. You can click column headings to change the message list's sort order.

More Help for Project Email

Manually copying/moving messages into a project can be time-consuming. Here are some tips for speeding things up:

- When you add a new project contact, the person's old email isn't added. On the Overview tab, click the Properties icon, click the Maintain tab, and click Apply Rules to existing messages.
- Create some Entourage *message rules* (Tools > Rules) to handle incoming and/or outgoing email. For example, you can automatically route all email received from or sent to a particular person into the project message folder.
- To make it easier to find existing messages to move to the project folder, filter the message list to show a project-related subject or sender.

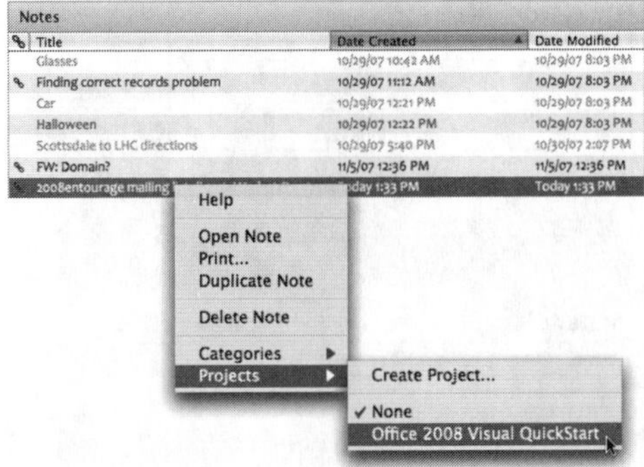

Figure 30.12 You can also Control-click any note, task, or calendar event to associate it with a project.

Adding Notes, Tasks, and Events

A project is also likely to have associated notes, tasks, and calendar events (such as appointments and meetings). It's simple to add any of these items to a project.

To add an Entourage note, task, or event to a project:

- *Do any of the following:*
  - From Notes, Tasks, or Calendar view, select a note, task, or event. Choose Edit > Projects > *project name*.
  - From Notes, Tasks, or Calendar view, Control-click a note, task, or event. Choose Projects > *project name* from the pop-up menu that appears (**Figure 30.12**).
  - On the Notes or Schedule tab of the Project Center, click Add to add an existing note, task, or event to the project. On these tabs, you can also click the New icon to simultaneously create a new note, task, or event and add it to the current project.

✔ Tip

- There are two types of Add and New icons on the Project Center tabs. Some—such as those on the Notes tab—are section-specific. That is, you simply click them to add or create an item. Others—such as those on the Overview and Schedule tabs—contain a drop-down menu with which you can specify the item type.

Adding Documents

Projects frequently rely on Office documents (presentations, worksheets, and word processing files), as well as documents from other programs, such as images, statistics, Acrobat PDFs, and desktop publishing publications. The Project Center allows *any* file to be associated with a project. By including key files in a project, you can quickly open them for editing or viewing.

To add a document to a project:

- *Do any of the following:*
  - ▲ On the Files tab of the Project Center, click the Add button. In the Add File dialog box that appears, select the file you want to add to the current project and click Open.
  - ▲ On the Overview or Schedule tab of the Project Center, click the Add button and choose File from the drop-down menu.
  - ▲ On the Schedule tab of the Project Center, click the New button and choose File from the drop-down menu. The Project Gallery appears. Select the type of new Office document you want to create, simultaneously adding it to the current project.
  - ▲ In Word, Excel, or PowerPoint, open the Toolbox by choosing View > Project Palette. To add the current document to a project (**Figure 30.13**), select the project from the drop-down menu at the top of the Toolbox and then click the Add current file icon (the plus). Click OK in the confirmation dialog box that appears (**Figure 30.14**).
  - ▲ Drag the original document icon (or its alias) into the Project Watch folder on the Desktop or into the files list on the Files tab of the Project Center.

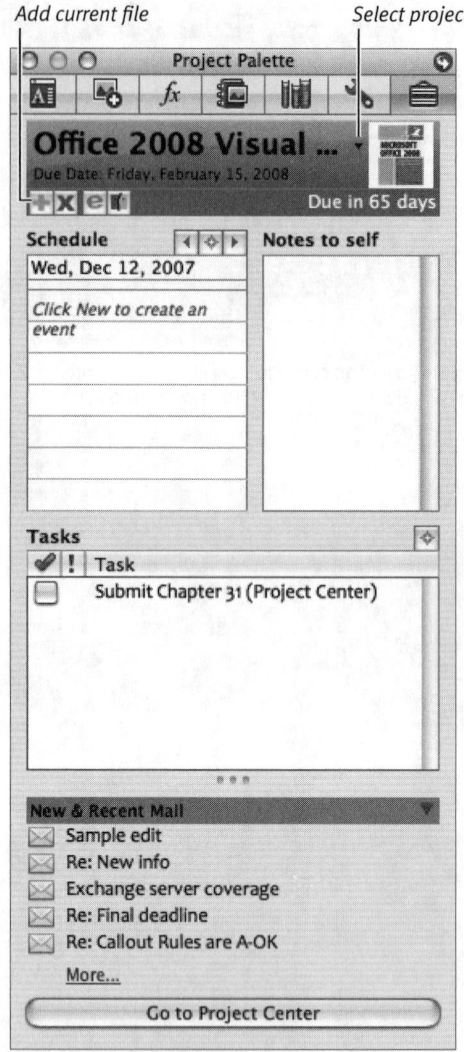

Figure 30.13 You can use the Project Palette to add the open Office 2008 file to a project.

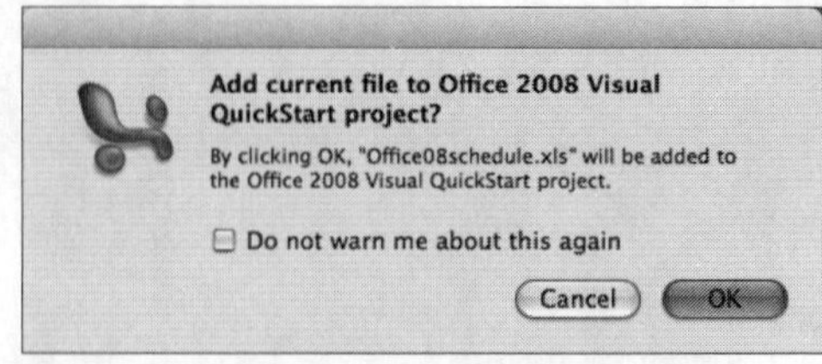

Figure 30.14 Confirm the file addition by clicking OK.

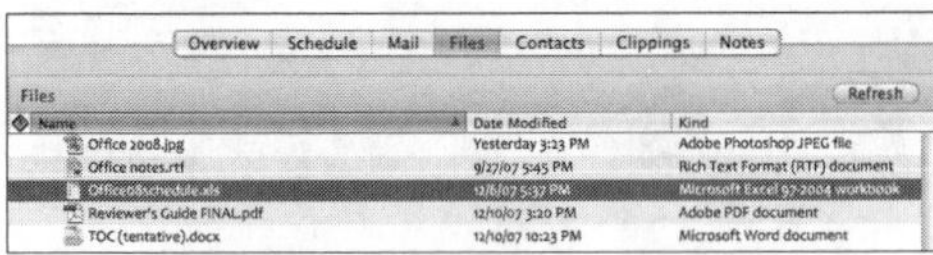

Figure 30.15 To open a project-related document, double-click its filename in the Files tab list.

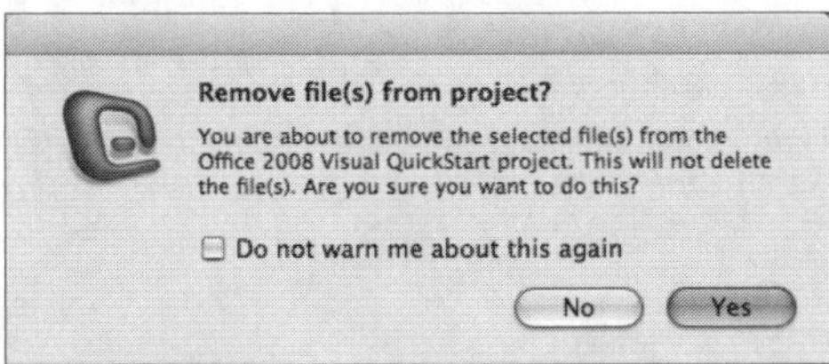

Figure 30.16 Click Yes to complete the file's removal from the project.

✔ Tips

- To open any project-related file, go to the Files tab of the Project Center and double-click the filename (**Figure 30.15**). Note that this technique will open *any* Project Center item, such as events, notes, email messages, and so on.
- If you believe that the file list has gotten out of synch with the contents of the Project Watch folder, click the Refresh button on the Files tab.
- To end the association between an added file and a project, select the file's name on the Files tab, click the Remove button at the bottom of the window, and click Yes to confirm the removal (**Figure 30.16**).

Adding Clippings

Scrapbook clippings can also be associated with a project. For information on adding items to the Scrapbook, see Chapter 1.

To add a clipping to a project:

1. In the Project Center, switch to the project's Clippings tab.
2. Click the Add button at the bottom of the window.
   The Add Clipping window appears (**Figure 30.17**), displaying a list of all items currently stored in the Scrapbook.
3. Select an item to add to the project, and then click Add.
   The clipping is added to the project. To view any clipping, select it in the list.

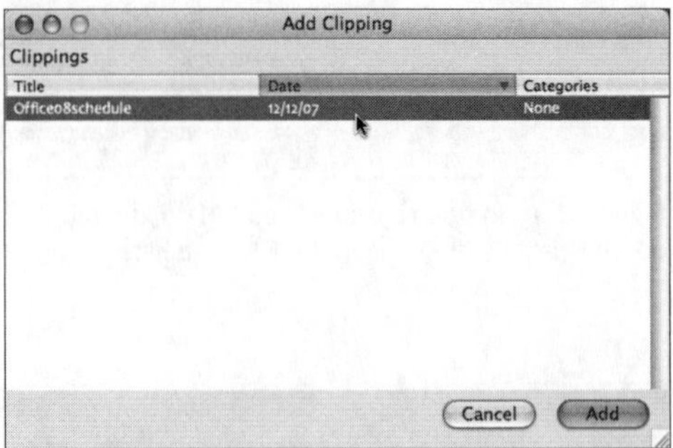

Figure 30.17 Select a Scrapbook clipping that you want to add to the project.

✔ Tips

- Click the Remove button to eliminate a selected clipping from the project.
- You can associate keywords with the currently selected clipping by typing them—separated by commas or spaces—in the Keywords area and clicking Apply (**Figure 30.18**). You can also add keywords in the Scrapbook. Because there's two-way communication between the Clippings tab and Scrapbook, it doesn't matter where you create the keywords.
- You can also add or remove project clippings from within the Scrapbook. Select a clipping in the Scrapbook, click the Projects icon in the Organize section, and select the project name from the drop-down list (**Figure 30.19**).

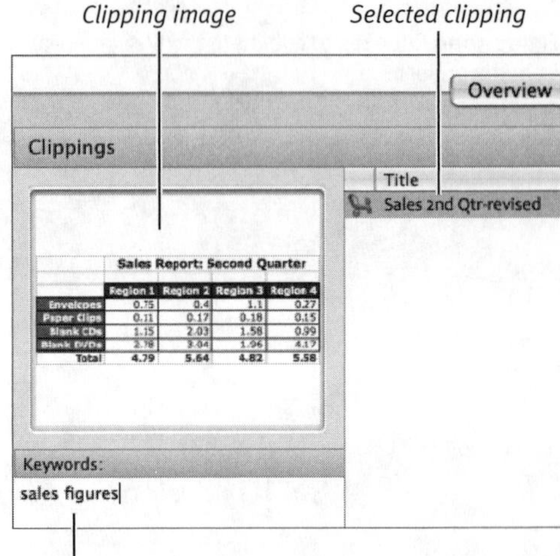

Figure 30.18 You can create keywords for a clipping.

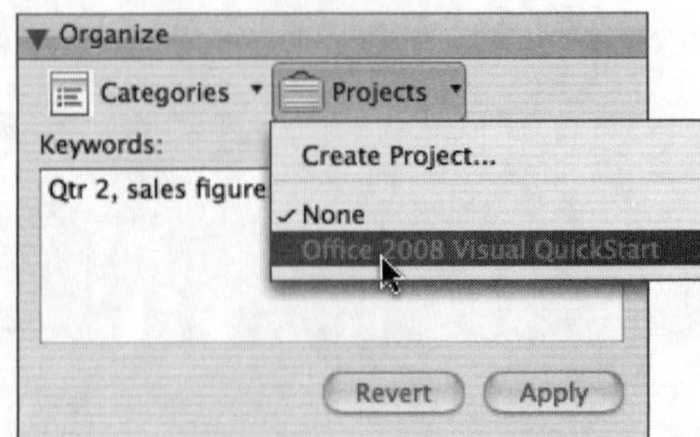

Figure 30.19 Select a project with which to link the clipping. Select None to remove it from all projects.

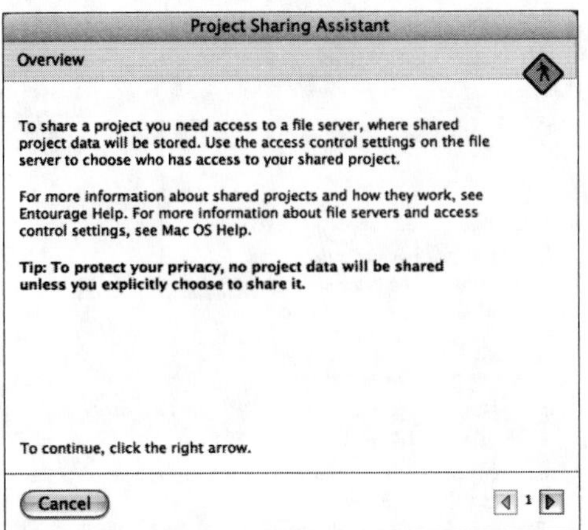

Figure 30.20 Use the Project Sharing Assistant to enable sharing for a project.

Sharing a Project

A project and its materials can be shared with others. In order to share a project, you and your colleagues must have access to a file server or iDisk account. Shared materials are moved from their original location to the specified shared location.

To share a project:

1. *Do either of the following:*
   - ▲ At the bottom of any Project Center tab, click the Share icon and choose Start Sharing Project.
   - ▲ Choose File > Share a Project.

   The Project Sharing Assistant appears (**Figure 30.20**).

2. Provide the information requested by the Project Sharing Assistant, such as the project you wish to share and the location of the file server. Click the right-arrow icon to move from one screen to the next.

✔ Tips

- To invite colleagues via email to join the current project, click the Share icon and choose Invite people to join project.
- To join someone else's project, choose File > Subscribe to a Project, select a project (.rge) file from the file list, and click Choose.
- Materials that you elect to share will be made available to other project participants. To set or change the sharing status of any project item, go to the Project Center, select the item, click the Share icon, and choose Share *item type* or Do Not Share *item type*.

Archiving a Project

To ensure that your project data is secure or to clear it from your hard disk at the project's conclusion, you can use the Project Center's backup/archive procedure.

To back up or archive a project:

1. In the Project Center, select the project and click the Overview tab. Click the Backup button at the bottom of the page.

   The Export wizard appears (**Figure 30.21**).

2. Ensure that the correct project is selected. If you wish, you can elect *not* to archive some project item classes by clearing their check boxes. Click the right-arrow icon.

   The Delete Archived Items? screen appears (**Figure 30.22**).

3. Click a radio button to indicate whether the project items should remain in Entourage (when performing a backup) or be deleted (when making an archive at a project's conclusion). Click the right-arrow icon to continue.

   If you elect to delete the items, you can click the check box to prevent the wizard from deleting any items that are associated with *other* projects or categories.

4. In the Save dialog box (**Figure 30.23**), select a location for the archive file, edit its name (if desired), and click Save.

   The project archive is created.

5. Click Done to dismiss the Export wizard.

✔ Tips

- You can also archive a project using the File > Export command.
- To restore an archived project, choose File > Import, select Import Entourage information from an archive or earlier version, select Entourage archive. (.rge), and then select the archive (.rge) file.

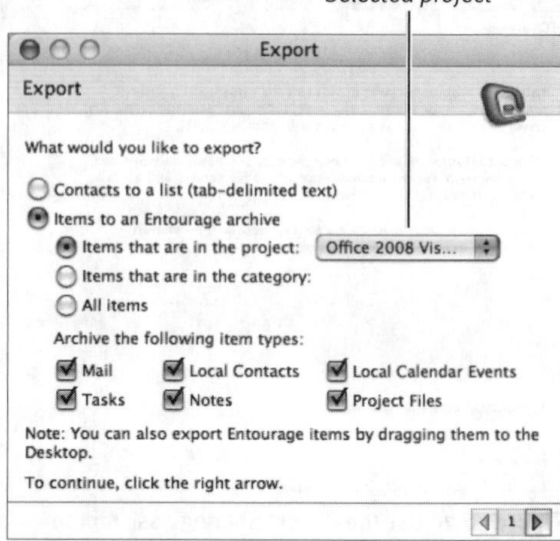

Figure 30.21 Select a project and specify the types of items to archive.

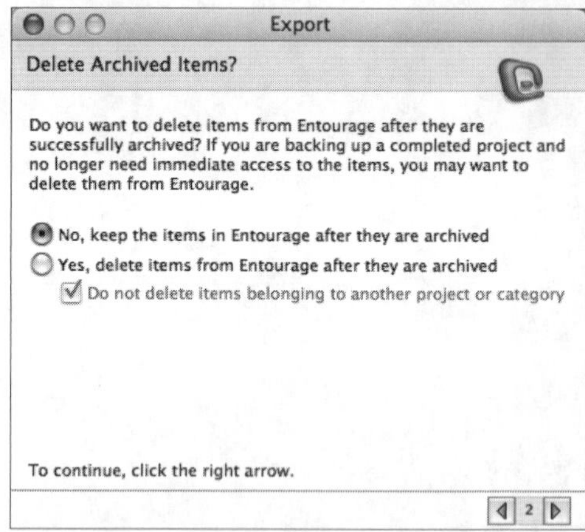

Figure 30.22 Following the archive procedure, you can delete or keep the data in Entourage.

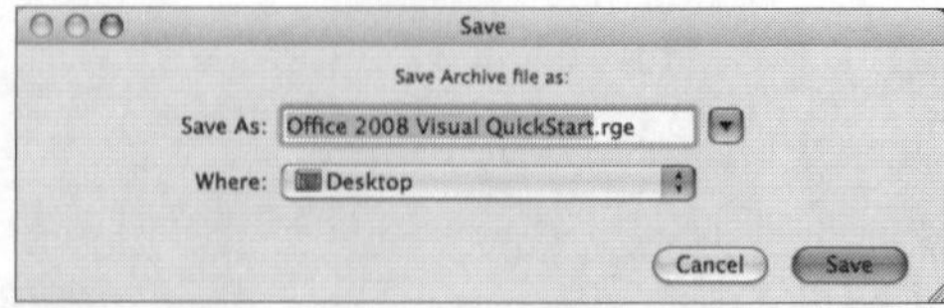

Figure 30.23 Select a location for the archive file, and then click Save.

31

Office 2008 and the Internet

In addition to using Entourage to handle email and newsgroup activities, Office has features that let you tap into the power of the Internet. This chapter shows you how to incorporate Internet links (called *hyperlinks*) in your documents, so you can direct readers to the Web to see a graphic, hear an audio file, or read additional information on a topic. For example, a Word letter about your summer vacation could contain a link to a Web site where you've posted pictures.

You'll also learn to perform these Internet-related activities:

- Without leaving Word, Excel, or PowerPoint, send the current document in email.
- Save any Office document or your Entourage calendar in HTML format so you can publish it on the Web. Because the resulting files can be viewed in any browser, you can also give or email them to people who don't use Office.
- Check for Office software updates.
- Visit Mactopia, the Macintosh section of Microsoft's Web site.
- Search the Web and the Encarta encyclopedia for useful reference material.

Working with Hyperlinks

Including clickable links (called *hyperlinks*) in an Office document is a handy way to enhance content. Clicking a hyperlink can launch a browser to display a specified Web page, open a document on your hard disk, or address a new email message.

To create a Web page hyperlink in a Word, Excel, or PowerPoint document:

1. Position the text insertion mark where you want to insert a hyperlink. Or select existing text or an object that you want to designate as the link.
2. Choose Insert > Hyperlink (⌘K).
   The Insert Hyperlink dialog box appears.
3. If it isn't selected, click the Web Page tab.
4. *Do one of the following:*
   - ▲ Type or paste the Web address in the Link to text box (**Figure 31.1**).
   - ▲ If you've recently linked to the address, select it from the drop-down list.
5. *Optional:* The text in the Display box is what will appear on the document page. By default, the Link to text is displayed. To specify different text, edit as desired.
6. *Optional:* When the cursor is rested over a hyperlink, a pop-up ScreenTip appears (**Figure 31.2**). By default, the Link to address is displayed. Click the ScreenTip button to customize the text that appears.
7. *Optional:* To link to a specific spot on the Web page (called a *bookmark* or *anchor*), click the Locate button. Note that the Web page designer must have already created the anchor. You can't arbitrarily select a link spot.
   In the dialog box that appears (**Figure 31.3**), select an anchor and click OK.
8. Click OK to create the hyperlink.

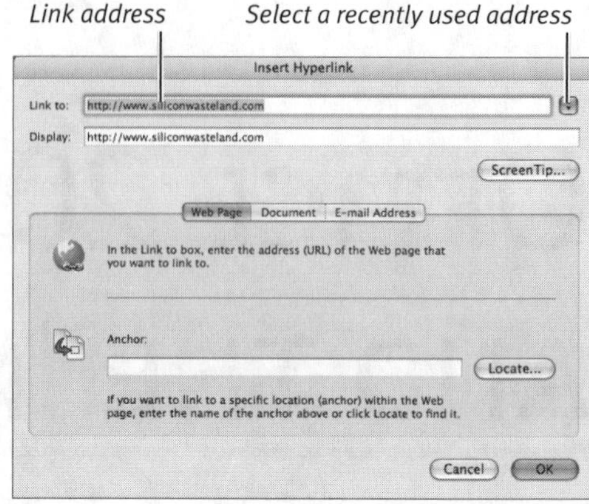

Figure 31.1 You can create a clickable link in the current document that will open a Web page, open a document on disk, or create an email message.

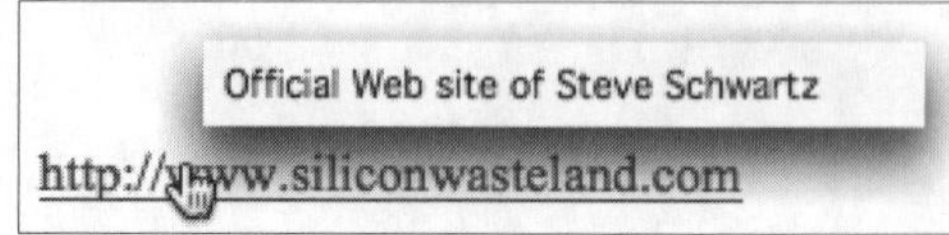

Figure 31.2 A ScreenTip automatically appears when you rest the cursor over a hyperlink.

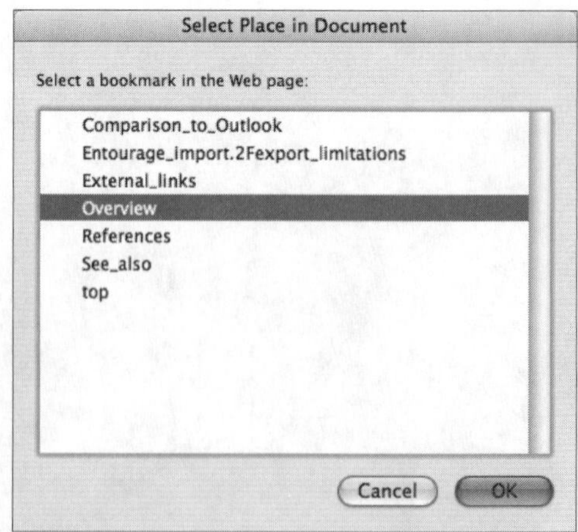

Figure 31.3 To link to a specific location on a Web page, select it from the named bookmarks in the list.

Document tab

Insert Hyperlink

Link to:

Display:

ScreenTip...

Web Page | Document | E-mail Address

Select a file to link to. Or, in the Link to box, enter the path to the file.

Select...

Anchor:

Locate...

If you want to link to a specific location (anchor) within the file, enter the name of the anchor above or click Locate to find it.

Cancel | OK

Figure 31.4 To create a link to another document on your hard disk, click the Document tab.

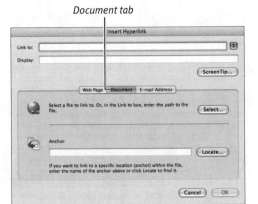

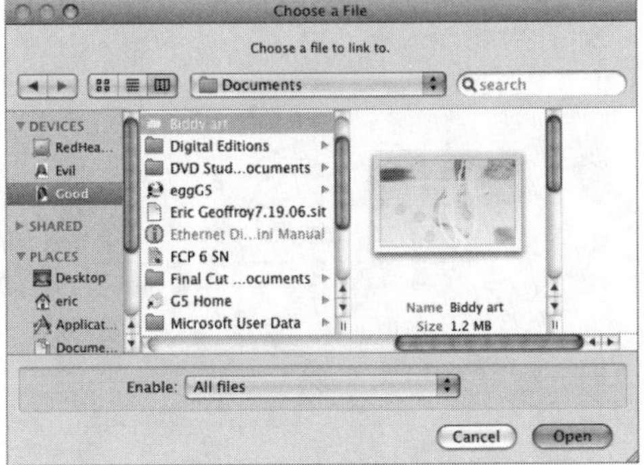

Figure 31.5 Select the document file to which you want to link (OS X 10.5/Leopard shown).

To create a document hyperlink in a Word, Excel, or PowerPoint document:

1. *Do one of the following:*
   - ▲ Position the text insertion mark where you want to insert a text link.
   - ▲ Select existing text or an object that you want to designate as the link.
2. Choose Insert > Hyperlink (⌘K).
   The Insert Hyperlink dialog box appears (see Figure 31.1).
3. On the Document tab (**Figure 31.4**), click the Select button.
   The Choose a File dialog box appears (**Figure 31.5**).
4. Select a file and click Open.
   To restrict listed files to one type, select a file type from the Enable drop-down list.
5. *Optional:* The text in the Display text box is what will appear on the document page. By default, the Link to text is displayed. To specify different text, edit as desired.
6. *Optional:* When the cursor is rested over a hyperlink, a pop-up ScreenTip appears (see Figure 31.2). By default, the Link to text (i.e., the file path) is displayed. Click ScreenTip to customize the pop-up text.
7. *Optional:* To link to a bookmarked spot in the document, click the Locate button. In the dialog box that appears, select a bookmark and click OK.
8. Click OK to create the hyperlink.
   When the link is clicked, the document will open in an appropriate program (if one is installed on the computer).

To create an email hyperlink in a Word, Excel, or PowerPoint document:

1. *Do one of the following:*
   - ▲ Position the text insertion mark where you want to insert a text link.
   - ▲ Select the text or object that you want to designate as the link.
2. Choose Insert > Hyperlink (⌘K). The Insert Hyperlink dialog box appears (see Figure 31.1).
3. Click the E-mail Address tab (**Figure 31.6**).
4. *Do one of the following:*
   - ▲ Type or paste the recipient's email address in the To text box.
   - ▲ Select an address from the Recent Addresses drop-down list.
   - ▲ To look up an address in your default email program, click Launch E-mail Application.
5. *Optional:* Enter a subject for the message in the Subject text box.
6. *Optional:* The text in the Display text box is what will appear in the email message. By default, the Link to text is displayed. To specify different text, edit as desired.
7. *Optional:* When the cursor is rested over a hyperlink, a pop-up ScreenTip appears (see Figure 31.2). By default, the Link to text is displayed. Click ScreenTip to customize the pop-up text.
8. When the settings are satisfactory (**Figure 31.7**), click OK. When the link is clicked, a new email message is generated in the user's default email program. It will be addressed to the designated recipient, use the specified Subject (if any), and be ready for the message text to be entered.

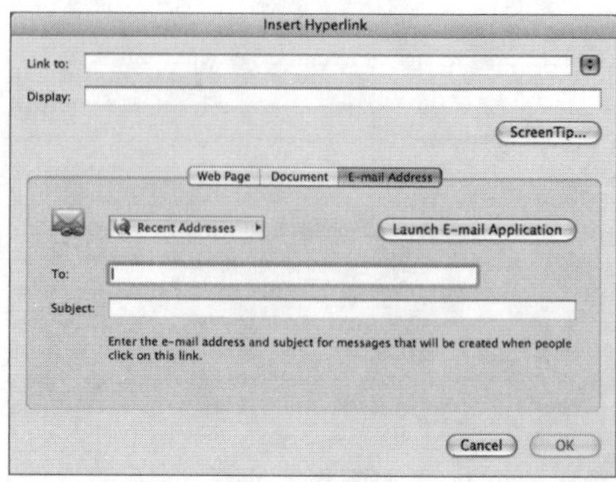

Figure 31.6 On the E-mail Address tab, enter the recipient's email address and the message's Subject.

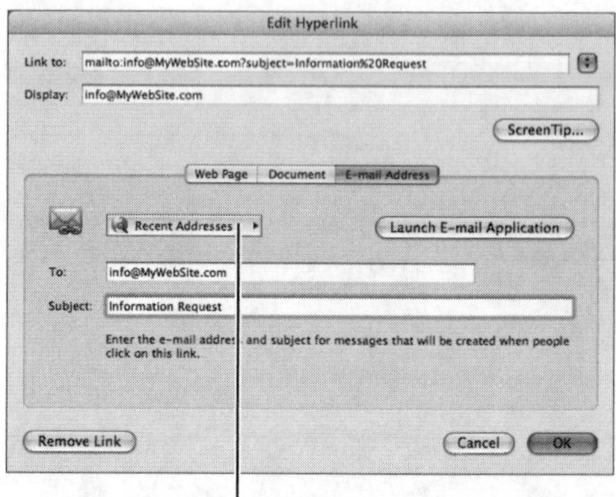

Figure 31.7 When an email hyperlink is clicked by someone reading the document, a message with the specified Subject will be sent to you (or another designated recipient).

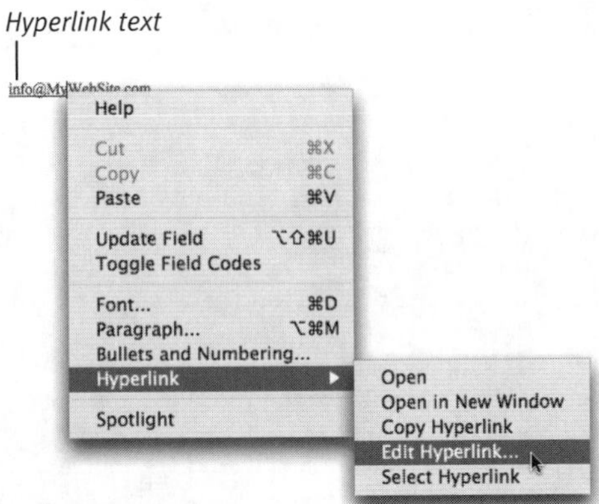

Figure 31.8 To modify a link, right-click it and choose Hyperlink > Edit Hyperlink.

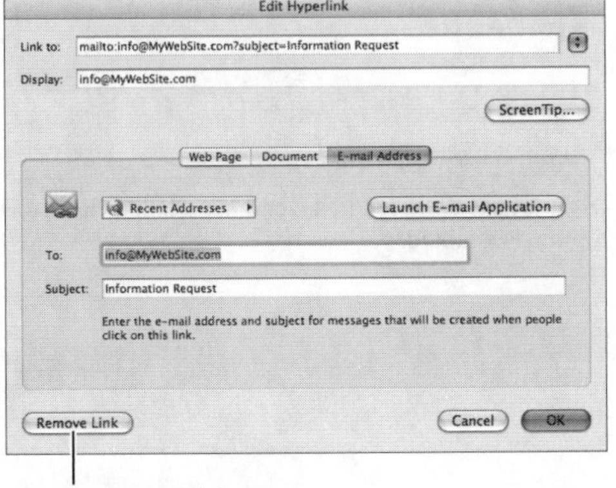

Figure 31.9 In the Edit Hyperlink dialog box, you can modify or remove an existing link.

To add a hyperlink to an Entourage email message:

◆ Type or paste the complete link address into the message. The following examples illustrate the proper syntax.

- ▲ `http://www.msn.com` (Web address)
- ▲ `ftp://ftp.microsoft.com` (FTP site)
- ▲ `mailto:roadrunner@cox.net` (email address)

Whether or not the link will be clickable depends on the capabilities of the recipient's email program.

To modify a hyperlink in a Word, Excel, or PowerPoint document:

1. *Do one of the following:*
   - ▲ Control-click the hyperlink text or object to reveal the pop-up menu. In Word or PowerPoint (**Figure 31.8**), choose Hyperlink > Edit Hyperlink. In Excel, choose Hyperlink.
   - ▲ Select all or part of the hyperlink. Choose Insert > Hyperlink (⌘K).

   The Edit Hyperlink dialog box appears (**Figure 31.9**).
2. Make the necessary changes and click OK.

To remove a hyperlink:

1. *Do one of the following:*
   - ▲ Control-click the hyperlink text or object to reveal the pop-up menu. In Word or PowerPoint (Figure 31.8), choose Hyperlink > Edit Hyperlink. In Excel, choose Hyperlink.
   - ▲ Select all or part of the hyperlink. Choose Insert > Hyperlink (⌘K).

   The Edit Hyperlink dialog box appears (Figure 31.9).
2. Click the Remove Link button.

   The link text or object remains but will no longer function as a clickable link.

✔ Tips

- When clicked, a Web or email hyperlink automatically launches the default Web browser or email program.
- A document hyperlink can be made to *any* document on your hard disk—not just Office documents. When clicked, the appropriate application will launch and open the specified document.
- When giving someone an Office file that contains document links to other files, be certain to also give them the linked-to documents.
- You can create a clickable table of contents in any lengthy Word document. First, assign a bookmark to every major heading. Then create a document hyperlink from each table of contents entry to the appropriate bookmark.
- You can also create a hyperlink by typing it directly into a document or by copying it from another source (such as the address box of your Web browser, a link on a Web page, or the body of an email message) and then pasting it into the document.
- For typed hyperlinks to be recognized in Word, you must set AutoCorrect to transform eligible text into links. Choose Tools > AutoCorrect, and click the AutoFormat As You Type tab. Ensure that Internet and network paths with hyperlinks (**Figure 31.10**) is checked, and click OK.
- For a Web page hyperlink to work when clicked, you must be on a computer that has an Internet connection.
- Deleting hyperlink text or a hyperlinked object simultaneously removes the link.

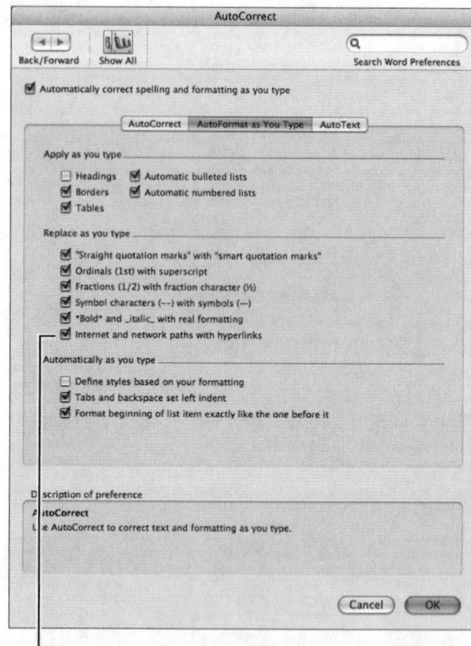

Figure 31.10 Word ignores typed hyperlinks unless this option is enabled.

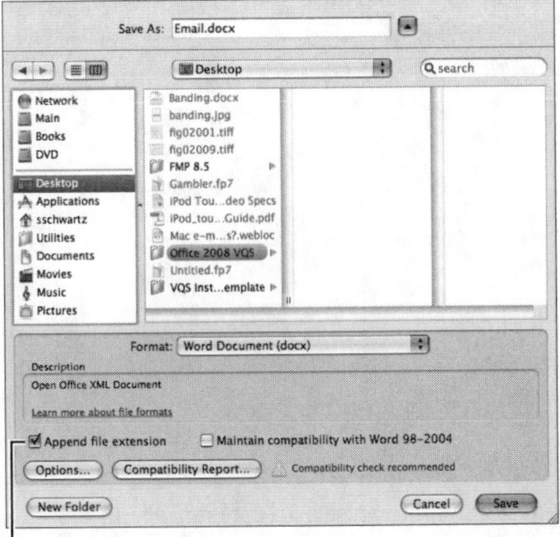

Add a Windows file extension

Figure 31.11 When sending attachments to Windows users, click the Append file extension check box to add the appropriate extension.

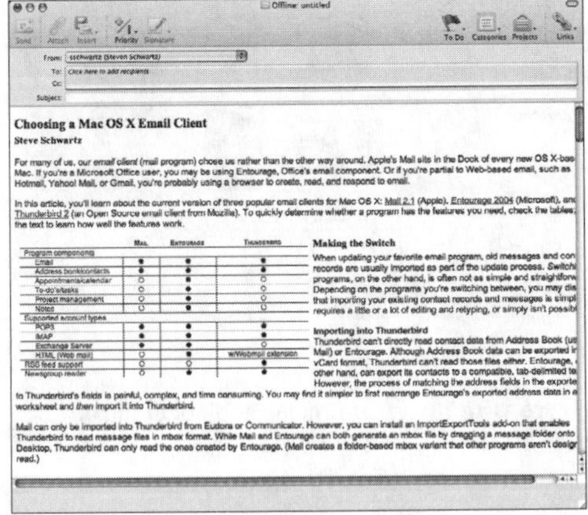

Figure 31.12 If a recipient doesn't have Word or Excel, you can send a document formatted as HTML.

- If multiple people use your computer, you may need to switch *identities*. Quit all Office programs, launch Entourage, choose Entourage > Switch Identity, and click Switch in the dialog box that appears. In the next dialog box, select your identity and click OK.

Emailing Office Documents

You can email any open Office document without leaving Office. Using the Send To command in Word, PowerPoint, or Excel, you can send any open document as an email attachment. In Word or Excel, you can elect to translate the document into a formatted HTML message. The latter option is most useful when a recipient doesn't have Office.

To email an Office document:

1. *Optional:* Choose File > Save As to save the document. If you intend to send it to a recipient who uses Windows, click the Append file extension check box (**Figure 31.11**).
2. *Do one of the following:*
   - ▲ Choose File > Send To > Mail Recipient (as Attachment).
   - ▲ Choose File > Send To > Mail Recipient (as HTML).

   Your default email program launches and creates a new message with the document attached or converted to an HTML message (**Figure 31.12**).
3. Specify recipients, write the message text (if sending a document as an attachment), and send the message.

✔ Tips

- When converting a document to HTML, carefully examine the generated message before sending it. Many Office documents are poorly suited for HTML conversion. If the results aren't true to the original document, you can use the File > Print command to create a PDF file that can be sent as an email attachment. (PDF files can be opened and viewed in Preview or Adobe Reader.)
- You can't edit an HTML message generated with the Send To command.

Other Internet Capabilities

Office 2008 has other Internet capabilities you may wish to explore. Here are some of the most interesting ones:

- You can create Web pages from Word, PowerPoint, or Excel documents using the File > Save as Web Page command, enabling you to publish the pages on the Internet or a company intranet. If you have friends or coworkers who don't use Office, they can view the resulting documents in any browser. For an example of saving an Office document as a Web page, see Chapter 19.
- You can use the File > Save as Web Page command in Entourage to save your calendar as a Web page (**Figure 31.13**). If you publish the page to a Web site, you and others can refer to the calendar from any Internet access point—while on vacation or a business trip, for example.
- Use the File > Web Page Preview command to quickly see how the current Word, PowerPoint, or Excel document will look if saved as a Web page.
- You can download clip art images from Office Online. In Word or Excel, choose Insert > Picture > Clip Art. In PowerPoint, choose Insert > Clip Art. Then click the Online button in the Clip Gallery window (**Figure 31.14**).

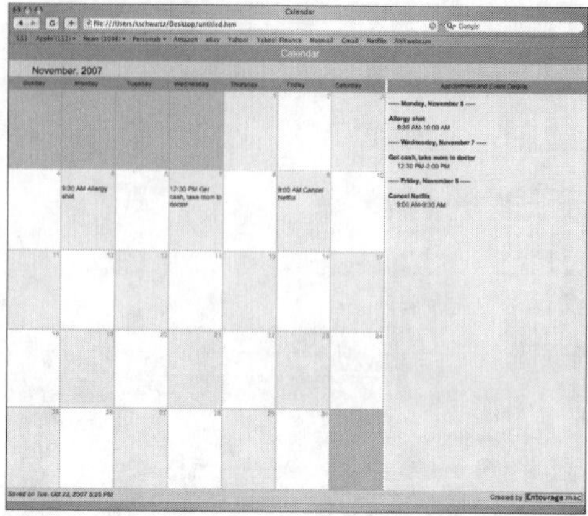

Figure 31.13 You can select a date range from your Entourage calendar and save it as a Web page.

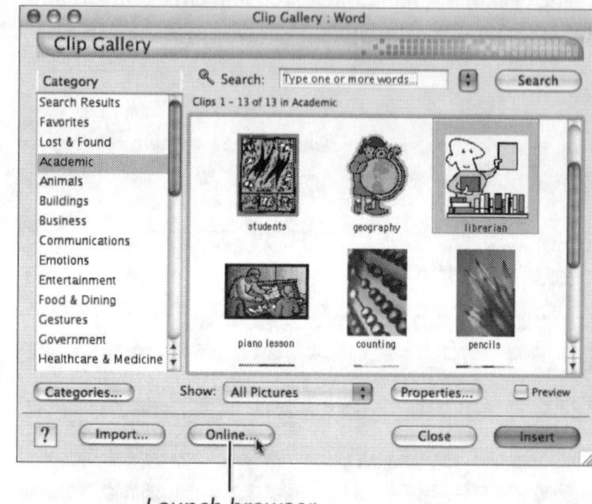

Figure 31.14 You can download additional clip art from Microsoft's Web site.

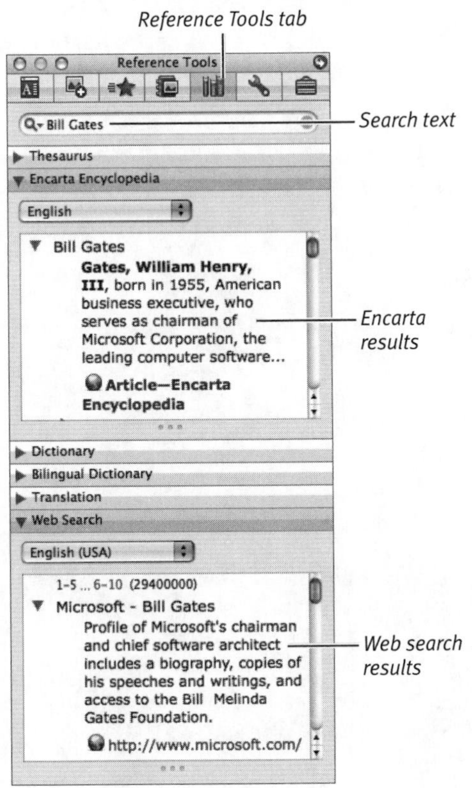

Figure 31.15 Enter a search string on the Reference Tools tab and examine the results.

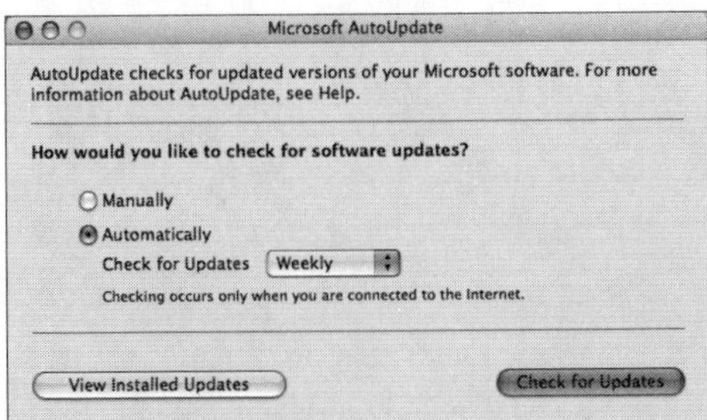

Figure 31.16 You can configure AutoUpdate to check for Office updates on a schedule or just run it manually whenever you wish.

- On the Reference Tools tab of the Toolbox (**Figure 31.15**), you can search the Web or consult the Encarta encyclopedia. If the Toolbox is visible, click the Reference Tools tab. Otherwise, choose View > Toolbox > Reference Tools or click the Toolbox icon on the Standard toolbar. Click the Reference Tools tab (if it isn't currently selected), enter a search string, and press Return.
- The Help menu has commands that open your Web browser to display information from the Internet:
  - Choose Help > Check for Updates to launch Microsoft AutoUpdate (**Figure 31.16**).
  - Choose Help > Visit the Product Web Site to view the Mactopia Web site in your browser.

INDEX

D

INDEX

E

F

INDEX

G

H

I

P

X

Y

Z